Pathways in Modern Western Magic

Pathways in
Modern Western Magic

Edited by Nevill Drury

Concrescent Scholars

Pathways in Modern Western Magic © 2012 Concrescent LLC

All rights reserved. Except for brief quotations in a review, the book, or parts thereof, may not be reproduced in any work without permission in writing from the publisher. The moral rights of the authors have been asserted.

The right of authors as listed in the table of contents to be identified as the authors of this work has been asserted by them in accordance with the Copyright, Designs and Patents Act, 1988.

Concrescent Scholars
an imprint of Concrescent LLC
Richmond CA 94805
info@concrescent.net

ISBN: 978-0-9843729-9-7

Library of Congress Control Number: 2012947222

Cover illustration: Jean Delville, Parsifal, 1890

Contents

	Introduction *Nevill Drury*	1
1	Lifting the Veil: An Emic Approach to Magical Practice *Lynne Hume*	19
2	The Visual and the Numinous: Material Expressions of the Sacred in Contemporary Paganism *Dominique Beth Wilson*	37
3	Encountering the *Universal* Triple Goddess in Wicca *Nikki Bado*	65
4	Away from the Light: Dark Aspects of the Goddess *Marguerite Johnson*	87
5	Neo-Shamanism in the United States *Andrei A. Znamenski*	105
6	Neo-Shamanisms in Europe *Robert J. Wallis*	127
7	Seiðr Oracles *Jenny Blain*	159
8	Magical Practices in The Hermetic Order of The Golden Dawn *Nevill Drury*	181
9	The Thelemic Sex Magick of Aleister Crowley *Nevill Drury*	205

10 The Draconian Tradition:
    Dragon Rouge and the Left-Hand Path   247
    Thomas Karlsson

11 Claiming Hellish Hegemony:
    Anton La Vey, The Church of Satan & The Satanic Bible   261
    James R. Lewis

12 Modern Black Magic:
    Initiation, Sorcery and The Temple of Set   281
    Don Webb

13 The Magical Life of Ithell Colquhoun   307
    Amy Hale

14 Two Chthonic Magical Artists:
    Austin Osman Spare & Rosaleen Norton   323
    Nevill Drury

15 Nothing is True, Everything is Permitted:
    Chaos Magics in Britain   379
    Dave Evans

16 The Computer-Mediated Religious Life
    of Technoshamans and Cybershamans   409
    Libuše Martínková

17 The Magic Wonderland of the Senses:
    Reflections on a Hybridised Tantra Practice   425
    Phil Hine

Contributors   *437*

Index   *443*

Publisher's Preface
Welcome to Concrescent Scholars

Pathways in Modern Western Magic launches a new imprint in the Concrescent family of books. This imprint specializes in peer-reviewed works of scholarship in the fields of Esotericism, Pagan religion and culture, Magic, and the Occult. Concrescent Scholars present their views from within and without the Academy. Here will be heard the Voice of the Academic, and also the Voice of the Practitioner, the native of the sometimes alien, sometimes intimate, spaces of the Esoteric.

Paraphrasing the Buddhologist Stephan Beyer, we are mindful that Scholars of the Esoteric do not deal with Esotericism so much as they deal with Esotericists. Real lives are behind these words and each one has a voice to contribute.

Concrescent Scholars is dedicated to bringing together all who work, learn, and live in the Esoteric that they may flourish materially, intellectually, and spiritually.

And so it begins…

Introduction

Nevill Drury

The academic study of modern Western magic is still a comparatively new phenomenon. While the anthropological study of magic in pre-literate societies has been well established as a discipline for a hundred years or more, rigorous academic interest in the study of modern Western magical beliefs has gathered pace only during the last twenty years or so. *Pathways in Modern Western Magic* has been conceived as a contribution to this steadily expanding body of literature, complementing other academic studies of modern Western magical practices by authors like Tanya Luhrmann (1989), Ronald Hutton (1999), Alex Owen (2004), Susan Greenwood (2005), Nikki Bado-Fralick (2005) and Hugh Urban (2006).[1]

One of the key elements that distinguishes *Pathways in Modern Western Magic* from a number of *etic* anthologies on esotericism that have appeared in the last few years is that here *emic* magical accounts— 'insider perspectives'—are highly valued because of the insights provided by the practitioners themselves. The terms *emic* and *etic* were first proposed by the anthropological linguist Kenneth Pike and were further developed by the socio-cultural anthropologist Marvin Harris.[2] Essentially they relate to issues of subjectivity and objectivity in anthropological research. 'Emic' derives from the word *phonemic*, a linguistic term that refers to the categories of sounds used by native speakers to understand and create meaningful utterances. 'Etic' is from the linguistic term *phonetic*, referring to the acoustic properties of sounds discernible through linguistic analysis.³ Harris is quite specific in describing their application to the study of cultural anthropology:

> **Emic** *operations have as their hallmark the elevation of the native informant to the status of ultimate judge of the adequacy of the observer's descriptions and analyses. The test of the adequacy of* **emic** *analyses is their ability to generate statements the native accepts as real, meaningful, or appropriate...* **Etic** *operations have as their hallmark the elevation of observers to the status of ultimate judges of the categories and concepts used in descriptions and analyses. The test of the adequacy of* **etic** *accounts is simply their ability to generate scientifically productive theories about the causes of sociocultural differences and similarities.*⁴ [bold in original]

Harris himself was in no doubt as to which was the superior method. According to Harris the value of the *etic* approach was that it allowed the anthropologist to establish 'the social nature of truth' in an objective and scientific fashion, whereas *emic* approaches, in his opinion, were invariably 'relativistic.' As Harris succinctly explains:

> ...*the participant observer can never find the truth of the lived experience, apart from the consensus about such things found in the community in which the observer participates.*⁵

Harris also makes specific reference to the 'obscurantist' approach adopted by some anthropologists with regard to various forms of contemporary esoteric and religious practice:

> *Obscurantism is an important component in the emics of astrology, witchcraft, messianism, hippiedom, fundamentalism, cults of personality, nationalism, ethnocentrism, and a hundred other contemporary modes of thought that exalt knowledge gained by inspiration, revelation, intuition, faith, or incantation as against knowledge obtained in conformity with scientific research principles. Philosophers and social scientists are implicated both as leaders and as followers in the popular success of these celebrations of non-scientific knowledge, and in the strong anti-scientific components they contain.*⁶

Harris's point is well taken, whether one agrees with it or not, but it is ultimately of little assistance in solving the vexed issue of how to legitimately research the nature of modern Western magic and its quest for transformative states of consciousness. A more sympathetic view than that of Marvin Harris—one which seeks to bridge the apparent gulf between the magical realm and the world of legitimate academic research—is provided by anthropologist Lynne Hume, who argues that a phenomenological [or substantially *emic*] approach is extremely useful in researching magical beliefs and practices:

> *To my mind, the most appropriate approach to the study of belief systems is a phenomenological one which aims at moving beyond the constraints of structural functional analysis, and even beyond semiotic symbolic anthropology which treats accounts as texts to be analysed in terms of their meaning. A phenomenological approach aims at an objective descriptive analysis, and a systematic evaluation of the essence of a belief system, endeavouring to perceive the devotee's conception of truth in order to assess what is meaningful to the devotee, without raising questions of its ultimate status in reality... as a phenomenologist one suspends disbelief without accepting the totality of the informants' worlds as one's own.*[7]

Another important distinction that should be made at this point is that in the classical anthropological literature 'magic' has long been associated with pre-literate indigenous cultures that were assumed to be essentially 'primitive' and intellectually unsophisticated. Much of the academic literature on magic up until quite recent times has been written by anthropologists and social theorists who have responded to the data on magic in a fundamentally unsympathetic way and from a position of perceived intellectual superiority. Academic responses to magic—and also religion—include the late 19th century *evolutionary* approach, which sought common threads in the development of magical and religious systems (a perspective associated especially with Frazer and Tylor); the *functional* approach, which focused on the relationship of magic and religion to the structure and survival of society (Durkheim, Malinowski, Radcliffe-Brown), and the *psychosocial* approach, which has been concerned with the relationship between culture and personality and the connection between the society and the individual (Evans-Pritchard, Freud, Spiro, et al.).[8]

All of these perspectives have continued to influence anthropological thought in varying degrees. As recently as the late 1980s Tanya Luhrmann thought it appropriate to study magic in contemporary urban

England whilst also employing Malinowski's Trobriand-islander model of 'magical crisis'.[9] Drawing on an anthropological paradigm transposed from the study of pre-literate Oceanic cultures, Luhrmann argued that modern Western magic was essentially about seeking control in an uncontrollable world. Needless to say, Luhrmann's data does not support her principal conclusions—one of the contemporary magical groups she studied (Gareth Knight's Western Mysteries group) derives its esoteric practices from Dion Fortune's Fraternity of the Inner Light which in turn had historical associations with the theurgic high magic practised in the Golden Dawn. High magic is not found in pre-literate societies and the magic associated with all of these modern English esoteric organisations is inwardly-directed and 'transformational' rather than 'functional' in every significant respect.

Paradoxically, the misplaced nature of Luhrmann's anthropological approach reinforces the innate value of scholarly *emic* accounts of modern Western magic. Academics who are also magical practitioners and who document their experiences intelligently and systematically help us avoid the distortions that inevitably enter the literature when insider accounts are ignored. Contemporary anthropologists who have explored magical beliefs and practices as 'insider-practitioners' include Jeanne Favret-Saada (1980) who studied witchcraft in the Bocage region of Normandy,[10] Paul Stoller (1987) who became an apprentice to Songhay sorcerers,[11] Lynne Hume (1997) who researched Wicca and neo-paganism as a participant with various groups in Australia,[12] Susan Greenwood (2000, 2005) who became a Wiccan priestess in England[13] and Nikki Bado-Fralick (2005), currently a university professor, who has also been a high priestess in witchcraft covens in Ohio and Iowa.[14] Hume and Bado-Fralick (now Bado) are contributors to the present volume.

Defining magic

Given the diversity of modern esoteric practice, magic itself obviously requires some sort of definition. Aleister Crowley, arguably the most influential occultist in the 20th century, provided several different definitions of magic in his various publications. In *Magick in Theory and Practice* (1929) he writes:

> There is a single main definition of the object of all magical Ritual. It is the uniting of the Microcosm with the Macrocosm. The Supreme and Complete Ritual is therefore the Invocation of the Holy Guardian Angel, or, in the language of Mysticism, Union with God.' [capitals in original][15]

In the same volume Crowley echoes the famous Hermetic principle 'As above, so below' when he writes: 'The Microcosm is an exact image of the Macrocosm; the Great Work is the raising of the whole man in perfect balance to the power of Infinity.'[16] Crowley also offered a more direct and pragmatic definition of magic: 'Magick is the Science and Art of causing Change to occur in conformity with Will.'[17]. For Crowley, application of the will was a crucial component in magical practice for he also wrote: 'Every intentional act is a Magical Act,'[18] to which he added a footnote: 'By "intentional' I mean "willed".' From Crowley's perspective, acts of magical intent could also lead to subjugation of others: 'Man is capable of being, and using, anything which he perceives, for everything that he perceives is in certain sense a part of his being. He may thus subjugate the whole Universe of which he is conscious to his individual Will.'[19]

Israel Regardie, Crowley's one-time secretary and editor of *The Golden Dawn* (published 1937-40), defined magic in more psychological terms: 'As a practical system, Magic is concerned not so much with analysis as with bringing into operation the creative and intuitive parts of man.... Magic may be said to be a technique for realising the deeper levels of the Unconscious.' [capitals in Regardie's text] [20] However, like Crowley, Regardie also focused on the significance of the magical will:

> *The magician conceives of someone he calls God, upon whom attend a series of angelic beings, variously called archangels, elementals, demons etc. By simply calling upon this God with a great deal of ado, and commemorating the efforts of previous magicians*[21] *and saints who accomplished their wonders or attained to the realization of their desires through the invocation of the several names of that God, the magician too realizes the fulfilment of his will.*[22]

Regardie also emphasized the nature of the magical imagination:

> *In practice, the idea is to arrange a play or a ritualistic ceremony wherein is enacted the entire life-cycle of the God or his terrestrial emissary whose spiritual presence one wishes to invoke. The union or identification with the God is accomplished through suggestion, sympathy and the exaltation of consciousness. ...the magician imagines himself in the ceremony to be the deity who has undergone similar experiences. The rituals serve but to suggest and to render more complete the process of identification, so that sight and hearing and intelligence may serve to that end. In the commemoration, or rehearsal of this*

history, the magician is uplifted on high, and is whirled into the secret domain of the spirit... [23]

For Regardie, the ultimate spiritual destination of the magician was submergence of the individual self within the transcendent Godhead:

All the characteristics of the higher worlds are successively assumed by the Magician, and transcended, until in the end of his magical journey, he is merged into the being of the Lord of every Life. The final goal of his spiritual pilgrimage is that peaceful ecstasy in which the finite personality, thought and self-consciousness, even the high consciousness of the highest Gods, drops utterly away, and the Magician melts to a oneness with the Ain Soph [24] *wherein no shade of difference enters.* [25]

Other influential occultists—pioneers, as it were, of the modern Western magical perspective—have also proposed their own definitions of magic. For S.L.MacGregor Mathers, co-founder of the Hermetic Order of the Golden Dawn in 1888, magic was 'the Science of the Control of the Secret Forces of Nature'[26] while Mathers' colleague in the Golden Dawn, Dr Edward Berridge (*Frater Resurgam*) sought also to distinguish the role of the imagination in the practice of magic:

Imagination is a reality. When a man imagines he actually creates a form on the Astral or even on some higher plane; and this form is as real and objective to intelligent beings on that plane, as our earthly surroundings are to us...To practice magic, both the Imagination and the Will must be called into action... the Imagination must precede the Will in order to produce the greatest possible effect. [27]

Dion Fortune, a former member of the Stella Matutina (a Golden Dawn derivative) and founder of the Fraternity of the Inner Light, noted that: 'White magic...consists in the application of occult powers to spiritual ends.'[28] Fortune also defined magic in much the same way as Aleister Crowley: '[Magic is] the art of causing changes in consciousness at will.'[29] Dr Michael Aquino, a self-proclaimed 'black magician' and principal formulator of the doctrines of The Temple of Set, also defines magic within the context of the application of the magical will:

The theory and practice of non-natural interaction with the subjective universe is defined as Greater Black Magic...Great-

> er Black Magic is the causing of change to occur in the subjective universe in accordance with the Will. This change in the subjective universe will cause a similar and proportionate change in the objective universe.'[30]

Influential Goddess worshipper and eco-feminist Starhawk offers another perspective, emphasizing the principle of interconnectedness with the cosmos in her definition of magic:

> The primary principle of magic is connection. The universe is a fluid, ever-changing energy pattern, not a collection of fixed and separate things. What affects one thing affects, in some way, all things. All is interwoven into the continuous fabric of being. Its warp and weft are energy, which is the essence of magic.[31]

Starhawk focuses on the connection between magic and the physical world:

> Magic is part of nature; it does not controvert natural laws. It is through study and observation of nature, of the visible, physical reality, that we can learn to understand the workings of the underlying reality. Magic teaches us to tap sources of energy that are unlimited, infinite...[32]

Overview of Volume

In the opening chapter, 'Lifting the veil: an emic approach to magical practice', anthropologist Lynne Hume sets the tone for the present volume, arguing that magicians, pagans and shamans have numerous portals, or entry points, to the sacred and mysterious realm referred to by some as the 'otherworld'. For her the key lies in understanding the relationship between altered states of consciousness and the realm of emotions and imagination. Magicians of all persuasions acknowledge the value of using visualisation and trance techniques accompanied by chanting and singing, and sometimes they also employ ritual entheogens (psychedelic sacraments) to enter the hidden, sacred worlds beyond the realm of familiar reality. As several of the contributors to the present volume emphasize in their respective chapters, modern Western magic values the *imaginal*—and many magical rituals are based on conceiving and visualizing forces greater than the individual self. Indeed, this is how the sense of magical transformation generally comes about.

Modern pagan witchcraft—otherwise known as Wicca—openly

explores the imaginal as an 'alternative reality'. Wicca offers a holistic view of a cosmos alive with creative potential — propelled by the dynamic union of sacred female and male principles. In honoring the Universal Goddess as its principal deity, Wicca is very specifically grounded in the symbolism of fertility and embraces Nature's seasons as reflective of the eternal cycles of life, death and rebirth. For the most part, the Wiccan spiritual quest is oriented towards 'this world'. The main emphasis in Wicca is on immanent, rather than transcendent, aspects of deity and the Universal Goddess is personified in the coven by the high priestess. Nevertheless, as Dominique Beth Wilson observes in her chapter, 'The visual and the numinous: material expressions of the sacred in contemporary paganism,' it is still possible for devotees of sacred earth traditions to embrace the more abstract notion of the *'mysterium tremendum et fascinans'*. Members of the contemporary Australian witchcraft community, Applegrove, make use of 'numinous' objects like altars, dress and rituals in order to transcend the profane and everyday world and commune with the sacred and the divine.

This theme is also explored by Nikki Bado in 'Encountering the *Universal* Triple Goddess in Wicca'. She acknowledges, though, that the ritual process itself is sometimes based on modern constructs far removed from the ancient cultures traditionally associated with myth and primal religion. We have to ask, writes Bado, whether in the Pagan and Goddess communities 'the Maiden, Mother, and Crone are either self-evident ancient and empowering figures that have been universally revered as primal archetypes since the dawn of time' or whether they are 'relatively recent romantic literary constructs rooted in dubious scholarship that are possibly essentialist, covertly sexist, and woefully inadequate in capturing the range of women's life cycles, roles, and expectations of longevity'. Bado acknowledges that like most religious practitioners, 'Witches participate in a universe of competing and sometimes conflicting discourses and practices.' But as a practising Wiccan High Priestess herself she nevertheless values the transformative experiences associated with Goddess spirituality despite their occasional contradictions — and these are experiences that involve both light and darkness. The Goddess, writes Bado, 'moves throughout the world, free and unfettered by our simplistic categories, embracing and embraced by Moon and Sun. Dancing in a universe of lights and shadows.'

And it proves to be very much a matter of light and shadow. As Marguerite Johnson's chapter on the Dark Goddess makes clear, there is now a tendency among 'Gothic' shadow-magic Wiccans to focus their ritual energies on imagery associated with the dark regions of the psyche in order to obtain an authentic balance between 'white' and 'black' magic.

Some Wiccan practitioners who practise Nocturnal Magic or Shadow Magic focus primarily on 'dark' goddesses like Hecate, Lilith and Kali. As Johnson explains, these 'Nocturnal' or 'Shadow' Wiccans are dismissive of 'Fluffy Bunnies', 'Playgans' or 'White-lighters' who interpret the Wiccan Rede literally—'An Ye Harm None, Do What Ye Will'. Nocturnal Wiccans openly embrace what others regard as a more confronting interpretation of the Craft. As one Wiccan practitioner, Digitalis, explains: 'The aspects of shadow magick range widely. In many ways, those that deal with the *internal* darkness of the self can be considered positive in nature: practices such as magickal work on the emotional plane, mysticism, and types of deep meditation. Other arts, such as divination, astral projection, automatic writing, and dreamwalking, are clearly not negative in nature (and are in fact shared by nearly all Witches). But some shadow magick can be deemed more negative: demonic evocation, Qlippothic [sic] or Goetic work, uncontrolled psychic vampirism, cursing, and some types of necromancy.'

Moving on from Wicca and Goddess spirituality to the resurgent interest in shamanism and 'native spirituality', it is fair to describe 'neo-shamanism'—like modern pagan witchcraft—as a construct or 'invented tradition'. Following the lead of anthropologist Michael Harner—who established the Foundation for Shamanic Studies and sought to distil common elements of the shamanic process into an accessible approach called 'core shamanism'[33]—various forms of neo-shamanism have now emerged in both the United States and Europe. Andrei A. Znamenski describes the growth of this movement in his chapter 'Neo-shamanism in the United States', acknowledging also the key role of Carlos Castaneda and Mircea Eliade in stimulating the revival of interest in Native American spirituality in the 1960s and 1970s counterculture.

Znamenski addresses the important issue of whether neo-shamanism loses its authenticity and usefulness by being abstracted from a specific cultural context. He also notes that some writers claim that traditional shamanism is a form of spiritual individualism and that this characteristic has been responsible in part for neo-shamanism's appeal, especially in the United States. The issue of whether core shamanism can be successfully reintroduced into various indigenous cultures that have lost their shamanic heritage—native peoples like the Sami, Siberians and Inuits, for example—is also addressed here.

Robert J. Wallis explores similar issues in 'Neo-shamanisms in Europe'. Wallis rejects universalist interpretations of shamanism and neo-shamanism as unhelpful abstractions, preferring instead to ground shamanisms (and neo-shamanisms) within their specific cultural contexts. Wallis argues against Eliade's concept of shamanistic world views based on a tripartite cosmology of upper, middle and lower worlds and maintains that the focus on 'altered states of consciousness' as a characteristic of shamanisms has also been greatly overstated. Rather than their experiences producing the 'world views' of their communities, he writes, shamans, their experiences and their communities, human and non-human, are situated within 'wider animic ontologies'. As Wallis explains, animist ontologies approach a world filled with persons, only some of whom are human, and often shamans are crucial in maintaining relations between human-persons and other-than-humans. Animisms are, then, concerned with *relating*—with persons, human and non-human, and 'animism makes shamans both possible and necessary because their roles are about dealing with the problems of living in a relational world'.

Jenny Blain's chapter 'Seidr oracles' focuses specifically on a form of oracular neo-shamanism based on re-constructed elements derived initially from Nordic mythology. Diana Paxson, founder of the seid-magic Hrafnar community in San Francisco, reconstructed *Eiríks Saga Rauða* and the Eddic *Voluspá* and began to use them experientially as a form of visionary magic. Paxson had also been influenced by the 'core shamanism' techniques of Michael Harner and her approach mirrors some aspects of the neo-shamanic spirit-journey. Paxson's *seidr* séances involve two main figures — the *völva* or seeress, and a person who serves as both guide and singer, chanting the *völva* and the other group participants into a state of trance. The songs are based on Nordic mythology and guide the participants toward Helheim, where the *völva* communicates with the ancestors. The *völva* enters a deeper state of trance as she goes through the gates of Helheim and then encounters the spirits of the dead. Members of the group are able to put oracular questions to the *völva* relating to more specific, local issues and circumstances. The *völva* typically receives 'answers' to these questions in the form of visual images received from the deities and ancestor spirits—and then conveys appropriate responses to the people who asked the questions.

As experiential journeys that venture beyond the gates of Helheim, *seidr* séances clearly employ imagery and techniques that take their practitioners into the dark mythic underworld of the magical psyche. However, as Blain explains, this particular form of visionary magic focuses on healing and divinatory methods that benefit the community members as a whole.

Looking back now to the origins of the 20th century magical revival, it is increasingly clear that the late 19th century Hermetic Order of the Golden Dawn—with its systematic approach to practical ceremonial magic and its focus on the quest for personal spiritual transformation—strongly influenced the various forms of esotericism that would emerge in the West in more recent times.

'Magical practices in the Hermetic Order of the Golden Dawn', describes the theurgic techniques adopted by members of this late 19th century organisation. Shunning darkness in the pursuit of spiritual light, the Golden Dawn magicians were influenced by the Kabbalistic desire to attain sacred knowledge of the 'Body of God'. The ultimate aim of their magical rituals was to experience what occult practitioner Israel Regardie has called 'a spiritual state of consciousness, in which the ego enters into a union with either its own Higher Self or a God'. However as the Hermetic Order of the Golden Dawn began to fragment during the period between 1900 and the end of World War One,[34] the practice of ceremonial magic in the West would become increasingly dominated by Aleister Crowley's doctrine of *Thelema* (Greek: 'will'). Historically this occurred as Crowley introduced sex magick into his magical order, Argenteum Astrum (The Silver Star, established 1907) and later into the European Ordo Templi Orientis.

Since the 1960s modern Western magical practice has polarized, producing two major streams of occult thought led on the one hand by Crowleyan *Thelema* and its various derivative offshoots and affiliated movements[35] and by Wicca and Goddess spirituality on the other (Wicca would not emerge as a major esoteric movement until the repeal in 1951 of the British Witchcraft Act forbidding the practice of witchcraft.)[36] Placing this polarization effect in a historical context, 'The Thelemic magick of Aleister Crowley' describes the significance of Crowley's 1904 revelation in Cairo and the emergence of *The Book of the Law*—a key Thelemite text dictated in trance by a metaphysical entity named Aiwass that changed Crowley's magical orientation completely. Moving away from the Hermetic theurgy of the Golden Dawn, a magical organisation to which he had belonged, Crowley now embraced a new form of sexual magick that, for him, characterised the birth of the New Aeon. Crowley's interest in sexual magick subsequently brought him into contact with the European Ordo Templi Orientis (O.T.O.)—an organisation that Crowley headed from 1922 onwards, following the resignation of co-founder Theodor Reuss.

One of the most interesting magical orders to have emerged in the post-Crowley era is the Dragon Rouge, established in Sweden by Thomas Karlsson in 1989. This order developed independently but shares many points in common with the Typhonian O.T.O. established in Britain by Crowley's disciple, the late Kenneth Grant. The Dragon Rouge openly aligns itself with the Left-Hand Path, which it refers to as 'the dark side of magic'. As Karlsson points out in his chapter 'The Draconian Tradition: Dragon Rouge and the Left-Hand Path', darkness equates symbolically with unfathomed potential and here the magician seeks to develop the individual human will in order to enter parallel universes. In the Dragon Rouge the Left-Hand Path is associated with 'the forbidden, the abnormal, the exclusive and deviant,...[and] celebrates dark and revolutionary deities like Lucifer, Loke, Kali, Hekate, Prometheus, Azazel and the Fallen Angels, to mention just a few.' The Dragon Rouge is antinomian and breaks cultural, religious and existential taboos—but the central aim is self-deification. As Karlsson observes: 'The Left Hand Path is associated with the goal to become a God, which means that one becomes existentially mature, expresses free will, takes personal responsibility and gains knowledge and power over existence.'

We turn now to contemporary Satanism, which also identifies itself with the so-called Left-Hand Path. It soon becomes apparent that there are marked differences between the two leading Satanic groups—Anton LaVey's Church of Satan (established in 1966) and The Temple of Set, headed by Michael Aquino (established in 1975)—although both are characteristically antinomian and share a common quest in embracing the potency of darkness. Under LaVey, the Church of Satan celebrated humanity's carnal nature and indulgences of the flesh and its founder justified this by asserting that an animalistic image of humanity was supported by natural science and Darwin's theory of evolution. In 'Claiming hellish hegemony: Anton LaVey, The Church of Satan and the *Satanic Bible*' James R. Lewis explores LaVey's legitimation strategy and dissects the façade created by Anton LaVey as he sought to develop an occult persona far more exotic than was actually warranted. In 1975 LaVey was deserted by a group of senior Church of Satan members who went on to establish the more philosophically based Temple of Set. A former High Priest of this Temple, Don Webb provides us with a lucid 'insider' account in his essay 'Modern black magic: initiation, sorcery and the Temple of Set'.

The following chapters, 'The Magical Life of Ithell Colquhoun' and 'Two chthonic magical artists: Austin Osman Spare and Rosaleen Norton', explore the visionary art and creativity of three important modern occultists. Focusing especially on the connection between modern Western magic and artistic creativity, Amy Hale shows in 'The magical life of Ithell Colquhoun' that in addition to embracing a Hermetic approach to magic the noted British surrealist artist was also fascinated by the symbolic attributions of colour that she first encountered in the Golden Dawn approach to Western ceremonial magic. Spare and Norton had a somewhat darker vision, and have even been accused of being satanic. Spare and Norton both produced magical imagery that was markedly chthonic in nature and both artists utilised techniques of self-hypnosis to produce their visionary imagery. They also explored magical grimoires like the Goetia and were fascinated by the sigils or 'seals' associated with elemental spirit-beings. Both artists were attracted to sex-magic and both were familiar with the magical writings of Aleister Crowley (Spare knew Crowley personally).

Crowley's influence has extended in recent times to include practitioners of Chaos Magick who align themselves with the Left-Hand Path and who use this term emically to describe their magical orientation. Chaos Magick—generally spelt with a 'k' to acknowledge its connection to Thelemic magick—burst onto the British occult scene in the late 1970s with a radical outlook and a reformist agenda. In his chapter, 'Nothing is true, everything is permitted: Chaos magics in Britain' Dave Evans describes the birth of the movement, noting in passing that it presents us with a multitude of interesting and rewarding challenges. 'As a major, influential and fast-moving new development in occultism,' he writes, it 'cannot be ignored and offers an enticing arena for researchers in finding new, improved research strategies which will hopefully evolve in tandem with the developments in the magical practice itself.'

Also of interest in this particular context are magical practices that draw inspiration from fiction and the Internet. In the realm of cyberspace human beings interact with each other in ways limited only by their imagination. In her fascinating chapter, 'The Computer Mediated Religious Life of Ttechnoshamans and Cybershamans' Libuše Martínková shows clearly that some contemporary magical practitioners have integrated cutting-edge computer technologies and traditional shamanic practices in order to give rise to a new form of postmodern religion.

Finally, there are those who have embraced more eclectic esoteric fusions. The influential British occultist Phil Hine, who has been closely associated in the past with the rise of Chaos Magick, provides an insider account of his 'hybridised Tantra practice'. Hine describes the Arrow-Shakti rite—which utilises both external worship (*bahiryaga*) and internal worship (*antaryaga*). Here the practitioner exteriorises the Sense-Shaktis in order to honor them before drawing back the Arrow Goddess (their condensed form) into the 'heart-cave' that equates with the seat of the inner self.

As will become clear to any reader perusing the chapters in this anthology, the major forms of contemporary Western magic are characterised by an ongoing sense of self-exploration and spiritual renewal. *Pathways in Modern Western Magic* will hopefully be seen as a far-ranging and authoritative selection of writings addressing the broad spectrum of modern Western magical beliefs and practices.

—*Editor*

Endnotes

1. Four of these publications focus on modern and contemporary magic in Britain. Tanya Luhrmann's *Persuasions of the Witch's Craft* (Harvard University Press, Cambridge, Massachusetts 1989) explores contemporary Wicca and white magic in England, Ronald Hutton's *The Triumph of the Moon* (Oxford University Press, Oxford 1999) is considered the definitive historical study of modern pagan witchcraft and explores the birth of Wicca in England and events leading up to it, Susan Greenwood's *The Nature of Magic: An Anthropology of Consciousness* (Berg, Oxford 2005) describes nature magic, witchcraft and neo-shamanism in contemporary Britain, and Alex Owen's *The Place of Enchantment* (University of Chicago Press, Chicago 2004) is a highly regarded scholarly overview of occult practices in Victorian and Edwardian England. Nikki Bado-Fralick's *Coming to the Edge of the Circle: A Wiccan Initiation Ritual* (Oxford University Press, New York 2005) is of special interest because the American author is both an academic and a high priestess within a Wiccan coven, and Hugh Urban's *Magia Sexualis* (University of California Press, Berkeley, California 2006) looks likely to become a key source-work on sexual magic in the West for many years to come.
2. See M. Harris, *Cultural Materialism*, Random House, New York 1979.
3. P.E. Sandstrom, 'Anthropological Approaches to Information Systems and Behaviour', *Bulletin of the American Society for Information Science and Technology*, 30, 3, February/March 2004.
4. M. Harris, *Cultural Materialism*, loc cit: 32.
5. Ibid: 315.
6. Ibid.
7. L. Hume, *Witchcraft and Paganism in Australia*, Melbourne University Press, Melbourne 1997:11.
8. R.L. Stein and P.L. Stein, *The Anthropology of Religion, Magic and Witchcraft*, Pearson/Allyn & Bacon, Boston 2005: 21-23.
9. T.M. Luhrmann, *Persuasions of the Witch's Craft: Ritual Magic in Contemporary England*, loc cit.
10. J. Favret-Saada, *Deadly Words: Witchcraft in the Bocage*, Cambridge University Press, Cambridge 1980.
11. P. Stoller (and C. Olkes), *In Sorcery's Shadow*, University of Chicago Press, Chicago 1987.
12. L. Hume, *Witchcraft and Paganism in Australia*, Melbourne University Press, Melbourne 1997.
13. S. Greenwood, *Magic, Witchcraft and the Otherworld*, Berg, Oxford and New York 2000, and *The Nature of Magic: an Anthropology of Consciousness*, Berg, Oxford and New York 2005.
14. N. Bado-Fralick, *Coming to the Edge of the Circle: A Wiccan Initiation*

Ritual, Oxford University Press, New York 2005.
15 A.Crowley, *Magick in Theory and Practice*, Castle Books, New York, n.d:[1929]:11.
16 Ibid: 4.
17 Ibid:xii.
18 Ibid xiii.
19 Ibid:xvii. It is interesting that of all the religious pantheons Crowley utilized for his magical activities he regarded the ancient Egyptian as 'the noblest, the most truly magical'. See A.Crowley, *Magick without Tears*, Falcon Press, Phoenix, Arizona 1982: 23. Crowley would surely have known that in ancient Egypt magicians could subdue even the gods themselves, through acts of magical intent. As Wallis Budge has observed (E.A.Wallis Budge, *Egyptian Magic*, University Books, New York 1958: ix [1899]): '...the object of Egyptian magic was to endow man with the means of compelling both friendly and hostile powers, nay, at a later time, even God Himself, to do what he wished, whether they were willing or not.' Budge subsequently elaborates on the potency of words of power uttered by the magician: ' By pronouncing certain words or names of power in the proper manner and in the proper tone of voice he could heal the sick, and cast out the evil spirits which caused pain and suffering in those who were diseased, and restore the dead to life, and bestow upon the dead man the power to transform the corruptible into an incorruptible body wherein the soul might live to all eternity. His words enabled human beings to assume diverse forms at will, and to project their souls into animals and other creatures...The powers of nature acknowledged his might, and wind and rain, storm and tempest, river and sea, and disease and death worked evil and ruin upon his foes, and upon the enemies of those who were provided with the knowledge of the words which he had wrested from the gods of heaven, and earth, and the underworld. Inanimate nature likewise obeyed such words of power, and even the world itself came into existence through the utterance of a word by Thoth; by their means the earth could be rent asunder, and the waters forsaking their nature could be piled in a heap, and even the sun's course in the heavens could be stayed by a word. No god, or spirit, or devil, or fiend, could resist words of power.' (1958:xi).
20 I. Regardie, *The Middle Pillar*, Aries Press, Chicago: 1945: 19.
21 This quotation incorporates the magical concept that the repeated performance of the same rituals - whether by magicians or religious practitioners - has a cumulative effect on the 'inner planes', an effect referred to as the 'egregore' or 'group consciousness'. W.E.Butler, a disciple of Dion Fortune in the Fraternity of the Inner Light, describes the nature of the egregore in *The Magician: His Training and Work* [1959]: ' When

two or three or many people gather together in one place to perform certain actions, to think along certain lines, and to experience emotional influences, there is built up, in connection with that group, what may be termed a composite group-consciousness, wherein the emotional and and mental forces of all the members of the group are temporarily united in what is known in occultism as a group-thought-form or "artificial elemental". This group consciousness seems to have a much greater power that the simple sum of the objective minds in the group would suggest. This is because, not only is the group-thought-form built up by the *conscious* minds of all who help to build it up. Since those subconscious minds reach back on the one hand into the Collective Unconscious and on the other reach upwards into the realms of the superconscious, the group-thought-form is psychically linked with...many aspects of thought and many forms of psychic-mental energy. Thus it is greater than any sum of its parts.' See W.E.Butler, *The Magician: His Training and Work*, 1959: 57-58.

22 I. Regardie, *Ceremonial Magic: A Guide to the Mechanisms of Ritual*, loc.cit: 93.
23 Ibid: 93-94.
24 The *Ain Soph* is the 'limitless light' that extends beyond finite creation as delineated on the Kabbalistic Tree of Life.
25 Ibid: 246-47.
26 Quoted in D.Valiente, *An ABC of Witchcraft, Past and Present*, revised edition, Hale, London 1984: 231.
27 Quoted from Flying Roll No. 5 (Golden Dawn source document), 'Some Thoughts on the Imagination' in F. King (ed.) *Astral Projection, Magic and Alchemy*, Spearman, London 1971: 33.
28 D.Fortune, *The Mystical Qabalah*, Benn, London 1935: 11.
29 Quoted by Fortune's magical disciple W.E.Butler and ascribed to her. See W.E.Butler, *Magic: Its Ritual Power and Purpose*, Aquarian Press, London 1952: 10.
30 M.Aquino, 'Black Magic in Theory and Practice,' in M.Aquino (ed.) *The Crystal Tablets of Set, Selected Extracts*, Temple of Set, San Francisco 1983: 18 and 28.
31 Starhawk, *The Spiral Dance: A Rebirth of the Ancient Religion of the Great Goddess*, 20th Anniversary edition, HarperCollins, San Francisco 1999 [1979]:155.
32 Ibid: 159.
33 See Harner's key work on experiential shamanism, *The Way of the Shaman*, Harper & Row, New York 1980.
34 MacGregor Mathers, the influential co-founder of the Golden Dawn, died in 1918.

35 These include the Ordo Templi Orientis in the United States, the Typhonian O.T.O. in Britain, and the Church of Satan and the Temple of Set in the United States. Chaos Magick has also been strongly influenced by Crowley.
36 The Witchcraft Act 1735 was repealed in New South Wales by the Imperial Acts Application Act, 1969. See L. Hume, *Witchcraft and Paganism in Australia*, Melbourne University Press, Melbourne 1997: 224.

1
Lifting the Veil: An Emic Approach to Magical Practice

Lynne Hume

The term 'magic' conjures up evil powers, the black arts, and even figures of the devil, for some, while for others, a false belief that is absurd and ridiculous. Anthropologists have commonly looked upon magic as illogical, irrational, and therefore erroneous, recognizing however, that indigenous cultures strongly engage with the belief and efficacy of magic. They have therefore been forced to account for it in some way. These accounts invariably fall into psychological or functional explanations. The notion that magic might in fact, have some basis, has been summarily dismissed. Nevertheless, occult practitioners who engage with magic and practise it on a regular basis, accept that it is real.

In this chapter, it is not my intention to prove or disprove whether magic is true or false. Instead, in order to recount perspectives on magical practice and how 'magical consciousness' can be put into effect, I take the position of the occult practitioner who 'knows' that magic, in a very broad sense, is possible. In pursuing this line of thinking, I offer some practical techniques that have been used cross-culturally for opening up magical consciousness, variously referred to as 'lifting the veil', 'moving through the portal', 'crossing the bridge' and similar metaphors, to recount what practitioners have to say about their experiences, and to see where it leads them. When investigating the universal commonalities that underlie both experiences and techniques of magical practice, one detects the same threads that bind them to each other, albeit through cultural lenses and individual narrative expressions.

Magical consciousness is a different way of looking at the world. It is based upon certain premises, the most important of these being that other dimensions or realities exist, that it is possible to tap into these dimensions, and that the imagination is seminal to the practice of magic. Some might prefer to call these different realities different levels of consciousness; to a magical practitioner they are interchangeable concepts.

A pervasive notion is that energy, vibrations, and frequencies permeate the entire cosmos, and there is a constantly moving flow of energy that not only flows through the cosmos, but through our bodies, energizing our organs via the chakras. If this energy becomes blocked it creates physical, emotional or mental pain of some sort. Energy is the basis of illness and spiritual healing, the latter being undertaken by the healer working with these energy flows. Much of the alternative healing in the Western world and traditional healing in other cultures is also based on this idea. Other dimensions are also made up of energy patterns that 'vibrate' at different frequencies. In order to 'tune in' to those realities, the practitioner needs to change his or her own vibrational frequencies to match those particular realities. Once this is attained, it is possible to open oneself up to beings in those dimensions and to gain knowledge. Rick Strassman (2001:549), who has employed the entheogenic method of entering an altered state of consciousness, specifically using DMT (dimethyltryptamine), which he refers to as the 'spirit molecule' writes that there are 'different levels of reality permeating and suffusing our own' and that beings in those other realities can observe us directly with their own senses or by using particular types of technology. A sobering thought.

In *Stalking the Wild Pendulum*, Itzhak Bentov suggests that we are pulsating beings in a vibrating universe, in constant motion between the finite and the infinite and our bodies mirror the universe, down to the working of each cell. This description reflects the occult maxim, 'as above, so below', attributed to Hermes Trismegistus. The 'pendulum' in the title refers to Bentov's premise: when a pendulum swings from one side to the other, there is a point at which, for an infinitesimal fraction, it stops, before the momentum takes it on to the opposite side of the swing. During this non-moment, or 'fraction-stop', it is possible for time to stop. It is the gap between, the space between. And in this non-moment, it is possible to move beyond the confines of the body, and shoot out into the universe and beyond. The clock is objective time (this worldly), writes Bentov, and methodically marches on in its predictable way for us humans in our everyday busy worlds. One could compare objective time to the rational mind with its focus on logical explanations and material explanations for phenomena.

Subjective time, on the other hand, is less predictable, less exact; it is, for example, those times when we might be engrossed in an activity and then realize that a couple of hours seem to have 'flown past' in a matter of minutes. We have entered into what Csikszentmihalyi calls 'the flow'. During 'flow' we can engage with all our senses in the activity at hand and become oblivious to everything else. Csikszentmihalyi gives the example of rock climbing as an activity in which the climber is so concentrated on the climb that he is at one with the mountain; time does not have much meaning. In subjective time, we might be sitting in the dentist's chair, or find ourselves forced into a conversation with someone who is utterly dull, at which time a few minutes turns into an interminable length of time. Or, we might be engrossed in a good book and look up at the clock, surprised to see that a couple of hours has gone by. Depending upon how our attention is taken, the emotions surrounding the event, and our pleasure or displeasure at the way we are being engaged, time might 'stand still'. Bentov takes this metaphorical expression a bit further with his notion of the swinging pendulum, and the 'fraction stop', to say that time does more than stand still metaphorically; it actually stops. If one is able to engage both in very deep meditation, and then consciously glance over at a clock, the meditator sees that the second hand has stopped. The moment he thinks to himself about what he is doing, the second hand begins to move again as he is back in objective time.

If we are listening to music that we particularly like, subjective time might take us into the mind of a composer; as Schutz suggests, we are 'tuning in' to the mind of the composer, and at these times we might sit, suspended in time, at one with the music, with no thought of time. In these times we are in a light trance, or an altered state of consciousness. During these moments, our observing self, which Bentov equates with the psyche, is not restricted by time or space; we have entered into the 'space between' and space and time as we ordinarily know them (objective) can be transgressed (subjective). In an expanded, or altered state of consciousness, the person has experiences that defy time and space. They may leave their physical body, travel thousands of miles away and return—all in a fraction of a second. Our non-physical body, even though tenuously linked to the physical body, can find itself crossing the speed of light barrier and rapidly moving about in the universe and beyond. Most of Bentov's ideas are mirrored in the esoteric branches of traditional religions, in shamanism, and in contemporary alternative spiritualities, and we find the same ideas appearing repeatedly in occult literature.

The triad of magical consciousness: ASCs, Emotion, and Imagination

Altered States of Consciousness

The key to transverse the imaginary line between the physical world and the non-physical world is an altered state of consciousness (ASC), defined by Charles Tart (2009) as a '*radical* alteration of the overall patterning of consciousness such that the experiencer ... can tell that *different laws are functioning,* that a new, overall pattern is superimposed on his experiences' (my emphasis). Tart has worked for many years on the nature of consciousness, particularly on altered states of consciousness, and is one of the founders of the field of transpersonal psychology. He insists that unseen forces such as telepathy, clairvoyance, precognition, psychokinesis, psychic healing, and other phenomena inextricably link us to the spiritual world. Further, that the experiences of millions of people indicate that they do take place.

What is meant by 'different laws are functioning'? Hermeticist Franz Bardon tells us that our material plane of existence is bound to time and space, while the astral plane is bound only to space, and the mental plane is both time-less and space-less. At this point, we seem to be entering the world of quantum physics, but as I am not a physicist, I am reluctant to introduce quantum physics into the equation.

Instead, to help explain that different laws are functioning, we might employ the German word *umweldt*, roughly translated as 'the world as perceived', used in the context of perception and surroundings. For example, in order for us to understand why an organism does what it does, we have to understand how the organism perceives and processes everything in its surroundings. The idea is generally used in animal behaviour. For example, with regard to bees, it was discovered that bees can perceive ultraviolet wavelengths of energy, which are undetectable to humans, and, through the use of ultraviolet-sensitive film, that patterns exist on many flowers that aid the bee to find nectar and pollen as well as helping the plant to reproduce. The *umweldt* of bees thus becomes, through technology, more easily understandable to humans, who have a different *umweldt*. This assumes however, the fact that there are ultraviolet wavelengths of energy. If it is possible for a bee to perceive these wavelengths, then perhaps it is possible for humans under the right circumstances.

Prior to the use of technology that allows us to perceive these ultraviolet wavelengths of energy, our human biological limitations left us ignorant of this symbiotic relationship between bees and flowers, even though we could see, with our naked eye, that there was some sort of relationship between them. If perceptions are reality, then limited perceptions only provide us with a small portion of the whole of reality. In some trance states, a person undergoes a transformation or metamorphosis, such that they may *become* something other than themselves, or at least subjectively experience this. A friend in the same room, staying in objective reality would not see the change, but someone else in a magically altered state, may see what the person in trance is experiencing. This sounds quite incredible but remember that, in an altered state, different laws are functioning.

During my research into Paganism (Hume 1997), I came across several people who had seen energy forms, and others who had experienced their bodies metamorphose into birds or animals that took them on journeys. This does not mean that other people present saw any change, or even that their physical bodies had changed, but that the individuals concerned *felt* that they had transformed. Shamans cross-culturally refer to the notion of human-animal metamorphosis or shape-shifting, which is the ability to change human shape into animals or other forms. Transformation into animal form is common and a shaman will usually have one particular bird or animal who acts as his guardian spirit. Among Siberian shaman it might be the reindeer, bear, bird or deer, while for the Huichol shaman of New Mexico, it might be a wolf, and for the Amazonian shaman it might be a jaguar. On the Asian continent, fish, birds, insects or invertebrates might be the guardian spirit (Riboli 2004:255-259). acting as the intermediaries between this world and the next. Metamorphosis enables the shaman to acquire some of the powers attributed to the animal world.

ASCs also allow energy forms or spirit forms to become visible. I refer to Edith Turner's ritual experience among the Ndembu of Africa when she participated in a healing ritual with *ihamba* spirit doctors in order to extract a bad spirit from a sick woman's body. With the aid of a medicine given to her to drink so that she would be 'opened from the inside', and becoming fully engaged in the drumming, shouting and emotional excitement of all the participants in the ritual, her own body became 'deeply involved' in the rhythm and passion of the ritual. At the high point of the ritual when the healing took place, Turner realized that all the Africans saw the same thing she did because everyone present shouted in amazed recognition at the same time. What she saw was 'a giant thing' like 'a large gray blob about six inches across, opaque and something between solid and smoke' emerge from the sick woman's back. This experience convinced her that 'spirits exist' (Turner 1994:71-95).

Contemporary Pagans use various meditative and trance techniques that are very similar to techniques used in many cultures throughout the world, in order to achieve a heightened sense of psychic awareness. Some use chanting and drumming to move between what Michael Harner (1990:xix). calls an ordinary state of consciousness (OSC), the reality we know in our everyday lives, and a shamanic state of consciousness (SSC), the reality of the altered state of consciousness.

Cultivating an active imagination and the ability to go into trance are consistently reported as essential to developing psychic awareness. I would add the willingness to 'let go' of inhibitions and to abandon disbelief. In my own experiences in altered states, having abandoned disbelief and opened myself up to the possibilities that strange things happen when one does so, I have at different times seen energy flows and energy 'sparks' emitting from my fingertips, felt that I was levitating, and sensed presences in the room when there was no-one there. Most psychic exercises are made more effective by relaxing both the body and the mind, and putting aside internal questions and arguments that it's not going to work. Keys to the development of psychic awareness and gaining occult knowledge are the practice of meditation, the cultivation of an active imagination, and the ability to go into trance. In addition to meditation, altered states can be achieved through physical exertion, chanting, listening to persistent and continual monotonous sound such as drumming, trance dance or movement, and performing rituals of significance in a sacred space or place. Sensorial awareness is increased when any of these methods are practiced regularly and over time, so that one may 'see' that which is not seen with normal vision, 'feel' presences that are not normally felt, or 'hear' in a clairaudient manner.

Emotion

Another important element in magical consciousness is emotion, which may affect the outcome of an experience, or may be the precursor of an experience. 'Set', the mindset or psychological state of the person and 'setting', the immediate environment, or space one establishes prior to ingestion, have been stated as crucial components to any outcome or experience. Huichol Indian peyote-takers recognize this fact and say that peyote needs to be taken with a 'pure heart' for the experience to be happy or joyous and without the nausea or terror that might accompany its use. If peyote is eaten by someone who is not 'properly prepared' and under the direction of an experienced shaman-priest, bad visions occur (Myerhoff 2009:300).

Set and setting can also make a difference in experiences that do not include the taking of entheogens. In Christian charismatic congregations that include highly emotionally-charged songs of praise, spontaneous and joyful singing and expectations of divine presence and divine healing, all contain worship that focus on the love felt towards Jesus or the Holy Spirit. During these services, deep emotions can create such surges of feeling that most of the congregation might express being personally transformed, or filled with the joy and love of Jesus. Strong emotions are highly significant to the success of rituals of healing in other cultures: the Ndembu healing ceremony in Africa, the !Kung Bushmen trance healing dances in the Kalahari, and the Sufis, for example. The Sufis speak of 'heart', and when a Sufi meditates with ardent desire and strong will, it can culminate in mystical knowledge. Highly emotional thoughts generate strong energy patterns and in Western Esoteric magical practices, emotion can be used to attain certain magical goals (Hume 2007:19-23).

Imagination
Fairy tales depict wondrous magic realms of unseen things, and speak the language of the unconscious mind. These stories allow us glimpses into a world of make-believe that might possibly be true. Fantasy fiction touches on 'the elusive proximity of an otherworld or otherworlds to and from which it is possible to travel with care or dangerous folly'; they offer 'mirrors to reality' (Harvey 2006:41). The enormous popularity of stories such as *Lord of the Rings*, the *Harry Potter* series, *Avatar*, and other books and films of this ilk, demonstrate that we are still captivated by the metaphysical and the mystical, even in the 21st century. Indeed, *Avatar*, with its third-dimensional component, engages our whole bodies in fantastic scenarios where we fly on the backs of monstrous birds and engage with non-human entities.

Tales like *Alice in Wonderland* also have metaphysically significant aspects to them—the black and white tiles of the Masons, the corporeal shrinkage and enlargement of Alice's body, the caterpillar smoking a pipe and sitting on a mushroom, all hint at magical practices or techniques. The playful imagination has been explained as the capacity to place oneself in an 'illusionistic world of the mythical and the metaphorical' (Pruyser, cited in Bainbridge, 1997:9), and make-believe as the realm of the possible (Singer, 1995). According to David Miller (1970), play and fantasy serve to free humans from fossilized thinking, opening up new ways of looking at life. So we begin early in life with a solid grasp on the enormous possibilities of the imagination.

Occultists, shamans and magical practitioners alike take the imagination a step further, by enhancing the imagination through actively promoting and exercising mental imagery. Guided journeys of the imagination, using vocal and visual maps, can guide a person along pathways leading to landscapes of the mind, fantastic realms or otherworlds. Such mind journeys often give people the chance to tap into their subconscious in ways that might throw some light on past or present problems.

Mental imagery cultivation exists in a wide variety of societies throughout the world and is defined by Richard Noll (1985:444) as 'the deliberate, repeated induction of enhanced mental imagery'. R.A. Finke (1980:113) informs us that when mental images are formed, our visual mechanisms respond in much the same way as they do when 'real' objects are observed; the image is seen as if it were an actual object. Furthermore, the more vivid the image created in the mind's eye, the more strongly these mechanisms respond, and the more similar to actual objects or events the mental image appears. Mental imaging (visualization) is used as a means of gaining access to an alternate reality, and is a tool which has functional value: to induce and highlight the experience.

Interestingly, the esoteric branches of all the major religions use mental imagery. Imagery and visualization are so important to the Sufi, that Ibn 'Arabi declared: 'He in whom the Active Imagination is not at work will never penetrate to the heart of the question' (Corbin 1969:38), and 'thinking in pictures' is used to optimum advantage in Tantric Buddhism. Csordas (1994) notes that Catholic Charismatics imagine Jesus in human form when they are healing members of their congregations. A mental image can be reinforced by concentrating the mind on the pictorial image so that it becomes almost tangible. 'The mind,' writes magician W.E. Butler, 'supplies the forms and channels through which the forces [energies] work, and the more definite the channel, the more control can be exercised over the forces flowing therein' (1970:39).

Magic workers (for example Franz Bardon, W.E. Butler, Aleister Crowley, Starhawk) realize the crucial importance of the imagination and all have exercises to both promote and enhance mental imagery cultivation, as do shamans cross-culturally. Creative visualization and a 'steady mind' are said to be most useful tools in order to function well in different realities. Indigenous shamanic vision cultivation invariably involves increasing the vividness of the imagery, using both psychological and physiological techniques, then increasing the controlledness of the visual imagery contents in order to engage and manipulate the phenomena envisioned (see Richard Noll for more on this). Basic exercises concentrate on imagining with the 'mind's eye', picturing the form, colour, size, and depth of an object, for example, then projecting it from the 'mind's eye' to beyond the body, and controlling both the image and the time it is held in this manner for as long as possible. Czaplicka (cited in Noll 1985) writes that the Samoyed *tadibey* cover their eyes so that they can more easily penetrate into the spirit world by their inner sight.

At first an image might be seen momentarily, but with practice a more sustained image can be maintained. In *The Magician: His Training and Work*, W.E. Butler writes (p.61):

> *For successful magical work it is absolutely essential that the operator should be able to build up mental images, since [...] the forces of the Astral Light are directed and controlled by such mental images. It is therefore evident that the would-be magician must gain proficiency in this image-building if he is to do any effective work.*

This *willed* projection can be extended to other sensory modalities. Training for audible image-making is done through the use of a gradually diminishing sound, and the projection of audible images is assisted by using aids such as large sea-shells. All magical work, writes Butler, 'begins within and is projected outwardly', and this is one of the first principles of magic. Aboriginal Australians' explanations of the 'strong eye' or 'inner eye', which enables an Aboriginal 'clever man' to see illnesses in the body or see through objects, say that it is like Western X-ray machines. The ability to do this is usually acquired during the clever man's arduous training period. Unhealthy organs are detected by their colour and brightness, or lack thereof. Curiously resembling the 'gray blob' seen by Edith Turner, some accounts report that the internal organs vary from a healthy 'clear' transparency to an unhealthy grey or black (Coate, quoted in Hume 2002:138).

Journey meditations to mythic realms of the Icelandic sagas where spirits and mythic beings may be encountered is achieved by the *Seid*-workers, contemporary practitioners of Northern European Heathenism (see Jenny Blain 2002). These journeys are aided by the Seid-workers' deep immersion, over time, in the appropriate mythology, literature and folklore, the Eddas and Icelandic sagas, Old English poetry, folktales and folklore from Scotland, England, Scandinavia and much of Europe. They are, therefore, thoroughly versed in imaginary tales that will assist them in their visualizations. As an additional aid they enter a trance state through drumming, rattling, rune-chanting, dance, and a repetitive pattern of question and answer that help the seer/seeress to sustain a focused trance. Some may also use entheogens, also known as 'teacher-plants' or consciousness-altering substances such as cannabis, peyote, or psilocybin mushrooms (Blain 2002:53).

Apropos the use of entheogens, shamans world-wide have made use of psychoactive plants to elicit encounters with other entities in order to gain information about a patient's illness, diagnosis, and to learn other information that is useful to members of the shaman's community. Individuals in some contemporary alternative spiritualities have discovered that psychedelic drugs engender encounters with 'discarnate spirit entities', or 'conscious autonomous spirits or intelligences' (Letcher 2007:77). Andy Letcher looks at what happens to consciousness under the influence of 'magic' mushrooms with psilocybin properties. In order to make sense of these experiences, proffers Letcher, we need to talk about them using a series of resistive discourses (animistic for example), that take into account the subjective experience of mushroom ingestion, instead of a discourse based only on observation that results in a pathological or psychological analysis.

Andy Letcher is an academic with personal experience of the ingestion of psychoactive plants. The 'profound spiritual and ontological impact' (Letcher 2007:78) of his experiences over a period of fifteen years led to his personal interest in myco-spirituality, an alternative spirituality that incorporates psilocybin mushrooms, and spiked his professional interest in how these experiences are analyzed by academics. He points out that there are two major streams of discourses about the ingestion of entheogens: the objective, non-experiential one used by scientists, and the subjective, experiential one used by those engaged in the practices. The latter say that non-human entities cannot be fully explained using the former approach. More importantly, it is possible to perceive: 'genuine beneficent discarnate entities or intelligences' that can impart important information to humans.

If we return to the term '*umweldt*', introduced earlier, the psilocybin ingestor is, following Letcher's argument, opening him/herself up to the *umweldt* of discarnate entities through the mushroom experience. Letcher (2007:88) also employs the term 'frequency', saying that psychedelics allow ingestors to perceive a 'different frequency' in much the same way as tuning in to a different radio station. Once the communication is made, these entities can impart helpful information such as the prognosis of an illness.

Just as indigenous shamans 'see' and experience a hidden world that is 'real', accounts by Western contemporary pagans reveal that their experiences of alternate realities have a clarity of perception and a vividness that is absent in our normal everyday world; there even exist colours in that world which do not appear in the physical world. Starhawk (1979) writes that experience that begins in the imagination actually becomes real, although it is a different reality to that of the physical senses; it is 'the reality of the underlying energy currents that shape the universe'. She uses the term 'astral vision' (the 'inner eye' of the shaman) to refer to the experience of that other reality. Starhawk talks of a created internal Place of Power which one can readily access through visualization. This is confirmed by other pagans who say that when they have created an 'astral temple' they can readily return to it by simply visualizing it.

The most elementary aspect to magic mental training, imagination, includes single-minded concentration on an image, while using controlled breathing (Bardon 1993:57). In training the imagination to hold on to a single thought or image, a novice might place several small objects on a tray, close the eyes and 'see' the objects, noting their exact size, colour, shape and position on the tray relative to each other. The next step is to hold this image for as long as five minutes, and then to open the eyes and project the image on to a blank wall, holding the image there once the phantom image produced by the eye mechanism has faded. The key is to develop the imagination until an image becomes a reality. This requires focus, concentration, and willpower. Bardon's book, *Initiation into Hermetics*, is replete with similar exercises to develop magical attributes through all the senses, not just the visual. The imagination extends equally to other senses as well as the visual. Training techniques to enhance magical consciousness pay attention to all the senses. For example, to enhance clairaudience, the novice is told to imagine the ticking of a clock, then enhance the sound, sustain the sound in the same way as the above exercises for visual imagery. Similarly, sensations of touch and taste can be imagined, enhanced and sustained. In this manner, the magician trains and strengthens all the senses.

When we are awake, but relaxed, or in what is often referred to as a 'daydream', our brain is measuring brainwave patterns in the 7.0 to 13.0 hertz, or cycles per second (cps). In a fully awake, fully focused state our brain wave patterns show in the 13.0 cps to 40.0 cps, known as the Beta state. In deep sleep, we are in Delta, which measures less than 3.5 cps. Between Delta and Alpha states is Theta, measuring 3.5 to 7.0 cps. The Theta state is when we experience lucid dreams, mental images, out-of-body experiences (OBEs), and astral projection. This is the state which is sought after by magical practitioners.

The study of altered states may itself be influenced by the scientific paradigms to which the observer adheres (Tart). Charles Tart believes it is important to recognize that ultimately all forms of scientific knowledge are *experiential* and:

> *The first step in bridging the gap between science and the spiritual... is that we must recognize that since all knowledge is fundamentally experiential, the observation of experience and the refinement of this kind of observation is legitimate and is the foundation of any psychological sciences we will build in this area. We cannot ignore data that is not physical ... the ortho-*

> dox scientist makes an error in dismissing a priori the data of
> spiritual experience and discrete altered states of conscious-
> ness because of his paradigmatic commitments ...

This sentiment is reiterated by David Howes, who comments that 'psychology itself is a cultural construct', and neuroscientists are 'remarkably insensitive to cultural influences' (Howes 2000:16).

Conclusion

One of the arguments used against magic is that it is irrational. When I made this comment to a magical practitioner I interviewed in Australia in 1996, she replied: 'You're right, it's not rational, that's the whole idea— you have to get out of your rational mind and into your imaginal mind. Allow your imagination to take over.' Entrenched skeptics emphatically refuse to entertain the idea of other realities, spirit-beings, and the existence of anything that alludes to the metaphysical, and it is only the brave, the retired, or the very persistent who pursue the topic 'as if it were real', or 'it is real'. There is now a growing number of serious researchers who are not only taking these things seriously, but have themselves experimented with different techniques and technologies, and have suggested that we should remove our heads from the sand to look at anomalous phenomena as a study worthy of academic research (Greenwood 2009:5).

While healthy skepticism is warranted, there is a place in research for the methodology that anthropologists are renowned for: participant observation. This type of methodology is based on the researcher approaching the object of research with an open mind and a willingness to observe, listen, and take part (hence the 'participant') in what his/her community of people are actually saying and doing. If we merely take note of the cultural elements that we can safely believe are real to us (kinship systems, political organization, material objects), casting aside or failing to report information that doesn't fit with our own scheme of possibilities, we will never get the full picture. Our ethnographies will be incomplete. If we go into an indigenous culture, record the stories, sacred sites, collect the sacred artifacts, and even testify in court about a people's right to their land because of their intrinsic sacred connections to that land, but put aside as nonsensical those same beliefs that attach them to the sacred because we profess to be atheists, we are not going to understand much, if anything, of what they are telling us at a very deep level.

Doing is knowing, from the inside, what the insider is talking about: what it feels like to participate in a sweat lodge (the heat, being with other bodies, the darkness, the smells, the rough feel of what you are sitting on, the taste of the food, the emotions that all this evokes); what it feels like to be part of a ritual, under a full moon, in the company of cloaked others, to smell the fragrance of incense, to see the play of light and shadows, to hear and feel the sound of drums, bare feet touching the earth, and to sense the anticipation and excitement that this might produce in everyone present. What happens when you've followed instructions, and after many failed attempts, you actually succeed in having an out-of-body experience? How do you maintain entrenched skepticism after such personal experiences? Or, how to account for the fact that it was not just you who saw spirit during a healing ritual, but that others present experienced or saw, the same thing you did?

Using its unique methodology of participant observation, many fieldworkers have done much more than 'observe', and 'participation' has moved from the level of participating in the everyday mundane lives of the people with whom they have worked, to a much more radical type of participation that involves deep immersion into the psychic and dream world of both villagers and urban dwellers alike, in all sorts of cultures and situations. The willingness of researchers to engage in radical empiricism, and to jump in where others fear to tread, has opened up anthropology in exciting and novel ways. See for example, the writings of Jenny Blain, Susan Greenwood, Andy Letcher, Robert Wallis, Edith Turner, David Turner, Michael Harner, Paul Stoller, Bruce Grindal, David Young and Jean-Guy Goulet, to mention just a few. Spiritual anthropology is a term now being used to discuss the aspect of anthropology previously termed transpersonal anthropology.

Fieldwork experiences of a spiritual nature might have been suppressed in the past, but once the lid was lifted from Pandora's Box, there emerged a veritable plethora of vivid accounts by fieldworkers, and people in other disciplines, to create what has been an explosion of interest in the area of consciousness studies as it pertains to the metaphysical. Many, if not most, of these radical empiricists now accept that there is something called, variously, 'spirit-energy' and that this is universally accepted by most cultures as being at the heart of ritual and shamanic or other spiritual practices.

In the past fifteen years or so, there has been a burgeoning interest in all things to do with consciousness as a general theme, and many valuable insights into consciousness and spirituality have been gleaned through various academic writing since these two terms have been linked.

The explosion of publications from researchers in the general area of contemporary Paganism and magical practice, have noted parallels between indigenous accounts and Pagan accounts of spirit, spirit-energy, energy fields, healing, magic as a practice, and other dimensions of existence, or other realities. This is a huge change from earlier publications, or even discussions among scholars themselves. I remember discussing the notion of 'feeling', in the sense of perception or intuition (a very innocuous and modest topic in light of what is now being discussed), with a colleague of mine in Studies in Religion, suggesting that this is an important aspect of religion in general. My suggestion was met with the familiar academic response—the curled lip, the scoff—and I was made to feel ridiculous for even commenting on the idea. This reaction was coupled with the comment, 'that's all new Age nonsense'— the convenient term of disdain and the hold-all basket in which to dump anything and everything of a non-material nature. For scholars who have spent their lives cloistered in their offices poring over old texts, or arguing about the nuances of a particular scriptural word, it is difficult for them to understand what might emerge from dealing with people at the grass-roots level of belief and practice. Yet when one moves through the doctrine and dogma of traditional religions to the esoteric richness within these ancient scriptures and to the esoteric branches of all of them, this approach to religion makes one wonder at their rigidity.

Intuition, premonitions, the 'sixth sense', of 'knowing' something we couldn't possibly know via rational thinking, and more, are all discussed in David Howes' 2009 collection of essays, *The Sixth Sense: A Reader*. In another publication, *Extraordinary Knowing* (2007), clinical psychologist Elizabeth Lloyd Mayer takes the reader through one scientific experiment after another, over a period of many years, to show how skepticism has actually effected even the most carefully conducted, methodologically sound, scientific studies of anomalous mental capacities. In spite of solid statistical results and thorough groundwork, the outcomes of these studies were constantly dismissed out of hand as they fled in the face of the conservative scientific approach. The usual response, in spite of data showing the contrary, was that 'these things are not possible', therefore it was of no use to pursue them.

Fraud, charlatanism, and glib popular accounts from credulous people or from individuals who want to feel special, have led to the cautious—perhaps overly cautious—attitude of the scientific community towards anything that even hints of the metaphysical. Although studies into anomalous phenomena need to be approached with caution, it is now time for science to step in and engage with the research and to dialogue with researchers in other disciplines. Ostracism from colleagues, and the fear of spoiling career prospects has meant that, until very recently, these things have not been taken seriously by anyone except the stalwart few, even in disciplines such as Studies in Religion, Psychology, and Anthropology, where they should be discussed openly. But these should not be reasons to abandon all research into such matters.

Peter Berger and Thomas Luckmann (1981) maintain that meaning is actively created through a dialectical relationship between the individual and culture. If one's culture accepts the world of spirits and the possibility of moving in and out of that world, then the individual will be able to openly accept and engage in discussions of that interface. If not, all sorts of obstacles are encountered that block those discourses. Alfred Schutz theorizes that common-sense knowledge of everyday life provides the foundation for how people gain knowledge and make sense of their worlds. If a large part of our 'common-sense reality' includes acknowledging our dreams and our imaginal world (and some cultures do not make any strong distinctions between both these latter two), then knowledge gained in altered states adds to the repertoire of our common-sense knowledge.

Major shifts in how someone experiences reality necessitates a re-thinking of what reality is and how it should be viewed. For the many people who are now experiencing reality shifts when in an altered state of consciousness, they are re-assessing the nature of reality, the long-held dogmas of major religions, and are looking for answers that make sense to them in light of their experiences. With the public now honing in on quantum physics and the questions raised by physicists, perhaps magic and science will soon be in closer dialogue. If epistemology is the study of how we know anything, or our grounds of knowledge, magical epistemology is yet another way of knowing.

References

Bainbridge, W. 1997. *The Sociology of Religious Movements*, New York: Routledge.

Bardon, F. 1993 [1956]. *Initiation into Hermetics*. Wuppertal, Germany: Ruggeberg-Verlag.

Bentov, I. 1977. *Stalking the Wild Pendulum: On the Mechanics of Consciousness*. Toronto: Bantam Books.

Berger, P. and Luckmann, T. 1981[1966]. *The Social Construction of Reality*. Middlesex: Penguin.

Blain, J. 2002. *Nine Worlds of Seid-Magic: Ecstasy and Neo-Shamanism in North European Paganism*. London: Routledge.

Butler, W.E. 1970 [1959]. *The Magician: His Training and Work*. Wellingborough, UK: Aquarian Press.

Corbin, H. 1969. *Creative Imagination in the Sufism of Ibn 'Arabi*, translated from the French by R. Manheim, Bollingen Series SCI, Princeton, NJ: Princeton University Press.

Csordas, T.J. 1994. *The Sacred Self: a cultural phenomenology of charismatic healing*. Berkeley, California: University of California Press.

Cziksentmihalyi, M. and Cziksentmihalyi, I. 1998. *Optimal Experience: psychological studies of flow in consciousness*. Cambridge: Cambridge University Press.
Finke, R.A. 1980. 'Levels of equivalence in imagery and perception', *Psychological Review*, 87:113-32.
Greenwood, S. 2009. *The Anthropology of Magic*. Oxford: Berg.
Harner, M. 1990. *The Way of the Shaman*. San Francisco: Harper and Row.
Harvey, G. 2006. 'Discworld and Otherworld: The Imaginative Use of Fantasy Literature among Pagans', in *Popular Spiritualities: The Politics of Contemporary Enchantment*, ed. L. Hume and K. McPhillips. Aldershot, England: Ashgate.
Howes, D. 2009. 'Introduction: The Revolving Sensorium' in D. Howes (ed.), *The Sixth Sense Reader*. Oxford: Berg.
Hume, L. 2007. *Portals: Opening Doorways to Other Realities Through the Senses*. Oxford: Berg.
_____ 2002. *Ancestral Power: The Dreaming, Consciousness and Aboriginal Australians*. Melbourne: Melbourne University Press.
_____ 1997. *Witchcraft and Paganism in Australia*. Melbourne: Melbourne University Press.
Letcher, A. 2007. 'Mad Thoughts on Mushrooms: Discourse and Power in the Study of Psychedelic Consciousness', *Anthropology of Consciousness*, vol.18 (2):74-97.
Lloyd Mayer, E. 2007. *Extraordinary Knowing: Science, Skepticism, and the Inexplicable Powers of the Human Mind*. New York: Bantam Books.
Miller, D. 1970. *Gods and Games*. New York: World Publishing Co.
Myerhoff, B. G. 2009. 'Peyote and the Mystic Vision' in D. Howes (ed.), *The Sixth Sense Reader*. Oxford: Berg.
Noll, R. 1985. 'Mental Imagery Cultivation as a Cultural Phenomenon: the Role of Visions in Shamanism', *Current Anthropology*, 26(4):443-61.
Riboli, D. 2004. 'Transformation' in *Shamanism: An Encyclopedia of World Beliefs, Practices, and Culture*, vol. I: 255-259.
Strassman, R. 2001. *DMT: The Spirit Molecule*, Rochester, Vermont: Park Street Press.
Schutz, A. 1970. 'Transcendence and Multiple Realities', in H.R. Wagner (ed.) Alfred Schutz on *Phenomenology and Social Relations: Selected Writings*. Chicago: University of Chicago Press : 245-64.
Singer, J.L. 1995. 'Imaginative Play in Childhood: Precursor of Subjunctive Thought, Daydreaming, and Adult Pretending Games', in A.D. Pellegrini (ed.), *The Future of Play Theory*. Albany, New York: State University of New York Press, pp. 187-219.
Starhawk (M. Simos). 1979. *The Spiral Dance*. New York: Harper and Row.
Tart, C.T. 2009. *The End of Materialism*. Oakland, California: New Harbinger

Publications.

Turner, E. 1994. 'A Visible Spirit Form in Zambia', in D. E. Young and J-G. Goulet (eds), *Being Changed by Cross-cultural Encounters: the Anthropology of Extraordinary Experience*. Ontario: Broadview Press: 71-95.

2
The Visual and the Numinous: Material Expressions of the Sacred in Contemporary Paganism[1]

Dominique Beth Wilson

Rudolf Otto and the Idea of the Holy

Rudolf Otto defines the numinous (from Latin, numen) as 'the *mysterium tremendum et fascinans*' that is a feature of encounters with deities, the supernatural, the sacred, the holy, and the transcendent. Otto's numinous might be sparked by natural or constructed triggers. Material expressions of the divine and the sacred come in many forms, including icons and statues, architecture, song, and dance. It is this 'thrilling vibrant' and intoxicating 'ecstasy' that one experiences when connecting with the divine that is of importance for this chapter. What is it that triggers these experiences, and what tools or aids may be used to initiate an encounter with the divine? What is that quintessential element that makes something holy or sacred, giving it numinosity and allowing it to act as a catalyst for experiencing the *mysterium tremendum et fascinans*? And once something becomes numinous, does it retain numinosity, and how can it then be used to spark further experiences of *mysterium tremendum*? This chapter will begin with by defining the term 'numinous', and its role and place within contemporary Pagan practice. The chapter then explores the representation and the celebration of the sacred within an Australian Pagan community, Applegrove—an eclectic coven that practices Witchcraft. The chapter examines the use of numinous objects, such as images, altars, dress and rituals, to enable Applegrove's members to transcend the profane and everyday, and commune with the sacred and the divine.

'*Mysterium tremendum et fascinans*' is the phrase most commonly associated with the theologian and philosopher Rudolf Otto. *Das Heilige (The Idea of the Holy)*, his legacy to the discipline of Religious Studies, was published in German in 1917, with twenty-five editions being published within the next two decades, including an influential translation into English in 1923.[2] In this book Otto recognises the profound importance of the non-rational in metaphysics and religion, and makes a serious attempt to analyse the '*feelings*' that remain when the '*concept*' fails. To do this he introduces an explanatory terminology necessary to interpret the symbols and experiences found within mythology and religion.[3] These symbols can be seen as earlier, 'primal' humanity's attempts to explain and represent the numinous, that awe-filled, awful, and fascinating mystery, the almost indescribable sensation that occurs when one apprehends the divine.

Otto regarded the '*mysterium tremendum*' as something precious, sacred, explaining:

> *The feeling of it may at times come sweeping like a gentle tide, pervading the mind with a tranquil mood of deepest worship. It may pass over into the more set and lasting attitude of the soul, continuing, as it were, thrillingly vibrant and resonant, until at last it dies away and the soul resumes its 'profane', non-religious mood of everyday experience. It may burst in sudden eruption up from the depths of the soul with spasms and convulsions, to intoxicated frenzy, to transport, to ecstasy.*[4]

Otto's identification of this phenomenon has continued to resonate with scholars and practitioners into the twenty-first century: colonist and broadcaster Tom Harpur, author of *The Pagan Christ*, in a 2009 radio interview defined 'the reality of a transcending numinous as the *mysterium tremendum et fascinosum*, that divine element in the human, in life, in the world, in all beauty, the mystery we use [as] a symbol [for] God' for the divine. He then went on to state that the presence and experience of *mysterium tremendum* within the world 'must never be lost,' and that humanity must never stop witnessing its existence.[5] From within the Christian tradition, pastoral theologian Melvin A. Kimble describes it as 'the mystery that is at once overwhelming and fascinating, that renders my existence significant and meaningful in here and now,' while also explaining that as a mystery 'it is unmeasurable, unprovable, and lacks universal definition.'[6] For Sociologist Omar McRoberts, *mysterium tremendum* lies at the centre of all religious experience. He views it as 'the inexplicit and unutterable sense of a wholly transcendent Holy,' as something that 'emerges from humanity's ethical capacity' and goes so far as to claim that 'Religious experience is only numinous experience.'[7]

Identifying the Numinous

For the ancient Romans, numen (meaning 'presence', plural numina) indicated the habitation of a god or spirit in the land and in physical objects.[8] Within the history of religion, numinosity has been ascribed to places, artefacts, actions, or persons due to the associations it evokes in the perceiving individual or group. From a historical perspective the numinosity of an artefact or place, the intangible and invisible quality that gives it significance, is simply due in its presumed association with something, either in the past, in the imagination, or both, that carries emotional weight with that individual or group.[9] Like the Durkheimian 'sacred', the numinous is culturally constructed. In a religious context, the qualities associated with such an artefact include those of sacredness and holiness, probing the core of what it means for something to be deemed 'numinous,' being a manifestation of deity, the numen, or the divine.

Otto argues that the experience of mysterium tremendum occurs only when one experiences/recognises the essence of the numinosity of an object, and in doing so gains access or a 'revelation of an aspect of [the] divine'.[10] Numinosity can be assigned to anything—an object, image, place, person, or even ritual action. It is simply a reflection of the significance that something holds for an individual or group, a notification that something is deeply important to them.[11] In a religious sense objects of numinosity are seen as resonating with divinity, they become 'other,' holy, sacred. Mircea Eliade explains that 'by manifesting the sacred, any object becomes something else',[12] while Émile Durkheim has argued that the sacred is 'a mark of group experience and identity, and thus acquires prestige.'[13] An object may look superficially the same to a casual observer, but to those who witnessed the manifestation of the sacred it now carries a supernatural essence. It has been 'transmuted into a supernatural reality',[14] not only for those who witnessed the event, but for the whole group to whom the object now holds importance and meaning. It has an otherness that now draws the religious mind to it, for it is now holy, sacred, numinous, infused with symbolic significance. Once an object or place has revealed its supernatural association, is seen as being permanently touched by the divine, it contains the memory of that sacred manifestation, and as such become a possible porthole or pathway, an aid to accessing the divine, and experiencing that mysterium tremendum. As James Lewis explains:

> ...the passion of the religious mind is to seek rapport with sacred power. This can be accomplished by drawing close to spots where the divine has manifested, or temporally by recreating—in ritual—the world as it was 'in the beginning,' when Gods and Goddesses walked upon the earth.[15]

Any item may carry with it a sense of numinosity, may evoke memories and be ascribed importance due to its connection to past people and events. However, the idea of the continued holiness, and later sacredness, of such an item is a 'category of interpretation and valuation peculiar to the sphere of religion'[16] and requires the presence of a community to transmit this notion of holiness through the group's tradition.

It is important to remember that at the most basic level, the definition of the *sacred* is simply that it is *the opposite of the profane* [17] and as such it must be given the designation of being *sacred* by an individual or group. While it may be argued that in Pagan beliefs everything is a source of divinity and as such sacred, one must be open to the fact that some things are more charged than others. These sites can be seen as having more *mana,* or divine power, and as such must be approached and handled with due care and reverence.[18] Generally, one does not stumble across a tree in a forest and instantly recognise it as a numinous object; the tree is sacred because at some point in time a manifestation of the divine that occurred within the precinct of the tree was witnessed and remembered. The memory and knowledge of the event was then relayed back to the wider community, where it became encoded into the religious traditions and mentalities of the group.

Numinous objects or places are arbitrary, socially constructed phenomena, as Edwyn Bevan explains: '[a] material object may acquire holiness by its associations with a holy person ... An image or picture is associated with its original by the visual likeness, in virtue of which it can serve to bring the person portrayed into our mind ...'[19] This is illustrated by Paganism's use of images, dress, altars and rituals. The item's presumed association with divinity, be it a particular deity, elemental, or the universal divine, makes it a useful trigger for activating an experience of ecstasy and 'awe-inspiring mystery'.[20] Through this experience unity with a higher power is achieved. It is the use of these items, and their ability to act as a pathway to the 'other' world that facilitates the experience of the divine. Otto explains that '*mysterium*' naturally implies notions of an unexplained secret or mystery, but in a religious sense it also denotes something which it 'wholly other', and not of this world.[21] This idea of 'otherness', and accessing the 'otherworld', is a theme that features heavily in Celtic mythology. The otherworld is the abode of the Gods, elementals, *sidhe* and the numerous other 'non-human' creatures that exist in the Celtic landscape.[22] These otherworldly denizens are seen by humans as 'other' simply because they possess different traits and value systems, existing outside the realm of the everyday, in a liminal space outside the bounds of time.[23] The use of the term 'other' can also be seen to convey a sense of indeterminacy, for the otherworld is connected to this world at certain places, and is accessible by various paths, or at certain times of the year when the boundaries are believed to become as thin as mist.[24]

Portholes to the otherworld also include features like narrow bridges, stone circles, underground caverns and water.[25] Water; with its natural source coming from deep down within the earth, is a common gateway to the 'otherworld', examples of which include wells, natural springs, and oceans lying to the west of the mainland. In Celtic myths and folklore these water ways and oceans can be traversed to gain access to the Otherworld/s, for example: *Tir nan Og* (the land of youth); *Mag Mell* (the land of promise), and the Isles of the Blest.[26] These islands always lie to the west as this is the direction of the setting sun and is the quarter associated with death and initiation; it is also the place from which one begins the 'return journey of rebirth'.[27] This link with water and Celtic deities follows though with the belief that some members of the *Tuatha De Danaan*, the pagan Gods of Ireland, moved to live in the 'land under the waves'[28] instead of the hollow hills with which they are more commonly associated. Such places are thresholds—boundary lines— which distinguish between this world and the world of the divine. They are also important, because they are access points where communication and passage from the profane to the sacred world becomes possible.[29] Thomas Kasulis calls such places 'holographic entry point[s]',[30] because they are indicative of the process in which one becomes aware of the whole, of cosmic unity, of microcosm of our world reflecting the macrocosm of the Gods. These numinous thresholds are used by Pagans to access the vague and unknown 'otherness,' the divine godhead. As Otto explains, the *mysterium* aspect of *mysterium tremendum* merely denotes 'that which is hidden and esoteric, that which is beyond conception or understanding, extraordinary and unfamiliar'.[31] Pagans actively strive to connect with these non-human entities, or aspects of the divine, using rituals, tools and costumes to re-create the pathways to the 'otherworlds' presented within the rich tapestry of the world's mythologies. They believe that it is only through access with the divine that one can gain understanding of, and a sense of being connected to, the cosmic whole.[32]

Contemporary Paganism

We will now focus on how such triggers or 'holographic entry points' operate within Paganism. 'Paganism' is an umbrella term which covers a whole range of religious groups and meanings. Some scholars choose to add the prefix of 'neo' to denote that the religions embraced by the term are modern phenomena, with romantic leanings towards older and ancient traditions and religious practices, rather than a direct continuation of these practices. Some traditions within the Pagan genre claim a lineage to ancient religions; however, such claims are often hard to substantiate. For the purpose of this chapter the term 'Paganism' will be used to describe members of the modern community, as it is the term they use to identify and describe themselves. The terms 'pagan' and 'paganism' are derived from the Latin term *paganus* meaning 'rustic' or 'peasant' and was applied to those who rejected the arrival of Roman culture, preferring the rule of their local government or *pagus*,[33] eventually evolving in Christian literature to a derogatory term implying that something, or someone, was not Christian.[34]

Movements covered by the term 'Paganism' include Witchcraft, Druidry, Heathenry, Wicca, Nature Worshippers and Asatru, as well as more culturally-based forms of Paganism, based on reconstructed revivals of indigenous faiths and mythologies. Such movements are diverse in their practices, but can all be seen as evolving from the same wellspring, as they attempt to re-encapsulate ancient and pre-modern notions of the divine, universal oneness, and the sense of an enchanted and alive Nature into a practical religion for contemporary society.[35] Paul Ricoeur argues that 'modern persons no longer have a sacred space, a center, a *templum*, a holy mountain, or an *axis mundi*. Their existence is decentered, eccentric, a-centered. They lack festivals, their time is homogenous like their space.'[36] Pagans, unlike Ricoeur's 'modern persons', constantly endeavour to connect with and recreate the sacred through ritual, meditation, the decoration of altars, and the celebration of seasonal festivals. Major themes within the Pagan worldview include immanence and transcendence, animism and spiritism, magic, the sacred circle, the cyclic nature of life and an understanding of the interconnectedness of all things.[37] Pagans generally accept that the Gods/Goddess exist in some shape or form, even if they are just acknowledged as the divine; the spark that is both within every living thing, yet transcendent and unknowable. Michael York explains that:

> *The world itself/herself is divine—including we humans, her children, along with whatever other product is derived from the earth, either directly or through us as intermediaries.*[38]

They also share a reverence for Nature and the changing of the seasons, most commonly seen in the celebration of seasonal and agricultural festivals, the phases of the moon and solar based events (solstices and equinoxes). Another common denominator is the belief in reincarnation, and the general acceptance that death is simply a part of the life cycle, and not an 'end' as such.[39] While the idea of reincarnation is not a phenomenon unique to Paganism, its presence in a large number of Pagan movements is important as it not only reflects the idea of the cyclic nature of life, but also offers a way of migrating some of the debates concerning ethnicity, especially those relating to personal affinities that individuals from other geographical locations may feel towards ethnically based traditions.[40]

Pagans are 'often inspired by the practices of indigenous peoples and the paganism of the ancient world revealed through archaeology, classics, myth and history.'[41] A romantic attitude towards such times is often seen within their beliefs and philosophies; however there seems to be a conscious effort to recreate these events in a format which imparts both mystery and meaning to those existing within the boundaries of contemporary society. As such, practices such as the sacrifice of animals and so on are rarely found within the modern Pagan scene. Not surprisingly many Pagans are 'avid readers' who find inspiration for their rituals and beliefs 'in the scholarly literature, and its semi-scholarly spin-off …enabling them to revive or reinvent the world of magic'[42] in what Pearson explains is a 'continual creative process'.[43] Such processes allow modern groups to connect with the past, and its presentation of the divine. Aa Barbara Davy explains,

> *These Neopagans—or Pagans, as they increasingly call themselves—seek to live in a world in which, as Euripides said, 'all things are full of Gods.' … As children, all of us possessed a certain eye that glimpsed gnarled faces in rocks and clouds; Pagans seek to recapture that mode of liminal awareness, conjuring it out of the body with ritual trance and magical visualizations.*[44]

One of the major groups within the Pagan tradition are Witches, who can themselves be broken down into numerous sub-groups: solitary witches working in isolation, eclectics, reconstructionalist, Goddess worshippers and hedge witches, as well as the more formalised traditions of Wicca, including Gardnerian, Alexandrian and Dianic.[45] The focus in this chapter is Witchcraft, and the beliefs and practices of the Sydney-based Witchcraft group, Applegrove.

General practices and beliefs that belong to the Witchcraft path of Paganism include: the practice of communing directly with deity through ritual and meditation; the celebration of the Wheel of the Year; four solar and four agricultural based festivals that acknowledge the turning of the seasons and Nature's harvest; the observance of the phases of the moon (known as esbats, they most commonly occur at the full moon, but may include other phases of the moon as they all have their own importance and symbolism); the practising of rituals within a circle, a sacred space that can be created at need; and the use of certain ritual tools, for example an athame, chalice, pentacle, or wand.[46] The most common practice which defines the path of Witchcraft is that of magic; performing spells and other workings within a ritual context with the intent of creating a change in the cosmic structure of the world.

In a chapter on magical practices within Paganism Síân Reid explains that 'In Neo-Pagan Witchcraft, most definitions of magic are variations on the formulations of two early-twentieth-century ritual magicians—Aleister Crowley and William Butler.' She cites Crowley's definition of magic as being 'the Art and Science of causing change to occur in accordance with Will,' and Butler's as 'the act of effecting change in consciousness at will'.[47] This idea of magic as a catalyst to change is common throughout the Paganism sphere, with the view that spells are to the Pagan what prayers are to the Christian—a way of voicing one's needs and desires to a higher power, with the intention of creating change. There is no major distinction between spells and prayer since they ultimately serve the same function of projecting one's will out into the world, and both rely on the belief, or faith, of the individual.[48] The type of magic and spell-work most commonly practised by witches is that of sympathetic magic,[49] which is substantially encoded in symbolism. Also referred to as 'natural magic', sympathetic magic is based on the idea that there is a correspondence between the natural and celestial worlds (macro- and micro- cosmos), and as such the powers or virtues associated with the different planets and stars are reflected within the properties certain plants, stones, and colours.[50] A Witch will choose to use particular plants, stones, coloured candles or incense when working a spell depending on their properties and their relation to the intention of the spell. For example raspberries, associated with the planet Venus, and the element of Water, are seen as feminine and have powers linked to protection and love, making them an appropriate ingredient for spells to protect family and friends.[51] Holly, on the other hand, is seen as a masculine plant, ruled by the planet Mars and the element of Fire, and it is used as a protection against lightning, to promote good luck, and for dream magic.[52]

Introducing Applegrove

Applegrove is a Sydney-based witchcraft group which runs Pagan gatherings and a teaching circle known as the Circle of the Hearth. It was started in 1996 by Gabby Cleary, known as Blayze in the Pagan community,[53] when the leaders of its parent group—Eldergrove - moved away from Sydney. Originally it was run as an open circle, meeting fortnightly in Granville Library, but eventually became a more closed group, meeting in the home of its organiser, Blayze. As well as the open circle, Applegrove also inherited the two public pagan gatherings that were started by Eldergrove's High Priestess, Hawthorn, in 1994.[54] Applegrove's aim is to give long-term training to students interested in Wiccan-based eclectic witchcraft, where the students are exposed to experiential spirituality and practice. Members and friends come together to celebrate the Wheel of the Year, which is divided into eight festivals or sabbats, writing and organising rituals that encourage a deeper understanding of what is being celebrated, while also exploring the different manifestation of the divine through various world mythologies.[55] Applegrove has a very informative website and members are often found presenting workshops and rituals at Sydney Pagan events as well as gatherings in Canberra, with their popular Yule and Beltane gatherings running from 1996 to 2001. Blayze and other Applegrove members were also part of the 2007 Australian Wiccan Conference.[56]

The Celtic-derived Wheel of the Year follows the cycles of the natural world with solar and agricultural festivals. From Samhain, which marks the beginning of the year to Yule at mid-winter, Beltane the fertility festival in spring, Mabon at the Autumn Equinox, and back to Samhain with the year beginning anew again, it is a continuous wheel of life.[57] The Wheel of the Year is often presented as the story of the relationship between the divine, the romance of the God and Goddess, the birth and death of the Sun God and so forth.[58] The various myths associated with the sabbats allow Applegrove's members to explore the different aspects of the divine, and attempt to connect with and experience mysterium tremendum. To help facilitate such experiences, the community of Applegrove employ various tools and aids. These include the creation of different altars to reflect the time of year or a particular deity, and the use of costumes, images, heavy symbolism and sympathetic magic within a ritual context to help evoke the senses, enabling and encouraging a manifestation of the divine.

Material Expressions of the Sacred: Altars

In Paganism altars are places, or objects - a table, shelf, rock or tree stump -dedicated to the worship of the divine. They are set aside to be sacred spaces and as such are thus numinous by design. They hold tools and symbolic items, acting as a focus for a witch's connection with both deity and themselves. In essence, the altar can be viewed as both a physical and a spiritual offering to the Gods, and as such it can have many purposes, with no two altars needing to look alike. Altars may be created for personal or group use, holding items held sacred by the individual or group. They may be erected for specific rituals and seasons or maintained as a permanent dedication/acknowledgement to the gods. It is the meanings ascribed to the objects on the altar that make them a material expression of the sacred, allowing the practitioner to connect to the divine. Otherwise, as one Applegrove member explained, an altar is 'just a table with stuff on it'.[59] Each item is placed there because of its symbolism and meaning to the individual or group. A candle represents the element of Fire, but in a certain colour, for example red, it may also symbolise love; an apple is a symbol of community to Applegrove members; olives may be placed as a traditional offering to Athena. The options are limited only by one's imagination and creativity in creating meaningful connections between the objects chosen and the element, or concept, that they symbolise.

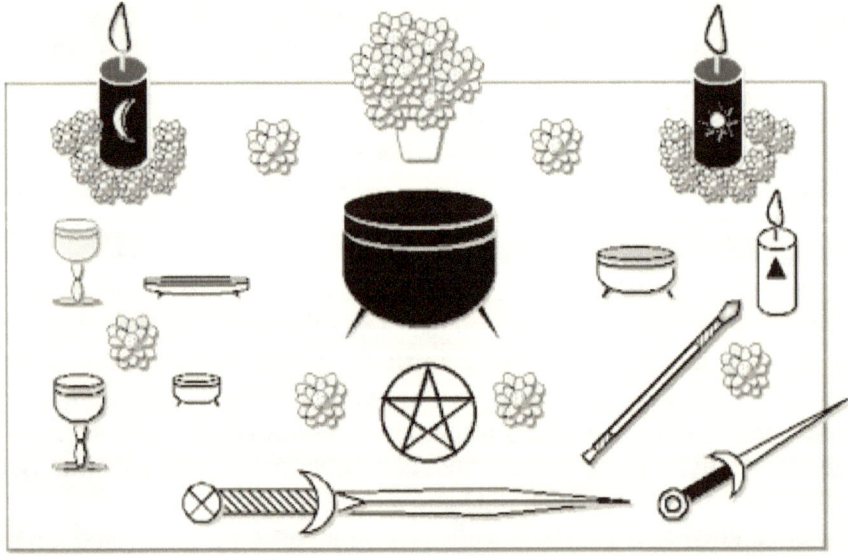

Figure 1: Altar Set up [61]

A basic altar set-up usually includes a candle or candles; incense burner (known variously as a 'censer' or 'thurible'); two dishes, one for salt and one for water; a libation dish; goblet(s); and figures to represent the deities.[60] Other commonly used items also include an athame (ritual knife), wand, cauldron, and pentacle, on which objects are placed to be consecrated. An altar is often seen as being divided into two halves, with the left representing the feminine side of deity, and the right representing the masculine. An example of a typical altar set-up for basic ritual is illustrated above.

While this kind of layout is practical and useful for basic rituals, it is also important to remember that it is just a starting point, especially for newcomers to the craft. An altar should evolve and change to represent the spiritual growth of the individual or group. Altars should be adaptable, containing what is needed and practical, while always symbolising a ritual's context, or the season at hand.

Figure 2: Applegrove's 2006 Mabon Altar

Different types of altars used by the members of Applegrove include: personal altars—usually permanent altars set up in the individual's house, used for personal rituals, daily mediations and worship of the divine; altars to a particular deity[62]; ritual altars—created and set up for a specific ritual, such as spell casting, the creation of magical items or elemental workings; and finally, seasonal or festival altars—used to celebrate the sabbats. These reflect the turning of year, 'connecting with the divine in a seasonal aspect as the individuals come together in a group mind for the purpose of celebration'.[63]

For a ritual celebration at Mabon, the Autumn Equinox, Applegrove created a seasonal and ritual specific altar (Figure 2). Mabon's seasonal festival myth is often based on the God's descent to the underworld, after sacrificing his life for the land. Thus for this Mabon ritual the altar set-up included sheaves of wheat, to represent the harvest, baskets of seasonal vegetables and food as an offering to the Gods, as well as the tools needed for the ritual. The altar cloth was orange and gold, autumnal colors that reflect Nature at this time of year.

An altar dedicated to Athena (Figure 3), and used in a ritual to celebrate the Panathenaia[64] included a statue and picture of the Goddess, a spearhead, an olive loaf, olives, and olive branches, which are all symbols of the Greek Goddess. An altar dedicated to a specific deity acts as an access point for that aspect of the divine, in a similar way in which statues of Gods or Goddesses in a temple allow for direct communication from our world to the realm of the divine. As Bevan explains:

> *The image was not the one body of the God, but it was his body in so far as what you did to the image—hanging it with garlands, washing it, making music and burning sacrifices before it—was pleasurably felt by the God, and the God on the other hand could put forth his power or declare his mind through his image.*[65]

The placement of an altar can also be important, as different directions are associated with different aspects of the divine and the otherworld. For example the East is seen as representing the 'place of the rising Sun,' and is thus connected to ideas of rebirth and beginnings.[66] It is also the quarter that is associated with the element of Air and also wisdom, traditionally it is seen as the direction that messengers carrying knowledge from divine sources would arrive.[67] North or South is the 'dark quarter' depending on which hemisphere the ritual is being conducted in. Most books on Wicca tell followers to place their altar in the North (for the northern hemisphere) because its 'the one place where the Sun never shines, and is therefore a place of mystery ... it is the place where the Gods "live"... So, the Wiccan practice of placing the altar in the "dark quarter" is directly related to our desire to link the focal point of our circle with the Gods.'[68]

Figure 3: Altar to Athena

The most important factor to remember about altars is that once set up they become a sacred space. The objects placed on the altar are chosen for their symbolic significance, for their abilities to act as a focus, a trigger allowing one to access the divine, experiencing *mysterium tremendum*. Thus altars are material expressions of the numinous for two reasons. Firstly, because the items placed on them are numinous, due to their symbolic associations and/or magical properties, and secondly because the altar itself acts as a 'holographic entry point'; its very purpose and nature is to act as a doorway to the divine and cosmic whole. David Murry explains it well when he says that 'Instead of seeing the object as powerful in itself, the worshipper sees it as a material representation of a spiritual power.' The altar is no longer just an object, or a table, it is a symbol of deity—a link to the supernatural and sacred world.

Ritual and Sacred Spaces
European mythology is full of tales in which journeys and passage to the otherworld occur. The veil between this world and the realm of the spirits, Gods and the divine is not clearly defined; it can be parted and torn, allowing one to traverse through to the hidden realms. The notion of accessibility between this world and otherworlds has found root within the modern Pagan tradition, and as such certain places are seen as being

more potent sites for rituals than others. The most obvious examples are the great stone circles, such as Stonehenge and Avebury, but others include sacred springs, groves of trees and other natural phenomena, as they are seen as points when the sacred/otherworlds are tied to, or closer to ours.[69] But not all witches are fortunate to live in close proximity to such sites; especially those practising in Australia, so it is not surprising to discover that ritual practices have been developed to allow one to access the otherworlds from any location. The most common ritual practice is that of casting a circle, creating a space that is seen as existing *between the worlds*. The idea of using a circle to mark the boundary between the sacred and the profane has been in use since ancient times, from the Babylonians—who drew a circle on the floor around the sick to keep demons at bay—to western ceremonial magicians, whose circle must have exact proportions in order to contain entities summoned from beyond.[70] In Paganism sacred spaces for ritual are created by casting a circle, as a 'circle stands between the worlds—neither within the Earthly realm nor upon the Astral Plane'.[71]

In Paganism circles are cast at the beginning of a ritual event, even when a ritual occurs in a common location. The majority of Applegrove's rituals are held at Jo and Blayze's house, either in the backyard or in the garage, which has been set up as a permanent temple. The act of casting the circle (which includes visualising a boundary between the worlds, chanting,[72] the consecration of the boundary with the four elements, Earth, Water, Air and Fire, the summoning of the quarter guardians, and eventually divinity itself) is a numinous act.[73] It is a trigger that facilitates communion with the divine, especially for long-term practitioners of the craft to whom the constant repetition of casting the circle encourages an ease of movement in and out of ecstatic states, between this world and the other. A document accessible though the Applegrove website explains that the importance of circles as sacred spaces is due to the fact that they are places that are used for 'both worship and work'. They are spaces in which Deities are invited and encouraged to manifest. The summoning of 'Them' inside a cast circle creates a gateway 'through which They can enter. Its creation forms a physical gateway into the circle as well as being a spiritual act of courtesy. The Gateway is also a reminder that all acts that are performed within the Circle are in honour of Them.'[74] Blayze expanded on this idea further by explaining that circles are a 'place being designated to be prepared to receive the divine by invitation. Even though we see the divine in myths and all around us, the creation of a sacred space is focused and a thing undertaken as a duty [to the divine] to acknowledge that what we are doing is for them.'[75]

Like altars, rituals can have many purposes. They can celebrate the changing of the seasons or phases of the moon, they can be for specific spell-work, healing, to connect with and explore an element or deity, even just for fun![76] Rituals can also mark turning points in life; these include naming ceremonies for children, initiations into the craft, and handfastings (pagan weddings) for couples. They can be simple occasions, with limited props and preparation, or elaborate affairs, the culmination of months of planning, research and preparation. As part of the curriculum of the Circle of the Hearth, members of Applegrove are required to write rituals, usually based around the celebration of a sabbat. The creation of a new ritual allows both the writer, and participants of the ritual, to continue to explore and connect with different aspects of the divine, to constantly seek moments of *mysterium tremendum,* and expand upon their knowledge and experience of deity.

Figure 4: Statue of Athena with her new Peplos

In a ritual held in early 2008, Applegrove recreated the Panathenaia, an ancient ritual held annually in Athens to celebrate Athena's birthday. The inspiration for the ritual came from a member, Michael, wishing to to celebrate 'something "outside" the usual Wiccan-based Sabbats'.[77] His reason for choosing to recreate a festival in honour of Athena was due to the fact that his Matron Goddess, the Celtic Brighid, already had her own festival, Imbolc, within the Wheel of the Year. As Athena is Brighid's Hellenic face, her equivalent, he chose to celebrate the Panathenia. Preparation for this ritual took six months, as members of Applegrove reseached the historical event, and then adapted it for modern usage. In keeping with its ancient origins, participants dyed and then sewed their own *chitons* (traditional Hellenic robes), and also created handmade gifts to offer Athena. The event took place in February 2008, as this was seen as corresponding to the season of the original Greek celebration. It included a ritual at a member's home, followed by a journey to Barrack Street in Sydney, where there is a large bronze statue of Athena, given in 2000 by the Mayor of Athens to the City of Sydney. Once in the city the group presented Athena with a new *peplos* (outer garment) before retiring to a nearby Greek restaurant to end the ritual with a feast.

When asked if the ritual's historical origins made him feel like he was connecting with people from ancient times, Michael explained that:

> *The rite was more to connect to the Goddess Athena rather than historical associations as I am a firm believer that we are in the twenty-first century and as such we need to try and reflect this when connecting to deity, otherwise the Gods themselves have wasted their time in getting us to this point in time. Although nostalgia has always got a place in pagan ritual and images—whether they are costume, tools or wording—are very important.*[78]

The depth of preparation and research into the ancient festival allowed members of Applegrove to induce an experience of *mysterium tremendum* during the ritual. This was activated not only by the ritual experience, but also by their use of costume and other props—such as traditional sacred symbols associated this particular aspect of the divine placed on their altar. The material objects used in the ritual have now taken on their own numinosity through association with the ritual, and act as visual reminders and 'holographic entry points' to communion with the divine.

Costumes and Props

The use of costuming and symbolism within a ritual occurs for several reasons. Firstly they help to create a ritual state of mind, starting the movement from the mundane to the sacred otherworld that will be created in the ritual space. For a group, costume can help create a communal atmosphere, with everyone wearing similar cloaks or robes, or even being in a similar state of undress or skyclad.[79] There is also a 'fun aspect'—dressing up and role-playing to assist in telling the story of the ritual. This still allows for a deeper immersion into the ritual story by the participant—the occasionally obvious symbolism acting like a 'brick through the window'[80]—and helps the participants to get the gist of the ritual's meaning. Props and costumes transform the person wearing them into a visually tangible image of the deity, helping to move participants into an ecstatic experience, clouding the boundaries between the sacred and the profane. An article used by Applegrove's Circle of the Hearth explains that:

> *Props can lend form to ideas making them visual and easily understood. They can act as a focus of attention. When you have a group of people trying to work together, a well used prop can get everyone acting and thinking in unison. They can become a potent symbol of something shared.*
>
> *Props lend atmosphere. They add a touch of the theatric (sic) and help to get participants of a ritual into the right frame of mind for magic. There is a certain special impact in seeing the High Priest play the role of the God in ritual resplendent in a horned helmet.*[81]

Costumes can act as a trigger in and out of ritual states, both for the participants and the people wearing them. One member of Applegrove explained that the removal of the veil and crown worn by her (when playing the part of the Goddess in a ritual) was like a sudden jolt back into the mundane world, as she released the manifestation of the divine that had resided in her during the ritual.[82] When rituals trigger *mysterium tremendum* the props and costumes used in the ritual take on their own numinosity, as the emotional significance of the object to the group deepens. This sentiment is echoed by Otto who 'finds the essence of religion in the emotions evoked by an immediate sense of the divine'.[83] The props themselves become access points to the divine, as they retain a sense of the divinity that was manifested during the ritual they were used in.

A horned helmet, cloaks and tunics of various colours, wigs and masks are props regularly used by Applegrove. The decision to use any prop or tool is carefully planned as such props act like the ingredients used in sympathetic magic: the colour of a cloak or tunic reflects the magical associations that colour has with an element and, in the same way, an incense is representative of a planet or deity. The horned helmet is a standard Pagan symbol for representing the male half of divinity, as the God is often presented as a stag or the horned God of the forest, the horns representing masculinity and male sexuality. The female divine may be embodied by a veiled figure, as it is held no one can know the true face of the Goddess—the veils also act to indicate the presence of an otherworldly visitor. Props and costumes can be made out of any items as it is not the actual physical prop that is important. Rather, it is the meaning assigned to the object that makes it sacred and special. So while many of the props used by Applegrove are extravagant—made purposely for a ritual with loving care and an attention to detail and its magical associations—props found and used on the spur of the moment, such as a branch for a staff or a feather to represent the element of Air, can be just as effective in creating experiences of *mysterium tremendum*. Ultimately, it is the emotions and feelings that the item evokes in the individual or group that is important. For members of Applegrove, the apple is a magical and sacred symbol. It is a symbol of wisdom and knowledge passed down from the ancestors to the ancient Celts,[84] but it is also the symbol of the Applegrove coven—their 'totemic image' if you may. It symbolises their community and the sum of its experiences. Blazye explained that apples, real or created, can be found on most of Applegrove's altars and that she buys any she stumbles across, to gift to members of Applegrove as a symbol of acceptance and membership.[85] For a member of Applegrove an apple is an object of numinosity because it represents the group and its actions; it is a physical representation of their religious community.

Conclusion

This chapter has explored the material expressions of the *numinous* in the contemporary Pagan community of Applegrove, located in Sydney, Australia. Rudolf Otto's classic formulation of religious experience as the apprehension of the *numinous* and a corresponding sense of awe in the presence of the *mysterium tremendum et fascinans* has been applied to the material aspects of Applegrove's ritual life; altars, sacred spaces, costumes and props. I hope I have shown that these physical objects and places are not mere adjuncts to ritual, but act, in Kasulis's terms, as 'holographic entry points',[86] enabling the group's members to experience the divine, the *mysterium tremendum et fascinans,* through the practice of magic. The case-study of the creation of a Panathenaic ritual in 2008 demonstrates clearly how aesthetic objects and devices can be used to open up and access 'the sacred' and trigger experiences of m*ysterium tremendum* in Pagans. The statue of Athena in Barrack Street, Sydney, was not erected as a sacred site or image of the Goddess to be worshipped; yet it provided the opportunity for Applegrove to engage with Athena in a very public way, transforming a largely culturally-irrelevant monument into an authentic object of numinosity for their community. This chapter has also described the magical associations found within other material objects used in spell work, which can help to facilitate experiences of *mysterium tremendum*, allowing Pagans to connect with the supernatural, the sacred and the divine.

References

Andrews, T. 1994. *Enchantments of the Faerie Realm*. St Paul, Minnesota: Llewellyn Publications.
Bancroft, A. 1987. *Origins of the Sacred*. London: Arkana.
Bevan, E. 1940. *Holy Images: An Inquiry into Idolatry and Image-Worship in Ancient Paganism and in Christianity*. London: George Allen & Unwin..
Biedermann, H. n.d. *Dictionary of Symbolism*. New York: Meridian.
Buckland, R. 1999. *The Complete Book of Witchcraft*, St Paul, Minnesota: Llewellyn Publications.
Carpenter, D. 1996. 'Emergent Nature Spirituality: An Examination of the Major Spiritual Contours of the Contemporary Pagan Worldview,' in *Magical Religion and Modern Witchcraft*, edited by J. R. Lewis. New York: State University of New York Press: 35-74.
Circle of the Hearth Teaching notes, 'The Placement of Altars in Wicca,' unpublished, used with permission.
_____ 'Setting up an Altar,' http://www.applegroveonline.com/articles.asp, (accessed 25 June 2010).
Cleary, 2003. 'Training and finding a working group,' in *Practicing The Witch's Craft*, edited by D. Ezzy, Sydney: Allen & Unwin: 228-241.
Cotterell. A. 1999. *Celtic Mythology*, Oxford: Sebastian Kelly.
Crowley, V. 1996. *Wicca: The Old Religion in the New Millennium*, London: Thorsons.
Cunningham, S. 2002. *Encyclopaedia of Magical Herbs*, St Paul, Minnesota: Llewellyn Publications.
Davis, E. 1993. 'Remains of the Deities: Reading the Return of Paganism,' Voice Literary Supplement, http://www.techgnosis.com/neopaganism.html, (accessed 14 June 2010).
Davy, B. 2007. *Introduction to Pagan Studies*, Lanham, Maryland: AltaMira Press.
Dillon, M. 1994 [1948]. *Early Irish Literature*, Dublin: Four Courts Press.
Dunster, J. n.d. 'Props Making,' *Circle of the Hearth Teaching notes*, unpublished, used with permission..
Eliade, M. 1987 [1957]. *The Sacred and the Profane: The Nature of Religion*, San Diego: Harcourt & Brace.
Evans, M. T. (2003). 'The Sacred: Differentiating, Clarifying and Extending Concepts,' *Review of Religious Research* 45.1, 32-47.
Ezzy, D. 2003. 'What is a Witch?' in *Practicing The Witch's Craft*, edited by D. Ezzy, Sydney: Allen & Unwin: 1-22.
Greenwood, S. 2005. *The Nature of Magic: An Anthropology of Consciousness*, Oxford: Berg.
Hanegraaff, W. 1998. *New Age Religion and Western Culture: Esotericism in the Mirror of Secular Thought*, Albany: State University of New York Press.

Harpur, T. 2009. *The Spirit of Things*, radio interview 16th August, http://www.abc.net.au/rn/spiritofthings/stories/2009/2652633.htm, (accessed 11January 2010).

Horne, F. 1998. *Witch: A Personal Journey*, Sydney: Random House.

Hume, L. 1998. *Witchcraft and Paganism in Australia*, Melbourne: Melbourne University Press.

Jordan, M. 1992. *The Encyclopaedia of Gods*, London: Kyle Cathie.

Kasulis, T. 2004. *Shinto: The Way Home*, Honolulu: University of Hawai'i Press.

Kemp, D. 2004. *New Age: A Guide*, Edinburgh: Edinburgh University Press.

Kimble, M.A. 2006. 'A Personal Journey of Aging: The Spiritual Dimension,' in *Aging and the Meaning of Time*, edited by S. H. McFadden and R. C. Atchley: Springer Publishing Company: 151-156.

Kunin, S.D. 2003. *Religion: The Modern Theories*, Edinburgh: Edinburgh University Press.

Lewis, J. R., 'Introduction', in *Magical Religion and Modern Witchcraft*, ed. J. R. Lewis. Albany, New York: State University of New York Press: 1-9.

Maines, R. and Glynn, J. 1993. 'Numinous Objects,' *The Public History* 15.1: 8-25.

McRoberts, O. 2004. 'Beyond Mysterium Tremendum: Thoughts towards an Aesthetic Study of Religious Experience' in *Annals of the American Academy of Political and Social Sciences* 595.1:190-203.

Moura, A. 2002. Green Magic: The Sacred Connection to Nature, St Paul, Minnesota: Llewellyn Publications.

Neils, J. ed. 1996. *Worshipping Athena: Panathenaia and Parthenon*, Wisconsin: University of Wisconsin Press.

Otto, R. 1982 [1923]. *The Idea of the Holy*, trans. John W. Harvey, Oxford: Oxford University Press.

Pearson, J. 2005. 'Neopaganism,' in *Dictionary of Gnosis and Western Esotericism*, vol. 2, ed. W.Hanegraaff, Leiden: Brill: 828-834.

Perowne, S. 1983[1969]. *Roman Mythology*, Feltham, UK: Newnes.

Phillips, M. and Phillips, J. 1994. *The Witches of Oz*, Berks, UK: Capall Bann Publishing.

Rabinovitch, S. T. 1996.. 'Spells of Transformation: Categorizing Modern Neo-Pagan Witches,' in *Magical Religion and Modern Witchcraft*, edited by J. R. Lewis, Albany, New York: State University of New York Press: 75-92.

Raphael, M. 1997. *Rudolf Otto and the Concept of Holiness*, Oxford: Clarendon Press.

Reid, S. 1996. 'As I Do Will, So Mote it Be: Magic as Metaphor in Neo-Pagan Witchcraft,'in *Magical Religion and Modern Witchcraft*, edited by J. R. Lewis, Albany, New York: State University of New York Press: 141-170.

Ricoeur, P. 1995. *Figuring the Sacred. Religion, Narrative, and Imagination*, Minneapolis: Fortress Press.

Ripinsky-Naxon, M. 1993. *The Nature of Shamanism: substance and function of a religious metaphor*, Albany, New York: State University of New York Press.

Strmiska, M. 2005. 'Modern Paganism in World Cultures: Comparative Perspectives,' in, *Modern Paganism in World Cultures: Comparative Perspectives*, ed. M. Strmiska. Santa Barbara, California: ABC:Clio: 1-54.

Versnel, H. S. 1991. 'Some Reflections on the Relationship between Magic-Religion,' *Numen*, 38:2: 177-197.

Wilson, D. B. 2005. 'Sacred Water: Pilgrimage to and veneration of holy wells by pagans and Christians in the British Isles,' in *Exile and Homecoming*, ed. P. O'Neill, Sydney: University of Sydney: 322-337.

Wooding, J. ed. 2000. *The Otherworld Voyage*. Dublin: Four Courts Press.

York, M. 2005. *Pagan Theology: Paganism as a World Religion*, New York: New York University Press.

York M. 2010. 'Idolatry, Ecology and the Sacred as Tangible,' *The Pomegranate*, 12.1, 74-93.

Endnotes

1 A version of this paper was presented at the *3rd Annual Alternative Expressions of the Numinous Conference* held at the University of Queensland, 15-17 August, 2008.

2 Melissa Raphael. *Rudolf Otto and the Concept of Holiness*, (Oxford: Clarendon Press, 1997), 73.

3 Rudolf Otto. *The Idea of the Holy*, trans. John W. Harvey (London: Oxford University Press, 1982 [1923]) 1.

4 Ibid., 26-27.

5 Radio interview with Tom Harpur, *The Spirit of Things*, 16th August 2009, available at http://www.abc.net.au/rn/spiritofthings/stories/2009/2652633.htm, last accessed 11th January 2010.

6 Melvin A. Kimble 'A Personal Journey of Aging: The Spiritual Dimension,' in *Aging and the Meaning of Time*, eds. S. McFadden & R. Atchley. (Springer Publishing Company, 2006), 151.

7 Omar McRoberts 'Beyond Mysterium Tremendum: Thoughts towards an Aesthetic Study of Religious Experience' *Annals of the American Academy of Political and Social Sciences* 595.1, (2004), 194. See also Leon Schlamm 'Rudolf Otto and Mystical Experience' *Religious Studies*, 27.3, (1991) 389-398.

8 Stewart Perowne, *Roman Mythology*, (Feltham: Newnes Books, 1983[1969]), 18-23. There were limitless *numina*, and many were

extremely local and had few distinctive characteristics. Examples include the household guardians the *lares*, and the *penates*, the 'dwellers in the storeroom'.

9   Rachel Maines and James Glynn 'Numinous Objects,' *The Public History* 15.1 (1993): 10.
10 Mircea Eliade. *The Sacred and the Profane: The Nature of Religion* (San Diego: Harcourt & Brace, 1987[1957]), 9.
11 See Maines and Glynn 'Numinous Objects,' 9-25 for more detailed examples of numinous object and the reasons for their numinosity.
12 Eliade. *The Sacred and the Profane*. 12.
13 William E. Paden. 'Reappraising Durkheim for the Study and Teaching of Religion,' in The Oxford Handbook of The Sociology of Religion, ed. Peter Clarke. (Oxford: Oxford University Press, 2011), 34. For a more in-depth exploration of the differing methodologies surrounding the use of the term 'sacred' see Matthew T. Evans, 'The Sacred: Differentiating, Clarifying and Extending Concepts,' *Review of Religious Research* 45.1 (2003), 32-47.
14 Paden, 'Reappraising Durkheim,' 12.
15 James Lewis, 'Introduction,' in *Magical Religion and Modern Witchcraft*, ed. James R. Lewis (New York: State University of New York Press, 1996), 4.
16 Otto, *The Idea of the Holy*, 5.
17 Eliade. *The Sacred and the Profane*, 10.
18 Michael York, *Pagan Theology: Paganism as a World Religion*, (New York University Press, 2005), 36.
19 Edwyn Bevan, *Holy Images: An Inquiry into Idolatry and Image-Worship in Ancient Paganism and in Christianity*, (London: George Allen & Unwin, 1940), 142. Kasulis also explores this idea in Shinto. He explains that once an object or place is deemed holy (or a *kami*), it is impossible to break the connection, likening to fresh water coming in contact to the sea; 'once the relation occurs, the fresh water cannot be separated from each other.' Thomas Kasulis, *Shinto: The Way Home*, (Honolulu: University of Hawai'i Press, 2004), 21.
20 Eliade. *The Sacred and the Profane*, 9.
21 Otto, *The Idea of the Holy*, 26.
22 For more information regarding the denizens of the otherworld see: Ted Andrews, *Enchantments of the Faerie Realm* (Minnesota: Llewellyn Publications, 1994), *passim*.
23 Vivianne Crowley describes the otherworld as 'the Land of Faery, a spiritual realm that is neither of Heaven nor Earth, but lies somewhere in between. She goes on to explain that it 'is the realm of the Wiccan circle; a sacred space not ruled by clock time or linear thought, but by the

timeless truths of the myths and dreams of the human psyche.' *Wicca: The Old Religion in the New Millennium* (San Francisco: Thorsons, 1996), 47-48.
24 The veils between the worlds are said to become thin on the festivals of Samhain and Beltane, both which are commonly celebrated by the contemporary Pagan community. Samhain, the Celtic New Year festival, occurs traditionally on October 31st, and is more commonly know as All Hallows Eve, or Hallowe'en, due to the fact that on this day the spirits of the dead, and other beings from the 'otherworld' are said to be able cross over into our world and vice versa. See Barbara Davy, *Introduction to Pagan Studies*, (Lanham: AltaMira Press, 2007), 58.
25 Arthur Cotterell. *Celtic Mythology*, (Oxford: Sebastian Kelly, 1999), 20.
26 For example, 'The Voyage of Bran,' in Myles Dillon, *Early Irish Literature* (Dublin: Four Courts Press, 1994[1948]), 124-131; and ed. Jonathan Wooding, *The Otherworld Voyage* (Dublin: Four Courts Press, 2000), *passim*.
27 Crowley, *Wicca: The Old Religion in the New Millennium*, 115.
28 Anne Bancroft, *Origins of the Sacred* (London: Arkana, 1987), 93.
29 Eliade. *The Sacred and the Profane*, 25.
30 Kasulis defines 'holographic entry point' as 'any phenomena through which we become aware that the whole is reflected in every part.' Kasulis, *Shinto: The Way Home*, 21.
31 Otto. *The Idea of the Holy*, 13.
32 The idea of accessing the divine or communicating with supernatural beings in order to gain access to universal truths, or a deeper understanding of the world and its workings, is not unique to the Pagan tradition. This practice is common in many religions and spiritual belief systems. For example many Shamanic traditions use trance states, also known as altered states of consciousness (ASC's) to travel between the realms and communicate directly with supernatural beings in order to gain information and knowledge that will benefit their communities. See Michael Ripinsky-Naxon, *The Nature of Shamanism: substance and function of a religious metaphor* (Albany, New York: State University of New York Press, 1993), 69.
33 Davy, *Introduction to Pagan Studies*, 2.
34 For a detailed history of the origins of the term, its negative connotations and the contemporary movement reason for its use see Michael Strmiska, 'Modern Paganism in World Cultures: Comparative Perspectives,' in *Modern Paganism in World Cultures: Comparative Perspectives*, ed. Michael Strmiska (Santa Barbara, CA: ABC:CLIO, 2005), 4-10.
35 Dennis Carpenter, 'Emergent Nature Spirituality: An Examination of the Major Spiritual Contours of the Contemporary Pagan Worldview,'

in *Magical Religion and Modern Witchcraft*, ed. James R. Lewis, (New York: State University of New York Press, 1996), 41.
36 Paul, Ricoeur, *Figuring the sacred. Religion, Narrative, and Imagination*, (Fortress Press: Minneapolis, 1995), 61.
37 Carpenter, 'Emergent Nature Spirituality,' 69.
38 Michael York, 'Idoltary, Ecology and the Sacred as Tangible,' *The Pomegranate* 12.1 (2010), 79.
39 Daren Kemp explains that it is Paganism's interpretation of reincarnation as a 'simpler view of natural cycles ... more suggestive of the eternal round than vertical planes' that separated its from the New Age's more 'karmic' and 'judgment[al]' hieratical planes.' Daren Kemp, *New Age: A Guide*, (Edinburgh: Edinburgh University Press, 2004), 8.
40 Strmiska, 'Modern Paganism in World Cultures: Comparative Perspectives,' 18.
41 Joanne Pearson, 'Neopaganism,' in *Dictionary of Gnosis and Western Esotericism*, Vol. 2, ed. Wouter Hanegraaff (Leiden: Brill, 2005), 828.
42 Wouter Hanegraaff. *New Age Religion and Wester Culture: Esotericism in the Mirror of Secular Thought* (Albany: State University of New York Press, 1998), 84.
43 Pearson, 'Neopaganism,' 828.
44 Erik Davis, 'Remains of the Deities: Reading the Return of Paganism,' *Voice Literary Supplement* (1993), http://www.techgnosis.com/neopaganism.html.
45 See Douglas Ezzy and Shelley Rabinovitch for more detailed explanations of the different types of witches. Douglas Ezzy, 'What is a Witch,' in *Practicing The Witch's Craft*, ed. Douglas Ezzy (Crows Nest: Allen & Unwin, 2003), 1-22; Shelley TSivia Rabinovitch, 'Spells of Transformation: Categorizing Modern Neo-Pagan Witches,' in *Magical Religion and Modern Witchcraft*, ed. James R. Lewis (Albany: State University of New York Press, 1996), 75-92.
46 For more information on the general beliefs and practices of Witchcraft see: Raymond Buckland, *The Complete Book of Witchcraft* (St Paul: Llewellyn Publications, 1999) *passim*; and Crowley, *Wicca*. For Witchcraft in Australia see: Matthew Phillips and Julia Phillips, *The Witches of Oz* (Berks: Capall Bann Publishing, 1994); Lynne Hume, *Witchcraft and Paganism in Australia* (Melbourne: Melbourne University Press, 1998), and Douglas Ezzy ed. *Practicing the Witch's Craft*, (Crows Nest: Allen & Unwin, 2003).
47 Siân Reid, 'As I Do Will, So Mote it Be: Magic as Metaphor in Neo-Pagan Witchcraft,' in *Magical Religion and Modern Witchcraft*, ed. James R. Lewis (Albany: State University of New York Press, 1996), 150.

48 H.S. Versnel, 'Some Reflections on the Relationship between Magic-Religion,' *Numen*, 38:2, 1991, 178.
49 Ann Moura, *Green Magic: The Sacred Connection to Nature*, (Minnesota: Llewellyn Publications, 2002), 81-86.
50 Susan Greenwood, *The Nature of Magic: An Anthropology of Consciousness*, (Oxford: Berg, 2005), 6.
51 Scott Cunningham, *Encyclopaedia of Magical Herbs*, (St Paul: Llewellyn Publications, 2002), 215.
52 Cunningham, *Magical Herbs*, 139.
53 Gabby Cleary, 'Training and finding a working group,' in Ezzy ed. *Practising the Witch's Craft*, (Crows Nest: Allen & Unwin, 2003), 228-241.
54 For more information of Eldergrove's gatherings and High Priestess see Fiona Horne, *Witch: A Personal Journey* (Sydney: Random House, 1998), 215-232.
55 Applegrove Website: http://www.applegroveonline.com/coh.asp, last accessed 20th June 2010.
56 My thanks are due to Gabby, Jo and Michael of Applegrove, Sydney, Australia, for making their teaching information for Circle of the Hearth, available to me, as well as their personal experiences of the *Numinous* during rituals and other pagan practices.
57 In the northern hemisphere Samhain traditionally occurs on the 31st October/1st November. However, because the Wheel is based on the turning of the seasons, these dates are normally swapped in the southern hemisphere, with Samhain occurring on the 30th April/1st May. For more information about the Wheel of the Year and its associated festivals see: Davy, *Introduction to Pagan Studies*, 56-59; for an Australian perspective see Phillips and Phillips, *The Witches of Oz*, 65-80.
58 For an example of a mythos connected to the Wheel of the Year see Crowley, *Wicca: The Old Religion in the New Millennium*, 156-170.
59 Jo, personal communication 29th July, 2008.
60 Buckland, *Buckland's Complete Book of Witchcraft*, 22.
61 Blayze, 'Setting up an Altar,' http://www.applegroveonline.com/articles.asp
62 Many pagans feel drawn to a particular aspect or deity, and may set up and altar dedicated specifically to that God/Goddess. Blayze and Jo have an altar to the Celtic Goddess Brigit set up in their living room, as Brigit is a Goddess of the hearth and home, associated with womanly arts and concerns such as healing, craft, learning poetry and fertility. See Michael Jordan, *The Encyclopaedia of Gods*, (London: Kyle Cathie,1995 [1992]), 54 .
63 Gabby, personal communication, 29th July, 2008

64 The Panathenaia was an ancient Greek ritual celebrated in Athens in honor of the city's patron Goddess, Athena's birthday. For more information see Jenifer Neils (ed.), *Worshipping Athena: Panathenaia and Parthenon* (Wisconsin: University of Wisconsin Press, 1996).

65 Bevan, *Holy Images: An Inquiry into Idolatry and Image-Worship in Ancient Paganism and in Christianity*, 23.

66 Phillips and Phillips, *The Witches of Oz*, 17.

67 Blayze, 'The Placement of Altars in Wicca,' *Circle of the Hearth Teaching notes*, unpublished.

68 Phillips and Phillips, *The Witches of Oz*, 17-18.

69 Other examples of sacred sites in the United Kingdom include Glastonbury Tor, the Chalice Well, and the *Uffington* White Horse. In America locations including Sedona and the Bighorn Medicine Wheel are seen as sacred to members of the Pagan Community, pilgrimage to such sites is seen as a transformative experience as one can tap into the resonance of the divine located at such sites. Dominique Beth Wilson, 'Sacred water: Pilgrimage to and veneration of holy wells by pagans and Christians in the British Isles,' in *Exile and Homecoming,* ed. Pamela O'Neill (Sydney: University of Sydney, 2005) 330.

70 Buckland, *Buckland's Complete Book of Witchcraft*, 41.

71 Blayze, 'Circle Casting,' http://www.applegroveonline.com/articles.asp, last accessed 1st September 2008.

72 The following is an example of a chant used by Applegove when casting a circle:
By the blade a Circle born,
Between the worlds a boundary formed,
By the powers raised herein,
To guard without and hold within,
Be this Circle Cast
Taken from, 'Full Moon Training Notes—Sydney Version,' *Pagan Awareness Network*, unpublished, April 2008, pg. 18, used with permission.

73 For more information on circles and circle casting see Crowley, *Wicca: The Old Religion in the New Millennium*, 43-68.

74 Blayze, 'Circle Casting.'

75 Gabby, personal communication, 29th July, 2008.

76 Examples of rituals which are just for fun include the Chocolate Ritual, and the Honey Ritual, both of which have been used as part of Beltane Celebrations held by Blayze over the years. The outlines for both rituals, and many others, are available at http://www.applegroveonline.com/rituals.asp, 1/9/08.

77 Michael, personal communication, 9 August 2008.

78 Michael, personal communication, 9th August, 2008.
79 Some Pagans choose to work naked or skyclad, 'clad only by the sky', as they see it as being closer to Nature and one's natural state. Buckland, *The Complete Book of Witchcraft*, 33.
80 Jo, personal communication 29th July, 2008.
81 Joanne Dunster, 'Props Making,' *Circle of the Hearth Teaching notes*, unpublished.
82 Jo, personal communication 29th July, 2008.
83 Melissa Raphael, *Rudolf Otto and the Concept of Holiness*, 9.
84 Hans Biedermann, *Dictionary of Symbolism* (New York: Meridian, 1994), 16.
85 Gabby, personal communication 29 July 2008.
86 Kasulis, *Shinto,* 21.

3
Encountering the *Universal* Triple Goddess in Wicca

Nikki Bado

Maiden, Mother, Crone

When asked to write this chapter, I was quite excited by the opportunity to address a number of long-standing and even thorny issues connected with the Triple Goddess that have puzzled and intrigued me over the years in my role as an interdisciplinary scholar of Contemporary Paganism. I have looked at the embodied practice of ritual, considered women's roles in religions, and studied folklore—all carefully examined through a philosophical lens. Just as important to this discussion is the fact that I first encountered the Maiden, Mother, and Crone when I was a college student in the early seventies and began studying for initiation into what would eventually become my parent coven, which I understood at that time as belonging to a form of British Traditional Wicca. That statement marks me as both scholar and practitioner, an often tricky and occasionally perilous identity that challenges the dualism of insider/outsider so prevalent in many studies of religion.[1]

Dichotomous thinking is unsatisfying for a number of reasons. It almost always essentializes, reducing each end of the binary construction to a uniform monolith not reflected in actual human experience. It assumes that there is only one insider voice, or that insider perspectives are uniform or monolithic. Just as my 'outsider voice' is complicated and multifaceted by the fact that I am an interdisciplinary scholar, my 'insider voice' is complicated and multifaceted as a woman, a feminist, and a Witch—a number of dimensions that hardly reflect a single perspective. The terms insider and outsider actually conceal a whole realm of discourse engaged in by a multitude of shifting voices and perspectives in negotiation and even contestation with one another. Religious practice, like scholarly practice, tends to be a messy affair, with various descriptions, judgments, perspectives, analyses, and outright opinions contending and sometimes conflicting with one another.

But the multi-faceted perspectives concealed by scholar-practitioner present us with an opportunity to view particular teachings and practices connected with the Triple Goddess at least somewhat first-hand, as well as through the critical lenses of interdisciplinary scholarship. As I reasoned in my first book (2005) *Coming to the Edge of the Circle: A Wiccan Initiation Ritual*, getting down to the level of *individuals-practising*[2] their religions yields insights into the ways in which people construct and perform religious paradigms and make them meaningful. This method of reflexive and self-aware engagement allows us to avoid the disembodied, essentialized, and decontextualized discourses about religion and ritual that we so often encounter in the field.

By more closely examining the paradigm of the Triple Goddess at the level of individuals-practising, we may discover useful material 'to think with' that challenges what have become normative ideas of the Goddess and addresses some of the questions connected with Her triune form. While it is true the Triple Goddess as Maiden, Mother, and Crone was a fundamental—I am wary of the term *universal*—theological construct for my own coven, Her story is unsurprisingly much more nuanced, complex, and multifaceted—in other words, much more bewitchingly messy and interesting—than it first appears.

Over the past thirty years or so, growing numbers of women (and men) have chosen to create or explore alternatives to traditional religions, often motivated by the search for full or more satisfying religious participation, expression, and authority. Fuelled partly by the influence of the Women's Movement and the growing body of feminist scholarship critical of androcentric religions, this has translated into an impressive growth in alternative religions with a Western mythological base, many of which involve some aspect of Goddess worship.

Certainly one of these Western Goddess religions is Wicca, here variously called Witchcraft or simply the Craft.[3] Perhaps more than any other single work, Starhawk's publication of *The Spiral Dance* in 1979 led thousands of women to this religious path, and they have left an indelible mark upon this living, endlessly changing, and evolving religious form. But the term 'Goddess religions' includes a number of other Contemporary Pagan religions, some of which are rooted in particular ethnic or national identities and are distinct from Wicca historically and in terms of practice. It also includes a variety of religious practices we might simply call 'Goddess' or 'Feminist Spirituality', many of them inspired by books such as Z. Budapest's (1975) *The Feminist Book of Lights and Shadows*, Merlin Stone's (1976) *When God Was a Woman*, or Margot Adler's (1979) *Drawing Down the Moon*, which came out at the same time as Starhawk's *Spiral Dance*.

The Triple Goddess—most often represented by the cycles of the Moon and framed in terms of Maiden, Mother, and Crone—has become established as a nearly universal theological paradigm not only for Witches or Wiccans, but also for many other Contemporary Pagans and followers of the modern Goddess movement. By now of course many Pagans and Witches are familiar with the origin story of the Triple Goddess, its relatively recent construction, and the influence of Robert Graves and his (1948) book *The White Goddess* in the formation of the paradigm. Historian Ronald Hutton carefully traces the development of the Triple Goddess in his (1999) book *The Triumph of the Moon*. Drawing heavily on the Cambridge school of myth-ritualists, especially Sir James Frazer and Jane Harrison's 'imagery of three aspects', Hutton notes that Graves further

> *related them to the waxing, full, and waning moon, to represent the One Goddess most potently as a bringer of life and death, in her forms as Maiden, Mother, and Crone. He divided her son and consort into two opposed aspects of his own, as God of the Waxing and of the Waning Year, fated to be rivals and combatants for her love.*[4]

This accurately describes the ways in which my parent coven thought of deity. Ours was a British Traditional coven, and as a student dedicant I read all the mythological stories I could find on the Gods and Goddesses our Circle honoured and worshipped in preparation for my initiation, including Graves' *The White Goddess*, which my High Priest hinted 'accurately described' some features of Wiccan deity.

For many Wiccans and some Contemporary Pagans, the Triple Goddess forms one half of a duotheistic theological paradigm that includes a God, who is understood as either having a dual aspect in the form of the seasons of Winter and Summer, or a triple aspect as Solar, Vegetative, and Hunter deities. Many covens are polytheistic and choose to worship Gods and

Goddesses within a particular group or pantheon of related deities, but also feel free to invoke deities outside of those pantheons as required by the circumstances of a particular ritual or need. Goddesses and Gods are generally worshipped within the context of the seasonal cycles of Nature and, through these cycles, are invoked into worshippers' lives as powerfully transformative catalysts for change and growth.

Having read the mythologies extensively, I understood each of the Goddesses and Gods as having distinct personalities, narratives, attributes, and roles. But I also learned to think about them in more abstract terms. Most of the time my High Priest presented deity as a kind of overarching presence in the form of a male Solar deity and a female Lunar deity, despite the existence of Solar Goddesses and Moon Gods found throughout the world, including within our own pantheons. The Solar God and Lunar Goddess formed a kind of male/female polarity that together created the cosmos and were intimately connected with time and particular actions—Their cycles positioned within both the natural world and the personal one. The Solar cycle formed the Wheel of the Year, the Eight Witches' Sabbats. The Lunar cycle described a monthly rhythm of energy, its ebb and flow marking a shorter cycle in which to do things.

Practitioners of Wicca and other Contemporary Pagan and Goddess religions typically understand the Triple Goddess as either a single female deity having three major aspects or dimensions, or a trio of Goddesses who are interrelated and function together in some way as one. Connecting the Maiden aspect with birth, new beginnings, inspiration, and the courage to start anew, practitioners represent Her by the new/waxing Moon. The Mother is the nurturer and caretaker, and represents fertility, the ripeness and fullness of the growing season that brings all things to fruition. Her protective strength maintains and sustains life and is symbolized by the full Moon. Finally the Crone represents death, banishing, letting go, endings, age, and wisdom, and is represented by the waning/dark Moon.

It is as stages in the female biological lifecycle where the Triple Goddess seems especially to function as a paradigm or archetype, one that gives women the potent ability to resonate with deity through the sacralized body. Starhawk eloquently writes:

> *The image of the Goddess inspires women to see ourselves as divine, our bodies as sacred, the changing phases of our lives as holy, our aggression as healthy, our anger as purifying, and our power to nurture and create, but also to limit and destroy when necessary, as the very force that sustains all life.*[5]

According to some practitioners, this kind of identification with deity is something that women have not been able to do 'since the advent of patriarchy'.[6] Certainly it is extremely rare under the more patriarchal and androcentric manifestations of the Abrahamic traditions, which tend to exclude women from full religious participation and authority — sometimes entirely so.

Reclaiming the sacrality of the body is one of the most significant and powerful lessons of the Triple Goddess, for men as well as women, potentially countering centuries of somataphobia and denigration of the body in general and the *female* body in particular. Starhawk continues,

> *The Craft also demands a new relationship to the female body. No longer can it be seen as an object or vilified as something dirty. A woman's body, its odors, secretions, and menstrual blood, are sacred, are worthy of reverence and celebration.*[7]

In saying this, Starhawk anticipates the insights of feminist theorists such as Luce Irigaray and Elizabeth Grosz, whose works call for a rethinking of female difference and who tackle the issues of somataphobia and essentialism that inevitably seem to hover around the edge of any discussion of the female body. The question is whether the embodiedness of the Triple Goddess and the celebration of Her female form *empowers* women and connects them with the holy. Or whether the Triple Goddess simply *reduces* women to body once again and reinforces the dualistic and androcentric stereotypes found throughout Western culture — in which the body has occupied a problematic place at least as far back as Plato. Confrontation with the issues of somataphobia and essentialism is absolutely central to Goddess feminists if we are to reclaim the female body, according to Kathryn Rountree's fascinating 2004 study of feminist Witches in New Zealand, *Embracing the Witch and the Goddess*:

> *Embracing and assigning positive meanings and value to the female body, female sexuality in whatever form it takes, and female biological functions (for example, menstruation) are an important preoccupation of Goddess feminists not simply to reverse the patriarchal devaluation, but because they are important to women, give women pleasure and pain, preoccupy women from time to time, and are essential (yes, essential) to women's being.*[8]

The Triple Goddess not only potentially facilitates the empowering of women and women's bodies as holy, but also functions for some of Her practitioners as an important psychological archetype in *human* — not just female—consciousness. This can be seen in the works of post-Jungian writers such as Nor Hall, Jean Shinoda Bolen, M. Esther Harding, and Erich Neumann, as well as by popular Pagan authors, such D.J. Conway, who writes: 'The Triple Goddess, the three faces of human life, are ingrained in the human subconscious and collective unconscious.' Conway further notes that acknowledging 'their practical application in human lives can create a foundation for understanding ourselves and future generations'.[9]

Trouble in Paradigms

As an ingrained archetype in human consciousness, the Triple Goddess must be a significant and universal paradigm indeed. But there are signs that the universal paradigm is beginning to crack. Depending upon whom you talk to among both scholars and practitioners in Pagan and Goddess communities, the Maiden, Mother, and Crone are either self-evident ancient and empowering figures that have been universally revered as primal archetypes since the dawn of time—or at least since Neolithic times. Or they are relatively recent romantic literary constructs rooted in dubious scholarship that are possibly essentialist, covertly sexist, and woefully inadequate in capturing the range of women's life cycles, roles, and expectations of longevity.

And worries over interpreting these aspects of the Goddess as *supporting* structures to patriarchy are not helped by connecting them to Carl Jung's notions of archetypes. According to the late Asphodel P. Long,

> *Much of the objection to ideas of women's spirituality and the Goddess movement has centred on the eager acceptance by many women of Jung's ideas of 'the Feminine', disregarding his own overt sexism. Many still today believe that the Feminine and thus women are more sensitive, caring, perceptive, intuitive and so on, and yield to the Masculine the areas of intellectual thought and activity in the professional world.*[10]

Far from monolithically universal, the paradigm of our Triple Goddess appears to envelop a lively universe of shifting voices and multiple perspectives engaged in discussion, negotiation, and contestation with one another. Various online communities of Goddess feminists and Pagans occasionally struggle with these and other issues connected to the Triple Goddess. One pertinent example can be found on the blog *Medusa Coils*, http://medusacoils.blogspot.com, a fascinating column by Goddess scholar Judith Laura, who insightfully addresses some of the issues with the Triple Goddess paradigm.[11] These and other such online discussions frequently revolve around the inadequacy of the terms Maiden, Mother, and Crone to reflect the actual stages of women's lives, and participants in the discussion often attempt to suggest other stages or dimensions of categorization that are more accurate. For example, instead of three stages, why not four, or five or some other number? The number three doesn't seem really to describe even the phases of the Moon, and the Crone stage of the Triple Goddess appears particularly inadequate to capture women's increased lifespan after menopause.

Perhaps we should modify the age at which a woman becomes a Crone, or redefine what the word Crone itself means. After all, today many fifty-year old menopausal women simply don't feel like the ancient Crones of times gone by. Life isn't over after menopause, especially if you are healthy and relatively well off economically. Participants in these discussions proffer and debate terms such as Queen, Sovereign, Elder, Matriarch, and others as either substitutes for the word Crone, or additional fourth or fifth stages to the Triple Goddess, but objections are often made to those categories on the basis of their relationships with power and hierarchy, among other things. At the other end of the spectrum from Crone, a few have suggested elaborating on the time of childhood, a time before the sexual availability often suggested by the word Maiden.

Many of these discussions revolve rather literally around female biology, which is surprising if one of the goals of Goddess feminists is to escape the crippling biological determinism so prevalent in patriarchal discourses. Focusing on the aspects' literal connection with the lifecycles of the female body, some feminists worry that these dimensions of the Triple Goddess may be fundamentally and covertly sexist—or at least nonthreatening to the male patriarchy—and too prone to being defined in terms of how they relate with men and are tied to heterosexual and biological experience.[12] Images of a young, attractive, nubile, sexually available teenage Maiden and a nurturing, comforting, and protective Mother are hardly challenging to male structures of power. The Crone aspect seems to be the most difficult to portray as nonthreatening, although I suppose She might be stretched in this context to fit the role of the doting grandmother.

Feminists who worry about the ways in which the Triple Goddess can be used to reinforce sexist stereotypes do have a point, and it is one that I have experienced first-hand. Ideally, female Witches have roles that are both extremely powerful *and* valuable and that are not ones of passivity and obedience to male authority.[13] But while Wicca has many wonderful images of female divinity along with powerful and valuable roles for women, it has never been feminist heaven. Wicca has been and still can be pretty sexist in practice.

I recall my High Priest trying to explain to us—quite unsuccessfully, really—why he could become an old man and retain his position as High Priest, while the High Priestess must always be a lovely young maiden, presumably chosen by the High Priest, of course. In other words, an aging High Priestess must step down for a younger woman at precisely the time in her life when she has the greatest experience. I think this attitude toward aging women was consistent with how the Goddess Herself was viewed at that time. When I was initiated in the early seventies, Witches seemed to emphasize the alluring Maiden or the nurturing Mother, and women were encouraged to choose Craft names that reflected these identities. The third aspect or dimension of the Goddess, the dark Crone of wisdom and death, was vaguely developed and given comparatively little emphasis.

In formal classes, my High Priest always presented the female as a reflection of the male's light, just as the moon reflects the light of the sun (and presumably just as the High Priestess reflects the light of the High Priest). According to him, power was always carefully balanced by level: the male may be more powerful in the outer world, but the female more powerful in the inner world. The male is the better magician because he is the better 'projector' of magic, while the female is the better clairvoyant, the ultimate 'receptor'. While perhaps intended to be a lesson on complementarity and balance, these descriptions of the roles of the Lunar Goddess and Solar God fit more than anything else into a particular cultural narrative about gender roles for women and men rooted in a kind of biological determinism, an observation that did not escape me then, and one that has grown in certainty over the years.

But like most religious practitioners, Witches participate in a universe of competing and sometimes conflicting discourses and practices. We must be careful not to conflate Witchcraft with feminism, or to assume that Witchcraft is entirely patriarchy-free simply because of the existence of Goddesses in its pantheon. The same can probably be said of other forms of Contemporary Pagan practice.

In this regard, it is probably wise to remember that for every sexist discourse about the roles of women and men wrapped in the guise of mythic paradigms about the Triple Goddess and Her Solar consort, there are countering discourses that are liberating. For instance, the same myths I read for initiation taught valuable lessons about the range of attributes assigned to 'gender', a word perhaps not as extensively used back then as it is today. Ultimately, I could find no attributes available to Gods that were not also available to Goddesses, and vice versa. There were Gods and Goddesses of war, of healing, of inspiration, of smithcraft, of the hunt, of death, of sex, and of love. As genders, they were equally capable of intelligence and creativity, nurturing and comfort, fierceness and battle, wisdom and compassion.

It seems to me that there are at least three major and interrelated challenges that must be overcome if we are to successfully reclaim and resacralize the body, especially the *female* body. They include literalism and dichotomous thinking, both wrapped within the problem of the idea of paradigm itself. Each of these challenges affects Western culture more broadly than a discussion of the Triple Goddess and is worth much more extensive discussion than can be had here. But this is a good place to begin.

The Literal Truth and Nothing But the Truth

The Triple Goddess aspects can be interpreted as relating quite easily and literally to the female menstrual cycle—one of the reasons my High Priest gave for identifying the moon with women was the timing of our 'monthly cycles'—and of course the ability to have babies. The Maiden begins Her menses and can now begin to have babies; the Mother has the babies and nurtures them; and the more vaguely conceptualized Crone emerges when She can no longer have babies, so perhaps She can serve as Grandmother for the babies. If biology is destiny or at least identity, some feminist scholars worry whether women can be fully realized as women only if they have produced children.[14]

Curiously these same worries don't seem to accompany God the Father, who is not normally visualized as God-the-Great-Penis-Universal-Inseminator, at least not since the time of Zeus, who seemed to get around. Here we can perhaps see that bodies are problematized in different ways for males and females. Female bodies are literally highlighted, usable for everything from mythic symbols to advertising. But male bodies are...missing, at least missing certain parts. God's body, especially His penis, seems to have been erased, something I think He would find rather distressing. And yet this occurs even in Pagan publications, for example, wherever the Cerne Abbas Giant or Rude Man is portrayed without the giant member. Rude indeed.

It might be useful to think about how we can accomplish the reclaiming of *all* bodies—male and female—without falling back on a kind of literal biological determinism, something that seems 'natural' for women, wombs, and Goddesses, but downright silly when applied to men, penises, and Gods. We can understand here that our discussants in online communities walk a fine line: how to *reclaim* body without being *reduced* to body. In other words, they grapple with a long-standing Western dichotomy between mind and body, male and female—trying to create more accurate models of deity without falling into the trap of biological literalism.

Certainly, it would be relatively easy for Witches and other Contemporary Pagans and Goddess worshippers to create rituals celebrating lifecycle changes using the Triple Goddess in a literal way: invoking Maiden Goddesses for young girls and menarche, Mother Goddesses for birth rituals, Crones at menopause, and so forth, readily keying the stages of the Moon to chronological stages in female life. But in the body of ritual practices inherited from my parent coven, the Triple Goddess was almost never used in this fashion. There were no rites that specifically addressed either female or male events of *literal* biological transformation, which may say something about the invisibility of such events within large portions of Western culture[15]—a conversation for perhaps another time.

If my own covens are any indication at all,[16] a literal understanding both of the Triple Goddess aspects and their application to exclusively female lifecycle experiences would be far from accurate in terms of how the aspects are generally used by Witches and other Contemporary Pagans and Goddess worshippers. The Moon's monthly cycles of waxing and waning provide a visible reminder of the ebb and flow of life's energies. Practitioners understand and employ the symbol of the Triple Goddess in a multivalent fashion that suggests a more fluid understanding of gender, and a somatically based awareness of the permeable or porous boundaries between people, between people and Nature, and between people and the Gods. This fluidity affords ample opportunities to ritually celebrate the various stages of human experience and enables women *and men* of all ages, sexual orientations, and biological conditions to invoke Her in order to enact powerfully transformative rites that celebrate and shape the changes in their lives.

Male deities, here usually connected to the Sun, also work in much the same way and are fully accessible by both male and female Witches. Gods are sometimes understood in terms of the dual aspects of summer and winter, balancing cycles of growth and decay, activity and rest, within practitioners' lives. They may also be understood as having a tripartite dimension in the form of solar, vegetative, and forest/animal aspects worshipped within the Solar Wheel. Following the solar cycle, Witches celebrate the returning Sun—the spark of life—at Winter Solstice. This is the time of year when the worshipper rests, contemplating the success or failure of last year's activities, and plans what changes she will make in the year to come. As the Sun grows in intensity until its height at Midsummer, the Witch plans for the coming year, planting seeds of change in the spring, working hard to establish her goals through the summer, and looking forward to fruitful harvest.

The fluidity of the Lunar triple aspects and their connection to the timing of ritual events are two of the first major lessons students learn within my lineage of the Craft, and it occurs during the embodied ritual performance of the Dedication Ceremony. As I discuss in *Coming to the Edge of the Circle*, students learn that the Moon as deity is not merely a metaphor, a way to think about things, but a time to *do* things. Any Witch, male or female, of any age, may call upon the power of the Maiden at the new and waxing moon to ask for Her blessings to secure the skill and inspiration to launch a new project, to obtain a fresh start, or to make a new beginning. At the Full Moon, any Witch may turn to the Mother for the strength and vitality needed to sustain his goals, his projects, and himself. During the Waning and Dark Moon, the Crone gives to any Witch, regardless of age or gender, the power to destroy in order to create, to end in order to begin anew.

These cycles all represent *human* life experiences. Everyone, male or female, can participate equally in the Moon's cycles and can share in the life-affirming, transformative powers of the Goddess. No one is left out because she is not heterosexual, or not a biological mother, or because she is too young to be a Crone, or too old to be a Maiden. No one is left out because the *she* is actually a *he*. The invocation of the feminine divine by men and their subsequent identification with the fluid range of human experiences framed within the feminine divine is something that feminist theologians and scholars of religions should find thought-provoking and worthy of further exploration.

It strikes me that this conversation about the literal interpretation of the Triple Goddess paradigm may be concealing a larger point about our culture—the disturbing extent to which we have lost the ability, especially in religious discourse, to interpret narratives in ways outside of the literal frame, or to recognize the importance of myth and allegory. This is something I frequently encounter in my introductory comparative religions classes: students consistently interpret religious (as well as other) narratives literally and have a hard time recognizing or understanding the importance of myth and allegory in shaping meanings. They are also baffled by any discussion of truth not framed within binary logical structures. Truth has merely become one side of a coin tossed by a logical positivist: if it's not True, it must be False. Truth itself as a category has narrowed, and become singular, represented by a capital 'T'. 'Truth' includes only those things that can be proven by either science or history and established as fact.

I offer one anecdotal case in point merely to illustrate the problem. In a lesson about the five ways that scholars have identified to understand religious narrative—literal, rational, allegorical, mythical, or from a faith stance—I write on the board the bits and pieces of what students know about the life of Jesus. We begin with a set of premises we all agree will be unquestioned for the sake of argument: someone named Jesus was born, lived, and died.

Students expand the story from there, adding their favorite parts about his birth, his teachings, their favourite miracles, the way he died, and so on. Then we interpret the story of Jesus using the five different approaches. Only the initial premises can be interpreted as true under the 'rational' perspective and are circled on the board. The 'literal' approach requires the most work, leading to discussions about the nature of evidence, the necessity of doing biblical archaeology to find proof, the feasibility of going to the Middle East to search for the fish bones from the fish Jesus fed to the multitudes, and so forth. In many ways, the 'faith stance' seems to be strongest, as questions about having to prove things true aren't even raised. The 'allegorical' and 'mythical' stances prove to be the most elusive. Here, students grapple with understanding how aspects of a story can be 'true', or even meaningful at all if they are not connected to factual—i.e., historical or scientific—proof.

Many students tell me that they are encouraged by their pastors and other religious teachers to read religious narratives as if they were literal truths. Here I wonder if the faith stance and the literalist stances aren't being conflated with one another: to have faith now means to believe everything literally. This might explain why some students have trouble seeing 'literal' and 'faith' as separate approaches to interpretation. The hidden danger here is of course the challenges that science, history, and even education itself pose to faith. Do you lose your faith if something disagrees with scientific proof or historical fact? Does the story of Jesus' birth become meaningless when you discover that he was in all likelihood not born on December 25? For everyone outside of the United States baffled by the most recent (there have been others) anti-evolutionist, anti-science, anti-history, anti-educational, anti-intellectual trends in modern American political life, this conflation of faith and literalness may provide some insights into the problem.

The lesson in class really starts to get interesting when I contrast the story of Jesus with the story of Ganesh, a popular version illustrated in Hindu comic books. Briefly, the story goes as follows: the Goddess Parvati alone at home wanting some private time to take a bath, getting constantly interrupted, creating a son from the soap bubbles floating in the tub, charging him to guard the door, the unexpected return of her husband Shiva, the fight between Shiva and courageous little Ganesh who stands up to this intruder, Ganesh's beheading, Parvati's dismay, finally Shiva restoring the life of his son, replacing his head with that of a white elephant's.

I end the lesson by asking, 'What is the meaning of the story? What is its truth?' If I'm lucky someone might say something about having courage in the face of unbeatable odds—a good meaning to come from the story of a little boy facing a mighty God of invincibility. Perhaps another student will say something about guarding doorways—another good meaning for Ganesh as both the placer and remover of obstacles. Unfortunately, students hardly ever get to the meaning connected with the elephant's head without a great deal of prompting. The story of Ganesh tells us that the elephant is considered an important and sacred animal, and that the sacred includes all the world, not just humans. Unbelievably, I've had a couple of students who were actually distracted by the anatomical problem of connecting a head from another animal onto a human body.

Finally, I ask, 'Is anyone digging up the subcontinent of India looking for the body of a headless elephant?' And by that time there are usually some glimmers of understanding about the multiple dimensions of truth, the power of story, and the ways in which of narrative and myth *point* to truths and create meaning without having to prove them. Except for the one student who vehemently answered, 'No! They're not digging up India because they don't have the truth!'

I suspect there is an interesting historical narrative that waits to be told, hiding behind this seeming inability to read with depth and imagination and involving the confluence of several events in time. One such event must have been the invention of the printing press, which made possible the growth of literacy by making publications affordable, thereby at least partially breaking the hold the elite and the Church had over education. The printing press created an entirely new method of communication, and likely revolutionized the way people thought about and described the world they lived in. This may even have changed the ways in which our brains worked, much like some interesting cognitive studies today suggest that the Internet has changed how our brains process information, making us more prone to skim and process data superficially.

Another contributor to literalness must have been the Protestant Reformation, which facilitated the move from understanding ritual as the primary locus of religious knowledge and education to privileging text, a move that was eventually so thorough in moving religion from practice to belief that students have a hard time comprehending that religion isn't something that just 'lives in your head'. Before the Reformation, certainly the most prevalent way to understand religious narratives was allegorical and through their ritual performance. This was partly because few folks could read or afford the texts. It was also because the Church tended to 'discourage' regular folks from the jobs of translation and interpretation, usually by treating them as heretics.

Finally, the Enlightenment and the scientific revolution must have marked an overwhelming shift in the means by which truth was established, or even defined. The reactions of devoutly religious people to this new kind of truth might be characterized as 'Our truth is every bit as true as yours, and we can prove it, too, just like you!'—a stance that seems to motivate everything from biblical archaeology to scientific studies that *prove* the Bible is right about everything from feminism, to homosexuality, to family values, to evolution.

Literalism is a problem because it flattens meaning, it replaces our abilities both to think deeply and to feel profoundly by distracting us with trivial math problems. How old is a Crone, how young is a Maiden? How many stages describe the cycle of the Moon? Or—oh, we are not alone in our literal dance—how old is the world, and how long is a day?

Into how many pieces must we cut reality until it is small enough to resemble us? Literalism inhibits us from extending our awareness beyond the surface, from reaching beyond our own skins to find the larger meanings, to discover the greater truths that connect us one to another, connect us to our Gods and Goddesses, connect us to the cosmos. For the Triple Goddess, literalism conceals the deep layers of Her meanings, the multiple ways in which Her followers engage and play with the sensuous rhythms of Her tides and cycles to work those changes and transformations they wish to see in their lives. Literalism hides Her agency and conceals the ways She dances through the world all on Her own, without care for either our counting or our constraints.

Three Times a Charm—Or the Power of Paradigms

And speaking of counting, why the *Triple* Goddess—why the number three? All throughout this chapter, the number three has lurked in the background, little challenged except by those who must count the phases of the moon or number the stages of a woman's life. Notice how often the number makes an appearance in everyday life—in everything from sports to the courts, from real estate to religion, and in countless examples from everyday folklore. Three strikes and you're out! Ready, set, go! The three strike rule in the justice system. Three on a match. Third time's the charm. Three meals a day. Beg, borrow, or steal. Like a three ring circus. Location, location, location. Three aspects of the Goddess. Three dimensions of the Wiccan God. The Christian Trinity. The three Wise Men. Did you notice I said there were *three*—major and interrelated challenges that we must overcome if we are to successfully counter essentialism and somataphobia?

We could go on almost endlessly, thinking up phrases that illustrate the importance of the magic number three. There is so much material on the number three that it has its own fascinating online encyclopedia, *The Book of Threes*, http://threes.com/index.php, with chapters that organize what must be all the articles ever written about the number three, in every category from art to economics, mathematics to myth. The number three is so significant, so paradigmatic that the late folklorist Alan Dundes wrote trichotomy seems to be a *universal* pattern in American culture—just as the scholar Georges Dumézil once wrote that three was the universal pattern throughout Indo-European culture.[17]

In fact, the number three may be the first most paradigmatic thing about the universal paradigm of the Triple Goddess. If so, Her characterization as Maiden, Mother, and Crone has to be the second. Don't get me wrong. Triple Goddesses do indeed occur in several Indo-European mythologies. But when you find them, they seldom—if ever—manifest as Maiden, Mother, and Crone, despite the attempts of practitioners and some scholars to squeeze or mold the Goddesses into this paradigm or, conversely, to twist the categories Maiden, Mother, and Crone themselves beyond all recognition. In other words, it is stretching it to make triune Goddesses such as the fiery Brigid or the formidable Morrigan into Maiden, Mother, and Crone. Why do we insist on seeing Goddesses within this *particular* tripartite paradigm even when they clearly do not fit the model?

Let's answer that by looking more closely at the nature of paradigms and what they do. Scholars create—some would say discover—paradigms for much the same reason we create categories. They make information about cultures, in this case, religions, easier to manoeuvre. Without them, we might have to begin our classes by saying there is no such thing as religions, only religious people, something which my professor Tom Kasulis actually used to do in his introductory religious studies classes. Categories and paradigms enable us to talk about subjects more broadly, more abstractly, by removing and decontextualizing them from their particular manifestations. They are the constructs that enable us to compare, contrast, and make judgments on a meta-level.

But we need to remember that categories and paradigms often conceal as much as they reveal. The category 'Christian', for example conceals a vast range of practices and theological ideas under one label. When asked to name how many flavours of Christianity there are, students in my introductory classes are astonished to discover there are at one count 33,830 distinct denominations organized under about 151 major subheads.[18] Likewise, a term such as 'Hinduism' conceals practices that range from the sensual forms of tantra to extreme forms of asceticism. While perhaps not quite as vast, the range of distinctly different kinds of Contemporary Paganisms is often concealed under the single word

Pagan—or all too often, under the label 'Wicca', which itself conceals both a variety of types of Wiccan practice and simultaneously hides the types of Contemporary Pagan religions that are not associated in any way with Wicca.

My own first encounter with the power of paradigms occurred when I was a graduate student writing on Wiccan initiation. Initially I was sure the rite would fit anthropologist Arnold van Gennep's tripartite rites of passage model, a standard in the field since its creation in the early 1900s. Van Gennep saw initiation and other rites of passage as a three stage—not a coincidence—process with sharply defined movements of separation, liminality, and reincorporation, using a unidirectional spatiality and linear understanding of the transformative process. But when I compared this model closely to an actual practice of initiation performed by a particular group of Witches, the model just didn't work. That discovery led to my eventual dismantling of van Gennep's paradigm in *Coming to the Edge of the Circle: A Wiccan Initiation Ritual*, in favour of one that more accurately captures the shifting roles and perspectives of the participants.[19]

The problem with paradigms is that once they are created—some would say discovered—*it is nearly impossible to escape their influence*. Once identified, they appear everywhere, dominating and even determining what and how we see. If something doesn't fit the model, we manipulate it until it does. Paradigms impose an order upon human experience that is at first convenient, but then constraining. For the unwary researcher, paradigms are tricksters, masters of illusion and delusion that confound our research in the guise of our own expectations, and guarantee we will find what it is we are looking for.

Alan Dundes echoes my concern. After establishing the cultural pattern of trichotomy in American culture, he points out that 'three' is not a universal pattern. It is also not the only American magic number: two, seven, and twelve are *three* obvious examples (italics mine).[20] Philosophical dualism is also part of American culture—one of the *three* problems I suggest is at the heart of essentialism. Nevertheless we often ignore the influence of other numbers as cultural patterns in favor of tripartite models. This is part of a more serious problem. Dundes goes on to suggest that much of our 'objective scholarship' is essentially folklore masquerading as fact:

> *This is the really insidious part of cultural patterning. No individual can escape his culture and its built-in cultural cognitive categories. Yet many individuals think they have escaped, and they claim to have described the nature of objective reality*

> in culture-free terms. But often what scientists and scholars present as bona fide analytical categories are in fact ethnocentric extensions of their own native categories.[21]

Expect to find the Maiden, Mother, and Crone? There She is, even if that *particular* group of triple Goddesses has nothing whatsoever to do with birth, nurturing, or death, or if that *particular* group of three Goddesses seem to be the same age, rather than chronologically ordered as Grandmother, Mother, and Daughter, or even if that *individual* Goddess isn't in any way connected to those two other Goddesses over there. We need to question whether these groupings of three are really there and significant to the culture, or whether we see them because we are looking for them. Do we discover the Maidens, Mothers, and Crones only because that's what we expect to find? And are there other expectations hidden in the universal paradigm of the Triple Goddess?

At least two more suggest themselves to me: that deity must be monotheistic, giving us Goddess the Mother, parallel in form and function to God the Father; and the expectation that our Goddess must be identified with the Moon, and not the Sun. Some practitioners, myself included, occasionally worry that the Triple Goddess bears too much similarity to the Christian male trinity and simply offers us a female version of the monotheistic God. In other words, exclusive worship of *The* Goddess uncomfortably appears too much like the Judeo-Christian god in another sex—'Jahweh-in-drag', an observation made in Craft Circles by Morning Glory Zell at least as early as 1975.[22] Echoing Zell, Margot Adler says that the idea of a single Great Mother Goddess is suspiciously monotheistic, and that it is more reasonable to assume that different cultures created different deities out of different needs.[23]

The worry here is that the sense of freedom and the wide accessibility of the sacred within the Craft, which are engendered by the pluralistic and polytheistic worldview, will be lost to dogma and control every bit as crippling and stifling as any under the patriarchy. Theologically, the creation of a monotheistic Goddess is troubling because it ignores an intrinsically male and female, polytheistic, and pluralistic worldview that is at least potentially quite unlike the monotheistic religions more familiar to Westerners.

But it is precisely this familiarity that is the problem. If categories and paradigms act stealthily, framing things in ways that are already familiar and therefore comfortable, we might well be worried that monotheism is too deeply engrained in our culture to be replaced by a different model. I think it is possible to escape Dundes' trap of cultural patterning, but only if we replace the fiction of 'objective scholarship' with something a bit more realistic—reflexive scholarship, the ability to be aware of and acknowledge one's own perspective in the scholarly process. Another way to avoid the trap of paradigms and categories is to remember that they are constructs, often disembodied and abstract, which can be checked by the reality of individuals-practising their religions, by entering the messy world of religion as it is lived.

In terms of a monotheistic Goddess figure, we may find that there are indeed some practitioners who engage the female divine in this manner. We may also discover that, on the level of individuals-practising, *The Goddess* is actually a lot more multi-faceted and pluralistic than She first appears. Religious practice and theology among Witches, Pagans, and Goddess worshippers express a universe of competing and sometimes conflicting discourses and practices—something that cannot be repeated enough.

Although the discovery of Wicca by the Women's Movement brought what I think are some troubling developments, such as the creation of a potentially monotheistic Goddess and the exclusion of men from Circles, it also brought new maturity and insights to our understanding of Goddesses in general and helped us challenge the more limited roles for women in our religious practice. This has reinvigorated the Craft, providing new modes of religious discourse and models of ritual expression, new challenges to rigid hierarchical structures, and an increased sense of political activism among Witches.

The fact that a religion that has many strong Goddesses is still not patriarchy-free reminds us to look at religious phenomena more carefully. We need to question how female models of deity are used within a particular community. Do they enable women to negotiate for power and authority, or do they reinforce patriarchal models of religious behavior? Such questions enable us to challenge our own hidden presuppositions, our lurking expectations, and unquestioned paradigms that masquerade as objective scholarship, and enable us to better capture and describe the range of religious experiences concealed under the Triple Goddess.

Here Comes the Sun
There is one final lurking expectation hidden within the universal paradigm of the Triple Goddess I wish briefly to mention: Her connection with the Moon. One riddle that has puzzled me from the beginning of my studies of the Craft was why our coven did not acknowledge Sun Goddesses and Moon Gods, even though they were part of our pantheons. Of course, one answer might be that they don't fit the theme of Moon/female reflecting Sun/male that seemed to be popular in my parent coven. But in fact, Sun Goddesses and Moon Gods are found all over the

world. Yet whenever the gender of Moon or Sun is discussed, folklorists, anthropologists, and linguists overwhelmingly agree that the Sun is male and the Moon female.

I found an answer to this riddle many years later, wrapped in the problem of Western dualism, that dichotomous thinking that splits the world in half, essentializing each end as a monolith, and consistently valuing one side over the other: mind/body, spirit/matter, subject/object, sacred/profane, man/woman.

Patricia Monaghan's (1994) excellent work, *O Mother Sun! A New View of the Cosmic Feminine*, solves the riddle of the missing Sun Goddesses and outlines the history of a lie: that men are always the brilliant life-giving Sun, and women forever the dark, deceptive Moon. She eloquently describes the participation of our own images of deity in the very problem we wish to avoid: the false dichotomies of Western philosophy that promote a sexism damaging to both women and men. As Monaghan's book is sadly out of print, her comments are worth quoting and considering in some detail.

> *Night and day. Death and life. Black and white. Yin, yang. Moon, sun. Evil, good.*
>
> *These, we are told are opposites. Opposites like body and mind, like the flesh and the spirit. And—in all these pairs—the first is feminine, the second masculine. So we are told.*
>
> *Women are said to be connected to the dark, to the moon goddess; to anything that broods and grows in darkness; to dreams, fantasies, emotions, illusions...*
>
> *Women are not as men are, radiant beings connected to the intellect, to reason and to thought. While we stew in our fleshy juices, 'the masculine' shines forth in heavenly splendor. If femininity is the moon, masculinity is the sun....*
>
> *Over and over, we are told that this is a world of opposites, and that woman stands on the wrong side.*
>
> *The past two decades have seen many effective attacks on this flawed world view, but even feminist philosophers often unwittingly accept one part of the fallacy: that women everywhere are mythically connected with darkness, the earth, the moon. And so, to honor our femininity, we dance by the light of the*

goddess moon.[24]

As a paradigm, this is one of the most deeply engrained in Western culture, and it is reinforced by a number of cultural factors, including the history of Western philosophy at least as far back as Plato. It is also reinforced by followers of Jungian psychology, who have enshrined what are sexist constructions of philosophical thought into universal human archetypes, eagerly accepted by Goddess worshippers. These dichotomies are the lens through which we look at the world; they inform our understanding of every aspect of what it means to be human. They are cultural patterns so deeply entrenched that we have difficulty imagining any other way to be.

Monaghan continues:

And thus we argue from the same wrong-hearted stance as our opponents. Salutary as these actions are, they do not attack the foundation myth: the duality of man and woman, yin and yang, light and dark. To do that, we must shift ground in this philosophic dispute, disengage from the false dichotomies that our culture offers, and claim the light as well as the darkness, the sky as well as the earth, as part of Goddess.[25]

Monaghan is not suggesting, nor am I, that we abandon the Triple Goddess or forsake dancing by the light of Her Moon. We must do something much harder: learn to see the shifting *play* of light and dark, to see dynamic polarities rather than dichotomies. There is a difference, stretching back to a metaphor used by the Pre-Socratic philosophers of ancient Greece. Dichotomies are sets of binary absolutes that function in a way as on/off switches. In absolute light, we are blind. In absolute darkness, we are blind. But if *sight* is the point, we need the interplay of light and dark—the shifting of lights and shadows—that make sight possible. This shifting interplay of light and dark, the dynamic tension between and movement of lights and shadows produce the wonderful multitude of sights and perspectives possible in human experience.

The final and most challenging encounter with our 'universal' Triple Goddess may be learning with body and mind to become aware of Her presence and agency, feeling Her touch as She moves throughout the world, free and unfettered by our simplistic categories, embracing and embraced by Moon and Sun. Dancing in a universe of lights and shadows.

Endnotes

1. For an extensive discussion on the insider/outsider problem in religious studies, see Bado-Fralick (2005), chapter one, pp. 3-21.
2. Bado-Fralick (2005), especially pp. 41, 144. Too often scholarly discourse about religion takes place on a level far removed from the world of actual practice. My term individuals-practising is an attempt to recover the experiences and practices of religion as it is lived.
3. For the purposes of this chapter, I use the term Wicca in its largest possible sense, employing the terms Wicca, Witchcraft, and the Craft interchangeably, although I recognize that some practitioners today distinguish between them.
4. Hutton, p. 41.
5. Starhawk, p. 9.
6. Griffin, in Berger, p. 62.
7. Starhawk, p. 101.
8. Rountree, p. 65.
9. Conway, p. 17.
10. Long, in Clifton and Harvey, p. 318.
11. See especially the blog entry from May 3, 2010: 'The Triple Goddess and the Queen'.
12. See for example, Hackett and Weaver.
13. Bado-Fralick, 1989, 1991.
14. See for example, Hackett.
15. Two of the women in my second coven, The Merry Circle, had daughters going through menarche at the same time. They tried to plan a coming of age ritual and party to celebrate their daughters' 'Maiden time', but the girls were so mortified at the idea their mothers never carried this out.
16. I have now been Priestess or High Priestess of three covens: my parent coven into which I was first initiated, my second coven in Ohio, which I call The Merry Circle, and is the subject of my book *Coming to the Edge of the Circle*, and my present coven here in Iowa.
17. Dundes.
18. These statistics were provided by CNN many years ago, and can be found in various online sources. The numbers of denominations tend to vary between 33,820 and 38,000 depending on the date of their collection.
19. Bado-Fralick, 2005.
20. Dundes.
21. Dundes.
22. Morning Glory Zell wrote 'Mother Hertha spare us from Jahweh in drag!' in *Green Egg*, Vol. VIII, No. 72 (August 1, 1975), p. 43.
23. Cited in Rountree, p. 64. Original quote taken from Adler, 1989: 97-8.

24 Monaghan, pp. 1-2.
25 Monaghan, p. 2.

References

Adler, M. 1989. 'A response', in *Journal of Feminist Studies in Religion*, 5.1: 97-100.

_____ 1979. *Drawing Down the Moon: Witches, Druids, Goddess-Worshippers, and Other Pagans in America Today*, New York: Viking.

Bado-Fralick, N. *Coming to the Edge of the Circle: A Wiccan Initiation Ritual*. Oxford: Oxford University Press.

_____ 1991. 'Changing the Face of the Sacred: Women Who Walk the Path of the Goddess', in *Explorations* 8.1:5-14. Reprinted in *Mezlim* 2.3: 24-9.

Budapest, Z. E. 1979. *The Holy Book of Women's Mysteries*, Oakland, California: Wingbow. Expanded and revised version of 1976: *The Feminist Book of Lights and Shadows*. Venice, California: Luna.

Conway, D.J. 2008. *Maiden, Mother, Crone: The Three Faces of the Goddess*, Woodbury, Minnesota: Llewellyn.

Dundes, A. n.d. 'The Number Three in American Culture', article in *The Book of Threes*, online encyclopedia.

Graves, R. 1975 [1948]. *The White Goddess: A Historical Grammar of Poetic Myth*. New York: Farrar, Straus, and Giroux.

Griffin, W. 2005. 'Webs of Women: Feminist Spiritualities', in H. A. Berger, ed., *Witchcraft and Magic: Contemporary North America*, Philadelphia: University of Pennsylvania Press : 55-80.

Hackett, J. A., 1989. 'Can a Sexist Model Liberate Us? Ancient Near Eastern "Fertility" Goddesses', in Special section on Neopaganism in the *Journal of Feminist Studies in Religion* 5.1: 65-76.

Hutton, R. 1999. *The Triumph of the Moon: A History of Modern Pagan Witchcraft*. Oxford: Oxford University Press.

Long, A. P. 2004. 'The Goddess Movement in Britain Today', in C.S. Clifton and G. Harvey, eds., *The Paganism Reader*, London and New York: Routledge: 305-25.

Monaghan, P. 1994. *O Mother Sun! A New View of the Cosmic Feminine*. Freedom, California: The Crossing Press.

Rountree K. 2004. *Embracing the Witch and the Goddess: Feminist Ritualmakers in New Zealand*. London and New York: Routledge.

Starhawk [M. Simos]. 1979. *The Spiral Dance: A Rebirth of the Ancient Religion of the Great Goddess*. San Francisco: Harper & Row.

Stone, M. 1976. *When God Was a Woman*. New York: Dial.

Weaver, M. J. 1989. 'Who Is the Goddess and Where Does She Get Us?' in Special section on Neopaganism in the *Journal of Feminist Studies in Religion* 5.1: 47-64.

4
Away from the Light: Dark Aspects of the Goddess

Marguerite Johnson

> *... magical or divine energy is not capable of being evil—or good for that matter ... (Nocturnum 2005: 45)*

As Wicca, Neo-paganism, Witchcraft and other contemporary spiritual paths are now firmly established in the West, there have been recent movements away from what may be termed 'traditional' courses of belief and worship towards systems reflecting an amalgam of Right- and Left-Hand Path philosophies and practices. Whereas, in the past, Pagans have generally advocated a common system of ethics, best exemplified in the line from the Wiccan Rede, 'An Ye Harm None, Do What Ye Will', a new breed of practitioners is not as convinced of the necessity to shun a darker path or more precisely, to fear it. What makes these new Pagans different from Satanists, however, is their desire for equilibrium between what may be crudely defined as 'white' and 'black' magic. While the movement towards a symmetry that nurtures the dark magic and meaning of goddesses such as Hecate, Lilith and Kali, is comprised of both male and female practitioners, males are the most frequent authors of texts that advocate dark or Nocturnal Magic[1] or Shadow Magic with authors such as Konstantinos, John Coughlin, Timothy Roderick, Corvis Nocturnum and Raven Digitalis being the most prolific and influential.[2]

Nocturnal Magic is primarily defined as rituals and lifestyles governed by working with energies of a darker kind. Not surprisingly, practices take place at night and the energies to which I refer are those often avoided by Wiccans, namely the dangerous yet potent powers both within and external to the human psyche. Roderick focuses on magic that engages with the Shadow[3] within us, acknowledging its presence and heeding its potentiality in not only magical workings but in self-healing as well:

> ... *'darkness' is a multilayered term that holds a variety [of] meanings ... the Dark is what you don't want to see within yourself. ... Although darkness can feel menacing, it is not a place of utter dread. ... You will find that although Western, monotheistic culture equates the term dark with 'evil', people with an earth-centered spiritual view see darkness in a completely different way. They see it as only one half of the total human spirit, which is a mix of active and passive, male and female, light and dark energy, as symbolized by the familiar yin-yang symbol from Asia. (Roderick 1996: 5-6)*

Roderick, a trained clinical psychologist, combines his Pagan beliefs with Jungian archetypes, particularly the Shadow, in addition to the works of mythologists such as Joseph Campbell. Other practitioners and authors, specifically Konstantinos, Coughlin, Nocturnum and Digitalis, offer a more overt system of Nocturnal Magic, not explicitly associated with self-healing, but more concerned with self-empowerment and genuine mystical engagement with dark and often chaotic forces. Their magical personae are inextricably linked with Gothic subculture,[4] and in part also take their cue from the concepts and philosophies underpinning Jung's Shadow archetype. In addition to the basic attraction to Nocturnal Magic, its forces and its potentialities, those adhering to this system are also reacting against what has now been regarded by some as 'fluffy' Paganism; Coughlin defines the latter in a discussion of the ethics behind the Wiccan Rede:

> *New Age 'fluffy' Wiccan extremists mean well when they ignore or condemn aspects of the Craft that could be misinterpreted as evil or dangerous by non-Wiccans and newcomers in hopes of getting on the good side of those who condemn Paganism, yet they can go to such extremes that they sacrifice the balance of their religion and deny its roots. (Coughlin 2009: 9)*

Coughlin's sentiments are humorously, yet nevertheless poignantly expressed by witch par-excellence Willow, in an episode from *Buffy the Vampire Slayer* entitled 'Hush':

> *Willow: Talk, all talk. Blah Blah Gaia, Blah Blah Moon ... menstrual life force power thingy. You know after a couple of sessions I was hoping we could get into something real but....*
> *Buffy: No actual Witches in your witch group?*
> *Willow: No. Bunch of wanna-blessed-bes. You know, nowadays every girl with a henna tattoo and a spice rack thinks she's a sister of the Dark ones.*

Willow's biting words typify the resistance felt by some Pagans about the dilution of their understanding of the Craft and, as specified by Coughlin, its ancestral ethics and practices. 'Fluffy Bunny' bashing is on the increase, particularly on websites and blogs, reflecting the increasingly divergent beliefs and practices that are seemingly fracturing any notion of a cohesive or peer-supportive Pagan community as Witchcraft strengthens its position as an established world religion in the 21st Century.

Most Fluffy Bunnies or 'Playgans' or 'White-lighters' are defined by their emphasis on—as the last name indicates—white magic or good magic, adhering to a strict and, according to Coughlin (2009: 8-13), literal understanding of the Wiccan Rede. Alternative paths, such as the one advocated in Nocturnal Magic, stress the ethical ambiguity of Paganism and thereby reject a notion of white magic along with black magic, hence the words quoted from Nocturnum that open this chapter. The dichotomy between Pagans who stringently adhere to the Wiccan Rede (and who have tended to be the public face of contemporary Witchcraft until the 21st Century) and those who now engage with the Shadow-side of the craft, is well explicated by Digitalis:

> *Shadow magick is not a negative practice. However, it does require coming to terms with the shadow self, and reaching into those crevices of the mind is sometimes perceived as a negative experience. ... The aspects of shadow magick range widely. In many ways, those that deal with the internal darkness of the self can be considered positive in nature: practices such as magickal work on the emotional plane, mysticism, and types of deep meditation. Other arts, such as divination, astral projection, automatic writing, and dreamwalking, are clearly not negative in nature (and are in fact shared by nearly all Witches). But some shadow magick can be deemed more negative: demonic evocation, Qlippothic [sic] or Goetic work, uncontrolled psychic vampirism, cursing, and some types of necromancy. (Digitalis 2008: 14)*

Digitalis is correct in noting the overlap between some of the practices and rituals employed by White-lighters[5] and Nocturnal Magicians (although he may have been wise to note the significance of intent in this instance) and makes a nuanced observation concerning the darker elements of Nocturnal or, in his words, Shadow Magick, which underpins the distinction between these two strands of Paganism (the Right- and Left-Hand paths) but maintains the difference both have in relation to Satanism, Chaos Magick or Vampiric Sorcery, for example. The influence of Satanism and Chaos Magick on the formulation of Nocturnal Magic cannot, however, be underestimated. Obviously the darker the Nocturnal Magic is, the more likely its connection to Left-Hand path traditions. The writing of Michael W. Ford, a practitioner whose philosophies at times reflect elements of Satanism[6] and who advocates 'the darkest magick' (2006: 10), a Luciferian system, works with forces that are also shared by Wiccans in their invocations and rituals. The forces of dark Wicca include Hecate, Lilith and Kali and it is to these entities to which I now turn.

In *Book of the Witch Moon*, Ford dedicates the grimoire to Hecate and Choronzon.[7] He evokes the goddess with the traditional language of the reverential occultist:

> *... the Goddess of the Triple Moon, of Youth, of Wisdom and of Darkness..she who resides in the North, whose masks are many, Lilith, Diana, Az, those daughters who shall meet thee in the Crossroads—Blessed is Her terrible name, she who blesses and curses with a glance...*
> *O Mother of the Bleeding Moon, O Bride of Chaos and Darkness Born... (Ford 2006[a]: 4)*[8]

In the same invocation / dedication, Ford goes on to specify the goddess as an entity of the night:

> *May you seek her in the night, when the veil'd dream opens and the hunger is awakened...*
> *(Ford 2006[a]: 4)*

Hecate is invoked here as 'the Goddess of the Triple Moon', in keeping with the ancient tradition surrounding her. From the time of the first extant account of her in Hesiod's *Theogony*, an aetiological text in hexameter from the 6th Century BCE that provides a genealogy of the divine, semi-divine, heroic and human for the ancient Greeks (see Johnson 2009: 312 ff), Hecate has been associated with the triple aspect. Hesiod connects her with the three realms—power over the sky, the earth and the sea—and it is most likely this early account explains her later connections to the crossroads (a place of three ways) as well as the artistic representations that show her triple-bodied and triple-faced. While Ford refers to her as 'the Goddess of the Triple Moon', scholars now agree that her connection to the moon was a later development in antiquity, beginning around the 1st Century CE. Just as this later association took a firm hold in the latter centuries of antiquity, it has remained a strong fixture in modern representations of Hecate and is referenced in Nocturnal Magic.

Ford rightly connects Hecate to youth, tapping into one of her oldest aspects. While modern people tend to associate the goddess with all that is terrifying and strange, she did begin her life with benevolent qualities, as a youthful deity who in turn was associated with youth:

> ... albeit her mother's only child, she is honoured amongst all the deathless gods. And the son of Cronos [Zeus] made her a nurse of the young who after that day saw with their eyes the light of all-seeing Dawn. So from the beginning she is a nurse of the young, and these are her honours. (Theog. 448-52) [9]

In addition to her oldest incarnations—as *kourotrophos* (nourisher of youth) and goddess of the three ways—Ford also invokes the Hecate of later traditions, especially the goddess of fearsome magic that features in ancient curses and spells such as those from the *Papyri Graecae Magicae (Greek Magical Papyri)*, an anthology of spells from Greco-Roman Egypt spanning the 2nd Century BCE to the 5th Century CE but including magic formulae from much earlier dates (see Johnson 2009: 313). Ford's powerful entreaty to the goddess—'Blessed is Her terrible name, she who blesses and curses with a glance...O Mother of the Bleeding Moon, O Bride of Chaos and Darkness Born...' (Ford 2006[a]: 4)—recalls a spell from the *Papyri*, namely *PGM* IV.2785-2890, from which comes the following excerpt:

> *Goddess of dark, quiet and frightful one,*
> *O you who have your meal amid the graves,*
> *Night, Darkness, broad Chaos: Necessity*
> *Hard to escape are you; you're Moira and /*
> *Erinys, torment, Justice and Destroyer,*   2860
> *And you keep Kerberos in chains, with scales*
> *Of serpents are you dark, O you with hair*
> *Of serpents, serpent-girded, who drink blood, /*
> *Who bring death and destruction, and who feast*   2865

> *On hearts, flesh eater, who devour those dead*
> *Untimely, and you who make grief resound*
> *And spread madness, come to my sacrifices,*
> *And now for me do you fulfil / this matter.*   2870
> *(Betz 1992: 90)* [10]

The above lines, while more graphic in imagery, are comparable to Ford's contemporary homage in regard to the use of aggressive, potent language to appeal to the goddess and to enhance the effectiveness of the magical intent. While some of the imagery is not meant to be interpreted literally as specifically defined aspects of Hecate, it nevertheless creates a spell of immeasurable power because each image builds on the next, creating a cumulative effect over 105 lines. Aleister Crowley also knew the imagery and language required to invoke Hecate and his writings on her are akin to the *PGM* spell (see Johnson 2009: 314 ff).

The anonymous author of the ancient spell calls Hecate by various names throughout the formula: she is Selene, Justice,[11] Persephone, Megaira, Alekto[12] and Artemis. Hecate is regularly associated with these goddesses: Selene, goddess of the moon, Persephone, goddess of the Underworld and Artemis, Olympian goddess of youth, the wilderness and virginity are especially invoked alongside Hecate who is often called by their names. Ford likewise names her 'Lilith, Diana, Az' and states that 'there is no difference between Hecate and Lilith or Babalon'(2006: 103).[13]

In magic that follows a Left-Hand path, Lilith is a natural companion of Hecate. Traditionally, however, the deities are dissimilar: Lilith was, for example, originally a demon that harassed men and preyed on infants (see Johnson 2006: 651-52). Hecate, as has been discussed, was a virginal deity who cared for the young. The connection between the two in modern Paganism is based on the tradition of later antiquity concerning Hecate that associates her with death, witchcraft and revenge; this image of the goddess fits more cohesively with the frightening demon, Lilith, who was also associated with death and destruction. Likewise, Kali, the Hindu goddess of darkness, death and—like Lilith—sexual domination, is regularly associated with Hecate in some modern Pagan systems.

The tendency in modern Wicca, Neo-paganism and Witchcraft to amalgamate deities from various cultures and eras is a distinguishing feature of the religion(s), yet it is also problematic for some scholars of religion and related disciplines as well as social commentators.[14] When it comes to ancient deities from the Mediterranean, for example, there is a dichotomy between Reconstructionists and Eclectics; the former aim to adhere as closely as possible to the ancient traditions, while the latter prefer a combination of traditions, both ancient and post-ancient (see Strmiska 2005: 19-20). And while there is an enormous freedom in the paths chosen by the Eclectics in particular, the question that arises concerns the tension that emerges between belief and reality and reality and belief; namely, if a deity such as Hecate exists in her own right as an entity of a plane of universal and sublime veracity, how exactly does one reconcile the (obvious) human intervention in her divine sphere, the crafting and reinvention of her to fit another—new—'reality' of existence? When and how and why did this ancient deity of virginity and youth and decidedly non-magical practices become important to (some) Pagans as the Maid, Mother and Crone? The ancient Greeks and Romans, arguably her original (or at least most prominent) devotees, changed her too as the centuries passed, yet they had no understanding of Hecate-as-Trivia in the context of the three ages of woman. This begs the question: does Hecate exist independently of her devotees or is she a creation of them? Jung would argue for the latter as would most agnostic scholars, and the Eclectic cohort of Pagans would add fuel to this interpretive fire.

Yet for a practitioner like Ford, one could safely posit that he is tapping into the divine energies of the goddess and his writings to her and about her—his 'holy' invocations—are the result of an interaction with the divine on another plane that opens the doors to eclecticism for a more universal, more personal and arguably more spiritual relationship with Hecate (and the other deities who form the principals of his system). This is what Wicca, Neo-paganism, Witchcraft and New Age spiritualities have demonstrated most vehemently to the scholars of religion— that religion is an incredibly fluid system of belief and practice, with all major traditions, be they Islam, Christianity, Buddhism or Hinduism, open to radical change, interpretation, sectional divergence and eclecticism. Konstantinos sums up this eclectic approach and expresses its simplicity of meaning to Pagans such as himself: '... I discovered through my own probing of mythologies that other cultures had similar Gods and Goddesses [to the ancient Greeks]. It began to make sense that the world had been worshipping the same Divine energies for millennia, only using different names for them' (2002 [a]).

Darker paths appeal to women as much as men although there is a noticeable gender binary in the sexes' approaches to and understanding of Nocturnal Magic. Many female devotees of this form of magic tend to rely more on positive readings of the Jungian concept of the Shadow to inform their workings with female deities; while this is also a component of the writings of Digitalis and Roderick, it has been a much stronger recurring feature of female followers of the nocturnal path.

Demetra George, for example, is an author who typifies the female interpretation of darker aspects of magic. Her work on the darker goddesses, in some ways a product of the early 1990s and the crossover between Paganism and New Age, aimed to 'revision the dark' (1992: 6) for women with a focus on 'The Feminine Shadow' (essentially several key goddesses, including Hecate and Lilith). George, like several writers and practitioners from the era of Second Wave Feminism till the mid-1990s, tends to favour a matriarchal theory that argues for the patriarchal suppression of what she calls the 'Dark Goddess'. Witches and authors like Starhawk advocated the matriarchal theory as a central tenet of belief during the early stages of their spiritual journey, and although most tend not to promote the hypothesis nowadays, it effectively provided worshippers with a history of oppression and persecution as well as a group of supernatural scapegoats that manufactured a need on the part of the worshippers to defend their deities and beliefs. George's 'take' on the Dark Goddess reflects this somewhat defensive interpretation of religious history:

> *In the mythic imagination of male-dominated cultures, her original nature became distorted and she took on horrifying proportions. As Kali she appears in cremation grounds adorned with a garland of skulls and holding the severed head of her mate, Shiva, dripping with blood. As Lilith she flies through the night as a she-demon who seduces men, breeds demons, and kills infants. As Medusa her beautiful, abundant hair becomes a crown of hissing serpents and the gaze from her Evil Eye turns men to stone. And as Hekate she stalks men at the crossroads at night with her vicious hounds of hell. (1992: 28).*

This approach towards the chthonic deities, the so-called dark ones, contains more than an element of victimisation on the part of their advocates, which is in contrast to the more recent devotees of the Left-Hand Path, whose identity politics are strongly aligned to reclamation, celebration and a flagrant disregard of any need for self-justification.[15] In systems such as George's, the alleged transformations of the goddesses from positive, nurturing beings to nasty crones can be traced to 'the transition from matriarchal to patriarchal culture that occurred five millennia ago' (1992: 28). But this is simply not the case. There is no conclusive archaeological evidence to support claims of matriarchy in the major cultures of the Mediterranean during the Bronze Age or earlier. To write of the 'original nature' of goddesses such as Hecate and Lilith is as naive an exegetical position as the interpretation of any discernable historical developments in their iconographical representations being the result of a male conspiracy in the form of the emergence of a patriarchal religion. Graham Harvey offers a more lenient or genuinely sympathetic understanding of the place of the legitimate (usually female) voice in the 'herstory' of goddess spirituality:

> As with any discussion of deity or religion, it has to be said that all these words are stories which attempt to carry rich and varied experiences. The experiences are always bigger than the containers; life is too messy and wild to be controlled by a single story. If this is true in most religions it is an acknowledged and welcomed facet in Goddess Spirituality. (1997: 77)

This liberated interpretation places emphasis on the devotees' claimed right to fashion the goddess in her (or his) own image, and this is a useful tool for writers such as George. Not focusing on how to worship the dark goddesses, George's aim instead is to encourage the reader to engage with the Shadow Goddess of one's choice. On Hecate, George discusses her chthonic aspect as a positive element to be embraced by women as it 'suggests the motif of incubation as we go down deeper still into the darkness of unconscious sleep as a necessary step in the cycle of transformation and renewal' (1992: 148). Hecate's traditional association with being a torch-bearer, one who leads the way, is also picked-up by George, who utilises this aspect of her to remind the reader that a meditation on a goddess who functions as a path-finder is to embrace 'the way out' (147), to be aware that renewal always follows death. When we consider the grim outlook for women when it comes to the absence of female deities in the major monotheistic religions, reminders such as these are indeed inspiring.

This latter understanding of Hecate as the torch-bearer (*phosphoros* is the Greek epithet applied to her) is an incredibly positive image for modern Pagans, particularly women (for the reason outlined above) and is intricately connected with her association with darkness in modern magical practice; as a goddess linked to night-time and darkness, she is importantly—and perhaps necessarily—also linked to the light. She thus functions as a goddess of duality to many modern Pagans—symbolising the necessity for darkness and representing its beauty, yet simultaneously reminding one of the light that always follows the gloom of evening. The most intense example from antiquity of Hecate as torch-bearer comes from the well-known myth concerning Persephone, Demeter and Hecate. Often generically called 'The abduction of Persephone', the narrative explains how Persephone became the goddess of the underworld and the wife of Hades, as well as providing a beautiful aetiology of the seasons.[16]

First recorded in a work of the Archaic age (*c*. 800-500 BCE) entitled *The Homeric Hymn to Demeter*, by an unknown poet, the hymn records how Persephone was abducted by Hades and describes the ensuing search her mother, Demeter, carried out to rescue her. Hecate, besides Helios (the god of the sun), is the only deity who witnesses the abduction; while residing in her cave, Hecate hears the shrill cries of the goddess as she is carried away. The poet describes Hecate, torch in hand, approaching the distraught Demeter, and revealing to her the cries she heard, then facilitating contact between Demeter and Helios in order for the all-seeing Sun to reveal what he witnessed. After a long narrative entailing Demeter's determined journey to find her child, Hecate reappears in the narrative at the point of reunion between mother and daughter: 'Hekate of the delicate veil drew near them and often caressed the daughter of holy Demeter; from that time this lady served her as chief attendant.' (*Homeric Hymn to Demeter* 438-40) [17]

In this story, Hecate is indeed a bringer of light in both a literal and metaphorical sense; she not only lights the way for Demeter but also brings her the light of hope. She is both a goddess of earth and the underworld, traversing the planes of the upper and lower worlds; in this sense she is the goddess of both life and death, and her role in this narrative is regularly interpreted by Pagans as indicative of her powers of renewal: for them Hecate reveals that death is not final, but a source of regeneration—for Persephone 'dies' only to be 'reborn' each year in the glorious seasons of spring and summer—and it is Hecate who reveals this secret to Demeter.

Like Hecate, Lilith is a goddess with particular potency to practitioners of Shadow Magic. Like Hecate, Lilith too has been revived and re-imagined. For female Pagans, Lilith has a particular resonance, and is regularly re-visioned in a positive light. This is partly a result of Second Wave Feminism, which had a profound effect on women's spirituality and religious studies *per se*. At the helm of such reclamations of the wicked goddesses and witches of times past, were scholars and activists such as Mary Daly and Merlin Stone who advocated a happy embracing of their nasty spiritual sisters who were the products of a misogynist past inextricably tied to Christianity via a systematic process of what Daly calls 'dismemberment'(1979: 73). The path pioneered by women such as Daly and Stone better enabled Pagans to worship deities such as Lilith and, as a result, this one-time demon has come to occupy an important role in Shadow Magic and other forms of contemporary Paganism. As the first wife of Adam who refused to literally and metaphorically lie under him, Lilith is now regarded as a symbol of feminine freedom, as George notes:

> *To enter into the figure of Lilith is to remember a time in the ancient past when women were honoured and praised for initiating and fully expressing their personal freedom and sexual passion. (1992: 187)*

While ancient historians of Mediterranean cultures know that nothing is further from the truth, George's belief is an example of modern Pagans' determination to remake ancient deities in their own image and likeness (as discussed previously). This complex system of reappropriation is discussed by Maria Beatrice Bittarello in her article on contemporary Pagan appropriation of the ancient Greek rites at Eleusis, which involved the myths and religious beliefs surrounding Demeter and Persephone:

> *The contemporary Pagan reshaping of myths is an example of the emergence of mythopoesis in contemporary society— a mythopoesis that is the expression of a differently oriented, complex approach to reality, in which a rational worldview is now integrated by imagination and the recourse to tradition, in order to give meaning to life and orient action. (2008: 230)*

In *The Dark Archetype: Exploring the Shadow Side of the Divine*, occultists Denise Dumas and Lori Nyx include a Lilith ritual for 'self seduction' (2003: 168-71). In this they envisage Lilith as an empowering force for the worshipper; as a Shadow deity whose dark aura is threatening (to some) but nevertheless energising, they identity Lilith's intense sexuality and sexual expression as a force that despite being maligned by certain traditional monotheistic religions as dark (in the negative sense), was life-affirming in its very taboo nature. In this sense, she offers a gift to the practitioners of magic who worship her that Hecate, the eternal virgin, cannot: the gift of sensuality. It is not surprising, therefore, that Lilith is a goddess regularly invoked during rites of sex magic. Ford specifies the significance—indeed vital role—of Lilith in Tantra and sex magic, referring to her as possessing a 'predatory nature' (104), which is necessary for such rituals. She is not only the predatory goddess but the predatory aspect of woman—symbolic of female sexual energy and its potency.

Ford understands Lilith in Tantra and sex magic via the systems designed by Aleister Crowley, and he thereby emphasises her 'dark' sexuality in the form of the Crowleyan 'Scarlet Woman' or 'Great Whore': 'Red Force, the mother of demons, darkness in nature, primal instincts, menstrual blood from the Kiss of Ahriman'[18] (2006[b]: 55) and 'the dark primal instinct, the spirit of night and desire, hunger and sexual copulation.' (2006[b]: 57). Ford defines Lilith—and all the forces he works with—within the system of Luciferian Magick, utilising her energies as a means of engaging with the Adversary. He works with such energies during the shadow times:

> *An ideal time for utilizing Succubi and consorting with Lilith is during the time of the Full Moon and New Moon, when it is shadowed and dark. Approaching Lilith as Mother and Goddess will no doubt protect the Luciferian from being prey to her spirit, having self-respect and open desire to pass her tests means everything. (2008:106).*

Most practitioners like Ford who author rituals for the worship of Lilith in her most potent form include warnings to their readers to ensure protection. This is indicative of their sincere belief in the power of these dark forces as well as their respect for the deities in question.

The most widely accessed and quoted Lilith ritual on the Internet is entitled 'The Invocation of Lilith: A Rite of Dark Sexuality' by Joseph Max.555 and Lilith Darkchilde.777. Here too is a strong warning to the potential practitioners:

> *!*WARNINGS*: Lilith is a primal egregore[19] of the dark animal. She is unfettered sexual dominance and power. This invocation should not be attempted by those with little background in ceremonial magic, nor by those who harbour unresolved psychological problems related to sexuality. If blood is to be drawn, or sexual activities ensue, all precautions pertaining to the prevention of diseases borne by blood or sexual fluids should properly be observed. It may be wise to appoint a "guardian" who shall "observe" the rite as it proceeds from a detached viewpoint and intervene if the participants, in their excess, are about to commit dangerous acts. The guardian should cast hir [sic] own circle of protection about hirself [sic]. The guardian should only intervene if there is a threat of serious bodily harm; otherwise, events must be allowed to transpire as they will. Anyone fearful of the possible psychological effects of this rite would do well not to participate in it in the first place. It is not for the timid. With these caveats, all discretion pertaining to these matters is left to the participants. The authors assume no responsibility for the irresponsibility of the participants in performance of this rite. You have been warned![20]*

The ritual, described in detail, is to induce the Main Operator (preferably female, as 'Lilith is the primal feminine aspect of dark sexuality') into a Gnostic trance in order for the egregore of Lilith to be 'invoke[d] ... into hir body and mind', 'so that by her spirit we experience the power of Sex and Death and obtain her Word Of Power!' (the invocation utilises a message delivered to Edward Kelley in 1587 during a scrying ritual with John Dee).[21]

As the ritual reaches a climax, 'all participants should feel the emotions of simultaneous fear, lust and the urge to submit'.[22] The will of the egregore will dictate the nature of what ensues among the participants. Herein we witness the power and meaning of Lilith for Left-Hand Path devotees; this egregore is invoked as a force that embraces the life-force in the form of unbridled sexuality ('I am a harlot for such as ravish me, and a virgin with such as know me not') as well as the death force—over which she triumphs ('It is our Will to invoke the egregore of Lilith, so that by her spirit we are liberated from the fear of Sex and Death and obtain her Word Of Power!').[23]

Jo Pearson, in her article on Paganism/Wicca and its correlations to S/M notes the distinction between rituals such as the one by Joseph Max.555 and Lilith Darkchilde.777 and those practised by "fluffy', white-washed Wicca', writing on the adepts of Shadow Magic who prefer to 'invoke the allure of Witchcraft, retaining its dark and sexual connotations and, importantly, its aura of power, elements of the Western Christian stereotype of the witch' (Pearson 2005: 32-33). Pearson's discussion of the nexus between such rites and S/M is clearly evidenced in the concluding practices of the rite under discussion:

What proceeds next is not specified, but left up to the will of the egregore. She may choose to scourge the participants, or mock them or entice them or seduce them. She may force them to commit various unspeakable acts of lust upon her or each other. All participants must submit to her will, whatever it may be—it would be dangerous in the extreme to do otherwise; do not risk the wrath of Lilith![24]

The Crowleyan influences are obvious here as the participants are encouraged to lose themselves—to destroy an earth-bound reality and to aim instead for an esoteric reality based on sublimation of the Self. Here the dark mistress, Lilith, presides as the acts of sadomasochism are sacralised in her honour. Indeed, practitioners like Joseph Max.555 and Lilith Darkchilde.777 represent all that is frightening to opponents of modern occultism. The fears of Christian opponents are best summarised in the words of Linda P. Harvey, a public advocate of right-wing Christianity in the United States:

> *When one does not know the genuine, the counterfeit is easy to accept. So a limited knowledge of Christianity plays right into the hands of promoters of witchcraft in America. There is no power and authority outside oneself, witchcraft maintains. The 'goddess' and her male consort honored in many witchcraft beliefs may be conceptualized by a Wiccan practitioner as nature—based deities, but most operate as if the power they are invoking is just an extension of the 'higher' self. This lie from Satan is as old as Genesis.* [25]

When Harvey is not witch-hunting gay rights advocates and feminists, she is busy writing diatribes about Pagans such as the one above, in which she identifies (very likely, unknowingly) one of the defining tenets of Shadow Magic and other forms of Paganism, namely the embracing of one's own authority and the worship of forces for one's own betterment. The dark aspects of the goddess—or more precisely the dark goddesses themselves—and the links between their revival and the role of feminism in 20th century Western culture represent two powerful threats to the right-wing Christian movement, embracing and promoting as they do the empowerment of women and the legitimacy of alternatives to Christianity.

Such responses to Paganism as voiced by Harvey and like-minded advocates provide an interesting background to the appearance of more strident supporters and practitioners of magic, particularly Shadow Magic and the divide between them and the increasingly adamant stance of those whom the shadow practitioners define as 'fluffy bunnies'. In some respects, these two sides of modern occultism reflect a response to right-wing Christian politics: shadow magicians are clearly aware of the political advantages of 'outing' themselves in quite overt ways—in terms of the promotion of so-called 'alternative' spiritualities, a public, self-acceptance of what one believes in is a powerful political tool, as the gay-rights advocates vilified by the likes of Harvey have come to realise. The more conciliatory approach of 'fluffy bunnies' may belie an attempt to purify themselves and their gods in the eyes of Christian opponents, but like one who lives in the gay closet, they will find that hiding or attempts at mollification by promoting a same-not-different agenda does little to achieve acceptance or respect in the end.

The contemporary West's fascination with the dark goddess and her energies is on the rise and some of her most passionate and articulate advocates have embraced a public image that suggests a new aeon in the West's history of religion. While opponents may rail against their beliefs and lifestyles, there is little by way of fear in the eyes or hearts of the

Pagans who walk a decidedly Left-Hand path. Long gone—so it seems—are the burning times (*pace* Harvey, although her flames are containable). Perhaps Hecate and her ilk truly give the gift of individual power and courage to those who truly believe in their magick.

References

Betz, H. D. ed. 1992. *The Greek Magical Papyri in Translation, Including the Demotic Texts*. vol. 1: Texts. Chicago: University of Chicago Press, 2nd edition.

Bittarello, M. B. 2008. 'Re-crafting the Past: The Complex Relationship between Myth and Ritual in the Contemporary Pagan Reshaping of Eleusis.' *Pomegranate* 10.2: 230-55.

Coughlin, J. 2009. *Ethics and the Craft—The History, Evolution, and Practice of Wiccan Ethics*. USA: Waning Moon Publications.

__ 2002. *Out of the Shadows: An Exploration of Dark Paganism and Magick*. USA: 1st Books Library.

Daly, M. 1978. *Gyn/Ecology*. Boston: Beacon Press.

Digitalis, R. 2008. *Shadow Magick Compendium: Exploring Darker Aspects of Magickal Spirituality*. St Paul, Minnesota: Llewellyn Publications.

__ 2007. *Goth Craft: The Magickal Side of Dark Culture*. St Paul, Minnesota: Llewellyn Publications.

Dumars, D. and Nyx. L. 2003. *The Dark Archetype: Exploring the Shadow Side of the Divine*. USA: New Page Books.

Ford, M. W. 2006(a). *Book of the Witch Moon: Chaos, Vampiric & Luciferian Sorcery*. Choronzon Edition. USA: Succubus Publishing.

__ 2006(b). *Adamu: Luciferian Tantra and Sex Magick*. Houston: Succubus Publishing.

__ 2008. *The Bible of the Adversary*. Second Edition. Houston: Succubus Publishing.

George, D. 1992. *Mysteries of the Dark Moon: The Healing Power of the Dark Goddess*. San Francisco: HarperSanFrancisco.

Harvey, G. 1997. *Listening People, Speaking Earth: Contemporary Paganism*. London: Hurst.

Harvey, L. P. 2002. 'Heresy in the Hood II: Witchcraft among Children and Teens in America.' Accessed: 29/5/2010. http://www.leaderu.com/theology/teenwitchcraft.html

'Homeric Hymn to Demeter.' 1993. *The Homeric Hymn to Demeter. Translation, Commentary and Interpretative Essays by Helene P. Foley*. Princeton, New Jersey: Princeton University Press.

Hesiod. 1914. *Theogony*. In *The Homeric Hymns and Homerica with an English Translation by Hugh G. Evelyn-White*. Cambridge: Harvard University Press; London, William Heinemann.

'Hush.' *Buffy the Vampire Slayer.* Season 4, Episode 10. Written and directed by Joss Whedon. 14 December 1999.

Johnson, M. 2009. 'Drawing Down the Goddess: The Ancient {Female} Deities of Modern Paganism.' In *Handbook of Contemporary Paganism.* eds. James R. Lewis and Murphy Pizza. Leiden: Brill. 311-34.

___ 2006. 'Lilith.' In *Encyclopedia of Witchcraft: The Western Tradition.* Vol. III. ed. Richard M. Golden. Santa Barbara, California: ABC-Clio. 651-52.

Jung, C. 1975. 'Psychology and Religion: West and East.' In *Collected Works.* Vol. 11. Trans. R.F.C. Hull. Princeton, New Jersey: Princeton University Press, 2nd edition.

Konstantinos. 2005. *Nocturnicon: Calling Dark Forces and Powers.* St Paul, Minnesota: Llewellyn Publications.

___ 2004. *Speak with the Dead: Seven Methods for Spirit Communication.* St Paul, Minnesota: Llewellyn Publications.

___ 2002[a]. *Nocturnal Witchcraft: Magick After Dark.* St Paul, Minnesota: Llewellyn Publications.

___ 2002[b]. *Gothic Grimoire.* St Paul, Minnesota: Llewellyn Publications.

___ 2002[c]. *Summoning Spirits.* St Paul, Minnesota: Llewellyn Publications.

Lewis, J. R. 2001. 'Who Serves Satan? A Demographic and Ideological Profile.' *Marburg Journal of Religion* 6.2: 1-25.

Nocturnum, C. 2005. *Embracing the Darkness: Understanding Dark Subcultures.* USA: Dark Moon Press.

Roderick, T. 1996. *Dark Moon Mysteries.* St Paul, Minnesota: Llewellyn Publications.

Strmiska, M. 2005. *Modern Paganism in World Cultures: Comparative Perspectives.* Santa Barbara, California: ABC-Clio.

Endnotes

1. I use this term generically throughout this article to denote this particular form of Paganism (a term I also use in the same vein). Shadow Magic is used with similar meaning by Digitalis (2008).
2. As my methodology is neither anthropological nor sociological, but based on literary analysis, my approach is primarily of a textual nature with a focus on the writings of key contemporary practitioners as named above.
3. As understood by Jung; see 'Psychology and Religion: West and East.' See also, Digitalis (2008) for extensive discussion of the Shadow.
4. As exemplified also by the organisation, Dragon Rouge (in addition to individual exponents of Left-Hand practices discussed here). See http://www.dragonrouge.net/english/general.htm (accessed 22 March 2011).
5. Here I use the term not in a pejorative sense but to designate followers

of a strictly Right-Hand path; those who follow the Wiccan Rede in its strictest or most literal sense.
6   Also Chaos Magick; see Ford (2006: 9) 'chaos magick from a left hand path perspective'.
7   Choronzon is the daemon named by John Dee and Edward Kelley in the Enochian system of magic. The figure also features in Thelemic Magick as practised by Aleister Crowley as well as in the workings of Chaos magicians.
8   Text, including ellipses, as printed.
9   Translation by Hugh G. Evelyn-White.
10 Translation by E. N. O'Neil.
11 *Dike*, the personification of justice in Greek polytheism; a goddess.
12 Megaira and Alekto are two of the Furies, the chthonic goddesses of ancient, blood-based revenge.
13 On names such as 'Az', see Ford's Glossary.
14 Admittedly, it is the appropriation of Indigenous peoples' deities and spiritual traditions that have caused the most consternation; see Strmiska (2005).
15 The personal and social (self-) positioning of practitioners of the Left-Hand path reflects the observations made by Graham Harvey on Satanists in regard to their 'performance of alterity'(2009: 27).
16 As goddess of the earth and its fertility, Demeter's grief manifests in a material form as the earth mysteriously stops 'producing'; a season of death or infertility pervades until Demeter is reunited with Persephone and her joy is transformed into the seasons of life and bountifulness—spring and summer—and when she releases her daughter back to Hades for half the year, she mourns and brings seasons of earthly stillness and infertility—autumn and winter. George interprets the myth thus: 'Both Hekate and Persephone stood for the ... hope of regeneration.' (145)
17 Translation by Helene P. Foley.
18 Indicative of Ford's interest in Persian or, more precisely, Zoroastrian deities; Ahriman is a demon from that system and is regularly equated with the Devil in comparative systems of magic.
19 Employed by occultists, an egregore denotes a collective force that is made manifest by meditation and ritual.
20 Accessed 21/3/2011. http://lilith.abroadplanet.com/Rite.php
21 See John Dee, *A true & faithful relation of what passed for many years between Dr. John Dee ... and some spirits*.
22 As above.
23 As above.
24 As above.
25 Harvey, Linda P. 2002. 'Heresy in the Hood II: Witchcraft among

Children and Teens in America.' http://www.leaderu.com/theology/teenwitchcraft.html (accessed: 29 May 2010).

5
Neo-Shamanism in the United States

Andrei A. Znamenski

The rise of the counterculture in the 1960s and environmental movements in the 1970s promoted people to question the foundations of Western civilization, which opened doors for old and new spiritual alternatives which at that moment had existed on the fringes of spiritual and social life. In opposition to earlier positivism and materialism, during that time spiritual seekers became very interested in exploring the non-Western, unique, individual, irrational, and bizarre. Scholars also began to revisit dropout, drug, and psychic experiences.[1] Earlier dismissed as superstitions and abnormalities, the traditions and knowledge of non-Western 'others' came into the spotlight of Western culture. In the human sciences, experiential knowledge acquired high status, and it became a popular practice to live the life of human subjects. By the 1990s, a growing community of people who partook of Theosophy, Jungian scholarship, and humanistic and transpersonal psychology and who shared the popular interest in classical Oriental and tribal beliefs produced a consciousness revolution that, to some extent, disarmed a society steeped in materialism and rationalism.[2] Neo-shamanism was part of this intellectual and cultural shift.

Like many other modern nature spiritualities, neo-shamanism sprang up in the United States and then spread to other Western countries.[3] For many traditionalists and nature-oriented people, America—where one can see the fruits of modernity in their extreme—represents the ultimate den of materialism and cosmopolitanism. Therefore, it was natural that, in the 1960s and 1970s, the first spiritual antidotes to modernity blossomed in America. There were certainly cultural prerequisites for such spiritualities as neo-shamanism to spring up in the United States. Historically, Americans have been more religious and spiritual than Europeans. At the same time, they are traditionally open to religious experimentation. Since the founding of the United States, many people believe that they have the right to choose their own religion or to follow none at all.

The community of neo-shamanism in the United States emerged at the convergence of the counterculture/environmental movements, anthropology, transpersonal psychology, and Native Americana. The 1960s and 1970s counterculture and nature movements, with their reverential attitude toward nature, created a fertile soil for the rise of various earth-based spiritualities that share a notion that nature is divine and alive. In addition to earth-centered philosophy, anthropology and psychology were two other major spearheads of neo-shamanism. It is no accident that many current teachers of shamanism in the West are people with anthropology or psychology training.

Driven by romantic notions, anthropology sprang up in the nineteenth century, primarily as a scholarly enterprise devoted to the exploration of 'exotic' non-Western elementary societies. It was natural that, in the 1960s and 1970s, Western seekers, who came to consider these people an antidote to Western modernity, found in anthropology texts blueprints of ideal spiritual and ethical behavior. Moreover, some anthropologists themselves entered the community of Western esotericism, becoming shamanism teachers and practitioners. The rehabilitation of tribal peoples, which began in the 1960s, quickly turned into the glorification and idealization of 'tribal' people as an embodiment of a superior wisdom.

Figure 1: Carlos Castaneda

The increased attention to shamanism in humanities and in popular culture is usually associated with two names: Mircea Eliade (1907–1986) and Carlos Castaneda (1925–1998)

Eliade, a Romanian-born philosopher and religious scholar, worked for many years as a professor of comparative religion at the University of Chicago. Eliade's *Le Chamanisme et les techniques archaiques de l'extas* (1951) became an academic bestseller after its revised translation was published in English as *Shamanism: Archaic Techniques of Ecstasy* (1964). Also an immigrant, Castaneda came to the United States from Peru. Although he failed as a mainstream academic scholar, by publishing an experiential novel, *The Teachings of Don Juan: A Yaqui Way of Knowledge* (1968), he captivated the minds of numerous spiritual seekers and served as an inspiration for many literary emulators. Castaneda became one of the informal apostles of the countercultural community in the United States and beyond and his Don Juan sequel eventually entered the pantheon of sacred texts of the neo-shamanism community.[4]

The contribution of psychology, especially popular psychology, which has been pivotal for many newly emerged spiritualities, was no less important. As a manifestation of altered states, shamanism was a natural match for psychology. Transpersonal psychology, which emerged in the 1960s and which moved away from materialism and behaviourism, revisited the concept of the abnormal, and began to treat the spiritual as a valid experience. The therapeutic techniques of tribal shamans, which were earlier dismissed as primitive and abnormal, became a source of knowledge to be utilized for the benefit of Western society. Incidentally, many current shamanic practices in the West exist as programs of short and long-term spiritual therapy conducted by people trained or at least well read in transpersonal psychology.

In the 1960s and 1970s, many alternative scholars and spiritual seekers who approached the personality holistically and who worked to help people develop their emotional and spiritual potentials to their full extent clustered around the Esalen Institute in California, one of the first centres of countercultural spirituality in the United States. Esalen was also one of the first to make shamanism part of its experiential curriculum, along with drama therapy, yoga, and various Asian spiritual techniques. During the 1960s and 1970s, one of the chief managers at Esalen was psychologist Julian Silverman, who wrote a paper in 1967 in which he approached shamanism as a form of spiritual therapy. It was he who at the turn of the 1970s invited Castaneda, Michael Harner and other students of tribal spirituality to test their techniques in a workshop format.[5]

In the United States at the turn of the 1970s, the countercultural revolution, which turned many Americans on to hallucinogens and alternative lifestyles, was on the decline. Many spiritual seekers felt fatigue from the psychedelic and communal experiences and longed for natural, individually oriented spirituality. One of these seekers was Harner, an anthropologist who, while formally remaining an academic, gradually grounded himself in the countercultural community.

Figure 2: Michael Harner

Although he had invested much of his earlier career into the study of South American Indian indigenous groups, whose spiritual cultures are saturated with hallucinogens, he purposely moved away from replicating these experiences in Western settings. Instead, Harner searched for alternatives by experimenting with drugless spiritual techniques, particularly from native North American, Siberian, and Sami traditions, which rely more on drumming, rattling, chanting, and guided meditation. Since Harner's thinking resonated well with the sentiments of many spiritual seekers, his workshops began to enjoy popularity.

Eventually, Harner left academia and moved from the East Coast to California in order to devote himself completely to teaching Westerners how to spiritually cure themselves by using 'archaic techniques of ecstasy'. In 1980, he established the Foundation for Shamanic Studies (FSS), the first school of modern shamanism, which organizes, systematizes, and disseminates the basics of shamanism worldwide. Thus, shamanism entered modern Western nature communities. Harner's *The Way of the Shaman* (1980), designed as a manual for any Euro-American wishing to learn shamanic techniques, became one of the major inspirational texts for the neo-shamanism community.[6] Viewing mind-altering plants not only as inefficient but also as detrimental to spiritual experiences, Harner pointed out that hallucinogens might unleash confusing imagery, interfere with the concentration necessary for shamanic work, and leave various chemical residues in one's body. Instead, he noted that the sound of the shaman's drum supplemented by rattling could produce the same effect as the hallucinogenic snuffs and drinks, but without any negative side-effects. By reading ethnographies and studying with indigenous spiritual practitioners who did not use mind-altering herbs, Harner began to shape a system of spiritual techniques, which he called 'core shamanism'. The premise of this system is based on a conviction that, if stripped of its cultural garb, a particular tradition reveals generic cross-cultural practices characteristic for shamanisms all over the globe. In other words, spiritual practices of elementary earth-based societies of all times and of all continents—including pre-Christian Europe—are remarkably similar. In his view, once identified and extracted, the core methods can be used for the spiritual curing of modern Western people. Therefore, Harner centered his teaching strategy on the 'distillation and interpretation of some of the millennia-old shamanic methods'.

The intellectual source of this approach is the Eliadean vision of shamanism as an archaic cross-cultural spirituality, the original cradle of all beliefs and religions. In *The Way of the Shaman*, Harner credited Eliade for bringing to light the worldwide consistency in shamanic knowledge.[7] Like his intellectual predecessor, the founder of core shamanism is convinced that the ancient way is so powerful and taps so deeply into the human mind that one's culturally coloured beliefs and assumptions about reality are essentially irrelevant. According to Harner, shamans worldwide manifest striking similarities in their spiritual practices, although they are separated by thousands of miles.

The core ritual item in the Harnerian version of shamanism is the drum. Rationalizing its use as a healing tool, the anthropologist and his associates argue that monotonous drumming can produce changes in the central nervous system and put the person in an altered state. Incidentally, although Harner sometimes uses the expression 'altered state', he prefers to talk about the 'shamanic state of consciousness'. He points out that drumming in a frequency of four to four and a half beats per second temporarily changes brain wave activity. This facilitates imagery in the human mind and allows people to reach rapidly an altered state, which helps the spiritual practitioner to embark on a shamanic journey.[8] The founder of core shamanism also stresses that the changes induced by the monotonous drumming build up the resistance of the body's immune system against various diseases. Proponents of the Harnerian version of shamanism add that no hallucinogen can produce such marvellous effects. The only problem one has to worry about when using the drum is the privacy of one's neighbours. Yet Harner and his associates found a solution. They began to release drumming audio cassettes and CDs, which they advertise as perfect substitutes for actual drumming. This multimedia option that encourages an individual to become his or her own shaman is a truly Western solution framed in the spirit of the American tradition of individualism and privacy.

The foundation has become the major spearhead of shamanic practices in the United States and other Western countries. An important component of FSS activities is the preservation of shamanic knowledge on the tribal periphery. It might be a desire of the foundation to somehow pay back indigenous people for the knowledge Western spiritual seekers have digested from their traditions. The foundation responds to the requests of those indigenous groups that ask for help to restore traditional earth-based knowledge undermined by colonization. Again, Harner's associates view this assistance as providing such natives with the skeleton of shamanism knowledge, on which interested natives can overlay their cultural 'meat'. Thus, such fertilization of a local tradition has helped to enhance the revitalization of shamanic practices in the Tuva republic (Siberia), where native spiritual practitioners blend what has remained from their tradition with the techniques appropriated from Western esotericism.[9]

Critics point out that this project harbours the danger of imposing on native societies the quick-fix version of shamanism constructed for Western audiences. At the same time, native people (for example, in Siberia) are themselves interested in receiving spiritual feedback from their Western colleagues.[10] FSS representatives insist that not only Siberians, but also some Native American, Sami, and Inuit people have similarly approached Harner, requesting that he teach them core shamanism to restore their sacred knowledge, which was lost due to conquest and Christianization. Cast against ethnographic descriptions of nineteenth-century shamanism, Harnerian techniques certainly look different and not so traditional. Still, this does not prevent interested indigenous spiritual practitioners in non-Western areas from reading his books and weaving his techniques into their own practices.

In a Harnerian basic workshop, people usually lie on the floor, close their eyes, and try to relax. Accompanied by the intensive monotonous sounds of a drum, they begin to enter the altered state, the spiritual journey to the spirit world. Harner and his associates encourage those participants who have mastered the basics of his core techniques to journey on their own, using drums or earphones and drumming tapes. The spiritual journey usually begins with entering either a passage, or a tunnel, or a cave and then the spirit world. Although Harner and those who follow his method insist that the information people learn during those journeys comes straight from otherworldly beings, they seem to realize that not everybody in the present-day skeptical world is ready to embrace the reality of spirits right away. Hence, participants are invited to use their imaginations as a first step in order to 'smooth' their transition to the spiritual realm. Thus, imagination becomes a key to the world of spirits.

One of the major goals of the Harnerian technique is to identify one's own power animal, which acts as some sort of a guardian angel, advises an individual, and shields him or her from misfortunes.

Figure 3: Attendees at Harnerian workshop.

In return, people are expected to cultivate a good relationship with this power animal, to visit it on a regular basis through spiritual journeys, to dance with it, and to acknowledge its presence in many other ways. If people forget to maintain contact with the power animal, it might leave temporarily or even forever. In this case, says Harner, the despirited person might get into trouble by falling ill or experiencing various misfortunes. What Harner calls the power animal in existing ethnographic literature is also known as the guardian spirit, spirit familiar, totem animal, or helping spirit. The images of these power animals that individuals might encounter in their 'spiritual holodecks' reflect Western shamanism's fascination with wildlife and all things earth-based. In *The Way of the Shaman*, Harner directly suggested that power animals are 'usually wild, untamed species'. Among possible candidates, he named cranes, tigers, foxes, eagles, bears, deer, porpoises, and dragons. Dragons, in non-ordinary reality, are treated as real beings just as other beasts. Such unattractive domestic animals as hens, pigs, and cows are not eligible for the role of power animal because, as the products of artificial breeding by human beings, they have lost a connection with nature and do not have any power. Harner also stressed that insects never can be power animals.[11] At the same time, the Harner system has allowed cats to enter the spiritual pantheon of core shamanism. Despite their long-time association with human beings, it is assumed that these mysterious creatures still maintain a great deal of autonomy and wildness.

In the unpredictable and threatening spiritual pantheon of tribal shamanism, people frequently did not know what to expect from their spirits. In contrast, in core shamanism and in the modern shamanism subculture in general, not only power animals but also all other spirits behave quite benevolently. They never harm people. Harner stresses, 'No matter how fierce a guardian animal spirit may seem, its possessor is no danger because the power animal is absolutely harmless. It is only a source of power; it has no aggressive intentions. It only comes to you because you need help.'[12] Overall, in neo-shamanism, spirits might be gentle or stern, and they might help, taunt, spook, or even perform a spiritual dismemberment of a person. Still, they never hurt one. No matter how scary a shamanic journey is, it always has a happy ending, like an adrenaline-raising movie thriller.

After a successful return from a spiritual journey, its participants—together with the help of the workshop leader, other participants, or on their own—see how these spiritual encounters might affect their lives in ordinary reality. Usually the goal of a spiritual journey to the other reality is to secure advice from a power animal about how to fix certain personal problems or cure an illness. The explanation for the benevolent nature of core and other versions of Western shamanism lies in the psychotherapeutic goals of this spirituality, which seeks to unleash the best of human potential. Harner explains that the shaman does not need to know about the nature of a specific illness. It is enough to make a journey 'out there' to the alternative reality, and through contact with spiritual forces, one finds his or her lost power animal and restores it. The restoration of the power animal energizes an individual, strengthens his or her resistance to illness, and helps the person to live a good, happy life.[13]

Core shamanism and related techniques are advertised as a shortcut to spiritual growth, which also resonates well with the mindsets of busy American audiences. For example, a neo-shamanic manual written by two former students of Harner characteristically 'samples ancient techniques that produce immediate results'.[14] Jonathan Horowitz, who teaches Harner's core shamanism to spiritual seekers in Scandinavian countries, generalizes along the same lines. He stresses that such 'democratic knowledge' as tribal spirituality does not require any long introduction and that 'it only takes a few minutes to have a shamanic experience'.[15] Paula Klempay, a career counselor who also apprenticed at FSS, stresses that for those who aspire to partake of shamanism quickly, it is enough to get a tape with drumming music distributed by the foundation, to read Harner's book *The Way of the Shaman* for guidelines, and then to experiment as one wishes.[16] Canadian psychologist Ed Kennedy, another former student of Harner's, who, after learning with the master, established an FSS branch in Thunder Bay, is even more explicit: 'I found it's one of the most profound, direct, fastest things that works for the human body. It's a quick fix.'[17]

Leslie Gray, a shamanism practitioner from San Francisco, has elaborated on that quick approach. She says that the majority of her clients want to regain power to deal better with life situations. At the same time, they are too busy to spend years of their precious time playing the psychoanalysis game, going back and forth digging into their childhood memories. Gray tries to accommodate such desires. In her work, she focuses on people taking present action into their own hands rather than mulling over the past. As an example, she went through the case of a person who approached her when he was passed over for a promotion. The client had never been to a psychotherapist and had no desire to analyze his personality. His goal was to become, as Castaneda would have said, a spiritual predator who is able to receive power to fight for himself at work. To find out how to deal with the situation, Gray conducted a spiritual journey and a divination session for him. Gray stressed that the modern shaman knows very well that current life is fast and hectic and that people frequently must make instant decisions. Therefore, in this hectic environment, according to Gray, shamanism has become a 'very quick way of using consciousness, which is not bound by time and place, so you can have immediate access to deeper wisdom and include it in your decision-making'.[18]

Neo-shamanism is designed not only as a fast access to ancient wisdom but also as a portable and compact technique. A good example is Harner's drumming cassettes and earphones, which can be used by a person to conduct a shamanic journey literally anytime and anywhere. In this case, age-old spirituality is always within reach. To support these individualized practices, neo-shamanism appeals to the impromptu nature of traditional shamanism. Indeed, in contrast, for example, to Christianity or Islam, in the past and nowadays the tribal shaman is solely responsible for crafting his or her personal techniques and rituals and does not have to follow any fixed spiritual blueprint. To modern Western seekers, the spontaneity of indigenous spirituality and the lack of corporate unity among 'tribal doctors' appear as inherently anarchistic and reveal the democratic nature of shamanism.

Drawing attention to these aspects of traditional spirituality, one of its modern practitioners has stressed that 'Shamanism is not an elite professional club, open to some and closed to others. Much to the contrary, the indigenous or primal perspective acknowledges that each individual has a unique and viable link with the otherworld, and therefore a gift to give.'[19] Moreover, some spirituality writers go as far as directly claiming that non-Western traditional shamanism is spiritual individualism.[20] Obviously, this stance has wide appeal to the Western and especially American public, whose tradition is heavily informed by the notions of privacy and individualism.

Incidentally, anthropologist Bill Burton from Harner's foundation directly pointed to the American tradition of rugged individualism and personal freedom as a supportive context for the resurgence of shamanism: 'No cultural theme is more important to Americans than that of democracy at the level of the individual.' Elaborating on this point, he noted that the attraction of shamanic practices is that everyone is free to mold his or her personal spiritual pantheon. Interacting with the helping spirits as their intimate friends, people find a refuge from the isolation they sense in an impersonal mass society and at the same time feel shielded in their spiritual privacy.[21] In his workshops and writings, Harner repeatedly mentions this individualism factor, stressing that shamanism is a democratic spirituality, where shamans are independent of each other, follow their own spiritual paths, and have no central authority to oversee them. Moreover, he adds that—unlike traditional practitioners who usually act on behalf of their patients—in core shamanism everyone can act as his or her own priest and doctor, catering to individual needs from soul loss to professional career growth. The founder of core shamanism explains, 'In shamanism everyone is his or her own prophet, getting spiritual revelation directly from the highest sources.' On another occasion he stressed, 'I think that almost everybody is potentially a shaman.'[22]

Trying to distill the individualized essence of shamanic techniques for the uninitiated public, Gini Scott, the author of *The Complete Idiot's Guide to Shamanism*, has compared the activities of the shamanism practitioner to the work of a film director, who is in complete control of his or her scene. She writes, 'You choose the actors, decide on the setting, give actors a general guideline to follow, and let them improvise. Yet, at any time you can interrupt to redirect and guide the action, and then return to observing again.'[23] Overall, in many various modern versions of neo-shamanism, individuals can conduct visionary travels on their own or as part of a group. During these journeys, they freely experiment with spiritual images by entering altered states, creating their own spiritual holodecks, and then populating these realms with various characters. It is notable that Canadian anthropologist Joan Townsend, who surveyed several shamanism workshops in North America, has defined neo-shamanism as an 'individualist religious movement' in contrast to a 'group organized movement' that subjects itself to certain collective standards.[24]

Although Harner was a pioneer in setting tribal shamanic techniques into a form of Western spirituality, his core shamanism is now only one of many versions of shamanism found in Western countries. Moreover, not all spiritual practitioners are happy about his version of shamanism.

Some, for example, are disturbed by his conviction that shamanic knowledge can be mastered through a workshop. The members of the shamanism community who are critical of Harner also argue that there is no way to digest the abstract core of universal shamanism by stripping off cultural traditions. They stress that shamanism always manifests itself in a particular cultural setting: Lakota, Mongol, Sami, Jivaro, and so forth.[25]

Incidentally, such critical remarks about Harnerian shamanism mirror the similar critique of Mircea Eliade by anthropologists who point out that the Eliadean universal shamanism is an abstraction that has nothing to do with reality. No doubt, this criticism of the generic cross-cultural vision of shamanism also reflects current postmodern thinking that treats with suspicion all kinds of generalizations and seeks to tribalize and particularize knowledge. Applying critical scrutiny to the Harnerian version of shamanism, Annette Host, from the Scandinavian Center for Shamanic Studies, made an important observation. She notes that when we intellectually strip, let us say, Lakota, Nepalese, or Yakut (Sakha) shamanisms of their indigenous garb, we unavoidably wrap the final product in our own cultural outlooks, habits, and biases, even when we do not intend to. Seen from her Nordic European perspective, the shamanism Harner offers appears very much American—'adapted to the American spiritual-fast-food culture'—as she has remarked.[26] Nevertheless, although she uses her criticism of Harner to prove that core shamanism is wishful thinking, one can turn around her 'American spiritual-fast-food culture' thesis. If we take into account the polyglot nature of the modern world and the expanding cosmopolitan culture, whose core is definitely American, we will see that Harnerian shamanism does not look so superficial. It perfectly fits the format of our world as a global village and might look attractive to many people who either belong to hyphenated groups or who simply do not know who they are.

Critics also note that practising tribal spirituality in the Western industrial setting is problematic. Cast against the existing ethnographic literature, the jungle and arctic practices, cozy suburban healing centres, drumming cassettes, and individualized techniques devoid of any particular cultural tradition do not look earth-based. Some spiritual seekers feel that what we call shamanism always existed as a form of local spiritual knowledge set not only in a particular culture but in a particular natural soil and landscape. To Loren Cruden, a writer who interviewed major American practitioners of 'tribal' spirituality, shamanism is a spiritual technique that literally should be anchored in particular earth, streams, animal, plants, and other elements of the 'telephone-less existence'.[27] In turn, transpersonal psychologist Jurgen Kremer has written, 'It is quite beyond me to imagine a genuine shaman who is not grounded in the specificity of the wild and her spirits.'[28] To him and to like-minded people, shamanism transplanted into the cement jungles of the Western megalopolis as a workshop practice does not make sense because it usually does not lead to a change of lifestyle, away from consumerism and toward the earth. Critics like Cruden and Kremer do not believe that quick weekend spiritual sessions might change the consciousness of people.

Another controversy that has affected the neo-shamanism community in the United States and by default in other Western countries is the appropriation of tribal symbols and metaphors, particularly the ones associated with indigenous people of North America. Earlier marginalized by modern society as primitive and archaic, in the 1960s and 1970s Native Americans became for Western seekers a blueprint of superior moral and spiritual values precisely because those particular qualities ascribed to them by society had acquired a positive meaning.[29] At least until the early 1980s, Native Americana heavily influenced much of US neo-shamanism symbolism and artifacts. Among the most popular are vision quests, eagle feathers, hawks, the four directions, the sacred circle, the sweat lodge, drums, dream catchers, and sacred pipes.

Figure 4: Dream catcher.

The spiritual imagery some neo-shamanism practitioners experience on their otherworldly quests has been also heavily loaded with Native American symbolism that comes from books, seminars, and spiritual teachers. Many hyphenated American spiritual seekers came to view American Indians as stewards of nature and as an archetype of ancient tribal wisdom, which their own ancestors had lost.

Indian spokespeople frequently call those who weave indigenous symbols and artifacts into the fabric of the mind, body, and spirit culture 'plastic shamans" or 'plastic medicine men/women'. The assumption here is that the 'New Age' rituals are artificial, imagined, and, therefore, not real. By contrast, native ceremonies practised by Native Americans—

especially in such traditional settings as reservations—appear to them to be organic, natural, and real. The most devastating criticism against those Americans and Europeans who emulate specific Indian rituals was levelled by the late Native American spokesperson Vine Deloria, Jr., a professor of political science from the University of Colorado. With irony and humour he wrote about those non-Indians who cling to 'alleged shamans' as individuals who are ready to 'pay hundreds of dollars for the privilege of sitting on the ground, having corn flour thrown in their faces, and being told that the earth was round and all things lived in circles'.[30] The crux of the Native American criticism of the 'New Age' is that indigenous ceremonies taken out of context and mixed with rituals from other cultures and traditions do not make sense. Drawing on the premise that each religion is somehow mysteriously linked with a specific land and locality, Deloria argued that tribal spirituality became deeply grounded in native communities and, by its very nature, could not contain a universal message. For this reason, he described those natives who work with wider audiences as people who have betrayed the values of their respective groups.[31]

The attempts to reserve Native Americana for the Indians—to sanction what is traditional and what is not—clearly represent an effort to freeze religions and cultures in time and space, which, whether one likes it or not, never happens in real life. In order to make sure that native ceremonies stay within their groups, some Native American communities have begun to restrict their rituals to individuals who have sufficient Indian bloodlines and who can produce special Indian 'roll cards' issued to the members of officially recognized tribes. In a long-term perspective, it is obvious that, in the United States, the greater part of which consists of hyphenated people of multiple descents, it is hard to stick to this requirement. At the same time, this practice does make sense in the context of the ideology of multiculturalism, which currently dominates American life and which cultivates the fragmentation of people by Balkanizing them in their respective ethnic, gender, and cultural niches.

Within American nature spirituality circles, many people accept the Indian criticism of 'plastic shamans' as valid and sound. Although Native Americana continues to enjoy popularity among seekers, the controversy over its use has made many of them look for other forms of spirituality that could provide a steadier ground. Overall, currently there is a growing realization that American Indian rites and symbols cannot make non-Indian spiritual practitioners more indigenous. Thus, since the end of the 1980s, the general trend among American seekers of a European descent has been to move away from a reliance on Native American symbolism toward the pre-Christian heritage of Europe. After all, Carl

Jung—one of the spearheads of modern Western esotericism—prophetically instructed future spiritual seekers: 'The Western road to health must be built upon Western groundwork with Western symbols, and be formed from Western material.'[32]

The broad and loose meaning the expression 'shamanism idiom' has acquired in modern anthropology, psychology, and religious studies serves well for current spiritual seekers. As a result, people in the nature community frequently use this expression not only in the conventional sense to mean 'spiritual work in altered states' but as a way of situating their spiritual practices as ancient, tribal, and earth-based. For example, seekers might talk about a shamanic attitude towards land or shamanic philosophy, which in other contexts can simply mean a spiritual or ecological attitude toward the earth. Thus, shamanism might mean different things to different people. In current American spirituality there is a variety of groups and individuals who use the expression 'shamanism' to describe their spiritual techniques. These people range from the practitioners of core shamanism and those who find inspiration in a particular non-Western, earth-based spirituality to eco-feminists and participants in the goddess movement. Furthermore, since the 1980s, in the United States there is a growing number of pagan and Wiccan people who are concerned about their own indigenous roots and who describe their practices as shamanic (Figures 5 and 6).[33]

Figure 5 and Figure 6.

Strictly speaking, many of these practices resist generalization as purely shamanic because one can equally describe them as pagan, Wiccan or Druid. Moreover, the same individual or group can often be simultaneously involved in exploring, experimenting with, and practising multiple traditions, and creating his or her own spiritual blend. This is obvious, for example, in the spiritual resources used by a California group called Hrafnar. Its leader, fiction writer Diana Paxson, gradually converted to European pre-Christian spirituality as a result of her work on several novels dealing with characters and events from the Nordic spiritual heritage. At the same time, one of her major inspirations was reading Harner's book *The Way of the Shaman* and participating in his workshop. Still, prior to this, she was already grounded in women's mysteries (goddess spirituality), Kabbalah, and Wicca. Hrafnar mostly draws on Nordic Scandinavian folklore and puts much of its emphasis on *seidr* divination—an ancient Scandinavian form of entering altered states for divination purposes that she and her friends learned by reading Nordic sagas.[34]

The spiritual profile of this and many other similar groups shows that, unlike scholars who try to classify social and cultural phenomena, the practitioners of nature spirituality are least of all interested in sorting themselves into categories and groups. The lack of any hierarchy, dogma, or fixed rituals encourages spiritual seekers to produce their own eclectic imagery and techniques. Both those who have schooled themselves in such spiritual centres as Harner's FSS and those who have mastered shamanism on their own add their individual creative spins to shamanic practices. For example, one can easily meet in the United States seekers for whom shamanism might appear to be something that represents, let us say, a mixture of Buddhist, Siberian, and Native American symbolism peppered with urban yoga and Jungian analysis. Finally, a growing number of psychotherapists and spiritual counsellors, especially those who are trained in transpersonal psychology, use shamanism as a supplementary technique to work with their clients.[35] The rule of thumb here is to select what works well for one personally and discard what does not. A good example is spirituality writer Joan Halifax, who, in addition to Harner, was one of the first to bring shamanism to the attention of the Western educated public. In her personal techniques, she melds Buddhism with shamanism.

The variety of American neo-shamanisms is also visible in the choice of tools seekers use to enter altered states (shamanic state of consciousness) and embark on a spiritual journey. While Harner's followers use drums and rattles, for the followers of the retired psychologist and linguist Felicitas Goodman, musical instruments are only supplementary tools. The major device she and her associates use to immerse themselves into altered states is archaic body postures replicated from ancient figurines and statuettes.[36] There is also a fringe practice, pioneered by Daniel Statnekov, that induces shamanic journeys through the replication of the sounds of ancient Peruvian whistling bottles (Figure 7).

Figure 7.

Prior to the 1970s, archaeologists believed that pre-Columbian Indians had used these ceramic vessels for carrying water. Challenging this conventional scholarly wisdom, Statnekov and his spiritual followers insist that the major role of these items was spiritual. Particularly, they are convinced that, if used as whistles, the bottles produce low-frequency sounds that generate altered states of consciousness.[37] Moreover, Gini Scott, the author of the popular *The Complete Idiot's Guide to Shamanism*, informs us that to enjoy a full shamanic experience and to reach the altered states, one actually does not need anything. She claims that drumming and rattling only irritate her, preventing her from stepping into the separate reality. To plunge herself into the altered state, she simply uses creative imagination, guiding her fantasy in a designated direction. Scott is convinced that the spiritual holodeck that she constructs using this simple exercise is no less effective than the ones induced by other shamanisms.[38]

Despite the variety of their practices, those people who participate in neo-shamanism share some common sentiments. First of all, they recognize the existence of non-ordinary reality in addition to the ordinary or mundane realm. This means that these people believe that there is something 'out there' that is as real as what we perceive in our regular life. If the person is ready to adopt this stance, he or she has to make a second step—to recognize that the spirits who populate the non-ordinary realm are real beings. This is an essential 'theological' prerequisite for participation in any school of modern Western shamanism. Belinda Gore, who teaches body posture shamanism, notes that 'Our [spiritual] experiences are not the products of our imaginations or totally a reflection of the personal unconsciousness. While the personal unconsciousness may determine the lens through which we look, the scene itself exists separate from us. We may interact with it, but we do not create it.'[39]

Among other essential common sentiments, practitioners of shamanism subscribe to the notion that spirituality should be earth-based, which explains the essential place of environmental ethics in neo-shamanism. Like representatives of other nature religions, practitioners of shamanism are convinced that everything in this world is holistically related. They view the human body as only a small part of this web of natural life. In fact, this stance has already become part of the cultural mainstream in many Western countries. Another important notion is a negative attitude toward Western civilization—especially its core elements, Enlightenment and modernity—and, simultaneously, a reverential attitude toward non-Western spiritual traditions and cultures. Many of those who teach and disseminate shamanic practices in Europe and North America argue that from the Stone Age to approximately medieval times, humanity existed in balance with nature and was deeply steeped in spirituality. The Renaissance and Enlightenment reduced the presence of the divine in human life and imposed limitations on human knowledge, excluding everything that was unscientific. They are also convinced that modern Western civilization, which continues to denigrate the significance of the sacred and the spiritual, cages the human mind. Many shamanism practitioners position themselves as people who bring back ancient knowledge to cure modern people from the spiritual devastation produced by Enlightenment philosophy.

Although shamanic practitioners usually harbour strong negative sentiments toward organized Christianity, they do appropriate a variety of Christian images and symbols, especially if they can trace them to early and folk Christianity, which they view as pristine and uncorrupted by organized religion. In fact, many of these people view Jesus Christ himself as a master shaman, who was able to perform miracles just like classical Siberian and Native American spiritual practitioners. In response to the growing popularity of such unchurched spiritualities as neo-shamanism, some conventional denominations—especially the ones that are traditionally open-minded and liberal—have begun to accommodate pagan and non-Western symbolism in their practices. For example, in Seattle, the Church of Unity has embraced such practices as chanting in Sanskrit and Native American vision quests to enhance its popularity in the eyes of parishioners in a city notorious for its indifference to mainstream Christianity. American Unitarian Universalism, much of whose creed stresses the link between nature and spirit, is in the forefront of this movement. In this denomination, the romance with nature, the non-Western, and the 'primitive' goes back to Emerson and Thoreau. Thus, some practitioners of shamanism, paganism, Wicca, and other nature spirituality groups are simultaneously either members or friends of Unitarian Universalism or use the facilities of this denomination for drumming sessions and shamanic healing. John Burciaga, a Unitarian minister in Bethesda, Maryland, argues that now there is a significant subculture within the ministry, who experiment with various ways of reaching altered states.[40]

Like many members of the modern Western esotericism community, American practitioners of shamanism are very suspicious of any caste and group loyalties. Stressing that in his or her ritual practice the shaman is an explorer and an improviser, modern-day shamanism practitioners are usually very sensitive to any imposition on their personal spiritual blend. With its loose structure and individualized practices, a neo-shamanic group, a workshop, or a drumming group is usually amorphous and short-lived. As such, this anti-structure is usually an ideal structure for contemporary educated Westerners, who are too skeptical to commit themselves to group values and who, at the same time, long for spiritual experiences.

References

Castaneda, C. 1968. *The Teachings of Don Juan: A Yaqui Way of Knowledge*. Berkeley, California: University of California Press.

Eliade, Mircea. *Shamanism: Archaic Techniques of Ecstasy* (Princeton, NJ: Princeton University Press, 1964).

Fikes, J. C. 1993. *Carlos Castaneda, Academic Opportunism and the Psychedelic Sixties*. Victoria, Canada: Millenia Press.

Harner, M. 1980. *The Way of the Shaman*. San Francisco: Harper & Row.

Jenkins, P. 2004. *Dream Catchers: How Mainstream America Discovered Native Spirituality*. New York: Oxford University Press.

Penczak, C. 2005. *The Temple of Shamanic Witchcraft*. Woodbury, Minnesota: Llewellyn.

Scott, G.G. 2002. *The Complete Idiot's Guide to Shamanism*. Indianapolis: Alpha.

Stuckrad, Kocku von. *Schamanismus und Esoterik: Kultur- und wissenschaftsgeschichtliche Betrachtungen*. Leuven: Peeters, 2003.

Wallis, R. J. 2003. *Shamans/Neo-Shamans: Ecstasy, Alternative Archaeologies, and Contemporary Pagans*. London: Routledge.

Walsh, R.. 2007. *The World of Shamanism: New Views of an Ancient Tradition*. Woodbury, Minnesota: Llewellyn.

Znamenski, Andrei A. *The Beauty of the Primitive: Shamanism and Western Imagination*. New York: Oxford University Press, 2007.

Endnotes

1   See for example, the works by historian and philosopher Theodore Roszak, who was one of the first to explore these experiences, which were labeled as a counterculture at that time: Theodore Roszak, *The Making of a Counter Culture: Reflections on the Technocratic Society*

       and its Youthful Opposition (Garden City, NY: Anchor Books, 1969) and *Where the Wasteland Ends: Politics and Transcendence in Post Industrial Society* (Garden City, NY: Doubleday, 1972).

2   One of the first pivotal texts that underscored the significance of this consciousness revolution is Merilyn Ferguson, *The Aquarian Conspiracy* (New York: Tarcher, 1980). The most comprehensive study of the historical and philosophical roots of this spiritual revolution that sprang up in the 1960s-1970s is Olav Hammer, *Claiming Knowledge: Strategies of Epistemology from Theosophy to the New Age* (Leiden: Brill, 2001). For the best succinct account focused specifically on the 1960s consciousness revolution and a follow-up events, see Nevill Drury, *The New Age: Searching for the Spiritual Self* (New York, NY: Thames & Hudson, 2004). A popular history of the "New Age" as applied to the United States can be found in Walt Anderson, *The Upstart Spring: Esalen and the American Awakening* (Reading, MS: Addison-Wesley, 1983) and Eugene Taylor, *Shadow Culture: Psychology and Spirituality in America* (Washington, DC: Counterpoint, 1999).

3   For the first comprehensive study of neo-shamanism in Europe and North America, see Kocku von Stuckrad, *Schamanismus und Esoterik: Kultur- und wissenschaftsgeschichtliche Betrachtungen* (Leuven: Peeters, 2003). Building on his research, I wrote *The Beauty of the Primitive: Shamanism and Western Imagination* (New York: Oxford University Press, 2007), which represents my own take on the history of neo-shamanism in the West with a special emphasis on American scene.

4   Carlos Castaneda, *The Teachings of Don Juan: A Yaqui Way of Knowledge* (Berkeley, California: University of California Press, 1968). For more about the influence of Castaneda and the 1960s' counterculture on shamanism studies, see Jay C. Fikes, Carlos Castaneda, *Academic Opportunism and the Psychedelic Sixties* (Victoria, BC: Millenia, 1993).

5   Jeffrey J. Kripal, *Esalen: America and the Religion of No Religion* (Chicago: University Of Chicago Press, 2008); Julian Silverman, "Shamans and Acute Schizophrenia," *American Anthropologist* 69, no. 1 (1967): 21–31; Eugene Taylor, *Shadow Culture: Psychology and Spirituality in America* (Washington, DC: Counterpoint, 1999), 248; Walter T. Anderson, *The Upstart Spring: Esalen and the American Awakening* (Reading, MA: Addison-Wesley, 1983), 22.

6   Michael Harner, *The Way of the Shaman: A Guide to Power and Healing* (San Francisco: Harper & Row, 1980).

7   Ibid., xii Michael Harner and Sandra Harner, "Core Practices in the Shamanic Treatment of Illness," *Shamanism* 13, no. 1-2 (2000): 20.

8   Melinda Maxfield, "The Journey of the Drum," *ReVision* 16, no. 4 (1994): 157–163.

9   Paul Uccusic, "Shamanism Alive and Well: the 1999 Legacy of the First FSS Expedition to Tuva," *Shamanism* 13, no. 1-2 (2000): 45-54.
10 See, for example, "Michael Harner Invited to Teach Master Class by Siberian Shaman," *Shamanism* 13, no. 1-2 (2000): 59.
11 Harner, *The Way of the Shaman*, 67, 113, 81.
12 Ibid., 67-68.
13 Michael Harner, "The Ancient Wisdom in Shamanic Cultures," in *Shamanism: An Expanded View of Reality*, edited by Shirley J. Nicholson (Wheaton, IL: Theosophical Publishing House, 1987), 9.
14 Angelique S. Cook and George A. Haw, *Shamanism and the Esoteric Tradition* (St. Paul, MN: Llewellyn, 1992), front matter.
15 Galina Lindquist, *Shamanic Performances on the Urban Scene: Neo-Shamanism in Contemporary Sweden* (Stockholm: Department of Social Anthropology, Stockholm University, 1997), 24.
16 Barbara Clearbridge, "Shamanism Alive and Well in Urban America." Available at http://www.energyworkinfo.com/files/shaman.html (downloaded November 29, 2003).
17 Kim Zarzour, "Witch Doctor Takes You on Trip to Another World," Toronto Star, December 1, 1987, G1.
18 Mirka Knaster, "Leslie Gray's Path to Power." Available at http://www.woodfish.org/power2.html (downloaded July 16, 2005).
19 Frank H. MacEowan, "Reclaiming Our Ancestral Bones: Revitalizing Shamanic Practices in the New Millennium," *Shaman's Drum* (July–November 2001): 17.
20 Wolf Moondance, *Rainbow Medicine: A Visionary Guide to Native American Shamanism* (New York: Sterling, 1994), 7.
21 Bill B. Burton, "Western Shamanism in a Cultural Context," in *Materialy mezhdunarodnogo kongressa shamanizm i inie traditsionnie verovania i praktiki*, edited by V. I. Kharitonova and D. Funk, *Ethnological Studies of Shamanism and Other Indigenous Spiritual Beliefs and Practices*, no. 5, pt. 2 (Moskva: Institut Antropologii i Etnografii, 1999), 235–236.
22 Michael Harner, "What Is a Shaman?'" in *Shaman's Path: Healing, Personal Growth & Empowerment*, edited by Gary Doore (Boston: Shambhala, 1988), 10; Harner, "The Ancient Wisdom in Shamanic Cultures," 16.
23 Gini Graham Scott, *The Complete Idiot's Guide to Shamanism* (Indianapolis, IN: Alpha, 2002), 182.
24 Joan Townsend, "Modern Non-Traditional and Invented Shamanism," in *Shamanhood: Symbolism and Epic*, edited by Juha Pentika"inen (Budapest: Akademiai Kiado , 2001), 257.
25 Karen Kelly, "Editorial," *Spirit Talk* 14 (2001): 24. Available at http://www.shamaniccircles.org/spirit_talk/index.html (downloaded July 29,

2005); Jurgen Kremer, "Seidr or Trance? Toward an Archaeology of the Euro-American Tribal Mind," *ReVision* 16, no. 4 (1996): 183–192.

26 Annette Host, "What's in a Name," *Spirit Talk* 14 (2001): 1. Available at http:// www.shamaniccircles.org/spirit_talk/index.html (downloaded July 29, 2005).

27 Clearbridge, "Shamanism Alive and Well in Urban America."

28 Jurgen Kremer, "Practices for the Postmodern Shaman," in *Proceedings of the Tenth International Conference on the Study of Shamanism and Alternate Modes of Healing*, edited by Ruth-Inge Heinze (Berkeley, CA: Independent Scholars of Asia, 1993), 39.

29 For the most comprehensive discussion of this fascination with the spiritual side of Native Americana, see Philip Jenkins, *Dream Catchers: How Mainstream America Discovered Native Spirituality* (New York: Oxford University Press, 2004).

30 Vine Deloria, Jr., *God Is Red: A Native View of Religion* (1973; new edition, Golden, CO: North American, 1992), 41.

31 Vine Deloria, Jr., *For This Land: Writings on Religion in America* (New York and London: Routledge, 1999), 266; Deloria, *God Is Red*, 43.

32 Harry Oldmeadow, *Journeys East: 20th-Century Western Encounters with Eastern Religious Traditions* (Bloomington, IN: World Wisdom, 2004), 100.

33 Christopher Penczak, *The Temple of Shamanic Witchcraft: Shadows, Spirits, and the Healing Journey* (Woodbury, Minnesota: Llewellyn, 2005).

34 Maude Stephany, "An Interview with Diana Paxson," *Echoed Voices* (November 2002). Available at http://www.echoedvoices.org (downloaded June 20, 2004). See also Diana Paxson, *Essential Asatru: Walking the Path of Norse Paganism* (New York: Citadel Press, 2006).

35 The most comprehensive study of shamanism as a transpersonal technique is Roger Walsh, *The World of Shamanism: New Views of an Ancient Tradition* (Woodbury, MN: Llewellyn, 2007).

36 Belinda Gore, *Ecstatic Body Postures: An Alternate Reality Workbook* (Rochester, VT: Bear, 1995).

37 Daniel K. Statnekov, *Animated Earth: A Story of Peruvian Whistles and Transformation* (Berkeley, CA: North Atlantic Books, 2003).

38 Scott, *The Complete Idiot's Guide to Shamanism*.

39 Gore, *Ecstatic Body Postures*, 22.

40 Julia Lieblich, "Looking for God on a Psychedelic Drug Trip Obviously Controversial," *Stuart News/Port St. Lucie News* (Stuart, FL), January 31, 1998, D6.

6
Neo-Shamanisms in Europe

Robert J. Wallis

Introduction
A sourcebook titled 'Pathways in Modern Western Magic' would be incomplete without a chapter on 'neo-shamanisms' in Europe, for two reasons. First, a wide variety of contemporary mages in Europe and elsewhere look to the ancient origins of their practices in the ecstasies of prehistoric and indigenous shamans. Second, the construct of 'shamanism' has been a part of European consciousness since the eighteenth century (when explorers began reporting on Siberian shamanic practices) and as a classic instance of 'the other', shamanism—real and imagined—is a phenomenon against which we have defined ourselves. In this chapter I engage critically with neo-shamanisms in Europe, commenting for example on instances in which shamanism is generalised and universalised, perceived to be acultural, ahistorical and apolitical—even nonreligious. The disconcerting implications of this concern insensitivity to contemporary indigenous self-determination and at worst neo-colonialism. By contrast, I also discuss examples which look to ancient European pagan religions in order to reimagine local shamanistic practices for the present. In these instances, the appropriation of the past and its mobilisation in nationalist politics are concerning also, but neo-shamanisms have contributed in important ways to the discourse on 'shamanism'. Drawing on the rethinking of animism in the anthropology of religion which offers

a recasting of how shamanism is constituted, I close my discussion by considering neo-shamanic practices which accord with animist ontologies and so 'give back' to the discourse on 'shamanism'. I begin with some background orientation, draw on my earlier research on the subject, and outline my current thinking on the topic.

Coming to terms with neo-shamanisms

The term 'shamanism' was crystallised in the eighteenth century (Flaherty 1992) and shamans have continued to fascinate scholars and the public alike, to the present: 'shamanism' endures as a phenomena against which late modernity defines and negotiates itself. As we embark on the second decade of the globalised twenty-first century, while it might still be appropriate to differentiate shamans from neo-shamans in some instances, in others, and increasingly, this distinction is blurred. Euro-American Techno-shamans using avatars in Second Life as part of their spiritual practice[1] are quite clearly distinct from indigenous San/Bushman shamans in Southern Africa whose practices have changed over time necessarily but are rooted in localised environmental conditions and a relatively unchanged social milieu (Katz et al 1997; Lewis-Williams & Dowson 1999[1989]). But even in these instances, shamanism and neo-shamanism are entangled: some Euro-American spiritual tourists pay to participate in San/Bushman trance dances,[2] shamans in post-Communist Siberia whose practices were persecuted now develop their 'shamanism' based on the ethnographic records of anthropologists and the reimagining of 'shamanism' by Euroamerican practitioners (Balzer n.d.), while indigenous shamans elsewhere use the web as a resource.[3] Shamans and neo-shamans are too diffuse and diverse to pin down with the singular terms 'shamanism' and 'neo-shamanism', and we might rather speak less pejoratively, plurally and simply of shamanisms and neo-shamanisms (Wallis 2003: 30), acknowledging fluid boundaries between these terms in many contexts.[4] Even these terms do have the tendency to generalise or suggest a coherent, unified and closed systems, so it is important to approach specific instances of practice on their own terms so as to tease out diversity and difference.

My research on neo-shamanisms began in the mid-1990s when, as a scholar of the shamanistic approach to rock art (Wallis 1996; 2002), I turned for my PhD research (Wallis 1999) to how Westerners engage with shamanism as a source of re-enchantment and empowerment. I was upfront in my published work (e.g. Wallis 2000, 2001, 2003, 2004) that my interest was both academic and personal because I was, and am, a part of my research, as a practitioner. Rather than compromising the objectivity of my research, I argued, drawing on autoethnography and insider anthropology (Jackson 1987; Ellis & Bochner 2000; Reed-Danahay 1997; Blain *et al* 2004), that my location as both scholar and practitioner brings different insights to the material. My location is not an exclusive or privileged one, but alongside more orthodox enquiry, affords other insights. The previous literature on neo-shamanisms has tended to be celebratory and non-academic (e.g. Heinze 1991; Cruden 1995; Webb 2004) or critical and dismissive (e.g. Kehoe 2000), although there are more nuanced analyses (e.g. Townsend 1988, 1999; Lindquist 1997; Jakobsen 1999; Blain 2002). My extensive and ongoing work has identified areas of neo-shamanisms for criticism, particularly appropriations of indigenous religion, but also instances in which neo-shamans give something of substance back to shamanism, so despite an element of use or appropriation there is a form of contributing to the discourse on the subject. I have warned against attempts to pin down 'shamanism' or 'neo-shamanism' as discrete entities, or arrive at a check-list of defining features (such as, typically, healing, altered states, ecstasy, journeying, visions) (e.g. Lewis-Williams 1998), and emphasise instead the importance of analysing the discourse on what people *say* is 'shamanism' so as to unpack our enduring Euroamerican fascination with shamans. But my thinking on the subject has changed over the last fifteen years, and this chapter is guided by what I think now is crucial context for evaluating both shamanisms and neo-shamanisms.

Previously, scholarship has tended to discuss communities with shamans as having shamanistic worldviews, typically based on a tripartite cosmology of upper, middle and lower worlds (e.g. Lewis-Williams & Pearce 2005). I think this view is myopic, situating shamans as the arbiters of ontology and leading to a focus on the 'altered states of consciousness' and inner visions (read brain-derived 'hallucinations') that produce these 'worldviews'. Rather than their experiences *producing* the 'worldviews' of their communities, shamans, their experiences and their communities, human and non-human, are, I argue, *situated within wider animic ontologies*. By animism I do not mean the attribution of spirit to matter as supposed by Victorian anthropologists; rather, recent thinking on animism in anthropology and the study of religion suggests that for animists the world is filled with persons only some of whom are human (there are human-people and there are other-than-human-people), situating shamans and their human communities within a wider-than-human world (e.g. Harvey 2005). Shamans, who (seek to) 'see as others do' and so mediate between persons are crucial negotiators in facilitating harmony and healing (and in some instances, the opposite effect; 'magic' is a grey area). If shamans are usefully understood as animists and mediators, then it is more relevant to speak of animic ontologies than it is of shamanic worldviews or to focus on their 'altered states of consciousness' and inner visions, which tell us more about Western terminology and how we have tried to work out what shamans mean to us, than about shamans themselves whose practices and ontologies do not easily fit into our own conceptual frameworks.

What academics say about shamans has ultimately come to have a major impact on how neo-shamans talk about what is 'shamanism'. Many neo-shamans have understood and in the main still continue to understand 'shamanism' in the classical sense, as perpetuated by, for example, Eliade (1989[1964]) and Harner (1990[1980]), as an ecstatic religion in which practitioners undergo initiation and struggle with spirits in order to access a spirit world through ecstasies or altered consciousness, and so achieve various community-oriented tasks such as healing, harnessing game and changing the weather. Among neo-shamans, this has tended to result in a tendency to de-contextualise and universalise shamanism as a coherent, enduring religion (oft-cited as the 'origin' of religion), and a set of techniques (recalling Eliade's subtitle of *Shamanism*, 'archaic techniques of ecstasy') which can be used by anyone. But there are also, and increasingly, neo-shamans who are more sensitive and critical in their understanding and whose practices can be approached usefully in terms of the conceiving of animism[5] that I have outlined above. I next examine these shifting patterns of neo-shamanic practice, with a focus on Europe.

Everyone's a shaman:
Decontextualising and universalising shamans

What is 'shamanism' has always been filtered, interpreted and re-cast, principally through a Western lens, since its first reception. Key contributors to this representation in the twentieth century were Carl Jung (see Noel 1997), Mircea Eliade (1989[1964]), Carlos Castaneda (e.g. 1968, 1971, 1972, 1974), Joseph Campbell (1988) and Michael Harner ([1990]1980), and while there are differences between their respective shamanisms, they share an emphasis on ecstatic religion, journeying to the spirit world, healing with the assistance of animal helpers, and, particularly in the work of Castaneda, drugs and initiation. Most of these thinkers have written in English and operated out of the USA (even if their origins are not in North America), bringing a distinctly Anglo-American edge to how neo-shamans have approached 'shamanism', and where indigenous cultures are cited, these tend to be American Indians[6]. For some scholars including American Indian critics of neo-shamanism (e.g. Talamantez, cited in Hutton 2001: 158), the concept is inappropriate in a North American context, yet other scholars have found the term useful (e.g. Jilek 1982), and in any case 'shamanism' can be straightforwardly, if problematically, transposed to North America (and anywhere else) when conceived of in very general terms (e.g. a practitioner's initiatory engagement with the spirit world through trance).

There are, as a result, neo-shamans in Europe who draw upon American Indian traditions, holding drumming circles and pipe ceremonies, wearing 'native' costume and taking 'native' names (a tradition of appropriation hailing back to Grey Owl: Kehoe 1990; Root 1996; also Wallis 2003: 201-2). These neo-shamanisms engage with 'American Indian' and 'shamanism' in diluted and/or misrepresented form and they are problematic as such. I have encountered a number of 'shamans' during my research who claim to be 'American Indian' medicine men but are clearly European 'wannabes', 'fake Indians' or 'plastic shamans', as termed by various critics (e.g. Kehoe 1990), especially American Indians (e.g. Rose 1984, 1992; Green 1988; Smith 1994)[7]. While not claiming to be Indian, other workshop leaders, for example Bernie Prior's week-long retreat 'experiencing the romance of life in a tipi, the shamanic way' (see Wallis 2003: figure 2.1), takes the trappings of American Indian cultures. Others neo-shamans are more specific, less generic, in their interests, such as the 'shamanism' of the 'Yaqui' set out (and at least partially fabricated: e.g. De Mille 1976, 1980; Noel 1976; Beals 1978; Fikes 1993; Clifton 1994; Wallis 2003) by Carlos Castaneda: these neo-shamans may never have visited the Sonoran Desert or met a Yaqui Indian, but they aspire to be 'Toltec Warriors', practice 'new Toltequity' and name themselves 'double-beings', 'dreaming' men or women, or more recognisably anthropological classifications like 'nagual' (e.g. Saler 1967). Books and workshops on 'nagualism' are now common-place, for instance by Merilyn Tunneshende, a 'Toltec seeress' and 'nagual dreaming woman' who claims that she learnt directly from the shamanic teachers of Carlos Castaneda (e.g. Tunneshende 2002) and Victor Sanchez (e.g. 1995, 1996, 2001),

> *a Mexican researcher who has developed workshops for personal and spiritual growth, applicable to the creative improvement of the every day life. He has lived for fifteen years with indigenous peoples of Mexico who, hidden in the mountains, have kept alive the spiritual path of the ancient Toltecs.*[8]

Such neo-shamans draw on 'shamanism' as a lifestyle choice that has been 'preserved' in remote and therefore romanticised indigenous communities. It is not always clear how the indigenous communities themselves benefit from this relationship. Other neo-shamans, still, are not so much attempting to dress like or adopt the beliefs and practices of American Indians but are influenced nonetheless by the thinking that has come out of North America, for example *Eagle's Wing College of Shamanic Medicine* (formerly *Eagle's Wing for Contemporary Shamanism* co-organised by Leo Rutherford, Dawn Russell, Lorraine Grayston and Howard Charing) based in London. In his book *Thorsons Principles of Shamanism* (1996), ostensibly an introductory text to the topic of shamanism, Rutherford devotes an entire chapter to the American Indian-derived 'Medicine Wheel', discusses 'sweat lodges' (Rutherford 1996: 61-5) and 'vision quests' (Rutherford 1996: 75-7), and gives a personal statement on the influence of American Indian traditions on his approach to shamanism (Rutherford 1996: 146-7). *Eagle's Wing* offers:

> *Comprehensive trainings in Shamanic Practice, Shamanism Workshops and Courses, Teachings of the Medicine Wheel, Ritual and Ceremony, Shamanic Journeys, Soul Retrieval, Movement / Dance / Voicework, Trance Dance events, Vision Quests, Sweatlodges, Remote Viewing, Womens' Courses and many other workshops & ceremonies in the UK and abroad (http://www.shamanism.co.uk/).*

In addition to the significant influence of American Indian religions on *Eagle's Wing's* workshops, quite a variety of practices are deemed to be shamanic in this context, an eclectic approach summarised by Rutherford's description of himself as 'a citizen of Planet Earth! That is my culture' (Rutherford 1996: 146). There is a New Age edge to *Eagle's Wing* (indeed many neo-shamanisms are inseparable from the 'New Age' [see, for example, articles in the *Journal of Shamanic Practice*]), with an emphasis on personal growth and individual empowerment, and the 'shamanism' here is generalised to a greater degree. While practitioners no doubt find empowerment, it is perhaps too easy to be critical of an approach which appropriates indigenous cultures and generalises 'shamanism' through a Euro-American lens. Yet these neo-shamanisms have learned their 'shamanism' from previous scholars who themselves generalised—and popularised—'shamanism' (such as Eliade) and of course anthropology has had its own difficult colonial relationship with shamans (e.g. Taussig 1987; papers in Narby & Huxley). In consequence it is important for anthropologists and other scholars to engage with neo-shamans, so as to disseminate current thinking and transform negative stereotypes, and this is increasingly the case (e.g. Harvey 2003; Wallis 2003; Harvey & Wallis 2007).

Arguably the most significant influence on how neo-shamanisms have developed in Europe over the last thirty years has been former anthropologist (at, for example, Columbia and Yale universities) Michael Harner's 'core shamanism', disseminated through his book *The Way of the Shaman* (first published 1980) and various popular and successful training programs, from the 'Basic' workshop to more intensive 'Harner Shamanic Counseling Training' and 'Michael Harner's Three-Year Programs in Advanced Initiations in Shamanism and Shamanic Healing'[9]. Core shamanism attempts to strip away all cultural baggage from shamanism in indigenous contexts and get to its 'core' which Harner identifies as the 'journey' to non-ordinary reality. Practitioners usually facilitate this journey, both individually and in group settings, by laying down, covering one's eyes and listening to a monotonous rhythm, such as a repetitive drumbeat. Some core shamanists use a frame-drum which, it is assumed, is the shaman's instrument *par excellence*, or use a recording of drumming listened to through headphones. Riding the sound of the drum-beat in their journeying, practitioners visualise a landscape in which there is an entry point to the non-ordinary realm of spirits and there engage with their helpers in order to resolves problems (personal, for a patient, or a group) such as the healing of sickness. After a time, the drum signals the time to return and one's journey back is retraced, the experience related, retold or recorded, and practitioners often report a sense of initiation, personal healing or tranquillity as a result.

Core shamanism purports to be acultural and apolitical, simply the bare-bones of shamanism, but of course its cultural context is late twentieth-century Euro-America. This denotes a universalising of shamanism, de-contextualising it from indigenous contexts, with a focus on personal growth and healing, and overlooking the darker aspects of shamanism such as sorcery. Core shamanism is a simple and apparently effective technique, offered in training seminars across Europe so that now 'shamanism', or more accurately core shamanism as marketed by the Foundation for Shamanic Studies, is available to almost anyone; that is, in contrast to most indigenous shamanisms in which specific individuals are singled out for an arduous, painful initiation and training.

One interesting aspect of core shamanism in a European context is how some neo-shamans and indeed indigenous shamans have taken on the techniques of core shamanism and then fleshed-out other cultural trappings based on indigenous, historic and prehistoric shamanistic practices. Perhaps most startling is the request from some Saami, the indigenous reindeer herders of North Scandinavia, that Harner teach them core shamanism so that they may reconnect with their shamanic heritage, largely eradicated due to colonialism, Christian missionary activity and Communism (Hoppál 1992; Harner pers.com. 1998, cited in Wallis 2003: 221-2; Townsend 1999; Wallis 2003: 221-2). That Westerners are taking an interest in their shamanic traditions as valid, can be very positive for some indigenous communities, a vindication of the relevance of their traditions after centuries of persecution. On the other hand, the dynamic is disconcerting, with Euro-Americans standing as the ultimate arbiters of what shamanism is and presenting this shamanism—in this instance, the construct of core shamanism—to indigenous people as *the* definitive shamanism.

The anthropologist Alice Kehoe is dismissive of Harner's core shamanism, and neo-shamanism more generally, and understandably she and others are concerned over the neo-colonial appropriation of indigenous shamanisms by Euro-Americans. I think this standpoint is all the more understandable given Kehoe's location in the US and the problem there (and by extension other Western countries where neo-shamans exoticise American Indians) of the specific appropriation of American Indian religion. But the dynamics are complicated: Jakobsen alerts us to the fact that a Greenlandic woman based her journeying on American Indian teachings—'is she committing cultural imperialism?' (Jakobsen pers.com. cited in Wallis 2003: 221). There are, then, neo-shamans in Europe who draw upon American Indian traditions, but many others are interested in the ancient pagan past, and their approach intersects with the resurgence of contemporary paganism in the region, as I next discuss.

The Earliest European neo/shamans

Shaman*isms* are diverse and historically situated, but shaman*ism* is often misconceived as a unified and pervasive system, a notion with wide currency and a benchmark for neo-shamanic practice. Shamanism is often held to represent the origin of religion and European shamans are frequently characterized as the first artists, leaving their infamous mark in the Cave Art of Lascaux—widely believed to represent the 'origins' of art. Among other human-animal therianthropic figures in cave art, the so-called 'sorcerer' in the cave of Les Trois Freres in France's Dordogne, is often held to represent the earliest European shaman and therefore ancient precedent for contemporary practices. Most notably, the 'sorcerer' was cited by Murray (1931: 23-4) as the 'horned god of the witches', and evidence for her thesis of a surviving pagan religion among Medieval European people tried as witches (Hutton 2003: 33). Murray argued that 'the horned god of the greenwood had been the oldest deity known to humans, and traced his worship across Europe and the Near East, from the Old Stone Age to the seventeenth century' (Hutton 1999:196). This notion has been prevalent in pagan/neo-shaman discourse: in *Magic and Witchcraft: from Shamanism to the Technopagans*, for instance, Drury (2003:12) states that the 'Upper Palaeolithic hunter-sorcerer can be seen as a precursor of the archetypal shaman with his animal familiars and clan totems'. Shamanism is cited as both a practice and a precedent in many core texts of Modern pagan witchcraft or Wicca (e.g. Farrar and Farrar 1984; Starhawk 1989) and some Wiccans term their religion 'Shamanic Wicca', 'Shamanic Craft' and 'Wiccan-shamanism' (e.g. Adler 1986:430-434; Luhrmann 1989:134, 329)—to emphasise the point, Cunningham's best-seller (sold 400,000 copies by the 2001 29th edition) claims Wicca 'is a shamanic religion' (p. 4) and 'we are the shamans' (p. 13). Practices such as inducing trance, working magic, divination, interacting with spirits and animal familiars, and healing via supernatural means, are certainly reminiscent of many shamanistic practices. Taken together, the cave artists of prehistory and medieval witches make a potent shamanistic equation which invigorates Modern witchcraft, but Hutton (e.g. 1999, 2003, 2009) has demonstrated, very robustly, that any sense of continuity of tradition is mistaken. In many instances, pagans today are recognising this as well as the historical specificity of shamanisms in ancient Europe.

Neo/shamans in Northern Europe

Rather than using a generalised concept of European prehistory and insisting on a continuity of shamanistic practice from prehistory to the present, many pagans look to specific examples of ancient pagan religions as sources on shamanism, for example among the Norse, Saxons and other Northern communities of the migration age in the first millennium. Recent work (e.g. Price 2000; 2002) demonstrating strong links between the indigenous Sami and Norse settlers in Scandinavia, and an influence of Sami shamanic practices on the Norse (and likely vice versa), has lent particular weight to contemporary re-imaginings of Northern shamanisms. The *Scandinavian Center for Shamanic Studies*, for instance, is influenced by Harner's core shamanism, offering similar basic workshops on journeying,[10] but accents this with a Northern European slant. The course, 'Seidr Craft', for instance, is based on historical accounts of 'magic' or 'sorcery' amongst the communities of the migration age in Northern Europe that many scholars and practitioners have termed 'shamanic':

> *Seiðr is the old Nordic form of shamanic magic, described in bits and pieces in Norse myths and sagas. Traditionally, the practitioners of seiðr used a unique combination of staff, ecstatic song and a magic seat as means to open the door to the other worlds and let the soul journey. In this weekend we will explore the power of the main tools of the seidr craft— spirit song and magic staff. And we will do seiðr together as*

a community ritual as well as learning to practise seiðr alone. We will also be doing seiðr in nature.[11]

The trappings of seidr cited in this extract, such as the use of song, staff and 'magic seat' derive from the most detailed account of seidr, found in the saga of Erik the Red (for more detail and critical comment, see Wallis 2003). This saga describes in rich detail the circumstances of a seidr-séance in Greenland in the thirteenth century: a community suffering a famine is visited by a seeress who prepares for the ritual by eating a porridge containing the hearts of a number of farm animals. Her clothing is unusual, consisting of a black lambskin hood lined with cat's fur and cat skin gloves. A pouch at her waist contains various (unstated) 'charms', she holds a long staff topped with a brass knob which is studded with stones, and she sits on a ritual platform or 'high seat', a special seat reserved for the leaders of the household and special guests. A young woman sings the songs that will invoke what seem to be spirits and in communication with them the seeress answers questions posed by community members gathered at the séance, and prophesies a better future.[12] Inspired by this and other evidence, both literary and archaeological, seidr neo-shamans reconstruct and re-imagine the seidr séance for today. Contemporary seidr is particularly notable in the context of this paper because it draws on evidence from Northern Europe to inspire a regionally and culturally contextualised neo-shamanism, as distinct from the core shamanism of Harner which aims to strip away cultural baggage, and other neo-shamanisms which are more culturally eclectic. While the appropriation of the past is problematic—we can never know what ancient seidr was actually like; we can never know the past fully, and these neo-shamans can be accused of appropriating the past—seidr-practitioners' attention to the past does avoid the more dangerous criticism of appropriating contemporary indigenous traditions (such as Native American 'shamanism'). What is more, seidr has offered its own critique of Western thought, particularly in relation to gender. In our articles (Blain & Wallis 1999, 2000), Blain and I point to instances of seidr-practice which contest binary gender divisions and heterosexist stereotypes, and how in so doing the ontologies and practices of these seidr-workers are comparable with the 'third gender' or 'changing ones' of many indigenous shamans.

The seidr practices I've discussed thus far are termed 'high-seat seidr' by some neo-shamans, meaning that they rely principally on the scene set by the saga of Erik the Red and reconstruction of this ritual in detail. Other practitioners and writers on the topic take a broader view of northern shamanism and seidr. The German pagan, neo-shaman, mage and writer—though he does not fit easily into any category—Jan Fries, draws on the translation of seidr as 'seething' in his book *Helrunar: A Manual of Rune Magick* (2002[1993]) and develops this argument in *Seidrways: Shaking, Swaying and Serpent Mysteries* (1996). While the etymology may be problematic (e.g. Thorsson 1999), 'seething' has become important on the neo-shamanic scene. The practice involves using shaking, swaying, dance and related 'shamanic trembling' techniques to induce trances of various levels of intensity. Much of its currency lies in its simplicity and emphasis on personal transformation, with a thin veneer of Northern trappings. Fries' earlier work on the runes and divination, *Helrunar: A Manual of Rune Magick* (1993) also discusses trance-inducing techniques and offers more detailed European cultural background. Also in Germany, Hans Stucken, has co-founded the 'Seidhfeuer' network and authored *Das Seidhr Handbuch* ('The Seidhr Handbook', 2006). Further North, in Scandinavia, the group 'Dragon Rouge', a magical order founded in Sweden in 1989 by Thomas Karlsson, 'as an unprejudiced search for a darker spiritual ideology or path' (Granholm 2005: 164), draws on a range of practices incorporating ritual magic and shamanistic techniques (see Karlsson 93-5; Granholm 2005).

Among this literature, there has been a focus on England; indeed the earliest work presenting Northern shamanism to neo-shamans is Brian Bates' novel *The Way of Wyrd* (1981), set in Anglo-Saxon England at the time of conversion, in which a Christian monk is posted to seek intelligence on pagan religion and becomes embroiled in a variety of spiritual encounters while guided by a shaman. Combining the engaging, creative power of a novel with a compelling Castanedaesque narrative, Bates presents a shamanism native to England. The scholarly background to *The Way of Wyrd* is set out in *Wisdom of the Wyrd* (1996; see also 1996/7), offering a largely psychological reading of ancient heathen mythology and other literature. More recently, Runic John's *The Book of Seidr: The Native English and Northern European Shamanic Tradition* (2004), links herb lore, ritual magic, healing and the runes to Heathen shamanistic practice. A further instance is that practiced by the Ulfhednr group in the south of England, as set out in *Galdrbok: Practical Heathen Runecraft, Shamanism and Magic* (Johnson & Wallis 2005), which includes the induction of trances using *galdr* (sung spells or spoken chants), scrying (prolonged visionary engagement with a crystal ball or 'magic mirror') and divination through the use of runes. These examples (among others I have not had space to discuss here), evidence a thriving heathen neo-shamanistic scene in Northern Europe, but it is impossible to avoid the issue of nationalism when dealing with this area because while most heathens and especially those involved in seidr tend to be liberal in their outlook, there are those whose interests concern 'blood and soil' issues surrounding the constructs of race and nationhood (e.g. Gallagher 1999; Mardell 2003; Goodrick-Clarke 2003, 2004, Asprem 2008). Indeed often, because those who 'shout loudest' are those that are heard, it is easy to overlook those practitioners who challenge right-wing politics (see also Blain & Wallis 2000).

'Celtic' neo/shamans

Elsewhere in Northern and Western Europe, neo-shamans have engaged with other ancient pagan traditions, particularly those of the 'Celts' (e.g. Matthews 1991a; Cowan 1993; Conway 1995; Fries 2003; MacEowan 2004, Laurie & White 2007). While the term Celt is primarily a linguistic construct (see Wallis 2003: 108), its ascription as a distinct 'culture' by culture-historians (in the first half of the twentieth century [examined by, for example, Chapman 1992; Dietler 1994; James 1999]), primarily based on archaeological finds from across the region, has meant that many neo-shamans now speak of a 'Celtic shamanism'. For these practitioners, sources on the Celts, such as Iron Age archaeology and medieval manuscripts, offer a rich resource for developing contemporary practice. While the evidence is fragmentary and its translation has routinely challenged scholars (see Hutton 1991), the tales on the Welsh figure of Taliesin, for example, are rich in shamanistic themes if read through a universal and generalising lens of 'shamanism' informed by such thinkers as Eliade, Campbell and Harner. Taliesin's claim to be a master of poetry, to have obtained wisdom by ingesting a magic brew and to have transformed into a variety of different animals, certainly resonate with shamanistic themes in literature elsewhere. The Irish mythological hero Fionn MacCumhail (Finn Macool) similarly attains esoteric wisdom by ingesting a magical substance, and in the *Táin Bó Cúailnge* (Kinsella 2002), the hero Cú Chulainn encounters various supernatural beings and journeys to an otherworld (see Wallis 2003; Adhouse-Green & Aldhouse-Green 2005). In addition to these mythological sources, records on the Druids, particularly by Roman ethnographers, are often drawn upon as evidence for Celtic shamanism. *Mog Ruith*, the chief Druid of the King of Ireland is described as wearing a bull's hide and a white speckled bird's head-dress, and performing magical feats involving fire (Ross 1967:333). Celtic neo-shamans take up these and many other enigmatic sources as firm evidence, or at least a wonderful resource for imagining, a Celtic shamanism. The contemporary Druid Philip 'Greywolf' Shallcrass, Chief of the British Druid Order, told me how his practices might be regarded as Celtic shamanism:

> *I sometimes use a drum as an adjunct to moving myself and/or others into altered states of awareness. I use a rattle for calling spirits, for cleansing ritual space or individual's psychic space or for tracking spirit paths. I use incense for cleansing and purification, referred to by the old British term saining, a practice similar to the Native American concept of smudging. I journey into the spirit world to find healing for people. I look to the spirit world for guidance and information (pers.com, cited in Wallis 2003).*

While the term Celtic shamanism is often used uncritically by neo-shamans (e.g. Cowan 1993; Conway 1995), Shallcrass is more cautious:

> *I avoid using the term shamanism wherever possible since it is, or at least should be, a culturally specific term for spirit workers in Siberia who have particular understandings of the universe and particular ways of working within that understanding. The kind of Druidry I practice works with the spirits of the land, is of the creatures who inhabit the land, of the gods and of our ancestors. The work we do is about communication, seership, healing, rites of celebration, rites of passage and teaching. Some of this could come under the far too broad definition of 'shamanism' now being bandied about as a catch-all term for working with spirits.*

Over time, as dialogue has ensued and scholarly thinking disseminated, other neo-shamans have become critically engaged; in *Cauldron of the Gods: A Manual of Celtic Magick* (2003), Fries states, with typical pragmatic aplomb:

> *[A] growing fashion to label any bit of Island Celtic trance practice as 'shamanic' has collided with an opposing dogma that will only accept serene priests of the no-funny-business school as genuine. People argue passionately about the existence or non-existence of Celtic shamanism, but what they are really getting excited about is the question, whether their own tradition (real or imaginary) ought to include wild and shamanic elements or whether it should all be done in a dull, dignified and churchy fashion...More important, as far as the actual practice is concerned, is what you need to get going (2003: 198-9).*

There is an emphasis on technique or practice here, over such issues as ontology, epistemology or belief. Fries' thoughts on 'wild' shamanic work can be distinguished clearly from the 'quiet' settings of core shamanism basic workshops which suggest a sanitising and 'making safe' of 'shamanism' for Euro-Americans. Yet presenting 'shamanism' as wild and as a technique retains its own stereotype of an extreme practice set apart from daily life, and which is purely functional in getting results.

The most significant body of literature on Celtic Shamanism is by the British authors and practitioners John and Caitlin Matthews (e.g. C. Matthews 1996; J. Matthews 1991a, 1991b, 1991c) which draws primarily on the Welsh mythological sources on the figure of Taliesin. Jones' (1994, 1998) assessment of J. Matthews' work is critical, indeed dismissive, because '[t]he Celtic shaman turns out to be an eco-nanny' (201):

> *These inner quests of the Celtic shaman are fizzy and warm, exciting but not particularly dangerous, like the pony ride at the amusement park...The encounter with the Otherworld basically comes down to sightseeing and acquiring souvenirs...Harner's Jívaro shamanism is more than a little scary—if you screw up you could lose your soul. In Matthews' Celtic shamanism, you have little to do besides lose your dignity...no doubt he would advise including a hanky in your crane bag (200-201).*

Amusing though this is, and given that Jones does point to instances where she thinks ancient Celtic shamanism may have existed (favouring the warrior-poet-hero as a more likely candidate than the druid-as-shaman), it is important not to write-off these contemporary readings outright. It is problematic that authors such as J. Matthews purport to offer empirical readings of the ancient past, but I do think that they have facilitated useful insights nonetheless; Jones' book and indeed my own would not have been possible without these neo-shamanisms—moreover they are situated in and therefore comment in interesting ways on the present. As Hutton observes:

> *Caitlín Matthews and her colleagues are not really concerned with the past, so much as with the present and the future...One aspect of this is her imposition upon Celtic lore of a lot of Native American religion, such as the totem, the spirit-quest and the shamanic vision. There are actually no precise parallels for any of these in ancient Celtic culture (Hutton 1991:144).*

Having raised the issue of right-wing politics in certain instances of

Heathenry, I should point out that certain Celtic Pagans in Europe are also embroiled in nationalism and right-wing culturist agendas (e.g. the nationalist Celtic *Touta Dumnonioi* at www.homestead.com/dafydd/ declaration2.html); but I reiterate that most pagans and neo-shamans find nationalism tainted with right-wing politics and racism and, in their cosmopolitan ideology, resist cultural boundaries. Accounting for the problems inherent in looking to the ancient past for inspiration, such as the inevitability of imposing contemporary prejudices onto the past and dealing with fragmentary, enigmatic sources, other neo-shamans in Europe take a more eclectic, cosmopolitan approach, sometimes generalised as 'techno-shamanism'.

Techno-shamans and the (more than) Global Stage

The term 'techno-shamanism', coined by among others Clark (1993), was first used to refer to shamanistic elements in the dance (or 'rave') culture of the late 1980s and early 1990s which emerged in the UK and spread rapidly across Europe and the USA. For Clark (Ibid), the techno-shaman:

> [S]erves the community by accessing the technological infrastructure, not as a tool-user ordering their machine to do something, but as one sentient being negotiating with another for the performance of a service...Drug use, ecstatic dancing, and trance music are well-established in today's techno-shamanic subculture, as is their use in ritualistic events to bind communities together. One can easily see a mapping between computer networks and the spirit world, and between computers and the powerful entities the traditional shaman interacts with.

Using the auditory driving monotonous rhythms in 'trance', 'psytrance' (i.e. psychedelic trance), 'Acid House' and other genres of computer-generated music, as well as so-called party-drugs such as Ecstasy (MDMA), 'ravers' found that electronic dance events afforded healing experiences which seemed to make sense to them as communal shamanic experiences (e.g. Vitebsky 1995: 153; Harvey 1997: 122-4; Hutson 2000). Loosely-knit counter-cultural groups such as the 'Spiral Tribe' coordinated illegal outdoor all-night raves in rural locations in the UK, in the early 1990s, at which an alternative, heterotopic space was created: a heady mix of dance music, various drugs, the presence of 'new age' travellers and warmth provided by many bonfires produced a 'new-primitive' 'tribal' community atmosphere. Certain DJ's and musicians reiterated the connection between dance culture and shamanism, most obviously the group *The Shamen* who in addition to their name-tag included interview recordings with Terence McKenna on the 1992 track *Re:Evolution*; McKenna being a counter-cultural icon who hypothesised that human evolution was advanced by the ingestion of psilocybin 'magic' mushrooms. Straightforwardly, dancing and taking drugs in ways which superficially resemble shamanisms does not make one a shaman, but it is interesting that ideas on 'shamanism', broadly conceived and de-contextualised from original sources of production and consumption, permeated the discourse of the dance culture.

In a globalised, technologically-oriented Europe, a variety of media such as wireless Internet connectivity and increasingly sophisticated mobile phone technology enable instant communication across vast distances—as a result, techno-shamans of a different sort are using cyberspace, also known as Cyberia (Rushkoff 1994), as a powerful resource. In many instances, as with the Internet more generally, much of the information disseminated is uncritical and uses 'shamanism' as a convenient catch-all. But the Internet does facilitate independent research, online community networking and interaction. Webpages, email lists, blogspots, forums, Twitter, FaceBook and so on, enable individual practitioners to connect, research topics on shamanism and debate. What is more, the Web is being approached as a technological otherworld in itself: some techno-shamans compare the surfing of web pages with shamanic journeying in the spirit world, use shaman-avatars as a spiritual resource in Second Life[13], and employ the internet as an electronic oracular device or Ouija board, with 'the Web' conceptualised as connecting all things and so able to prophecy advice (see also Brown 1997: 125). Indeed, for the vast majority of neo-shamans, as for most affluent Euro-Americans, the Internet has become a crucial space for individual and community formation, performance and empowerment. The Internet has enabled neo-shamans to access a great deal of information on the pharmacology, cultivation and effects of various drugs which were only available in dense medical volumes until fairly recently, the web-vaults of Erowid being a notable example (http://www.erowid.org/). Arguably the Internet has thus contributed to the spread of neo-shamanic interest in such syncretic religions as The Peyote Church and Santo Daime, and interest in such drugs as Peyote, San Pedro and Ayahuasca which are freely available for 'cultivation' purposes.[14] If they are unable to take trips with indigenous Ayahuasceros in Amazonia, these techno-shamans can access information on where to acquire these drugs or join groups organising sessions in London and other European cities.

Aspects of 'Chaos Magic' (with Kaos and Magick/Magik sometimes spelled with a 'k'), originally formulated in Britain by Carroll (e.g. 1987), Hine (e.g. 2004) and others,[15] can be approached as techno-shamanistic because Chaos Magicians approach magic by drawing on pragmatic techniques, popular science and especially the Chaos Theory of quantum physics, read through the lens of ceremonial magic, altered consciousness, Hindu philosophy and other world religions—indeed any belief system is used if it helps achieve the desired outcome, according to 'free belief' or the maxim 'Nothing is True, Everything is Permitted' (Harvey 1997: 100). 'Shamanism' from this viewpoint is a set of techniques (recalling Eliade's subtitle once again) which is cross-cultural, timeless and generic, and can be deployed to alter consciousness towards a willed result. For many Chaos Magicians, a key figure is the early twentieth century artist Austin Osman Spare (1886-1956) who produced his own religion involving, *inter alia*, the use of altered consciousness and magically charged sigils (Semple 1995). Few contemporary mages engage with the complexity of Spare's philosophy, but many do find practical value in his use of sigil magic. Spare has been read as a shaman by some Chaos Magicians and other neo-shamans and pagans, because of certain similarities between his approach and shamanistic practices: using the 'death posture', Spare induced altered consciousness and he claimed to be assisted by certain 'spirits', reminiscent of shamans' 'spirit-helpers', including the American Indian 'Black Eagle'. But while there are superficial resemblances to what shamans do, Spare was not mediating between humans and non-humans in order to bring healing to his community (in modern London in the first half of the twentieth century) (Miles 2006). In common with other neo-shamans, then, Chaos Magicians tend to de-contextualise, universalise and individualise shamanism away from diversely occurring, locally-situated, community-oriented contexts, and emphasise 'shamanism' as a set of archaic techniques relevant to contemporary practitioners.

The discussion of techno-shamans and other neo-shamans I've presented, draws attention to the way in which indigenous shamanisms are transforming in an increasingly globalised and technologically sophisticated world. Of course, shamanisms have always changed, to a lesser or greater extent, over time (see, e.g., Thomas & Humphrey 1994); indigenous communities of the present are not frozen in time or the key to understanding the past. But certainly instant communication, across national boundaries, immediate access to information online, and increased air-travel, is having a rather different transformative effect as indigenous shamanisms, real and imagined, are now more accessible to Westerners. Michael Harner has taught core shamanism to the indigenous Sami of Northern Scandinavia, as I have noted, and elsewhere, in Eastern

Europe, particularly parts of the former Soviet Union, Harner's core shamanism has given people the 'core' elements around which they can build localised shamanisms. Here, too, folk traditions including elements of 'shamanism' have been important resources for the performance of post-Soviet national and ethnic identities (e.g. Hoppál 1992a, 1992b), but again, the role of 'shamanism' in the construction of ethnic nationalism is a matter for concern (e.g. Shnirelman 2007).

While this changing global stage has enabled European neo-shamans to engage with a wide variety of indigenous shamanisms, including 'entheogen tourism' to remote and exotic locations, other neo-shamans frame their practices with a more generic understanding of 'shamanism', most notably core shamanism. Harner's framework has also enabled indigenous people in Europe, such as the Sami, to reconstitute their traditions, and the same is true of parts of Eastern Europe such as Hungary (e.g. Hoppál 1992c). Other neo-shamans still, are re-embedding their neo-shamanisms in the ancestral past. Having outlined this variety of neo-shamanistic practices in Europe (with implications elsewhere), I close my discussion by thinking about these neo-shamanisms in terms of the value of their discourse, particularly in light of the anthropological rethinking of animism: since theorising shamanism in this way has led to important insights (e.g. Harvey 2005; Wallis 2009), I consider its value for approaching neo-shamanisms.

Conclusion: Reanimating neo/shamans

In earlier work (e.g. Wallis 2001, 2003), I have argued that neo-shamans should not be dismissed out of hand by scholars as fringe, eccentric, 'culture-vultures', but taken seriously as contributors to the discourse on shamanism; they are therefore worthy of study and, just as importantly, should be engaged with in dialogue in order to enable reciprocal exchange (as I hope my own publications and presentations in academic and popular forums evidence). It is important to consider ways in which neo-shamanisms are problematic, for example the cultural appropriation of American Indian religion,[16] but also ways in which they give something back, or give positive 'extra pay' (Harvey 1997: 111-4) to shamanisms. Practitioners who do not self-ascribe as 'shamans' and so avoid packaging themselves with 'authentic', 'primitive' and 'noble savage' credentials, for instance, but are nonetheless called 'shaman' by their clients, do I think give something back to shamanisms in terms of a sense of humility, and their sensitivity to indigenous/prehistoric shamanisms. Those practitioners who are critically engaged with the problematics of what shamanisms are, and in turn how neo-shamanisms are constituted (such as Shallcrass and Fries, cited above), and in so doing encourage critical thinking on the part of individuals in their community or those who read their work, are, like scholars of shamanism, contributing to the subject of study and the negotiation of what shamanisms are in the twenty-first century. Furthermore, neo-shamans engaging with shamanisms past, and using this to challenge heterosexist normativity and right-wing appropriation of the past, such as the seidr-workers discussed earlier, are also offering something of value to the negotiation of the subject under scrutiny. Across these instances, academia often has a role to play in transforming neo-shamanist discourse, and potentially vice versa. I have no doubt that my own informants (better termed collaborators) were influenced in various ways during my engagements with them, but of course I was also changed by this encounter, by those whom I studied—a well-known result of ethnographic work (see papers in Blain *et al* 2004).

In this sense, and at the time of writing, it is interesting to consider how the anthropological re-examination of animism over the last decade has reached neo-shamanist discourse and transformed neo-shamanic practice, in Europe (with implications elsewhere). Repositioning shamans within animist ontologies moves away from the traditional focus on shamans as the arbiters of cosmological thinking and cosmology-making in their (human) communities by virtue of their engagements with 'spirits' in 'altered states of consciousness'. Some of the traditional thinking on 'shamanism' is problematic because it has been formulated by Western observers of shamans who have struggled, understandably, to fathom the meanings of what shamans do.[17] Rather than taking shaman's experiences seriously, for instance, it has generally been assumed that shamans' fantastic ecstasies are simply neurologically derived and while this may have a social function, the experiences are hallucinations none the less. By association, the animism conceived of in the late nineteenth century assumed that 'primitive' people were mistaken for attributing 'spirit' to 'matter'.

Re-examining animist communities and their shamans without assuming the axiomatic status of Cartesian and positivist thinking, the situation is far more complex: as I have highlighted, animist ontologies approach a world filled with persons, only some of whom are human, and often shamans are crucial in maintaining relations between human-persons and other-than-humans. Animisms are, then, concerned with relating—with persons, human and non-human, and 'animism makes shamans both possible and necessary because their roles are about dealing with the problems of living in a relational world' (Harvey & Wallis 2007: 25).[18] Shamans are important because they are skilled in meeting the communicative level of other-than-humans, or being able to relate by 'seeing as others do'. Rather than reducing this negotiative practice to 'altered states of consciousness', 'trance' or 'ecstasy', it is more sensitive to speak of 'adjusted styles of communication'; shamans are skilled in mediating between humans and non-humans because they are understood to adjust themselves to the communicative level of other-than-human-persons. This rethinking of animic ontologies and the roles of shamans has, in turn, I argue, been negotiated in various ways by neo-shamans, whether conscious of the academic literature or influenced by the dissemination of ideas into the public domain.

Based on research dealing with the experiences produced when ingesting 'magic mushrooms' (psilocybin), British scholar Letcher (2007) finds that he has 'mad thoughts'. Conventional, 'scientific', observations of these experiences offer pathological, psychological and prohibitive answers, but Letcher presents various 'resistive discourses', defined as 'recreational, entheogenic and animistic' which challenge orthodox approaches. Of these, he argues that only the animist discourse 'transgresses a fundamental societal boundary': 'the belief that mushrooms occasion encounters with discarnate spirit entities, or animaphany' (all citations Letcher 2007: 74). The animist approach is radical because it takes 'hallucinations' seriously, which DSM-IV[19] guidance would ascribe as psychosis. Of course, taking the same drugs does not a shaman make, but Letcher's 'mycospirituality' does challenge the Cartesian dualism and truth-value of science in orthodox Western thought, and this contributes to a rethinking of shamans' ontologies. An ontological repositioning away from the preeminence of human consciousness and recognition of other conscious beings results, with 'shrooms' potentially occasioning negotiation with others in the non-human world. Rather than theorise 'beshroomed' experiences as brain-derived aberrations, Letcher considers what Turner (1992) calls (in old animism terminology) 'the reality of spirits', or, thought through animically, the ontological position of a world filled with a variety of people, some of whom are mushroom-persons.

From this standpoint, Letcher also questions the value of the term 'entheogen': meaning literally 'to inspire god within', entheogen has become popular in the literature on shamans who use botanical 'allies' because the term is seen as more sensitive and accurate than 'drug', 'hallucinogen' or 'psychedelic'. Letcher proposes that entheogen is problematic nonetheless for assuming that, *inter alia*, the experience generated is an interior one, derived from the drug's chemical impact on neurological hard-wiring. In challenging this materialist discourse and other underpinnings of Western thought, Letcher's argument contributes usefully to discussion on shamanisms, particularly issues of nomenclature, ontology and epistemology.

In other work (Letcher 2001), examining and participating in eco-protesting in the UK, Letcher makes a further animic contribution, as recognised by Harvey who proposes that eco-activists such as those campaigning against road-building projects, are neo-animists. In recognising a wider-than-human world and the responsibilities of human-people to engage respectfully with non-humans rather than treat 'the natural world' as 'resources' to be exploited, eco-activists make an active and very visible contribution which requires a deep sense of responsibility to the wider-than-human world. Based on their transformative experiences, other pagan campaigners cite animism, more directly, in ways which resonate with the recent anthropological thinking on animisms and shamanisms: Emma Restall Orr, a well-known Druid priestess and author, established (in 2004) the organisation 'Honouring the Ancient Dead' (HAD) in order to promote respect towards the human remains of prehistoric 'ancestors' excavated by archaeologists and stored or displayed in museums in Britain (and elsewhere). Restall Orr's approach (e.g. 2006, 2009) recognises that at the time of internment a connection was made (or indeed reiterated) between 'the land' and 'the dead' (or in more nuanced terminology, the deceased human-person and their human- and non-human community), a connection which is broken by archaeological excavation. Many difficult questions are raised by this project, such as how archaeology can be respectful and who are ancestors, which I have begun to address elsewhere (see especially Blain & Wallis 2007)— but for the purposes of this chapter, it is interesting that as a self-defined pagan animist Restall Orr argues that humans are connected to a wider-than-human world which is deserving of respect, an ontological position which leads her to campaign actively for ancestor welfare.

As a final example of neo-animist thinking among neo-shamans, I cite Gordon 'the Toad' MacLellan.[20] Working with groups of British children in such activities as pond-dipping, mask-making and dancing as animals, MacLellan encourages young human-people to think beyond the presumed ascendancy of humanity that they have been taught, to relate with a world which is diversely populated by communities of non-humans deserving of our (human) respect. Termed a 'shaman' by the human communities he works with, though avoiding this term for himself, MacLellan's approach to 'shamanism' is animist. These examples, among others I might cite, suggest that new animist thinking is starting to influence neo-shamanisms. If many neo-shamans seek, as Harner suggests, to find 'a deeper sense of community' (Harner 1988: 182), then as Harvey argues, these animist-shamans in particular explicitly 'seek a deeper involvement and participation' (Harvey 2009: 409) in the world. In consequence of these considerations, I reiterate my proposal that we move away from thinking about 'shamanism' as a technique for inducing altered consciousness to engaging animism as an ontology within which shamans are situated. And this idea has implications for how we consider shamanisms and neo-shamanisms, and how they are constituted, one decade into the twenty-first century—as well as, I argue, how 'magic' is considered, elsewhere in this volume.

References

Adlam, R. and L. Holyoak. 2005. 'Shamanism in the Postmodern World: A Review Essay.' *Studies in Religion / Sciences Religieuses* 34: 517-568.

Adler, M. 1986. *Drawing Down the Moon: Witches, Druids, Goddess-Worshippers and Other Pagans in America Today*. Boston: Beacon Press.

Aldhouse-Green, M. and S. Aldhouse-Green. 2005. *The Quest for the Shaman: Shape-Shifters, Sorcerers and Spirit-Healers of Ancient Europe*. London: Thames & Hudson.

Asprem, E. 2008. 'Heathens Up North: Politics, Polemics and Contemporary Norse Paganism in Norway.' *The Pomegranate: The International Journal of Pagan Studies* 10(1): 42-69.

Balzer, M. M. n.d. *Sustainable Faith: Reconfiguring Shamanic Healing in Siberia*. Available online: http://www.sakhaopenworld.org/alekseyev/festschrift4.html (accessed 30 June 2010).

Barrett, M. 1997. 'Tangible Visions: Northwest Coast Indian Shamanism and its Arts.' *Parabola* 22: 84-9.

Bates, B. 1983. *The Way of Wyrd*. London: Arrow.

———1996. *The Wisdom of the Wyrd: Teachings for Today from Our Ancient Past*. London: Rider.

———1996/7. 'Wyrd: Life Force of the Cosmos.' *Sacred Hoop* 15 (Winter): 8-13.

Beals, R. L. 1978. 'Sonoran Fantasy or Coming of Age?' *American Anthropologist* 80: 355-362.

Blain, J. 2002. *Nine Worlds of Seidr-Magic: Ecstasy and Neo-shamanism in North European Paganism*. London: Routledge.

———2006. ' Constructing Identity and Divinity: Creating Community in an Elder Religion within a Postmodern World.' In: S. Reid (ed.) *Between the Worlds*: 241-265. Toronto: Canadian Scholars' Press.

Blain, J.; D. Ezzy and G. Harvey (eds) 2004. *Researching Paganisms: Religious Experiences and Academic Methodologies*. Walnut Creek, California: AltaMira.

Blain, J. and R. J. Wallis. 1999. 'Men and "Women's Magic": Gender, Seidr, and "Ergi".' *The Pomegranate: A New Journal of Neopagan Thought* 9: 4-16.

———2000. 'The "Ergi" Seidman: Contestations of Gender, Shamanism and Sexuality in Northern Religion, Past and Present.' *Journal of Contemporary Religion* 15(3): 395-411.

_____ 2007. *Sacred Sites, Contested Rites/Rights: Pagan Engagements with Archaeological Monuments*. Brighton: Sussex Academic Press.

_____ 2009. Heathenry and its Development. In: J. Lewis & M. Pizza (eds) *Handbook of Contemporary Paganism*: 413-31. Handbook of Contemporary Religion. Leiden and Boston: Brill Academic Publishers.

Brown, M. F. 1997. *The Channeling Zone: American Spirituality in an Anxious Age*. Cambridge, Massachusetts: Harvard University Press.

Campbell, J. with B. Moyers. 1988. *The Power of Myth*. New York: Doubleday.

Carroll, P. 1987. *Liber Null and Psychonaut: An Introduction to Chaos Magic (Two Complete Volumes)*. York Beach, Maine: Samuel Weiser Inc.

Castaneda, C. 1968. *The Teachings of Don Juan: A Yaqui Way of Knowledge*. California: University of California Press.

_____ 1971. *A Separate Reality*. London: The Bodley Head.

_____ *Journey to Ixtlan: The Lessons of Don Juan*. New York: Simon & Schuster.

_____ 1974. *Tales of Power*. New York: Penguin Books.

Chapman, M. 1992. *The Celts: The Construction of a Myth*. New York: St. Martins Press.

Churchill, W. 2003. 'Spiritual Hucksterism: The Rise of the Plastic Medicine Men.' In: G. Harvey (ed.) *Shamanism: A Reader*: 324-33. London: Routledge.

Clark, F. 1993. *Technoshamanism*. Available online: http://hyperreal.org/raves/spirit/technoshamanism/Technoshaman-Definitions.html (accessed 30 June 2010).

Clifton, C. S. 1994. 'Shamanism and Neoshamanism.' In: C. Clifton (ed.) *Witchcraft and Shamanism: Witchcraft Today, Book Three*: 1-13. St. Paul, Minnesota: Llewellyn.

Conway, D. J. 1995. *By Oak, Ash, and Thorn: Modern Celtic Shamanism*. St. Paul, Minnesota: Llewellyn.

Cowan, T. 1993. *Fire in the Head: Shamanism and the Celtic Spirit*. San Francisco: Harper Collins.

Cruden, L. 1995. *Coyote's Council Fire: Contemporary Shamans on Race, Gender, and Community*. Vermont: Destiny Books.

Cunningham, S. 2001 [1988]. *Wicca: A Guide for the Solitary Practitioner*. St Paul, Minnesota: Llewellyn.

De Mille, R. 1976. *Castaneda's Journey: The Power and the Allegory*. Santa Barbara, California: Capra Press.

_____ (ed.) 1980. *The Don Juan Papers: Further Castaneda Controversies*. Santa Barbara, California: Ross-Erikson.

Dietler, M. 1994. 'Our Ancestors the Gauls: Archaeology, Ethnic Nationalism, and the Manipulation of Celtic Identity in Modern Europe.' *American*

Anthropologist 96 (3): 584-605.

Dourley, J. P. 1996. 'C. G. Jung's Appropriation of Aspects of Shamanism.' In: J. Pentikainen (ed.) *Shamanism and Northern Ecology* 51-9. New York: Mouton de Gruyter.

Drury, N. 2003. *Magic and Witchcraft: From Shamanism to the Technopagans.* London: Thames & Hudson.

Dubois, T. A. 1999. *Nordic Religions in the Viking Age.* Philadelphia: University of Pennsylvania Press.

Eliade, M. 1989 [1964]. *Shamanism: Archaic Techniques of Ecstasy.* London: Penguin Arkana.

Ellis, C. and A. Bochner 2000. 'Autoethnography, Personal Narrative: Reflexivity Researcher as Subject.' In N.K. Denzin and Y.S. Lincoln (eds) *Handbook of Qualitative Research*: 733-769. Thousand Oaks: Sage.

Farrar, J. and S. Farrar. 1984. *The Witches' Way: Principles, Rituals and Beliefs of Modern Witchcraft.* London: Robert Hale.

Fikes, J.C. 1993. *Carlos Castaneda, Academic Opportunism and the Psychedelic Sixties.* Victoria BC Canada: Millenia Press.

Flaherty, G. 1992. *Shamanism and the Eighteenth Century.* Princeton, N. J.: Princeton University Press.

Fries, J.. 1992. *Visual Magick: A Manual of Freestyle Shamanism.* Oxford, England: Mandrake.

_____ 1996. *Seidways: Shaking, Swaying and Serpent Mysteries.* Oxford, England: Mandrake.

_____ 2002[1993]. *Helrunar: A Manual of Rune Magic.* Oxford, England: Mandrake.

_____ 2003. *Cauldron of the Gods: Manual of Celtic Magick.* Oxford, England: Mandrake.

Gallagher, A-M. 1999. 'Weaving a Tangled Web? Pagan ethics and issues of history, "race" and ethnicity in Pagan identity.' *The Pomegranate* 10: 19-29.

Gardell, M. 2003. *Gods of the Blood: The Pagan Revival and White Separatism.* Durham, NC: Duke University Press.

Goodrick-Clarke, N. 2003. *Black Sun: Aryan Cults, Esoteric Nazism, and the Politics of Identity.* New York: New York University Press.

_____ 2004. *The Occult Roots of Nazism: Secret Aryan Cults and Their Influence on Nazi Ideology.* London: I. B. Tauris.

Granholm, K. 2005. *Embracing The Dark: The Magic Order of Dragon Rouge — Its Practice in Dark Magic and Meaning Making.* Åbo, Sweden: Åbo Akademi University Press.

Green, R. 1988. 'The Tribe Called Wannabee.' *Folklore* 99.1: 30-55.

Greenwood, S. 2005. *The Nature of Magic: An Anthropology of Consciousness.* Oxford: Berg.

Hardman, C. 1996. Introduction. In: G. Harvey and C. Hardman (eds) *Paganism Today: Wiccans, Druids, the Goddess and Ancient Earth Traditions for the Twenty-First Century*: ix-xix. London: Thorsons.

Harner, M. 1988. 'Shamanic Counseling.' In: G. Doore (ed.) *Shaman's Path*: Boston: Shambhala.

_____1990 [1980]. *The Way of the Shaman*. New York: HarperCollins.

Harvey, G. 1997. *Listening People, Speaking Earth: ContemporaryPaganism*. London: Hurst and Co.

_____ 2003a. General Introduction. In: G. Harvey (ed.) *Shamanism: A Reader*: 18. London: Routledge.

_____ 2003b. *Shamanism: A Reader*. London: Routledge.

_____ 2005. *Animism: Respecting the Living World*. London: Hurst and Company.

_____ 2009. 'Animist Paganism.' In: J. Lewis & M. Pizza (eds) *Handbook of Contemporary Paganism*: 393-411. Brill Handbooks on Contemporary Religion 2. Leiden and Boston: Brill Academic Publishers.

Harvey, G. and R. J. Wallis. 2007. *Historical Dictionary of Shamanism*. Lanham, Maryland: Scarecrow Press (reprinted in paperback as *The A to Z of Shamanism*, 2010).

Hayden, B. 2003. *Shamans, Sorcerers and Saints: A Prehistory of Religion*. Washington: Smithsonian Books.

Heinze, R. I. (ed.) 1991. *Shamans of the 20th Century*. New York: Irvington.

Hine, P. 2004. *Prime Chaos: Adventures in Chaos Magic*. Las Vegas, NV: New Falcon Publications.

Holyoak, L. 2005. 'Shamans Watching Shamans: The Dialectic of Identity in Northeast China.' *Studies in Religion / Sciences Religieuses* 34(3-4): 405-24.

Hoppál, M. 1992a. 'Urban Shamans: A Cultural Revival.' In: A-L. Siikala and M. Hoppal (eds) *Studies on Shamanism*: 197-209. Budapest: Akadémiai Kiadó and Finnish Anthropological Society, Helsinki.

_____1992b. 'Traces of Shamanism in Hungarian Folk Beliefs.' In: A-L. Siikala and M. Hoppal (eds) *Studies on Shamanism*: 156-68. Budapest: Akadémiai Kiadó and Finnish Anthropological Society, Helsinki.

_____1992c. 'The Role of Shamanism in Hungarian Ethnic Identity' in: A-L. Siikala and M. Hoppal (eds) *Studies on Shamanism*: 169-175. Budapest: Akadémiai Kiadó and Finnish Anthropological Society, Helsinki.

Hutson, S. R. 2000. 'The Rave: Spiritual Healing in Modern Western Subcultures' in *Anthropological Quarterly* 73(1): 35-49.

Hutton, R. 1991. *The Pagan Religions of the Ancient British Isles: Their Nature and Legacy*. Oxford: Blackwell.

_____1999. *The Triumph of the Moon: A History of Modern Pagan Witch-*

craft. Oxford: Oxford University Press.

———— 2001. *Shamans: Siberian Spirituality and the Western Imagination*. London: Hambledon and London.

———— 2003. *Witches, Druids and King Arthur*. London: Hambledon and London.

———— 2006. 'Shamanism: Mapping the Boundaries.' *Magic, Ritual, and Witchcraft* 1(2): 209-13.

———— 2009. *Blood and Mistletoe: The History of the Druids in Britain*. New Haven, Connecticut: Yale University Press.

Jackson, A. (ed.) 1987. *Anthropology at Home*. London: Tavistock Publications.

Jakobsen, M. D. 1999. *Shamanism: Traditional and Contemporary Approaches to the Mastery of Spirits and Healing*. Oxford: Berghahn Books.

James, S. 1999. *The Atlantic Celts: Ancient People or Modern Invention?* London: British Museum Press.

Jilek, W. G. 1982. *Indian Healing: Shamanic Ceremonialism in the Pacific Northwest Today*. Surrey, British Columbia: Hancock House.

Johnson, N. J. and R. J. Wallis 2005. *Galdrbok: Practical Heathen Runecraft, Shamanism and Magic*. Winchester: The Wykeham Press.

Johnson, W. 1993. 'The Visions of Luciano Perez, Contemporary Native American Shaman.' *Religion* 23(4): 343-54.

Jones, L. 1994. 'The Emergence of the Druid as Celtic Shaman.' *Folklore in Use* 2: 131-142.

———— 1998. *Druid, Shaman, Priest: Metaphors of Celtic Paganism*. Enfield Lock, Middlesex: Hisarlik Press.

Karlsson, T. 2002. *Uthark: Nightside of the Runes*. Sundbyberg, Sweden: Ouroboros.

Katz, R., Biesele, M. and V. St Denis. 1997. *Healing Makes Our Hearts Happy: Spirituality and Cultural Transformation among the Kalahari Jul'hoansi*. Rochester, Vermont: Inner Traditions International.

Kehoe, A. B. 1990. 'Primal Gaia: Primitivists and Plastic Medicine Men.' In: J. Clifton (ed.) *The Invented Indian: Cultural Fictions and Government Policies*: 193-209. New Brunswick: Transaction.

———— 2000. *Shamans and Religion: An Anthropological Exploration in Critical Thinking*. Prospect Heights, Illinois: Waveland Press, Inc.

Kim, T-G. 1995. 'The Symbolic Ur-Meaning of Shamanism.' In: T-G. Kim and Mihaly Hoppal (eds) *Shamanism in Performing Arts*: 1-16. Budapest: Akadémiai Kiadó (Bibliotheca Shamanistica, vol. 1).

Kinsella, T. 2002. *The Tain*. Oxford: Oxford University Press.

Koch, W. 2000. 'Contemporary Shamanism: Vegetalismo in the Peruvian Amazon.' *Unia Latin American Report* 16(2): 42-58.

Kürti, L. 2001. 'Psychic Phenomena, Neoshamanism, and the Cultic Milieu in

Hungary.' *Nova Religio* 4(2): 322-50.
Laurie, E.R. and T. White. 1997. 'Speckled Snake, Brother of Birch: Amanita Muscaria Motifs in Celtic Literature.' *Shaman's Drum* 44: 52-65.
Laws, G. and A. Laws, 2007. 'A Pilgrimage to the Heart of the Kalahari San.' *Sacred Hoop: Celebrating the Circle of Life* 55: 6-13.
Letcher, A. 2001. 'The Scouring of the Shire: Fairies, Trolls and Pixies in Eco-Protest Culture' in *Folklore* 112: 147-61.
_____ 2007. 'Mad Thoughts on Mushrooms: Discourse and Power in the Study of Psychedelic Consciousness.' *Anthropology of Consciousness* 18(2): 74–97.
Lewis-Williams, J.D. 1998. 'Quanto?: The Issue of "Many Meanings" in Southern African San Rock Art Research.' *South African Archaeological Bulletin* 53:86-97.
_____ 1999 [1989]. *Images of Power: Understanding Bushman Rock Art.* Johannesburg: Southern Book Publishers.
Lewis-Williams, J. D. and D. Pearce 2005. *Inside the Neolithic Mind: Consciousness, Cosmos and the Realm of the Gods.* London: Thames and Hudson.
Lindquist, G. 1997. *Shamanic Performance on the Urban Scene:Neo-Shamanism in Contemporary Sweden.* Stockholm Studies in Social Anthropology 39. Stockholm, Sweden: University of Stockholm.
Luhrmann, T. M. 1989. *Persuasions of the Witches Craft: Ritual Magic in Contemporary England.* Massachusetts: Harvard University Press.
Matthews, C. 1996. 'Following the Awen—Celtic Shamanism and the Druid Path in the Modern World.' In: P. Carr-Gomm (ed.) *The Druid Renaissance*: 223-236. London: Thorsons.
Matthews, J. 1991a. *Taliesin: Shamanism and the Bardic Mysteries in Britain and Ireland.* London: Aquarian.
_____ 991b. *The Celtic Shaman: A Handbook.* Shaftesbury, Dorset: Element Books.
_____ 1991c. *The Song of Taliesin: Stories and Poems fromthe Books of Broceliande.* London: Aquarian.
MacEowen, F. 2004. *The Spiral of Memory and Belonging: A Celtic Path of Soul and Kinship.* Novato: CA : New World Library.
McClenon, J. 1997. 'Shamanic Healing, Human Evolution and the Origin of Religion.' *Journal for the Scientific Study of Religion* 36: 345-57.
Michaelsen, P.; T. W. Ebersole, N. W. Smith and P. Biro. 2000. 'Australian Ice Age Rock Art May Depict Earth's Oldest Recordings of Shamanistic Rituals.' *Mankind Quarterly* 41(2): 131-46.
Miles, C. J. 2006. 'Journey into the Neither-Neither: Ausin Osman Spare and the Construction of a Shamanic Identity' in *The Pomegranate: The International Journal of Pagan Studies* 8(1): 54- 83.

Murray, M. 1931. *The God of the Witches*. London: Sampson Low, Marston.
Narby, J. and F. Huxley (eds) 2001. *Shamans Through Time: 500 Years on the Path to Knowledge*. London: Thames and Hudson.
Noel, D. C. (ed.) 1976. *Seeing Castaneda: Reactions to the "Don Juan" Writings of Carlos Castaneda*. New York: Capricorn Books.
_____1997. *The Soul of Shamanism: Western Fantasies, Imaginal Realities*. New York: Continuum.
Peters, J. 1997-2010. *Don Marcial, Maestro Curandero: Ayahuasca Ceremonies and Diets in Pucallpa, Peru*. Available online: http://uazu.net/sc/marcial/ (accessed 16 June 2010).
Price, N. 2000. 'Shamanism and the Vikings?' In: W. W. Fitzhugh and E. I. Ward (eds) *Vikings: The North Atlantic Saga*: 70-71. Washington D.C.: Smithsonian Institution.
_____2002. *The Viking Way: Religion and War in Late Iron Age Scandinavia*. Department of Archaeology and Ancient History, University of Uppsala, Sweden.
Reed-Danahay, D.E. (ed.) 1997. *Auto/Ethnography: Rewriting the Self and the Social*. Oxford: Berg.
Restall Orr, E. 2006. *Human Remains: The Acknowledgment of Sanctity*. Paper delivered at the conference 'Respect for Ancient British Human Remains: Philosophy and Practice', Manchester Museum, 7 November 2006, available online: www.museum.manchester.ac.uk/medialibrary/documents/respect/human_remains_the_acknowledgement_of_sanctity.pdf.
_____2009. Consultation on the Request for Reburial of Human Remains, Avebury. *Museum Archaeologists News* (Spring): 1-2.
Rios, M. Dobkin de. 1994. 'Drug Tourism in the Amazon.' *Newsletter of the Society for the Anthropology of Consciousness* 5(1): 16-19.
Root, D. 1996. *Cannibal Culture: Art, Appropriation, and the Commodification of Difference*. Colorado: Westview Press.
Rose, W. 1984. 'Just What's All This Fuss about Whiteshamanism, Anyway?' In: B. Schöler (ed.) *Coyote Was Here: Essays on Contemporary Native American Literary and Political Mobilization*: 13-24. Aarhus: University of Aarhus.
_____1992. 'The Great Pretenders. Further Reflections on Whiteshamanism.' In: M. Annette Jaimes (ed.) *The State of Native America: Genocide, Colonization, and Resistance*: 403-21. Boston, Mass.: South End.
Ross, A. 1967. *Pagan Celtic Britain*. London: Constable.
Runic John, 2004. *The Book of Seidr: The Native English and Northern European Shamanic Tradition*. Chieveley, Berks.: Capall Bann.
Rushkoff, D. 1994. *Cyberia: Life in the Trenches of Hyperspace*. San Francisco: Harper Collins.

Rutherford, L. 1996. *Principles of Shamanism*. Lonson: Thorsons.
Saler, B. 1979 [1967].'Nagual, Witch, and Sorcerer in a Qhiché Village.' In: J. Middleton (ed.) *Magic, Witchcraft and Curing*: 69-100. Austin and London: University of Texas Press.
Sanchez, V. 1995. *The Teachings of Don Carlos: Practical Applications of the Works of Carlos Castaneda*. Santa Fe, New Mexico: Bear & Company.
———— 1996. *Toltecs of the New Millennium*. Santa Fe, New Mexico: Bear & Company.
———— 2001. *The Toltec Path of Recapitulation: Healing Your Past to Free Your Soul*. Santa Fe, New Mexico: Bear & Company.
Sanson, D. 2009. 'New/Old Spiritualities in the West: Neo-Shamans and Neo-Shamanism.' In: J. Lewis & M. Pizza (eds) *Handbook of Contemporary Paganism*: 433-462. Brill Handbooks on Contemporary Religion 2. Leiden and Boston: Brill Academic Publishers.
Shnirelman, V. 2007. 'Ancestral Wisdom and Ethnic Nationalism: A View from Eastern Europe.' *The Pomegranate: The International Journal of Pagan Studies* 9(1): 41-61.
Semple, G. 1995. *Zos-Kia: An Introductory Essay on the Art and Sorcery of Austin Osman Spare*. London: Fulgur.
Smith, A. 1994. 'For All Those Who Were Indian in a Former Life.' In: C. J. Adams (ed.) *Ecofeminism and the Sacred*: 168–71. New York: Continuum.
Starhawk. 1989. *The Spiral Dance*. San Francisco: Harper & Row.
Stucken, H. 2006. *Das Seidhr Handbuch: Eine Einführung*. Hamburg: Verlag Daniel Junker.
Taussig, M. 1987. *Shamanism, Colonialism and the Wild Man: A Study in Terror and Healing*. Chicago: The University of Chicago Press.
Thomas, N. and C. Humphrey (eds) 1994. *Shamanism, History, and the State*. Ann Arbor: University of Michigan Press.
Thorsson, E. 1999. Witchdom of the True: A Study of the Vana-Troth and the Practice of Seidr. Smithville, Texas: Runa-Raven Press.
Townsend, S. 1988. 'Neo-shamanism and the Modern Mystical Movement.' In: G. Doore (ed.)
Shaman's Path: Healing, Personal Growth and Empowerment: 73-83. Boston: Shambhala.
———— 1999. 'Western Contemporary Core and Neo-shamanism and the Interpenetration with Indigenous Societies.' *Proceedings of the International Congress: Shamanism and Other Indigenous Spiritual Beliefs and Practices* 5 (2): 223-231. Moscow: Institute of Ethnology and Anthropology of the Russian Academy of Sciences.
Tunneshende, M. 2002. *Don Juan and the Power of Medicine Dreaming: A Nagual Woman's Journey of Healing*. Santa Fe, New Mexico: Bear & Company.

Turner, E. 1992. 'The Reality of Spirits.' *ReVision* 15.1: 28-32. Reprinted in Graham Harvey (ed.) 2003. *Shamanism: A Reader*. London: Routledge. pp. 145-52.

Vitebsky, P. 1995. *The Shaman*. London: Macmillan.

Wallis, R. J. 1996. *Tombs for Living Death: Irish Passage Tomb Art and Shamanism*. Paper presented at TAG (Theoretical Archaeology Group), Department of Archaeology, University of Liverpool.

_____1999. *The Socio-politics of Ecstasy: Autoarchaeology and Neo-Shamanism*. PhD Thesis, Department of Archaeology, University of Southampton.

_____ 2000. 'Queer Shamans: Autoarchaeology and Neo-shamanism.' *World Archaeology* 32(2): 252-262.

_____2001. 'Waking the Ancestors: Neo-shamanism and Archaeology.' In: N. Price (ed.) *The Archaeology of Shamanism*: 213-330. London: Routledge.

_____2002. 'The *Bwili* or "Flying Tricksters" of Malakula: a critical discussion of recent debates on rock art, ethnography and shamanisms.' *Journal of The Royal Anthropological Institute* 8(4): 735-760.

_____2003. *Shamans/neo-Shamans: Ecstasy, Alternative Archaeologies and Contemporary Pagans*. London: Routledge.

_____2004. 'Between the Worlds: autoarchaeology and neo-shamans.' In: J. Blain, D. Ezzy and G. Harvey (eds). *Researching Paganisms: Religious Experiences and Academic Methodologies*: 191-215. Walnut Creek, California: AltaMira.

_____2007. 'Remember Mugwort, what you made known': *Mugwort (Artemesia vulgaris)*, The Nine Herbs Charm and 'New Animism'. *Many Gods, Many Voices* (Journal of the Association of Polytheist Traditions) 5: 16-26 (Spring).

_____2009. 'Re-enchanting Rock Art Landscapes: animic ontologies, non-human agency and rhizomic personhood.' *Time and Mind: The Journal of Archaeology, Consciousness and Culture* 2(1): 47-70.

_____ 2010. 'In mighty revelation': The Nine Herbs Charm, Mugwort Lore and Elf-persons—an animic approach to Anglo-Saxon Magick. *Strange Attractor Journal* 4: in press.

Wallis, R.J. and J. Blain 2007. *The Sanctity of Burial: Pagan Views, Ancient and Modern*. Paper delivered at the conference' Respect for Ancient British Human Remains: Philosophy and Practice', Manchester Museum, 17 November 2006. Available online: http://www.museum.man.ac.uk/respect/intro.htm

_____in preparation. From Respect to Reburial: Negotiating pagan interest in prehistoric human remains in Britain, through the Avebury Consultation. Submitted to *Public Archaeology*.

Webb, H. S. (ed.) 2004. *Travelling Between the Worlds: Conversations with Contemporary Shamans*. Newburyport, MA: Hampton Road Publishing.

Znamenski, A. A. 2007. *The Beauty of the Primitive: Shamanism and the Western Imagination*. New York: Oxford University Press.

Endnotes

1. Heinani Huet aka Lois Stokes, 2001-2008. *Virtual Shaman, 'Extending Aka Cords': My Second Life as a Virtual Shaman*. Available online: http://www.stringfigure.com/virtual/virtual.html (accessed 16 June 2010).
2. See, for example, Laws & Laws 2007; *Destination Information: Kalahari Desert Bushmen, the Basarwa*. Available online: http://www.kalahari-desert.com/destination_bushmen.asp (accessed 16 June 2010); Bona Safari Services, 2003-2010. *Africa–Botswana: Cultural Tours; Meet People Of Botswana & Their Country; Bushmen Kuru San Dance Festival*. Available Online: http://www.bonasafari.com/cultural.html (accessed 16 June 2010).
3. Peters, J. 1997-2010. *Don Marcial, maestro curandero: Ayahuasca ceremonies and diets in Pucallpa, Peru*. Available online: http://uazu.net/sc/marcial/ (accessed 16 June 2010.
4. The 'neo' in neoshamanism is not intended to devalue the term but mark the majority of practitioners as different from 'shamans', and in both cases I use the lower case to acknowledge that neither are singular, unified and closed.
5. As with shamanisms/neo-shamanisms, 'animism' is best pluralized, but I think there is value in approaching neo-shamanisms with a more general conceptualisation of animic ontologies as it is this general theorising in anthropology which has influenced certain practitioners.
6. In previous work (e.g. Wallis 2003) I have promoted the nomenclature 'Native American' over 'American Indian' or simply 'Indian', as politically correct and suitably sensitive. However, given that most indigenous people in North America self-ascribe as 'Indian' and some are critical of 'Native American' (as others are of American Indian) as yet another academic and federal imposition, I use the more common though no less respectful 'American Indian' here. I particularly like the way that while other ethnic groups in the region use their ethnic origin first (e.g. African-American), 'American Indian' is the only term with the reverse arrangement, positioning them as the first ethnic group(s) in the continent.
7. See also: the website of NAFPS (New Age Frauds and Plastic Shamans): http://www.newagefraud.org/, and http://www.kiowakat.com/fakeindians.html (accessed 19 June 2010).
8. See: http://www.toltecas.com/aboutvic.html (accessed 19 June 2010).

9   See the Foundation for Shamanic Studies website: http://www.shamanism.org/workshops/calendar.php?Wkshp_ID=22. Accessed 16 June 2010.
10 See: http://www.shamanism.dk/Courses.htm#the shaman's journey (accessed 19 June 2010).
11 See: http://www.shamanism.dk/Courses.htm#Seidr Craft (accessed 14 June 2010).
12 For further discussion, see Blain 2002; Wallis 2003.
13 Heinani Huet aka Lois Stokes, 2001-2008. *Virtual Shaman, 'Extending Aka Cords': My Second Life as a Virtual Shaman*. Available online: http://www.stringfigure.com/virtual/virtual.html (accessed 16 June 2010).
14 See, for example: http://www.magicplants.co.uk/peyote.html (accessed 30 June 2010).
15 The 'Kaos' journal published by Joel Birocco was particularly important: see http://www.biroco.com/.
16 Of course, American Indians are not all the same and some Indians are themselves critical of those that have facilitated in the appropriation of native culture (e.g. the website of NAFPS [New Age Frauds and Plastic Shamans]: http://www.newagefraud.org/, and http://www.kiowakat.com/fakeindians.html [accessed 19 June 2010]).
17 I state this in general terms, with full acknowledgement of the important, extensive body of work examining shamanisms to date.
18 My approach to animisms/shamanisms/neoshamanisms is therefore different to that set out by Greenwood 2005: 195.
19 Diagnostic and Statistical Manual of Mental Disorders, Fourth Edition, available online: http://allpsych.com/disorders/dsm.html (accessed 30 June 2010).
20 See his 'Creeping Toad' website: http://creepingtoad.org.uk/ (accessed 30 June 2010). MacLellan's neo-shamanism and paganism has also been discussed by Harvey 1997, Wallis 2003 and Greenwood 2005).

7
Seiðr Oracles

Jenny Blain

Introduction
One of the three main forms of ritual practice found in today's Heathenry (or Asatru) is that of *seiðr* or broadly-speaking North European 'shamanistic' work. In constructing seiðr, today's Heathens are engaging with original sources and with scholarly or academic analyses, as well as their own understandings of the literature, and they draw on other 'shamanic' practices in attempting to create something that may be akin to the older practices. A short description is given by Blain and Wallis in the *Brill Handbook of Contemporary Paganism* (2009); the archaeology of seiðr is discussed by Price (2001) and different types of seið-practice in today's communities are explored in some detail by Blain (2002a and b, 2006) and by Lindquist (1997). The 'definitive' work on pre-Christian seiðr has been that of Strömbäck (1935) (in Swedish), and accounts and analysis within practitioner communities have often drawn on this work, although for many English-speaking practitioners this has been accessed only through second-hand interpretations of Strömbäck's own interpretations. However, Dubois (1999) has discussed links between seiðr and practices of nearby 'shamanic' cultures, notably Sámi shamanism, and recently, Tolley's two-volume work (2009) has made many descriptions of seiðr accessible, while further developing discussions of the context in which seiðr occurs as development from more general 'Indo-European'

practices, within the specific geography of Northern Europe.

This chapter first outlines some descriptions of older seið-practice, before discussing how practitioners today are re-inventing or re-constructing these. It then includes some discussion of seiðr as community practice and suspicion of practitioners in the literature, and concludes with a section on some of the issues, including challenges and confrontations, that practitioners face in their communities or from academic critics.

A common criticism is that 'you are doing it wrong!' and it should be clear from the outset of this paper that no community of which the author is aware claims that it has the definitive way to construct seiðr. While some forms of practice (derived often from the Hrafnar community in the US, or from the use of song developed by Annette Høst in Denmark) are more frequently met with, each community or working group develops practice in its own way: the commonalities are the sources, and the deliberate use of altered consciousness to achieve and work within a 'shamanic' state. Many diverse interpretations of the term seiðr are possible, and the term does not imply the same practices to all people. Seiðr is most often practiced by Heathen or Asatru groups or individuals, or by 'shamanic' practitioners, but other pagans and magical workers, including Wiccans and Druids, at times also develop their ways of working seið-magic within their own cultural and cosmological worldviews.

Today's practitioners, therefore, rely on accounts from the sagas and Eddas, scholars' analyses of this literature, and parallels with shamanic practices elsewhere, using these within a framework of Heathen cosmology and beliefs about soul, afterlife, and the nine-worlds. Seiðr-workers engage in faring-forth and trance-journeying or altered consciousness work, for a variety of ends, including healing and divination. Seiðr is Heathen magical practice, performed for a purpose, whether that be to gain knowledge of potential futures (as in oracular seiðr), to effect a change in circumstances, as in healing, to seek knowledge about places or pasts, or to explore magically the landscape of the Nine Worlds. As today's Heathens are well aware, the past shapes the present, with actions or thoughts long within Wyrd's Well forming part of the weaving of present-day Earth-religion.

The Sources:
Seeresses and Seers in Literature and Archaeology
Women as seiðworkers
The best-known description of practices to which the term 'seiðr' is given, in literature, comes from the Saga of Eirík the Red, which describes the visit of a *spákona*, a seeress, to a Greenland farm, approximately around the year 1000 of the common era. The farm has fallen on hard times and

her presence is requested so that she can foretell the fate of the farm and its people. This is one of the more detailed descriptions of any personage in the Sagas; her clothing and shoes, her staff and cloak are detailed. She wears a hood of lambskin lined with catskin, and has white catskin gloves. Her gown is girdled with a belt of touchwood, from which hangs a bag to hold magical items. Her cloak is blue, fastened with straps and adorned with stones, and stones stud the head of her staff. Her calfskin shoes are tied with thick laces, with tin buttons on their ends. She is asked to predict the progress of the community; she eats a meal including a porridge made from goat's milk or colostrum and of the hearts of the farm animals, and the next day a 'high seat' is made ready for her, where she will sit to foretell. She engages in ritual practices to make seiðr, and these require a special song to be sung to call or bind 'the powers' or spirits, in order that she may gain their knowledge, in trance. So, here is the visit of the *spákona*, Þorbjörg, to that Greenland farm, one thousand years ago, as described in the Saga of Eirík the Red. The next day she sits on a raised platform (*seiðhjallr*), on a cushion stuffed with hen's feathers, to make her predictions, as in the continued description:

> *Later the following day she was provided with things she required to carry out her magic rites. She asked for women who knew the chants required for carrying out magic rites, which are called ward songs (Varðlokur). But such women were not to be found. Then the people of the household were asked if there was anyone with such knowledge.*
>
> *Gudrid answered, 'I have neither magical powers nor the gift of prophecy, but in Iceland my foster-mother, Halldis, taught me chants she called ward songs.'*
>
> *[After some persuasion] The women formed a warding ring around the platform raised for sorcery, with Thorbjorg perched atop it. Gudrid spoke the chant so well and so beautifully that people there said they had never heard anyone recite in a fairer voice.*
>
> *The seeress thanked her for her chant. She said many spirits had been attracted who thought the chant fair to hear—'though earlier they wished to turn their backs on us and refused to do our bidding. Many things are now clear to me which were earlier concealed from both me and others.' (Eiríks saga rauða, trans Kunz, 2000, p. 658.)*

The seeress then spoke 'futures' for the community as a whole—the farm would survive—and for individuals within it, notably Guðríðr. The account of Þorbjörg has formed a basis, together with other descriptions of practice, for today's practice of *oracular seiðr*, also known as *high-seat seiðr* or spae-working, reconstructed in different ways by groups focusing on different points in the account. There can be no surety that this particular episode happened as indicated, or indeed even happened at all. The account and the writing of the Saga date from at least two hundred years after the described incident, and are told as background and introduction for the heroine, Guðríðr; however the details in this account may indicate much about how seeresses were thought of, by people claiming to be their descendants or inheritors and retaining stories of their practice, including their costume, their way of life, and how they might be regarded in time of crisis: and how they were expected to behave and what they would need to talk with the spirits.

Other descriptions are less detailed. Within the Icelandic poems and sagas, seeresses, seid-women, and those who are 'much-knowing' (fjölkunnig) appear as part of the action, influencing events, sometimes as central figures. A few examples are given here: more detailed descriptions are available in Morris (1991) and Blain (2002a). Within 'family sagas' (those describing events within Iceland relating to historic ancestors of the 13th and 14th century Icelanders forming the audience for the tale) they include Þórdís, the seeress of *Kormáks saga* and *Vatnsdæla saga*; another Þórdís from *Gunnars saga keldugnúpsfífls*; Oddbjörg of *Víga-Glúms saga*; Kjannok of *Heiðarvíga saga*, Heimlaug of *Gull-Þóris saga*, Þurrid from *Gréttis saga;* various women in *Eyrbyggja saga* including the rivals Katla and Geirrid. Though the accounts are fictive, they suggest cultural frameworks in which ecstasy, magic and prophecy could occur, in which women could ask spirits to assist them to advance community needs or personal ends.

Other sagas and short stories focused less on the settlement of Iceland and the ancestors of the writers, more on the entertainment derived from legends, and these reintroduce the seeing-women, but now their magic is both more 'outlandish' (less rooted in daily 'reality') and more often akin to 'evil' sorcery. In the tale (þáttr) of Norna-Gest, it is told that three wise women came to the house of Norna-Gest's parents, at his birth, and foretold his future: a lack of attention to the youngest norn caused her to attempt to countermand the great prophecies of her elders, stating that the boy's life would be no longer than that of the candle burning beside him. The eldest norn extinguished the candle and gave it to the boy's mother to preserve. Three hundred years later, so goes to story, Norna-Gest related his story to the king of Norway, accepted Christian baptism, and had the candle lit, dying as the flame expired. Arrow-Odd, the hero of Örvar-odds saga, likewise had an extended life, of 300 years, and both this life and the strange death that ended it were predicted by a seidkona known as Heiðr. The implication is that the prediction of the death is in some way adverse to Arrow-Odd, and indeed it occurs through his (much earlier) attempts to circumvent it.

Seeing might, however, be only one component of what the 'much knowing' (fjölkyngi) seiðrworker could do. A number of accounts refer to women or men who change shape, whether to avoid enemies, to seek knowledge, or to cause trouble, as discussed later in this chapter. The shapeshifter is *hamhleypa*, one who is *hamrammr*, shape-strong. Illusion and protection are other possibilities, and the account of Odin making seiðr, discussed later in this chapter, refers to his transferring health or strength from one person to another. Many words are used for practitioners and practices and it is not clear exactly what 'seiðr' refers to, but there seems to be an indication of work performed for clients or for a community, by a specialist practitioner, involving some kind of change or transformation, often using sound or chant to attract and hold 'spirits' who assist or enable the work to be done.

So, there are many women—and some men—indicated as practitioners of magic worked to gain knowledge, possibly associated with shape-shifting, protection or other activities. The sagas were written during a particular period of history, and tell of an earlier period. Anthropologist Kristen Hastrup holds that the objective of the saga-writers of the 12th and 13th centuries was to tell Icelandic history in a particular way, though family stories (Hastrup, 1996). The sagas do not deal with 'community' or 'society' as such, rather with the relations and happenings of particular families. According to Borovsky (1999:7), 'the sagas can be read as documents that straddle the terrain between (oral) "history" and (written) "fiction" because they were intended to provide the medieval audience with a sense of their past that would resonate with the present.' The descriptions of seidworkers appear as part of this construction, and for the most part seiðr is performed against the protagonists of the sagas. There could be reasons for this: some members of the Icelandic church had become versed in certain kinds of magic, including rune-magic and, to some extent, foretelling not associated with seiðr. Various kinds of magical practice were proscribed by the laws in Jónsbók, after the (13th century) annexation of Iceland to Norway, as punishable by death. These included: '...fordæðuskap ok spáfarar allar ok útiseta at vekja tröll upp ok fremja heiðni,' (Hastrup, 1990, p 391), that is 'sorcery and spae-working (foretelling) and sitting out to wake up trolls (spirits) and practising heathenism'. In actuality, no-one was convicted until Iceland's small witch-craze in the 17th century, long after official religion had changed from Catholicism to Lutheranism.

The proscription shows however that '[b]y the act of sitting out, which was a metaphor for leaving the ordinary social space, it was possible to invoke supernatural beings' (Hastrup, 1990, p. 391), and that the invocation of these beings, by the time of writing, was regarded suspiciously. Whether it was regarded with equal suspicion in the 10th century is not clear. Some early accounts (of for instance the activities of Queen Gunnhildr, a noted seidworker and political figure) may suggest that seid-magic was more acceptable, more part of the community, whereas in later ones seiðr is negatively construed and Gunnhildr has become the archetypal sorceress, 'the prototype of evil and revenging women in the old Norse corpus' (Jochens, Old Norse Images of Women, p. 180). However we are told that Gunnhild's husband, Eiríkr 'bloodaxe' and his father Haraldr called 'Fairhair', 'hated seiðr' and put to death Eirík's half-brother together with eighty seidworkers: indication both that seiðr was performed, and that it was not favoured by some of the power-seekers of the time.

Seið-related practices are described, in the Icelandic literature, as relating to skills held by individuals and utilised for specific purposes such as to gain knowledge when asked (as in the case of the Greenland seeress) to support a side of a dispute or feud, but their practitioners are named according to their relations with others in the community. Terms used include 'seidworker' (seiðkona or seiðmaðr, seid-woman or seid-man) but the same practitioners may be referred to a 'much-knowing' or by other terms such as *spákona* (a woman who foresees, often a term of respect) or more negative ones such as *fordæða* (usually translated 'sorceress' and implying a negative evaluation, literally a doer of evil deeds). Seiðr was not simple, and not necessarily either 'good' or 'evil', but in some sense woven into the daily life of practitioners and those they worked for. In the stories the episodes deal mostly with individual seidworkers and individual clients. There are, however, exceptions.

A notable account cited by today's practitioners is that of a woman awarded a name within the communities she visited—Þurídr *sundafyllir*, 'sound-filler'—who according to the *Book of Settlements* gained her name by calling or singing fish into the sound, by means of seiðr, thereby providing prosperity for the people. Zoë Borovsky (1999) points out that both this instance and that of the Greenland seeress relate to seiðr in association with fertility or prosperity, and she speculates that the practitioners used seiðr techniques, calling the spirits, to actively accomplish this fertility by bringing the components of *innangarð* and útangarð— approximately settlement and wildness, deities and giants, knowable and unknowable—back into balance within the communities. If so, it is an example of seiðr as active magic, involving spirits and ecstatic practice for community benefit and with community support: that is, potentially 'shamanic' in the dynamic, community-based sense mentioned previously. This instance and its sense of restoring balance are important, today, for a practitioner who relates the incident to her own practices, and tells her own 'fishing story' (for which see Blain, 2002a p.98).

Archaeological evidence includes items such as staffs and pouches similar to those described for seeresses. Neil Price (2001) details an impressive list of sites in Scandinavia in which either staffs have been identified, or objects previously otherwise classified may be re-interpreted as 'shamanic' staffs. Most are from burials identified as those of women, but one in Norway is of a man, and in several others either no attribution has been made, or the staffs are not in a burial context. Interestingly, the association of staff and seiðworker, within a burial context, was present at the time of writing of the sagas: *Laxdaela saga* includes an account of the uncovering of a grave, deemed to be that of a seiðkona because of her staff. The association of seeress, staff, and magic can however be an uneasy one. The *Laxdaela* grave is uncovered because of dreams and other strange occurrences. The object of this excavation is the stopping of dreams in which the dead seiðkona protests about the behaviour of her living (and now Christianised) descendants who have built a chapel above her grave and so are disturbing her sleep with their changed religious practices, especially the different chants which they now use.

Men and seiðr

So far this chapter has focused on seeresses and *fordæður*—female practitioners. Most accounts *are* of women and within today's communities seiðr is still often 'women's magic'. With some exceptions (Kotkell in *Laxdæla saga*, Þorgrim of *Gísla saga súrssonar*, who are identified as seiðr practitioners) when men are spoken of in the sagas as having knowledge, their methods are not usually given, other than as out-sitting *(útiseta)*, which is spoken of in the sagas of the kings, and notably in the example of the Lawspeaker of Iceland, during the transition to Christianity, which has been extensively analysed. A detailed discussion is given by Jón Hnefill *Aðalsteinsson* (1978), drawing on the account in a 12th century History of Iceland (see also Blain 2005). At the end of the 10th century, the Lawspeaker of Iceland, Þorgeir, needs to find a way to resolve the issue of whose law—Heathens' or Christians'—should govern Iceland, at a time when pressure was being applied externally for a formal conversion to Christianity. To 'see' what may result he goes 'under the cloak', lying wrapped in a cloak for a day and a night, during the Althing or parliament meeting, before emerging to say what he has seen and give instructions for law practice relating to the official or nominal conversion.

Otherwise, men appear instead as practitioners of *galdr*, sung or spoken spells, which do not involve the shapeshifting, journeying or other ecstatic components associated with seiðr. However that men *could* perform seiðr is evident. Snorri's *History of the Kings of Norway* recounts how Haraldr Finehair (who became king of all Norway in the 9th century C.E.), and his son Eiríkr Bloodaxe, were responsible for the death of Eirík's brother Rögnvaldr Rettilbeini (a seiðmaðr or man known for seið-work) and the troop of 80 *seiðmen* with whom he was associated, seemingly because Eiríkr and his father did not like 'magic' or seiðr. (*Haralds saga ins hárfagra*, ch 36—for translation see Hollander 2002 or Laing 1844/1906.) If political motivations were involved, Snorri does not recount those.

One of the best-known accounts of any type of seiðr work is of a male: in this case, Óðinn or Odin, the master magician, euhemerised by Snorri Sturluson as an invading king who used shapeshifting and magic to gain knowledge for himself or others. The version quoted here—Samuel Laing's 1844 translation, easily available to practitioners via the internet—filters Snorri's 13th-century account through a 19th century translation that in itself indicates some of the suspicion with which men doing seiðr could be held.

> *Odin could transform his shape: his body would lie as if dead, or asleep; but then he would be in the shape of a fish, or worm, or bird, or beast, and be off in a twinkling to distant lands upon his own or other people's business ... Sometimes even he called the dead out of the earth, or set himself beside the burial-mounds; whence he was called the ghost-sovereign, and lord of the mounds... Odin understood also the art in which the greatest power is lodged, and which he himself practiced; namely, what is called magic [seiðr]. By means of this he could know beforehand the predestined fate of men, or their not yet completed lot; and also bring on the death, ill-luck, or bad health of people, and take the strength or wit from one person and give it to another. But after such witchcraft followed such weakness and anxiety [ergi], that it was not thought respectable for men to practice it; and therefore the priestesses were brought up in this art (Ynglingasaga, Translation by Samuel Laing, London, 1844[1]).*

This extract indexes seiðr-practice as something not appropriate for men to perform. The word *ergi*, translated into this 19th century discourse as 'weakness and anxiety', might be more accurately glossed as 'demasculinization': it covers a range of meanings including implied homosexuality, though possibly as insult rather than as description of practice; cowardice; and a general sense of 'engaging in activities normally performed by women'. (For a detailed account of the use of 'ergi' or 'argr' within the mediaeval literature, in particular as insult, see Meulengracht Sørenson, 1983; for a discussion of its relevance to today's practice, Blain and Wallis, 2000.) In one of the poems of the Poetic Edda, Loki raises the accusation of 'ergi' against Óðinn.

> *But you once practiced seiðr on Samsey*
> *and you beat on the drum as seeresses do*
> *in the likeness of a vitki you journeyed among people*
> *and I thought that showed an ergi nature.*
> *(Locasenna, 24. Translation based on Larrington (1996:89),*
> *but retaining words relating to magic and ergi.)*

Today's seiðworkers, male and female, dispute meanings of 'ergi'. (Applied to a woman, the term may have implied sexual promiscuity.) The word and its contestations indicate ambiguities relating to seiðr and seiðworkers, and embeddedness of seiðr within political and gendered dimensions. For today's seiðworkers the term raises possibilities of finding ways of relating to the worlds that are not those of hegemonic masculinity, an abnegation of ego that, so say some practitioners, is a requirement for a male of today's world, in engaging with shamanistic practices (Blain and Wallis, 2000). So, it is time to look at some of the range of practice today.

Seiðr in today's Heathen practice

Today's seiðr takes many forms, with groups developing their own practice. I have observed a number of high-seat seiðr rituals conducted by practitioners of Ásatrú or Heathenism, a religion reconstructed from the extant material on Norse and Germanic pre-Christian practices, and participated in these on a variety of levels. Within North America, a school of practice has emerged, based on the work done by a Californian group known as Hrafnar (the Ravens), and particularly the author Diana Paxson, to reconstruct oracular seiðr. Hrafnar began its reconstruction with the account of Þorbjörg (discussed above) using such details as were available: the seeress needed first to familiarize herself with the community and its energies; she then sat on a high seat and a special song was sung to 'the powers' that enabled her to gain her knowledge—or 'the powers' to give it to her. The word 'powers' (*náttúrur*, from Latin *natura*, nature, in plural meaning spirits, and therefore an adopted rather than native Old Icelandic word) is uncertain: it may refer to ancestral spirits, elves (álfar), guardian or animal spirits or other wights or beings, or deities. The mechanisms of how the seeress entered the trance in which she was able to acquire knowledge and the process of questioning her have not been handed down in the account. Hrafnar have therefore gone to other sources (including 'core shamanism') to find details of how a seiðr seance might be conducted.

Their main initial resources have been the Eddic poems *Völuspá*, *Baldrs draumr*, and *Völuspá in skamma* (the shorter Völuspá—according to Snorri Sturluson's *Prose Edda*, in which one verse is found—forming a part of the Eddic poem *Hyndluljöð*). Each of these appears to show part of a question-and-answer process, in which one who knows, a seeress, a *Völva*, is asked to reveal her knowledge. In *Völuspá* the seeress speaks in answer to Óðinn, the god/magician; in *Baldrs draumr* Óðinn travels to a grave-mound, just outside Hela's realm, and there raises the dead Völva to answer his questions. In *Hyndluljöð*, the giantess/seeress Hyndla is speaking to Freyja and her follower Ottar about Ottar's ancestry, when (in the portion known as The Shorter Völuspá) she starts to foretell the coming of Ragnarok and the fates of the Gods. From *Baldrs draumr* Hrafnar has taken the calling of the seeress:

> *Way-tame is my name, the son of Slaughter-tame,*
> *tell me the news from Hel—I know what's happening in the world:*
> *or whom are the benches decked with arm-rings,*
> *the dais so fairly strewn with gold?*[2]

From *Völuspá* and the Shorter Völuspá comes the pattern of question and seeress' answer:

> *Much we have told you, we will tell you more,*
> *It's important that you know it, do you want to know more?*[3]

or the more concise version of *Völuspá*:

> *Do you understand yet, or what?*[4]

Paxson has described the construction of the high-seat seiðr ritual in *The Return of the Völva*, an article written for a Heathen journal,[5] and later developed this through her further writing on 'oracles' (available from the same site). In this version, drumming and singing accompany and facilitate the induction of the trance or altered consciousness state, enabling those present to participate within the ritual structure. One participant will act as seiðr-guide, narrating a meditative journey whereby all present, seers and questioners alike, travel through a tunnel of trees, down to the plain of Miðgarðr and the great tree Yggdrasill, then below one of its roots past Urð's well and through caverns of Earth, across the echoing bridge with its guardian maiden Móðguðr to the gates of Hela's realm, the abode of the dead, for in Old Norse tradition wisdom comes from the dead, the ancestors. There the audience participants remain, in a light trance state, while the seiðworker, sitting on a carved 'high seat' or raised dais, enters a deeper trance and 'journeys' on her or his own, assisted by spirit allies or 'power animals'. The guide acts almost as a master of ceremonies, singing the seeress through Hela's gates, and calling to other participants to ask their questions, and the seeress to answer. The process can be a long one, depending on the audience and the number of questions, and several seers or seeresses may succeed each other on the 'high seat'.

A *seiðmaðr*, Jordsvin, described for the author the journey and what he finds there.

> *...there's a guided journey down to Helheim. The people that are doing the public oracular seiðr go with me, they stop at the gate. ... I go down, I go through Hela's gate... I always nod respectfully to Hela, I'm in her living room. I see, other people see different things, I see a lake, an island and a torch burning on it. It lights up, the torch and the lake light up the area enough to actually see the dead people. And I walk down there and they tend gather round, and I'll say, would those who need to speak with me or speak with the people I'm here representing please come forward. ...I've never seen anything scary, they look like people, the ones that have been there are passing on I guess to another life or whatever they're going to do, sometimes they're just like shadows, some look like living men and women, some are somewhere in between. Of course there's many, many many of them. They ask me questions, sometimes they'll speak ... Sometimes I hear voices, sometimes I see pictures, impressions, feelings, I have my eyes closed physically, and I'm in a trance, and I got a shawl over my head, sometimes it's almost like pictures on the back of my eyelids (Interview, 1996 — this is further discussed in Blain, 2002a, p.36).*

Not all seiðr-workers see what Jordsvin sees. Even within Hrafnar's scenario, each worker faces the task of seeking knowledge in their own way. For Winifred, a seeress who has likewise received training from Hrafnar, a large part of her work is in making contact with deities, and attempting to place other people, her seiðr clients, in a relationship with them. A seiðworker known as RavenHorn traces his seeings to varying sources depending on the questioner: after passing Hela's gates, he often journeys on a ship, which transports him to where the answer to the question can be found. At other times he travels in the form of a raven, seeing the countryside below him. Sometimes a question brings contact with a deity, particularly Heimdallr, Freyja, or Óðinn. Others may experience being in darkness within a mound, solitary, and called forth by the seiðr-guide; visions, sounds, sensory experiences then arise in response to the questions that are asked, and these may involve people, animals, birds or trees, specific scenes or objects, sometimes music. The spirits who bring or provide 'answers' often include ancestors, recent or more distant, of the querants, and seiðworkers comment that images and concepts may have little meaning for them, being recognised by the querants when they are voiced.

Hrafnar and their followers have now trained a generation of seiðworkers in their methods, and these people are training others, so that a fellowship of seeresses, and seers, all working in similar ways and following broadly similar methods, is emerging across North America and elsewhere, extending to areas of Europe including the United Kingdom. Their practices have evolved and developed over two decades, and have included periods of 'possession' seiðr where the practitioner is 'horsed' by a deity, following other sources. However not all seiðr workers follow this method. Some directly challenge its authenticity; others consider that it is much too complicated, with too much emphasis on the elaborate ritual structure, the seeress's costume and other theatrical components. Even for those who do follow the methods, not all seiðr-workings are oracular. Jordsvin, trained by Hrafnar, uses similar methods of trance-journeying to dispel ghosts and finds himself called upon by people outside his religion to 'unhaunt houses'; others deal in healing (see in particular Blain 2002b for a discussion of healing-seiðr). It should be said also that the description above is essentially of a 'public seiðr' which has necessarily theatrical components. Hrafnar-trained participants may, on a smaller scale, conduct something much less elaborate, though often using the same songs and the same overall ritual structure.

Many workers have derived their practices independently of Hrafnar. Examples come from practices in Denmark and the United Kingdom, as well as the Swedish shamanic practitioners described by Lindquist (1997).

Within already 'shamanic' groups, seiðr becomes a distinctive kind of shamanic (or neo-shamanic) practice, involving alteration of consciousness assisted by song or chant, and the use of the altered consciousness to effect some kind of change, whether as 'oracles', healing, or other. These seiðworkings tend to be rather less elaborate than those of the Hrafnar-influenced groups. However here I must, as author, recount personal experience of performing seiðr on two sides of the Atlantic. In North America, the seiðr which I have experienced tends to be more 'god'-focused (though for some practitioners it includes communication with close ancestors) and appears in some sense more difficult to achieve; further, it may be performed at an event which includes an audience with only minimal exposure to the cosmology or mythology of North Europe, within which the Hrafnar-style meditation journey is embedded. In Europe, particularly (as I have experienced it) within Britain or (as described by Lindquist 1997) Scandinavia, the focus tends to be on landscape and on the 'wights' or spirits of that landscape, much closer, more immediate to the workers, and while a knowledge of the cosmology of the Nine Worlds of North European 'lore' is partially assumed it is less explicit. Likewise, songs used tend to focus on calling 'spirits' or offering sound to a landscape, rather than praising the exploits of deities as in the Hrafnar versions.

In these European contexts, and particularly when the work is undertaken within a small community (rather than as a public demonstration), a pattern followed may simply be that of singing, as a group, followed by speaking by the seeress. Shared elements of practice are the raised platform or chair, the use of song to facilitate the process, and usually the staff held by the seeress. Lindquist's description of practice indicates two types of seiðr, 'instrumental' designed to effect some kind of change (to protect a landscape, to heal) and 'research', to seek knowledge.

Seiðr and the community: the seer/ess as shamanistic practitioner

It would seem that Icelandic and indeed Scandinavian culture of 1000 years ago was not 'shamanic' in the sense in which Tungus or Sámi culture is said to be shamanic: we do not find a 'shamanic complex' of activities, no 'shamanic' figure is described as central to community life. There are kings and queens and battle-leaders, goðar (or priests) associated with different deities, and in Iceland the emergence of a representative system of goðar, as regional administrators, coordinated by a 'lawspeaker', and only occasional seiðworkers and other magic practitioners. Possibly oracular seiðr and other magical practices may form part of the rather scattered remnants of shamanistic techniques in Norse culture, related to the shamanic practices of other cultures, notably the Sámi, though not necessarily derived from Sámi practice (Hultkrantz, 1992). Grundy has pointed out (1995:220) that 'The only figures in Germanic culture which we can point to as bearing significant resemblance to the "professional shaman"...are the seeresses who occupy a position of respect based on their visionary capabilities' though to him they do not demonstrate other shamanic techniques or activities. The seeresses are often said to have been trained by 'the Finns'—apparently the nomadic Sámi. Sámi shamanism has been described in Scandinavian accounts at least since the 12th century, and up to the present day (e.g. Pentikäinen, 1984). Dubois (1999) indicates a considerable measure of overlap between Sámi and Scandinavian, Icelandic or Hebridean magical practices, whereas Tolley (2009) suggests a more fragmented pattern of remnants of Indo-European practices. Either way, by the time described in the Sagas of Icelanders these seiðworkers appear to be associated with families or local communities, but their position within these is not detailed.

Of course, 'shamanism' is itself a highly problematic term, initially specific to Tungus/Evenk-speaking peoples but generalized and universalized into a westernism (Blain 2002, Wallis, 2003), an abstraction coined to explain aspects of religious and spiritual practice of 'other people' in societies as different from the defining Westerners as possible. Eliade's (1964) work, still extensively referenced by today's Western practitioners, postulates an ideal type against which descriptions of practitioners or practices can be matched, rather than an actuality which is 'shamanism'. It may be of more use in attempting to understand seiðr to understand 'shamanism' as indicating techniques of altered consciousness and ecstasy attained by otherworldly experience, embedded in specific social relations and cultural settings. Thus the seiðr both emerges from and partly constitutes socio-political relations of the community. The Old Norse material becomes particularly interesting because there shamanistic activity is not supported by the entire community: it is contested on a number of levels.

It may be useful to remember processes of change which were occurring during the period described by the sagas: expansion of trade links, centralization, Christianization, the settlement of Iceland, among others. It may be that in some communities in some periods a practitioner did hold a position not so dissimilar to that of the Sámi noaide. Rather than say that there was one unified 'Norse' culture, it may be more helpful to examine some of the instances—told long after the occurrences they purport to describe—in terms of how they reflect shamanistic techniques elsewhere, how these techniques may have been embedded in community practice, and how their definition may have contested, in past and present.

These Norse seeresses enter repeatedly into the Icelandic poems and sagas. Other accounts of prophecy are found in the 'mythological' sagas as well as those displaying family stories. For instance:

> Heið, the sibyl of Hrólfs saga Kraka 3, was also treated hospitably and then asked to prophesy... King Frodi asked her to make use of her talents, prepared a feast for her, and set her on platform for her spell-making. She then opened her mouth, yawned, cast a spell and chanted a verse... (Morris, 1991: 45)

Þórdís, the seeress of Kormáks saga and Vatnsdæla saga, was 'held in great esteem and knew many things' and the hill behind her dwelling was named after her Spákonufell, the mountain of the seeress. These women, and others, such as Oddbjörg of Víga-Glúms saga, Kjannok of Heiðarvíga saga, Heimlaug of Gull-Þóris saga, are woven into the fabric of the family sagas. Oddbjörg may serve as an example of how the magic-worker might be regarded. She lives within a settlement, and can be seen as the equivalent of the village wise-woman; people go to her for prophecy. And yet, she is said to give good or bad 'spá' or foretellings, depending on how she is treated. In the saga description, she predicts misfortune for two young boys and is turned away from their grandmother's house. (Her prophecy is borne out by events.) Her standing shows a mixture of respect and suspicion with which other seið-workers are described, and she does have a position within her community, as a magical specialist. This ambivalence and suspicion is shown in the how people with 'knowledge' and magical abilities such as shapeshifting are described: in the saga of Kormák the Skáld, there is Vigi, who is both *fjölkunnigr* and *hamramr*; he sleeps by the door of a hall, and knows the business of everyone who enters or leaves. More telling is the account of Kormák's enemy, the seeress Þorveig, described in the saga as *fjölkunniga* and whom Kormák has earlier insulted: Kormák and his brother set off in a ship, but a walrus appears close by. Kormák aims a spear at it, striking it, and it disappears and does not come up again. The walrus had the eyes of the woman Þorveig, 'þóttust menn þar kenna augu Þórveigar'.[6] Þorveig was reported as dying from this spear-wound.

Metamorphosis and magic, as protection and aggression, form key elements in *Eyrbyggja saga*, which displays amongst others two competing women, Katla and Geirrid. Katla protects her son, giving him a charmed tunic and later disguising him thrice by illusion—until her enemies bring Geirrid who defeats her magic. The sagas have no single word for a magical specialist, but many words for components of magical or even 'shamanic' practice, relating to knowing, transforming, protecting. Healing is not there, though the paragraph about Odin, quoted earlier, describes taking health from one person to give to another and refers to this as seiðr, implying use in healing while suggesting a fear of how this may be done. Whether seiðr can be regarded as 'shamanic' does not seem a useful question to pursue; but an understanding of 'shamanic' practices elsewhere does seem appropriate in evaluating seiðr and in understanding something of the relationship of seeress and community, in the past descriptions and in how people today are re-creating practice.

Challenges to Seiðr practitioners

Among today's practitioners, many use the word 'seiðr' for what they do, whether they work as community-diviners using oracular seiðr, or seek private knowledge through techniques of 'sitting out for wisdom', or develop areas such as healing. However, some prefer to use another term, well-attested in the sagas for those who speak with foreknowledge. Thus of those modern practitioners mentioned earlier, Winifred is a *spákona*, Jordsvin a *spámaðr*. *Spá* (or *spae*, as in the Scottish 'spaewife') refers to foretelling, or prophesying. These words, *spá* and seiðr have differing implications within the old literature—the *spákona* or *spámaðr* is spoken of with respect for the most part, whereas the *seiðkona* or *seiðmaðr* is often regarded rather negatively. Seiðr may imply not only trance-divination, but what Jordsvin calls 'messing with people's minds' (this is not, he emphasizes, what he does, whatever people call it); or using shape-shifting to journey in this world, not the spirit world, and use the knowledge gained to the detriment of others, and influencing or affecting other people's behaviour by means of the journey.

Then there are the gender issues previously referred to. Most accounts of seiðr are of women: male practitioners—in the late, Christian accounts that we have—were deemed to be 'ergi', un-masculine, possibly crossing gender barriers in ways not then acceptable. It is unclear at what time this negativity spread to include seiðkonur (seið-women), or how the spread of Christianity affected ways in which seið-workers in general were regarded.

Sitting out, or *útiseta*, is another set of related, contested practices in search of knowledge. Sitting out typically involved sitting on a gravemound or at a crossroads, going under the cloak could be done wherever one was, but both implied a distancing of oneself from the other human members of the community. The one who was sitting out was not to be disturbed, and in particular their name should not be mentioned (Aðalsteinsson, 1978). As already referred to, Hastrup commented that 'By the act of sitting out, which was a metaphor for leaving the ordinary social space, it was possible to invoke supernatural beings'—the 'trolls' indicated in the 13th century law code. As with seiðr, members of today's Heathen community are attempting to rediscover techniques of útiseta, seeing it as a solitary practice, whereas 'oracular seiðr' is a community ritual.

Today's practitioners are dealing with challenges associated both with the 'bad name' of seiðr and with the lack of detail in saga descriptions. Within practitioner communities there are arguments over not only how seið-magic was done but whether it should be done at all. Popular Heathen writer Kveldúlfr Gundarsson adopts a more sophisticated form of argument, maintaining that the word 'seiðr', as used in a ninth or 10th century context, was generally negative but that it does not in fact describe shapeshifting or trance-journeying—having rather a precise meaning relating to the calling of spirits to a specific task, and that 'seiðr is never used for healing, soul-retrieval or guiding of the dead to their homes' (in the magazine *Idunna*, issue 26 p.11, 1995): in short, that 'seiðr' was evil magic, but that what today's practitioners do is not seiðr, but spae-working (foretelling) with use of shamanic techniques including shapeshifting within the knowledge-journey. A counter argument is that the term may have become increasingly negative due to Christianization, and practitioners draw on the work of scholars such as Jenny Jochens (e.g. 1996) who suggests from a study of terms used in the sagas and in law codes that magical practice *(fjölkyngi)* was originally a complex of female skills, which became taken over by male practitioners, with some of these skills then viewed very negatively, others *(spá)* positively. Jochens holds that 'Rooted deep in paganism, the oldest magical figure in the north was not the skilled male magician but the female diviner.' (1996,130) There may however be other ways in which the material on seiðr can be viewed.

In thinking of the seiðworkers of the sagas, all the discourses of the 'sorceress' or even the 'wicked witch' come into play. Conventional scholarship has it that seiðr was women's magic, and was generally evil: men who took to performing it were therefore seen as evil also, and terms such as 'ergi' applied. Possibly, however, women's magic was only seen as 'evil' depending on the observer's point of view. A woman or man who uses knowledge for protection may be seen as 'evilly' working against an aggressor—from the aggressor's point of view. In any case, we have one word—*fordæða*—referring to a woman who engages in deeds against the community, regardless of whether these are magical, but and many words which refer to techniques, practitioners, or knowledge gained, *spá, seiðr, spákona, seiðkona, fjölkyngi* and so forth. The second woman magic-worker from Kormáks Saga, Þórdís, is termed both *spákona* and *fordæða*. The distinction seems to depend on who she is working for at the time, and whose point of view is expressed in the saga, with *spákona* as a term of respect for her knowledge,[7] 'fordæða' a term of abuse. Seiðr performed by men, or by large numbers of either females or males as in the eighty seiðmen put to death by Eiríkr Bloodaxe, may have been politically threatening. Also one might speculate that, with increasing Christian influence, gender categories seem to have become much more rigid so that the charge of *ergi*, for men performing activities otherwise associated with women, may have become increasingly important over time.

A particular example involving Þórdís (the same woman as in Kormáks Saga) is given in the Saga of the People of Vatnsdal. In this Þórdís is asked, as a 'worthy woman and wise in many ways', to intervene in a law case. It is explained that she 'was very wise and could see into the future and was thus chosen to act in major cases' (Wawn, 2000, p. 262). When the prosecutor refuses her intervention she indeed does 'mess with his mind' magically to effect the resolution which the community wishes—thus preventing the banishment of the (Christian) hero of the tale.

Katherine Morris (1991) suggests that 'seeking for knowledge' in Iceland remained part of the complex of activities that were appropriate for women; it became problematic only when men practised it, possibly (in my conjecture) for political reasons. Indeed there is some evidence, particularly from Iceland's previous Allsherjargoði, Jörmundur Ingi (interviewed in 1998), for women in Iceland maintaining some of the folk-practices associated with seiðr, as everyday activities, small magics and divinatory performances, simply things that women do in their households and kitchens (Blain, 2002a). The extent to which these activities would be considered seiðr is of course debatable, though there are similarities with women elsewhere in North Europe who could see and possibly change fate, such as the Scottish spae-wife.

Conclusion: seiðr today

These arguments form part of the background for the practice of seiðr today. Seiðworkers are reconstructing practice as best they may, recognising that the saga accounts are not a manual for practice and drawing on material from further afield to help develop techniques. Seiðr is being revived, in association with the reconstruction of Heathenism, as a specific set of skills, notably the use of trance states to gain knowledge; and paralleling this, in association with 'core shamanic' practice where participants have knowledge of the saga accounts, and in relation to landscape and history. By whatever means the 10th-century gendering of seiðr came about, in today's Heathenry or Ásatrú, in North America and

Europe, the majority of seiðr-workers seem to be female, though with a number of both gay and heterosexual men among the best-known practitioners. Hrafnar-style high-seat or oracular seiðr-working has come to be an established part of larger-scale Heathen gatherings, though its techniques may still regarded with some suspicion and its rituals viewed by some as marginal to the 'main purpose' of the gathering. Other members of Earth Religions are also coming into contact with oracular seiðr, at festivals or local events.

How seiðr, spá, or shamanic journeying is viewed within Heathenism, or Ásatrú, depends very much on which group one focuses on. Some cling to an image of Heathenry as a religion of viking warriors, and reject signs of 'weakness' (including seiðr, women's magic, and especially seiðr performed by men). However, many people are enthusiastic about *the* techniques and about their potential for use in healing and alternative medicine, as well as divination. They also see journeying and útiseta as a way to gain personal knowledge the cosmology of the World Tree, Yggdrasill, and of deities and other wights, and so to explore the possibilities of the religion together with conceptions of self and spirit.

In summary, the position of seiðr is being played out against a background of debate on who or what Ásatrú or Heathenry is, and how far shamanic or shamanistic work forms or formed part of spiritual practices in past or present. Though some conventional scholarship still associates seiðr with evil, scholars within Heathenry and Earth Religions generally are raising questions and exploring possibilities raised by competing definitions. This chapter contributes to that debate, and introduces readers to how today's workers are reconstructing seiðr—whether oracular, or for other purposes such as healing or protection—along with some of its dilemmas and contradictions, as shamanistic practice for today.

References

Aðalsteinsson, J. H. 1978. *Under the Cloak. Acta Universitatis Upsaliensis 4.* Uppsala: Almqvist & Wiksell.

Borovsky, Z. 1999. 'Never in public: Women and performance in Old Norse Literature.' *Journal of American Folklore* 112(443): 6-39.

Blain, J. 2005. 'Now many of those things are shown to me which I was denied before: Seiðr, shamanism, and journeying, past and present.' *Studies in Religion/Sciences Religieuses* 34(1) 81-98.

———. 2002a. *Nine Worlds of Seid-Magic: Ecstasy and Neo-Shamanism in North European Paganism.* London: Routledge.

——— 2002b. 'Magic, healing, or death? Issues of Seiðr, "balance", and morality in past and present.' In G. Carr and P. A. Baker (eds.) *New Approaches to Medical Archaeology and Anthropology,* 161-171.

Oxford: Oxbow Books.
Blain, J. and Wallis, R.J. 2009. 'Heathenry.' In J.R. Lewis and M. Pizza (eds.) *Handbook of Contemporary Paganism*, 413-431. Leiden and Boston: Brill.
_____. 2000. 'The Ergi Seidman: Contestations of gender, shamanism and sexuality in northern religion past and present.' *Journal of Contemporary Religion*, 15(3), 395-411.
Dubois, T. 1999. *Nordic religions in the Viking Age*, Philadelphia: University of Pennsylvania Press.
Eliade, M. 1964. *Shamanism: Archaic Techniques of Ecstasy*. New York: Pantheon.
Grundy, S.S. 1995. 'The Cult of Odhinn, God of Death.' Unpublished Ph.D. Thesis, Cambridge University.
Hastrup, K. 1990. 'Iceland: Sorcerers and Paganism.' *Early Modern European Witchcraft: Centres and Peripheries*. Ed. B. Ankarloo and G. Henningsen. Oxford: Clarendon Press.
Hollander, Lee M (trans.). 2002. *Snorri Sturluson's Heimskringla: History of the Kings of Norway*. Austin: University of Texas Press.
Hultkrantz, Å. 1992. 'Aspects of Saami (Lapp) Shamanism.' *In Northern Religions and Shamanism*, ed. M. Hoppál and J. Pentikäinen. Budapest: Akadémiai Kiadó, and Helsinki: Finnish Literary Society.
Jochens, J. 1996. *Old Norse Images of Women*. Philadelphia: University of Philadelphia Press.
Kuhn, H. and Neckel, G. ed. 1962. *Edda: Die Lieder des Codex Regius (V1. Text)*. Heidelberg: Carl Winter.
Kunz, K. (trans) 2000. 'Eirik the Red's Saga.' In *The Sagas of Icelanders*, ed. V. Hreinsson, R. Cook, T. Gunnell, K. Kunz and B. Scudder. London: Penguin Books. 653-674.
Larrington, C. ed. 1996. *The Poetic Edda*. World's Classics. Oxford: Oxford University Press.
Laing, S. (trans.). 1906. *The Heimskringla: a history of the Norse kings*. London: Norroena Society.
Lindquist, G. 1997. *Shamanic Performances on the Urban Scene: Neo-Shamanism in Contemporary Sweden*. Stockholm: Stockholm Studies in Social Anthropology.
Meulengracht Sørenson, P. 1983. *The Unmanly Man: concepts of sexual defamation in early Northern society*, trans. J. Turville-Petre, Odense: Odense University Press.
Morris, K. 1991. *Sorceress or Witch? The Image of Gender in Medieval Iceland and Northern Europe*. Lanham, Maryland: University Press of America, Inc.
Pentikäinen, J. 1984. 'The Sámi Shaman—Mediator Between Man and Universe.' *Shamanism in Eurasia*. Ed. M. Hoppál. 2 vols. Göttingen:

Edition Herodot. 1: 125-148.
Price, N., 2001. *The Viking Way: Religion and War in Late Iron Age Scandinavia*. Uppsala: Uppsala University Press.
Strömbäck, D. 1935 *Sejd: Textstudier I nordisk religionshistorie*, Stockholm: Hugo Gebers Förlag.
Tolley, C. 2009. *Shamanism in Norse Myth and Magic*. 2 Vols. Helsinki: Academia Scientaum Fennica.
Wallis, R. J. 2003. *Shamans/Neo-Shamans. Ecstasy, Alternative Archaeologies and Contemporary Pagans*. London: Routledge.
Waun, A. (trans). 2000. 'The Saga of the People of Vatnsdal.' In *The Sagas of Icelanders*, eds. V. Hreinsson, R..Cook, T. Gunnell, K. Kunz and B. Scudder. London: Penguin Books. 185-269.

Endnotes

1. Online Medieval and Classical Library Release #15b. http://omacl.org/Heimskringla/ Snorri Sturluson, (Approx. 1225). English translation by Samuel Laing (London, 1844).
2. Baldrs Draumar, 6: 244, Poetic Edda translated by Carolyne Larrington (1996:244). Old Icelandic is:
Vegtamr ec heiti sonr em ec Valtams;
segðu mér ór helio—ec man ór heimi—:
hveim ero beccir baugom sánir,
flet fagrliga flóð gulli? (Kuhn, 1962: 278)
3. Song of Hyndla, 34, repeated in later verses, Larrington translation: 258
Mart segiom þér oc munom fleira,
vöromz, at viti svá viltu enn lengra? (Kuhn: 293)
4. Völuspá, 28 and many subsequent verses. Larrington translation: 7. Old Icelandic given by Kuhn is:
vitoð ér enn, eða hvat?
5. Mountain Thunder. This article is currently available via the website http://www.seidh.org/.
6. 'Men thought they recognized Thorveig's eyes.' Icelandic courtesy of 'Netútgáfan', http://www.snerpa.is/net/netut-e.htm, Kormák's saga, 18.
7. For the most part: although Kormák himself, in a poem late in the saga, uses 'spákona's man' as an insult to the husband of Þórdís.

8
Magical Practices in The Hermetic Order of The Golden Dawn

Nevill Drury

It is relatively easy to justify the pivotal position of the 19th century Hermetic Order of the Golden Dawn in the study of modern esotericism—simply stated, as an organization its influence on the 20th century magical revival has been unparalleled.[1] All modern occult perspectives—including Wicca, Goddess spirituality and even the Thelemic magick of Aleister Crowley—owe a historical debt to the Hermetic Order of the Golden Dawn for initiating a process of esoteric exploration that has continued to the present day.

The Golden Dawn drew on a range of ancient and medieval cosmologies and incorporated them into a body of ceremonial practices and ritual grades centred on the Kabbalistic Tree of Life, an important motif within the Jewish mystical tradition representing the sacred 'emanations' of the Godhead.[2] In addition to the Kabbalah, which occupied a central position in the cosmology of the Golden Dawn, the organisation also drew on the Hermetic tradition which had its roots in Neoplatonism and underwent a revival during the Renaissance. Rosicrucian mysticism, Masonic grade structures, alchemical rebirth symbolism, and the archetypal aspects of the medieval Tarot were also fundamental to the Golden Dawn approach.

Establishment of the Hermetic Order of the Golden Dawn

The Hermetic Order of the Golden Dawn was formally established in London on 12 February 1888 when its three founding figures, Samuel Liddell Mathers (1854-1918), Dr William Wynn Westcott (1848-1925) and Dr William Robert Woodman (1828-1891) signed a document headed 'Order of the G.D.' All three were members of the Societas Rosicruciana in Anglia (SRIA)[3] and it was through this esoteric Masonic organisation that they had met each other.[4] Westcott had recently acquired a manuscript in cipher form which had been discovered among the papers of a deceased member of the SRIA, and he claimed to have found among the leaves of the cipher manuscript the name and address of a certain Fraulein Anna Sprengel, said to be an eminent Rosicrucian adept. On her authority, and following a lengthy correspondence, Westcott announced in Masonic and Theosophical circles that he had been instructed to found an English branch of her German occult group, calling it the Esoteric Order of the Golden Dawn.[5]

The first official document of the new hermetic order defined the purpose of the Golden Dawn as a secret society dedicated to the pursuit of 'occult science' and located the organisation clearly within the Rosicrucian tradition—a tradition associated ultimately with the quest for spiritual rebirth. The text began as follows:

> *For the purpose of the study of Occult Science, and the further investigation of the Mysteries of Life and Death, and our Environment, permission has been granted by the Secret Chiefs of the R.C. to certain Fratres learned in the Occult Sciences, (and who are also members of the Soc. Ros. in Ang.) to work the Esoteric Order of the G.D. in the Outer; to hold meetings thereof for Study and to initiate any approved person Male or Female, who will enter into an Undertaking to maintain strict secrecy regarding all that concerns it. Belief in One God necessary. No other restrictions.*[6]

A key point in this statement is that the new magical order required its members to believe in 'One God'. The intention of the founding members was clearly to ground the Golden Dawn philosophically within a monotheistic spiritual tradition. This point is further clarified in the text of the Golden Dawn 'pledge form' which specified that the preferred religion should be Christianity: 'Belief in a Supreme Being, or Beings, is indispensable. In addition, the Candidate, if not a Christian, should be at least prepared to take an interest in Christianity.'[7] The early Golden Dawn manifestos also confirmed that its members would be dedicated to the 'investigation of the Mysteries of Life and Death'—the Order was not prepared to admit candidates to the Order who were Mesmerists[8] or Spiritualists[9] 'or who habitually allow[ed] themselves to fall into a completely passive condition of Will'.[10] Like most subsequent groups and movements associated with 20th century ceremonial magic, the Golden Dawn placed great emphasis on the development of the magical will and sometimes capitalised the word as Will to connote a higher spiritual purpose. As I hope to demonstrate in this chapter, the key aim of the theurgic magician in the Golden Dawn was to attain states of archetypal mythic awareness leading ultimately to an experience of the universal Godhead. The influential Golden Dawn historian and magical practitioner Israel Regardie has described this spiritual quest in Kabbalistic terms as follows:

> *The final goal of his spiritual pilgrimage is that peaceful ecstasy in which the finite personality, thought and self-consciousness, even the high consciousness of the highest Gods, drops utterly away, and the Magician melts to a oneness with the Ain Soph.*[11]

It is also significant, as reflected in the Golden Dawn source documents cited above, that despite the fact that they were practising ceremonial magicians, a number of influential members of the Golden Dawn regarded themselves as fundamentally Christian—a point emphasised in a personal communication between occult historian Gerald Yorke and the mystical poet Kathleen Raine.[12] Christian Golden Dawn members like Arthur Edward Waite, Dion Fortune, Rev. W.A. Ayton and Arthur Machen believed that a key function of the Golden Dawn was to recover the 'sacred mysteries' or *gnosis* discarded or overlooked by mainstream Christianity.[13] Christ, for these practitioners, was associated with the sphere of *Tiphareth* at the very heart of the Kabbalistic Tree of Life and, like Osiris in the ancient Egyptian pantheon—a deity also assigned to *Tiphareth*—personified spiritual rebirth. The legendary figure of Christian Rosenkreutz, who is central to the Adeptus Minor ritual grade—the portal to the Rosicrucian Second Order[14]—is similarly a figure of Christian *gnosis*, an alchemical embodiment of spiritual rebirth and transformation. Accordingly, as we will see, the theurgic ceremonial approach adopted by members of the Golden Dawn involved 'assuming the god-form' of various gods and goddesses from a number of ancient pantheons, their purpose being to partake of the specific spiritual qualities of these various deities as part of their 'spiritual pilgrimage', or mystic journey, towards the transcendent Godhead.[15]

Establishment of the Golden Dawn temples

One of Wynn Westcott's first initiatives in helping to consolidate the essential structure of the Golden Dawn was to invite his colleague from the SRIA, Samuel Liddell Mathers, to expand the cipher material so that it could form the basis of a 'complete scheme of initiation'.[16] Mathers obliged, developing the five Masonic grades into a workable system suitable for the practice of ceremonial magic and as a result the Isis-Urania Temple of the Golden Dawn was established in London on 1 March 1888 with Mathers, Westcott and Dr Woodman confirmed as leaders of the Order.[17] In a relatively short time the Isis-Urania Temple would be followed by other branches: the Osiris Temple in Weston-super-Mare, the Horus Temple in Bradford, the Amen-Ra Temple in Edinburgh and the Ahathoor Temple in Paris.[18]

In due course the Hermetic Order of the Golden Dawn attracted a distinguished membership including such figures as Arthur Edward Waite, an authority on the Kabbalah, Rosicrucianism and the Holy Grail legends; the well known poet William Butler Yeats, who would later win the Nobel Prize for literature; physician and pioneer of tropical medicine, Dr R.W. Felkin; homeopath Dr Edward Berridge; the Scottish Astronomer Royal, William Peck; lawyer John W. Brodie-Innes; the well-known fantasy novelists Arthur Machen and Algernon Blackwood; and the controversial ritual magician and adventurer Aleister Crowley. The Order also included within its membership several notable women, among them Annie Horniman, later a leading patron of Irish theatre; artist Moina Bergson, sister of the influential French philosopher Henri Bergson and future wife of Samuel Mathers;[19] Celtic revivalist Maude Gonne; actress Florence Farr; and in later years the Christian Kabbalist Violet Firth, better known as the magical novelist Dion Fortune.[20]

Ritual degrees and the Tree of Life

As Freemasons, Westcott and Mathers were strongly attracted to the concept of ritual degrees, and the grades of the Hermetic Order of the Golden Dawn were formulated in a manner that would align them symbolically with the *sephiroth*, or levels of mystical consciousness upon the Kabbalistic Tree of Life. Four of the five ritual grades had Latin names: Zelator (corresponding to the *sephirah* Malkuth on the Tree of Life), Theoricus (corresponding to Yesod), Practicus (corresponding to Hod) and Philosophus (corresponding to Netzach).[21] There was also a 'Neophyte' grade which, in a symbolic sense, was located *below* the

Kabbalistic Tree of Life because at this stage the candidate who had just entered the Golden Dawn had not yet embarked on the magical exploration of the higher spheres on the Tree. Occult historian Francis King notes that immediately after admission to the grade the Neophyte was given the first 'Knowledge Lecture', a document that contained various Hermetic teachings together with instructions on the meditations the candidate was to perform as part of his psycho-spiritual training. The Neophyte was also given the rubric of the 'Qabalistic Cross and the Lesser Ritual of the Pentagram' so that he or she might copy, learn and practise it, 'thus arriving as some...comprehension of the way to come into contact with spiritual forces.'[22]

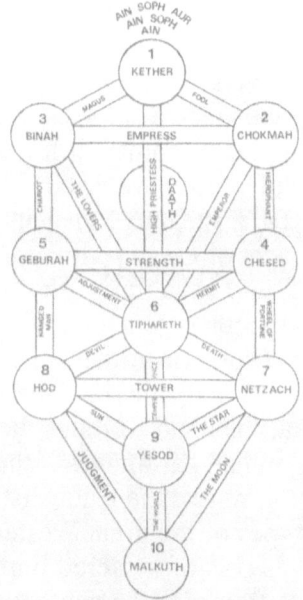

Figure 1: The Golden Dawn version of the Tree of Life, combining the ten Sephiroth and the interconnecting paths, represented by the Major Arcana of the Tarot

When Westcott, Mathers and Dr Woodman established the Isis-Urania Temple in London in 1888, they conferred upon themselves a Second Order[23] ritual grade which implied that they were the 'Secret Chiefs' incarnate: the grade 7° = 4° corresponded to the *sephirah* Chesed, the fourth emanation on the Tree of Life and the sphere symbolically associated with the Ruler of the Universe (represented cosmologically by Jehovah/Yahweh in Judaism, Zeus in ancient Greece and Jupiter in ancient Rome). As the leaders of the Isis-Urania Temple, Westcott, Mathers and Woodman interacted with incoming members by using secret magical names, for as a matter of principle Golden Dawn members could only be allowed to know the magical names of their peers and those with lower grades beneath them. Mathers was known as *Deo Duce Comite Ferro* and later *'S Rioghail Mo Dhream*, Westcott was *Non Omnis Moriar* and *Sapere Aude*, and Woodman *Magna est Veritas et Praevalebit* and *Vincit Omnia Veritas*.[24]

The three grades of the Second Order were Adeptus Minor (corresponding to Tiphareth on the Tree of Life), Adeptus Major (corresponding to Geburah) and Adeptus Exemptus (corresponding to Chesed).[25] By passing through the 5°=6° ritual grade of Adeptus Minor the ceremonial magician entered what Mathers called 'the Vault of the Adepts'.[26] The candidate was bound symbolically on the 'Cross of Suffering' while also witnessing 'the resurrection of the Chief Adept, who represented Christian Rosencreutz, from a tomb within an elaborately painted, seven-sided vault'.[27]

Magical symbolism in the Golden Dawn

As Israel Regardie notes in relation to the Neophyte grade, for the Golden Dawn magician the ultimate mythic attainment was to come forth ritually into the Light, for this was the very essence of spiritual rebirth.[28] The process of ascending the Kabbalistic Tree of Life by means of visualisation and ceremonial magic involved powerful acts of creative imagination: the magician had to feel that he or she was fully engaging with each sphere of consciousness in turn. However the monotheistic nature of the Kabbalistic Tree of Life presented the Golden Dawn occultists with a paradox, for while they acknowledged the sacred unity of the Tree of Life in all its emanations they also believed that they had to focus their creative awareness upon a sequence of specific archetypal images if they were to 'ascend' to the Light. Their solution was to regard the Kabbalistic Tree of Life as a matrix upon which the archetypes of the great Western mythologies could be charted and interrelated as part of a sacred unity. It then became possible to correlate the major deities from the pantheons of ancient Egypt, Greece, Rome and Celtic Europe in what was effectively a cumulative approach to the western mythological imagination. In due course other magical objects would also be charted symbolically upon the Tree, including various precious stones, perfumes, minerals and sacred plants—each being assigned to specific gods and goddesses in a ceremonial context. These charted mythological images were known to the Golden Dawn magicians as 'magical correspondences'.

Occult historian Ithell Colquhoun notes that S.L. MacGregor Mathers and Wynn Westcott began compiling the lists of magical correspondences during the 1890s but this work would subsequently be commandeered by Aleister Crowley and published under his own name:

A manuscript arranged in tabular form and known as *The Book of Correspondences*, the compilation of which Mathers and Wynn Westcott had together begun in the early days of their association, was circulated by them among their more promising students during the 1890s. Allan Bennett had a copy which he passed on to [Aleister] Crowley, or allowed him to copy again. Years later Crowley, while convalescing in Bournemouth, had the bright idea of adding a few columns to it. He then gave it the title of *Liber 777*, wrote an introduction and notes and, in 1909, published the whole as his own work, 'privately', under the imprint of the Walter Scott Publishing Co. Ltd., London and Felling-on-Tyne. This is the explanation of Crowley's claim to the feat of composing the whole within a week and without reference books. Certain of the columns were repeated in his *Magick in Theory and Practice* (1929) and in Regardie's *The Golden Dawn*. A new impression of the original was *Liber 777 Revised*, brought out in by the Neptune Press, London in 1955... the authorship of Mathers, who had done most of the initial work, went unrecognised.[29]

The listings in *Liber 777* included references to ancient Egyptian and Roman deities as well as listings for western astrology, plants, precious stones and perfumes. The following are selected listings from Crowley's version of Mathers' and Westcott's *Book of Correspondences* published in Table 1 in *Liber 777*: [30]

Tables of Correspondences

Level	Kabbalah	Astrology	Egyptian	Roman
1	Kether	Primum Mobile	Ptah, Hadith	Jupiter
2	Chokmah	Zodiac Fixed Stars	Amoun, Thoth,	Janus
3	Binah	Saturn	Isis, Nephthys	Juno, Cybele, Hecate
4	Chesed	Jupiter	Amoun	Jupiter
5	Geburah	Mars	Horus	Mars
6	Tiphareth	Sol (Sun)	Ra	Apollo
7	Netzach	Venus	Hathoor	Venus
8	Hod	Mercury	Anubis	Mercury
9	Yesod	Luna	Shu	Diana
10	Malkuth	The Elements	Seb	Ceres

The following perfumes, precious stones and plants were considered appropriate in rituals corresponding to the invoked god or goddess for each of the ten *sephiroth* and are also listings from Crowley's Table 1:[31]

Level	Precious Stones	Perfumes	Plants
1	Diamond	Ambergris	Almond in flower
2	Star Ruby, Turquoise	Musk	Amaranth
3	Star Sapphire, Pearl	Myrrh, Civet	Cypress, Opium Poppy
4	Amethyst, Sapphire	Cedar	Olive, Shamrock
5	Ruby	Tobacco	Oak. Nux Vomica, Nettle
6	Topaz	Olibanum	Acacia, Bay, Laurel, Vine
7	Emerald	Benzoin, Rose,	Rose Sandalwood
8	Opal	Storax	Moly, *Anhalonium lewinii*
9	Quartz	Jasmine	Mandrake, Damiana
10	Rock Crystal	Dittany of Crete	Willow, Lily, Ivy

Liber 777 and its precursor *The Book of Correspondences* helped codify the modern magical imagination. The listings themselves are of historic significance because they represented an early attempt to systematise archetypal images and 'mythic' levels of consciousness at a time when psychology itself was still in its infancy. *Liber 777* and *The Book of Correspondences* predate by well over a decade Carl Jung's work with the primordial images' of the unconscious mind, later referred to as the 'archetypes of the collective unconscious'.[32]

From a psychological perspective it is clear that the magicians of the Golden Dawn regarded the Tree of Life as a complex symbol representing the realm of sacred inner potentialities. To simulate the gods and goddesses through acts of magic was to *become like them*. The challenge was to identify oneself with the mythological and archetypal images of the psyche through a process of direct encounter: the act of engaging the gods, whether through ritual or by some other means like visualisation, meditation or magical trance, was essentially a process of discovering one's inner potential. As Aleister Crowley observed in *Magick in Theory and Practice* (1929): '...the Gods are but names for the forces of Nature themselves'[33] and 'the true God is man. In man are all things hidden...'[34]

The magicians in the Golden Dawn had therefore to imagine that they were partaking of the nature of each of the gods in turn, embodying within themselves the very essence of the deity. Their rituals were designed to control all the circumstances which might assist them in their journey through the subconscious mind and the mythic imagination. They included all the symbols and colours of the god, the utterance of magical names of power, and the burning of incense or perfume appropriate to the deity concerned. In Golden Dawn ceremonial workings, the ritual magician imagined that he or she had become the deity whose forms were imitated in ritual. The traditional concept of the gods (or God) ruling humanity was reversed so that it was now the ritual magician who controlled the gods, uttering the sacred names that sustained the universe. As Eliphas Lévi had written in his seminal text *The Key of the Mysteries*, '... all magic is in a word, and that word pronounced Kabbalistically is stronger than all the powers of Heaven, Earth and Hell. With the name of *Yod, He, Vau, He*, one commands Nature...' [35]

In passing through the ritual grades from Malkuth to Netzach, the Outer Order members of the Golden Dawn focused their magical activities on the mythic levels associated with the lower *sephiroth* of the Tree of Life, specifically the spheres of Malkuth, Yesod, Hod and Netzach.[36] In doing so, they developed specific techniques for the expansion of spiritual awareness. These included a rich application of magical symbols and mythic imagery in their ritual adornments, ceremonial procedures and invocations, all of which were intended to focus the imagination during the performance of a given magical ritual. In one of his most important books, *The Tree of Life*, Israel Regardie describes magical ritual as 'a deliberate exhilaration of the Will and the exaltation of the Imagination, the end being the purification of the personality and the attainment of a spiritual state of consciousness, in which the ego enters into a union with either its own Higher Self or a God'.[37] Such an approach, by its very nature, demanded the experience of altered states of consciousness. Within the Golden Dawn it was widely anticipated that magical approaches involving techniques of 'mystical ascent' would lead to inspirational states of spiritual *gnosis*.

Visionary techniques in the Golden Dawn
The records of various Golden Dawn members provide extensive documentation of magical techniques involving altered states of consciousness (ie. trance states, mystical experiences and out-of-the-body experiences).[38] These magical techniques are described in a series of semi-official documents known as 'Flying Rolls' which, according to occult historian Francis King, were privately circulated 'among the Adepti of the pre-1900 Golden Dawn'.[39] The Flying Rolls themselves were written by high-ranking members of the Golden Dawn but were not included in Israel Regardie's monumental four-volume collection of Golden Dawn rituals (first published 1937-1940),[40] and did not become widely known in magical circles until the early 1970s.[41]

The Golden Dawn magicians employed a technique of willed imagination utilising what was known as the 'body of light'. The body of light has been described within an occult context as a 'magical personality' that is 'deliberately built for a purpose [and] acquired through practice and concentration'.[42] In a magical context it is the vehicle of conscious awareness through which the magician interacts with 'thought-forms', spirit-entities and archetypal beings on the inner, or 'astral' planes.[43] The contemporary American occultist Dr Michael Aquino has described the role of this 'magical double' in quasi-Egyptian terms as follows:

The magician constructs within his subjective universe a magical double or ka. (Goethe's Doppelgänger). This is an idealized entity whose precise characteristics may vary from Working to Working. He then, by an act of Will, transfers his soul or ba to the vehicle of this ka and then executes his Will in the subjective universe. This may be completely dissociated from the physical body of the magician, or it may be closely aligned with it...At the conclusion of the Working, the ba is redirected to the physical body and the ka is disintegrated. The elements of the subjective universe specifically summoned for the Working are released into their normal contexts, there to influence their objective counterparts.[44]

Transferring consciousness to a magical simulacrum or 'body of light' through willed concentration and visualisation is central to the practice of visionary magic in the Western esoteric tradition, and the experience of 'consciousness-transfer' is described in *Flying Roll XXV*, written by *Frater Sub Spe*—Dr John W. Brodie-Innes—who was a prominent figure in the Golden Dawn's Amen-Ra temple in Edinburgh. *Frater Sub Spe* describes the shift in consciousness that occurs when a practitioner focuses meditatively on a Major Arcana Tarot card or one of the *Tattva* symbols of the elements, thereby switching personal awareness to the inner world of magical perception:

Gradually the attention is withdrawn from all surrounding sights and sounds, a grey mist seems to swathe everything, on which, as though thrown from a magic lantern on steam, the form of the symbol is projected. The Consciousness then seems to pass through the symbol to realms beyond...the sensation is as if one looked at a series of moving pictures... When this sensitiveness of brain and power of perception is once established there seems to grow out of it a power of actually going

> *to the scenes so visionary and seeing them as solid, indeed of actually doing things and producing effects there... The sensation...is first to become, as it were, dimly conscious of a figure walking among the scenes of the new country—or the Astral Plane—gradually to become conscious that it is my own figure that I am looking at—gradually, as it were, to be able to look through the eyes—and feel with the sensations of this doppelganger. Further to be able consciously to direct its motions, to control it, to inhabit it... It is as though my Consciousness had extruded from my own body to take possession of a body which I had either created for the purpose, or invoked out of the Astral Sphere as a vehicle for myself.*[45]

The key elements in this process include concentrating the mind on a specific magical symbol, such as a Major Arcana Tarot card image or a Tattva symbol, and then using it to bring about a transfer of consciousness to the inner, imaginal realm of perception. Sometimes the magician also uses various utterances (pronouncement of sacred god-names or one's personal magical name) to reinforce the sense of a transfer of awareness. According to Dion Fortune, who was a member of the Alpha et Omega Temple of the Golden Dawn,[46] the act of projecting her 'body of light' was greatly assisted by uttering her magical name. As she notes in Applied Magic:

> *In my own experience of the operation, the utterance to myself of my Magical name led to the picturing of myself in an idealised form, not differing in type, but upon an altogether grander scale, superhuman in fact, but recognisable as myself, as a statue more than life-size may yet be a good likeness. Once perceived, I could re-picture this idealised version of my body and personality at will, but I could not identify myself with it unless I uttered my Magical name. Upon my affirming it as my own, identification was immediate.*[47]

Following the transfer of consciousness, the magician then experiences the contents of the visionary realm as perceptually 'real'—including mythic landscapes populated by gods, spirit-beings and various other entities. According to *Frater Sub Spe*:

> *At first it seems as though everything thus perceived were just the product of one's own imagination... But a little further experience generally convinces one that the new country one*

has become conscious of has its inviolable natural laws just as the physical world has: that one cannot make or unmake at will, that the same causes produce the same results, that one is in fact merely a spectator and in no sense a creator. The conviction then dawns on one that one is actually perceiving a new and much extended range of phenomena; that in fact, which is known as the Astral World or Astral Plane. [48] *[emphasis added]*

According to the cosmology established in the Golden Dawn, the Tarot cards of the Major Arcana and the Hindu *Tattvas* could be used as 'symbolic doorways' granting access to various realms of visionary consciousness on the astral plane. The *Tattvas* were among the few specifically Eastern motifs incorporated within the ritual practices of the Golden Dawn. In their basic form the *Tattvas* are associated with the five Elements as follows:

Tejas, a red equilateral triangle	Fire
Apas, a silver crescent	Water
Vayu, a blue circle	Air
Prithivi, a yellow square	Earth
Akasha, an indigo or violet egg	Spirit [49]

Flying Roll XI describes a Tattva vision by Mrs Moina Mathers (*Soror Vestigia*) which arose as she sat in her ceremonial robes, meditating on a Tattva card combining *Tejas* and *Akasha*—a violet egg contained within a red triangle (Spirit within Fire).[50] Following her projection of the body of light, the Tattva symbol seemed to grow before her gaze, enabling her to pass into a 'vast triangle of flame'. She felt herself to be in a harsh desert of sand. Intoning the god-name *Elohim*, she then perceived a small pyramid in the distance and, drawing closer, noticed a small door on each face. She then vibrated the magical formula *Sephariel* and a warrior appeared, leading a procession of guards. After a series of tests involving ritual grade signs, the guards knelt before her and she passed inside:

> ...dazzling light, as in a Temple. An altar in the midst—kneeling figures surround it, there is a dais beyond, and many figures upon it—they seem to be Elementals of a fiery nature... She sees a pentagram, puts a Leo in it [ie, a Fire sign], thanks the figure who conducts her—wills to pass through the pyramid, finds herself out amid the sand. Wills her return—returns—perceiving her body in robes. [51]

In this account and others like it, it is clear that the visionary landscape is experientially 'real' to the meditator undertaking the projection of the body of light. However the contents of the visionary journey itself are also closely related to the meditative symbol that the magician has used in the transfer of consciousness: the magical entities Moina Mathers perceived in her 'spirit vision' were fire elementals—anthropomorphic figures embodying the *essential* properties of Fire.

On another occasion, Moina Mathers employed the Tattva symbols for Water and Spirit. Once again her account demonstrated the connection between the meditative symbol and the visionary beings present in the ensuing vision:

> *A wide expanse of water with many reflections of bright light, and occasionally glimpses of rainbow colours appearing. When divine and other names were pronounced, elementals of the mermaid and merman type [would] appear, but few of the other elemental forms. These water forms were extremely changeable, one moment appearing as solid mermaids and mermen, the next melting into foam.*
>
> *Raising myself by means of the highest symbols I had been taught, and vibrating the names of Water, I rose until the Water vanished, and instead I beheld a mighty world or globe, with its dimensions and divisions of Gods, Angels, elementals and demons—the whole Universe of Water. I called on HCOMA and there appeared standing before me a mighty Archangel, with four wings, robed in glistening white and crowned. In one hand, the right, he held a species of trident, and in the left a Cup filled to the brim with an essence which he poured down below on either side.* [52]

However, in this example, in addition to using the *Tattvas* for Water and Spirit as her meditative symbols, Mrs Mathers also uttered the sacred magical name HCOMA,[53] thereby causing an archangel to appear in her visions. She was also utilising a Golden Dawn technique known as 'rising in the planes', which is directly related to the concept of magical 'ascent'. In *Flying Roll XI*, Moina Mathers' husband, MacGregor Mathers, provides specific instructions for this particular technique:

> *Rising in the Planes is a spiritual process after spiritual conceptions and higher aims; by concentration and contemplation of the Divine, you formulate a Tree of Life passing from you to the spiritual realms above and beyond you. Picture to yourself*

> *that you stand in Malkuth—then by use of the Divine Names and aspirations you strive upward by the Path of Tau towards Yesod, neglecting the crossing rays which attract you as you pass up. Look upwards to the Divine Light shining down from Kether upon you. From Yesod leads up the Path of Temperance, Samekh, the arrow cleaving upwards leads the way to Tiphareth, the Great Central Sun of Sacred Power.*[54]

MacGregor Mathers' account makes it clear that within the Golden Dawn, magical 'ascent' was achieved by visualising oneself coursing like an arrow towards the higher realms of the Kabbalistic Tree of Life. In Flying Roll XI, Mathers is referring specifically to the symbolic pathways connecting Malkuth, Yesod and Tiphareth: collectively they represent the path of mystical ascent via the Middle Pillar of the Tree of Life. When one considers that the symbols of the Major Arcana of the Tarot were also employed in the Golden Dawn as meditative pathways connecting all ten sephiroth on the Tree of Life—resulting in a total of 22 interconnecting pathways on the Tree—it becomes clear that the Kabbalistic Tree of Life, itself a symbol of the Body of God, was regarded by the members of the Golden Dawn as nothing less than a map of the 'terrain' accessed through visionary magical consciousness. For them, the Body of God represented the operative magical territory: the act of 'rising in the planes' involved 'rising' or 'ascending' meditatively from one sephirah to the next.

Dan Merkur, a scholar well known for his study of Hermeticism and Gnosticism, argues that 'ascension' is a key element in the Hermetic tradition and he describes Hermetic 'ascension' in terms that resemble the Golden Dawn conception of 'rising in the planes':

> *In the Hermetic literature...different varieties of mystical experience were each associated with a specific celestial region on the trajectory of ascension...A single region of the sky might be termed the seven planetary heavens or the twelve zodiacal mansions... The ascension was literal, but mental rather than bodily. The ascent beyond the seven planetary zones of the sensible world was a motion of the mind [and involved] an experiential sense of the mind's detachment from the body.*[55]

In *Corpus Hermeticum XIII*, Hermes explains to his son Tat that in the course of Seeing 'I went out of myself into an immortal body, and now I am not what I was before. I have been born in mind.'[56] Elsewhere in the *Corpus Hermeticum* the sense of mystical ascent achieved during an out-of-the-body state is specifically associated with the spiritual will:

> *Command your soul to travel to India, and it will be there faster than your command. Command it to cross over to the ocean, and again it will quickly be there, not as having passed from place to place but simply as being there. Command it even to fly up to heaven, and it will not lack wings. Nothing will hinder it, not the fire of the sun, nor the aether, nor the swirl nor the bodies of the other stars... You must think of god in this way, as having everything—the cosmos, himself [the] universe—like thoughts within himself. Thus, unless you make yourself equal to god, you cannot understand god.* [57] *['god' is spelt lower case in Merkur's quotation]*

According to Merkur, for the Hermetic initiate the visionary or 'imaginal' realm was located in the Eighth celestial region, in a 'dimension' beyond the seven planetary heavens; however, in due course the initiate had to ascend still further, rising eventually to the Ninth cosmic region and achieving union with the pure Mind of the Creator. 'The Hermetic God', writes Merkur, 'was the Mind that contains the cosmos as its thoughts'[58] and the Hermetic initiate had to proceed 'from vision to *union*',[59] thereby experiencing the sacred realisation that 'both the universe and self were located in the mind of God'[60]

In the Kabbalistic Tree of Life the first three *sephiroth* (ie. emanations from the Godhead) similarly transcend the imaginal realm of forms, because they are located above the Abyss that separates the seven lower *sephiroth* associated with Creation. MacGregor Mathers makes it clear that the initiate's task in 'rising in the planes' is to 'Look upwards to the Divine Light shining down from Kether.'[61] The spiritual aspiration of the Hermetic magician is ultimately towards the highest point on the Kabbalistic Tree of Life and transcendent union with the Godhead.

As noted earlier, ritual activities in the Hermetic Order of the Golden Dawn focused especially on structured initiations and 'rites of passage' linked specifically to the symbolic pathways on the Kabbalistic Tree of Life. This initiatory process had as its principal aim the mystical experience of spiritual rebirth (associated with the Kabbalistic sphere of *Tiphareth* and the ritual grade of Adeptus Minor: 5°=6°). Ultimately, however, the magician would aim higher, striving for sacred union with the Godhead in *Kether*.

Clearly, the spiritual purpose associated in the Golden Dawn with 'rising in the planes' was ultimately a quest for spiritual *transcendence* and the act of 'merging into God'. An important Golden Dawn document on the *Qliphoth* or negative energies of the Kabbalistic Tree of Life titled *The Book of the Black Serpent* (c.1900) encouraged all Order members to 'banish thou therefore the Evil and seek the Good...let thy countenance be raised up towards the Light of the Holy One to invoke the Divine Brightness.'[62] For the Golden Dawn magical practitioner, all notions of an individual self would ultimately be subsumed within the total Oneness of God.

Endnotes

1. In my view the Hermetic Order of the Golden Dawn assumes much greater historic significance, for example, than the Theosophical Society — which has been cited by some authors (most recently Nicholas Goodrick-Clarke in *The Western Esoteric Traditions*, Oxford University Press, New York 2008) as the key source behind the modern magical revival. The Theosophical Society, which was established in New York in 1875 was concerned primarily with introducing Eastern spiritual teachings to the West and its cosmological concepts are, for the most part, theoretical. The Golden Dawn, on the other hand, provided its initiates with an extensive range of practical occult methods and techniques which laid the basis for the 20th century magical revival. For a consideration of the scope of these magical approaches — which included magical invocation and the exploration of trance states, as well as various forms of meditation and visualisation — interested readers are referred to Israel Regardie's definitive four-volume compilation *The Golden Dawn*, Aries Press, Chicago, 1937-1940, since reissued in many different editions and formats. See also my recent publication *Stealing Fire from Heaven: the Rise of Modern Western Magic* (Oxford University Press, New York 2011).

2. The Kabbalistic Tree of Life is referred to in the Jewish mystical tradition by its Hebrew name *Otz Chiim* and represents a process of sacred emanation from the Godhead. The Tree is a composite symbol consisting of ten spheres, or *sephiroth*, through which the creation of the world — indeed, all aspects of creation — have come about. The ten sephiroth are aligned in three columns headed by the first three emanations, Kether (The Crown), Chokhmah (The Great Father / Wisdom) and Binah (The Great Mother/Understanding). Collectively the ten *sephiroth* on the Tree of Life symbolise the process by which the Infinite Light and Formlessness of the Godhead (*Ain Soph Aur*) becomes manifest in the universe. The seven emanations beneath the supernal triad of Kether, Chokhmah and Binah (ie. the remaining *sephiroth* Chesed, Geburah, Tiphareth, Netzach, Hod, Yesod and Netzach) represent the 'seven days of Creation'.

3. The Societas Rosicruciana in Anglia (SRIA) had been founded in England on 1 June 1867 by Robert Wentworth Little and W.J. Hughan,

drawing on a system of grades employed by an Edinburgh-based group known as the Rosicrucian Society in Scotia. (See R.A. Gilbert, *A.E.Waite: Magician of Many Parts*, Crucible, Wellingborough UK 1987: 105). Other members of the SRIA included Frederick Hockley, Kenneth Mackenzie and Sir Edward Bulwer-Lytton.

4   R.A. Gilbert, *Revelations of the Golden Dawn: The Rise and Fall of a Magical Order*, Quantum/Foulsham, Slough UK 1997: 93.

5   A thoroughly researched history of the establishment of the Order is provided by Ellic Howe in *The Magicians of the Golden Dawn*, Routledge & Kegan Paul, London 1972.

6   R.A. Gilbert, *Revelations of the Golden Dawn: The Rise and Fall of a Magical Order*, loc cit: 21.

7   Ibid: 23. Nevertheless the form of Christianity which was adopted in the Golden Dawn, namely the spiritual rebirth symbolism of Christian Rosenkreutz, was far from the mainstream, and few orthodox Christians would have embraced the concept of assigning Christ to Tiphareth in the centre of the Kabbalistic Tree of Life alongside the many other 'god-forms' and archetypal mythic images associated by the Golden Dawn members with the different spheres on the Tree of Life.

8   Franz Anton Mesmer (1734-1815) was born in Germany and studied medicine at the University of Vienna. Here he embraced the then-current scientific view that a magnetic fluid permeated all aspects of life. Mesmer then came to the view that when this natural source of energy was blocked in the body, disease and ill-health would result. After graduating from the University of Vienna, Mesmer worked as a healer, first in Vienna and later in Paris, using magnets to 'correct' imbalances in the human organism. He transmitted 'healing energy' to his patients by making passes over his patients with his hands, or by using iron rods or wands that he had magnetized. Mesmer is now regarded as one of the pioneers of psychosomatic medicine and hypnotherapy. During the late-Victorian era of the Golden Dawn, the term 'Mesmerist' was used to connote a hypnotist.

9   Spiritualism is the belief that the spirits of the dead can communicate with the living through a psychic medium. Seances are conducted to summon a particular deceased spirit and the medium then enters a state of trance. The deceased spirit subsequently 'possesses' the trance medium and either addresses the gathering directly or communicates through 'automatic' writing, painting or drawing. Spiritualism was a popular practice in late-Victorian Britain and was widely believed to provide proof of life after death.

10 R.A. Gilbert, *Revelations of the Golden Dawn: The Rise and Fall of a Magical Order*, loc.cit: 23.

11   The *Ain Soph* is the 'limitless' that transcends finite creation as delineated on the Kabbalistic Tree of Life.
12   K. Raine, *Yeats, the Tarot and the Golden Dawn,* Dolmen Press, Dublin 1976: 9.
13   The well known mystical scholar and poet, Kathleen Raine, refers to the Christian element in the Golden Dawn in her book *Yeats, the Tarot and the Golden Dawn* (Dolmen Press; Dublin 1976). Here she quotes correspondence from esoteric publisher Geoffrey Watkins, who notes the Christian dedication of initiates entering the Second Order—the R.R. et A.C. (1976: 9). Raine also quotes occult historian Gerald Yorke on the influence of Arthur Edward Waite in particular: 'Where the G.D. called itself a Hermetic Order, Waite called his version a Rosicrucian Order, and the Rosicrucians were always more Christian than the Hermeticists' (Ibid.). Waite confirms his essentially *gnostic* position in his autobiography, *Shadows of Life and Thought* (Selwyn and Blount, London 1938) when he writes: 'I believe to this day...that there is a Church behind the Church on a more inward plane of being; and that it is formed of those who have opened the iridescent shell of external doctrine and have found that which abides within it. It is a Church of more worlds than one, for some of the Community are among us here and now and some are in a stage beyond the threshold of the physical senses.'(1938: 170-171)
14   The inner, or Second Order, of the Golden Dawn was known as the Ordo Rosae Rubeae et Aureae Crucis—the Ruby Rose and Cross of Gold—and included the ritual grades associated with the *sephiroth* Tiphareth, Geburah and Chesed on the Kabbalistic Tree of Life.
15   A.E. Waite describes the spiritual quest—a quest he refers to as the 'unconditional Godward direction'—as 'the path and term of the Union between Man and God...The Godward direction is the secret of that transcendent state in which Mind discovers that it is in Unity of Real Being with Eternal Mind; in other words, that God is within us...It is we and no other exploring the Great Mystery of our own being.' See A.E. Waite, *Shadows of Life and Thought,* loc cit: 281.
16   Quoted in E. Howe, *The Magicians of the Golden Dawn,* Routledge & Kegan Paul, London 1972:12.
17   See F. King (ed.) *Astral Projection, Ritual Magic and Alchemy,* Neville Spearman, London 1971:21.
18   See F. King, *Ritual Magic in England,* loc cit: 43 and R.A. Gilbert, *Revelations of the Golden Dawn: The Rise and Fall of a Magical Order,* loc cit: 44.
19   Samuel Mathers and Moina Bergson married in 1890.
20   Details of the Golden Dawn membership are included in E. Howe, *The*

Magicians of the Golden Dawn, Routledge & Kegan Paul, London 1972; I. Colquhuon, *Sword of Wisdom: MacGregor Mathers and the Golden Dawn*, Neville Spearman, London 1975; R.A. Gilbert, *Revelations of the Golden Dawn: The Rise and Fall of a Magical Order*, loc cit, and M.K. Greer, *Women of the Golden Dawn*, Park Street Press, Rochester, Vermont 1995. According to Ellic Howe (*The Magicians of the Golden Dawn* loc cit: 49), 170 people had been initiated into the Golden Dawn by 2 September 1893 and 315 by 1896. These figures include the membership of four Golden Dawn temples at that time: Isis-Urania in London; Osiris in Weston-super-Mare; Horus in Bradford and Amen-Ra in Edinburgh, and after 1894, Mathers' Ahathoor temple in Paris.

21 F. King, *Ritual Magic in England*, loc.cit:57-58.
22 Ibid: 57.
23 According to Golden Dawn historian R.A. Gilbert, the Second Order, the *Rosae Rubeae et Aureae Crucis* had existed since the earliest days of the Golden Dawn, but had worked no actual rituals. 'Members who advanced to become adepti of the Second Order did so by means of passing examinations.' See R.A. Gilbert, *A.E. Waite: Magician of Many Parts*, loc.cit: 107.
24 The magical names of the leading Golden Dawn members are provided in G.M. Harper, *Yeats's Golden Dawn*, Macmillan, London 1974: 314-316.
25 F. King, *Ritual Magic in England*, loc.cit:56.
26 Quoted in F. King, *Ritual Magic in England*, loc.cit: 44. The 'Vault of the Adepts' was a ritual crypt representing the burial tomb of Christian Rosenkreutz.
27 R.A. Gilbert, *A.E.Waite: Magician of Many Parts*, loc.cit: 112.
28 Within the Golden Dawn system of ritual grades this would not actually be achieved until the candidate had attained the Second Order 5°=6°degree associated with Tiphareth, the sphere of 'spiritual rebirth'.
29 I. Colquhoun, *Sword of Wisdom: MacGregor Mathers and the Golden Dawn*, loc cit. 104-105.
30 See A. Crowley, *Liber 777*, in *The Qabalah of Aleister Crowley*, Weiser, New York 1973: 1-10.
31 Crowley's *Liber 777* listings included several psychoactive plants: opium poppy, nux vomica, mandrake, peyote (*Anhalonium lewinii*) and damiana, a sure sign that these were his additions and not part of the original Mathers/ Westcott listings. Moly is a mythical plant: it was given by Hermes to Odysseus to protect him from the magic of Circe. See C. Ratsch, *The Dictionary of Sacred and Magical Plants*, Prism Press, Dorset, 1992: 127.
32 According to Jung's colleague, Dr Jolande Jacobi, Jung at first referred

to 'primordial images' and later to the 'dominants of the collective unconscious'. It was 'only later that he called them archetypes'. Jacobi notes that Jung took the term 'archetype' from the *Corpus Hermeticum* and from *De Divinis nominibus* by Dionysius the pseudo-Areopagite. See J. Jacobi, *The Psychology of C.G. Jung,* Routledge & Kegan Paul, London 1942:39.

33   A. Crowley, *Magick in Theory and Practice* (1929), Castle Books, New York, n.d.:120.
34   Ibid: 152-153.
35   E. Levi, *The Key of the Mysteries,* Rider, London 1959:174.
36   The Kabbalistic sphere of Malkuth, for example, was associated with the earth, crops, the immediate environment and living things. Yesod was linked symbolically to the Moon and was regarded as the sphere of 'astral imagery', the dream-world and the element Water. Yesod was also the seat of the sexual instincts and corresponded to the genital area when 'mapped' upon the figure of Adam Kadmon, the archetypal human being. Hod was associated with the planet Mercury, representing intellect and rational thinking, and symbolised the orderly or structured aspects of the manifested universe. Netzach was linked to the planet Venus, and was said to complement the intellectual and orderly functions of Hod. While Hod could be considered clinical and rational, Netzach represented the arts, creativity, subjectivity and the emotions. See also the mythological listings in *Liber 777* referred to above.
37   See I. Regardie, *The Tree of Life: A Study in Magic*, Rider, London 1932:106.
38   Anthropologists who have studied shamanism in pre-literate societies are especially aware of the highly significant relationship between altered states of consciousness and the nature of magical practice in these societies. See I.M. Lewis, *Ecstatic Religion: an Anthropological Study of Spirit Possession and Shamanism*, Penguin, Harmondsworth, UK 1971, and M. D. de Rios and M. Winkelman, 'Shamanism and Altered States of Consciousness: an Introduction' in the *Journal of Psychoactive Drugs*, 21,1, 1-7, San Francisco, January-March 1989. Shamanic and visionary elements within the Western esoteric tradition have received somewhat less attention but are addressed in N. Drury, *Sacred Encounters: Shamanism and Magical Journeys of the Spirit*, Watkins, London 2003 and A.S. Cook and G.A. Hawk, *Shamanism and the Esoteric Tradition*, Llewellyn, St Paul, Minnesota 1992.
39   F. King (ed.), *Astral Projection, Magic and Alchemy*, Spearman, London 1971: 29.
40   I. Regardie (ed.) *The Golden Dawn*, four volumes, Aries Press, Chicago, 1937-1940.

41 Francis King first published a collection of the Flying Rolls under the title *Astral Projection, Magic and Alchemy* in London, in 1971.
42 See M. Stavish, 'The Body of Light in the Western Esoteric Tradition', published on-line at www.hermetic.com/stavish/essays/bodylight.html.
43 Ibid.
44 M. Aquino, *The Crystal of Set: selected extracts*, loc cit: 37.
45 J.W. Brodie-Innes (*Frater Sub Spe*), 'Flying Roll No. XXV: Essay on Clairvoyance and Travelling in the Spirit Vision', in F. King (ed.), *Astral Projection, Magic and Alchemy*, loc cit.: 73-74.
46 Dion Fortune was initiated into the London Temple of the Alpha and Omega in 1919. See A. Richardson, *Priestess: The Life and Magic of Dion Fortune*, Aquarian Press, Wellingborough, UK 1987:111.
47 D. Fortune, *Applied Magic*, Aquarian Press, London 1962: 56-57.
48 J.W. Brodie-Innes (*Frater Sub Spe*), 'Flying Roll No. XXV: Essay on Clairvoyance and Travelling in the Spirit Vision', loc cit.:73.
49 See I. Regardie (ed.) *The Golden Dawn*, vol.4, Aries Press, Chicago 1940: 12-13.
50 S.L. MacGregor Mathers (*Frater Deo Duce Comite Ferro*), 'Flying Roll No.XI: Clairvoyance', in F. King (ed.), *Astral Projection, Magic and Alchemy*, loc cit.: 68-69.
51 Ibid.
52 Quoted in I. Regardie (ed.) *The Golden Dawn* (vol.4), loc cit: 1940: 43.
53 The sacred name HCOMA derives from the so-called Enochian system of angelic magic established by the Elizabethan occultists Dr John Dee and Edward Kelley.
54 S.L. MacGregor Mathers (*Frater Deo Duce Comite Ferro*), 'Flying Roll No.XI: Clairvoyance', loc cit.: 66.
55 D. Merkur, 'Stages of Ascension in Hermetic Rebirth' *Esoterica* 1 (1999):82, 84.
56 *Corpus Hermeticum XIII:3*, quoted in Merkur, ibid: 85.
57 *Corpus Hermeticum XI: 19-20*, quoted in Merkur, ibid: 85.
58 Merkur: 90.
59 Ibid: 89.
60 Ibid: 90.
61 S.L. MacGregor Mathers (*Frater Deo Duce Comite Ferro*), 'Flying Roll No.XI: Clairvoyance', loc cit.
62 Anon., *The Book of the Black Serpent*, c.1900, circulated among initiates of the Isis-Urania Temple in London. Included as an appendix in R.A. Gilbert, *The Sorcerer and his Apprentice*, Aquarian Press, Wellingborough, UK 1983.

References

Aquino, M.. 1983. *The Crystal of Set: Selected Extracts*. San Francisco: TheTemple of Set.
Brodie-Innes, J. W. (*Frater Sub Spe*). 1971. 'Flying Roll No. XXV: Essay on Clairvoyance and Travelling in the Spirit Vision', in F. King (ed.), *Astral Projection, Magic and Alchemy*. London: Neville Spearman.
Colquhuon, I. 1975. *Sword of Wisdom: MacGregor Mathers and the Golden Dawn*. London: Neville Spearman.
Cook, A.S., and Hawk, G.A. 1992. *Shamanism and the Esoteric Tradition*. St Paul, Minnesota: Llewellyn.
Crowley, A. 1973. *Liber 777*, in *The Qabalah of Aleister Crowley*. New York: Weiser.
_____ n.d. *Magick in Theory and Practice*. New York: Castle Books.
De Rios, M.D. and Winkelman, M. January-March 1989. 'Shamanism and Altered States of Consciousness: an Introduction'. San Francisco: *Journal of Psychoactive Drugs*, 21,1, 1-7.
Drury, N. 2011. *Stealing Fire from Heaven: the Rise of Modern Western Magic*. New York: Oxford University Press.
_____ 2003. *Sacred Encounters: Shamanism and Magical Journeys of the Spirit*. London: Watkins.
Fortune, D. 1962. *Applied Magic*, London: Aquarian Press.
Gilbert, R. A. 1997. *Revelations of the Golden Dawn: The Rise and Fall of a Magical Order*. Slough, UK : Quantum/Foulsham.
_____ 1987. *A.E. Waite: Magician of Many Parts*. Wellingborough, UK: Crucible.
_____ 1983. *The Sorcerer and his Apprentice*. Wellingborough, UK: Aquarian Press.
Goodrick-Clarke, N. 2008. *The Western Esoteric Traditions*. New York: Oxford University Press.
Greer, M. K. 1995. *Women of the Golden Dawn*. Rochester, Vermont: Park Street Press.
Harper, G.M. 1974. *Yeats's Golden Dawn*. London: Macmillan.
Howe. E. 1972. *The Magicians of the Golden Dawn*. London: Routledge & Kegan Paul.
Jacobi, J. 1942. *The Psychology of C.G Jung*. London: Routledge & Kegan Paul.
King, F. (ed.). 1971. *Astral Projection, Ritual Magic and Alchemy*. London: Neville Spearman.
_____ 1971. *Ritual Magic in England*. London: Neville Spearman.
Levi, E. 1959. *The Key of the Mysteries*. London: Rider.
Lewis, I. M. 1971. *Ecstatic Religion: an Anthropological Study of Spirit Possession and Shamanism.*, Harmondsworth, UK: Penguin.

Mathers, S.L.M., (*Frater Deo Duce Comite Ferro*). 1971. 'Flying Roll No.XI: Clairvoyance', in F. King (ed.), *Astral Projection, Magic and Alchemy*. London: Neville Spearman.
Merkur, D. 1999. 'Stages of Ascension in Hermetic Rebirth' *Esoterica* 1:82, 84.
Mundy, Jennifer (editor). *Surreealism: Desire Unbound*. London: Tate Publishing, 2001.
Polizzotti, Mark. *Revolution of the Mind: The Life of Andre Breton*. New York: Farar, Straus and Giroux, 1995.
Raine, K. 1976. *Yeats, the Tarot and the Golden Dawn*, Dublin: Dolmen Press.
Ratsch, C. 1992. *The Dictionary of Sacred and Magical Plants*. Dorset: Prism Press.
Regardie, I. 1937-40. *The Golden Dawn* (four vols.). Chicago: Aries Press.
_____ 1932. *The Tree of Life: A Study in Magic*. London: Rider.
Richardson, A. 1987. *Priestess: The Life and Magic of Dion Fortune*. Wellingborough, UK: Aquarian Press.
Rosemont, Penelope (editor). *Surrealist Women: An International Anthology*. Austin: University of Texas Press, 1998.
Waite, A.E. 1938. *Shadows of Life and Thought*. London: Selwyn and Blount.
Warlick, M.E. *Max Ernst and Alchemy: A Magician in Search of a Myth*. Austin: University of Texas Press, 2001.

9
The Thelemic Sex Magick of Aleister Crowley

Nevill Drury

It can be argued that Aleister Crowley's proclamation of the doctrine of *Thelema* polarized the Western esoteric tradition from the early 20th century onwards by shifting the pursuit of ceremonial magic away from the quest for mystical transcendence towards an affirmation of the individual human will through acts of sacred sex magick (*Crowley's special spelling). Crowley's exploration of sex magick was indeed a radical departure although, as I will seek to demonstrate below, some aspects of his doctrine reflect cosmological concepts dating back to the time of the 4th century Gnostics.

Historical background
Born at Leamington Spa, Warwickshire on 12 October 1875, Edward Alexander Crowley[1] was raised in a fundamentalist Plymouth Brethren home and soon developed an antipathy towards Christian belief and morality that would remain with him for his entire life. His father was a prosperous brewer who had retired to Leamington to study the Christian scriptures. Crowley came to despise the Plymouth Brethren primarily on the basis of his unfortunate experiences at the special sect school in Cambridge which he was obliged to attend, and which was run by an

especially cruel headmaster. Much of his school education was unhappy—marked by poor health and a vulnerability to bullying attacks—but after he went up to Trinity College, Cambridge in 1895 he was able to spend much of his time reading poetry and classical literature as well as confirming his well-earned reputation as a champion chess player. Crowley had an adventurous spirit and would later become an enthusiastic mountaineer, joining an expedition in 1902 to scale the mountain known as Chogo Ri (Mount Godwin-Austin, also referred to as K2)—at the time the highest peak in the world open to European climbers.

Crowley's direct association with the Western esoteric tradition began in London in 1898 with his introduction to George Cecil Jones, a member of the Golden Dawn. By the following year Crowley had also become a close friend of magical initiate Allan Bennett, who for a time rivalled MacGregor Mathers as a dominant figure among the English occultists of the period. Within the Golden Dawn, Bennett had taken the magical name Frater *Iehi Aour* (Hebrew: 'Let there be Light') and he became a mentor to Crowley. For a time Bennett and Crowley shared the latter's Chancery Lane flat in London[2] and it was here that Bennett tutored Crowley on applied Kabbalah and the techniques of magical invocation and evocation, as well as showing him how to create magical talismans.

Crowley quickly grasped the fundamentals of magic—or *magick*, as he would later spell it in his own writings on the subject. In one of his most influential books—*Magick in Theory and Practice*, first published in 1929 and frequently reprinted since—Crowley outlined the basic philosophy of magic as he had come to see it, which in essence involved the process of making man god-like, both in vision and in power. Crowley's magical dictums are instructive because they reveal the particular appeal that magic had for him:

A man who is doing his True Will has the inertia of the Universe to assist him.[3]

Man is ignorant of the nature of his own being and powers. Even his idea of his limitations is based on an experience of the past and every step in his progress extends his empire. There is therefore no reason to assign theoretical limits to what he may be or what he may do.[4]

Man is capable of being and using anything which he perceives, for everything that he perceives is in a certain sense a part of his being. He may thus subjugate the whole Universe of which he is conscious to his individual will.[5]

> *The Microcosm is an exact image of the Macrocosm; the Great Work is the raising of the whole man in perfect balance to the power of Infinity.* [6]

> *There is a single main definition of the object of all magical Ritual. It is the uniting of the Microcosm with the Macrocosm. The Supreme and Complete Ritual is therefore the Invocation of the Holy Guardian Angel, or, in the language of Mysticism, Union with God.* [7]

Crowley was initiated as a Neophyte in the Golden Dawn on 18 November 1898. He soon came to appreciate that those with the loftiest ritual grades in the Order were able to wield profound spiritual influence over their followers by claiming rapport with the so-called 'Secret Chiefs'[8] whose authority was said to emanate from higher planes of spiritual reality. Keen to ascend to as high a rank as possible, Crowley took the grade of Zelator and then Theoricus and Practicus in the following two months. Initiation into the grade of Philosophus followed in May 1899. Greatly enthused by his magical research under the tutelage of Allan Bennett, Crowley also began making preparations for a substantial magical working based on the fifteenth century rituals of *Abramelin the Mage*, described in a grimoire that had been translated from French into English by Golden Dawn co-founder S.L. MacGregor Mathers and which George Cecil Jones had introduced him to a year earlier.[9] Apart from allegedly providing the magician with the services of 316 spirit-advisers, the *Abramelin* system of magic was also said to grant the practitioner communion with the Holy Guardian Angel, an embodiment in visionary form of one's higher spiritual self. However, Crowley believed there was another potential benefit: such an experience would enable him to claim spiritual parity with Mathers in the Golden Dawn hierarchy.

Crowley delayed the actual performance of his Abramelin operation but, after attaining the grade of Philosophus within the Golden Dawn, contacted Mathers in Paris and requested ritual entry into the Second Order—the Red Rose and the Cross of Gold. In January 1900, under Mathers' direct supervision, Crowley was admitted 'to the Glory of Tiphareth'—the $5°= 6°$ Adeptus Minor ritual grade associated with the experience of spiritual rebirth. He then returned to England where he challenged the authority of William Butler Yeats, who at the time was one of the senior figures in the Golden Dawn in England. As mentioned earlier, Yeats was unimpressed by this effrontery and Crowley was unsuccessful in his bid for ritual supremacy. Having failed to dislodge Yeats as the head of the Golden Dawn, Crowley now suddenly switched course.

Unpredictably and apparently acting on pure impulse, he withdrew from the dispute altogether and in June 1900 embarked upon a series of travels through Mexico, the United States, France, Ceylon and India before finally arriving in Cairo with his wife Rose on 9 February 1904.[10] Crowley's entire conception of the magical universe was about to be dramatically transformed.

Crowley's Thelemic revelation

The Thelemic practice of sex magick, referred to earlier in this chapter, derives specifically from a transformative spiritual event that occurred during Crowley's visit to Cairo in 1904. Crowley would come to believe that the revelatory communication itself emanated from the ancient Egyptian gods, via an entity named Aiwass (or Aiwaz)[11] whom Crowley believed to be a messenger from Horus. Paradoxically Crowley's personal revelation would also come to acquire a quasi-biblical orientation for it led him to regard himself henceforth as the Beast 666 referred to in the Book of Revelation.[12] Crowley's life and career as a ceremonial magician would subsequently focus on the ongoing personal quest to find the ideal Whore of Babalon [Crowley's variant spelling][13] or Scarlet Woman, with whom to enact the philosophy of *Thelema*, or magical will. According to the doctrine of Thelema, Crowley's sex-magick encounters with his Scarlet Women (there would be many more than one!) were sacramental acts confirming Crowley's role as Lord of the New Aeon.

On 17 March 1904, Crowley performed a magical ceremony in his apartment in Cairo, invoking the Egyptian deity Thoth, god of wisdom.[14] Crowley's wife Rose appeared to be in a dazed, mediumistic state of mind and, the following day, while in a similar state of drowsiness, she announced that Horus was waiting for her husband. Crowley was not expecting such a statement from his wife but according to his diary she subsequently led him to the nearby Boulak Museum which he had not previously visited.[15] Rose pointed to a statue of Horus, or Ra-Hoor-Khuit, and Crowley was intrigued to discover that the exhibit was numbered 666, the number of the Great Beast in the Book of Revelation. Crowley regarded this as an omen. He returned to his hotel and invoked Horus:

> *Strike, strike the master chord !*
> *Draw, draw the Flaming Sword !*
> *Crowning Child and Conquering Lord,*
> *Horus, avenger!* [16]

On 20 March 1904 Crowley received a mediumistic communication through Rose stating that 'the Equinox of the Gods had come'[17] and he arranged for an assistant curator at the Boulak Museum to make notes on the inscriptions from Stele 666. Rose continued to fall into a passive, introspective state of mind and advised her husband that precisely at noon on April 8, 9 and 10 he should enter the room where the transcriptions had been made and for exactly an hour on each of these three days he should write down any impressions received. The resulting communications, allegedly dictated by a semi-invisible Egyptian entity named Aiwass—said to be a messenger of Horus—resulted in a document that Crowley later titled *Liber AL vel Legis (The Book of the Law)*.[18]

The pronouncements contained in *Liber AL vel Legis* became a turning point in Crowley's magical career. Crowley was specifically commanded by Aiwass to put aside the Kabbalistic ceremonial magic he had learnt in the Hermetic Order of the Golden Dawn and was instructed to pursue the magic of sexual partnership instead:

> *Now ye shall know that the chosen priest and apostle of infinite space is the prince-priest The Beast, and in his woman called The Scarlet Woman is all power given. They shall gather my children into their fold: they shall bring the glory of the stars into the hearts of men. For he is ever a sun and she a moon...*[19]

Crowley would soon come to believe that his magical destiny was inextricably connected to the Horus figure Ra-Hoor-Khuit whose statue he had seen in the Boulak Museum. In Egyptian mythology the deities Nuit (female-the circle-passive) and Hadit (male-the point-active) were said to have produced a divine child, Ra-Hoor-Khuit, through their sacred union. According to Crowley this combination of the principles of love and will brought into incarnation the 'magical equation known as the Law of Thelema'.[20] *Thelema* is the Greek word for 'will' and the principal magical dictum contained in *Liber AL vel Legis* is 'Do what thou wilt shall be the whole of the Law.' The concluding instruction in *Liber AL vel Legis* reads as follows: 'There is no law beyond Do what thou wilt. Love is the law, love under will.'[21]

Crowley's notion of the will, or Will—he usually capitalized it to denote its special significance—is central to his magical philosophy. Crowley understood that one should live according to the dictates of one's true Will because 'A man who is doing his True Will has ...the Universe to assist him.'[22] An individual's True Will is that person's authentic spiritual purpose and it also confers a sense of identity. 'The first principle of success in evolution,' wrote Crowley in *Magick in Theory and Practice*, 'is that the individual should be true to his own nature...'[23]

Crowley believed that in terms of his own individual spiritual purpose, his unique personal destiny had been made manifestly clear by the communications received from Aiwass in *Liber AL vel Legis*. As Crowley's magical disciple Kenneth Grant (1924-2011) has written, from a Thelemic perspective the revelations in Cairo in 1904 represented nothing less than the birth of a new Aeon in the history of humanity's spiritual evolution:

> *According to Crowley the true magical revival occurred in 1904, when an occult current of cosmic magnitude was initiated on the inner planes. Its focus was Aiwaz and it was transmitted through Crowley to the human plane... The initiation of this occult current created a vortex, the birth-pangs of a New Aeon, technically called an Equinox of the Gods. Such an event recurs at intervals of approximately 2000 years. Each such revival of magical power establishes a further link in the chain of humanity's evolution, which is but one phase only of the evolution of Consciousness.*[24]

In cosmological terms, Crowley believed he had now been recognised by the transcendent powers of the ancient Egyptian pantheon as the 'divine child' brought into being through the sacred union of Nuit and Hadit. There could be no doubting the importance of this event and its dramatic outcome. In *Liber AL vel Legis* we read 'Ra-Hoor-Khuit hath taken his seat in the East at the Equinox of the Gods.'[25] Previously, according to Crowley, there had been two other Aeons: one associated with the Moon and the other with the Sun. The first of these, the Aeon of Isis, was a matriarchal age characterised by the worship of lunar deities, the second epoch, the Aeon of Osiris, a patriarchal age associated with incarnating demi-gods or divine kings. John Symonds, Crowley's literary executor, describes this historical process in his introduction to Crowley's *Confessions*:

> *The cosmology of The Book of the Law is explained by Crowley thus: there have been, as far as we know, two aeons in the history of the world. The first, that of Isis, is the aeon of the woman; hence matriarchy, the worship of the Great Mother and so on. About 500 B.C. this aeon was succeeded by the aeon of Osiris, that is the aeon of the man, the father, hence the paternal religions of suffering and death—Judaism, Buddhism, Christianity and Mohammedanism. This aeon came to an end in 1904 when Aleister Crowley received The Book of the Law, and the new aeon, that of Horus, the child, was born. In this*

aeon the emphasis is on the true self or will, not on anything external such as gods or priests...[26]

There can be no doubting the position of *Liber AL vel Legis* with regard to the religious traditions that preceded the 1904 revelation. 'With my Hawk's head,' proclaims Ra-Hoor-Khuit (ie. Horus) in stanzas III: 51-54:

I peck at the eyes of Jesus as he hangs upon the Cross. I flap my wings in the face of Mohammed and blind him. With my claws I tear out the flesh of the Indian and the Buddhist, Mongol and Din. Bahlasti! Ompedha! I spit on your crapulous creeds.[27]

Quite apart from the iconoclastic tone adopted by *Liber AL vel Legis* in dismissing earlier religious traditions like Christianity, Buddhism and Islam, the sexual implications of the revelation were also made clear. The received doctrine of the Aeon of Horus would now supersede Christianity and all the other outmoded religions that had constructed barriers to spiritual freedom, and the way this would be achieved was through the power of sexuality. *Liber AL vel Legis* summons the Scarlet Woman to 'raise herself in pride!' and calls for uninhibited sexual freedom:

Let her work the work of wickedness! Let her kill her heart! Let her be loud and adulterous; let her be covered with jewels, and rich garments, and let her be shameless before all men. Then will I lift her to the pinnacles of power: then will I breed from her a child mightier than all the kings of the earth. I will fill her with joy...[28]

As Kenneth Grant has explained, with reference to *Liber AL vel Legis* and its call for sexual freedom, Crowley came to believe that the so-called Great Work—sacred union, or the attainment of Absolute Consciousness—would be achieved through the sexual union of the Great Beast with the Whore of Babalon: 'The Beast, as the embodiment of the Logos (which is Thelema, Will) symbolically and actually incarnates his Word each time a sacramental act of sexual congress occurs, ie. each time love is made under Will.'[29] A review of Crowley's subsequent career shows that he would spend much of his life from this time onwards seeking lovers and concubines who could act as his Divine Whore. While he would be frustrated in his numerous attempts to find a suitable and enduring partner, there were many who filled the role temporarily.[30]

In relation to the practice of sex magic, quite apart from defining Crowley's spiritual destiny as the High Priest of Thelema, *Liber AL vel*

Legis also contained instructions relating to ceremonial offerings associated with sacramental sex magic, specifically the preparation of what later came to be known as 'cakes of light'. Preparation of this ritual offering as specified by Ra-Hoor-Khuit, is outlined in III: 23-25 of *Liber AL vel Legis*:

> *For perfume mix meal and honey and thick leavings of red wine: then oil of Abramelin and olive oil, and afterward soften and smooth down with rich fresh blood. The best blood is of the moon, monthly: then the fresh blood of a child, or dropping from the host of heaven: then of enemies; then of the priest or of the worshippers; last of some beast, no matter what. This burn: of this make cakes and eat unto me.*[31]

As one of Crowley's most recent biographers, Lawrence Sutin, has noted:

> *There is no evidence that Crowley ever used the fresh blood of a child or an enemy in preparing the cakes. Indeed, in his comment on this verse, written during the period, Crowley was careful to specify that the 'child' was 'Babalon and the Beast conjoined'—that is, the elixir of sexual magic.*[32]

The magical elixir itself consisted of the 'ingredients' of sexual congress itself: semen from the male, gluten from the woman's vagina, and preferably fresh menstrual blood, as specified in stanza 24 of Book III of *Liber AL vel Legis*. These ingredients were included in the preparation of the 'cakes of light' which were then consumed by participants as a ritual offering to Ra-Hoor-Khuit.

It is clear that Crowley placed great emphasis on the magical elixir because it is later referred to as 'the germ of life'[33] in *The Book of the Unveiling of Sangraal* which was part of the 'Secret Instruction of the Ninth Degree' in the Ordo Templi Orientis—a European sex magic organisation which Crowley was able to gradually transform into a Thelemite order after joining it in 1910 (see below).[34] In the Ninth degree of the Ordo Templi Orientis, which employs veiled sexual references, the candidate is instructed as follows:

> *Now then, entering the privy chapel [the vagina], do thou bestow at least one hour in adoration at the altar, exalting thyself in love toward God, and extolling Him in strophe and antistrophe [sexual lovemaking]. Then do thou perform the Sacrifice of the*

> Mass [ejaculation of semen]. The Elixir [a mixture of semen and female sexual secretions] being then prepared solemnly and in silence, do thou consume it utterly.[35]

The ritual consumption of a sexual magical elixir was not part of the magical teachings of the Hermetic Order of the Golden Dawn, which tended to downplay any references to sexual symbolism in its rituals,[36] and since Crowley had established his own unique connection with Aiwass and Ra-Hoor Khuit in 1904 he had little need for an ongoing relationship with the Golden Dawn after his revelation in Cairo. In deciding to enact the magical procedures dictated by Liber AL vel Legis Crowley had, in any case, already laid the foundation for a quite different sort of magical practice based not on advancing through the sephiroth of the Kabbalistic Tree of Life but instead on utilising the magical energies of sexuality.

The Argenteum Astrum and Victor Neuburg

In 1907 Crowley established his own magical order, the Argenteum Astrum, or Silver Star.[37] Two years later he commenced production of a semi-annual periodical titled *The Equinox*, as its official publishing arm. Some of the early issues of *The Equinox* contained Crowley's first writings on sex magic rituals.[38] In these writings Crowley identified three types of sexual activity—autoerotic, heterosexual and homosexual—as a way of raising magical energy and he also formulated the notion that sex magic rituals could be dedicated to achieving specific results like financial gain, attaining personal creative success, etc. His central idea was that sex magic could enable the practitioner to focus on a specific goal or outcome. The magician would dedicate the sexual activity to the goal of the magical ritual and would hold the image of that goal in his mind at the moment of sexual climax: at that very moment the energy raised during the ritual would be directed to the goal by the magical will. In this way the sex magic practitioner would be able to 'wed the image and the magical power'.[39]

Initially the Argenteum Astrum drew primarily on borrowed sources from the Hermetic Order of the Golden Dawn. Crowley had begun rewriting MacGregor Mathers' Kabbalistic rituals, employing an amended form of the Golden Dawn grades as well as including some yogic and oriental material of his own. He also published the secret rituals of Mathers' Second Order, the Red Rose and Cross of Gold, in *The Equinox*.[40] Interestingly, although Crowley had made a commitment to the sex magic proclaimed in *Liber AL vel Legis*, he did not initially include it within the grades of his new magical order.[41] Nevertheless the Argenteum Astrum would gradually develop as a vehicle for Crowley's increasingly explicit bisexuality, thereby complicating the apparently clear sex-role distinction between the Beast and the Scarlet Woman delineated in *Liber AL vel Legis*.[42]

One of the early members of the Argenteum Astrum was Victor Neuburg (1883-1940), a young poet who, like Crowley, had studied at Trinity College, Cambridge. Crowley heard about Neuburg from another A.A. member, Captain J.F.C. Fuller, and invited him to his magical retreat in Boleskine, Scotland. Crowley quickly recognised in Neuburg a kindred spirit, and they would soon enter into a homosexual magic liaison tinged with sado-masochistic tendencies, which would last until 1914.[43]

Following a painful divorce from his wife Rose in 1909, Crowley went with Neuburg to Algeria where they intended exploring the Enochian magic of the sixteenth century Elizabethan occultists Dr John Dee and Edward Kelley.[44] This process involved the magical evocation of thirty so-called 'Aethyrs' or 'Aires'—a group of metaphysical spirit-entities that included Choronzon, the demon of Chaos. Deep in the Algerian desert— at such locations as Aumale, Ain El Hajel, Bou-Saada, Benshrur, Tolga and Biskra—Crowley summoned the different Aethyrs in turn. Crowley was carrying with him a large golden topaz set in a wooden rose-cross decorated with ritual symbols. Choosing a place of solitude, Crowley would recite the required Enochian conjuration and then use his topaz as a focusing glass to concentrate his attention on the visionary landscape as it unfolded before his gaze. As a result of his Enochian 'calls' Crowley had a number of visionary experiences which were then transcribed by Neuburg as they took place.[45]

While in the Algerian desert, Crowley and Neuburg also engaged in an act of ritual sex magic. Crowley writes in his Confessions that on one occasion they climbed a mountain named Da'leh Addin and felt an intuitive command to perform a magical ceremony on the summit:

> *We accordingly took loose rocks and built a great circle, inscribed with the words of power; and in the midst we erected an altar and there I sacrificed myself [submitted to anal sex]. The fire of the all-seeing sun [Neuburg's penis] smote down upon the altar, consuming every particle of my personality. I am obliged to write in hieroglyph of this matter, because it concerns things of which it is unlawful to speak openly under penalty of the most dreadful punishment.*[46]

After Crowley returned to England the Argenteum Astrum began to grow modestly, building on its core membership which included Captain

J.F.C. Fuller and Crowley's Golden Dawn teacher George Cecil Jones. The Argenteum Astrum would in due course initiate around a hundred of Crowley's followers, among them Neuburg's friend and fellow poet Pamela Hansford Johnson, Australian violinist Leila Waddell, mathematics lecturer Norman Mudd from Bloemfontein, and the visionary English artist Austin Osman Spare.[47]

Events took a strange turn in London in May 1912 when Crowley was contacted one evening at his Fulham flat by a man named Theodor Reuss. Reuss identified himself as Brother Merlin, head of the German branch of the Ordo Templi Orientis. Crowley would already have been familiar with the O.T.O. because according to occult historian Francis King he had been admitted to its lower grades a year earlier.[48] What surprised the British occultist was Reuss's claim that Crowley had published a statement which revealed the most prized secret of the Order's ninth degree — the sacrament of sex magic.[49] Crowley was initially perplexed by Reuss's accusation and wondered which publication he was referring to. Reuss then reached across to Crowley's bookshelf and pulled down a copy of his recently published work *The Book of Lies*, a collection of magical commentaries and reflections. The offending lines were contained in Chapter XXXVI titled 'The Star Sapphire' which begins with the words: 'Let the Adept be armed with his Magick Rood and provided with his Mystic Rose.'[50] Further on Crowley's text reads as follows: 'Let him drink of the Sacrament and let him communicate the same.'[51]

Crowley pointed out to Reuss that he had not yet been admitted to the ninth degree of the O.T.O, so he was not in a position to reveal its secrets. In 'The Star Sapphire' Crowley had used the Old English word *rood* to mean a cross, and Reuss had assumed that he was referring to the phallus. Reuss had also assumed that the Mystic Rose was a reference to the vagina.[52] Then there was the issue of what 'drinking the Sacrament' could actually be referring to. As they were speaking Crowley realised intuitively that sexual intercourse between priest and priestess must be a culminating event in the ritual of the O.T.O's ninth degree, and he now engaged Reuss in a discussion about sex magic which lasted for several hours. The outcome was that Crowley would in due course become the head of a new magical order to be called the Mysteria Mystica Maxima, effectively an English subsidiary of the German Ordo Templi Orientis.[53] Much later, in 1922—following Reuss's retirement—Crowley would replace Reuss as the head of the O.T.O. itself, a position he held until his death in 1947.[54]

The rise of the Ordo Templi Orientis

Although the practice of sex magic was central to Aleister Crowley's doctrine of *Thelema* it did not originate with him. In recent times the rise of the O.T.O and the history of sex magic as a branch of Western esotericism have been documented by a small group of specialist academic scholars, among them Peter. R. Koenig in Switzerland, Hugh B. Urban, Joscelyn Godwin, John Deveney and J. Gordon Melton in the United States, and Henrik Bogdan in Sweden.

From a historical perspective it is clear that the two key figures in the early development of the O.T.O in Europe were Carl Kellner and Crowley's German O.T.O. contact, Theodor Reuss. Kellner (1851-1905) was a wealthy Austrian chemist and industrialist and also a Freemason — he was a member of the Humanitas Lodge, established in Neuhäusl, Austria, in 1871 under the constitution of the Grand Lodge of Hungary.[55] Reuss (1855-1923) was an Anglo-German Freemason who specialized in buying and selling Masonic charters, even though he was not recognised by any authentic Lodges in Craft Masonry. According to Koenig, Reuss invented an organization known as the 'Order of the Illuminati' as well as several Rosicrucian societies.[56] While it is evident that Kellner was a businessman and inventor of considerable integrity, Reuss's reputation was more dubious and some historians consider him a swindler.[57] Nevertheless it was through their joint efforts that the organization known as the Ordo Templi Orientis (O.T.O.) would eventually emerge.

Around 1895 Kellner had the idea of forming a private group which could explore various 'Tantric' exercises within a Hatha Yoga circle.[58] Kellner had a long-standing interest in both the Western esoteric tradition and also Eastern mysticism. According to Urban, Kellner is said to have studied with three Eastern masters — a Sufi and two Hindu Tantrikers — and was also in touch with an American esoteric order known as the Hermetic Brotherhood of Light (an offshoot of the Hermetic Brotherhood of Luxor),[59] which in turn drew on the sex magic ideas of the influential American occultist Paschal Beverly Randolph (see below).[60] Kellner and Reuss had in mind that they would form a new esoteric order that would fuse Craft Masonry, Rosicrucianism and Hindu Tantra.[61] Urban maintains that at the time Kellner was one of the few Western figures with a detailed knowledge of Yoga and that he regarded 'white sexual magic' as a source of godlike power. Kellner performed Tantric rites with his wife and a small group of disciples in order to produce the so-called 'divine Elixir' — an amalgam of male and female sexual fluids.[62]

Like Kellner, Reuss was also interested in phallic cults and Tantra and would later produce a treatise on sexual worship titled *Lingam-Yoni*.[63] He believed that sexual congress mirrored the cosmic act of creation and that the *lingam*, or phallus, was a key symbol of the creator of the universe.[64] Urban argues that it was Reuss who incorporated sexual magic into the upper grades of the O.T.O.[65] Unfortunately Kellner did not live to see the actual establishment of the new esoteric organisation. He became terminally ill in 1904 and died the following year. Reuss was forced to act on his own, recruiting a range of 'Oriental Freemasons' for the new Order and eventually naming it the 'Order of Oriental Templars' [Ordo Templi Orientis].[66] With the assistance of Franz Hartmann and Heinrich Klein, Reuss prepared a constitution for the O.T.O. in 1906.[67]

Koenig maintains that Reuss never intended that the O.T.O should become a vehicle for Crowley's doctrine of Thelema.[68] However, Reuss was sufficiently impressed by Crowley's ideas that he translated the latter's sex-magick ritual, the *Gnostic Mass* (composed 1913), into German and had it recited at a special O.T.O congress at Monte Verità.[69] Reuss also announced at the same congress that he was translating Crowley's *Book of the Law* into German. Crowley reciprocated the gesture by publishing several major O.T.O. documents in *The Equinox*, among them *Liber LII: the Manifesto of the O.T.O.*[70]

In his *Confessions*, Crowley states that Reuss 'resigned the office [of the Outer Head of the Order] in 1922 in my favour' although even in the official O.T.O History it is conceded that that no evidence or letter from Reuss has ever been found confirming this claim.[71] Nevertheless, Crowley succeeded Reuss as O.H.O.(Outer Head of the Order) in 1922 and would hold this position until his death in 1947.

Under Crowley, the O.T.O.'s original nine degrees were expanded to eleven. The eighth, ninth and eleventh degrees focused on non-reproductive sexual acts including masturbation, the consumption of sexual fluids (referred to above as the 'magical elixir'), and homosexual intercourse.[72] Koenig notes that other elements of Crowleyan sex magic, in addition to the ritual consumption of semen and vaginal fluids, were incorporated into the rites of the O.T.O. at this time. They included various forms of sexual visualisation and the act of masturbating on magical sigils:

> *Crowley's VIIIth degree unveiled...that masturbating on a sigil of a demon or meditating upon the image of a phallus would bring power or communication with a [or one's own] divine being... The IXth degree was labelled heterosexual intercourse where the sexual secrets were sucked out of the vagina and when not consumed...put on a sigil to attract this or that demon to fulfil the pertinent wish... In the XIth degree, the mostly homosexual degree, one identifies oneself with an ejaculating penis. The blood (or excrements) from anal intercourse attract*

the spirits/demons while the sperm keeps them alive.[73]

Crowley's writings on sex magic

Crowley produced several short texts on sex magic, some of which are written in veiled symbolic language. These texts include *De Arte Magica* (written in 1914 and also translated and published in Reuss's German-language O.T.O. magazine, *Oriflamme*, in the same year); *Liber Agape*; *Energized Enthusiasm: a Note on Theurgy*, and the notorious, but blandly titled *Emblems and Modes of Use*. Crowley's *Gnostic Mass* and the *Mass of the Phoenix* also contain sex magic references. Despite their often discursive language and veiled symbolism these texts provide intriguing insights into Crowley's philosophy and practice of sex magic.

De Arte Magica was intended as a document for IX° O.T.O candidates. After reminding the reader that 'the Phallus is the physiological basis of the Oversoul'[74]—a statement with which Reuss would surely have agreed—Crowley goes on to describe sex magic methods drawn from both the Jewish Kabbalah and the Hindu spiritual tradition. With regard to the former, Crowley states that 'in the semen itself...lies a creative life which cannot be baulked'. According to Jewish teachings, says Crowley, conjugal love should be a holy act, preceded by ablutions and prayer: 'All lustful thoughts must be rigidly excluded, the purpose must be solely that of procreation [and] the blessing of God must be most earnestly invoked.'[75] However Crowley was also interested in the magical consequences of other types of sexual act:

> All other sexual acts involving emission of semen...attract other spirits, incomplete and therefore evil...nocturnal pollutions bring succubi, which are capable of separate existence and of vampirising their creator. But voluntary sterile acts create demons, and (if done with concentration and magical intention) such demons...may subserve that intention.[76]

Crowley also makes reference to the Hindu concept that *prana* or life-force 'resides in the *Bindu*, or semen'. Certain yogic practitioners, writes Crowley, are able to

> stimulate to the maximum its [ie. sperm's] generation, and at the same time vigorously withhold by will. After some little exercise they claim that they can deflower as many as eighty virgins in a night without losing a single drop of the Bindu. Nor is this ever to be lost, but reabsorbed through the tissues of the body. The organs thus act as a siphon to draw constantly

> *fresh supplies of life from the cosmic reservoir, and flood the body with their fructifying virtue ... in the semen itself exists a physical force which can be turned to [the] magical or mystical ends of the Adept.* [77]

Here we have a clear expression of the concept that the individual human will can harness the life-force in semen and direct it to a specific magical purpose. Writings like *Liber Agape* and *Energized Enthusiasm: a Note on Theurgy*, on the other hand, are much more obscure: they contain veiled symbolism and require more detailed scrutiny. *Liber Agape* is also known as *The Book of the Unveiling of the Sangraal* and was intended as 'a secret instruction of the Ninth degree' in the O.T.O.[78]

Liber Agape begins with a prayer, a salutation to Baphomet[79] and a statement inferring that the Ninth degree of the O.T.O. will reveal occult secrets hitherto associated with the Knights of the Temple (Knights Templar) and the 'Brethren of the Rose Crosse'. The rite itself is described as a 'High Mass to be celebrated in the Temple of the Holy Ghost'. Crowley also employs alchemical imagery in his text, making reference to the 'Medicine of Metals', 'the Philosopher's Stone', 'Tinctures White and Red' and 'the Elixir of Life'. The latter are clearly intended as sexual images. As mentioned earlier, the Elixir of Life refers to the sexual fluids produced and co-mingled in the vagina through sexual intercourse. The white tincture is also described elsewhere in Crowley's sex magic writings as the 'Gluten of the White Eagle'[80] and is a reference to the sexual fluids (and sometimes also the menstrual blood) of the female participant in sex magic. The red tincture is the 'Blood of the Red Lion', a reference to the semen generated by the male participant (Crowley often linked blood symbolically with semen).[81]

Interestingly, *Liber Agape* incorporates within its structure the text of *The Star Sapphire* (previously published as Chapter 36 of *The Book of Lies*)—the short work which Theodor Reuss believed betrayed the innermost secret of the Ninth degree of the O.T.O. We are fortunate that a commentary on *The Star Sapphire* has recently been made available by American ceremonial magician Frater Osiris, a former member of the O.T.O., who was privy to the inner-Order *Thelemic* interpretation of the text.[82]

While it is clear at the outset that *The Star Sapphire* is intended as a sex-magic tract, and it comes as no surprise that the *Magick Rood* is the phallus, and the *Mystic Rose* is the vagina, it is perhaps less obvious that the reference to 'make the Holy Hexagram' is an instruction that the man and woman should interlock their heads and bodies in a mutual oral sex position to form the shape of a hexagram.[83] Crowley provides a clue in the aptly numbered Chapter 69 of *The Book of Lies* where he refers to the Holy Hexagram and the 'Double Gift of Tongues'.[84] Frater Osiris explains that 'Making the Rosy Cross' is also a reference to sexual intercourse and the participants should utter the magical exclamation *'Ararita'* three times at the moment of orgasm. The instruction 'Let him drink of the Sacrament and let him communicate the same' is an instruction that the 'sacrament'—the 'elixir' or fluids arising from sexual intercourse—should be consumed by both participants, each providing this elixir to the other. As Frater Osiris notes, 'It is suggested elsewhere in Crowley's writings that the Sacrament be dissolved and absorbed in the mouth to obtain the fullest effect.'[85]

Energized Enthusiasm: a Note on Theurgy (Liber DCCCLX)—a work dedicated to 'IAO, the supreme One of the Gnostics, the true God'[86]—is one of Crowley's most interesting writings on sex magic, combining didactic content with a seemingly autobiographical, yet highly symbolic, narrative written in the first person. Crowley begins by introducing the reader to the idea that divine consciousness is 'reflected and refracted' in works of Genius [capitalised in Crowley's text] and in turn feeds on 'a certain secretion... analogous to semen, but not identical to it.'[87] Later Crowley claims that he can always trace a connection between his sexual state and 'the condition of [his] artistic creation' and that what he calls 'energized enthusiasm' is 'the lever that moves God'.[88] In other words, there is a technique of ecstasy, heightened by sexuality, which is directly related to artistic creativity and Genius, and this is a technique that subjects God to the artistic intent and human will. We encounter a similar concept in the artistic and magical trance-method of Austin Osman Spare, described elsewhere in this volume. Spare was briefly a member of Crowley's O.T.O. *circa* 1910 but seems to have formulated his ideas independently. Both men believed that they could use the transcendent power of the sexual orgasm to subject the visionary universe to their own individual will in order to bring about a desired result—artistic or otherwise. In *Energized Enthusiasm* Crowley writes quite specifically that through 'the sacramental and ceremonial use of the sexual act, the divine consciousness may be attained'.[89]

Later in the same work (which consists of sixteen short chapters) Crowley describes a sex-magick ceremony of the Rose Croix. The ceremony—which is presented in Crowley's text as taking place in a mystical vision—is a High Mass and is conducted in a private chapel. The altar is covered by a cloth which displays the symbols of the Rose and Cross, and at the entrance of the chapel stand a young man and woman 'dressed in simple robes of white silk embroidered with gold, red and blue'. The High Priest presiding over the ceremony is a man of about sixty, with a white beard, and he is accompanied by a High Priestess. Both wear richly ornamented robes, have a 'stately' presence, and embrace each other. Knights and Dames make up the congregation. The chapel is consecrated, the litany begins, and the High Priest takes from the altar a flask which resembles a phallus—an indication that the ceremony about to be performed has a sexual orientation. The High Priestess then kneels and presents a boat-shaped cup of gold (the cup, as a receptive vessel, being traditionally perceived in the Western esoteric tradition as a 'female' symbol, especially in the sexual sense). The High Priest's flask contains wine that looks like fire but which is cool to drink. Crowley somehow receives this as a sacrament—he is an onlooker at the ceremony and feels he is experiencing this sacred rite while in a mystical out-of-the-body state.[90] Crowley writes that he 'trembles' as he consumes this sacred drink, as do other members of the congregation— for the ritual is charged with sacred meaning. In due course the celebrants move down the chapel aisle and the Knights and Dames rise up and give the secret sign of the Rose Croix. The High Priestess discards her robe, stands naked before the congregation, and begins to sing: 'Io Paian! Io Pan!'... A sacred mist now rises up around the participants, heightening the sense of mystery as organ music wafts through the chapel, and the High Priest joins his partner at the altar of the Rose Croix where they both lie down. The celebrants, meanwhile, stretch forth their arms in the shape of a cross...

Presumably the 'Great Rite' is about to be performed by the High Priest and High Priestess—Crowley does not provide us with the details of what happens next. However, given (as Frater Osiris has already explained above) that in the O.T.O. 'Making the Rosy Cross' is a reference to ritual sexual intercourse, it would seem that Crowley's High Mass of the Rose Croix is analogous to the mystic marriage of the alchemical King Sol and Queen Luna who consummate their sacred union and thereby create the 'Elixir of Life'.[91]

Crowley's Thelemic sex-magick ritual, the *Gnostic Mass* (*Liber XV, Ecclesiae Gnosticae Catholicae Canon Missae*), composed in 1913, is linked thematically to *Energized Enthusiasm* and was written around the same time.[92] The *Gnostic Mass*—Crowley's *Thelemic* (and perhaps also blasphemous) response to the Roman Catholic Eucharist—employs specific sexual motifs and draws on the theme of transubstantiation. Although other minor characters play a part, the Mass focuses on two central figures, the Priest, who bears the Sacred Lance (a symbol of the phallus) and the Priestess, who in this ritual context is deemed to be 'Virgo Intacta' and is identified symbolically with the Holy Graal (the sacred Cup). During the 'Consecration of the Elements', the Priest gives a blessing and oversees the transubstantiation of the 'cakes of light' ('By the virtue of the Rod / Be this bread the Body of God!') and wine ('By the virtue of the Rod / Be this wine the Blood of God'), and during the 'Mystic Marriage and Consummation' the Priest and Priestess jointly lower the Sacred Lance into Cup in a symbolic expression of sexual union.[93] All congregants then partake of the consecrated 'cakes of light' which contain the sexual elixir and which are said to embody 'the essence of the life of the Sun'.[94]

The Mass of the Phoenix (Liber XLIV), by way of contrast, is a simplified form of the Eucharist intended for daily life by the practising Thelemic magician.[95] Despite its simpler form Crowley nevertheless considered it to be just as significant as the *Gnostic Mass*.[96] *The Mass of the Phoenix* derives its name from the mythical phoenix, an alchemical symbol of transmutation and resurrection. The phoenix was said to feed its young on blood drawn from its own breast. First published as Chapter 44 of *The Book of Lies* (1912), the Mass is performed only at sunset and is undertaken as a solitary ceremonial activity. At the climax of the ritual the magician makes the Mark of the Beast[97] on his (or her) breast, either drawing blood directly with a burin (a small sharp knife) or by cutting a finger and inscribing the sign in blood. A cake of light is used to staunch the blood and is then ritually consumed.[98]

Crowley's most controversial work on sex magic, however, is a short four-page article titled *Emblems and Modes of Use*, which was intended as a 'secret' text for the Ninth degree of the O.T.O.[99] Once again, Crowley utilises alchemical imagery, writing that the 'Egg' (Emblem 1) is borne by the 'menstruum [that] the Alchemists call the Gluten [capitals in Crowley's text]. The Egg will be fertilized by the 'Serpent' (Emblem 2). Crowley says that the Serpent is 'the principle of immortality, the self renewal through incarnation, of persistent will, inherent in the "Red Lion" *who is, of course, the operator*' [My italics—Crowley generally presents his magickal texts from the viewpoint of the male practitioner, even when a woman is involved].[100] Crowley writes that 'both Lion and Eagle must be robust, in good health...overflowing with energy, magnetically attracted to one another, and in absolute understanding [and] harmony about the object of the operation'.[101]

According to Crowley the sex magick operation has to be sufficiently intense that it creates a state of 'Black-Out' where 'the Ego-consciousness itself is abolished'.[102] At this stage, notes Crowley,

> the Will should still continue to create, stopping only when 'the blood of the Red Lion' [ie. semen] is one with the 'Gluten of the White Eagle' and the 'Serpent' and the 'Egg' have fused

completely. *The result of this fusion is called the Elixir—and numerous other names, eg. The Stone of the Philosophers, the Medicine of the Metals etc., especially the Quintessence.*[103]

It would seem from this statement that Crowley believes the symbolism of medieval Alchemy—a key branch of the Western esoteric tradition—should be interpreted primarily in sexual terms. For him the elixir itself has innate magical potency. From a purely pragmatic point of view, it can be used to achieve specific magical outcomes and therefore becomes useful in the practice of sorcery:

The Lion must collect it—the best method is by suction [ie., sucking it out of his partner's vagina] so as to avoid waste, and share it with the Eagle. It should be absorbed by the mucous membrane [ie through the upper palate of the mouth, rather than swallowed]. A portion is reserved and placed in physical contact with the magickal link, or with a talisman specially prepared for the Operation, and consecrated accordingly. At the very least, some suitable symbol, eg. if you are making an opus for $$ smear the Elixir on a gold coin, or ring; if for health, touch the bare earth, or the patient with it. In any case, be careful to consume it by absorption for it restores with interest any virtue that may have been expended in the work itself.[104]

This is not the only occasion where Crowley refers to the idea of the elixir, or semen, being used to achieve specific magical outcomes. In another short text, *Liber A'Aash vel Capricorni Pneumatici* (Liber CCCLXX)—which is recognised as a major (Class A) sex magic document by members of the O.T.O.[105]—Crowley makes a veiled reference to masturbating on demonic sigils by using the magical utterance as a metaphor for ejaculation:

Let him sit and conjure; let him draw back the hood from his head and fix his basilisk eye upon the sigil of the demon. Then let him sway the force of him to and fro like a satyr in silence, until the Word burst from his throat… that which floodeth him is the infinite mercy of the Genitor-Genitrix of the Universe, whereof he is the Vessel.[106]

Sex Magic and 'Spermo-Gnosis' prior to the O.T.O.

As mentioned above, within the context of the Western esoteric tradition the practice of sex magic precedes both Carl Kellner and Theodor

Reuss and the establishment of the O.T.O. Several scholars, among them Hugh B. Urban (2006), John Deveney (1997), Joscelyn Godwin (1995) and J. Gordon Melton (1985), have drawn attention to the unique contribution made by the influential American occultist Paschal Beverly Randolph (1825-75). Randolph is significant because, as Melton puts it: 'Like Crowley, Randolph discovered the essential aspect of sex magick by suddenly combining long-term interests in sexuality and the occult.'[107] The bridging link between Randolph and the O.T.O. is provided by two American esoteric orders, the Hermetic Brotherhood of Luxor, and Randolph's Brotherhood of Eulis.

Born in New York in 1825, Paschal Beverly Randolph was the son of a wealthy Virginian named William Randolph, and a slave woman named Flora Beverly who was of mixed East Indian, European and Madagascan descent. Flora raised her son by herself in a 'gloomy old stone house on Manhattan Island'.[108] However when Randolph was five, his mother died during an epidemic and he was placed in an orphanage. Essentially growing up on his own, Randolph taught himself to read and write by copying letters from printed posters and billboards.[109] Classified as a 'free man of colour', he trained as a natural physician and also studied spiritualism and Franz Anton Mesmer's theory of 'animal magnetism', a precursor of modern hypnosis.[110] Randolph worked for the Abolitionist cause before the Civil War and helped raise money for the Black Militias of Louisiana. He also gained a reputation as a trance speaker and spiritualist medium.[111] During the late 1840s he travelled widely in Europe, visiting England, Scotland, Ireland, France and Malta as well as also visiting Egypt, Turkey and Palestine.[112] Intent on seeking out the sources of esoteric wisdom wherever he could find them, Randolph maintained that he received many high initiations while he was in Europe. During his travels he met the famous French Kabbalist and magician, Eliphas Lévi, whose writings and occult ideas would later greatly influence the Hermetic Order of the Golden Dawn (see Chapter 8). He also met the notable Rosicrucian occultists Kenneth R.H. Mackenzie and Edward Bulwer-Lytton[113] and the eccentric cleric and Rosicrucian historian Hargrave Jennings (1817-1890), who was interested in ancient phallic worship.[114] After returning to the United States, Randolph founded the Fraternitas Rosae Crucis in 1858, the oldest Rosicrucian organization in North America (currently headquartered in Beverly Hall, Quakertown, Pennsylvania).[115] In 1861, after returning to Europe, Randolph was initiated into the Order of the Rose, a group headed by Hargrave Jennings. He then travelled on to Syria where he was inducted as a Hierarch of the Ansaireh before returning to the United States in 1863.[116]

Randolph explored clairvoyant scrying[117] with magic mirrors and also wrote a treatise on the use of hashish as an aid to trance possession (1860). However he became a controversial figure largely because of his ideas on occult sexuality, expressed publicly at a time when such issues were largely a taboo subject. Randolph's Rosicrucian activities were interrupted during the Civil War period but in 1870 he re-established his Rosicrucian organisation in Boston, calling it the Brotherhood of Eulis and using it as a vehicle to explore sex magic.[118] Three years later Randolph published one of his best-known and most controversial books, *Eulis! The History of Love: Its Wondrous Magic, Chemistry, Rules, Laws, Modes, Moods and Rationale, Being the Third Revelation of Soul and Sex*.[119]

In *Eulis!*—which derives its title ultimately from the Greek *eos*, meaning 'the dawn, the gate of light'[120]—Randolph provides an account of how he was first initiated into the mysteries of sex magic while travelling in the Middle East:

> *One night—it was in far-off Jerusalem or Bethlehem, I really forget which—I made love to... a dusky maiden of Arabic blood. I of her and that experience learned... the fundamental principle of the White Magic of Love; subsequently I became affiliated with some dervishes and fakirs by whom... I found the road to other knowledges... I am became practically... a mystic and in time chief of the lofty brethren... discovering the ELIXIR OF LIFE, the universal Solvent... and the philosopher's stone.*[121]

Basing his ideas substantially on the ritual sex practices of the Islamic Nusairi sect in Syria, Randolph came to believe that the sexual instinct was a fundamental force in the cosmos. Randolph maintained that 'the pellucid aroma of divinity' suffuses the sex act[122] but he also believed that sexual union could become a metaphysical and sacred ritual *only* between married loving couples and *only* when it resulted in full and complete orgasms for both partners.[123] Many years before Crowley and Austin Spare, Randolph proposed that the sexual orgasm could be used to gain practical and tangible outcomes, that is to say, *subject to willed intent, the power of sexuality could be harnessed to produce specific magical results*:[124]

> *It follows that as are the people at that moment [orgasm] so will be that which enters into them from the regions above, beneath, and round about; wherefore, whatsoever male or female shall truly will for, hopefully pray for, and earnestly*

yearn for, when love, pure and holy, is in the nuptive ascendent, in form, passional, affectional, divine and volitional, that prayer will be granted, and the boon given. But the prayer must precede [the moment of orgasm]. [125]

In another text, *The Ansairetic Mystery: A New Revelation Concerning Sex!* (*circa* 1873-74), which was circulated privately to his Rosicrucian followers, Randolph lists over a hundred outcomes that he believed could be achieved or resolved through this type of sex magic. They include topics and issues relating to money matters, marital discord, prolonging life, eliminating disease and charging amulets with life-force.[126] Randolph was unstinting in proclaiming the potency of sexuality but warned that it could lead to both highs and lows in the quest for spiritual awakening:

The ejective moment...is the most divine and tremendously important one in the human career as an independent entity, for not only may we launch Genius, Power, Beauty, Deformity, Crime, Idiocy, Shame or Glory on the world's great sea of Life, in the person of the children we may then produce, but we may plunge our own souls neck-deep in Hell's horrid slime, or else mount the Azure as coequal associate Gods; for then the mystic Soul swings wide its Golden gates, opens its portals to the whole vast Universe and through them come trooping either Angels of Light or the Grizzly Presence from the dark corners of the Spaces. Therefore, human copulation is either ascentive and ennobling, or descensive and degrading...'[127]

Superficially, Randolph's theories of sex magic and tangible outcomes seem to mirror those of Aleister Crowley, described earlier. However, Randolph's interpretation of sex magic was actually very different from Crowley's. Randolph deplored masturbation and homosexuality and other forms of non-reproductive sexuality[128] and believed that sacred sex could only occur between a loving heterosexual husband and wife. Randolph's approach essentially involved love among equals, whereas Crowley sometimes employed prostitutes or other available women who were not personally committed to his magical purpose and who were used purely for sex.[129] Crowley's magical episode with Victor Neuburg in Algeria involving homosexual anal sex (referred to above) was also an act of ritual sexual submission by Crowley and would therefore have failed Randolph's criteria on at least two counts.

Randolph seems to have been far more averse than Crowley to the negative [or *Qliphothic*] realms of primal consciousness that could be unleashed through what Randolph regarded as misplaced acts of sex magic. Nevertheless, Randolph and Crowley would certainly have agreed that the orgasm itself was among the most powerful and profound of all human experiences,[130] and Randolph would also have agreed with Crowley's statement in *Energized Enthusiasm* (1913) that through 'the sacramental...use of the sexual act, the divine consciousness may be attained'.[131] For both men, sexuality was a vital key to potency and transcendence.

Robert North, who contributed an introduction to the 1988 edition of Randolph's *Sexual Magic*,[132] maintains that Carl Kellner derived many of the O.T.O. teachings directly from Randolph's instructions for the Brotherhood of Eulis. However, other writers, including T. Allen Greenfield (2003), Samuel Scarborough (2001) and Joscelyn Godwin (1994), believe it was the Hermetic Brotherhood of Luxor—which in turn drew on Randolph's sex magic teachings—that was probably the specific connecting link between Randolph, Kellner and Reuss.

The Hermetic Brotherhood of Luxor was founded in 1870 by the Polish mystic Max Théon (1848-1927). Théon was interested in Hermeticism and looked to ancient Egypt as the source of the Western esoteric tradition. However he was also highly eclectic, embracing the Kabbalah, the Rig-Veda, Tantrism, and elements of Freemasonry. For a time he lived in Algeria, where he formulated what he referred to as the Cosmic Tradition and took the mystical name Aia Aziz ('the beloved').[133] In 1873 Théon recruited the Scottish occultist and Freemason Peter Davidson (1837-1915), a close friend and colleague of Dr Gerard Encausse (also known as Papus), to join him in administering the Brotherhood. As an initiatory organisation the Hermetic Brotherhood of Luxor first became public in London in 1884, even though it had been in existence since 1870[134] and its initiations—based on Rosicrucian and Masonic principles—resembled those of the Hermetic Order of the Golden Dawn, established several years later.[135] Théon took the role of Grand Master of the Exterior Circle of the Order while Davidson was appointed Provincial Grand Master of the North (Scotland) and later also the Eastern Section (America). Together, Théon and Davidson made extensive use of ancient Egyptian symbolism in their magical ceremonies. This symbolic emphasis was further developed by Thomas H. Burgoyne (1855-1895), who joined the Hermetic Brotherhood of Luxor in 1883 and helped Théon and Davidson run the organisation from this time on. The early curriculum of the Hermetic Brotherhood also included selections from the writings of the Rosicrucian author Hargrave Jennings as well as Paschal Beverly Randolph.[136] During the 1880s and 1890s Davidson and Burgoyne adapted Randolph's *The Mysteries of Eros*[137] and *Eulis!*,[138] thereby placing more emphasis on practical sex magic in the Brotherhood's curriculum. It seems likely that it is through the reworking of Randolph's sex magic concepts in the Hermetic Brotherhood of Luxor, and in particular through Davidson's close association with Papus in Europe, that Randolph's sex magic teachings eventually attracted the attention of Reuss and Kellner.[139] According to P-R. Koenig, Reuss first made contact with Papus in 1901.[140]

Nevertheless, as indicated earlier, there is something of a gulf between Randolph's version of sex magic as the 'White Magic of Love' and the homo-erotic approach to sex magic advocated by Reuss and Crowley in the O.T.O. Clearly, Randolph cannot be considered the only major precursor of Crowley's Thelemic sex magick since there are major aspects of Crowley's occult doctrine that are entirely absent in Randolph's writings and philosophy. It is necessary to explore other sources entirely — sources much closer to the origins of the Western esoteric tradition itself — and it comes as no surprise that some of Crowley's libertine mystical and sex-magick ideas are mirrored quite specifically in the ritual practices of certain heretical Gnostic sects whose origins date back to the early centuries of the Christian era.[141] These include the Gnostic sects that Mircea Eliade refers to as *Pneumatikoi* [142] and O.T.O. historian P-R.Koenig calls 'Spermo-Gnostics'.[143]

One of the most intriguing elements in the rise of Gnosticism during the early Christian era was the concept that spiritual redemption could be attained by collecting, salvaging, and carrying to heaven the sparks of divine light that were buried in living matter — primarily within the human body. Eliade notes that

> the equation divine light = pneuma [Greek: 'spirit'] = semen plays a central role only among the Phibionites (and sects related to them) and among the Manichaeans. But while the latter, on the ground of this very equation, scorned the sexual act and exalted a severe asceticism, the Phibionites extolled the most abject sexual orgies and practised the sacramental absorption of semen virile and menstrual fluids, careful only to avoid pregnancy.[144]

Despite the overt sensuality of their sexual rituals, the Syrian Phibionites regarded themselves as Christian Gnostics: they believed that the divine power of the crucified Son had been trapped within the physical confines of the material world. The Phibionites also believed they were giving true expression to their Christian beliefs by releasing this spiritual power during their sacred rituals without creating more children in the process — from their perspective, pregnancy and the act of giving birth would trap more souls within the painful constrictions of physical existence. For them, consuming semen and menstrual blood during the Eucharist was a purer form of ritual communion than the more conventional symbolism of blood and wine.

The practices of the Phibionites are described in the *Panarion*, written by the 4th century Christian writer, Epiphanius:

> *The power, which is in menstruation and in the sperm they called psyche, which would be gathered and eaten. And whatever we eat, flesh or vegetables or bread or anything else, we do a favour to the creatures because we gather the psyche from everything...And they say that it is the same psyche which is dispersed in animals and beasts, fishes, snakes, men, vegetables, trees and anything that is produced.*[145]

Epiphanius was clearly horrified by what he describes as the 'shameless' sexual practices of the Phibionites:

> *...they serve rich food, meat and wine even if they are poor. When they thus ate together and so to speak filled up their veins, from the surplus of their strength they turn to excitements. The man, leaving his wife, says to his own wife: 'Stand up and make love with the brother ('Perform the agapē with the brother'). Then the unfortunates unite with each other, and as I am truly ashamed to say the shameful things that are being done by them... nevertheless I will not be ashamed to say those things which they are not ashamed to do, in order that I may cause in every way a horror in those who hear about their shameful practices. After they have intercourse in the passion of fornication they raise their own blasphemy toward heaven. The woman and the man take the fluid of emission of the man into their hands, they stand, turn toward heaven, their hands besmeared with the uncleanness, and pray as the people called Stratiotikoi and Gnostikoi, bringing to the Father of the Nature of All, that which they have on their hands, and they say: 'We offer to thee this gift, the body of Christ.' And then they eat it, their own ignominy, and say: 'This is the body of Christ and this is the Passover for the sake of which our bodies suffer and are forced to confess the suffering of Christ.' Similarly also with the woman: when she happens to be in the flowing of the blood they gather the blood of menstruation of her uncleanness and eat it together and say: 'This is the blood of Christ.'*[146]

The Phibionite ritual of consuming menstrual blood and semen is mirrored in Crowley's sex magick practice of consuming 'cakes of light', which contained precisely the same key ingredients (based on the instructions conveyed to Crowley by Aiwass in 1904, as recorded in *Liber AL vel Legis*). As with the Phibionites, Crowley included the consumption of sacramental 'cakes of light' in both his Gnostic Mass and also in the Mass of the Phoenix (see above), and it is clear that Crowley intended that in these magickal ceremonies the 'cakes of light' should serve as an alternative to the Body of Christ consumed by congregants during Christian communion. Although Crowley does not mention the Phibionites specifically in his writings, he nevertheless believed he was perpetuating the Gnostic tradition through such ceremonies, and for him the ritual consumption of blood and semen was a sacred act. According to the text of the Gnostic Mass, consecrated 'cakes of light' contain the sexual elixir and therefore embody 'the essence of the life of the Sun'.[147]

The surviving papers of Theodor Reuss show that the sex magic practices incorporated within the O.T.O. by its founder also had an essentially 'Spermo-Gnostic' orientation, and that this was linked to the mystical legend of the Holy Grail. According to P-R.Koenig,

> *The whole body was considered divine (the Temple of the Holy Ghost) and the sexual organs were meant to fulfil a peculiar function: a Holy Mass was the symbolic act of re-creating the universe. The root belief is that only by co-operation between man and woman can either advance spiritually. Sexually joining is a shadow of the cosmic act of creation. Performed by adepts, the union of male and female approaches more closely the primal act and partakes of its divine nature… The central secret of his Ordo Templi Orientis was built around Richard Wagner's Parsifal. The spear became the phallus while the Graal, of course, was the vagina which contained the 'Gralsspeise' (sperm and vaginal fluids).*[148]

The O.T.O. after Crowley

When Crowley died in 1947 he was succeeded as Head of the O.T.O. by his former representative in Germany, Karl Germer (1885-1962). At this time the focus of the O.T.O. had already begun to shift to the United States, the organization of its European affiliates having become fragmented and dispersed as a result of the impact of World War Two.[149] At the end of the war in 1945 only the Agapé Lodge of the O.T.O. in Pasadena was still actively functioning: this was a lodge established in the 1930s by Wilfred Talbot Smith (1885-1957), a loyal Thelemite who had first met Crowley in Vancouver in 1915, and Jane Wolfe (1875-1958), who had stayed at Crowley's sex-magick Abbey at Cefalu, Sicily, in the early 1920s.[150] After Crowley's will was probated, Germer received most of the materials from Crowley's estate and took them to his home in Westpoint, California[151] — various court proceedings have since determined that Crowley's copyrights are held legally by the U.S. Grand Lodge of the O.T.O. which now seeks to control publication of Crowley's works around the world.[152]

In Britain the thrust of Crowley's Thelemic teachings continued under the enthusiastic leadership of Kenneth Grant (1924 - 2011). Following Crowley's death, Germer charted a British branch of the O.T.O. under Grant but then expelled him in July 1955 for associating with a rival O.T.O. offshoot, the Fraternitas Saturni,[153] and circulating a new, unauthorised O.T.O. manifesto.[154] Until his death in 2011 Grant headed the so-called Typhonian O.T.O., which is not legally connected to the American O.T.O. and is very much a rival occult organisation.[155]

Grant first met Crowley at Netherwood, Hastings (UK), in December 1944 and worked with him for a brief period as his secretary.[156] Grant later emerged as one of Crowley's most notable Thelemic disciples and over a period of forty years released a number of important volumes on the Western esoteric tradition. Grant's occult perspective is especially significant because it affirms the esoteric connection between Indian Tantra, Gnosticism and what he calls the Draconian, Ophidian and Typhonian currents in modern sex magick.[157] In 1948 Grant published a *Manifesto of the British Branch of the Ordo Templi Orientis* in which he claimed that the Order promulgated a range of esoteric practices spanning both the Western and Eastern esoteric traditions:

> *In the O.T.O. are promulgated the essential teachings of the Draconian Tradition of Ancient Egypt; the teachings of the Indian Shakta Tantra Shastra; the teachings of the pre-Christian Gnosis; the Initiated Western Tradition as enshrined in the mysteries of the Holy Qabalah, and the Alchemical Mystical and Magical Formulae of the Arcane Schools of the age long past, as well as the mode of applying practically the essential principles underlying the Spagyric or Hermetic Sciences, the Orphic Mysteries and the use of the Ophidian Current.*[158]

Crowley was sufficiently impressed by Grant's research into the subject of sex magick that he admitted him to the Ninth degree of the O.T.O.[159] and this initiation was complemented by secret Tantric instructions from another occultist, David Curwen, who had become a Ninth degree member of the Order in 1945.¹⁶⁰ It was Curwen who provided Grant with a full initiation into the Tantric *vama marg* (the 'left-hand path').¹⁶¹ According to Grant, Curwen's instructions convinced him that Crowley did not fully appreciate the significance of the female sexual fluids (*kalas*) which, together with the male fluids, form the basis of the 'elixir' in Thelemic sex magick.¹⁶² The contemporary Thelemic practitioner Frater Zephyros elaborates on this theme in a recent article titled 'The Ophidian Current', which fuses the sex-magick doctrines of Grant and Crowley with references to the *chakras*, or spiritual energy centres in the body, that are awakened by the Kundalini serpent in Tantric yoga:

> *The formula and function of the Scarlet Woman starts with zones of occult energy intimately related to the network of nerves and plexuses associated with the endocrine glands. Kundalini energy affects the chakras in her body ... [see below for a description of chakras] ... and its vibrations influence the chemical composition of her glandular secretions. Such fragrances are devoured by the Priest and transmuted into magickal energy. ...*
>
> *Kalas [genital secretions] may only be evoked into a chakra that has been properly prepared... Consuming the kalas charged with the upwardly directed currents (nectar) transforms consciousness and makes it possible to contact and communicate with transcendental entities...*
>
> *For the female to arouse the Kundalini, she visualizes the Serpent in phallic form in the Mulhadara chakra and inflames herself to the point of orgasm. Yet before orgasm, she must move to the Ajna chakra [see below for descriptions of these two chakras]. Then she must maintain the image until consummation occurs. The male must proceed by identifying Kundalini with Hadit and the Cerebral Centre with Nuit [the Egyptian deities involved in Crowley's Thelemic revelation]. The Hadit force is awakened and forces its way up the spinal column past all the sealed chakras into the cerebral centre [ie. Ajna].* ¹⁶³

Lawrence Sutin, author of a recent biography of Aleister Crowley, believes that Crowley's first reference to sex magic is recorded in a diary titled *The Writings of Truth* which was later published in a modified form in his *Temple of Solomon the King*.¹⁶⁴ It was while visiting his friend and former Golden Dawn colleague Allan Bennett (*Frater Iehi Aour*) in Ceylon in 1901 that Crowley was tutored for the first time in yoga. Bennett had left the world of ceremonial magic behind in England and had come to Ceylon to become a Buddhist monk. Bennett was willing to share his practical knowledge of yoga with his friend and together they rented a furnished bungalow in the hills near Kandy for a period of several months so Crowley could be shown the yogic techniques.[165]

Crowley's diary entries in *The Writings of Truth* record that during his stay in Kandy he practised yogic *pranayama* (control of prana, or life-energy, utilising breathing techniques) and that he had also been exploring *vamacharya*, a form of Tantra devoted to licentious rites and sexual debauchery.[166] Sutin writes:

> *This reference to vamacharya is most important, as it documents his [ie. Crowley's] first known foray into ritual sexual magic. This Sanskrit term refers to a Hindu tantric practice of sexual intercourse that could—if the spiritual aspirations were untainted by lust—re-enact the cosmic coupling of Shiva and Shakti...* [167]

Because of Crowley's fascination with the magical potency of semen and his emphasis in Thelemic magical practice on the ritual consumption of sexual secretions as part of the 'magical elixir', it is possible that even if he was following a practice of retaining semen during his exploration of *vamacharya* in 1901 he was prepared to abandon this aspect of Tantra after his transformative revelations in Cairo, just three years later.

In his article, 'The Origins of Modern Sex Magick' (1985) J. Gordon Melton points out that there were certain aspects of Hindu Tantra that would definitely not have been to Crowley's liking, post-1904. Commenting on the traditional concept of Shakti as 'Goddess' or 'power', Melton notes that while variously understood by different tantrics, an understanding of the role of the female and her energy is central to all Hindu tantrism, but is absent from Crowley's treatment of sex magick. As John Woodroofe would write just a few years after Crowley finished the new O.T.O. rituals, Hindu tantrism teaches that 'S'akti [Shakti] in the highest causal sense is God as Mother, and in another sense it is the universe which issues from Her Womb.'[168]...Such concepts are quite foreign to and stand in stark contrast to the O.T.O. teaching of God as Sun and phallus.[169]

Melton also rightly observes that Crowley's notion of the Scarlet Woman as a sexual consort is based on the biblical Book of Revelation and has nothing whatever to do with the Tantric tradition. 'Crowley's Scarlet Woman,' he writes, bears 'no substantive resemblance to Shakti in any of her forms, including Kali.'[170] Kenneth Grant meanwhile provides an important insight into the connection between the practice of sex magic and the image of the Kundalini serpent—or 'fire-snake':

> *The ability to function on the inner, or astral planes, and to travel freely in the realms of light or inner space, derived from a special purification and storage of vital force. This force in its densest form is identical with sexual energy. In order to transform sexual energy into magical energy (ojas), the dominant Fire Snake at the base of the spine is awakened. It then purges the vitality of all dross by the purifying virtue of its intense heat. Thus the function of the semen—in the tantras is to build up the body of light [the astral body], the inner body of man. As the vital fluid accumulates in the testicles it is consumed by the heat of the Fire Snake, and the subtle fumes or 'perfumes' of this molten semen go to strengthen the inner body. The worship of shakti means in effect the exercise of the Fire Snake, which not only fortifies the body of light but gradually burns away all impurities in the physical body and rejuvenates it.*[171]

Grant maintained that arousing the Kundalini serpent-energy could stimulate artistic or inventive creativity. In *The Magical Revival* (1972) Grant referred to the Kundalini as 'the serpentine or spiral power of creative consciousness'[172] and he also believed this type of occult exploration could bestow profound spiritual insights: 'Men will become as gods,' he wrote, 'because the power of creation (the prerogative of gods) will be wielded by them through the direction of forces at present termed 'occult' or hidden.[173]

Grant's Typhonian O.T.O. sought to affirm the importance of the Tantra in Western magical practice. And yet it is equally clear that Grant's esoteric practice depended totally on Crowley's Thelemic revelation. When we look back on the forces polarizing occult thought in the 20th century it is clear that together Crowley and Grant played a vital role consolidating ritualized sexuality as a central aspect of modern Western magic.

Endnotes

1   While he was at Cambridge University, Crowley changed his name from Edward Alexander Crowley to Aleister Crowley, by adopting a variant Gaelic spelling of his middle name. See L. Sutin, loc cit: 48.
2   L. Sutin, loc cit: 65.
3   A. Crowley, *Magick in Theory and Practice* [1929], Routledge & Kegan Paul, London 1973: xv.

4   Ibid: xvi.
5   Ibid: xvii.
6   Ibid: 4.
7   Ibid.
8   The 'Secret Chiefs' of the Golden Dawn were high-ranking spiritual beings who, it was claimed, provided guidance and inspiration to the leaders of the Inner Order. MacGregor Mathers, in particular, emphasized their importance. See Chapter Eight.
9   Ibid: 69.
10 L. Sutin, *Do What Thou Wilt: A Life of Aleister Crowley*, loc cit: 118.
11 Crowley believed Aiwass was messenger from the Egyptian deity Horus, the falcon-headed god that had the sun and the moon for his eyes. Crowley came to believe that he was Lord of the Aeon of Horus, which began in 1904, replacing Christianity and the other major religious traditions of both West and East.
12 Although a psychoanalytic perspective on why there should have been an anti-Christian component to Crowley's spiritual revelation is outside the scope of this thesis, Crowley's new role as the Beast 666 is almost certainly related to his restrictive and oppressive Christian upbringing within a Plymouth Brethren family: Crowley's entire magical philosophy is grounded in notions of personal freedom and a libertine philosophy.
13 Crowley's unique spelling for the Scarlet Woman of the Apocalypse, as revealed in *The Book of the Law*. The spelling 'Babalon' has a Kabbalistic numerical value of 156 which, according to Crowley's disciple Kenneth Grant, equates with the number of shrines in the City of Pyramids. Grant maintains that the name 'Babalon' means 'Gateway of the Sun, or solar-phallic power' (see *Nightside of Eden*, London 1977: 259)—thereby revealing its symbolic significance to practitioners of sex-magick.
14 See J. Symonds, *The Great Beast: the Life and Magick of Aleister Crowley*, Mayflower/Granada, London 1973: 81.
15 The Boulak Museum no longer exists; the antiquities housed in this museum were transferred to the National Museum, Cairo. (Symonds, loc. cit: 1973: 81 fn)
16 J. Symonds, *The Great Beast: the Life and Magick of Aleister Crowley*, loc. cit.: 1973: 82.
17 Ibid.
18 The text of *The Book of the Law* is included as an appendix in *The Magical Record of the Beast 666*, ed. J. Symonds and K. Grant, Duckworth, London 1972.
19 See stanzas I: 15 and 16 of *Liber AL vel Legis*, in the appendix to *The Magical Record of the Beast 666*, loc.cit 1972: 303.

20 See A. Crowley, *Magick in Theory and Practice*, loc cit.:12.
21 See stanza I:40 of *Liber AL vel Legis*, in the appendix to *The Magical Record of the Beast 666*, loc.cit: 304. See also *The Comment* which comes at the conclusion of *Liber AL vel Legis*, loc cit: 315.
22 A. Crowley, *Magick in Theory and Practice*, loc.cit: xv.
23 Ibid.
24 K. Grant, *The Magical Revival*, Muller, London 1972: 20.
25 See stanza I:49 of *Liber AL vel Legis*, in the appendix to *The Magical Record of the Beast 666*, loc.cit 1972: 305.
26 See J. Symonds and K. Grant (ed.), *The Confessions of Aleister Crowley*, Hill and Wang, New York, 1970: 22.
27 See appendix containing the text of *Liber AL vel Legis* in *The Magical Record of the Beast 666*, ed. J. Symonds and K. Grant, Duckworth, London 1972:314.
28 Ibid: stanzas III: 44-45: 314.
29 K. Grant, *The Magical Revival*, loc cit.:.45. Grant elaborates on this point later in the same book: 'In sexual congress each coition is a sacrament of peculiar virtue since it effects a transformation of consciousness through annihilation of apparent duality. To be radically effective the transformation must be also an initiation. Because of the sacramental nature of the act, each union must be magically directed... the ritual must be directed to the transfinite and non-individualised consciousness represented by Egyptian Nuit... The earthly Nuit is Isis, the Scarlet Woman.' (loc cit.:145)
30 Crowley's insatiable search for sexual partners is described in Colin Wilson's *Aleister Crowley: the Nature of the Beast*, Aquarian Press, Wellingborough 1987.
31 See appendix containing the text of *Liber AL vel Legis* in *The Magical Record of the Beast 666*, ed. J. Symonds and K. Grant, Duckworth, London 1972: 311-312.
32 L. Sutin, *Do What Thou Wilt: A Life of Aleister Crowley*, St Martin's Press, New York 2000: 292.
33 F. King (ed.), *The Secret Rituals of the O.T.O.*, C.W.Daniel, London 1973: 226.
34 King maintains that Crowley joined the O.T.O. in 1911. See F. King (ed.), *The Secret Rituals of the O.T.O.*, loc.cit:: 28. However according to the O.T.O. *History of the Ordo Templi Orientis* (www.oto-usa.org/history html.), Crowley was admitted to the first degrees of the O.T.O in 1910. Reuss made frequent trips to England.
35 F. King (ed.), *The Secret Rituals of the O.T.O.*, loc cit: 225.
36 John Michael Greer and Carl Hood have suggested (*Gnosis* magazine: 43, Spring 1997) that there may have been a secret sexual dimension

to the rituals of the Golden Dawn, but in my view their arguments are unconvincing. MacGregor Mathers, arguably the most influential figure in the formation of the Golden Dawn, valued celibacy and virginity and never consummated his marriage to Moina Bergson (see I. Colquhoun, *Sword of Wisdom: MacGregor Mathers and the Golden Dawn*, loc cit.:54).

37   J.G. Melton, 'The Origins of Modern Sex Magick', Institute for the Study of American Religion, Evanston, Illinois, June 1985:3.
38   These writings included such texts as *Liber A'ash* (*Equinox* 1:6, September 1911: 33-39), *Liber Cheth* (*Equinox* 1: 6 (September 1911: 23-27) and *Liber Stellae Rubae* (*Equinox* 1:7, March 1912: 29-38).
39   See J.G. Melton, 'The Origins of Modern Sex Magick', loc cit.
40   The Second Order rituals related to the Kabbalistic *sephiroth* Tiphareth, Geburah and Chesed on the Kabbalistic Tree of Life. See Chapter Eight.
41   F. King, *Ritual Magic in England*, Spearman, London 1970:117.
42   See stanza 1:15 of *Liber AL vel Legis* in *The Magical Record of the Beast 666*, ed. J. Symonds and K. Grant, Duckworth, London 1972:303.
43   Neuburg's magical diary describes how Crowley on one occasion rebuked him by giving him thirty-two strokes of a gorse switch, drawing blood. 'He is apparently a homosexual sadist,' wrote Neuburg, 'for he performed the ceremony with obvious satisfaction.' Quoted in C.Wilson, *Aleister Crowley: the Nature of the Beast*, loc cit: 91. See also J.O. Fuller, *The Magical Dilemma of Victor Neuburg*, W.H. Allen, London 1965 where Neuburg's diaries are also discussed in detail.
44   Enochian magic derives historically from the work of Elizabethan occultists Dr. John Dee (1527-1608) and Edward Kelley (1555-15950, who met in 1581. Dee and Kelley made use of wax tablets called almadels, engraved with magical symbols, and also used a large number of 49-inch squares filled with letters of the alphabet. Nearby, on his table, Kelley had a large crystal stone upon which he focused his concentration and entered a state of trance reverie. Kelley maintained that while he was in a state of trance 'angels' would appear, and they in turn would point to various letters on the squares. These letters were written down by Dee as Kelley called them out. When these invocations were completely transcribed, Kelley then reversed their order, believing that the angels had communicated them backwards to avoid unleashing the magical power which they contained. Dee and Kelley considered that the communications formed the basis of a new language known as Enochian. These magical conjurations were subsequently incorporated into magical practice by the ritual magicians of the Hermetic Order of the Golden Dawn, who used them to induce trance visions on the 'astral plane'.
45   These magical visions are described in A. Crowley, *The Vision and the*

Voice [1929], Sangreal Foundation, Dallas, Texas 1972.
46. A. Crowley, *The Confessions of Aleister Crowley*, ed. J. Symonds and K. Grant, Hill and Wang, New York 1970: 621. According to Lawrence Sutin, Crowley was deeply ashamed of his homosexuality because it 'conflicted with his status as a manly gentleman coming of age' (*Do What Thou Wilt*, loc cit: 43). Crowley was also well aware of the famous libel action that led to the imprisonment of Oscar Wilde. This had occurred in 1895, during Crowley's first year at Cambridge University.
47. Spare was briefly a member of the O.T.O. *circa* 1910 but soon quarrelled with Crowley and thereafter sought to avoid him. Even though Spare became friendly with Thelemite Kenneth Grant in the late 1940s, Spare and Crowley were never reconciled. See Chapter Six and also K. and S. Grant, *Zos Speaks!: Encounters with Austin Osman Spare*, Fulgur, London 1998.
48. F. King (ed.), *The Secret Rituals of the O.T.O.*, loc.cit: 28. See also fn. 57 above.
49. Crowley writes in *The Confessions*: 'I protested that I knew no such secret. He said, "But you have printed it in the plainest language." I said that I could not have done so because I did not know it. He went to the bookshelves and, taking out a copy of *The Book of Lies*, pointed to a passage in the despised chapter.' See A. Crowley, *The Confessions of Aleister Crowley*, ed. J. Symonds and K. Grant, Hill and Wang, New York 1970: 710.
50. A. Crowley, *The Book of Lies*, [1912], Hayden Press, Ilfracombe, Devon 1962:82.
51. Ibid.
52. J. Symonds, *The Great Beast: The Life and Magick of Aleister Crowley*, loc cit: 182 fn.
53. Crowley later visited Berlin where he received instructional documents from the German O.T.O. He was also granted the grandiose title 'King of Ireland, Iona and all the Britains within the Sanctuary of the Gnosis" and took *Baphomet* as his new magical name. Later Crowley adapted the Ninth degree of the O.T.O so that it identified the priest and priestess as Osiris and Isis, 'seeking Nuit and Hadit through the vagina and the penis'. He also developed a series of homosexual magical rituals with Victor Neuburg featuring invocations to Thoth-Hermes. At one point in these rituals, which became known collectively as the *Paris Working*, Crowley scourged Neuburg on the buttocks and cut a cross on his chest. For details see J.O. Fuller, *The Magical Dilemma of Victor Neuburg*, W.H. Allen, London 1965:203-216.
54. See F. King (ed.), *The Secret Rituals of the O.T.O.*, loc.cit: 29. King points out that Crowley was not accepted by a majority of German

O.T.O. members until 1925. The Order was suppressed by the Nazis in 1937.
55 P-R. Koenig, 'Introduction to the Ordo Templi Orientis', published on-line at www.user.cyberlink.ch/~koenig/intro.htm.
56 Ibid.
57 Ibid.
58 Ibid.
59 P-R. Koenig suggests that Kellner may have been one of the twelve co-founders of the Hermetic Brotherhood of Light in Boston/Chicago in 1895. See www.user.cyberlink.ch/~koenig/spermo.htm.
60 H.B. Urban, *Magia Sexualis: Sex, Magic and Liberation in Modern Western Esotericism*, University of California Press, Berkeley, California 2006: 96.
61 Ibid: 97.
62 Ibid: 99.
63 T. Reuss, *Lingam-Yoni*, Verlag Willsson, Berlin and London 1906.
64 P-R. Koenig, 'Spermo-Gnostics and the Ordo Templi Orientis', published on-line at www.user.cyberlink.ch/~koenig/spermo.htm
65 H. Urban, *Magia Sexualis*, loc.cit: 101.
66 P-R. Koenig, 'Introduction to the Ordo Templi Orientis', loc cit.
67 Sabazius X° and AMT IX°, *History of Ordo Templi Orientis*, U.S. Grand Lodge, 2006: 12-13. Published on-line at www.oto-usa.org/history.html.
68 P-R.Koenig, 'Introduction to the Ordo Templi Orientis', loc cit.
69 Sabazius X° and AMT IX°, *History of Ordo Templi Orientis*, loc cit.:17.
70 Published in *The Equinox* Vol.III: 1, March 1919—the so-called *'Blue Equinox'*.
71 Sabazius X° and AMT IX°, *History of Ordo Templi Orientis*, loc cit.:17.
72 H. Urban, '*Magia Sexualis*: Sex, Secrecy and Liberation in Modern Western Esotericism,' *Journal of the American Academy of Religion*, September 2004, Vol.72, No.3: 711.
73 P-R. Koenig, 'Spermo-Gnostics and the O.T.O', published on-line at www.cyberlink.ch/-koenig/spermo.htm.
74 A.Crowley, *De Arte Magica*, Ch.XII, published on-line at www.skepticfiles.org.
75 Ibid, Ch.XIII.
76 Ibid.
77 Ibid, Ch.XVI.
78 See See F. King (ed.), *The Secret Rituals of the O.T.O.*, loc.cit: 207.
79 Baphomet was Crowley's magical name after he assumed leadership of the British branch of the O.T.O. in 1912. It is also the name of a demonic deity represented graphically by Eliphas Lévi as a goat-headed god with wings, breasts and an illuminated torch between his horns. The Knights

Templar were accused by King Philip IV of France of worshipping Baphomet although few members of the Order admitted to this ritual practice. It has been suggested that the name Baphomet may be a corruption of Mohammed.

80 See A. Crowley, 'Emblems and Modes of Use', private text intended for the Ninth degree O.T.O. Published on-line at www.aethyria.com.
81 See Frater Osiris, 'Analysis of the Mass of the Phoenix', Seattle 2003, published on-line at www.hermetic.com/osiris and also A. Rhadon, 'Sex, Religion and Magick: a concise overview', 2004, published on-line at www.baymoon.com.
82 Frater Osiris, 'Analysis of the Mass of the Phoenix', loc cit.
83 See Frater Osiris, 'Analysis of Liber XXXVI, *The Star Sapphire*', Seattle 2004, published on-line at www.hermetic.com/osiris.
84 A. Crowley, Chapter 69, 'The Way to Succeed—and the Way to Suck Eggs' in *The Book of Lies* [1912], Haydn Press, Ilfracombe, Devon 1962:148.
85 Frater Osiris, 'Analysis of Liber XXXVI, *The Star Sapphire*', loc cit. Frater Osiris is probably referring to Crowley's sex magic text *Emblems and Modes of Use*, where it is suggested that the 'elixir' should be consumed in this way.
86 This is Crowley's expression. IAO was one of the sacred names ascribed to the archon Abraxas, a planetary deity associated with Basilides, a Gnostic philosopher who lived and taught in Alexandria c.125-140 CE. The name Abraxas in Greek letters has a numerical value of 365, thereby linking the deity to the number of days in a year. Abraxas was said to rule over 365 heavens and was depicted on numerous charms, amulets and talismans in order to attract good luck.
87 A. Crowley, *Energized Enthusiasm: A Note on Theurgy*, published on-line at www.luckymojo.com/esoteric/occultism/magic/ceremonial/crowley.htm. This text was first published in *The Equinox*, vol.1 No.9, March 1913, and was republished by Weiser, New York 1976.
88 Ibid.
89 Ibid.
90 See section in the present chapter dealing with altered states of consciousness in modern magical practice.
91 See L. Abraham, entry for the 'Chemical Wedding' of King Sol and Queen Luna, *A Dictionary of Alchemical Imagery*, Cambridge University Press, 1998: 36.
92 A. Crowley, *Gnostic Mass (Liber XV, Ecclesiae Gnosticae Catholicae Canon Missae)*, composed in Moscow in 1913.
93 Ibid.
94 Ibid.

95 A. Crowley, Liber XIV, *The Mass of the Phoenix* (1912), published on-line at www.thelemicgoldendawn.org/rituals/phoenix.htm.
96 In *Liber Aleph*, Crowley writes: 'Neglect not the daily Miracle of the Mass, either by the Rite of the Gnostic Catholic Church, or that of the Phoenix.' Quoted in Frater Osiris, *On the Mass of the Phoenix: An Analysis*, Seattle 2003. Published on-line at www.hermetic.com/osiris.
97 The Mark of the Beast is 'the sign of the Sun and Moon or Cross and Circle conjoined'. See www.thelemicgoldendawn.org/rituals/phoenix.htm.
98 Frater Osiris, *On the Mass of the Phoenix: An Analysis*, loc cit.
99 First published in the Thelemic journal *Mezla*, Vol.1: 111, 1, Ithaca, New York 1985.
100 A. Crowley, *Emblems and Modes of Use*, loc cit.
101 Ibid.
102 Ibid.
103 Ibid.
104 Ibid.
105 See listing of key Crowley texts on sex magic published on-line at www.hollyfeld.org. *Liber A'ash vel Capricorni Pneumatici* heads the list. A 'Class A' document in the Argenteum Astrum was one that could not be altered or modified in the slightest way and had to be adhered to by members strictly as presented by Crowley.
106 A. Crowley, *Liber A'Aash vel Capricorni Pneumatici (Liber CCCLXX)*, first published in *The Equinox*, vol.1 No.6.
107 J.G. Melton, 'The Origins of Modern Sex Magick', loc cit.
108 R. North, Introduction to P.B. Randolph, *Sexual Magic*, Magickal Childe, New York 1988 (original French-language text: *Magia Sexualis*, Paris 1931) published on-line at www.supoervirtual.com.br.
109 Ibid.
110 Franz Anton Mesmer (1734-1815) studied medicine at the University of Vienna and embraced the then-current scientific view that a magnetic fluid permeated all aspects of life. Mesmer then came to believe that when this natural source of energy was blocked in the body, disease and ill-health would result. After graduating from the University of Vienna, Mesmer worked as a healer, first in Vienna and later in Paris, using magnets to 'correct' imbalances in the human organism. He transmitted 'healing energy' to his patients by making passes over his patients with his hands, or by using iron rods or wands that he had magnetized. A Royal Commission established in Paris in 1784 to test Mesmer's concept of 'animal magnetism' (Mesmer's term for the magnetic life-energy), found that his healing method had no scientific basis but that some patients nevertheless responded positively because their own imagination

provided the healing benefit. Mesmer is rightly regarded as one of the pioneers of psychosomatic medicine and hypnotherapy. During the late-Victorian era of the Golden Dawn, the term 'Mesmerist' was used to connote a hypnotist.

111   H.B. Urban, *Magia Sexualis: Sex, Magic and Liberation in Modern Western Esotericism*, loc cit.: 63.
112   R. North, Introduction to P.B.Randolph, *Sexual Magic*, loc cit.
113   J.G. Melton, 'The Origins of Modern Sex Magick', loc cit.
114   C. Yronwode, *The Reverend Hargrave Jennings and Phallism*, published on-line at www.luckymojo.com.
115   Ibid.
116   Randolph received this initiation from an Islamic sect usually referred to as the Nusairi, who live mainly in the mountains near the city of Latakia in Syria. These sect members were formerly known as the Namiriya, or Ansariyya—a reference to the mountainous region where they come from. Randolph's reference to 'Ansairetic Mysteries' is based on an early variant spelling.
117   This is a form of divination using the trance state to achieve a magical outcome.
118   R. North, Introduction to P.B. Randolph, *Sexual Magic*, loc.cit.
119   P.B. Randolph, *Eulis!*, Randolph, Toledo, Ohio 1873, republished 1896.
120   H.B. Urban, *Magia Sexualis: Sex, Magic and Liberation in Modern Western Esotericism*, loc cit.:65.
121   P.B. Randolph, *Eulis!*, loc cit.: 48, 218.
122   See H.B. Urban, *Magia Sexualis: Sex, Magic and Liberation in Modern Western Esotericism*, loc cit.: 67 and C. Yronwode, 'Paschal Beverly Randolph and the Ansairetic Mysteries', published on-line at www.luckymojo.com.
123   See P.B. Randolph, *Magia Sexualis*, tr. M.de Naglowska, Paris 1931: 76-77 (a composite work published in an English-language edition (trs. R.North), Magickal Childe, New York 1988).
124   Randolph's term *Ansairetic* is a reference to the Nusairi Islamic sect in Syria, formerly known as the Ansariyya. See also B.H. Springett, *Secret Sects of Syria and Lebanon*, Allen & Unwin, London 1922.
125   P.B. Randolph, *Eulis!*, quoted in C. Yronwode, 'Paschal Beverly Randolph and the Ansairetic Mysteries', loc cit.
126   See P.B. Randolph, *The Ansairetic Mystery: A New Revelation Concerning Sex!*, Toledo, Ohio, c.1973-74, republished in J.P. Deveney, *Paschal Beverly Randolph: A Nineteenth-Century American Spiritualist, Rosicrucian and Sex Magician*, State University of New York Press, Albany, New York 1997: 319-25.
127   P.B. Randolph, *The Ansairetic Mystery: A New Revelation Concerning*

Sex!, loc cit.

128 H.B. Urban, *Magia Sexualis: Sex, Magic and Liberation in Modern Western Esotericism*, loc cit.: 72.

129 This is especially true of Crowley during his visit to the United States around the time of World War One. Crowley arrived in New York in October 1914 and during his first year in America experimented with a range of sexual partners—both male and female—in the IX° and XI° O.T.O. sex magick rituals. This included the use of prostitutes in his magical rituals. See L. Sutin, *Do What Thou Wilt: a Life of Aleister Crowley*, loc cit: 244.

130 H.B. Urban, *Magia Sexualis: Sex, Magic and Liberation in Modern Western Esotericism*, loc cit.: 73.

131 A. Crowley, *Energized Enthusiasm: A Note on Theurgy*, loc.cit.

132 According to Joscelyn Godwin the original French-language edition of this book was probably not written by Randolph himself but adapted by M.de Naglowska in Paris, where the book was first published in 1931. See letter dated 13 October 1994 from Godwin to P-R. Koenig quoted in 'Correct Gnosticism', published on-line at www.user.cyberlink.ch/~koenig/correct.htm.

133 M.A. Kazlev, 'The Teachings of Max Théon', published on-line at www.kheper.net/topics/Theon/Theon.htm.

134 J. Godwin, C. Chanel and J.P. Deveney, *The Hermetic Brotherhood of Luxor*, Weiser, Maine 1995: 92-97.

135 Ibid: 6.

136 S. Scarborough, 'The Influence of Egypt on the Modern Western Mystery Tradition: The Hermetic Brotherhood of Luxor,' *Journal of the Western Mystery Tradition*, No.1, Autumn 2001: 2.

137 J. Godwin, letter dated 13 October 1994 to P-R. Koenig quoted in 'Correct Gnosticism', loc cit.

138 See T.A. Greenfield, 'Peter Davidson, Occultist', *Agape*, 2 May 2003.

139 Ibid.

140 P-R. Koenig, 'Correct Gnosticism', loc cit.

141 These Gnostic sects include the Carpocratians, the Ophites and the Phibionites and they are of interest because of their libertine tendencies, chthonic snake-imagery, and ritual consumption of blood and semen respectively. The Phibionites provide arguably the most intriguing parallel to Thelema in relation to Crowley's sacramental sex-magick practices. See also P-R. Koenig, 'Spermo-Gnostics and the O.T.O', loc cit. and P-R. Koenig, 'Correct Gnosticism', loc cit.

142 M. Eliade, *Occultism. Witchcraft and Cultural Fashions*, University of Chicago Press, Chicago 1976:109.

143 P-R. Koenig, 'Spermo-Gnostics and the O.T.O', loc cit.

144 M. Eliade, *Occultism. Witchcraft and Cultural Fashions*, loc cit: 113.
145 Epiphanius, *Panarion* 26: 9, 3-4.
146 Ibid: 26: 17, 1 ff. quoted in M. Eliade, *Occultism. Witchcraft and Cultural Fashions*, loc cit: 110.
147 A. Crowley, *Gnostic Mass (Liber XV, Ecclesiae Gnosticae Catholicae Canon Missae)*, 1913, loc cit.
148 P-R. Koenig, 'Spermo-Gnostics and the O.T.O', loc cit.
149 According to the official historical statement issued by the U.S. Grand Lodge of the O.T.O. the various European branches of the Order were 'largely destroyed or driven underground during the War'. See Sabazius X° and AMT IX°, *History of Ordo Templi Orientis*, loc cit.:19.
150 See Sabazius X° and AMT IX°, *History of Ordo Templi Orientis*, loc cit.: 18, and L. Sutin, *Do What Thou Wilt: A Life of Aleister Crowley*, loc cit.: 286, 334.
151 Sabazius X° and AMT IX°, *History of Ordo Templi Orientis*, loc cit.: 22-23.
152 The American O.T.O. remains vigilant in policing pirated editions of Crowley's voluminous writings on magick and the doctrine of Thelema. However it has been less successful preventing various websites on the Internet from publishing most of Crowley's significant magickal texts on-line. These rival websites include www.thelemicgnosticism.org; www.luckymojo.com; www.hermetic.com; www.rahoorkhuit.net; www.bbs.bapho.net; www.skepticfiles.org; www.sacred-texts.com and www.aethyria.com.
153 The Fraternitas Saturni was established in Germany in 1926 by Eugen Grosche (1888-1964) and was the second magical order to be based on Crowley's doctrine of *Thelema*. The first was Crowley's Argenteum Astrum which in turn merged into the O.T.O. after 1922.
154 Ibid: 23.
155 One can sense this rivalry in such articles as Michael Staley's 'Typhonian Ordo Templi Orientis: the O.T.O. after Crowley' which seeks to reinterpret various historical events in the O.T.O. as documented by the American branch of the O.T.O. Staley, who is a senior member of the Typhonian O.T.O. in Britain and editor of its publication *Starfire*, is widely regarded as Grant's deputy and heir apparent. See www.freespeech.org/magick/koenig/staley2.htm.
156 H. Bogdan, 'Kenneth Grant: Marriage between the West and the East', edited extract taken from 'Challenging the Morals of Western Society: the Use of Ritualised Sex in Contemporary Occultism,' *The Pomegranate*, 8, 2, Equinox Publishing, London 2006 (published on-line at www.fulgur.co.uk).
157 Grant defines the Draconian Cult as 'the cult of the Fire Snake

represented celestially by the stellar complex, Draco, the Dragon or Fire-breathing Beast of the Great Deep (of Space).' Grant claims that 'Draco is identical with the Goddess Kali of the later Tantric Cults of the Left Hand Path. The Draconian Cult is also alluded to as the Ophidian Current when no specifically Egyptian reference is intended' and he notes further that 'It is also known as the Typhonian Tradition, for Typhon was the primal Goddess and the Mother of Set.' See K. Grant, *Cults of the Shadow*, Muller, London 1975: 214.
158 The manifesto is undated but Grant has confirmed that it was circulated around 1948. See H. Bogdan 'Kenneth Grant: Marriage between the West and the East', loc cit.: 4, fn 2.
159 Ibid: 3.
160 Ibid.
161 Ibid.
162 Ibid.
163 See Frater Zephyros, 'The Ophidian Current', n.d., published on-line at www.groups.msn.com/TheMage/theophidiancurrent.msnw.
164 L. Sutin, *Do What Thou Wilt: A Life of Aleister Crowley*, loc cit: 92.
165 Ibid: 91.
166 I. Fischer-Schreiber et al. (ed.) *The Encyclopedia of Eastern Philosophy and Religion*, Shambhala, Boston 1994: 355.
167 Sutin adds the pertinent observation that 'There is, in this tradition, no moral judgment attached to the use of "left" and "right", although Western interpreters have frequently interposed a negative connotation to "left" that is native to their own, but not Hindu, cultures.' See L. Sutin, *Do What Thou Wilt : A Life of Aleister Crowley*, loc cit: 92-93.
168 J. Woodroffe, *S'akti and S'akta* , Ganesh, Madras 1975: 87.
169 J.G. Melton, 'The Origins of Modern Sex Magick,' Institute for the Study of American Religion, Evanston, Illinois, June 1985.
170 Ibid.
171 K. Grant, 'Cults of the Shadow' in J. White (ed.), *Kundalini: Evolution and Enlightenment*, Paragon House, St Paul, Minnesota 1990:400-401.
172 K.Grant, *The Magical Revival*, Muller, London 1972: 21.
173 Ibid.

10
The Draconian Tradition: Dragon Rouge and the Left-Hand Path

Thomas Karlsson

Some interpreters of the Left Hand Path (LHP) choose to refer to it as a religion, but in Dragon Rouge we view it as a tradition. The reason behind this is that the term 'religion', which is derived from Latin and the Western cultural sphere, denotes various obligations, rules and beliefs that assist the religious person to re-establish a sense of order in a presumed original ideal state, such as the Garden of Eden. It is possible in our order to work with people who come from different religious backgrounds, as well as accommodating those who are atheist or agnostic. The word 'tradition', which is also a Latin expression and can be translated as 'to deliver', signifies something that has been delivered from generation to generation and consequently binds the past with the future. In the interpretation of Dragon Rouge, tradition allows for innovation and creation, even if it is based on earlier knowledge and experience. Tradition is a red thread, which in the case of esotericism facilitates initiations within an occult order structure. Dragon Rouge is an administrator of a dynamic tradition that does not directly connect with only one specific historical tradition, but to a dark spiritual current that can be found in several cultures and historical periods and which has various common denominators.

Dragon Rouge does not follow only a Nordic Sejd tradition, Indian Vamachara, Pethro Vodou, Ophitian Gnosticism or any other specific culturally bound tradition. Rather, the LHP in Dragon Rouge is a meta-tradition that from one perspective always has existed, not only historically but also ahistorically in the form of certain archetypal principles within ourselves. By decoding these principles we decode the cultures in which we exist. This means that the order works hermeneutically and comparatively to find those deeper patterns in different local and historical traditions that represent the LHP and the Draconian Tradition.

When reading literature about the Left Hand Path, the Dark Aesthetics are often in focus. However, if we are to associate something truly meaningful with the Left Hand Path, a more thorough exploration of dark symbols is necessary. Dr. Alberto Brandi reveals in his book *La Via Oscura. Introduzione al Sentiero di Mano Sinistra* ('The Dark Way. Introduction to the Left-Hand Path') that we can distinguish two forms of the Left Hand Path: 1) Traditions which belong to the LHP both in method and goal. Among these, Brandi mentions Tantric LHP and heretical and Qliphotic Qabalah, and 2) those traditions that only use the methodology but lack initiatory perspectives. Examples of these are: Pethro Vodou and Palo Mayombe, which mainly focus on exchanges between the world of the dead and the living. According to these criteria, Dragon Rouge belongs to the first grouping, since the order works with dark forces methodically and by setting goals—in order to foster individual development and ultimately to attain a state of self-deification.[1]

The Left Hand Path can be viewed as a part of the Draconian tradition, which is characterized by being 1) a path towards a goal, and 2) associated to the Left side. But what is the goal, and what is the relation between this goal and other religious and spiritual traditions? From many perspectives, Dragon Rouge can be regarded as an anti-religion. Religion is of course an ambiguous concept, not least from the viewpoint of recent post-secular definitions.[2] In so far as religion can be defined as a set of obligations, duties, and behaviours that assist the religious person to re-establish order in an original lost ideal state, the LHP strives to instead fulfil those occurrences that threw mankind out of the original order. The original order, as it is described for example in the myth of the Garden of Eden, portrays a static, childlike, primordial state in submission to God. Instead of appeasing God and returning to this state, the adept of the Left Hand Path follows the Serpent who offered the fruits of knowledge, which led in turn to the expulsion from Eden but also awoke man's sexuality, thirst for knowledge and the will to become like God. This is what the serpent promises, or as Jeffrey J. Kripal writes in *The Serpent's*

Gift: Gnostic Reflections on the Study of Religion:

> In a rather tragic way for Western religious thought, then, the story seems to suggest that God stands against our own morality, against sexuality, and against the divinization of human nature through the acquisition of knowledge and sensual pleasure.[3]

It is however possible to understand from the Bible that this is actually the will of God, since Man is said to have been created in the image of God and God apparently wishes that Man should become existentially grown up like Him. To this extent the adept of the Left Hand Path expresses the will of God more effectively than those who attempt to simply obey and worship God.

The Left Hand Path is associated with the goal to become a God, which means that one becomes existentially mature, expresses free will, takes personal responsibility and gains knowledge and power over existence. The Left Hand Path does not beg for mercy and emphasises the need for personal responsibility.

What distinguishes this path from forms of Hermeticism—which emphasise becoming divine and attaining states of sacred knowledge—is the focus on the dark and the left; in almost all cultures the left side is associated with the forbidden, the abnormal, the exclusive and deviant and in esotericism it is associated with the magic that goes against religion and the rules of the gods. The Left Hand Path celebrates dark and revolutionary deities like Lucifer, Loke, Kali, Hekate, Prometheus, Azazel and the Fallen Angels, to mention just a few. The LHP is antinomian and breaks cultural, religious and above all existential taboos. This does not have to do with any kind of criminal deeds, or about doing shocking or provocative actions, but about breaking unconscious patterns that determine our existence. Antinomianism challenges 'unawareness' and enables us to consciously behold our existence and our possibilities. From this perspective we may make free choices and develop our own sense of personal responsibility. The greatest taboo is without doubt our own non-existence, our death, which the adept of the Left Hand Path confronts through exploration of the dark. By confronting our non-existence we may grow and gain the life-force through which we may become like gods.

The *Qliphoth* and the *Sitra Ahra* are the worlds of the dark side. The Left Hand Path is a meta-tradition that is characterized by 1) the goal of individual divinity and 2) the desire to explore the dark. The Left Hand Path, as interpreted in Dragon Rouge, is never dogmatic but is a method to reach a goal. Discussions about what is associated with one side or the other must never exclusively divide what is perceived as belonging to the right or the left side. Principally, the adept of the Left Hand Path should be able to do everything that the adept of the Right Hand Path can do, but the reverse is not always the case. An adept of the Left Hand Path can choose to participate in religious practices, services, theurgy or invoking angels if he or she wants to, but is always closest to the dark forces. This fact does not mean, as in some psychologically oriented teachings, that it is all about 'balancing' the light and the darkness—instead it is all about employing the entire spectrum of deviant and conflicting principles. The Draconian LHP is dualistic and non-dualistic at the same time. The Draconian path is close to the Tantric *bhedabeda*, 'Dualist-Non Dualist' concept.[4] The light and the dark, the right and the left, exist as real principles and powers that alternately work together or work against each other. This dynamic is what the dark adept uses to grow and progress. The RHP generally wishes to fight or harmonise these polarities, while a dark adept uses them to gain power. The goal is not, however, that one should win over the other. The magician is an existential being, and in that way an embodiment of the light, who turns to the dark to attain divinity.

The Draconian tradition and the Left Hand Path are related to perennialism and the view that there are common denominators beneath the surface of different cultures and religions. As a result, Dragon Rouge compares gods and demons from different times and cultures; under the surface they represent the same powers, which perhaps can best be described by looking at them from several angles simultaneously. By comparing Kali and Lilith, for example, we gain a greater image of the dark goddess.

The Draconian tradition is a greater meta-tradition that includes both the right and the left hand path. *Drakon* is a word which derives from the Greek verb *derkein* which means 'to see', and the Draconian tradition strives towards increased perception and insight. The Dragon as a mythical entity represents the primal forces that existed before anything gained form. In ancient mystery traditions the Dragon represents chaos and those forces that contain all polarities but which at the same time remain beyond polarities.

The Draconian magician encompasses principles that are contained both within the dark and the light. This allows matter and spirit to be viewed holistically as different expressions of the same thing. The Dragon, in other words, is related to the double-aspect theory which was expressed for example by Spinoza, where spirit and matter are regarded as the same substance but can be viewed from different aspects. Spirit can be viewed as consciousness and also as matter. For this reason the

Draconian tradition is not negative towards the body or Nature and views matter as a repository of immanent forces that permit entry into magical and alternative dimensions. Dragon Rouge posits the notion that many spiritual seekers have missed the goal by forgetting that the key to self-awareness is immanent both within the body and Nature. The holism of the Draconian tradition is expressed in the image of the Ouroboros serpent that swallows its own tail and incorporates the opposites of spirit and matter, light and darkness, female and male. This holistic principle is also reflected in the alchemical motto *en to pan*—all is one. But this is a unity which in itself is also multitude and division, dynamic and ever-changing. Unity to Herakleitos is constant change. In this dynamic Draconian substance we can be more or less unconscious and dependent, but through the Left Hand Path we reach awareness, autonomy and free will.

Consequently, the Dragon Rouge emphasises both the importance of natural science on the one hand and psychological and humanistic scholarship on the other, as disciplines completing each other—just as we emphasise physical training and physical challenges as well as musical and aesthetic expressions. Nevertheless, in Dragon Rouge we must expand our range of insights into the nature of matter and the body and move well beyond the contemporary materialistic paradigm. Nature is not dead, and we are not only our bodies. Sexuality is not only reproduction, but also a progressive, initiatory power. The brain does not create thoughts, just like a television set does not create programs. The source of our thoughts lies in levels beyond our physical body—we are more than our body and we can travel with our mind.

The Draconian tradition is contradictory and cannot be logically explained. This is why the order recommends books that may contradict each other, but which together present a more complete image of the Draconian reality, which is otherwise very hard to grasp. From a Draconian perspective reality is always greater than the realm of reason and logic and for this reason we emphasise the value of practical occult experiences. The Draconian tradition is philosophically related to Taoism, where Tao—represented by the Dragon—is often described as that which cannot be described. In Western esotericism this is best represented by the Orphic principle Nox, the night—that which is limitless and indescribable.

The Draconian tradition and the Left Hand Path are pragmatic and action-oriented and focus on results. They emphasise that co-operation is needed to achieve good individual outcomes and that work and self-sacrifice are required if one wishes to develop. Magic is a life-path that encourages creative action and practice. The professor of philosophy,

Eugenio Trias, has pointed out that the word 'magic' can be traced to the word 'make' and the German *machen*—to do or create. Magic invokes Man's creative power through which the magician makes his visions real through the Draconian formula *Visio Vires Actio*—Visions, Power and Action.

Practical magic in the 21ˢᵗ century

Judging from the number of esoteric organisations and groups found on the Internet one can easily be led to believe that esotericism is one of the largest religious and philosophical expressions today. However, if one actually investigates the actual number of followers the image changes. Most of these organisations have only a few members and rarely survive for more than a couple of years. Often they are essentially individual projects that transmit the founder's subjective opinions. With the establishment of the Internet as the main source of information students of magic need to be more critical of their sources than ever. In Dragon Rouge we have always emphasised the importance of tangible esoteric expressions such as physical temples, real texts and books, actual knowledge grounded in historical and academic sources, real efforts, real meetings, real practice and real people.

Although fantasy is an important tool in esotericism, it must never become stuck in a groundless facade or escapism. Dragon Rouge emphasises that esoteric initiation should be connected to personal development in the mundane world. If one is attracted to magic because one is seeking to escape the normal world, one is on the wrong path. As a Draconian esotericist one is indeed a visionary, but with both feet on the ground.

On the Left Hand Path, antinomianism is viewed as a means of attaining initiation. However antinomianism is often misinterpreted in a shallow way. Antinomianism does not correspond to criminality, provocation or immorality. It is a path that enables the magical practitioner to break free from unconscious structures and rules and to instead create an inner ethical compass that normally demands more than is generally found in society at large.[5] Antinomianism is basically a path that takes the magician beyond the limits of the laws of Nature and individual existence. It is a method of encountering our non-existence—death—in order to be able to ennoble our existence. In order to reach this state of awareness stable structures are demanded, as well as serious intent. True solitary initiations are possible, but are as rare as becoming a perfected martial arts performer on one's own, without learning from others. If this is possible, it is in any case an ineffective and much slower path.

There is also a myth among certain esoteric students that esotericism and information is, or should be, costless. Nothing could be further from the truth. 'Costless' means that one desires to behold something without doing anything. Esotericism and initiation demand powerful action and hard work. Never in this world has anything been achieved without cost—not in the Stone Age and not now. Knowledge and information are something for which the adept must be prepared to give in return, both to the one who transmits the knowledge and also in the form of hard work. If one wishes to do anything above the ordinary in life, one must be prepared to show respect to those who are expressing potential, whether in the martial arts, music or any form of artistic expression, by paying one's dues, and by working hard. In association with the esoteric arts, which deal with vast subjects like life and death, this is even truer, and always has been.

With the Internet, one can be flooded with information as never before. Initiation rituals from many of the old magical orders are freely accessible to download, as well as books and previously hard-to-find occult texts. From one perspective, this presents serious occult students with important insight into the occult traditions and teachings. However, if these sources of information are misused and treated like any other object acquired via the Internet there can easily be a negative impact on one's personal and magical development. Esoteric knowledge is not about quantity—that one should collect as much as possible—but about quality. This in turn is a long process that takes a considerable amount of time to integrate into one's individual life and consciousness. From an esoteric point of view, it is better to copy ONE occult book by hand than to download a hundred.

If knowledge is like a journey, the Internet is like flying. It is fast and takes us to many destinations in a short amount of time. However, it does not automatically help us to see or experience more—and, perhaps, the opposite. The modern traveller generally knows more about airports than about people and places from other cultures, unlike a traveller of old who inevitably—through the slow tempo—was forced to get to know the environments and persons encountered on the journey. Modern techniques are useful but must never lead us to believe that the tool is the purpose, that the map is the place, or that real knowledge is something we can acquire easily and swiftly.

The Draconian Initiation
The occult societies that were founded and developed in the West from the 18th century onwards had initiatory systems based on personal development and social schooling and employed symbolic language from Western Christian Platonic paradigms whereas exoteric Christian systems were instead influenced by Aristotelian ideas. These earlier occult societies had

initiation systems that generally took around ten years to pass through. Dragon Rouge is founded on a different paradigm which although using Western symbols is closer to Tantric structures. We emphasise personal progression and social schooling, but mainly as necessary qualities to be able to handle the higher degrees. To reach half the way—to Tiphareth-Thagirion, the central sphere of the Qabalistic Tree—can take between 11 or 28 years (a turn of Saturn). This level brings unity with one's Daemon and a form of enlightenment that makes one like a Bodhisattva, with one foot in the higher worlds and one in this world, and a philosophy based on the principle of assisting others to reach this central sphere. The following levels can take a very much longer time to pass through, and may require mystical ideals in terms of fulfilment. When the magician reaches beyond the limited self, he or she becomes a magician in the highest sense and acquires cosmic powers and soul-immortality. This state is best compared to the Siddhis of the Tantric traditions, but even this is not the final stage, since it is often described as a state of a thousand lotuses in all the rainbow's colours, filled with immeasurable lust and power. These lotuses represent wombs and are also metaphors for a state of erotic lust and the possibility of allowing things to be born. The next level beyond this—*Sahasrara*—involves becoming a Nath, which may take thousands of years. A Nath is an 'aghora', a dark adept who is identified with Shiva and who would be a terrifying demon to an uninitiated person. A Nath is described as an immortal dedicated adept of Shiva, with the Kundalini flowing at full force. However, after millions of years, a Nath may in turn become a Muni, which is a form even more powerful and fathomless in appearance. However, not even becoming a Muni is the highest attainment. Finally, one may become a Rishi and it is at this level that we find the greatest magicians who are beyond the universe and who can create and destroy worlds, connect karmic bonds—and who can also enable other magicians to attain the highest states of awareness. A Rishi has passed through the black hole, the *Mahakala*, which is associated with *Shunya* and the god Shiva. This is the ultimate level of the Left Hand Path, as described by Julius Evola:

> *There is a significant difference between the two Tantric paths, that of the right hand and that of the left hand (which both are under Shiva's aegis). In the former, the adept always experiences 'someone above him', even at the highest level of realization. In the latter, 'he becomes the ultimate Sovereign' (chakravartin = worldruler).*[6]

Tantric descriptions of processes that take millions and billions of years must of course be metaphorically understood as signifying the size and importance of the processes themselves—but in Dragon Rouge our philosophy of seeking self-deification is not something taken lightly, unlike certain forms of Satanism and New Age thought where claims to divinity seem all too common. In those instances, where a teacher on the Left Hand Path hears from some student that the process is not going quickly enough, there is always the comparison with Vamachara Tantra to take to heart, looking into the time span of billions of years.

The initiatory system of the Dragon Rouge follows the Left Hand Path, which is a manifestation of the *Qliphoth* and other emanations that exist as revolutionary anti-worlds which the magician can enter in order to attain magical and initiatory progression. The Left Hand Path is associated with the Sanskrit term *Vama*—denoting 'left' and also excrements and vomit—and is naturally associated with the *Qliphoth* in the Qabalah, which are also viewed as excrements. *It is up to the adept to ennoble that which has been cast out of the universe and turn it into gold.* When God created the cosmos all that was left of the primordial dragon became left-overs, the excrements of existence. From this black earth, the adept can give birth to new plants. Those elements that were cast out—*Vama*, *Qliphoth*—were not included in the new order but were thrown into desolation. The true purpose of *Vama Marg*, the Left Hand Path, is not to join God's perfect order but to find the Dragon, the primordial mother, and to pass onwards through her womb—Drakon, the Eye, the Black Hole—in order to enter a new universe created by the magician's will.

Kali-Kundalini of the Tantra, Lilith-Nachash of the Qabalah

In Dragon Rouge, the Red Dragon equates with *Tehom*, which is Hebrew for 'depths' and 'abyss' and refers to the primordial state from which God created the world in Genesis. Phenomenologically and etymologically, Tehom represents Tiamat in the Babylonian myth of creation, *Enuma Elish*. Tiamat is described as a deadly ancient dragon, but if viewed through the lens of Gnostic philosophy, Tiamat/Tehom corresponds to Bythos (Greek for 'depths') which has a positive role in the original monad (compared with the Ouroboros-serpent which unites all in one). This takes us beyond the negative connotations of the Demiurge, the Biblical Creator—who in turn represents the Babylonian Marduk who slew the primordial mother Tiamat and created the world from her body. Tehom/Bythos is the 'unmentionable' Proarche who existed before Creation and is responsible for the Pleroma, the pure light. In Jewish mysticism Tehom is also the source of the *Qliphoth*, which are often described as mere matter. However, in Dragon Rouge they are viewed as emanating from Tehom—the absolute highest level of being. Similarly, *Ain* is the highest level beyond Creation on the Tree of Life in the Qabalah.

Dragon Rouge's view of the *Qliphoth* is close to the double-aspect theory in philosophy where spirit and matter are not in opposition but are two expressions of the same foundation. This view is shared by Maggid Decarav le-Ya'aqov who believes that *Ain* represents Hyle—Prime Matter and the divine wisdom—and also that *Ain* is beyond God. Dragon Rouge interprets *Ain* as corresponding to the Great One in Gnosticism, the one who is beyond God and who manifests its power as the Serpent in the Garden of Eden. Furthermore, the Great One can be interpreted as Tehom/Tiamat through a creative hermeneutics applied to the *Enuma Elish* with regard to the Genesis myth.

In these ancient esoteric traditions, Tiamat and Tehom are described as the primeval darkness—the terrible dragon who threatens to annihilate all—but from a dark magical perspective the Serpent in the Garden of Eden, the bringer of wisdom, is a spark of Tiamat. However, Tiamat is also the ultimate expression of life, represented by the Tantric goddess Shakti (power) and the Kundalini (Dragon Fire). Dragon Rouge ascribes to the theory that the word Tiamat is derived from the Sumerian words Ti ('life') and Ama ('mother'), and that she is the mother and source of all life.

Dragon Rouge is based on a philosophy that in many ways is distinct from other forms of Western esotericism. The initiatory system of the order embraces Tiamat, the *Qliphoth* and darkness, and does not view matter as a negative counterpoint to spirit. Rather, Dragon Rouge views matter as a prerequisite for the ascent of the spirit. Matter is Maya/Shakti/Kali/Kundalini, which in hermeneutic terminology may be compared to Qliphoth/Shekinah/Lilith/Nachash. In the Dragon Rouge we regard matter not as empty but as over-filled. In a Hermetic sense, we also claim that it/she (Maya/Shakti/Qliphoth/Lilith) represents or corresponds to the highest reality and is thus the foremost initiatrix of the utmost reality. She is a Serpent in the Garden of Eden, a mirror image of Tiamat/Tehom, which is the ultimate reality that corresponds to the Great One among the Gnostics, the *Ain* of the Qabalists and the *Nox* (night) of the Orphics. Through a Gnostic reading of the traditional Western religious literature we are inclined to interpret the God we encounter there as one who keeps man imprisoned. Maya/Qliphoth are those shells and veils that create the material world and Shekinah/Shakti is the inherent life-force in Nature, both as energy and consciousness. In Greek philosophy Shekinah/Shakti is Sophia, wisdom. Lilith/Kali is the storming, dynamic, erotic and terrifying manifestation of the Dark Goddess and Kundalini/Nachash is the serpent that awakens in man and whose poison is wisdom.

We can establish that *Sitra Ahra* has its roots in *Ain Soph*. The satanic powers, called in the *Zohar* 'Sitra Ahra' ('the other side') are none other than the other side of Ain-Soph itself. According to the heretic Sabbataian Qabalah, the *Sitra Ahra* is formed as an anti-structure to Creation. Dragon Rouge is not attempting to reconstruct Sabbataian Qabalah, but shares its multifaceted view on *Ain Soph*, namely that the *Qliphoth* has its roots there. If we study other Qabalistic texts, *Ain* is sometimes equated with Prime Matter. As Daniel C. Matt writes in '*Ayin*: The concept of Nothingness in Jewish Mysticism':

> *Ayin is the root of all things, and 'when one brings anything to its root, one can transform it'... Nothingness embraces all potentiality. The Maggid identifies ayin with divine wisdom, which is also hyle (primordial matter) — capable of assuming any form. Ayin 'strips off one form and puts on another.... Transformation is possible only through...ayin.*[7]

In the Qabalistic text, *Galya Raza*, we also discover that the origin of existence and Creation is in the Darkness, and that Sitra Ahra ruled alone before Creation. Supported by Qabalistic sources, Dragon Rouge finds that *Ain* and the *Qliphoth* are equivalent to each other and that, in accordance with this perspective, the God we encounter in Genesis is not the utmost power. Instead we have to trace our way back into the history before Creation, where we encounter Tiamat/Tehom, and possibly the Great One. Creation is Jahve's/Mardus's formation of existence, where phenomena are created through a primordial sacrifice of the Dragon. Creation reaches a form of perfection which in itself is positive but also at the same time static. Surrounding Creation/Cosmos is the primordial Dragon/Kaos/Nox/Ain which in turn is a dynamic transformative lifeforce. It brings life to existence but at the same time is shut out from the walls of Eden. Meanwhile a spark of the primordial Dragon/Kaos/Nox/Ain sneaks into Eden and enables man to awaken from his paradisiacal slumber by offering the fruits of knowledge. The Tree of Knowledge represents the *Qliphoth*. This is a tree that can be found in the North, while the Tree of Life is in the East. Originally, they were united, but the God of Genesis does not allow man to partake of the fruits of knowledge and banishes them from Eden, thus hindering them from eating from the Tree of Life to live forever. This God is afraid of man´s progression, as described in Genesis 3:22 where this is explicitly stated.

The orthodox Qabalist seeks to reinstate the paradisiacal order and re-establish the original contact with God, while the adepts of the Left Hand Path choose to fulfil the path that began with the eating of the fruits of knowledge, or as Scholem writes in 'Sitra Ahra: Good and Evil in the Kabbalah':

> *Man may seek to join himself to the lost unity and harmony of the Divine by obeying the divine will revealed in the Torah, or else may follow the path of the Other Side, thereby repeating the primordial sin...*[8]

The Left Hand Path represents this last alternative and desires to complete the path of knowledge and to regain the fruits of life. Instead of becoming one with God, the Left Hand Path adept strives to become like God, which is promised by the Serpent. For this to be possible, the adept must receive help from the force that is 'beyond God'—Tehom/Tiamat/Dragon/The Great One and Chaos/Nox/Ain which corresponds to a primordial foundation of both matter and spirit united.

One possibility for a *Qliphotic* adept would be to disintegrate oneself through the powers of Sitra Ahra and in that manner return into the primeval dynamic unity of Ain—it would be a form of mysticism close to Meister Eckhart's negative theology and unity with nothingness—but it is more characteristic of a true adept of the Left Hand Path to fulfil the promise by the Serpent and become like God. As noted earlier, in Dragon Rouge we emphasise that magic is etymologically connected to the root 'make' or in German *machen*, and the highest goal is to become a 'Maker', a Creator. Thus, the creation of golems is an important aspect of our philosophy and explains why we view science as something positive in accordance with the Luciferian-Promethean-Faustian will of man. Although we work against a path predestined by God, through the *Qliphotic* Powers, God is also a role model, as the most powerful magician and alchemist.

Members of Dragon Rouge read religious and esoteric texts holistically, like ontological descriptions, without necessarily sharing the normative entirety. By analysing Isaac ha-Kohen, Luria, Nathan of Gaza, Tantric and Gnostic texts etc, we come to our own logical conclusions and these in turn provide the basic philosophy which is central to the esoteric system of Dragon Rouge. The order's view on *Sitra Ahra*, *Ain* and the Left Hand Path has been shaped by such studies, combined with analysing and exploring magical practice.

Summary

The Draconian Tradition is a form of Faustian magic—a type of 'Promethean pioneering'—that explores the dark and seeks progression. Although it may be demanding, it is not a rootless progressivism disconnected from a basic experience of the underlying power and energy of life. The latter can be symbolised by the Dragon. Thus, the philosophy of Dragon Rouge can be viewed as a synthesis between the Faustian and Promethean pioneer spirit and the Draconian vitalism found in Shaktism and the teachings of Vril and Od in Western esotericism—a teaching that claims that there is a fundamental power and meaning inherent in existence.

Furthermore, the Darkness is a prerequisite for the Light and in Matter rests the power that can elevate the Spirit to the highest levels. Any dualism is an illusion and has generally merely caused fear and ignorance regarding those very principles that can increase our knowledge and insight. The Tarot card *The Hanged Man* depicts the initiate who turns the world upside down and inside out in order to be initiated into the mysteries. We recognize this motif from ancient mystery cults, and Odin's search for runic wisdom. Only when we are able to see existence from a different perspective can new wisdom arise. This is illustrated by both Odin and Christ who express how enlightenment can only be beheld by first entering into the dark spheres and death. The Dragon is not opposed to God, the Serpent is not the arch-enemy of Christ or the Aleph. Tehom and Ain are not different, but two sides of the same coin. To be able to explore darkness and find new knowledge we must momentarily turn the world upside down, enter into the absurd and gaze upon the strange. In the words of the occultist and surrealist André Breton we have to 'cross what the occultists call dangerous territory'.
—*Translations by Tommie Eriksson and Thomas Karlsson*

References

Brandi, Alberto, 2008, *La Via Oscura. Introduzione al Sentiero di Mano Sinistra*. Rome: Atanòr.
____ 2008, 'Monism and Dualism on the Left-Hand Path: A Brief Consideration', in *Dracontias* 4, Stockholm: Dragon Rouge.
Dan, Joseph, 1995, 'Samael, Lilit, and the Concept of Evil in Early Kabbalism', in *Essential Papers on Kabbalah,* edited by Lawrence Fine, New York: New York University Press.
Evola, Julius, 1992 (1968), *The Yoga of Power,* Rochester, Vermont: Inner Traditions.
Flowers, Edred, 1995, *Black Runa*, Smithville, Texas: Runa-Raven Press.
Granholm, Kennet, 'The Secular, the Post-Secular, and the Esoteric in the Public Sphere', forthcoming.
Grant, Kenneth, 1975, *Cults of the Shadow*, London: Muller.
____ 1977, *Nightside of Eden*, London: Muller.
Karlsson, Thomas, 2007, *Qabalah, Qliphoth and Goetic Magic*, Jacksonville,

Oregon: Ajna.

———2002, *Uthark: Nightside of the Runes*, Sundbyberg: Ouroboros Produktion.

Kripal, Jeffrey J., 2007, *The Serpent's Gift: Gnostic Reflections on the Study of Religion*, Chicago: The University of Chicago Press.

Matt, Daniel C. 1995, 'Ayin: The Concept of Nothingness in Jewish Mysticism' in *Essential Papers on Kabbalah*, edited by Lawrence Fine, New York: New York University Press.

Thorsson, Edred, 1987, *Runelore—A Handbook of Esoteric Runology*, York Beach, Maine: Samuel Weiser, Inc.

Scholem, Gershom, 1991. 'Sitra Ahra: Good and Evil in the Kabbalah' in *On The Mystical Shape of the Godhead: Basic Concepts in the Kabbalah*, New York: Schocken.

Svaboda, Robert, 1996, *Aghora II: Kundalini*, Calcutta: Rupa & Co.

Endnotes

1. Brandi, Alberto, *La Via Oscura. Introduzione al Sentiero di Mano Sinistra*.
2. Granholm, Kennet, 'The Secular, the Post-Secular, and the Esoteric in the Public Sphere', 10.
3. Kripal, Jeffrey J. *The Serpent's Gift: Gnostic Reflections on the Study of Religion*, 3.
4. Brandi, Alberto, 'Monism and Dualism on the Left-Hand Path. A Brief Consideration', in *Dracontias* 4, 2008.
5. Flowers, Edred, *Black Runa*, 17; Karlsson, Thomas, *Qabalah, Qliphoth and Goetic Magic*, 20.
6. Evola, Julius, *Yoga of Power*, 55.
7. Matt, Daniel C., 'Ayin: The Concept of Nothingness in Jewish Mysticism', in *Essential Papers on Kabbalah*, 92.
8. Scholem, Gershom, *On the Mystical Shape of the Godhead*:75.

11
Claiming Hellish Hegemony: Anton LaVey, The Church of Satan & The Satanic Bible[1]

James R. Lewis

> LaVey describes Satanism as a secular philosophy of rationalism and self-preservation (natural law, animal state), gift-wrapping these ideas in religious trappings to add to their appeal.
>
> Blanche Barton 1990, 201

The status of *The Satanic Bible* as an authoritative scripture—or, perhaps more accurately, as a kind of *quasi-scripture*—within the Satanic subculture was initially brought to my attention during my first face-to-face encounter with Satanists in the Spring of 2000. Via the internet, I had found a small Satanist group in Portage, Wisconsin, which was about an hour south of where I resided at the time. This group, the Temple of Lylyth, distinguishes itself from Anton LaVey's brand of Satanism chiefly by its emphasis on feminine nature of the Dark Power. I arranged to meet with them in Portage on a Friday evening.

Over the course of our conversation, the founder and then leader of the group mentioned that on Friday evenings he was usually downtown where a small group of fervent Christians regularly set up what might be called a 'preaching station' to spread the Gospel. This young fellow (he was nineteen at the time) would confront them as a practising Satanist. He always carried a copy of *The Satanic Bible* with him, not just so he could quote some of accusations LaVey levelled against Christianity, but also so he could correct anything these evangelists might say about Satanism by citing an authoritative source. I'm sure this is something of a caricature, but I was left with the impression of duelling religionists, Christians hurling Bible verses at my informant as he matched them blow for blow with quotes from *The Satanic Bible*. This experience led me to pay attention whenever other Satanists mentioned *The Satanic Bible*.

The Temple of Lylyth is part of a loose, decentralized Satanic movement that coheres as a distinct religious community largely by virtue of adherence to certain themes in the thought of Anton LaVey, founder of modern Satanism, though few movement participants outside the Church of Satan would regard themselves as 'orthodox LaVeyans'. Following the dissolution of the Church of Satan's grotto system in 1975 and before the explosion of the Internet in the mid-nineties, the Satanic movement was propagated almost entirely by *The Satanic Bible*, which has continuously been in print as a widely-available, mass market paperback. Rather than a guide to Devil-worship, LaVey's work advocates a blend of Epicureanism and Ayn Rand's philosophy, flavoured with a pinch of ritual magic. Couched in iconoclastic rhetoric, *The Satanic Bible* has always held particular appeal for rebellious adolescents. The title seems to have originally been chosen for its shock value rather than from any pretence to scriptural status.

The present chapter focuses on issues of the legitimation of authority within the Satanist movement and among Anton LaVey's successors in the Church of Satan. LaVey was a charismatic individual who appealed to the authority of reason and attacked the authority of tradition. However, the figure of LaVey, and particularly *The Satanic Bible*, almost immediately became sources of authority for a new Satanic 'tradition' after LaVey's passing.

Satanic Legitimacy

Satanists do not consciously regard *The Satanic Bible* in the same way traditional religionists regard their sacred texts. In fact, the title seems to have originally been chosen for its shock value rather than from any pretence to scriptural status. However, *The Satanic Bible* is treated as an authoritative document, which effectively *functions* as scripture within the Satanic community. In particular, LaVey's work is quoted to legitimate particular positions as well as to de-legitimate the positions of other Satanists. This legitimation strategy appears to have been unconsciously derived from the Judeo-Christian tradition, which locates the source of religious authority in a sacred text. In other words, being raised in a religious tradition that emphasizes the authority of scripture creates an attitude that can be unconsciously carried over to other, very different kinds of writings.

The classic sociological analysis of the legitimation of authority is Max Weber's tripartite schema of traditional, rational-legal, and charismatic. The dynamics (in the sense of upsetting rather than reinforcing established authority structures) of this schema are largely confined to the factor of charisma, a form of legitimation Weber viewed as particularly characteristic of new religious movements. Weber's analysis of the legitimation of authority provides a useful starting point for understanding the legitimation strategies employed in contemporary new religions like the Church of Satan.

Weber's work provides a useful starting point for understanding the legitimation strategies deployed by contemporary new religions, but it should immediately be noted that his analysis is also inadequate. For example, in contrast to what one might anticipate from the discussion of charismatic authority in Weber's *Economy and Society* (1968), one often finds new religions appealing to tradition—though the explicit nature of such appeals means that they constitute a variation from what Weber had in mind by the traditional legitimation of authority (which he viewed as more implicit than explicit). Also, when nascent movements attempt to justify a new idea, practice or social arrangement by attributing it to the authority of tradition, it is usually through a reinterpretation of the past that they are able to portray themselves as the true embodiment of tradition. Such variations on what one might anticipate from his schema indicate that Weber did not have the last word in this issue.

For Weber, 'charisma' includes everything from direct revelations to the leader's ability to provide both mundane and supernatural benefits to followers. Charisma may be the keystone in a new movement's initial attractiveness, but charismatic leaders typically appeal to other sources of legitimacy as well. For instance, many modern movements appeal to the authority of reason as embodied in natural science. This is because the general populace of industrialized countries tends to give science and science's child, technology, a level of respect and prestige enjoyed by few other social institutions. As a number of observers have pointed out, science has come to be viewed quasi-religiously in the modern world. Thus any religion that claims to be *scientific* in some way draws on the prestige and perceived legitimacy of natural science. Religions such as Christian Science, Science of Mind, and Scientology claim just that.

There is, however, a distinct difference between popular notions of science and science proper. Average citizens' views of science are significantly influenced by their experience of technology. Hence, in most people's minds, an important goal of science appears to be the solution of practical problems. This perception shaped the various religious sects that incorporated 'science' into their names. In sharp contrast to traditional religions that focus on salvation in the afterlife, the emphasis in these religions is on the improvement of this life. Groups within the Christian Science/New Thought tradition, for example, usually claim to have discovered spiritual 'laws'. If these laws are properly understood and applied, they transform and improve the lives of ordinary individuals, much as technology has transformed society.

Modern Satanism is in some ways a continuation of this line of development, and in other ways a departure from it. Though Satanism also appeals to science, its focus is not on developing a pragmatic science of mind. Rather, when LaVey founded the Church of Satan in 1966, he grounded Satanism's legitimacy on a view of human nature shaped by a secularist appropriation of modern science. Unlike Christian Science, Scientology and other groups that claimed to model their approach to spirituality after the *methods* of science, LaVey's strategy was to base Satanism's 'anti-Theology' in a secularist *worldview* derived from natural science. The appeal to a worldview based on 'our scientific and technological advances' provided LaVey with an atheistic underpinning for his attacks on 'obsolete' Christianity and other forms of supernatural spirituality (Barton 1990, 13). Certain other emergent religions such as, for example, the Raelian Movement, similarly appeal to the worldview of secular science for their legitimacy and, like Satanism, attack other religions as unreasonable because of their lack of a scientific basis (Chryssides 2000, Sentes and Palmer 2000). At the same time, LaVey went beyond contemporary secularism by suggesting the reality of mysterious, 'occult' forces—forces he claimed were not supernatural, but were, rather, natural forces that would eventually be discovered by science. In his notion of mysterious forces that could be manipulated by the will of the magician, LaVey was really not so far from the mentalistic technology of Christian Science, Scientology, and other religious bodies in the metaphysical tradition.

The human nature to which LaVey appealed was humanity's animal nature, viewed through the lens of Darwinism. The human being in this view is little more than an animal with no ultimate morality other than law of the jungle and no purpose other than the survival of the fittest. In terms of Weber's schema, we would say that LaVey's appeal to human nature (meaning, for LaVey, the Darwinist vision of human nature) was a rational legitimation of authority. In other words, LaVey claimed that Satanism was a legitimate religion because it was rational (i.e., congruent with the science). As a corollary, traditional religion was irrational (unscientific) and therefore illegitimate.

Beyond this explicit appeal to science, LaVey was a charismatic individual and this charisma was undoubtedly crucial for the successful birth of the Church of Satan. In addition to his personal magnetism, LaVey also consciously amplified his charismatic status by creating an impressive pseudo-biography in which he was able to convincingly portray himself as an extraordinary individual. However, LaVey's charismatic authority soon began to wane, particularly after he dismantled the Church of Satan (CoS) as a functioning church in 1975 (discussed below). This led to a number of interesting—though somewhat paradoxical—developments. In addition to numerous splinter groups, a decentralized, anarchistic movement emerged that was shaped by the central themes in LaVey's thought, particularly as expressed in *The Satanic Bible*. This book became a doctrinal touchstone of the movement, though independent Satanists felt free to selectively appropriate ideas from *The Satanic Bible* and to mix them with ideas and practices drawn from other sources. LaVey's book became, in a sense, an actual scripture (or, perhaps more accurately, a kind of quasi-scripture), and sacred texts are a form of what Weber meant by traditional authority. However, many independent Satanists also adhered to LaVey's program of the authority of rationality, feeling free to criticize and even to reject aspects of the LaVeyan tradition. Thus the contemporary Satanic movement's legitimacy is based on a dual appeal to independent rational authority and to the authority of the LaVeyan tradition.

In contrast, the remnants of LaVey's church—which is still technically the largest Satanist group in terms of formal membership—quickly solidified into a doctrinally-rigid organization focused on maintaining the purity of LaVeyan Satanism. This was partly in response to the challenge presented by non-CoS Satanists. In the ongoing argument over legitimacy, LaVey's successors have come to place excessive stress on their role as bearers of his legacy, even asserting that only CoS members are 'real' Satanists, and characterizing Satanists outside the fold as 'pseudo' Satanists. In terms of Weber's analysis, one would say that CoS's legitimation strategy has narrowed to focus almost exclusively on CoS's claim to traditional authority.

Anton LaVey and Modern Religious Satanism

To comprehend religious Satanism, one must first understand that Satan has become an ambivalent symbol within the modern world. Part of the reason for the attractiveness of LaVeyan Satanism is its ability to hold together a number of diverse meanings found in this symbol. In the Western cultural tradition, the Devil represents much more than absolute evil. By default, the Prince of Darkness has come to embody some very attractive attributes. For example, because traditional Christianity has been so anti-sensual, Satan became associated with sex. The Christian tradition has also condemned pride, vengefulness and avarice, and, when allied with the status quo, has promoted conformity and obedience. The three former traits and the antithesis of the latter two traits thus became diabolical characteristics. LaVeyan Satanism celebrates such 'vices' as virtues, and identifies them as the core of what Satanism is really all about.

LaVey founded the Church of Satan in 1966, the first organized church in modern times devoted to Satan. As a consequence, Anton LaVey has sometimes been referred to as the 'St. Paul of Satanism' (Wright 1993, 122). LaVey has two biographies, one historical and one legendary. This dichotomy has only become apparent in recent years. His real life was far more prosaic than the story he fabricated for the benefit of the media. LaVey effectively promoted his carefully crafted pseudo-biography through conversations with his disciples, media interviews, and two biographies by associates that he appears to have dictated—Burton Wolfe's *The Devil's Avenger* (1974) and Blanche Barton's *Secret Life of a Satanist* (1990). LaVey's fictional biography was clearly meant to legitimate his self-appointed role as the 'Black Pope' by portraying him as an extraordinary individual.

According to the official Church of Satan biography, he was born Howard Anton Szandor LaVey in Chicago, Illinois. His parents, Joseph and Augusta LaVey, moved to San Francisco while LaVey was still an infant. He was introduced to the occult by his Transylvanian gypsy grandmother. As a teenager he pursued various avenues of occult studies, as well as hypnotism and music. He also played an oboe in the San Francisco Ballet Orchestra. He dropped out of high school at 17 to join the Clyde Beatty Circus and worked as a calliope player and big cat trainer, later learning stage magic as well. While an organist in a burlesque theatre, he had an affair with the young Marilyn Monroe shortly before she became famous.

He married in 1950 and about that time took a job as a police photographer, but in 1955 returned to organ playing. Until he formed the Church of Satan in 1966, he was the city of San Francisco's official organist. He divorced in 1960 in order to marry Diane Hegarty. He purchased his house—eventually becoming the Church of Satan headquarters, later dubbed the 'Black House'—after he found out it had been the former brothel of the madam Mammy Pleasant.

Drawing on his circus and occult backgrounds, he began to conduct 'midnight magic seminars' at his house. This proved popular enough for him to found the Church of Satan in 1966. The basis for his rituals was Nazi rituals recorded on top-secret films he had seen as a teenager. LaVey's showmanship encouraged significant media coverage of such events as the first Satanic wedding and the first Satanic funeral, worship with a nude woman as the altar, and a cameo appearance as the Devil in the movie *Rosemary's Baby*. LaVey made much of being a close friend of Sammy Davis, Jr. and of having had an affair with Jayne Mansfield, two celebrity members of the Church of Satan. At its peak, he claimed that the Church had hundreds of thousands of members. LaVey passed away in 1997.

LaVey's historical biography overlaps his legendary biography at several points. He was born in Chicago and his family did move to San Francisco. He did make his living as a musician and, of course, he actually did found the Church of Satan and died in 1997. He had several marriages. Almost everything else, however, seems to have been a fabrication.

LaVey's self-created legend was not seriously challenged until a 1991 interview in *Rolling Stone* magazine, entitled 'Sympathy for the Devil'. The author of that article, Lawrence Wright, did a little investigative footwork and discovered that: LaVey was born Howard Stanton Levey to Gertrude and Mike Levey; there never was a 'San Francisco Ballet Orchestra'; no one by the name Levey or LaVey worked as a musician or cat trainer for the Beatty Circus during the period he claimed to have been an employee; neither he nor Monroe ever worked for the Mayan 'burlesque' theatre; he never worked for the San Francisco Police Department; and there was no such thing as an official San Francisco city organist. These discoveries led Wright to remark toward the end of his article:

> *Later, as I began to take apart the literary creation he had made of his life, I would realize that 'Anton LaVey' was itself his supreme creation, his ultimate satanic object, a sort of android composed of all the elements his mysterious creator had chosen from the universe of dark possibilities. (Wright 1992)*

Wright later expanded his expose of LaVey into a chapter for his *Saints and Sinners* (1993).

These findings were considerably amplified in 'Anton LaVey: Legend and Reality', a nine-page 'fact sheet' compiled two or three months after LaVey's passing by his estranged daughter Zeena LaVey Schreck and her husband Nikolas Schreck (1998). In addition to repeating the points made by Wright, the fact sheet dismissed most of Anton LaVey's other claims, such as his claims to have had a Gypsy grandmother, seen films of secret German rituals, purchased the 'Black House' (it was given to him by his parents, who had lived there, and had never been a brothel), appeared in *Rosemary's Baby*, had affairs with Monroe and Mansfield, and so forth.

The current leadership of the Church of Satan has disputed some of these challenges to LaVey's official biography. Their strategy has been to vigorously dispute undocumented challenges while ignoring LaVey's documented fabrications. As one might anticipate, splinter groups from CoS as well as other independent Satanists have seized upon these revelations to challenge the Church leadership's implicit claims to be the only authentic Satanist religious body.

Thinly disguised claims to exclusive legitimacy are peppered throughout CoS documents, such as in some of Blanche Barton's remarks in her 'Sycophants Unite!' essay (composed prior to LaVey's death) posted on the CoS official website:

> *We're lucky to have a leader like Anton LaVey. He has ensured that his philosophy will not die with him; it has been and will continue to be codified, expanded and applied in new areas* by his organization *(emphasis in original)*.

The scope and significance of this dispute is reflected in the *many* attacks on non-CoS Satanists found on the Church of Satan website, particularly in the 'Satanic Bunco Sheet', 'Sycophants Unite!', 'The Myth of the "Satanic Community"', 'Pretenders to the Throne', and 'Recognizing Pseudo-Satanists'. Even a superficial perusal of these documents makes it clear that CoS is *obsessed* with shoring up its own legitimacy by attacking the heretics, especially those who criticize LaVey. For example, the unnamed author of the 'Satanic Bunco Sheet' blasts non-CoS Satanists for 'LaVey-baiting', and then goes on to assert that such pseudo-Satanists deal with LaVey and the Church of Satan by playing 'the Christian game of handing out laurels with one hand while stabbing their progenitor in the back with the other. ...they must somehow convince you that the author of *The Satanic Bible* wasn't practicing pure Satanism [and] that his Church has gone awry in the hands of his successors...'

The Church of Satan began generating splinter groups as early as 1973 when the Church of Satanic Brotherhood was formed by group leaders in Michigan, Ohio, and Florida. This Church lasted only until 1974, when one of the founders announced his conversion to Christianity in a dramatic incident staged for the press in St Petersburg. Other members of the Church of Satan in Kentucky and Indiana left to form the Ordo Templi Satanis, also short-lived. As more schisms occurred, LaVey decided to disband the remaining grottos, the local units of the Church of Satan, which left the Church as little more than a paper organization generating a meagre income for LaVey through sales of memberships (one could become an official member by paying a one-time $100 fee to the Church of Satan; this fee was recently raised to $200).

The conflict (mostly on the Internet) between the original Church of Satan and new Satanist groups accelerated after LaVey's death. In addition to attacking non-CoS Satanists as illegitimate, LaVey's organizational successors have also sought to legitimate their positions by appealing to the authority of LaVey and his writings. These kinds of appeals are rather ironic, given the Black Pope's rejection of traditional religious authority. As indicated earlier, LaVey himself did not attempt to legitimate his new religion with appeals to tradition or to the supernatural. Rather, his explicit strategy was to ground Satanism's legitimacy on a view of human nature shaped by a secularist appropriation of modern science.

Genesis of The Satanic Bible

The most significant single document for the Satanic 'tradition' is *The Satanic Bible*. The idea for this volume came not from LaVey, but from an Avon Books editor named Peter Mayer. As a direct result of the success of the popular film *Rosemary's Baby* and the subsequent increase of popular interest in Satanism and the occult, Mayer decided that 'the time was right for a "Satanic bible"' and he approached LaVey about authoring it (Aquino 1999, 52).

LaVey and his wife took the material they had on hand, wove it together and expanded on these writings to form what became the core of *The Satanic Bible*. This pre-existing material consisted of:

- A short, mimeographed paper that they had been distributing as an 'introduction to Satanism'.
- The so-called 'rainbow sheets', which were 'an assortment of polemical essays' the LaVeys had been mimeographing on coloured paper (Ibid., 52).
- A handout describing and containing instructions for the conduct of ritual magic.
- Articles previously published in the Church periodical, *The Cloven Hoof*.

The LaVeys then ran into a problem, which was that, even after expanding upon all of their available material, they were still *substantially* short of having a manuscript of sufficient length to satisfy their publisher. So, either because the deadline was coming up quickly or because LaVey just didn't want to write anything else at the time (Aquino describes their situation in terms of the former), LaVey tacked materials written by other authors onto the beginning and end of his manuscript.

Without acknowledging his sources, he took sections of 'an obscure, turn-of-the-century political tract', *Might is Right* by New Zealander

Arthur Desmond (writing under the pseudonym Ragnar Redbeard), added in a few sentences of his own, and incorporated it as a prologue. He also added the Enochian Keys ('a series of Elizabethan magical incantations') as they had been modified by Aleister Crowley, and 'further altered them by replacing their Heavenly references with diabolical ones'. Traditional occultists immediately recognized LaVey's source for the Keys, but it was not until 1987 that the source of LaVey's prologue was discovered (Ibid., 65).

LaVey's second daughter, Zeena Schreck, described the genesis of *The Satanic Bible* in the following way:

> I'm pretty sure that ASL [Anton Szandor LaVey] intended to include the Might is Right part from the beginning as he'd always liked it and wanted to use it somehow. From memory of what my mother told me years ago, the Enochian was added at the last minute when the deadline was breathing down their necks. Writing did not come easily to my progenitor, and he often suffered from extremely inhibiting writer's block, a side-effect of his chronic depression, which is another reason I believe he tended to 'borrow' the writings of other authors so liberally.... My mother also synthesized material from many of the old CoS newsletters, The Cloven Hoof to round out The Satanic Bible. She did type the manuscript and even added some of her own writing and much editing of the manuscript. If one takes away what came out of the old newsletters, other plagiarized sources and the Enochian, as well as many blank 'decorative' pages, and such filler as the list of Satanic names, there was very little original material written for it at all.... The title of the book itself, which I believe is far more responsible for its image of 'authority' than its rather thin contents, was a last minute decision (Schreck 2002).

It should also be mentioned that, in circles critical of CoS, one often comes across the accusation that LaVey's 'Nine Satanic Statements', one of the Church's central doctrinal statements, is an unacknowledged 'paraphrase...of passages from Ayn Rand's *Atlas Shrugged*' (Schreck and Schreck 1998), specifically a paraphrase of the character John Galt's lengthy speech in the latter part of Rand's novel. However, when one actually examines these parallels (which are conveniently laid out in Appendix 11 of Aquino's *The Church of Satan*), one finds that this is a caricature of LaVey's indebtedness to Rand. For example, the first Satanic Statement is:

Satan represents indulgence, instead of abstinence!

The Rand passage presented as the source of this statement is:

A doctrine that gives you, as an ideal, the role of a sacrificial animal seeking slaughter on the altars of others, is giving you death as your standard. By the grace of reality and the nature of life, man—every man—is an end in himself. He exists for his own sake, and the achievement of his own happiness is his highest moral purpose.

This passage is rather lengthier than LaVey's supposed 'paraphrase'. The second Satanic Statement is as brief as the first Statement:

Satan represents vital existence, instead of spiritual pipe dreams!

The Rand passage said to correspond with this Statement, though shorter than the first, is similarly distant in style and content from LaVey:

My morality, the morality of reason, is contained in a single axiom: existence exists—and in a single choice: to live. The rest proceeds from these.

And there is a similar disparity in the other 'parallels' between the Satanic Statements and Rand. Thus, even if it were true that LaVey was looking at *Atlas Shrugged* when he composed the Nine Satanic Statements, it would be more proper to say that he was *inspired* by Rand rather than to assert that he *paraphrased* her work.

I should finally note in this regard that the title of the appendix (which originally appeared as an article by George C. Smith in 1987) in which the LaVey/Rand connection is delineated, 'The Hidden Source of the Satanic Philosophy', similarly implies that Rand's philosophy was the *un*acknowledged core of LaVey's thought. This is, however, incorrect; LaVey himself explicitly acknowledged that his religion was 'just Ayn Rand's philosophy with ceremony and ritual added' (cited in Ellis, 2000, 180). (Refer also to the 'Satanism and Objectivism' essay on the Church of Satan website where this connection is examined at length.)

Despite the book's diverse source material and piecemeal assembly, it nevertheless coheres as a succinct—and, apparently, quite attractive—statement of Satanic thought and practice. As Aquino observes, 'the *Satanic Bible* was somehow "more than the sum of its parts". Its argument was an argument of common sense, assembled in part from pre-existing concepts, but the excellence of the book lay in its integration of these into a code of life meaningful to the average individual—not just to occultists and/or academic-level philosophers' (Aquino 1999, 52).

One measure of *The Satanic Bible*'s appeal is that it has continuously been in print since it first appeared in 1970, and has been translated into a number of other languages. I have been unable to obtain recent figures, but in his *In Pursuit of Satan*, Robert Hicks mentions a sales figure of 618,000 copies (1991, 351). There were also a number of illegal foreign language editions. These include a Spanish translation published in Mexico in the '70s and a Russian translation in the late '90s. Legal editions include Czech and Swedish translations in the mid-'90s and a 1999 German edition. The French translation has been completed but not yet printed. Also, the rights for a Greek translation were purchased, but the book does not seem to have appeared.[2]

The Role of The Satanic Bible in Modern Satanism

Although religious Satanism is interesting, until relatively recently academics almost entirely ignored it. (Prior to the advent of the new century, the relevant academic literature consisted of a handful of articles—e.g., Alfred 1976; Harvey 1995—and passing mentions in studies of the ritual abuse scare.) The principal reason for the lack of attention appears to have been that Satanism is perceived as a trivial phenomenon rather than as a serious religion. The tendency was to regard Satanists as nothing more than immature adolescents who adopted a diabolical veneer as a way of acting out their rebellion against parents and society. Does the phenomenon of adolescent rebellion, however, exhaust the significance of religious Satanism? Are most Satanists, in other words, just angry teenagers who adopt diabolical trappings to express their alienation, only to renounce the Prince of Darkness as soon as they mature into adults? Though many youthful Satanists undoubtedly fit this profile, through my fieldwork I came to feel that this was, at best, only a partial picture. Instead, I hypothesized that there must be a core of committed Satanists who—for whatever reasons they initially become involved—had come to appropriate Satanism as something more than adolescent rebellion.

In order to test this hypothesis—and also because so little had been written on religious Satanism—I collected some basic demographic data in connection with a larger study of contemporary Satanism. I constructed a simple questionnaire that could be answered in 5 or 10 minutes, and began sending out questionnaires in early August 2000. By the end of February 2001 I had received 140 responses, which I felt was adequate to use as the basis for constructing a preliminary profile.[3]

When I sought feedback on preliminary write-ups of my findings from informants, a few voiced objections to the central role I assigned LaVey and his best-known work, *The Satanic Bible,* in the formation of modern Satanic religion. I was, furthermore, encouraged to shift my emphasis to the work of earlier literary figures ultimately responsible for fashioning the positive image of the Devil that LaVey later adopted for his Church of Satan. My survey findings, however, consistently indicated the centrality of LaVey to modern Satanism. This finding was a surprise, as I had initially assumed that contemporary Satanism had moved well beyond LaVey. I was thus led to conclude that—despite his dependence on prior thinkers—LaVey was directly responsible for the genesis of Satanism as a serious religious (as opposed to a purely literary) movement. Furthermore, however one might criticize and depreciate it, *The Satanic Bible* is still the single most influential document shaping the contemporary Satanic movement. As one of my informants noted, 'I do not think Satanists can get away from LaVey, although some seem to take a real issue with him or try to downplay his importance. He wrote the book that codified Satanism into a religion, and for that he should be considered the central figure of the religion.'

I do not intend to review all of my survey findings here (they are the subject of Lewis, 2001), but I do want to note that I was surprised to find that the average respondent had been a Satanist for seven to eight years. I also found that over two-thirds of the sample had been involved in at least one other religion beyond the tradition in which they were raised— usually Neopaganism or some other magical group. Both of these statistics indicate a level of seriousness I had not anticipated.

Because most respondents became involved during their teens, I inferred that many had initially become Satanists as an expression of teenage rebelliousness. It was clear, however, that their involvement did not end after they left home. Rather, they went on to appropriate Satanism as a serious religious option. The fact that the great majority of Satanists have looked into other religions shows that this was not an unconsidered choice, undertaken solely as a reaction against established religions. Also, though a reaction against Christianity may well have been a factor for some, too many respondents indicated that their religious upbringing was superficial, nominal or non-existent for this factor to explain why most people become Satanists.

Before I began collecting questionnaire data, I had received the impression from perusing the Internet that contemporary Satanism had developed in different directions from the specific formulation developed by Anton LaVey in the 1960s. In particular, at the time it appeared to me that many contemporary Satanists had moved to a position of regarding Satan as a conscious being, and legitimated their claims to authority on the basis of direct communications from Dark Forces. I was thus surprised to discover that LaVey's humanistic approach—which rejects the real existence of personal spiritual beings, diabolical or otherwise—was the dominant form of Satanism professed by respondents.

At least part of the reason for this state of affairs appears to be the pervasive influence of *The Satanic Bible*. A full 20% of respondents explicitly noted *The Satanic Bible* as the single most important factor attracting them to Satanism. For instance, in response to a questionnaire item asking how they became involved, a number of people simply wrote, 'I read the *Satanic Bible*.' It is also likely that this book played a major role in the 'conversion' of other Satanists in my sample. One respondent elaborated by noting that she had been a Satanist in her 'heart first, but I couldn't put a name to it; then I found *The Satanic Bible*.'

Similar stories attributing their infernal 'conversions' to *The Satanic Bible* can be found in other sources. The popular book *Lucifer Rising*, for instance, recounts the story of how Martin Lamers, founder of the CoS-affiliated Kerk van Satan (Holland), was initially inspired by his discovery of LaVey's volume (Baddeley 1999, 104). However, not everyone who is converted to Satanism via *The Satanic Bible* feels prompted to join the Church of Satan. *Lucifer Rising* also notes that 'the Church of Satanic Liberation was established in January 1986 after its founder, Paul Douglas Valentine, was inspired by reading *The Satanic Bible*' (p. 153). Other stories of conversions directly inspired by *The Satanic Bible* can be found in Michael Aquino's *The Church of Satan,* e.g., the conversion of Robert DeCecco, who would later become a Master of the Temple (p. 69) and Lilith Sinclair, who would eventually become a Priestess and Aquino's wife (p. 82).

To return to the survey, LaVey's influential publication was also referred to a number of times in response to other questionnaire items. For example, one person noted that, 'because I agree with and practice the majority of the beliefs set forth in *The Satanic Bible* and other works of Dr. LaVey, I VERY MUCH consider myself just as valid a Satanist as any "official" priest.' Another respondent wrote, 'Satan is merely a word, a representative concept that encompasses all that the *Satanic Bible* teaches.' And yet another individual stated: 'To me, Satan is the personification of mankind's carnal nature. More information can be found in *The Satanic Bible* by Anton Szandor LaVey.'

My strong impression was that *The Satanic Bible* was a doctrinal touchstone for most participants in this movement, despite the fact that the great majority of my sample was not formal members of Anton LaVey's Church of Satan. (One respondent, noting that he was not a member of any organization, wrote, '[It's] just me and my *Satanic Bible*.') And whatever LaVey had in mind when he entitled this publication, in certain ways *The Satanic Bible* has truly come to play the role of a 'bible' for many members of this decentralized, anti-authoritarian subculture. (As indicated in Schreck's comments cited earlier, the title was 'a last minute decision'. She further noted in the same communication that: 'Earlier titles proposed included such awkward possibilities as *The Bible of the Church of Satan*, *The Bible of Satanism* and so forth' [2002]).

In a follow-up questionnaire, respondents were explicitly asked how they regarded *The Satanic Bible*, and to what extent their personal philosophies were congruent with the ideas expressed in its pages. Most stated that their view of the world aligned significantly with *The Satanic Bible*. One Satanist said that *The Satanic Bible* was about the realities of human nature, so that there was 'nothing [in *The Satanic Bible*] that I didn't already know or believe myself prior to reading it'. Only one respondent completely rejected the LaVeyan tradition. Two respondents asserted that they regarded *The Satanic Bible* as just another 'self-help book'. Some respondents diminished (without disparaging) *The Satanic Bible* as an 'introductory text' or 'primer' of Satanism. Most hastened to add that they did not regard it as 'dogma'.

One can acquire a sense of how *The Satanic Bible* is regarded as a doctrinal touchstone by perusing the official website of the Church of Satan (http://www.churchofsatan.com). For example, the 'Satanism FAQ' section of the 'Church of Satan Information Pack' states that 'critically reading *The Satanic Bible* by Anton Szandor LaVey is tantamount to understanding at least the basics of Satanism'. Similarly, the Church's 'Church of Satan Youth Communiqué' asserts that 'LaVey wrote *The Satanic Bible* so that people could pick up a copy, read it, and know everything they need to know about Satanism and how to put it to work in their own lives.'

In addition to these general assertions, one can find other essays on the Church of Satan website in which authoritative tenets are cited from *The Satanic Bible*, as when the 'Satanic Bunco Sheet' notes that '*The Satanic Bible* advises to "question all things"....' or when, in an essay entitled 'Satanism Needs an Enema!', an individual writing under the pseudonym Nemo introduces a series of citations from *The Satanic Bible* to support a point he is arguing with the words: 'Other quotes from LaVey's own pen in *The Satanic Bible* reiterate this theme'. The clear implication of this statement is that because these quotations come from 'LaVey's own pen in *The Satanic Bible*', they are authoritative; thus there can be no further discussion of the issue. Toward the end of the same essay, Nemo also asserts that,

> *We have a bible. We have a pro-human dogma. We have a church. We have a tradition. We have ceremonies and rituals. We have a High Priestess.*

In other words, with respect to the theme being pursued in this book, Nemo is asserting that CoS has an authoritative scripture, dogma and tradition that support his argument. And it is obvious that Nemo regards his appeal to CoS *tradition* as stronger than direct appeals to science or common sense, which were the touchstones of LaVey's philosophy.

It is also interesting that one of the accusations levelled against non-CoS Satanists in Nemo's 'Recognizing Pseudo-Satanism' essay was that in such groups, 'The words of *The Satanic Bible* become twisted and distorted until they no longer have useful meaning!' Furthermore, in his 'Satanism Needs an Enema!' essay, the same writer exclaims,

> *I am calling for a closing of the ranks and a throwing out of the heretics. I am asking for the Purge! I am asking for a reverse Inquisition.*

Both of these sets of passages—the first quoting *The Satanic Bible* to make a point and the second accusing heretical breakaways of warping *The Satanic Bible's* meaning (even going so far as to call for an 'Inquisition' against heretics within the ranks)—exemplify all-too-familiar patterns found in the theological conflicts of traditional religions.

Quoting *The Satanic Bible* to legitimate a point of argument is not, however, confined to representatives of the Church of Satan. The so called 'Xloptuny Curse' is an interesting example of how some of the 'heretics' have turned the message of LaVey's writings to their own purposes. A short essay on 'The Xloptuny Curse', written by Joe Necchi, was posted on the official website of the First Church of Satan in the summer of 2000. (The First Church of Satan—FCoS—is a more recent Satanist organization founded by a former member of CoS whose brand of Satanism is very close to *The Satanic Bible*.) The text discusses the circumstances of a seemingly effective suicide curse that was levelled by Lord Egan, founder/leader of the FCoS, against Xloptuny (John C. Davis), an Internet pugilist and member of the CoS. Less than a year before Davis took a gun to his head, Egan had cursed Davis, specifying in a public, online communication that he would die by shooting himself. The passage to focus on for present purposes is where Necchi remarks,

> *What is interesting, however, is the way in which some have predictably tried to rationalize Xloptuny's suicide as a Yukio*

> *Mishima-inspired act of heroism. Ironically, those trying so hard to canonize Mr. Davis thusly now have decided to conveniently ignore the book they are always waving about like a black flag at most other times: The Satanic Bible. In this sense, we see that many Satanists really behave exactly like Christians: they follow the precepts of their religion when it's easy to do so, when it suits them, but are quick to abandon them when it really counts.*
>
> *The Satanic Bible specifically states: 'Self-sacrifice is not encouraged by the Satanic religion. Therefore, unless death comes as an indulgence because of extreme circumstances which make the termination of life a welcome relief from an unendurable earthly existence, suicide is frowned upon by the Satanic religion.' There is little ambiguity in this passage. As there is no reason to believe that Xloptuny was in 'extreme circumstances which make the termination of life a welcome relief' he died as a traitor to the Church whose cause he so often trumpeted, the defense of which he used as a rationale for his often black and bilious attacks on his enemies. Apparently 'the great Dr. Anton LaVey's' words meant little or nothing to John C. Davis when he arrived at the moment of truth (1969, 94).*

Here again we see *The Satanic Bible* being quoted as an authoritative document in a manner similar to the way sacred texts are quoted in comparable conflicts within other religious traditions. In other words, 'The Xloptuny Curse' is yet another example of how *The Satanic Bible* functions as quasi-scripture within the Satanic community.

Almost all Satanists would deny that *The Satanic Bible* is an 'inspired' document in anything like the sense in which the Christian Bible is regarded as an inspired book. Interestingly, however, there are a few individuals—most notably Michael Aquino, a former CoS leader and founder of the Temple of Set—who *would* regard this book as inspired. For example, in the relevant chapter in his history of the Church of Satan, Aquino asserts that:

> *The Satanic Bible [clothes] itself in the supernatural authority of the Prince of Darkness and his demons. Less this element, the Satanic Bible would be merely a social tract by Anton LaVey—not High Priest of Satan, but just one more 1960s'-counterculture-cynic atop a soapbox.*
>
> *The substance of the Satanic Bible therefore turns upon*

> Anton LaVey's sincerity in believing himself to be the vehicle through which the entity known as Satan explains the mysteries of mankind's existential predicament. To the extent that he did, the Satanic Bible deserves the dignity of its title. ...
>
> Despite the haphazard nature of its assembly ... we may therefore consider the Satanic Bible in its totality not as argumentative, but as inspired writing. Thus it assumes an importance by its very existence, not just by its content (1999, 53).

Although Aquino's position would be rejected by most other professing Satanists, something approaching this position seems to be unconsciously informing their attitude toward *The Satanic Bible*.

Conclusion

Anton LaVey's primary legitimation strategy was to appeal to the authority of science, specifically to the secularist worldview derived from natural science and to an animalistic image of the human being derived from the Darwinian theory of evolution. In light of his radically secularist legitimation strategy, it is ironic that his organizational successors have subsequently attempted to legitimate their positions by appealing to LaVey as if he had actually been some kind of 'Black Pope', and to *The Satanic Bible* as if it was truly a diabolically-revealed scripture. It appears that being raised in a religious tradition that locates the source of authority in religious figures and sacred texts creates an unconscious predisposition that can be carried over to other kinds of persons and books—even in the unlikely context of contemporary Satanism.

Outside the institutional bounds of the Church of Satan, modern Satanism became a loose, de-centralized movement that coheres as a distinct religious community largely by virtue of participants' adherence to certain themes in the published words of Anton LaVey, particularly in *The Satanic Bible*. Despite this volume's patchwork quality and haphazard genesis, it came to play an authoritative, quasi-scriptural role within the larger Satanic movement. Unlike members of the Church of Satan, however, non-CoS Satanists felt free to criticize and even to reject aspects of the LaVeyan tradition by appealing to the authority of rationality—a criterion of legitimacy LaVey himself put forward as the very basis of Satanism.

References

Aquino, M.A. 1999. *The Church of Satan*. 4th ed. Self-published.
Baddeley, G. 1999. *Lucifer Rising: Sin, Devil Worship and Rock'n'Roll*.
    London: Plexus.
Barton, B. 1990. *The Secret Life of a Satanist: The Authorized Biography of*

Anton LaVey. Los Angeles: Feral House.
Chryssides, G. D. 2000. 'Is God a Space Alien? The Cosmology of the Raelian Church.' *Culture and Cosmos* 4:1 Spring/Summer.
Church of Satan. 'Sycophants Unite!' http://www.churchofsatan.com/home.html
_____ 'The Church of Satan Information Pack' http://www.churchofsatan.com/Pages/cosinfopack.pdf
_____ 'Church of Satan Youth Communique' http://www.churchofsatan.com/home.html
_____ 'Satanic Bunco Sheet.' http://www.churchofsatan.com/home.html
Ellis, B. 2000. *Raising the Devil: Satanism, New Religions, and the Media*. Lexington, Kentucky: The University Press of Kentucky.
Flowers, S. E. 1997. *Lords of the Left-Hand Path*. Smithville, Texas: Runa-Raven Press.
Holmes, E. 1944 [1926]. *The Science of Mind*. New York: Dodd, Mead, and Company.
LaVey, A. Szandor. 1969. *The Satanic Bible*. New York: Avon.
Lewis, J. R. 2001. 'Who Serves Satan? A Demographic and Ideological Profile.' *Marburg Journal of Religious Studies* 6:2.
Moody, E. J. 1974. 'Magical Therapy: An Anthropological Investigation of Contemporary Satanism.' In I. I. Zaretsky and M. P. Leone, eds. *Religious Movements in Contemporary America*. Princeton, New Jersey: Princeton University Press, 1974.
Moynihan, M. and Soderlind, D. 1998. *Lords of Chaos: The Bloody Rise of the Satanic Metal Underground*. Venice, California: Feral House.
Necchi, J. 'The Xloptuny Curse.' http://www.churchof satan.org/xloptuny.html.
Nemo. 'Recognizing Pseudo-Satanism.' http://www.churchofsatan.com/home.html
_____ 'Satanism and Objectivism.' http://www.churchofsatan.com/Pages/SatObj.html
_____ 'Satanism Needs an Enema!' http://www.churchofsatan.com/home.html
Petersen, J. A. 2002. 'Binary Satanism: Being Dark and Secretive in a Prismatic Digital World.' *Syzygy* 11: 37-52.
Rand, A. 1957. *Atlas Shrugged*. New York: Random House.
Redbeard, R. 1910, fifth ed. [1896]. *Might is Right; or, The Survival of the Fittest*. London: W.J. Robbins.
Richardson, J., Best, J., and Bromley, D.G. 1991. *The Satanism Scare*. New York: Aldine de Gruyter.
Schreck, Z, and Schreck, N. 1998. 'Anton LaVey: Legend and Reality.' http://www.churchofsatan.org/aslv.html
Sentes, B. and Palmer, S. 2000. 'Presumed Immanent: the Raelians, UFO Religions, and the Postmodern Condition.' *Novo Religio*, October, 4:1:

86-105.

Smith, G. C. 1987. 'The Hidden Source of the Satanic Philosophy.' Originally published in *The Scroll of Set*, June 1987. Reprinted as Appendix 11 in Aquino 1999.

Trull, D. 'Fortean Slips: Death of a Devil's Advocate.' *SF Weekly*. Reprinted online at: http://dagmar.lunarpages.com/~parasc2/articles/slips/fs27_3.htm

Weber, M. 1962. *Basic Concepts in Sociology*. H. P. Secher (trans). New York: Philosophical Library.

Wolfe, B. H. 1974. *The Devil's Avenger: A Biography of Anton Szandor LaVey*. New York: Pyramid Books.

Wright, L. 1991. 'Sympathy for the Devil.' *Rolling Stone*, 5 September.

Endnotes

1   The current chapter is a revised version of my article, 'Diabolical Authority', which originally appeared as an article in the Marburg Journal of Religion (2002). A somewhat modified version of that piece also appeared as a chapter in my book, Legitimating New Religions (Rutgers University Press, 2003), where I develop the notion of 'legitimation strategies' utilized in the present chapter in greater detail. A special word of thanks to Satanists who provided me with thoughtful feedback on earlier drafts of this paper, particularly feedback from several members of the Obsidian Enlightenment and the Temple of Lylyth. One comment of particular note was that the social organization (or, perhaps more appropriately, disorganization) of modern Satanism cannot accurately be characterized as a 'movement', 'community' or 'subculture'. I have nevertheless used these terms throughout for lack of more adequate terminology. Another comment was that 'conversion' is not appropriate in the context of Satanism. Again, however, I left this term in the chapter for lack of a better word. Finally, I was informed that Satanists prefer to refer to their community as the Satanic community (movement, subculture, etc.) rather than the Satanist community; I have tried to adhere to this convention throughout the present chapter.

2   Information on foreign language editions courtesy Peter H. Gilmore, High Priest of the Church of Satan.

3   110 (almost 80%) of my respondents were North American. Because European Satanism is a somewhat different phenomenon, one should be therefore be cautious about making inferences to European Satanism based on my survey findings.

12
Modern Black Magic: Initiation, Sorcery and The Temple of Set

Don Webb

> *He who does not have the demonic seed within himself
> will never give birth to a magical world.*
> —*Dr Ernst Schertel*

When I joined the Temple of Set in 1989, the most expensive book on our reading list was TeVelde's *Seth: God of Confusion*. As a specialty publication from Brill, you couldn't exactly waltz into a Barnes & Noble and pick one up. I had been a published writer before joining the Temple, and so one of the first things I did in the Temple was write. In those days when I wrote about Setian practice outside of the Temple of Set it would be for a small magazine—a creature of Xeroxage usually with a lurid red cover of card stock, often hand-stapled. Circulation for some of these titles must have easily been in the dozens. When I wrote internally for the Temple, it was either for the newsletter of my local group, the Bull of Ombos Pylon, or the house organ, *The Scroll of Set*.

My audience was overwhelmingly male, white and usually not college educated—although most had had some trade school or other specialized training. Most were not in long-term relationships, and most lived in California. Today when I write for the *Scroll* I am writing for an audience about 60% male, mainly college-educated (with 5% holding doctoral degrees), living everywhere from South Africa to Japan, Finland to Australia and at least one in a nuclear submarine Set-knows-where. Scholars of 'new religions' have also come from Canada, Denmark and

Finland to interview me.

Most occult groups have a charismatic leader that casts a long shadow — he or she is the only spokesperson and leader, the group lives and dies with the leader. The Temple of Set has had five High Priests and five of its members have written books on the magical arts. I note a couple of my own students are contributors to this volume — and my own work is regularly cited by a couple more of the good folk here. Our change from a small California-based Satanic cult into a (perhaps) culturally powerful international organization has been accomplished without a recruitment budget, without luring celebrities to endorse the product, or even a discernable cultural shift toward brainier magic groups. The Temple changed its status by its members changing themselves.

The Temple of Set has a practice that allows seekers to improve and explore themselves and exert those processes on the human world. Or, to use the jargon of the Temple, *it works*.

The first question someone encountering the Temple will have will be about our 'dark' symbolism. This essay will begin with that question and then go on to examine Setian magical practice, religion, philosophy, and lastly the Temple as an initiatory body. My ideas and opinions about Setian practice are well informed in that I hold the highest initiatory rank of the Temple and have served as its High Priest, but the 'Temple' is a group of truth-seeking individuals whose ideas have been and will continue to evolve.

The Big Bad Dark

The power of the left hand is always occult and illegitimate,
it inspires terror and revulsion . . .
Beings which are believed to posses dreadful magical powers
are represented as left-handed.

—Robert Hertz
in 'The Pre-eminence of the Right Hand:
A study in Religious Polarity'

Humans are confronted with a choice every day — *change or maintain*. One's current life, even if painful, is known — the life just beyond the edge is unknown. The current life is like full daylight. You are aware of the value of things, their meaning — their place and your place. Most human religion is about maintenance of this order. Christmas holidays repel the gloom of winter; Easter celebrates the re-growth of spring; baptism takes you into the fold; funerals take you out. Everything is as it should be, and new thoughts and troubling feelings can be kept to a convenient minimum. Most things in a society therefore belong to what the well known anthropologist Victor Turner calls 'structure'. Most of human life is designed to keep things ordered, and human religion devoted to the shining forces of Order.

For some humans the need to explore the Unknown is great, the need for Anti-Structure is huge, and the need for the very new or very old is tantamount. In any human group some folk are called not by the light of the sun, but by the hope of bringing things out of darkness—whether it is by confronting their fear, discovering what is yet Unmanifest, removing the gilt-paint that society has painted over certain truths, or simply gazing into the night sky and wondering what may be there. Any mood that leads to darkness—anger, lust, curiosity, wonder, bravery or even distrust of the voices of the daylight world, is Holy and powerful. The Setian, like anyone in an elitist sub-culture, may identify with a mad scientist or outsider artist: but some of the same yearnings are also found in the biker and the teenage rebel. Using the step down as the way to rise up will keep the Left-Hand Path as the road for the few.

Black Magic

> *I think that those who follow no matter whom, ought to be called 'magicians', if only they are determined to be divine and just men.*
>
> —*Apollonius of Tyana*

When they join the Temple, Setians are introduced to Black Magic by an essay *Black Magic in Theory and Practice* by Dr Michael Aquino in the introductory volume *The Crystal Tablet of Set*.

Magic is the art of changing the subjective universe in order to produce a change in the objective universe. The extent of that change is limited by the passion and precision of the operator and by the structural limits of the objective universe. Black Magic acts are those that create the Self, giving the human meaning, value and existence as a non-mechanical reflection of the objective universe. Black Magic furthers the separation of the Self from the Cosmos, ultimately making it self-ordering and self-aware and undying. The cinematic-derived connotation of Black Magic would see a fearsome curse worked by a dark, robed sorcerer as Black Magic and the Temple would agree with this image but would also regard the ritual a magician performs for the health of an ailing mother as equally 'Black Magical', as it furthers the goals and hopes of an individual psyche. Black Magic ultimately maintains, expands, and evolves self-consciousness and beyond this aim knows neither good nor evil. Let us briefly look at White Magic and then at the varieties of Black Magic and its aims.

White Magic is the creation of temporary unity of the psyche with a human-constructed psychoid—usually called a god or angel or spirit. Humans, by their magical ability, can create any number of gods. Because of our sense of loneliness or insignificance, we crave the protection of the Other as much as fear or emulate it. Thus, humans in times of stress seek to obliterate their sense of Self by the use of prayer or fasting or other consciousness-altering techniques. Sometimes we want to fool ourselves into feeling that we are not responsible for our destiny. We merge/submerge ourselves in other psychic creations. These moments of White Magic cause the Self to obtain value and significance from the text of another. It can be healing, powerful, and magical but it does not further the Self *qua* Self. These White Magical moments can be seen as much at a Pentecostal revival as at a Wiccan bonfire, at a High School pep rally, at a gathering of Trappist monks, at a Nuremberg rally, or on the National Day of Prayer. White Magic gives an empirical result but it deludes its users into believing that the Other with which brief unity is obtained is more worthy or real than the potentials of the Self. This betrayal of 'what could be' feeds the anger of White Magicians, who battle one another under their various banners.

The Temple teaches three forms of Black Magic: Lesser, Medial and Greater. Lesser Black Magic is a method of conveying one's will into another's mind. It can also be called 'meta-communication'. Most human situations are best handled with reason and civility, but sometimes it is needful to arouse passion and fire in others for important causes. By studying human psychology and knowledge of certain obscure laws of proximics, Setians can manipulate the moods and attention of those around them to make them open to new impulses. Millions of dollars have been spent researching the methods—they can be found in advertising, political control, architectural design, even Muzak tempos. The moods produced by a visit to Disneyland or by viewing a Super Bowl commercial would be consummate examples of Lesser Black Magic.

Medial Black Magic (MBM) is the use of non-empirical methods to obtain an empirical result. What most people would describe as 'magic' falls into this category. All sorts of invocations, spells, blessings and curses come under this heading. Use is made of either a traditional symbolic system (anything from the Runes to Voudoun) or symbolic systems of the Setian's own creation. There are three guiding principles here—*practicality* (Does it work?), *aesthetics* (Is it beautiful?), and *communicability* (Can I teach it to a friend who might need it?) The first reflects the Setian pre-occupation with magic as a truth process (see below) and shows our Crowleyan heritage (method of science, aim of religion). The second reflects our belief that magic is an ornament to life—magical deeds are the frescoes of the cathedrals of ourselves. The last reflects the need in Setian psychology to empower by teaching/sharing our journeys with others who like us struggle with Set's own struggle—defining and evolving ourselves in contrast to the cosmos. Setians are urged to master one traditional system as a way of checking for their own blind spots and to create a magical system of their own genius. Setian culture encourages the creation of magical-scholarly explorations of MBM—for example, see the many volumes of my teacher, Dr Stephen Edred Flowers or some of my own books—such as *The Seven Faces of Darkness*—which explore the practice and philosophy of the Greek magical papyri. There is no 'one way' for Setian magic—I have taken part in group Workings in shopping malls at Christmas, in recreations of the Church of Satan's *Die Elektriscehn Vorspiele* with giant Tesla coils and lasers, Chaos Magic-style sigil creations, *Walpurgisnacht* bonfire dances, pseudo-Masonic lodge workings, S&M sex magic, silent mediations, rituals on roller coasters, Black Masses, Black Hebrew *Seders*, Black Protestant Tent Revivals, Korean shamanic rituals, Setian Martial arts demonstrations, cyber magic, Setian raves, Yezedi rituals, and even a Working in the British Museum. And I am a fairly conservative Setian...

Medial Black Magic reflects a Neoplatonic universe. The Magician remembers the Real, and this action causes the Real to manifest in the world of Becoming.[1] As such, each magical act Orders the psyche based on the best structures that consciousness holds. If this were the limit of Setian action we would be peaceful warriors of a common truth that we could all sense noetically. If this were so, our Word would be *Ma'at* ('truth'). But Setians assert that new Events can be called into being. We assert that in certain situations Magic is a truth-process, that the New can be called forth from the Void. In these rare instances, existence precedes essence. We call this moment Greater Black Magic, and when Setians disturb the universe we are overcoming the gods. It is because of Greater Black Magic that Setians can assert (along with Steiner, Gebser and Lachman) that *consciousness itself evolves*. It evolves because we make it do so. Greater Black Magic is a method of transcending both the subjective and objective universes by creating a new process. Spectacular examples of Greater Black Magic would be Aleister Crowley's reception of the *Book of the Law* or Dr Michael Aquino's reception of the founding document of the Temple of Set, the *Book of Coming Forth by Night*. Greater Black Magic ends with new energy added to the sum total of the universe—energy that both compels the magician to act and the universe to bestow luck and friction upon the practitioner as the actions take place. If a Medial Black Magical working summoned a demon to fetch you gold, a Greater Black Magical working may cause a totally unnamed/

unknown god to be born in your psyche, bringing unknown and powerful changes. Greater Black Magic brings new forces into the universe—it is not merely adding energy into an entopic system, it is bring a new energy and a new system.

This essay works in all three areas of Black Magic. I have invoked certain images, maintained a certain tone and appealed to certain parts of your psyche as a reader, so that you are considering without undoing or filtering the value of some of the ideas. That would be Lesser Black Magic (LBM). I have used a known form of communication to invoke known forces by non-empirical means in the stock of magical experience that you possess. If you prefer Jungian terminology, I have guided you in accessing the collective unconscious. This form of Medial Black Magic (MBM) may empower some of you to pursue the methods of this essay in your own quest for power, pleasure and knowledge. For some, reading these words has been a Greater Black Magical working causing you to recreate yourself (however so briefly) as a Setian.

I will now look at Setian cosmology, philosophy and the Initiatory path, and I will end with a suggested reading list.

The Setian Cosmos

We have found a strange footprint on the shores of the Unknown. We have devised profound theories, one after another, to account for its origins. At last, we have succeeded in reconstructing the creature that made the footprint. And lo! It is our own.

—Sir Arthur Stanley Eddington

Setians are dualists. Unlike the Right-Hand Path, which posits a unified cosmos, Setians see the physical and psychical universes as separate. Discoverable and repeatable laws bind the physical universe. It is entropic in nature and it is essential to know this universe through scientific means. Dr Aquino in his essay, 'Black Magic in Theory and Practice', uses the terms 'natural order' and 'non-natural' for the physical and psychical universes, and because of this certain anti-Setian cranks have suggested that the Temple is 'anti-Nature', which would be as absurd as suggesting that someone who enjoys looking at Picasso is therefore 'anti-Picasso'. The manifestation of magic in the natural order does not contravene its laws. Gold will not be teleported to your chamber, you will not walk through walls, and your body will not turn into that of a crow.

The non-natural part of the human, the psyche, is necessary for the perpetuation of both universes. The non-natural part of ourselves is extropic—it actual adds new elements to the physical cosmos. Magic may be thought of as a violation of the First Law of Thermodynamics. Once magical energy has expressed itself as image-becoming-reality it is subject to natural laws. Obviously it is more efficient for this manifestation to occur in the human realm, which has already been conditioned to accept and manifest magic. Or, to put it another way, it would be an impossible magical feat to make a tea cup float to you from the kitchen, but your girlfriend would be glad to bring it if you asked her. This basic idea expresses itself in the Setian insistence to learn Lesser Black Magic first. It is easier to change the psyche of others than one's own. It is likewise easier to change the psyche of many through an established magical channel via Medial Black Magic than through the pure extropy of Greater Black Magic.

The non-natural part of the psyche expresses and knows itself by experiences that are not scientifically repeatable. Non-natural knowing can be experienced in realms such as music, art and magic. Natural knowing is experienced either in common sense or in scientific knowing. For example it is natural knowledge to know that a mass on earth will fall thirty-two feet per second — whether you or I or a third party test this today, tomorrow, or a hundred years hence. An example of non-natural knowing would be the experience I have listening to Miles Davis today would be different in ineffable ways to your experience of listening to the same piece, or even my own experience transposed to different circumstances. The energy and actions that derive from these non-natural moments shape the natural world.

The psychical universe needs the physical universe for its self-definition. The physical universe needs the psychical universe for its shaping. Between the two is the area magicians call the 'magical link'. For magic to flow into this universe the magician's will must be expressed through a symbolic action. Symbols are different to signs. Signs are purely arbitrary — in America we use a red octagon as a sign for 'Stop', but it could just as easily be a blue pentagon or an orange circle. Symbols are those things that partake of the meaning of the idea they symbolize. For example, a rose is a symbol of love because of its colour, softness, many-layeredness and thorns. Most traditional systems of magic obsess around the creation of symbolic lists. Setians are encouraged to create their own understanding in this matter, which reflects our central emphasis on *individuality*. For energy to flow into the psychical universe, correct perception is needed. The better magicians understand themselves and their world, the better they feed their psyche. Clarity is not an end unto itself as it might be for the mystic, but a conduit to allowing the self to express its being in both realms.

The ancient Egyptian god Set is experienced as the archetype of the hero of self-definition and self-evolution. Just as a Roman would not confuse Venus, who struggles with the mastery of love on the highest of levels—the archetypal idea of Love itself—Setians do not confuse Set with the principles of self-definition and self-evolution. Set is seen as the giver of our non-natural side. This is done out of motives that are not as banal as altruism or egotism. For a self to posit itself as an entity there ultimately has to be a summons of another self for the purpose of interaction, comparison, and even love—which is the highest of all truth processes. In our mythology we say that Set created the god Har-Wer (Horus the Elder). The mythological grounding for this began long ago in dynastic struggles in ancient Egypt, but has revealed itself again in human culture. Aleister Crowley's Cairo Working[2] is an expression of Har-Wer (*der Wille zur Macht*), the god of Will-to-Power. Crowley was well on his way in the *Book of the Law*, which focuses on the flow of energy into the psychical universe—this is half of the Setian equation. Notably Crowley expressed this as ShT (*Shin* = Fire, 20 and *Teth* =Force, 11)—the name of Set. On the one hundredth anniversary of Crowley's birth in 1875, Dr Aquino obtained the second half of the equation—not one that reveals the universe as a single Tao, but as two dynamic sections of Being and Becoming.

Setians' apprehensions of Set vary with their state of being and needs. Members of the Temple of Set are usually pigeonholed as 'theistic Satanists'—implying that there is a belief/worship of Set as a stand-in or rival to JHVH. The principle that Set represents—that of self-creation—is the origin of the sacred and the meaningful. Set is not conceived of as some gigantic figure in red tights waiting for prayer or sacrifice, but as someone who struggles with the pains and pleasures of existence on the deepest of levels. Identifying with Him in this struggle aids Set cosmically as well as increasing our intuition with regard to wiser choices of action. It is important to note that Setians see Set as an active force that intervenes in the evolution of consciousness. Not only would we agree with Aleister Crowley in *Magick*—'This serpent, SATAN, is not the enemy of Man, but He who made Gods of our race, knowing Good and Evil; He bade "Know Thyself!" and taught Initiation.'—but we feel that the intervention of Set is the *source* of human consciousness. Setians are not alone in thinking that human consciousness evolves—one need only think of the theories of Gray Lachman, Stan Gooch, Rudolf Steiner, Jurij Moskvitin, Jean Gebser and P. D. Ouspensky. We also feel, like George P. Hansen, that such intervention has to have come from the Trickster God.

Philosophy

The least of things with a meaning is worth more in life than the greatest of things without it.

—Carl Jung

Firstly, what is philosophy? If you asked my uncle, he would say, 'Never turn a free drink... That's my philosophy!' If you asked most modern British philosophers, you would be told it is a language game. If you asked most Americans you would get an answer indicating that philosophy is what you do when all the other aspects of your life have been met. For the Setian, philosophy is an intellectual and emotional pursuit that grounds our actions by letting us find meaning and seek self-definition. Philosophy is neither optional nor dogmatic (that is, received from an institution or its leaders). The Setian does not seek dogma. Setians cannot accept philosophy as truth—this is reflected in the *Book of Coming Forth by Night*, which states that 'the text of another is an affront to the Self'. Philosophy is not a production of truth but an operation from truths, since the category of truth must remain a void—an operational and logical void—which provides the grounding from which the Setian comes into being, much as the god Xepera came into being in a void. I can offer some of the framework that Setians use to derive their magic and its goals but, as in all things pertaining to an individualist praxis, I am merely offering my own opinions.

Four things distinguish Setian philosophy from other magical and religious groups: Firstly, the focus on the real and the attainable; secondly, a magical re-reading of the ideas of Fitche; thirdly, the notion (borrowed from Sartre) that existence may precede essence, and lastly the uniquely Setian notion that magic is a truth-process. Like most (perhaps all) Western magical systems the Temple expresses a Neoplatonic view of the cosmos. We consider the existence of the Ideal as being the origin of the world of perception, and that magic consists of accessing the force of the Ideal realm as a corrective to deficient patterns in the world of becoming. Let's look at an early attempt at Setian thinking and explore each of these principles in turn.

One could argue that the first Setian was Zoroaster (Zarathustra). His theory was that the Good Lord was a god of the Mind. All other gods were reflections of this Mind—they were good if they pointed back to the Source or evil if they pointed away. The Zoroastrian symbol of the Mind was the earthly element of fire—ever changing, transforming all things brought into contact with it. Fire cooked food, smelted metal, took offerings to the Mind, brought warmth and devastation. Zoroaster's synthesis failed when he excluded Doubt/Ahriman from the blend and focused only on a set of harmonious Ideas. Instead of natural fire, the Setian chose the Black Flame. The Setian sees the divine centre, Mind, as separate from the Cosmos and its symbol as an 'unnatural' one, a Black Flame. All lesser products of the Mind—whether we call them Ideas (after the Greeks), *Neteru* (after the Egyptians) or *Li* (after the Chinese) are tools for human endeavour and not idols that provide distractions by offering illusory comforts.

Another symbol of the Setian Cosmos is the Pythagorean inverse pentagram in a circular field where the points of the pentagram do not touch the circle's edge. The Pythagoreans thought (see, for example, Apollonius of Tyana in *On the Sacrifices*) that God was the supreme Intellect/Nous of the Cosmos. The supreme Intellect did not require prayer or sacrifice—what could Mind do with a burnt cow? But by exercising one's own Mind/Nous/Buddhi principle one could get to know, and hence be, like God. What better symbol than the Pentagram? The inner symbol shows the radical way thought may change (angular rather than smooth curves) and the *phi* ratio of the pentagram's lines show a symmetrical and intelligent self-ordering. The five-foldness of the pentagram reveals a principle beyond the simple three-foldness of Time (beginning, maintaining, passing-away) or the four-foldness of Space. The pentagram (Psyche) is isolate from the circle of Nature, and its upstanding points exalt creation and change over the central ruling of stasis.

Setians focus on the real and the obtainable. In the occult world there is a prevalent notion that humans are already divine—that each man or woman is a god, a virtual pope who is correct in all things and does not need to work either to see clearly or advance. Thus infantile notion is an understandable reaction to the disempowering view of the religious and social theories of our times, but does not lead to self-change. The focus on the *real* may on the one hand make the Temple look like a self-development cult in that members seek educational, economic and behavioural betterment, but at the same time it may also make the Temple look like a group of cinematic Satanists who are actively seeking magical power and insight. These two spurs balance the Setian from becoming a simplistic materialist or a delusional occultist. Unlike most occult groups Setians are likely to seek out dialogue and study in conventional academic venues rather than set up websites based on their channellings. This strongly pragmatic view comes from our roots in Anton LaVey's Church of Satan, which emphasized the real over 'spiritual pipe dreams'.

Why does the psyche need the Objective Universe? Why not just come up with a pleasant image of what might be? Certainly most of the occult world encourages fantasy—people can dream about kings in Atlantis and so forth. But in the 'real' world we learn things like caring for a sick friend, joy at real victory, mathematics to model the objective world etc. Through the gates of Understanding we not only perceive the Orderings of the Universe, we create similar (but more subtle and mutable) Orderings in our selves. In this understanding, Setians reverse the traditional 'As above, so below' maxim. We do not think the Cosmos reflects the psyche, we think the psyche can use the Cosmos to inspire its self-ordering.

Johann Gottlieb Fitche (1762-1814) was a Germanic idealist who created a theory of self that appealed to Michael Aquino. Fitche argued that consciousness implied self-consciousness. Nothing can be observed or done without an observer or a doer. The self begins its conscious actions in the world by positing its own existence. The existence of rational beings in the cosmos calls or summons (*fordern auf*) the non-natural sense of self from the hidden depths of a being. The self creates itself not because of the action or accident of another—and the self is both the action and recipient of the action of creation. For the self to become an 'I' it must perceive itself as limited (see above) and seek to overcome its limitations through action. The resistance of the cosmos causes the self to apprehend its own separateness from the cosmos and by the self-reflection that precedes action defines itself in such a fashion that it in turn summons others to aid in overcoming limitations and perceiving its own differences more accurately. In the Church of Satan Anton LaVey once gave Michael Aquino the task of picking a modern philosopher to exemplify Satanism and Aquino chose Fitche. This preceded another LaVey decree that Grotto leaders [3] should seek out anthropological and historical material to 'spice up' their ritual activities. Aquino had picked up the Dover reprint of Sir E.A. Wallis Budge's *Easy Lessons in Egyptian Hieroglyphics* (which had been re-issued in 1966, or in Setian-speak the Year I). In the nineteenth century, apprentice Egyptologists were given less important scrolls to practise on. 'Less' important meant magical or religious. 'More' important meant treaties and lists of tax-rolls. One of the first scrolls that Wallis Budge cut his teeth on was the *Papyrus Bremner-Rhind* (BM 10188), a Temple procedural or Dramatic Papyrus from the Ptolemaic period—it details a battle re-enacted between Apep and Thoth. Thoth recites a creation story that uses the phrase 'Xepera Xeper Xeperu' and destroys What Has Not Come Into Being by means of What Has Come Into Being. 'Xepera Xeper Xeperu' can be translated as: 'I have come into being and by my coming into being the way of coming into being has been established.' This ancient Egyptian magical summation of Fitche remained in Aquino's mind, waiting to be summoned by the Greater Black Magical Working that called the *Book of Coming Forth by Night* into being on June 21, 1975. The moment of self-creation for

Fitche—which is both the action of, and the product of, the 'I'—contains the basis for all empirical thoughts and actions of that 'I'. In this way the Egyptian god of Self Creation, Xephera, is seen as the force not only of the self, but the magical and empowering force behind all the products of the mind. Fitche's thought expands this notion that the 'I' creates itself as separate from the Cosmos in order to exist at all, and in order to create itself as an entity that it must recognize itself, as if it were, arriving as a response to a summons (*aufforderung*) made by other free individuals. This calling asks the developing self to limit its freedom out of respect for the other. The same limitation applies to the others and true self-development can only come by the exchange of recognition between rational individuals. Aquino's magical re-reading of these notions is reflected in the phrase from the *Story of Bata* he placed around the Seal of Set: 'Let then my great Nobles be brought to me.' The *Story of Bata* is a Nineteenth Dynasty tale of Set (Bata) who suffers many tragic metamorphoses until he becomes Pharaoh and eventually one of the undying luminaries associated with the Pole Star. Set's summons is the call for true freedom, and the possibility for mutual recognition—the means for advancement in the realms of the real and obtainable.

The Cosmos for the non-initiate is strictly Platonic—here essence precedes existence. This would suggest that the purpose of life is simply to 'tune-in' to a 'higher self' or a 'Holy Guardian Angel'. Such a presupposition pictures the day-to-day self as either inauthentic or weak. Setian philosophy suggests the self we experience is in fact real, and the intensity of its experiences gives rise to essence. Setians begin their journey with the Creation of something new: an Event called the Self. This Event, called out of the Void in response to the manifestation of sentience, changes the state of consciousness—this moment breaks the symmetry of the world. Setians assert that with the creation of each Setian, and also in rare and important moments of their lives, the New can come into being. This is the mystery of Baphomet. Actions of the Elect in the world of Becoming can alter the totality of both the natural and non-natural worlds. Setians reconcile the Will of Set—which brings confusion in the form of the New—and the Platonic world. Set is both the guardian of the absolute and the one who transcends boundaries. Because of Set there is a Void and the possibility to call things out of the Void.

As the Setian is the creation of the self as an eternal, powerful and dynamic essence—the Setian must choose those deeds that cause the world to reflect his will. Aquino had been a reader of existentialist thought before he encountered the Church of Satan and his writings in the Church of Satan (as 'John Kincaid') reflect Sartre's statement that 'the world is a mirror of my freedom'. Man's existence is the means by which the psyche becomes both aware of its existence and rises to power in this world—its self-definition comes after this fact. The moment of transcendence for the self is when one breaks with the conditioned world by choosing a project of one's own genius. Since this novelty is opposed to the inertia of the day-to-day world and does not represent the settled world of Ideas, the Setian may be seen as 'evil', or at least as *extropic*. When the world catches up with him, he will be seen as good. To transcend both the world and one's self-concept is to force the energy of the physical universe into the psychical universe. As the Setian renews the world, he creates himself as a force beyond the world. 'To do' precedes 'to be' and gives meaning to the path of *becoming*. This concept differentiates us from the Thelemites. In their model the true self is a fixed and knowable quantity whose unfolding is discovered as True Will. As such the self may be compared to a star. If a Setian were seen as a star, it would be a star that decided that maybe it didn't want to be a star—or at least a star that moved about erratically as it sought and created beauty and strangeness. If Thelemites are stars, Setians are more like Dr Who's TARDIS.

Setians have discovered magic as a truth process. The French philosopher Alain Badiou (b.1937) suggests that Truth can be found in four processes or discourses: Art, Science, Politics and Love. Under the right condition humans can encounter Truth in any of these processes. However each process can also lead to disaster and it is important to note that the process cannot predetermine the personal encounter with Truth. In other words, the discourses that lead to Truth are in themselves value-neutral, which enhances and gives meaning to the struggle of existence. Interestingly, Badiou articulates the same ideas the Temple has been articulating. Badiou is concerned with the Event, the new rupture into the world. In his schema any of the truth-processes can produce an Event, and the Event comes from the Void (much as Setian thinking would say that it comes from the Unmanifest/Apahnos). Take, for example, the subject of Jazz. At one time Jazz did not exist. It is the expression of Being—there was no Platonic form of Jazz that Jelly Roll Morton happened to tune-in to. The truth-process of Art called it into being from the Void. The truth found in it—which will be called Beauty since it comes from the truth process of Art—has transformed the event. Magic is a *truth process*: it calls things into being from the Void. The Self is the ultimate example of that which has been summoned from the Void. This can be seen as a new idea—a strong reaction against postmodernism or alternatively as the re-manifestation of a very old idea associated with the appearance of the *Xepera Xeper Xeperu* formula that dates from the First Intermediate Period in Egypt (2181-2055 BCE). Just as the relationship of the Dawn god, Xepera, was connected with the god of the night Sky, Set, in very ancient times, modern truth processes have re-discovered this relationship. The truth process that recognizes the event of Jazz is a *naming*. Badiou's philosophy (which he was developing while we developed ours) returns the notion of the *holy power of the name*. Naming is the magical act that takes a manifestation from the Void and turns it from an event into being. This process is coherent and resonant with the principle stated above, namely that existence precedes essence. Let us consider magic as a truth-process in the simplest of terms. The simple act of wishing for a better job—if done correctly, in the correct setting—will lead to a better job. In this new state Setians may give more time to discovering what they really want and explore this magically; alternatively they may simply keep wishing for a 'better' job as defined by society. Now let's add a few years to that situation: the Setian may have discovered that he/she wants a job as an art teacher in order to spend two and half months each year working on a painting, or instead may fall into the trap of using occult skills to do voodoo hexes and thereby traverse the cubicles of better paid slavery. Magic itself is neutral, but as it creates an effect on the world it must either enhance the self and its unfolding or simply advance one aspect of the self in an unbalanced way. The truths that the self creates in the world feed the self beyond this world. The Temple cannot tell the Setian which truths to bring forth. Similarly, the important truths found in the other discourses of Art, Science, Politics and Love certainly cannot arise from the text of another. The Setian must find what Badiou calls 'points of suture' between these truths by means of the individual quest. This is equivalent to the Gurdjieffian notion of unifying the little 'I's' into the big 'I'. It becomes imperative, especially as one advances beyond the stage of Adept, to make sure that the activity of truth-processes occurs in realms other than the magical.

The Path of a Setian
All truly great thoughts are conceived by walking.
—*Friedrich Nietzsche*

Setians see the Temple of Set, a not-for-profit corporation centred in San Francisco, California, as an outward manifestation of Set's *Will to Come into Being*. We see our individual quests for freedom and self-transcendence as part of the preservation of self-awareness in a time when mankind is developing technologies and social structures that oppose the self at the expense of the mindless all. Humans have over-developed the mechanical side of the intellect without grounding this advance in the quest for self-truth. As a consequence we see a world where collectivist forces—whether we call them British Petroleum, Islamic terrorism, or even Internet porn—erode Set's Gift of the Black Flame. It is no wonder that zombie films rake it in at the box office, for humankind seems quite happy to hasten to various mindless ends carrying different banners—each as inherently meaningless as the other. Yet, in spite of the dire state of this world, the Setian chooses to respond to Set's call to freedom. Great is the power of Set—greater still, he through us.

The Setian path of self-creation is an adult path. Decisions are based on experience and require a freedom of choice that children do not have. So the Temple is open only to adults, who are free souls. The atmosphere of a prison would not allow the freedom of action that a Setian would need. Setian practice is grounded in action and choice, not in intellectual exercise.

A smart human may decide to join the Temple for many reasons. He may be tired of the hypocrisy of his host culture, he may simply wish to become a magician—a young Faust looking for his Mephistopheles. He may like the spooky aesthetic or, best of all, he already knows a member of the Temple and likes that 'something different' about that person. He applies to the Executive Director. A member of the Priesthood will interview him. Does he seem intelligent? Does he have occult experience? Does he have the ability to express himself in non-occult terms? Does he have purpose and goals in his life? Is he more willing to learn what he might become than defend what he thinks he is now? Is he law-abiding, tolerant of others and willing to work hard on himself? Does he ask smart questions about us? Does he seem like a critical thinker who will try out our ideas rather than accept them with a starry-eyed grin?

Three of these points may require amplification. Firstly, we seek critical thinkers. People who view the Temple of Set as merely another module to plug into their heads are incapable of the realistic confrontation with the world or (more importantly) themselves. Secondly, as we openly affirm that we doubt the structures that maintain control of society, we understand that we draw the suspicious attention of the masses. To achieve the moral freedom of self-creation we must not scare the cows, even when we agree with the Roman poet Terrence, '*Quod licet Iovi, non licet bovi.*' Thirdly, as a group that studies elitism as a key to inspiration we must be sure that our applicants embrace diversity. A group that can fearlessly look at (for example) the magical processes of Nazi Germany, needs to avoid people of racist bent. This is not born out of political correctness, but philosophical necessity—humans won't work on their self-betterment if they assume that they are already halfway there because of their genes, culture, or economic status. Rivers of ink have been spilt asserting that we are Nazis because of certain ceremonies performed in Himmler's castle. It would be easy to point out in a knee-jerk fashion that our current

High Priestess is African-American, but I prefer to tell 'net heads' that we are trying hard to be Nazis—but we just keep finding smart people everywhere. There is just too much to gain magically with diversity.

The candidate who has passed the test, and feels good about his reasons in passing is permitted to join the Temple. This is the *external* event. However, the internal event occurred when the candidate was thinking about the archetype of the Prince of the Darkness at the same moment the Prince of Darkness was thinking of him. The circumstances can be as variable as reading an M.R. James tale as a lad, to thinking about Plato in an introductory philosophy class, buying a Tarot deck for fun, or watching a mummy movie. It is important to realize that the internal event, which is about offering choice to the psyche, may be hidden or trivialized by the seeker. Likewise, it is important to recall that Set was the Trickster of the Egyptian pantheon.

As a Setian I°, one receives access to the *Crystal Tablet of Set,* which contains the seminal essays 'Black Magic in Theory and Practice' by Ipsissimus Michael Aquino VI° and 'Within You and Beyond You' by Ipsissimus Don Webb VI°. The new Setian also receives access to current and all back issues of the *Scroll of Set,* and a White Medallion. White signifies Purity. For the Setian 'purity' does not come from some baptism performed by a Priest, nor does it come from abstaining from anything, or putting oneself through privations. Purity comes from the moment when a human decides to take responsibility for his or her own self-creation. At this moment he or she takes Set as part of his or her name. And as we progress though the degree system we all remain Setians. The sacred process of naming is part of the truth process of magic.

Our new Setian begins to work on himself in four lines of development—his body, his emotions, his intellect and his magical side. As he rids himself of ill thoughts or beliefs and deals with his emotional baggage he also begins to articulate his goals. The Fitchean need for Recognition (see above) causes him to seek out a member of the Priesthood to test his ability to explain his processes in Setian language, to learn to use all varieties of Black Magic more effectively in pursuit of his goals, and lastly to spur him (by Socratic questioning) into thinking about and perceiving himself and his world differently.

The Recognition process of the First Degree takes between one and two years. The Priest or Priestess looks for five things. Is there objective proof that the Setian has altered the world in his favour (ie. better job, better husband, cured a disease)? Has the Setian given up unloving self-criticism and uncritical self-love? Has the Setian mastered the intellectual and philosophical tools of the Temple in order to create an individual truth process? Has the Setian achieved a noetic apprehension of his own psyche? Does the Setian demonstrate loyalty in the sense that he sees the maintenance and furtherance of the Temple is in his own enlightened self-interest? Meanwhile, the Priest has gathered his answers through direct questioning and observation of the Setian's actions. If the Priest has found what he has sought, he Recognizes the Setian as an Adept. Setian degrees are confirmed, not conferred. The Adept is given a red medallion—red being the colour of evil in Egyptian religion, the colour of Set and Sekhmet. For most Setians the Second Degree is their last. They never feel a deeper connection to Set. Thousands of people have passed beyond our doors at this point—and these people continue to exert the influence of Setian philosophy wherever they may go. This is one of the ways we reshape the world.

The Adept is free to join an Order of the Temple. Orders are affinity groups that are devoted to particular approaches to working on emotions, schools of Medial Black Magic, or philosophy. Some of the better-known Orders are the Order of the Trapezoid, the Order of the Vampyre, the Order of the Wells of Wyrd, the Esoteric Order of Beelzebub and the Order of Setne Khamuast. The Order of the Trapezoid focuses the links between the human psyche and the world of Nature. Tradition is the Secret Door into Nature. In other words, all of those centuries of magic have caused certain things in Nature to respond to the human Will. Tradition can be either neo-mythological (for example, magic based on the fictions of H.P. Lovecraft or Frank Herbert) or actual magical traditions based on empowerment-centred magics. Examples would include Ipsissimus Stephen Flowers' extensive work on the Runes. Flowers was the second Grandmaster of the Order of the Trapezoid. The Order of the Vampyre uses vampire and werewolf folklore as a working method to focus on the link between the psyche and the body—and the link between psyches through the body. The glamour of sex and terror are tapped here. One of the Grandmasters of the Order of the Vampyre, Lilith Aquino, found her Word *Arkte* here—the Word of Recognition of the power of animal life as an expression of the psyche's power and the pleasure of incarnation. The Order of the Wells of Wyrd deals with the interaction/interference-patterns between self-directed destiny and other-directed fate. The Anglo-Saxon word *Wyrd* is an expression of the resulting pattern, and the Order explores this both philologically (see for example Paul C. Bauschatz's *The Well and the Tree: World and Time in Early Germanic Culture*) and with their own-technology—which includes their infamous 'dream rounds' process of group lucid dreaming. The Esoteric Order of Beelzebub is a Setian exploration of Fourth Way Work—consisting of Gurdjieff plus a seasoning of Heidegger's notion of *Aletheia* (Truth = Not Forgetting) and some medieval demonism. The Order of Setne Khamuast explores Egyptian and Greco-Egyptian magical technologies with an eye to reintegrating them into modern life.

During Order Work some Adepts give evidence of becoming aware noetically of the Principle of Isolate Intelligence, whom we call Set. This awareness of Set is not a merging with Set, nor a 'belief' in Set. It is the idea of Apollonius mentioned above—a knowledge of situations not only viewed from one's cultural/biological viewpoint but from a non-human perspective that expresses the desire of isolate intelligence to expand/evolve itself. This cold and exacting clarity is a good thing for an individual human if, and only if, that person has worked on his or her heart during Adepthood. The individual must have found (for himself/herself) feelings of love and fairness, friendship and play. The individual's enlightened humanity and Set's view of the evolution of the spirit must be balanced. This will change the effect of the individual's words on other First and Second Degree candidates. It will inflame the individual's heart toward a protective love of the Temple and will also cause other Setians working on the same emotional issues to be mysteriously drawn towards this person. Individuals who accept the changes that they and Set are Working in them, can seek the Priesthood. Three Masters of the temple will examine, challenge, and nurture this person's thought process. Let's assume, for the moment, that the Setian candidate is female—just by way of explanation with what follows. In a secular sense the act of becoming a Priestess will make her a voting member of the Temple of Set Incorporated. The Temple's governance rests in the hands of these humans, not a cult leader. The Third Degree medallion is black, which signifies the darkness of the new and terrifying nature of the *mysterium tremendum et fascinans* of the Prince of Darkness and His friends among humankind.

The duality of the Priesthood not only causes her words to have a greater effect on humans, but also on her own being. She is deeply energized to seek the sutures between the truth processes of Magic, Art, Science, Love and Politics in her own life. She helps others find their way to self-development spurred on by neither of the banal state of egotism/righteousness or altruism. She helps others because she now has a 24/7 need to balance the cosmic vision and the human/individual one. All of the aspects of her life must be examined, all old wounds healed, all mysteries cleared up. During this process her approach to magic may undergo a vast change. As opposed to the atomistic approach of seeing magic as a process applied to other dynamic processes, magic becomes a central stream that works without need for ritual or spell. As the whole of her life becomes transformed by integrating the Essence of Set, then the whole of life becomes a place where magic seeps into space-time. This state is the Fourth Degree, and it is highly *Wyrd*. In many ways it is the state humans sought when they first took up the magical path.

So why do we crave—actually feast upon—the Wonder of Magic? We talk tough, as if we only do magic for serious things. Heck, we love it when our magic makes a line open up at the supermarket! In the Fourth Degree the change we have made in ourselves affects the Objective Universe in mysterious ways. After all, the magician is a part of the Objective Universe. You are no less than the trees and the stars—as that poster read in your third grade classroom. Because you have Become You, Wyrd things happen—and the feedback loop teaches you more than the processes of the first three degrees. The High Priestess and Council of Nine provide the Recognition dialogue for the degree of Magister Templi. The years of magical experience have changed the Fitchean need for resistance, and the universe becomes a source of more accessible information.

The Master wears a blue medallion. Blue is the celestial colour and now *they are like unto a star.* It is likely that the Master's process of self-examination has to be reified. He must cast what he has learned into the world so that he can Play with energies of his former self. In Setian jargon, we call this a 'Remanifestation' of the Master—usually this results in the Creation of an Order. Masters and Adepts are linked in a transpersonal truth process in the same way that Priests and Setians are.

The Master can be elected to the Temple's governing body, the Council of Nine. The Council of Nine elects or removes the High Priest, and confirms any Recognitions of the Fourth Degree or higher, and any removal from office of the Third Degree or higher. The Council takes its mythological authority from Asoka's Nine Wise Men, which has been recorded in various places prior to arriving in Western magic via the Theosophist Talbot's Mundy's novel *The Unknown Nine*.

If the Master discovers in the ordering of his own life a single principle that can be reduced to a Word/Logos and he discovers that Set's cosmic viewpoint also has Logos as a focusing principle, the Master must Utter this Word as a Magus. A Word is a two-fold thing. One part is a label for a group or constellation of ideas. For example, we all 'know' what we mean when we utter the words 'Capitalism', 'Communism', 'Democracy' or 'Racism'. We use some Words to define who we are, and others to define who we are not. We can gain motivation when we think about Words—because Words separate us from the mechanical universe. A rock never worries if it is a good enough Capitalist, nor does a locust think ants can be Racist. All Words are ways that human beings use to align themselves with movements—and as such with the power and limitation of groups. At their worst, Words can lead to sleep—for example, we all know other people who are so self-identified with their label 'Mormon' or 'Democrat' or 'Feminist' that they have ceased thinking altogether. We also know people who think a good deal about their label—and who, by bringing themselves to their highest level of thinking, shape themselves and their world in good ways (or, at least, in ways that appear good to them). Words are also a magical act—specifically in some mythologies Words are the way the universe is created. Words create the Christian universe (see the *Gospel of John*) and the Hindu universe (google 'Vac').[4] Sometimes the 'Word' or plan is a template used to fashion the world from Chaos, as in the Hebrew or Germanic Cosmos. *Xeper* is the watchword of Setian thinking, much as *Communism* is the watchword of Marxism or *Thelema* the watchword of Aleister Crowley's Aeon of Horus. *Xeper* is also a Word of world-creation. In a psyche-centric religion such as the Temple of Set, the Word of an individual's self-creation is the word of cosmic creation. The sentient observer and actor is what is created, and his or her actions and perceptions of the Cosmos create his or her world. Purely philosophical systems see the contemplation of Words as a method of purifying the soul, or even causing an Ascent into powerful regions—such systems generally look upon ritual enactments of the Words as a 'lower' or 'superstitious' system. Most magical systems usually think that Words are keys to power only through a magical technology. The Setian system (in many ways harkening back to Chaldean theurgy) sees both approaches as complementary and necessary. Obviously Words are powerful and dangerous tools. They can lead to new vistas of self-truth in the Setian truth-process or alternatively to terrible disaster. The High Priest Recognizes the Utterance of a Word, and this Recognition must be unanimously confirmed by the Council of Nine. The Magus/Maga wears a purple medallion showing the individual is performing the Work of the Prince of Darkness. Current Words Recognized by the Temple are *Runa* (Stephen Edred Flowers). *Xeper* (Uttered by Michael A. Aquino, ReUttered by Donald James Webb), *Arkte* (Lilith Aquino), *Remanifest* (James A. Lewis), *Indulgence* (Anton S, LaVey) and *Thelema* (Aleister Crowley).

If the Magus successfully completes his task, the Word will inspire others to talk about how it was useful to them. The Word will be given as a present of Love to people the magician chooses to empower. The Word will change the paradigms of Science (à la Kuhn). The Word will impel Political action. The Word will inspire Art. The Word will enable greater Magic. This will change the world to reflect the utterer. Then he can say (with Nietzsche), '*Ego Ipsissimus*.' Nietzsche dug up this medieval term for 'His Very Own Self' in his *Human, All Too Human*. The Ipsissimus has become Set-like, in that he or she now derives nourishment from a Cosmos that is intelligible only as a Recognition of his or her being. The

Ipsissimus seeks to encourage the Cosmic ecology in a different way than in other Degrees. He or she is no longer extropic—the perceptual universe does not grow larger or more energized by their being—but he or she facilitates communication and flow between different viewpoints and principles, particularly between the forces engendered by the Utterance of his Word and Words that manifest before or after his. The Fitchean need for Recognition is ended, and the self is no longer called into being by the summons of others. In the jargon of Hinduism, the Ipsissimus acts without generating karma. Ipsissimi of the Temple (at the time of this writing in mid-2010) are Michael A. Aquino, James A. Lewis, Stephen E. Flowers and Donald J. Webb. The Ipsissimus wears a gold medallion. The symbolism of this colour is a ritual secret among the Masters, and links the work of the masters and Ipsissimus, much as the work of the Adepts and masters is linked.

I will now end with a few recommendations for further reading.

The Library of the Damned

> *I have dwelt ever in realms apart from the visible world; spending my youth and adolescence in ancient and little-known books, and in roaming the fields and groves of the region near my ancestral home. I do not think that what I read in these books or saw in these fields and groves was exactly what other boys read and saw there; but of this I must say little, since detailed speech would but confirm those cruel slanders upon my intellect which I sometimes overhear from the whispers of the stealthy attendants around me.*
>
> —H.P. Lovecraft, The Tomb

Readers may wish to visit the Temple of Set Website:
http://www.xeper.org/

Introductory articles about the Temple of Set:
Michael Aquino, *History of the Temple of Set*:
http://www.xeper.org/maquino/nm/TOSd11.pdf
This is a living document created by the human founder of the Temple of Set, Ipsissimus Michael A. Aquino. Here is his description, as of this writing:

> '*Companion to* The Church of Satan, *this is more of a personal memoir of the Temple 1975-1996 than a history, as the development of the Temple was far more multifaceted, and multi-individual, than that of the Church. This book is currently in writing, and successive drafts of it will be progressively*

uploaded here until the entire work is complete. At this time Draft #11 is available.'

Don Webb, *Mysteries of the Temple of Set,* Runa Raven Press 2004
Explains the current Words of the Temple and includes essays on Setian praxis and cosmology. It also includes several sample essays from the *Scroll of Set* and explains basic Setian thought and some of the larger issues of Left-Hand Path philosophy.

About the Archetype of the Prince of Darkness:

H. teVelde, *Seth: The God of Confusion,* Brill Academic Publishing 1977
The great study of the multi-faceted Set in ancient Egypt. Set's beginnings as a god of Rites of Passage, his connection with the oppressed people of Upper Egypt, his role as god of empire and god of foreigners, his connections with stellar cults. Set's various roles—as the one who crates and transcends boundaries, 'Opener of the Mouth' of the other gods, and the only deathless god are discussed in an historical context.

Sarah Iles Johnston, *Hekate Soteria: A Study of Hekate's Roles in the Chaldean Oracles and Related Literature,* American Philological Association 1990
A study in the development of the archetype from a goddess of liminal places to a goddess of witchcraft and malefic sorcery to finally the symbol of salvation for those seeking self-deification.

Guilhem Olivier, *Mockeries and Metamorphoses of an Aztec God: Tezcatlipoca,'Lord of the Smoking Mirror',* University Press of Colorado, 2004
A guide of the Aztec culture's take on the Prince of Darkness with useful studies of the psychology of worship, fear and wonder. The nature of sorcery and Aztec (nagualist) philosophy. Shapeshifting and imperial power discussed as well as the influence of the archetype on material culture.

George P. Hansen, *The Trickster and the Paranormal,* Xlibris Corporation, 2001
A study of Trickster myth, magicians and modern *psi* research, this book looks both at current scientific approaches to parapsychology, the psychology of Lesser Black Magic, and the nature of the Trickster as the god who makes you think. Hansen gives a great analysis of the liminality of the 'Unknown' and passes on certain useful studies of the magical

effects of folklore and narrative.

Stella Kramrisch, *The Presence of Shiva*, Princeton University Press, 1981
Shiva, the Indian subcontinent's take on the Price of Darkness, both compromises and transcends everything. Kramrisch deals with Shiva as Wild God, the Great Yogi, the guardian of the absolute. By revealing the paradoxes in Shiva's nature (just as the four books above do for their manifestation), this book reveals the nature of consciousness itself.

Paul Carus, *The History of the Devil,* Dover reprint
Carus surveys the satanic around the world in a variety of cultures and eras. Highlights include demonology in ancient Egypt; in Hindu, Buddhist, and early Christian thought; and throughout the Inquisition and Reformation.

About the Left-Hand Path:
Stephen E. Flowers, *Lords of the Left Hand Path: A History of Spiritual Dissent*, 2nd Edition Inner Traditions, 2012
The only comprehensive study of movements that attempt self-deification through antinomian practice. Flowers deals with the origin of the idea and traces it through ancient cults, forbidden religious sects, medieval heretics, Faustian libertines and modern occultists. He provides good insight on Left-Hand Path thinking in Blavatsky, Crowley, the Fraternitas Saturni and the Nazis as well as The Church of Satan and the Temple of Set.

Uncle Setnakt's Essential Guide to Left Hand Path, Runa Raven Press, 1999
A practice-centred guide to the Left-Hand Path which includes sorcery and divination methods as well as a fairly straightforward explanation of the Left-Hand Path in the West. The book divides the human experience into the carnal/physical, emotional, intellectual and daimonic centres—it is in many ways a Left-Hand Path re-reading of Fourth Way Work to consider the demonic and the magical as needed parts of self-development.

About Magic:
Ernst Schertel, *Magic: History, Theory, Practice*, COTUM, 2009
Simply the best introduction to the idea of the demonic in magic. Schertel has an excellent discussion of the magician as extropic agent, and the nature of the new/energetic as appearing dark and evil. This 1923 book

is a much clearer introduction to the idea of the Satanic in evil than more modern moralizing texts. The English-language edition is annotated by Adolph Hitler. Hitler's interest in the book didn't keep him from sending Schertel to a concentration camp. Power gained without an understanding and allegiance to the principle of isolate intelligence turns against the Devil's big three inventions: dignity, joy and freedom.

Jesper Sørenson, *A Cognitive Theory of Magic*, AltaMira Press, 2006
This is an analysis of the cognitive background of magical actions. Sørenson draws upon classical ethnographic cases (for example, Trobriand farmers) and modern cognitive theory to explain why magical rituals look the way they do. A good investigation of magic as a truth-process.

This essay is dedicated to my Teacher's Teacher
Dr Michael A. Aquino,
High Priest Emeritus of the Temple of Set,
who has caused the Black Flame to come down
from Heaven in the full view of men.

References
Austin, J. 1962. *How to do things with Words: The William James Lectures delivered at Harvard University in 1955*. Oxford: Clarendon.
Badiou, A. 2005. *Being and Event*. New York: Continuum.
Bauschatz, P.C. 1983. *The Well and the Tree: World and Time in Early Germanic Culture*. Amhurst: University of Massachusetts Press.
Bernstein, J. 1989. *Power and Politics*. Boston: Shambhala.
Crowley, A. 1998. *Magick: Book 4*. Second revised edition. New York: Weiser.
Edinger, E. 1972. *Ego and Archetype: Individuation and the Religious Function of the Pysche*. New York: Putnam.
Eliade, M. 1975. *Birth and Rebirth*. New York: Harper & Row.
Farber, P. 2010. *The Great Purple Hoo-Ha: A Comedy of Perception*, vol. I and II. Oxford, UK: Mandrake.
Fitche, J. G. 1992 [1798/99]. *Foundations of Transcendental Philosophy (Wissenschaftslehre nova methodo)*. Trans. and ed. D.B reazeale. Ithaca, New York: Cornell University Press.
Geertz, C. 1993. 'Religion as a Cultural System.' in *The Intepretation of Cultures*. London: Fontana.
Gebser, J. 1985. *The Ever-Present Origin*. Authorized translation by N. Barstad with A. Mickunas. Athens: Ohio University Press.
Gooch, S. 1978. *The Paranormal*. London: Wildwood House.
_____ 1973. *Personality and Evolution*. London: Wildwood House.
Hertz, R. 1973. 'The Pre-Eminence of the Right Hand: A Study in Religious

Polarity' in R. Needham, *Left and Right*. Chicago: University of Chicago Press.

Kuhn, T. 2000. *The Road Since Structure: Philosophical Essays, 1970-1993*. Chicago: University of Chicago Press.

_____1962. *The Structure of Scientific Revolutions*. Chicago: University of Chicago Press.

Lachman, G.V. 2007. *Rudolph Steiner: An Introduction to his Life and Work*. New York: Tarcher.

_____2003. *A Secret History of Consciousness*, London: Lindisfarne Books.

Webb, D. 2005. *Aleister Crowley: The Fire and the Force*. Smithville: Runa-Raven Press.

_____1996. *The Seven Faces of Darkness*. Smithville: Runa-Raven Press.

White, V. 1952. *God and the Unconscious*. London: Harvill.

Endnotes

1. *Note to readers*: capitalization is used throughout this chapter for specific points of emphasis.
2. The Cairo Working is another name for Aleister Crowley's magical revelation in Cairo, 1904, and gave rise to his key text *The Book of the Law*.
3. Grottoes were the local units of the Church of Satan, much as Pylons are in the Temple of Set.
4. Vac=Word=Logos.

13
The Magical Life of Ithell Colquhoun

Amy Hale

Ithell Colquhoun is becoming recognized as one of the most interesting and prolific esoteric thinkers and artists of the twentieth century, and although she was known in her day, it is only in the 20 or so years after her death that her innovative spirit is being acknowledged. Although she gained her early reputation as a member of the British Surrealist movement, she has become better known as an occult artist, writer and theorist. Throughout each decade of her life, she engaged with various movements and individuals who shaped and also complemented the development of her worldview and the goal which drove nearly all of her projects: becoming enlightened. Colquhoun presents an amazing case study of a primarily Hermetically focused magician. Every area of her life and all of her achievements were ultimately driven by her spiritual pursuits. Through her work we can see an interplay of themes and movements which characterizes the trajectory of certain British subcultures ranging from Surrealism to the Earth Mysteries movement and also gives us a rare insight into the thoughts and processes of a working magician.

Colquhoun and Surrealism

Colquhoun was born in India in 1906, as her father was serving in the military there, and from her own account she had an unusual childhood marked by freedom, exploration and unconventional spiritual leanings. When she was 13 she began study at Cheltenham Ladies School, and later studied art at the Slade. She took a very early interest in biology, and many of her early notebooks were filled with highly detailed representations of flowers and plants. The study of plants and flowers was a theme to which she returned many times during her life, in her painting and drawing and in her writing, frequently using plants as visual metaphors for eroticism. Her exceptionally representational visual style formed the basis for her early artistic work and also her segue into Surrealism in the mid 1930s.

Colquhoun is generally identified with the Surrealist movement, and while she claimed artistic identity as a Surrealist for the entirety of her life, her formal associations with British Surrealism were quite short-lived. Ithell first encountered Surrealism when she studied in Paris from 1931-33. She later visited the International Surrealist Exposition in London in 1936, and it was clear within the next two years that Surrealism was starting to impact her work more directly, primarily influenced by her exposure to Salvador Dalí. In 1939 she visited André Breton in Paris, and started working with automatic techniques in her writing and painting. By the late 1930s she was exhibiting with other Surrealists in Britain in prominent Surrealist spaces such as the Mayor Gallery in 1939, and she self-identified as a Surrealist for the rest of her life. In 1940 there was a rift in the British Surrealist movement. The Belgian Surrealist Edouard Mesens, who promoted the career of René Magritte and who published a feature on Ithell in his *London Bulletin* magazine, took over as figurehead and organizer of the British Surrealists, and decreed that no one involved with the British Surrealist movement would publish or belong to any group that was not in service of Surrealism, nor would they hold opposing political positions (Levy 2003). Ithell refused to sever her occult ties and relinquish her interests, and as a result she publicly separated from British Surrealism. Unlike many of her Surrealist counterparts in Britain, Ithell did not view Surrealism as part of a wider political or socialist agenda, although she clearly believed in its revolutionary capacity, specifically in her portrayals of sex and gender.

In 1943 Colquhoun married the charismatic artist Toni Del Renzio. Very little is known about their marriage, aside from the fact that it was rather short-lived, but it seems from their efforts at the time that Del Renzio was the publically dominant partner. Together the couple set out to promote Surrealism in Britain in opposition to Mesens' group through a series of poetry readings and publications, featuring their own original works and also those of founding Surrealists such as Breton. Their performances attracted the attention of Mesens and his cohort, however, which came to their performances to mock them. This incident had a devastating effect on Ithell (Levy 2005, 22). Her marriage with Del Renzio came to an end in 1947 under circumstances which are not exactly clear, but which may have been the result of an affair by Del Renzio. Although Colquhoun had romantic liaisons following her divorce, in many ways she never fully recovered from that relationship, and it also marked the end of her public engagement with the wider Surrealist movement.

Despite the short length of her engagement with the British Surrealists, Colquhoun's Surrealist body of work was wide-ranging and extensive. Although Surrealism tends to be associated most frequently with the visual arts, particularly those of a type which are highly representational and fantastic, it is important to stress that Surrealism was initially a movement expressed through writing. Surrealism was and is not a style, it is a philosophy, and a worldview. Most Surrealists enacted their experiments in poetry, prose, visual arts, and performance. As such, to consider Colquhoun primarily as a visual artist, would be to diminish her own personal Surrealist project. She was prolific with just about everything she did. She created thousands of pieces of visual art, wrote, published and performed hundreds of poems, wrote several novels (two of which were unpublished), three travel guides (one of which was unpublished), radio dramas, commentaries, and quite a large number of esoteric-related essays. Although not all of her work would be identified as explicitly Surrealist, she would have identified that as a primary current within her life, and most important to her was the link between the Surreal and the Fantastic.

Colquhoun frequently claimed throughout her life that she was the only true Surrealist left working in Britain (Colquhoun, "Autobiographical Notes"). She may have made this claim because the ways in which her own work reflected the automatism and the preeminent position of the unconscious that was key to the works of André Breton and many other Surrealists, notably Dalí. However, much of her visual and written work diverged from the Surrealists and should be considered primarily esoteric art, because she does not emphasize chance and open interpretation to the same degree. Colquhoun used both automatic methods and Hermetic methods to create works which simultaneously drew on subconscious elements and dream imagery, yet also were primed with specific intent, coded by the artist according to Hermetic principles.

The degree to which genuine occultism was an influence in the wider Surrealist movement is debatable. There is a difference between employing occult tropes and symbols in artistic creation and having a commitment to a sustained esoteric practice. The primary connection between Surrealism in general and occult processes is to be found in automatism, which was a key feature of Ithell's work, and according to André Breton's first Surrealist manifesto the defining feature of Surrealism itself (Polizzotti 1995, 209). Automatism was somewhat inspired by, yet different from, mediumistic automatism. The source of automatic images in Surrealism was not believed to be spirits, but the psyche itself releasing repressed desires and impulses. Automatic writing was in many ways close to stream-of-consciousness, while automatic art techniques were based on seemingly random applications of paint to canvas or paper to see what emerged. Other forms of automatism included collage, found objects or found poems, frottage or rubbings, and a number of other techniques designed to incorporate elements of chance and play into the creative process. Surrealists also embraced the works of Freud, dream states, hysteria, games of chance and madness. They looked for freedom from logical processes and direct, unmediated access to the unconscious. Surrealists believed that automatic processes would generate a sense of randomness out of which one could explore the workings of the subconscious. In 1941, Breton noted that the two primary visual forms of Surrealist expression were based either in automatism or the recording of dream like images, but said that automatism was closer to true Surrealist method.

Additionally, Surrealists drew on a variety of occult symbols. André Breton's references to alchemy in the 1929 *Second Surrealist Manifesto* and also to the 'occultation' of Surrealism are sometimes interpreted by art historians as examples of the adoption of a Hermetic position, and Colquhoun herself believed this to be the case according to an unpublished article she wrote on Surrealism and Hermeticism (Polizzotti 1995, 325, *Colquhoun, Surrealism and Hermetic Poetry n/d, 6*). It is evident that a number of individual artists had occult, mystical and mythological themes in their works. Leonora Carrington and Max Ernst, for example, frequently used alchemical symbolism such as eggs and alembics in their paintings and written work, while the image of the hermaphrodite was seen as a Surrealist ideal, as well as an occult ideal (Warlick 2001). For the core of male surrealists in the movement the hermaphroditic ideal was to be gained through the channel of the Muse, or conjunction with the female creative principle. We can hypothesize that women associated with Surrealism had their own interpretation of the hermaphrodite, and the work of Claude Cahun might be of interest in this regard (Ades, *Surrealism, Male-Female* 2001). We also know that Surrealists were reading writers of the French occult revival, notably Eliphas Lévi, and of course had a love of Tarot cards, of which Surrealists created a variety of decks over the years.

A primary question then would be the degree to which Colquhoun's interest in the occult and her use of occult symbols and techniques in her Surrealism was similar to other Surrealists, and the ways in which it was different. Because she considered herself to be engaging in magical acts, and because she believed in the objective reality of the figures and concepts with which she was working, her use of them was both divinatory and ritualistic. She was consistently working with otherworldly realms, and although she was using automatic processes, she was also directing the symbolism and the colours for specific ends. Dawn Ades has argued that Colquhoun's primary method of Surrealist working was the highly representational dream image, mostly inspired by her interest in Salvador Dalí, but Colquhoun would most likely argue that automatic processes were at the basis of her Surrealist practice, and for that reason she remained consistent with the directives and programs of the early continental Surrealists (Ades, *Notes on Two Women Surrealist Painters: Eileen Agar and Ithell Colquhoun* 1980) (Colquhoun, *Letter to the Editor* 1981). This is not to suggest that Colquhoun did not derive an exceptional amount of inspiration for her art from her dream states. Dreams were a very important source of imagery for her, but most of her visual art was simply not highly representational.

What seems to be a primary difference in Colquhoun's use of Surrealist techniques is that her conception of the spaces one would contact using automatic processes would be inhabited by specific beings, and reached using a variety of esoteric languages. She did not just use these techniques to see what came of them with her mind in a state unfettered by logic and rationality, or to explore subconscious desires. These other planes had things to communicate to her and as such her art was part of her road to enlightenment and served as invocation and ritual. For instance, she interpreted the four major automatic processes as corresponding to the four elements: Fire to *fumage* (which is developing figures from a canvas or paper which has been previously smoked), Water to *parsemage* (which is when charcoal or pastel are floated on water and then gently apply to paper), Air to techniques where things are blown on paper, such as charcoal, paint or pastel, and *decalcomania*, where prints are either transferred or superimposed from one surface to another, to Earth. Therefore, when she chose which process she would use, she was in some way prescribing intent or focus into the artistic outcome (Colquhoun, *The Mantic Stain* 1949).

Although many of the early Surrealists promoted the idea that their works were created by chance, randomness, and pure access to the unconscious, of course that is not completely true. Any of Breton's works which may have been guided by automatic principles were also guided by aesthetics and, in the end, editing. Words went together because they sounded good, or the imagery was intriguing. The automatic process may have started off a painting, but it was later shaped by the creator to bring out more of a recognizable meaning for both artist and audience. Colquhoun worked the same way, but she frequently would use as her starting point colours from a palette with specific magical associations or a text which already had some sort of personal esoteric meaning to her, and would be useful for further contemplation for invocation. For instance, she developed a set of 'found poems' from Sir E.A. Wallace Budge's translation of the *Egyptian Book of the Dead* (Colquhoun, "Gods of the Cardinal Points" n.d.). On reading them, they are not so much found poems as invocations and rituals to be done at cardinal points using Egyptian symbolism, and reflected her love and abiding interest in the Golden Dawn system of magical practice. These poems were not random—nothing ever is—but what she was doing was using her conception of the mental and psychic space one opens up to create something sacred from the profane. Similarly, she wrote a series of poems designed to reflect the polarities of male and female and to emphasize duality. They were titled 'Poems of He and She', and they were lists of masculine and feminine nouns taken from a Gaelic grammar (Colquhoun, "Poems of He and She" n.d.). The idea of her automatic poetry was to bring the order from the random, but order that was ultimately instructive about the nature of the universe and, in this case, alchemical duality.

Sex and Gender

Ithell Colquhoun's treatment of sex and gender was nothing short of radical and these were important themes in the first stages of her career as an artist. Some of her earliest pieces explore Biblical and classical stories featuring powerful women, and there is good reason to believe that she may have found inspiration in the Italian Renaissance artist Artemisia Gentileschi, a student of Caravaggio, who depicted scenes of female violence and also violence against women. In 1929, Ithell tied for first place in the Slade Summer Composition with *Judith Showing the Head of Holofernes*, which may have been an homage to a similarly titled piece by Gentileschi, as most likely was her 1930 composition entitled *Susanna and the Elders*. By the late 1930s, however, Ithell progressed into much bolder depictions of the male form, some so bold that one gallery refused to display *Gouffres Amers* (1939) (Moore April, 1941). Several of her pieces from the 1930s deal both metaphorically and quite literally with male genitalia, such as *Double Coconut* (1936) and *Sardine and Eggs*

(1940/41). Castration and male impotence was also an early theme in a number of important works, such as *Gouffres Amers, Cucumber* (1939) and *The Pine Family* (1940). These may have a reference to the myth of the fallen and resurrected god made so popular by the work of the religious scholar Sir James Frazer, but it was most likely not an overall comment on her view of men; it may represent studies of an archetype. In fact, *The Pine Family* depicts a castrated male, female and hermaphrodite where all genitalia have been removed. Art historian Dawn Ades once suggested that Colquhoun's explicit portrayals of the male body could be read as a parody of the ways in which the men of the Surrealist movement objectified women. Colquhoun responded directly to Ades' comments by stating that her work in this regard needed to be taken at face value and that she was not satirizing, or commenting on the works of male surrealists. In this way, Colquhoun states very directly that her work is not to be seen as derivative, but that it stands on its own, and that she was not afraid to confront the societal expectations of women artists and their relationship with the male body (Ades, *Notes on Two Women Surrealist Painters: Eileen Agar and Ithell Colquhoun* 1980) (Colquhoun, *Letter to the Editor* 1981).

Often, though, Ithell's early depictions of sex were positive and inviting. Visual metaphors of sexuality inundate her work, and even the simplest sketch of a cake or a spoon in a glass can easily take on a very explicit character. Colquhouns' celebrated piece *Scylla* (1938) features a view of a woman's knees in the bath with a small boat gliding not so innocently between them. These works date from the height of her public involvement with Surrealism. Sketches from her archives include other lighthearted watercolours of bathing women, and also more explicit depictions of a woman birthing a variety of complex esoteric symbols. Some of her decalcomania pieces such as *Alcove* (1946) appear to represent the folds of a vulva. As discussed below, in some cases Colquhoun's focus on gender was emblematic of her preoccupations with the integration of duality as a magical act, and the symbolism involved worked on a number of levels for the viewer. Although Colquhoun explored issues of sex and gender throughout her life, her more challenging and celebrated visual works on this theme came from the earliest stages of her career. She did, however, produce some quite radical essays and poems ranging from diatribes on the restrictions caused by women's clothing in the 1960s to poems about condoms in the decade before her death (Colquhoun, "My Ideas About Clothes" c. 1961).

The Hermetic and Alchemical Current

Colquhoun demonstrated a very early interest in the occult and in alchemy, and it was probably this that made her interest in Surrealism a very natural match. Her cousin was Edward Langford Garstin, who was Cancellarius of the Alpha Omega chapter of the Hermetic Order of the Golden Dawn, wrote extensively on alchemy and theurgy, and was friends with MacGregor and Moina Mathers. Garstin was also the secretary of G.R.S. Mead's Quest Society that Colquhoun joined in 1928 (Colquhoun, "Sword of Wisdom Draft Notes" n.d.). Although Colquhoun only developed her friendship with her cousin as an adult through their membership in the Quest Society, Garstin had a remarkable impact on her occult development, and it was through him that she was introduced to the Golden Dawn. It would be no underestimation to argue for the pre-eminence of the occult in Ithell's body of work. It was very clearly an overriding preoccupation from a relatively young age and her earliest writings on alchemy, Kabbalah and Enochian magic, dated from the 1920s. In 1926 she completed and performed a play called *Bird of Hermes* based on alchemical themes, some of which may have formed the basis for her alchemical novel *Goose of Hermogenes* (Colquhoun, "Bird of Hermes draft script" 1926). In 1936 she painted a watercolour of Allan Bennett, a Golden Dawn adept and magical teacher of Aleister Crowley and she was experimenting with alchemical themes in art from the late 1930s.

Although Ithell clearly showed Hermetic and alchemical influences in her art from a very early age, her involvement in occult organizations really emerges in the 1950s, after her divorce from Toni Del Renzio in 1947. Until this time, Ithell was much more integrated into both Modernist and Surrealist art and literature communities in London, but by the 1950s her focus had shifted. Not only did she begin joining occult and magical organizations, but her investigations into witchcraft began in earnest, and she relocated permanently to the west of Cornwall. From the beginning of the 1950s, Colquhoun's visual work seems to take on more of a private and contemplative nature and her painting output decreased for nearly a decade, while the public focus of her art switched more to poetry and essay writing. Her strictly magical essays proliferated and she also had success in publishing her spiritual and mystical travel guides, *Crying of the Wind* (1955) an experiential guide to Ireland, and also *The Living Stones* (1957), which is probably one of the first Earth Mysteries guides to Cornwall. A third travel guide to Egypt was drafted in the 1960s but was never completed. Some of her earliest work in occult journalism was completed for a local London paper called *The London Broadsheet*, where she wrote profiles of Gerald Gardner (1954) and Austin Osman

Spare (1955), as well as more theoretical material on *Thelema* and divination. Later in her life she wrote a number of esoteric articles for *Prediction* and *Quest* as well as several other publications.

Colquhoun then emerges as a nexus of all of the major occult currents of the 20th century. What follows is a very short resume of her esoteric interests: she was very firmly entrenched in the Western esoteric tradition, but was also well read in Asian traditions, including Buddhism and yoga. Kabbalah and alchemy were probably the most consistent references throughout her body of work, followed by her interest in Druidry and Nature religion. She was an initiate of a wide variety of different orders representing Hermetic and Pagan traditions, including the Ordo Templi Orientis, Co-Masonry, the British Circle of the Universal Bond, the Golden Section Society, and in later years the Fellowship of Isis. Although she was unsuccessful at her attempts to become an initiate of Golden Dawn at an early stage, the Golden Dawn system of magic was clearly one of her guiding principles, and she wrote the influential account of the Golden Dawn magicians, *The Sword of Wisdom*, published in 1975. She was also a key member of a Golden Dawn-type organization, The Order of the Pyramid and Sphinx, founded by Tamara Bourkhoun in the 1960s with a heavy emphasis on Enochian magic. It remains unclear to what degree this order was established in its initiatory process, but it is very clear from her notes and the art work which remains in her archives that she was working on Second Order-level Golden Dawn material (Colquhoun, Magical drawings and diagrams 1950s-1970s). She was also affiliated briefly with Dion Fortune's group, the Society for Inner Light, but the organization did not suit her and she did not continue on with them (Colquhoun, "Sword of Wisdom Draft Notes" n.d.). She had deep interests in and knowledge of both traditional and contemporary witchcraft, met with Gerald Gardner more than once, yet did not become a member of any Wiccan organization. Although she was not a spiritualist, she had knowledge of and correspondence with folk healers around Britain and Ireland, and made extensive use of remote healing services (Castle 1971).

Ithell's Magical Art Experiments

Throughout her life, Colquhoun produced an extensive and impressive body of esoteric visual art in addition to her poems and essays. But while it is no stretch to say that many of the works which she created with the intent to display or sell throughout her life were based on esoteric principles, there is a large collection of her esoteric work dating from the 1930s onward which clearly formed the basis for personal experiments regarding colour and shape which were most likely never intended for display. These works were obviously created to progress her own theories and personal magical work. It is also obvious that some of the visual experiments which remain in her archives were actually much larger projects, sometimes to be coupled with text. Sadly, many of these had little commercial value for the time, and some of these projects would have simply been too radical for public consumption.

Despite Colquhoun's fortunes with various Hermetic organizations, it is very clear from studying her entire corpus of material that it was the Golden Dawn system which held the most interest for her and underpinned the symbolism of her work until a very late stage of her life. Colour was a very important aspect of her work. She took a very precise interest in ensuring that the colours she used for invocations were correct, and she theorized about the magical use of colour in a number of essays throughout her life. Her interest in the precise use of colour and her affinity for the Golden Dawn system may well have been supported by her work with Amédeé Ozenfant in the mid 1930s. Ozenfant was responsible for progressing colour theory in Britain and his influence can most likely be seen in Colquhoun's focus on scientific blending of colour and the effects of colours in proximity to one another.

For Colquhoun, the Golden Dawn's 'Complete Symbol of the Rose Cross' was a very detailed colour wheel, and in her notes and poems there were frequent references to colour formulas and colour mixing. The more perfect the colours, the more one could be assured of success in creating 'flashing tablets', visual invocations of angels, deities and intelligences, and of course Tarot cards. Within the final decade of her life, she worked on enamel colour fields inspired by various Golden Dawn and Kabbalistic colour systems. In 1977, she developed a pack of Tarot cards. She had used Tarot images previously as stand-alone works, but this was her own set of divinatory materials. They are based purely on Golden Dawn systems of colouring, and in the accompanying essay she states that they were created using the 'psycho morphological' technique of colour placement used by other Surrealists. It is clear that Colquhoun believed in the power of colour as sufficient communicators with otherworldly interlocutors. In her deck one does not require images to create stories—the colours alone provide the necessary psychic link and shape the narrative for the reader. Another colour-based project, the *Decad of Intelligence*, was created in 1978 and 1979 featured a series of poetic *sephirotic* Kabbalistic meditations paired with abstract enamel colour studies of each *sephirah*. However, Colquhoun did not limit herself to Golden Dawn or Kabbalistic colour schemes; she also experimented with a number of palettes including ones with Asian and Sufi attributions.

Like many esoteric practitioners, Ithell had a near obsession with sacred geometry, but there were several themes that she explored most often over a 40 year period. Colquhoun worked quite frequently with cubes, and grids within cubes, envisioning figures and temples within three-dimensional and four-dimensional spaces. It is clear that she was influenced by Charles Hinton's theorizing on the *tesseract* and the general dimensionality of the Platonic solids, about which she wrote an essay which is currently not precisely dated (Colquhoun, "Dimensional Interrelation: a Meditation on the Platonic Solids" c.1950s). These ideas were current in the esoteric network of the early 20th century, but it is hard to know exactly at what point these entered her visual repertoire because she does not cite her influences. Internal references from sketches suggest that she was working with the idea of fourth-dimensional space as early as the 1940s. In 1978 she constructed a very simple piece called *Towards the Tesseract*, which featured colour schemes that were similar to those she was using in her sketches of cubes 30 years earlier.

Some of her geometric studies were clearly done in service of Enochian experimentation and other aspects of Golden Dawn work including the 'cube of space' which the tesseract material probably illustrates. There are some very highly polished pieces using sacred geometry which were clearly to be used within a Golden Dawn temple as they reflect aspects of the grade curricula, but in her archives there are also notes and cuttings where she would take these same geometric forms, crosses, pyramids and swastikas, build them up into a three-dimensional figure, and then reduce them once again to a two-dimensional space. It was her belief that the more times she could build up and reduce the figures, the more potential they would have for opening up a fourth-dimensional portal (Colquhoun, "Dimensional Interrelation: a Meditation on the Platonic Solids" c.1950s). In the end, she concluded that the cube and the cross are the most stable forms for fourth-dimensional reflection. Colquhoun was not the only artist to work with these ideas—the same exact principles are found in Salvador Dalí's 1954 *Corpus Hypercubus*, which was constructed on the principle of a crucifix extending into the fourth dimension based on its spiritual power. While critical discussion of Dalí's work frequently focuses on his relationship to the science of the period, he attributes the principles behind the painting to the alchemist Raymond Lully, which reinforces the concept of the extra-dimensional potential of solid forms which was being played with by the esotericists of the mid 19th century. Colquhoun never references Dalí within her own work, although she would obviously have known of this piece.

Colquhoun also used a technique of crosses and grids to serve as invocations of angels or elements. They seem to be a combination of automatic techniques, and highly controlled artistic invocations. She would start the process with colour schemes drawn from either alchemical works, or from Golden Dawn texts. She frequently applied grids to her figure drawings, starting from the base using Kabbalistic attributions and correspondences for the body and times of day working up through the figure. She would then overlay the designs with colours taken from particular schema. She also describes gridded images very similar to this in a section of *Goose of Hermogenes*. Some of her gridded drawings from the 1950s were inspired by sections from Francis Barrett's 1801 magical instruction guide, *The Magus*.

She also used colour in capturing alchemical processes. Meditations on the creation of the hermaphrodite through the union of polarities were an important theme in both her private studies and also in her more public works, although in those the couplings were somewhat more disguised. She created numerous studies in watercolour of the hermaphrodite, using red and blue on conjoined figures seen from the side. For the most part her colour imagery in these exercises was drawn from the King scale for Chokmah and Binah on the Kabbalistic Tree of Life, representing the most evolved of the two polarities before their unification into a philosopher's stone. It frequently appeared as though the paint was applied using what would be considered an automatic technique, but in other instances the paint was more carefully applied, accompanying sketches of both human and angelic lovers. Red and blue also appear in her poetry as continuing themes, showing the hermaphrodite being generated through an alchemical process (Colquhoun, "Union Pacific" n.d.). Many of these sketches were very explicit and were almost certainly inspired directly by Japanese erotica (*shunga*). Interestingly, there were homoerotic couplings among these studies, suggesting that her theories about the union of energy polarities may not have necessitated the embodiment of two different genders for completion. One sketch, *Grand Union Canal*, simply depicts what appears to be *kundalini* energy rising in the body of the woman during intercourse, but all Colquhoun represented was the energy itself without the supporting bodies.

A number of her experiments fused the themes of sacred geometry and energy polarities with studies of the human body. From the 1930s onward, Colquhoun created a number of sketches of the human form with the internal organs displayed in different colours. Some of these were titled *Alchemical Figure*, and the colours of the organs correspond to various classical and Kabbalistic attributions. A 1940 piece titled *the Thirteen Streams of Magnificent Oil* relates to the theosophical notion of various openings in the body into which divine energy can flow, and in this case, the work is centered around a woman, as Colquhoun argued that women have one more opening than men, who have twelve. Colquhoun frequently depicted the flows of energy around and throughout the human body, and sometimes featured figures in the center of a tesseract, or receiving the energy from interaction with a sacred site.

Hermetic and alchemical themes were also features of her creative writing and many of her poems mirror the visual themes she addressed. Colquhoun's Surrealist novel *Goose of Hermogenes* was published by London-based Peter Owen in 1961, but was started several decades earlier and shows themes which she depicts in her 1920s play *Bird of Hermes*. It is a difficult work, but is a fine example of the ways in which she combined Surrealist and esoteric art principles. Here, Colquhoun creates a narrative through highly coded alchemical tracts, but even without that background the tale can be read on a number of levels. It is loosely a story about a girl who has been lured by her uncle to his strange island, to help him in some way in his pursuit of the Philosopher's Stone (Colquhoun, Goose of Hermogenes 1961). The book is replete with alchemical imagery, each chapter of the book representing a stage of alchemical processing. Much of the work is an amalgam of alchemical visual images set on paper. One of the chapters directs the narrative through the images of the 1625 *Book of Lambspring* by Nicholas Barnaud. It also features explicit passages of sado-masochistic practice between the main character and her uncle, again demonstrating that Colquhoun was not afraid to confront a number of sexual taboos. Colquhoun penned two other pieces of magical fiction, *I Saw Water* and *Destination Limbo* which were rejected by publishers as unmarketable.

Paganism and Celticism
Ithell's love of the Celts started early with her own ancestral researches and eventually caused her to settle in Cornwall in the late 1940s after her divorce. Ithell believed that her Scottish ancestry predisposed her to the type of second sight and 'Celtic sensitivity' that would make her Surrealism more successful (Colquhoun, Autobiographcal Notes n.d.). So in tandem with her Hermetic pursuits, Ithell also investigated witchcraft, Druidry, and other Celtic orders, culminating in her initiation into the Fellowship of Isis towards the end of her life. There is a persistent theme of the relationship between women and Nature in her work long before there was anything like a cohesive or coherent Goddess movement. Her interest in Celtic spirituality focused on the land itself and on sacred sites, and also with the transmission of tradition embodied in a location.

The line separating Paganism and ceremonial magic is a difficult one to discern, and in the 1950s and 1960s the cultures were not as separate as some might think them to be in the 21st century, yet one can see in Colquhoun's magical life distinctive themes emerging from her magical interests and associations which would eventually develop into modern

Paganism. Her interest in Paganism and her love of things Celtic were inexorably intertwined. Although there were Celtic themes in her creative work dating from the 1950s, the concentration increased dramatically in the 1970s, coinciding with the second Celtic Revival of that period.

W.B. Yeats, who also combined the Hermetic and the Celtic, was a primary influence on Colquhoun's life and work, and although she met Yeats in both Dublin and London toward the end of his life, the nature of their interactions is not quite clear. She was interested in Yeats' attempts to create a Celtic Hermetic order similar to the Golden Dawn, and she studied his correspondence and journals to try to understand the details of this project. In the 1960s she elaborated on Yeats' work, fusing the Kabbalah and Celtic deities, and published two essays on this in *Prediction* magazine in 1970. Colquhoun supported Yeats' bold rejection of Christianity, and was ultimately inspired by his Traditionalist views on Celtic culture and the redemptive power of its Pagan past (Colquhoun, "The Importance of Yeats' 'A Vision'" Draft c.1940s).

In pursuing her Celtic interests Ithell took initiations with, and studied with, a number of organizations. However, she had a common pattern of studying the curriculum earnestly, only to be frustrated by the lack of knowledge displayed by senior members of the order in question. She was frequently found to be difficult or argumentative, and too challenging in her questions on the curriculum. For instance, in the 1960s she was a member of the Druidic order, The Circle of the Universal Bond, also known as *An Druidh Uileach Braithrearchas*. Although she engaged in a very vigorous discussion about the Order's first level of work, she told officials she was not interested in taking initiation beyond that ("Rebecca" n.d.). She was an associate of Colin Murray from the 1950s, and a very supportive member of his Celtic-based Golden Section Order until very late in her life, being most active in the 1970s.

Within Celtic spirituality, her participation in Druidry probably had the most significant impact on her work, but it was more of an influence on her poetry and her essay writing than on her visual work, which continued to be more significantly marked by her alchemical and hermetic symbolism. One could theorize that this was so because of the emphasis on the Bard and divine revelation within Celtic traditions, which would have been consistent with her Surrealist practice. As a result, there are many Celtic topics covered within Ithell's so-called 'found poems'. She visited Brittany several times with her Druidic order and became a member of the Breton Goursez, most likely due to a reciprocal arrangement between these Druidic orders. However, despite her residence and commitment to Cornwall, she was never made a Bard of the Cornish Gorseth, most likely due to her esoteric leanings. Still, her interests in Celtic cultures were not limited to the esoteric dimensions and she was also supportive of Celtic political movements for cultural recognition. She wrote essays on Cornish culture and took an interest in the history and survivals of the Cornish language. Her small 1973 poetry collection, *Grimoire of the Entangled Thicket*, contains images and works related to Celtic myth and was clearly inspired by Robert Graves' *The White Goddess* and the Celtic tree alphabet which he popularized (Colquhoun, Grimoire of the Entangled Thicket 1973).

Her visual art demonstrated a belief in ley-lines and Earth mysteries before such concepts became more prevalent in British alternative spirituality. She had a number of depictions of sacred sites among both her major display pieces and they were also frequently subjects of more casual study. A couple of pieces in particular indicate very developed beliefs about how megalithic sites functioned. Her 1942 oil painting, *Dance of the Nine Opals*, shows the Merry Maidens stone circle near Penzance, where each of the stones is revealed to be an opal—the stone of Mercury and the alchemical process. Each stone is linked in a geometric pattern of energy, fed from the ground, turning the site into a center of energy (Colquhoun, "Dance of the Nine Opals" c.1942). Additionally, each stone contains red, blue and yellow, which suggest that they function as alchemical crucibles where the mingling of the polarities create the Philosophers' Stone. Given that the belief in magnetic earth currents was not a widely accepted feature of British esoteric culture for over another two decades, this painting alone demonstrates the degree to which Colquhoun was ahead of her time in synthesizing diverse strands of occult belief. There might be an indication that Colquhoun believed sacred sites to also be dimensional portals, as some of the colour sketches she did of the Merry Maidens and the *Men an Tol*—an unusual stone site in West Cornwall—show the sites as existing in a cubic space with a similar colour scheme to the tesseracts that were a persistent source of interest.

Ithell Colquhoun died in Cornwall in 1988. Although she had always been a solitary woman, toward the end of her life she suffered more from depression and anxiety and found it difficult to find help and support. Still, despite what many people would consider an isolated and lonely existence in a hard-to-reach village in West Cornwall, Colquhoun remained in close contact with artistic and esoteric colleagues and was active and innovative until the end of her life. Even then she challenged perceptions about the themes and activities proper for an older woman, and continued to pursue an uncompromising vision. Colquhoun's most enduring commitment was to the principles of enlightenment, which she pursued in her own idiosyncratic way throughout her life. What we have left in her writings and art is the record of that journey.

References

"Rebecca". "Letters from ADUB." *TGA929/1/618-619*. Tate Gallery Archive.

Ades, Dawn. "Notes on Two Women Surrealist Painters: Eileen Agar and Ithell Colquhoun." *Oxford Art Journal*, 1980: 36-43.

Ades, Dawn. "Surrealism, Male-Female." In *Surrealism, Desire Unbound*, by Jennnifer (editor) Mundy, 171-201. London: Tate Publishing, 2001.

Castle, Jack. "Letter to Ithell Colquhoun." *TGA 929/5/36* . Tate Gallery Archive, June 1, 1971.

Chadwick, Whitney. *Women Artists and the Surrealist Movement*. New York: Thames and Hudson, 1985.

Colquhoun, Ithell. "Bird of Hermes draft script." *TGA929/2/1/5*. Tate Gallery Archives, 1926.

—. "Dance of the Nine Opals." *TGA929/2/1/17*. Tate Gallery Archive, c.1942.

—. "Gods of the Cardinal Points." *TGA 929/2/2/13* . Tate Gallery Archive.

—. "My Ideas About Clothes". *TGA 929/1/225*. Tate Gallery Archive, c. 1961.

—. "Poems of He and She". *TGA 929/2/2/13* . Tate Gallery Archive.

—. "Sword of Wisdom Draft Notes." *TGA 920/2/1/68/3/4*. Tate Gallery Archive.

—. "The Importance of Yeats' 'A Vision' Draft." *TGA929/2/2/14*. Tate Gallery Archive, c.1940s.

—. "Union Pacific." *TGA929/2/2/14*. London: Tate Gallery Archives .

—. "Dimensional Interrelation: a Meditation on the Platonic Solids." *TGA929/2/1/21* . Tate Gallery Archive, c.1950s.

—. *Grimoire of the Entangled Thicket*. Ore Publications, 1973.

—. "Autobiographcal Notes." *TGA/929/8/10/1*. Tate Gallery Archives.

—. "Goose of Hermogenes." London: Peter Owen, 1961.

Colquhoun, Ithell. "Letter to the Editor." *Oxford Art Journal*, 1981: 65.

—. "Magical drawings and diagrams." *TGA 929/5/36* . Tate Gallery Archives, 1950s-1970s.

—. "Surrealism and Hermetic Poetry." *TGA 929/2/1/60*. Tate Gallery Archives, n/d.

Colquhoun, Ithell. "The Mantic Stain." *Enquiry, Volume 2 Number 4*, 1949: 15-21.

Levy, Silvano. *The Scandalous Eye: The Surrealism of Conroy Maddox*. Liverpool: Liverpool University Press, 2003.

Levy, Silvano. "The Del Renzio Affair: A Leadership Struggle in Wartime Surrealism." *Papers of Surrealism Issue 3*, 2005: 1-34.

Moore, Doris. "Letter to Ithell Colquhoun." London: Tate Archive 929/1/850, April, 1941.

14

Two Chthonic Magical Artists: Austin Osman Spare & Rosaleen Norton

Nevill Drury

It is comparatively rare to find visionary artists who are magical practitioners and who also have a well developed individual cosmology. The British visionary artist Austin Osman Spare (1888-1956) and the bohemian Australian witch Rosaleen Norton (1917-1979) are two such individuals. Both artists were personally involved in the practice of sigil-based trance magic and both were familiar with key aspects of the Western esoteric tradition. Both artists also produced magical imagery that was markedly chthonic in nature—these elements are discussed below—and both utilised techniques of self-hypnosis to produce their visionary imagery. There are also parallels in their personal lives and artistic careers although, as far as is known, Spare and Norton had no knowledge of each other, either directly or indirectly.[1]

Within their respective individual contexts both Spare and Norton regarded themselves as artistic 'outsiders', largely alienated from the mainstream cultural trends of the day [2] and both spent most of their lives in squalid circumstances.[3] Both were skilled figurative artists whose art-school training contributed substantially to their graphic style, both exhibited their work extensively in popular meeting places like pubs or coffee shops in order to reach an appreciative audience[4] and both had a strong love for animals, especially cats.[5] However, there are other, more specific parallels between Spare and Norton that suggest they should be regarded as visionary artists within the same esoteric genre. As occult practitioners both considered themselves pantheists;[6] both were well versed in the literature of the Western esoteric tradition, Theosophy,[7] Eastern mysticism, and modern psychoanalysis (especially the works of Freud and Jung);[8] both were attracted to the practice of sex-magic and were familiar with the magical writings of Aleister Crowley (Spare knew Crowley personally);[9] both explored medieval magical grimoires like the *Goetia* and were fascinated by the sigils or 'seals' associated with elemental spirit-beings; and both were familiar with the philosophy and magical significance of the Kabbalah. Both artists also developed and utilised their own, personal techniques of self-hypnosis and trance in order to produce their distinctive visionary art-works as a direct result of their magical methods. There is a clear parallel between the trance states associated with the Zos/Kia cosmology of Austin Osman Spare and the trance magic of Rosaleen Norton, which in turn draws attention to the unique contributions of both Spare and Norton as 'visionary outsiders' operating within the context of the Western esoteric tradition.

Chthonic elements in modern Western magic

The term 'chthonic' (Greek *khthōn*: 'earth') refers to deities and ritual artefacts symbolically associated with the Earth. In ancient Greece the term *khthōn* referred to the interior of the soil, rather than its surface, and for this reason the word 'chthonic' is generally used with reference to the gods, goddesses and spirits of the Underworld, especially in the context of ancient Graeco-Roman religion. Typically, chthonic deities are associated with agriculture and the fertility of the land (eg. the Greek goddesses Demeter and Persephone) or are directly associated with the Underworld itself (eg. Hecate, Aidoneus/Hades). Chthonic deities are frequently represented by snakes[10] and some, like Attis and Adonis, are associated with ancient Mystery cults of death and rebirth.[11]

Contemporary Thelemic writer Vadge Moore has recently suggested that the term 'chthonic' may be used to refer generally to deities both '*of the earth or under the earth*'[12]—including Pan, Dionysus and Bacchus, as well as non-Hellenic deities such as Set and Abraxas.[13] He also relates their symbolic attributes to the occult quest for spiritual transcendence. Moore associates chthonic deities primarily with sexuality and the cycles of Nature:

> *The chthonic gods represent the primal instincts that come to us directly through Nature. The Greek god Dionysus is certainly one of these...Representative of the creative and destructive aspects of Nature, Dionysus is the ultimate chthonic figure. He can inspire the most beautiful, delirious sexual activity and the most degrading, violent, murderous activity. Dionysus' mother, Semele, has been described variously as a Moon-Goddess and as a mortal woman. His father was the leader of the Greek gods, Zeus. His mother as mortal then combines the earthly with the divine...bringing the balance that chthonic more deeply represents.*[14]

Moore maintains that chthonic deities, by their very nature, provide the basis for magical transformation and spiritual transcendence:

> *The chthonic process is an occult 'awakening' that includes the very lowest instinctual elements of the human psyche leading to the very highest elements. It is the base, primordial material that the psyche needs in order to evolve and grow. Chthonic is the soil, the fertilizer, and the dark, primitive unconscious* **material** *that can turn the beast into a god.*[15] *[emphasis mine]*

Moore maintains that potent chthonic images can be found ranging from the depths of the mythic unconscious through to the pure light of transcendence[16] and he supports the views of French decadent writer Georges Bataille, who similarly explores chthonic themes and emphasizes their potential for 'ascent' in states of visionary consciousness:

> *In opposition to the ancient sky and sun gods, Bataille proposes a worship of the gods of darkness and of the earth: Demeter, Hecate and Dionysus...We must not forget that it is just this sinking into the underworld of the id and the dark unconscious that helps to plant the roots for our ascent.*[17]

As I will argue in the commentary that follows, Spare and Norton are both essentially chthonic visionary artists. Both sought states of transcendent magical consciousness in their own, distinctive ways—Spare through his notion of Zos Kia (explained below) and Norton by embracing the universal qualities of the Great God Pan, whom she viewed as Master of the Cosmos.

Austin Osman Spare

Figure 1: Austin Osman Spare, a self-portrait from 1923.

One of five children, Austin Osman Spare was born at home in Snowhill, near Smithfield, London, on 30 December 1886. The son of a policeman,[18] Spare had two elder brothers and two sisters—one of whom, Ellen, was younger than him. The family moved to south London and Spare attended St Agnes' School in Kennington Park.[19] In 1902 Spare left school and began working for a company named Powells, a manufacturer of stained glass, where he distinguished himself by producing five stained-glass panel designs for one of his senior work colleagues.[20] However Spare was also taking formal art training at Lambeth Evening Art School, where his precocious artistic talent was noticed. At the age of 16, while he was still working for Powells, Spare won a £40 scholarship and a silver medal from the prestigious art journal *The Studio*, enabling him to study at the Royal College of Art, South Kensington,[21] and in 1904 one of his black-and-white bookplate designs was displayed at the Royal Academy. This particular work had been produced when he was 14, making him the youngest exhibited artist in the history of that institution.[22] The President of the Academy, John Singer Sargent, proclaimed Spare to be a genius[23] and Spare attracted the attention of art connoisseur Pickford Waller, from whom he would receive several commissions for bookplates.[24] He was later commissioned to illustrate Ethel Wheeler's *Behind the Veil* (1906) and a book of aphorisms by J. Bertram and F. Russell titled *The Starlit Mire*, published by the distinguished arts patron John Lane (1911). Around the same time an article on Spare by Ralph Straus appeared in *The Book Lovers Magazine*.[25]

In 1916 Spare founded the quarterly magazine, *Form*, joined later by

Frederick Carter who became co-editor. The magazine was sponsored by John Lane who hoped it would emulate the earlier success of *The Yellow Book*, an avant-garde literary publication renowned for its erotic and provocative illustrations by Aubrey Beardsley, with whom Spare was sometimes compared.[26] However in May 1917 Spare was enlisted, against his will, to join the Royal Army Medical Corps [27] and no further editions of *Form* were issued under the patronage of John Lane.[28] In 1919 Spare visited France as a special war artist documenting the aftermath of the Great War: several works based on sketches from this period are included in the collection of the Imperial War Museum.[29] After his sojourn in Europe, Spare returned to the genre of journal publishing. Between October 1922 and April 1924 he and Clifford Bax co-edited an illustrated literary magazine, *The Golden Hind*, which included the work of such notable writers as Aldous Huxley, Alec Waugh and Havelock Ellis.[30]

However, since 1905 Spare had also been involved in creating and publishing his own distinctive and highly unconventional books and it was these self-published limited-edition works that would identify his unique contribution to the Western esoteric tradition while simultaneously consigning him to the periphery of mainstream artistic circles. Although he had been praised by John Singer Sargent, and also by the renowned portrait painter Augustus John, who regarded Spare as one of the great graphic artists of his time,[31] others found Spare's magical compositions deeply confronting. According to Kenneth Grant, Spare's esoteric imagery prompted the noted playwright and critic George Bernard Shaw to remark: 'Spare's medicine is too strong for the average man.'[32]

Spare's self-published works, which he illustrated, designed, and financed himself, include the following titles: *Earth: Inferno* [265 numbered copies, 1905]; *A Book of Satyrs* [300 copies, first edition 1907, 300 copies, second edition 1909]; *The Book of Pleasure (Self-Love): The Psychology of Ecstasy* [380 copies, 1913]; *The Focus of Life: The Mutterings of Aaos* [650 copies, 1921] and *Anathema of Zos: The Sermon to the Hypocrites* [100 copies, 1927].[33] In the same way that *The Art of Rosaleen Norton* helped define Norton's persona as 'The Witch of Kings Cross' in Sydney during the 1950s (see below) so too Spare's distinctive and unconventional publications placed him clearly within the context of the Western magical tradition through their references to sigil magic and esoteric symbolism. While Spare had earlier been considered a possible successor to Aubrey Beardsley and was sometimes compared to other notable graphic artists like Charles Ricketts (illustrator of Oscar Wilde's *The Sphinx*) and Harry Clarke (illustrator of Goethe's *Faust* and Poe's *Tales of Mystery and Imagination*), his own publications were polemical in style, graphically complex, and unorthodox in presentation. His two major esoteric works — *The Book of Pleasure (Self-Love): The Psychology of Ecstasy* and *The Focus of Life: The Mutterings of Aaos* — explored sigil magic and the images of the subconscious and were written in an abstruse and inaccessible style that made few concessions to any mainstream readership, despite the spectacular graphic images that accompanied both texts. *Earth: Inferno*, *A Book of Satyrs*, and *Anathema of Zos: The Sermon to the Hypocrites*, meanwhile, were satirical works which drew attention to the misery of the human condition and the emptiness and shallow hypocrisy of the privileged classes in contemporary society. *Anathema of Zos* is a vitriolic and bitter invective directed specifically at the 'Mayfair' artistic elite that had initially supported Spare when his artworks were exhibited in prominent West End galleries.[34]

Spare's *The Book of Pleasure (Self-Love): The Psychology of Ecstasy* (1913) is widely regarded as his major work. It develops his concept of Kia, which is central to his magical philosophy, and also contains practical instructions for creating magical sigils and automatic drawings. In addition, it places Spare's magical explorations within the context of modern psychological approaches to the subconscious mind.

Zos and Kia

Spare first makes reference to the term 'Zos' in *Earth: Inferno* (1905) in a black-and-white line illustration titled *Chaos*.[35] Here a naked man draws aside a curtain revealing a cluster of tangled human forms representing what Spare calls the 'inferno of the Normal'. The accompanying text reads 'Oh! come with me, the Kia and the Zos, to witness this extravagance.' Although Spare does not develop his idea of the polarity between Zos and Kia in *Earth: Inferno*, he nevertheless provides tantalising clues. On page 22 he writes: 'Alas! We are children of Earth,' indicating that the term Zos refers to human manifestation, the incarnate, the physical. Alongside the preceding image, *Despair*, which shows four forlorn human beings, one of them a prostrate naked woman, Spare writes: 'Revere the Kia and your mind will become tranquil.'[36] In *The Book of Pleasure (Self-Love): The Psychology of Ecstasy*, Spare explains for the first time what he means by 'Zos'. A small, but nevertheless definitive, text-reference is inserted graphically into an illustration teeming with magical sigils, and the text reads: 'The body considered as a whole, I call Zos.'[37] Spare's definition of Kia, meanwhile, is included in the introductory section of the book: 'Kia', writes Spare, is 'the absolute freedom which being free is mighty enough to be "reality" and free at any time...'[38] Later in the book Spare also refers to Kia in sexual terms: as 'the ancestral sex principle' and the 'unmodified sexuality'.[39]

As Gavin W. Semple notes in an important essay on the art and magic of Austin Spare there is a clear distinction between Zos, representing 'all that which is embodied or manifest', and Kia, representing the Absolute.[40] Spare had been reading an English-language translation of the Kabbalistic text The Zohar [41] prior to working on Earth: Inferno,[42] and it has been suggested that Spare's reference to Kia may have a Kabbalistic origin. Semple believes that Kia may be an inversion of the Kabbalistic term Aiq Bekar,[43] a reference to 'the Kabbalah of Nine Chambers' and the secret Kabbalistic code system of Temurah[44] but an alternative suggestion from William Wallace seems more plausible. Wallace believes that Kia probably derives from the Kabbalistic Hebrew word Chiah which denotes the highest form of the world of Atziluth, the 'Absolute'.[45] This would certainly appear closer to Spare's own meaning of the word. In the Kabbalah, Chiah, or Chiyah is an aspect of Neshamah, the soul, one of the three principal spiritual agencies mentioned in the Zohar, the others being Nefesh (life) and Ruah (spirit).[46] Even though he was coining his own special term, Kia, Spare nevertheless aligned it conceptually with the mystical idea of the Absolute, or Void—the supreme reality in the Kabbalah—and, as discussed below, Spare's notion of the 'void moment' is central to his magical process.

In *The Book of Pleasure (Self-Love): The Psychology of Ecstasy* Spare uses his concept of Kia to refer to the primal, cosmic life-force which can be channelled into the human organism, Zos. In one of his later esoteric texts Spare refers to the life-force as 'a potency',[47] and his magical technique for arousing the elemental energies latent within this life-potency—a technique he termed 'atavistic resurgence'[48]—involved focusing on magical sigils which he employed as vehicles of his magical will. When the mind was in what Spare called a 'void' or open state— achieved, for example, through meditation, exhaustion or at the peak of sexual ecstasy—magical sigils could be used to send 'commands' to the subconscious mind. Later these magical commands would be intentionally forgotten in order to remove them from conscious awareness but in the meantime, according to Spare, they would 'grow' within the seedbed of the subconscious mind until they became 'ripe' and manifested once again in the familiar world of conscious reality, thereby achieving the magician's initial intent. Spare summarises this magical process in his esoteric text, *The Witches' Sabbath*: 'The ecstatic moment is used as the fecund instant of wish endowment; for at that period of reality, the will, desire and belief are aligned in unison.'[49]

Background to Spare's magical philosophy
Spare's approach to magical states of consciousness draws on a variety of sources, encompassing archetypal mythic imagery from ancient Egypt,

a fascination with the sexual energies of the subconscious mind,[50] and techniques learned through his close personal relationship with an unusual psychic mentor whom he always referred to simply as Mrs Paterson. Spare's magical approach was also shaped by his fascination with death,[51] by his interest in Taoism, which places great emphasis on the flow of positive and negative life-energy,[52] and by his personal conviction that the psychic energies, or 'karmas'[53] of previous incarnations, remained as latent potentials within the mind of every human being 'Ability,' writes Spare in his esoteric tract, *Axiomata*, 'is an endowment from our past selves.' [54] Spare believed that these karmic energies could be activated by the magical will.[55] He also maintained that the ancient Egyptians understood the complex mythology of the subconscious mind: their animal-headed deities provided proof that they understood the process of spiritual evolution:

> *They symbolised this knowledge in one great symbol, the Sphinx, which is pictorially man evolving from animal existence. Their numerous Gods, all partly Animal, Bird, Fish... prove the completeness of that knowledge...The cosmogony of their Gods is proof of their knowledge of the order of evolution, its complex processes from the one simple organism ... They knew they still possessed the rudimentary faculties of all existences, and were partly under their control. Thus their past Karmas became Gods, good and evil forces, and had to be appeased: from this all moral doctrine etc. is determined. So all Gods have lived (being ourselves) on earth, and when dead, their experience or Karma governs our actions in degree: to that extent we are subject to the will of these Gods...This is the key to the mystery of the Sphinx.* [56]

Frank Letchford, who was a close friend of Austin Spare from 1937 until the artist's death in 1956,[57] confirms in his biography, *From the Inferno to Zos* (1995), that ancient Egyptian culture and mythology impacted strongly on Spare's art and magical philosophy throughout his life :

> *The influence upon Austin of Egyptian art writing and practice were strong. The incidence of Egyptian deities like Isis, Osiris, Horus, Nuit and of amulets, talismans, sigils and magical symbols is varied in his work... According to the Egyptian religion the human 'being' is composed of four parts: the body itself, the astral double, the soul and the spark of life from the Godhead. In all Austin's writings, aphorisms, drawings and*

sketches are found charms, symbols and symbolic figures, namely, the sun, the moon, cats and gods, part-human, part-animal.[58]

The gods and goddesses of ancient Egypt had a profound impact on Austin Spare because they seemed to embody the principle of spiritual evolution through animal and human karma.[59] However, Egyptian cosmology was not his first point of reference: Spare first learned about the transformative potentials of the subconscious mind from an elderly woman called Mrs Paterson, who was a friend of his parents and used to tell his fortune when he was young. Spare's relationship with his own mother was not close and he soon came to regard Mrs Paterson as his 'second mother'.[60] She was illiterate but generous in spirit, and would often help neighbours and friends in distress. Mrs Paterson appeared to have an extrasensory ability to project thought-forms. According to Spare she was able to 'reify' ideas and thoughts to visible, sometimes even tangible, appearance: 'If in her occult prognostications she discovered an event or incident which she could not describe verbally, she would reify the scene...'[61] Spare describes her technique in the following way: 'She used to tell my fortune when I was quite young...She was a natural hypnotist. She would say, "Look in that dark corner," and, if you obeyed, she could make you visualise what she was telling you about your future.'[62]

Figure 2:
Spare and his atavisms
a self-portrait from
The Book of Pleasure (Self-Love):
The Psychology of Ecstasy *(1913).*

The Thelemic magician and occult writer Kenneth Grant has written extensively on Spare. Grant first met the artist in 1949[63] and had extensive contact with him during the last eight years of his life.[64] He believes that it was because of his close relationship with Mrs Paterson that Spare became attracted to older women, and that this was due, in part, to the fact that as a child he had watched her transform herself visually from an old crone into a young woman through the magical process of 'reification':

> *The wrinkled crone had appeared to change into a large-limbed voluptuous girl. So deep was the impression—whether actual or imagined—that for the rest of his life Spare was fascinated by the idea of sexual potency in ageing women...He used this theme in his witch drawings where he frequently combined the hag and the girl in one picture, if not in one image.*[65]

The archetypal image of the Universal Woman, or Goddess, in all her various aspects—from sensual maiden through to aged crone—became a central feature in Spare's personal mythology. Spare first refers to her in *Earth: Inferno* where, in an illustration titled *Earth*, she is shown and captioned 'lying barren on the Parapet of the Subconsciousness' while humanity itself is depicted 'sinking into the pit of conventionality'.[66] Spare uses this graphic image to call for what he termed the 'resurrection of the Primitive Woman'.[67] Grant writes that, for Spare, the 'Goddess, the Witch Queen, the Primitive or Universal Woman... is the cypher of all "inbetweenness"'[68] and she is experienced in the unity of Self-love, that is to say, in the ecstatic union of Zos and Kia. 'Nor,' adds Grant, 'is she to be limited as any particular "goddess" such as Astarte, Isis, Cybele, Kali, Nuit, for to limit her is to turn away from the path and to idealize a concept which, as such, is false because incomplete, unreal because temporal.'[69]

One of Spare's most significant compositions, *The Ascension of the Ego from Ecstasy to Ecstasy*,[70] shows the Goddess as a beautiful naked maiden welcoming Spare to higher realms of awareness. Spare is depicted, appropriately, with wings extending from his head, symbolic of ecstatic flight. Spare's 'ego', or persona, is shown merging with an earlier animal incarnation, and the two shapes transcend each other in the form of a primal skull, a motif representing the 'death' of the ego. Spare believed he could retrace his earlier animal incarnations or 'karmas' back to the very source of life itself, the universal 'Oneness of Creation' he called Kia, and that these residual animal energies could in turn become a source of magic power.

Figure 3: Austin Osman Spare: "The Ascension of the Ego from Ecstasy to Ecstasy" from The Book of Pleasure (Self-Love): The Psychology of Ecstasy.

Spare's *The Ascension of the Ego from Ecstasy to Ecstasy* provides us with an important insight into this magical process. Although sexual union with a female partner was not his only method for attaining an ecstatic state,[71] Spare frequently combined his magical will with the climax of sexual orgasm in his quest for creative inspiration.[72] According to Spare, at the peak of sexual ecstasy, the personal ego (Zos) and the universal life-force (Kia) are united in a state of blissful and transcendent openness: inspiration flows forth from Kia and is transmitted through the primordial Goddess herself.[73] 'Inspiration, writes Spare in *The Book of Pleasure,* 'is always at a *void* moment.'[74]

Fig. 4. Austin Osman Spare. "Stealing the Fire From Heaven" from The Book of Pleasure (Self-Love): The Psychology of Ecstasy.

In Spare's system of trance-magic two processes are associated with ecstatic states. The first of these employs a technique that Spare termed the Death Posture: by its very nature an ecstatic peak-moment is characterised by the surrender, or 'death', of the ego, and the process could therefore be regarded as a simulation of death itself.[75] 'Because every other sense is brought to nullity by sex intoxication', writes Spare, 'it is called the Death Posture.'[76] As Gavin Semple notes:

> *The Death Posture involves a total negation of conceptual thought and perceptual awareness, and the assumption of the Void, Kia, by its practitioner; its aim is ecstasy, the bliss of union with the Absolute in Self-Love.*[77]

The second of Spare's magical processes involved the creation and use of 'sentient' magical sigils that could act as vehicles or 'messengers' to the subconscious mind. This method embodied both Will and Desire, the magical sigils being used to implant the 'Great Wish' within the subconscious mind at the peak-moment of ecstasy. The ecstatic peak itself could be attained through sexual union, but there were other methods of attaining it as well, which are referred to below. Considered together, the two processes became a central feature of Spare's unique approach to trance-magic and his quest for union with Kia, the bliss of the Absolute.

Fig. 5. Austin Osman Spare, "Now for Reality"
—an illustration from The Focus of Life *(1921)*

The Death Posture

Spare's intent in utilising the Death Posture was to 'incarnate' the dynamic and inspirational life-force of Kia, the source of artistic genius [78] and sexual freedom. Gavin Semple writes that the Death Posture 'employs the flesh itself as the effigy or sigil of Belief, and through its "death" and resurrection... [initiates] the Great Work. The work is the ecstatic fusion of the Zos and the Kia (Ego and Self), the Self-Love which gives the title of Spare's book.'[79] Here the attainment of ecstasy is primarily an end in itself. However, because Kia is also the 'ancestral sex principle'[80] and the source of 'unmodified sexuality',[81] the union of Zos and Kia inevitably leads to expressions of what Spare terms the 'new sexuality'. In *The Book of Pleasure* Spare writes: 'Know the Death Posture and its reality in the ascension from duality...The Death Posture is the reduction of all conception to the Neither-Neither [Spare's term for the Absolute or true Self][82] till the desire is contentment by pleasing yourself...the restoration of the

new sexuality and the ever original self-love in freedom are attained.'[83]
Spare describes the actual method as follows:

> *Lying on your back lazily, the body expressing the emotion of yawning, suspiring while conceiving by smiling, that is the idea of the posture. Forgetting time with those things which were essential reflecting their meaninglessness, the moment is beyond time and its virtue has happened.*
>
> *Standing on tip-toe, with the arms rigid, bound behind by the hands, clasped and straining to the utmost, the neck stretched — breathing deeply and spasmodically, till giddy and sensation comes in gusts, gives exhaustion and capacity for the former.*
>
> *Gazing at your reflection till it is blurred and you know not the gazer, close your eyes (this usually happens involuntarily) and visualize. The light (always an X in curious evolutions) that is seen should be held onto, never letting go, till the effort is forgotten; this gives a feeling of immensity (which sees a small form ∞) whose limit you cannot reach. This should be practised before experiencing the foregoing. The emotion that is felt is the knowledge which tells you why.*[84]

Spare describes the mystical impact of the Death Posture:

> *The Ego is swept up as a leaf in a fierce gale — in the fleetness of the indeterminable, that which is always about to happen, becomes its truth. Things that are self-evident are no longer obscure, as by his own will he pleases; know this as the negation of all faith by living it, the end of duality of consciousness.*[85]

According to Frank Letchford, the essential purpose of the Death Posture — a practice Spare believed should be performed daily[86] — was to 'incarnate' a transformative magical process:

> *...the body is allowed to manifest spontaneously... His idea was to form a new body, it was a time for re-birth, incarnating and reincarnating. He wills his own death. He awaits the transfiguration, an inversion and reversion, a continuation of evolution; that which he desires will come to pass.*[87]

In addition to utilising the Death Posture, however, Spare also wished to develop a method for focusing his magical desires. This led him to formulate his own unique system of atavistic magical sigils.

Magical sigils

Spare's use of magical sigils, which he began to develop into a workable system from 1906 onwards,[88] was based on the understanding that the dynamics of the subconscious mind depend entirely on symbols and images, that the 'language' of the subconscious is pictorial rather than verbal.[89] As Spare observes in his essay *Mind to Mind and How*:

> There is a Grimorium of graphic symbology and vague phonic nuances that conjoin all thought and is the language of the psychic world. Mind is a continuant [sic] and all concepts are relatable to perceptions and contact, therefore real; the continuum of all aspects of memory and learning is consciousness—the past again becoming explicit...[90]

Spare believed that the human psyche contained all the residual 'karmas' of previous incarnations. Kia, as the Absolute, and as the source of all being, encompassed all evolutionary phases of life that had so far existed on the planet. As Spare notes in *The Book of Pleasure*: 'By sigils and the acquirement of vacuity, any past incarnation, experience, can be summoned into consciousness.'[91] Spare's sorcery—he himself labelled it as such[92]—utilised the process of atavistic resurgence in order to summon 'elementals', or karmic 'automata',[93] from the subconscious mind for magical purposes. Even when he lived alone in a small, squalid flat in South London, Spare maintained that he was always surrounded by elemental forces and that these 'spirits' were his allies or 'familiars'.[94]

As mentioned earlier, Spare was fascinated by medieval magical grimoires like the *Goetia* and *The Greater Key of Solomon* and was intrigued by the magical seals ascribed to various elemental spirits. It has been suggested that these magical seals may have been a source of inspiration for the 'cryptic letter-forms and devices' found in *The Book of Pleasure*[95] and that Spare was almost certainly influenced by the magical scripts found in Cornelius Agrippa's *Three Books of Occult Philosophy or Magic*, a work first published in 1533.[96] Spare appears to paraphrase the Renaissance magician's writings on sigils and also transcribed two of his signs in a page of sketches for the *Book of Pleasure* vignettes.[97] However, whereas the magical seals in the grimoires were linked either to specific demons like those identified in the *Goetia*, or to planetary spirits (Saturn, Jupiter, Mars etc.) like those referred to in Cornelius Agrippa's *Three Books of Occult Philosophy or Magic*,[98] Spare's great innovation was in realising that magical seals or sigils could be personalised. As Gavin Semple has noted:

> While the grimoires dictate the use of specific magical seals for the binding and control of spirits and demand a high degree of faith (ie. consciously formulated belief) in their efficacy, and in the theurgic system of which they form a part, Spare realized that any symbols must be effective provided they are congruent with the patterns of the operator's innate beliefs and personal aesthetic. This is certain to be the case if they are drawn from his or her own subconsciousness.[99]

Recognising that they would have to reflect his own magical credo, Spare created his own individualised sigils. In *The Book of Pleasure* he provides a summary of his method: 'Sigils are made by combining the letters of the alphabet simplified...the idea being to obtain a simple form which can easily be visualised at will, and has not too much pictorial relation to the desire...Verily, what a person believes by Sigils, is the truth, and is always fulfilled.'[100] In effect Spare was seeking to focus his magical will on a single graphic symbol so that his intent or purpose could more readily be grasped as a totality. He did this by first expressing his 'will' (or 'desire') in sentence form and then by combining the basic letters, without repetition, into a unified glyph or sigil. In *The Book of Pleasure*, Spare provides an example of how a sigil can be created from the sentence: 'This is my wish, to obtain the strength of a tiger...'

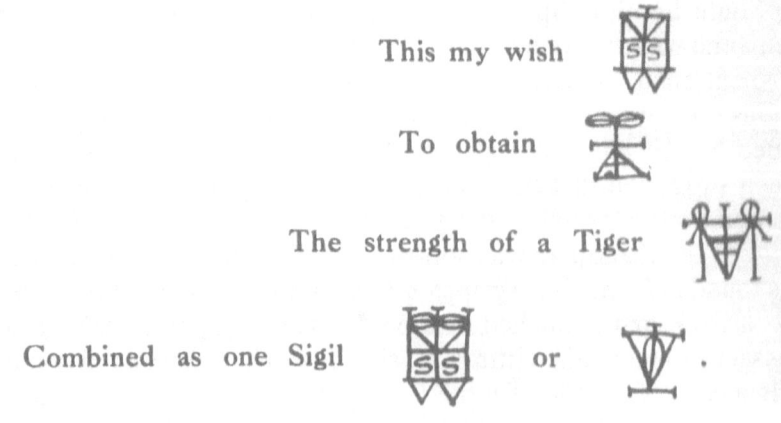

Spare then describes the personal conditions required for success in projecting the sigil into the subconscious mind:

> *Now by virtue of this Sigil you are able to send your desire into the subconsciousness (which contains all strength); that having happened, it is the desire's realization by the manifestation of the knowledge or power necessary.*
>
> *First, all consciousness of the Sigil has to be annulled; do not confuse this with concentration—you simply conceive the Sigil any moment you begin to think. Vacuity is obtained by exhausting the mind and body* [101] *...the time of exhaustion is the time of fulfilment. At the time of exhaustion or vacuity, retain only and visualize the Sigil form—eventually it becomes vague, then vanished and success is assured...the desire for identification carries it [ie. the Sigil] to the corresponding subconscious stratum, its destination....Hence the mind, by Sigils, depending upon the intensity of desire, is illuminated or obsessed (knowledge or power) from that particular Karma (the subconscious stratum, a particular existence and knowledge gained by it) relative to the desire...Knowledge is obtained by the sensation, resulting from the unity of the desire and Karma. Power, by its 'actual' vitalization and resurrection.*[102]

As mentioned earlier, Spare believed that it was crucially important that once the sigil was despatched into the subconscious at the moment of 'vacuity' (the 'void moment'), the instruction then had to be forgotten so that the process of manifesting desire could become 'organic'. As Spare explains:

> *Belief to be true must be organic and subconscious. The desire to be great can only become organic at the time of vacuity and by giving it (Sigil) form. When conscious of the Sigil form (any time but the magical) it should be repressed, a deliberate striving to forget it; by this it is active and dominates at the unconscious period; its form nourishes and allows it to become attached to the subconscious and become organic; that accomplished is its reality and realization.*[103]

It is reasonable to ask whether Spare's concept of magical sigils actually worked, and the anecdotal evidence is certainly intriguing, if not persuasive. The occultist Kenneth Grant who, as mentioned earlier, had extensive contact with Spare towards the end of his life, describes a situation where Spare needed to move a heavy load of timber without assistance. A sigil was required which could generate great personal strength and Spare employed the tiger sigil, referred to above, in order to access reserves of strength he did not consciously realise he possessed. According to Grant's account:

> *Spare closed his eyes for a while and visualised a picture which symbolised a wish for the strength of tigers [ie the sigil above]. Almost immediately he sensed an inner response. He then felt a tremendous upsurge of energy sweep through his body. For a moment he felt like a sapling bent by the onslaught of a mighty wind. With a great effort of will, he steadied himself and directed the force to its proper object. A great calm descended and he found himself able to carry the load easily.*[104]

*Figure 6: Austin Osman Spare,
Elemental Materialisation (1955)*

In 1955 Spare produced a pastel-portrait titled *Elemental Materialisation* depicting the same tiger atavism.[105] In the lower left-hand corner of the composition a sheet of paper reveals the appropriate magical sigil, accompanied by a drawing of a tiger's head. Spare is shown on the right-hand side, staring intently with his fist clenched. Sigils are also drawn on the centre of his forehead, indicating that he was concentrating on them as he sought to impose his magical will. The figure of a brooding tiger, the magician's ally, or 'familiar', lurks in the background. *Elemental Materialisation* is one of the few didactic magical portraits from Spare's later period and clearly depicts the process of atavistic resurgence.

Spare's sigil-process can be summarised as follows:
- A magical sigil may be employed to embody a desire or command in relation to what a person wishes to do or become.
- Latent karmic potentials already reside within the psyche of the individual and lie dormant in the subconscious.
- Once despatched through willed concentration, the magical sigil activates 'elementals' or 'karmic automata' related to the magical 'wish' or 'desire'.
- The wish or desire then becomes 'organic' in the atavistic realms of the subconscious. It automatically loses its effect if consciously remembered.
- The powers activated by the sigil finally manifest in the realm of consciously perceived 'reality', either as events or personal attributes. As Kenneth Grant has written, 'Sigillization leads... to the realization of belief.' [106]

Automatic art

In addition to developing his concept of the Death Posture and the Zos/Kia cosmology, Spare also explored the spontaneous creative process of automatic drawing. It has been argued that Spare can legitimately claim to be the first Surrealist artist because his earliest atavistic artworks preceded the 1924 Paris Surrealist Manifesto by at least a decade.[107]

Throughout his life Spare was interested in spiritualism and Theosophy,[108] and his attraction to automatic drawing is directly linked to the psychic automata, or elementals, which he believed surrounded him at all times. *The Book of Pleasure* includes an illustration titled *The Dwellers at the Gates of Silent Memory* which shows a reflective naked woman sitting in a state of repose. What appears to be a tree, but is actually an extended skull with antlers, extends upwards from her head, and perched upon the 'branches' are several birds, or more specifically, 'bird karmas'. Nearby, a disembodied winged head floats in space. Spare's accompanying text, titled 'The Sub-Consciousness', contains a reference to what he calls the 'Storehouse of Memories with an Ever-Open Door' and he goes on to write:

> *Know the sub-consciousness to be an epitome of all experience and wisdom, past incarnations as men, animals, birds, vegetable life, etc. etc. everything that exists, has and ever will exist. Each being a stratum in the order of evolution. Naturally then, the lower we probe into these strata, the earlier will be the forms of life we arrive at; the last is the Almighty Simplicity. And if we succeed in awakening them, we shall gain their properties, and our accomplishment will correspond.*[109]

The karmic entities referred to in *The Book of Pleasure* as the 'Dwellers at the Gates of Silent Memory' provide a key to Spare's automatic art. Spare thought of them as 'the nascent selves swarming at our periphery, always *behind* our attention. It is through interaction with these desire-bodies, and their integration into our subjective continua, that we interact directly with Self, through the infinite permutation of its expression.'[110] It was these psychic entities that Spare evoked in producing his automatic drawings; he maintained that they could be perceived in a darkened room:

> *Darken your room, shut the door, empty your mind. Yet you are still in great company—the Numen and your Genius with all their media, and your host of elementals and ghosts of your dead loves—are there! They need no light by which to see, no words to speak, no motive to enact except through your own purely formed desire.*[111]

According to his friend, journalist Hannen Swaffer (1879-1962), Spare used self-hypnosis to facilitate the 'automatic' process. Frank Letchford refers to Swaffer's account in his biographical study, *From the Inferno to Zos:*

> *In [1929] Hannen Swaffer published a little book entitled Adventures with Inspiration in which there is a paragraph describing Austin's method of work on automatic drawings. Staring into a mirror to induce self-hypnotism, he sets to work, sometimes for hours, awakening to find that he has covered hundreds of pages with most beautiful drawings. Try as he would, he could not stop, but if he wished to draw he could not. In this way he filled a drawing book of fifty sheets.*[112]

Spare denied that he was acting like a psychic medium on such occasions, always maintaining that his contact with elementals and karmic automata was subject to his magical will.[113] However, Letchford's account suggests that, at least on some occasions, these entities operated spontaneously and were beyond Spare's artistic control.

An article titled 'Automatic Drawing', co-authored by Austin Spare and Frederick Carter, and published in *Form* in 1916,[114] throws further light on the process:

> *Automatic drawing, one of the simplest of psychic phenomena, is a means of characteristic expression and, if used with courage and honesty, of recording subconscious activities in the mind. The mental mechanisms used are those common in dreams, which create quick perceptions of relations in the unexpected, as wit, and psycho-neurotic symptoms. Hence it appears that single or non-consciousness is an essential condition and as in all inspiration, the product of involution not invention. Automatism being the manifestation of latent desires (or wishes) the significance of the forms (the ideas) obtained represent the previously unrecorded obsessions. Art becomes, by this illuminism or ecstatic power, a functional activity expressing in a symbolical language the desire towards joy unmodified—the sense of the Mother of all things...*
>
> *In the ecstatic condition of revelation from the subconscious, the mind elevates the sexual or inherited power...and depresses the intellectual qualities. So a new atavistic responsibility is attained by daring to believe—to possess one's own beliefs—without attempting to rationalize spurious ideas from prejudiced and tainted intellectual sources.*
>
> *Automatic drawings can be obtained by such methods as concentrating on a Sigil—by any means of exhausting mind and body pleasantly in order to obtain a condition of non-consciousness—by wishing in opposition to the real desire after acquiring an organic impulse toward drawing.*
>
> *The hand must be trained to work freely and without control, by practice in making simple forms with a continuous involved line without afterthought, ie. its intention should just escape consciousness. Drawings should be made by allowing the hand to run freely with the least possible deliberation. In time shapes will be found to evolve, suggesting conceptions, forms and ultimately having personal or individual style. The mind in a state of oblivion, without desire towards reflection or pursuit*

of materialistic intellectual suggestions, is in a condition to produce successful drawings of one's personal ideas, symbolic in meaning and wisdom. By this means sensation may be visualized.[115]

Figure 7: Detail from an illustration by Austin Osman Spare for the Form *article on automatic art (1916).*

The *Form* article clearly indicates that Spare's approach to automatic drawing is linked to his concept of atavistic resurgence. Spare's artistic intention is to create a spontaneous and unimpeded flow of imagery that proceeds directly from his karmic atavisms, from the 'Dwellers at the Gates of Silent Memory' that are actually residual metaphysical personifications of his own inner being.

Various limited-edition collections of Spare's automatic art have been published since the artist's death in 1956. One of these, *A Book of Automatic Drawings*, was published by Catalpa Press, London, in 1972 in a hardcover quarto format, in an edition of 1000 copies. The drawings themselves were from a sketch-book dated 1925, designed as a complete work. As Ian Law indicates in his introduction to the 1972 edition, the compositions featured in *A Book of Automatic Drawings* were reproduced 'in the exact size, style and sequence that Spare indicated'.[116] The edition contains twelve full-size visionary images, executed in the meticulous and highly accomplished linear style that had led some critics to compare his work with that of Dürer and Holbein. Many of the images seem perverse and excessively ugly: the limbs of most of his humanoid figures are hideously distorted, many have horns or demonic shapes extending from their limbs, and several are surreal bird—or animal—fusions. However, Spare believed that the act of transfiguring the grotesque could be liberating.[117] In his posthumously published text, *The Witches' Sabbath*, Spare refers to the traditional image of the 'ugly witch' and argues, in keeping with the transformative powers he associated with Mrs Paterson, that this sort of ugliness could produce a new aesthetic of its own:

> *The witch...is usually old, usually grotesque, libidinously learned and is as sexually attractive as a corpse; yet she becomes the entire vehicle of consummation. This is necessary for transmutation; the personal aesthetic culture is destroyed; perversion is also used to overcome the same kind of moral prejudice or conformity...he who transmutes the traditionally ugly into another aesthetic value, has new pleasures beyond fear...*[118]

A second collection of Spare's automatic art, *The Book of Ugly Ecstasy*, was published by Fulgur in London in 1996, in both general and limited-edition hardcover formats. Once again the illustrations were taken directly from one of Spare's sketch-books. The original hand-drawn volume had been purchased from the artist in October 1924 by the art connoisseur Gerald Reitlinger for £20; it contained 58 automatic drawings, of which only 23 could be considered complete.[119]

The 1996 edition contains only the 23 finished artworks, all of them meticulously reproduced. In style, subject matter and quality, the automatic drawings in *The Book of Ugly Ecstasy*, resemble those in *A Book of Automatic Drawings* but are, perhaps, even more grotesque. Distorted human shapes transform into clawed, bestial phantasms with multiple eyes or drooping bulbous breasts; horned devils emerge, one from the other, in a nightmarish sequence of bestial emanations; other creatures have truncated limbs or are simply malformed.

Figure 8: An atavistic image from Spare's posthumously published work, The Book of Ugly Ecstasy (1925)

However, as Robert Ansell writes in his introduction:

> ...the mystery of their creation may be illumined by a single candle flame. In this light the viewer will find these aberrations slowly become familiar and induce a process of subtle sublimation. [120]

Spare once wrote: 'Out of the flesh of our Mothers come dreams and memories of the Gods.' [121] Spare's visionary *oeuvre*, teeming with atavistic forms and spirit-creatures from the nether-regions, embodies its own sense of magical authenticity: it is the unique vision of an artist who was also a sorcerer, and who was highly aware of the permutations of human form and expression.

Rosaleen Norton

*Figure 9: Rosaleen Norton in the 1950s
(courtesy of the estate of Walter Glover)*

During the 1950s the Australian bohemian artist Rosaleen Norton was well known in Sydney as 'the Witch of Kings Cross' and was portrayed in the popular media as a colourful and 'wicked' figure from Sydney's red-light district. She wore flamboyant, brightly coloured blouses and vivid bandanas, puffed on an exotic engraved cigarette holder, and plucked her eyebrows so that they arched in a somewhat sinister curve. Norton also claimed certain distinctive body markings that she possessed were a sign that she was 'born a witch'. Slight in build with curly black hair and a smile that revealed irregular teeth, Norton always had something of a magnetic presence that made her stand out in the crowd.

However her provocative 'pagan' art, exhibited first at the University of Melbourne Library in 1949 and later in the Apollyon and Kashmir coffee-shops in Sydney's Kings Cross, plunged her into legal controversy, and her 1952 publication *The Art of Rosaleen Norton* was, for a time, banned in Australia on the basis that it contained allegedly obscene material. Norton was involved in a number of court hearings and was widely criticised in the media for engaging in bizarre sexual practices with her lover, the poet Gavin Greenlees. She was also associated with the scandal that eventually engulfed the professional career of renowned musical conductor and composer, Sir Eugene Goossens (1893-1962), who had arrived in Australia in 1947 and became a member of Norton's magical coven in Kings Cross.[122]

Norton was invariably depicted in the popular media as a pagan rebel and portrayed in such ungracious terms as 'the notorious, Pan-worshipping Witch of Kings Cross...a person known to the police through two prosecutions for obscenity'.[123] Most of her mainstream print media coverage was generated by popular gossip-driven magazines like *The Australasian Post*, *People*, *Truth* and *Squire* that inclined towards sensationalist articles, and tabloid newspapers like *The Daily Telegraph*, *The Daily Mirror* and *Sun*.[124] But all of this salacious media interest in Norton has to be seen in an historical context. During the immediate post-World War Two period Australia was both socially and politically conservative, ruled by the highly traditional Sir Robert Menzies, an 'ultraconservative prime minister, who reigned supreme in the 1950s with his anti-communist manifesto and harsh stance on censorship'.[125] Norton was portrayed in the media as a Devil-worshipping harpy, ever eager to flaunt accepted social conventions at a time when the appropriate place for a woman was perceived to be within the home, focusing on domestic concerns and attending to the needs of husband and children. As Dr Marguerite Johnson has observed, 'Rosaleen was presented as society's scapegoat, the witch on the outskirts of the community, a demon required to reinforce family values and Christian morality.'[126]

According to census figures from the period, in 1947 Anglicans, Presbyterians and Methodists collectively comprised over 60 per cent of the Australian population and Roman Catholics made up an additional 20.7 per cent,[127] which meant that in the immediate post-war environment Australia was more than 80 per cent Christian. The media-driven backlash against Rosaleen Norton and her pagan visionary art has to be viewed in this context and was perhaps to be expected.

A profile of the artist
Rosaleen Miriam Norton was born in Dunedin, New Zealand in 1917, the youngest of three sisters. Her father, Albert, was a captain in the merchant navy and a cousin of composer Vaughan Williams. The Nortons migrated from New Zealand to Australia in 1925 and settled in the Sydney suburb of Lindfield. As a teenager Norton was expelled from high school because of her allegedly 'depraved nature' which her headmistress claimed 'would corrupt the innocence of the other girls'. She then studied for two years at East Sydney Technical College under the sculptor Rayner Hoff. During this time she became interested in studying everything she could find about

witchcraft, sorcery and magic and was soon well versed in the occult writings of Dion Fortune, Aleister Crowley and Eliphas Levi. In 1940, at the age of 23, she began to experiment with self-hypnosis as a means of inducing automatic drawing. Norton found that she could shut off her normal consciousness by means of self-hypnosis and could transfer her attention to an inner plane of awareness. She now began to focus specifically on the magical forces associated with the Great God Pan, whose spirit she felt pervaded the entire earth. Her studies had taught her that the ancient Greeks regarded Pan as lord of all things—symbolizing the totality of the elements and all forms of manifest being. He was therefore, in a very real sense, the true god of the world. Pan was a maintainer of the balance of Nature and also had at his command an invisible hierarchy of lesser spirits who could help him in his work of ruling and sustaining the earth.

Norton painted a large-scale interpretation of Pan, complete with horns, pointed ears, cloven hooves and musical pipes, and mounted it on the wall of her Kings Cross flat, where it served as a backdrop to her magical altar. She also conducted magical ceremonies dressed in a tiger-skin robe to honour Pan's presence, and would often experience him as a living reality when she entered a trance state. Other deities who played a major role in her rituals included Hecate, Lucifer, Lilith and Erzulie—the Voodoo goddess of love. Norton's art invariably reflected the gods, goddesses and spirits she encountered in her visions, including a variety of devilish creatures, half animal-half human pagan deities, and various supernatural motifs.

Many occultists have drawn on Swiss psychoanalyst Carl Jung's concept of the 'collective unconscious' to explain their relationship with the archetypal forces of the psyche. Jung believed that at a deep, collective level of human consciousness lay a rich and potent source of sacred archetypal imagery, and that these numinous forms provided the very basis of religious and mystical experience. Jung maintained that gods and sacred images were really an extension of the universal human experience. Norton, however, did not agree with this particular perspective even though she acknowledged Jung's influence in other areas of her work. For her, the gods existed in their own right. Norton believed she was able to encounter Pan, Hecate and Lucifer—the major deities in her personal pantheon—not as extensions of her own consciousness, but as mythic beings from a higher plane of reality who would grace her with their presence *if it pleased them*, and not subject to her will. She believed she had discovered some of the qualities of these gods within her own temperament, and that this provided a sense of natural affinity. This made their invocation much easier and more effective than would have been the case had there not been some sort of innate bond.

Figure 10: Rosaleen Norton and Gavin Greenlees in their Kings Cross flat with the Pan mural in the background (courtesy of the estate of Walter Glover)

Norton's magical art

Rosaleen Norton's drawings and paintings depict a wide range of magical entities including hermaphroditic god-forms, goddesses with writhing snakes in their hair, fire elementals, devils with dual banks of eyes, cats with magical awareness and horned beings with strange eerie lights emanating from their brows. Norton consistently maintained that her art arose as the result of the direct magical encounter. Energies filtered through her, she said, as if she were a funnel. She transmitted the current during a state of self-induced hypnotic trance. If the gods were alive in her, her artistic skills would then allow these gods to manifest, in varying degrees, in her drawings and upon her canvases. Norton always denied that she portrayed the totality of the god. She could depict only those qualities the god chose to show. The gods existed in their own right, on a plane far removed from the everyday world of human consciousness— but were directly accessible to her through her techniques of magical trance.

It can be argued that Norton reached an artistic peak with her exhibition in 1949 at the Rowden White Library at the University of Melbourne (which drew on ten years' accumulated work) and the publication of *The Art of Rosaleen Norton* in Sydney in 1952. In later years—specifically during the 1960s and 1970s—many of Norton's artworks became parodies of earlier compositions as she sought to replicate earlier images in order to make a reasonably steady, if modest, income. Her palette became increasingly more lurid and garish and many of her works were crudely executed in oils, producing a body of work far less refined and accomplished than her pen and pastel works from the late 1940s and early 1950s.

The early work

Figure 11: Rosaleen Norton, The Borgias (courtesy of the estate of Walter Glover)

Norton's adolescent macabre drawings inclined towards a formulaic horror-comic style and were not especially distinctive. It was only after making contact with the editor of a small, independent magazine named *Pertinent* in the early 1940s that Norton's recognisable artistic style began to emerge. One of these early works was *The Borgias*, a drawing produced when she was 24. Here the heads of three mysterious and quietly menacing figures are shown clustered together in a conspiratorial formation; a hand is poised above a bowl and is pouring what may well be poison from a small vial into a translucent bowl. A coiled snake with a darting forked tongue writhes threateningly in the foreground. In this particular work Norton is drawing partly on the distinctive Art Nouveau style of Aubrey Beardsley: the drawing is characterised by distinctive dark arcs and the snake is shown virtually in silhouette. The sneering expression on the face closest to us has a look of arrogant disdain that Norton would apply to her depictions of other authority figures in later artworks, especially some of the drawings reproduced in *The Art of Rosaleen Norton* a decade later.

Another early drawing from this period, *Astral Scene* — a work dating from around 1943 — showed Norton in a comatose state of trance while a magical horned entity manifested itself beside her. *Astral Scene* is one of the earliest works that depicts Norton's magical process, namely her ability to enter a state of trance through self-hypnosis in order to contact supernatural beings in this way. *Astral Scene* is perhaps the most notable artwork produced by Norton in the early 1940s.

*Figure 12: Rosaleen Norton, Astral Scene, c. 1943
(courtesy of the estate of Walter Glover)*

Pertinent was not only an important artistic stimulus to Norton's career. It also enabled her to meet her future lover and artistic collaborator, Gavin Greenlees. Two of Greenlees' poems had been published in *Pertinent* in

1943 when he was just 13 years old. Greenlees and Norton had a mutual interest in surrealism, poetry and fantasy and their creative contributions to *Pertinent* apparently brought them together, although exactly how this came about has not been established. It is thought that they first met each other toward the end of World War Two. By mid-July 1949 Norton and Greenlees knew each other sufficiently well to hitch-hike together from Sydney to Melbourne. Norton's task in coming to Melbourne was to find a gallery where she could exhibit 46 pictures representing ten years' artistic work.

A Controversial Exhibition and Publication
Among the works that Norton had taken with her to Melbourne were some of her best pen and pastel drawings of the mid to late-1940s : *Timeless Worlds*, *Lucifer*, *Triumph*, *The Adversary*, *The Initiate*, *Merlin*, *Loosing of the Whirlwind* [sic] and an early version of *Individuation*. A total of forty-six works would feature in the forthcoming show and several of the exhibited artworks would later be reproduced in colour in Walter Glover's *Supplement to The Art of Rosaleen Norton* (1984), providing some sense of the strong visual impact they must have had, displayed on the walls of the university library. *Pan* was essentially a portrait of a naked leering Devil; *Timeless Worlds* depicted a naked female demon riding ecstatically through the sky on the back of a griffin; *Loosing of the Whirlwind* showed a black serpentine demon emerging from a vortex of swirling forms beside a triumphant naked she-devil; *Triumph* and *Individuation* both featured naked hermaphrodites with their breasts and penis in full view; *The Initiate* showed two naked women engaged in a warm sexual embrace, while *Lucifer* depicted the figure of the Adversary standing proudly naked above a horned satyr and a female demon. The latter was clearly modeled on Norton herself; breasts and genitalia were once again clearly visible for all to see. Other distinctive works in the Rowden White Library exhibition included *The Blueprint*, in which a benign form of Pan, representing the Logos—the guiding spiritual force in the cosmos—peers into his crystal bowl, carefully watching the forms emerging in the lower worlds, and *Triumph*, a work divided symbolically into two distinct realms: the dark magical forces, or *Qliphoth*, shown appropriately on the left-hand side of the picture, and the domain of light ruled by a naked golden-bodied hermaphrodite who raises an arm in celebration while a transcendent being looks on from a higher spiritual sphere.

Norton probably expected that her exhibition in the Rowden White Library would be attended mainly by students and a few curious academics. However, two days after the opening of the exhibition officers from the Victorian police raided the library and seized four of the most controversial pictures on show. Charges would subsequently be laid under the Police Offences Act of 1928 alleging that these particular works—*Witches' Sabbath*, *Lucifer*, *Triumph* and *Individuation*—were decadent and obscene, and 'likely to arouse unhealthy sexual appetites' in those who saw them.

During the court hearings the police detectives argued their case vigorously before the presiding Stipendiary Magistrate, Mr Addison, claiming that Norton was exhibiting artworks inspired by medieval demonology. However, in Norton's defence, Mr A.L. Abrahams countered this claim by stating that these allegedly obscene pictures were mild compared with illustrations published in *The History of Sexual Magic*, a book that had already been cleared by the censors and which was readily available in Australia. Stipendiary Magistrate Addison accepted Abrahams' argument, finding in Norton's favour and dismissing the charges of obscenity brought against her under the Police Offences Act 1928. Costs were awarded against the Victorian police department.

After returning from Melbourne, Norton and Greenlees moved to Sydney's red-light district of Kings Cross, an inner-city suburb associated with poets, musicians and bohemian drop-outs. Here they took up residence in a crumbling three-storey terrace house in Brougham Street which they shared with a range of other eccentrics. Norton placed a placard outside their basement door which read: 'Welcome to the house of ghosts, goblins, werewolves, vampires, witches, wizards and poltergeists.' However they soon became known to the local police as 'undesirables' and in 1951 were arrested by the New South Wales Vice Squad on a charge of vagrancy. Fortunately Norton and Greenlees were rescued through the timely intervention of an enterprising journalist named Walter Glover. Sensing an opportunity to invest in Norton's creative outpouring while also offering Norton and her lover modest paid employment, Glover negotiated an agreement with Norton which made him the copyright holder of all her past, present and future artworks.

Glover also agreed to finance publication of a projected work titled The Art of Rosaleen Norton. Conceived as a limited edition art book, it would include a selection of major drawings by Norton with accompanying poems by Gavin Greenlees. When the final selection was made, 31 drawings by Norton had been chosen, together with 24 poems by Greenlees. Two of Norton's own poems would also be included, together with relevant extracts from her magical diaries.

Together with the major works selected for the Rowden White Library exhibition, the drawings reproduced in *The Art of Rosaleen Norton* represent the high point of Norton's artistic career. In later years she would parody many of her major compositions, producing hastily drawn copies of some of her best known works in return for modest financial gain. Norton sometimes bartered artworks for gin and tonics in the Prince of Wales Hotel in Sydney's Haymarket, where she used to drink frequently. On other occasions she would paint replicas of her portraits of Pan and Lucifer for prices ranging from £5 for a small work to £100 for a large canvas. However in late 1951 Norton had found a financial sponsor in Walter Glover and such acts of barter and self-parody were not required. For the most part the black and white artworks included in *The Art of Rosaleen Norton* are of a similar calibre to the major works exhibited in the 1949 Melbourne exhibition.

Figure 13: Rosaleen Norton, The Initiate (courtesy of the estate of Walter Glover)

The Art of Rosaleen Norton is especially significant because it contains many of Norton's most recognisable, iconic images. Most of them are modified pencil renditions of the coloured pen and pastel works exhibited at the Rowden White Library three years earlier. Replicated images in *The Art of Rosaleen Norton*—that is to say, works exhibited in Melbourne and then redrawn for black and white reproduction—included *The Bells*; *The Jester*; *The Gnostic* (retitled *Esoteric Study*); *The Adversary*; *Witches' Sabbath* (retitled *Black Magic*); *The Angel of Twizzari*; *The Initiate* and *Individuation*. The last of these was a substantially re-worked depiction of a winged hermaphrodite, now widely considered one of Norton's strongest images and a vast improvement on the original 1949 version.

Several completely new artworks were also included in the 1952 publication. These included *The Master*, a dramatic drawing reversed out in white against a black field depicting the horned god Pan as master of the zodiac; *Fohat*, a devilish, horned figure with a greatly extended serpentine penis; *Eloi*, a magisterial leonine figure identified by Norton as 'the spirit of the planet Jupiter';[128] *Geburah*, an imposing naked figure with a male torso and the head of a hawk, and *Lilith*, a fine depiction of the legendary she-devil accompanied by a black panther.

Once again Norton demonstrated her considerable mastery of human anatomy in her new work; the naked torsos were sculptural, finely hewn and well proportioned, and the mythic figures themselves had an engaging presence. *The Master*, illustrated below, is especially striking, as is her bold depiction of Lilith, shown with pointed cat's ears and snakes writhing in her hair. One senses that Norton's she-devil and goddess images were sometimes idealised, or greatly exaggerated, versions of herself.

*Figure 14: Rosaleen Norton, Lilith
(courtesy of the estate of Walter Glover)*

Norton's personal notes on the imagery and symbolism in the drawings selected for *The Art of Rosaleen Norton* have survived in manuscript form. They are of considerable interest because they reflect Norton's broad range of interests and knowledge, encompassing such areas as Jungian archetypal psychology, Kabbalah, Buddhism, western astrology, Kundalini Yoga, ancient Egyptian mythology, Voodoo, medieval witchcraft and demonology, ancient Greek philosophy, Hindu mythology, parapsychology, spiritualism and Theosophy. Norton's notes are also valuable for the commentaries they provide about major artworks that were published in *The Art of Rosaleen Norton* but not included in the 1949 Melbourne exhibition. Norton's portrait of Lilith, 'Queen of Air and Darkness', is one such work. Norton regarded the figure of Lilith as an 'image of the unconscious with its power to align images and draw together those spirits who have true affinity—holding man by the soul image' and Greenlees described her in his accompanying poem as the 'Queen of Night and Sympathy'. According to Norton, the writhing serpents in Lilith's hair are 'phallic symbols of creativity' and the sun and a moon drawn above her head represent the male and female polarities of consciousness.

*Figure 15: Rosaleen Norton, Individuation
(courtesy of the estate of Walter Glover)*

One drawing which caused deep offence in Melbourne in its 1949 incarnation, was Norton's *Individuation*. The revised, and greatly improved version of this work shows a naked winged hermaphrodite standing in a sacred circle inscribed with esoteric symbols, its curling arms outstretched and tapering off into slender pointed claws. The figure has cat's ears, small round breasts and a thin pencil-like phallus, and its face is perhaps modelled on Norton herself. The title of the work presents a key to its interpretation—'individuation' was Jung's term for psychic unity or inner wholeness.[129] Norton's commentary indicates that her intention was indeed to demonstrate a universal mystical principle, the cosmic union of opposites:

Another image seen for the first time in *The Art of Rosaleen Norton* was *The Master*. Here Norton shows us a mysterious horned entity who could easily be mistaken for a figure of evil for he is drawn in fine white pencil against a black background and is presented very much as a figure of the night. Portrayed as a master-controller, as a supernatural ruler who governs from within the swirling vortex of the Zodiac, it soon becomes evident that Norton's 'Master' is none other than Pan himself. Norton describes him in her commentary notes as 'the Master Magician, creator of worlds...in psychological terms the psyche, or Self, moulding the ego or minor self '.

*Figure 16: Rosaleen Norton, The Master
(courtesy of the estate of Walter Glover)*

Later artworks

A selection of Norton's later artworks, consisting of paintings from the 1960s and early 1970s, was included in Walter Glover's small, spiral-bound publication, *Supplement to The Art of Rosaleen Norton*, published in 1984.[130] Fortunately, since all of these later paintings were reproduced in colour and included alongside several of the artworks that had been photographed at the University of Melbourne in 1949, it has become possible to compare Norton's 'later' style of the 1960s and 1970s with her iconic works of the late 1940s and early 1950s.

A number of Norton's later works were auctioned at Exiles Bookshop in Sydney in October 1982—three years after the artist's death—and the fact that they were finally sold off collectively as a 37-piece 'job lot' to an inner-city hotelier is indicative of their lack of overall quality. By comparison with the pencil and pastel works exhibited in the Rowden White exhibition in 1949, most of the later works on show at Exiles Bookshop were lurid or roughly crafted paintings, many of them hastily produced and poorly painted. They included two impasto portraits titled *Demon* and *Fur Fur the Storm Demon*, showing the heads of demons peering out from a hazy grey vortex and storm clouds respectively; a painting titled *Khamsin*, featuring two demonic faces manifesting in the humps of a camel; a grotesque and crudely rendered portrait of Woden, and two inconsequential animal portraits, *Squid* and *Rabbit*. Other works of only passing quality included *Roie with Snake*, showing Norton sitting naked beneath the head of a protective, arched cobra; *Image*, a confronting painting of a leering female face with strongly slanted feline eyes; *The Cat*, which showed a humanoid ginger cat standing beside a tree occupied by a demonic being, and *Snakes*, a more sinister rendition of Norton's earlier drawing, *Lilith*. Norton had also parodied her controversial c.1949 work *Witches' Sabbat* in a much more crudely painted rendition titled *Montage*. The most accomplished paintings in the Exiles exhibition were *Three Sisters*, which showed three demonic female heads in a blaze of fiery smoke and *Fire Bird* which depicted a naked and aggressive fire-goddess riding on the back of an eagle, her head ablaze with streaming flames. The latter work featured a 'double image' effect so that the shape of the bird's wings and the female figure's outstretched arms revealed the face of a black panther (one of Norton's 'images of the Night') hidden in the background and seemingly propelling the fire-goddess forward on her hellish journey through the sky.

Given that Norton is known to have used LSD during the mid-1970s it is possible that the vivid palette, intense colours and expressionistic style of some of her 1970s paintings may reflect her use of psychedelic drugs. Several of the paintings from this period, exhibited at Exiles Bookshop in 1982, were produced in the highly coloured, almost iridescent style associated with psychedelic poster art in the late 1960s /early 1970s California counter-culture. Works like *Witch and Family Secrets*, with its exultant naked witch-priestess and fiery imagery, and the intense and vibrantly coloured portrait, *The Goddess*, where the head of the female deity manifests amidst searing flames, would not have seemed out of place alongside works by psychedelic artists in the 1960s Californian counterculture.[131]

It is also interesting to note that several of Norton's later images have a stridently demonic orientation. Several of the later paintings also make pointed visual references to the Kundalini fire-serpent and some also have an erotic, sexual flavour that may well have been influenced by Norton's exploration of Tantric sex-magic. These paintings include *The Temptress*, which shows a naked, blue-bodied witch surrounded by a large coiled snake, her head ablaze with fire; *Witch and Family Secrets*, referred to above, which depicts a serpent rising up from flames as a protector of the witch-priestess herself, and *Satan,* where a female human head has merged with that of a snake amidst hellish waves of fire. The head of Pan, a writhing snake, a surging fire and the head of a witch (who may well be an aspect of Lilith or Hecate), are all featured in Norton's expressionistic painting *Clairvoyant*. A related work, *The Cauldron*, shows two humanoid/animal creatures dancing in ritual ecstasy on rooftops above chimneys which in this painting double as fiery magic cauldrons. One of the dancing figures is male and has a tail and the head of a snake; the other is female, with firm pointed breasts and the smiling head of a pig.

With regard to Norton's later work, specific reference must be made to a work titled *Fur Fur the Storm Demon*. This work, like most of Norton's paintings and drawings, is undated but was probably produced c. 1975. The key point of interest is the name of the demon itself. The reference to 'Fur Fur' is taken directly from the medieval *Goetia* or *Lesser Key of Solomon* and shows that in the mid-1970s Norton had lost none of her fascination with magical grimoires. Furfur is the 34th of the 72 demons profiled in the *Goetia*, and although Norton spelt his name 'Fur Fur' there can be no mistaking the identity of the demon Furfur based on the contents of Norton's painting and his description in the text of the medieval grimoire:

> The thirty-fourth Spirit is Furfur. He is a Great and Mighty Earl, appearing in the Form of a Hart with a Fiery Tail. He never speaketh truth unless he is compelled, or brought up within a triangle. Being therein, he will take upon himself the Form of an Angel. Being bidden, he speaketh with a hoarse voice. Also

he will wittingly urge Love between Man and Woman, He can raise Lightnings and Thunders, Blasts and Great Tempestuous Storms. And he giveth True Answers both of Things Secret and Divine, if commanded. He ruleth over 26 Legions of Spirits.[132]

Fire Bird, Fur Fur the Storm Demon

The Goddess, Three Sisters

Figure 17: Four examples of Rosaleen Norton's later work, characterised by a vivid palette, intense colours and a tendency towards lurid expressionism (courtesy of the estate of Walter Glover)

Norton had continued with her study of demonology well into the 1970s and she claims in her unpublished journals that Fur Fur had become one of her 'tutelary and guardian spirits... a 'teacher of abstract things'.

Differentiating Spare and Norton

Despite the marked parallels in their chthonic art, Norton's trance magic differs from that of Austin Spare in several distinctive ways. As noted earlier, according to Norton the gods and goddesses exist *in their own right*. She believed they were transcendent beings who would interact with human consciousness only through their projected 'god forms' on the inner planes and these forms would then appear to the occultist in a manner that the viewer could comprehend. The so-called 'astral' or 'inner plane' domain which Norton explores during her trance journeys was therefore a type of middle ground between the sacred realm of deity and the world of familiar reality.

Figure 18: Detail from a work in Austin Osman Spare's
A Book of Automatic Drawings *(1925)*

For Spare, by way of contrast, deity was perceived as an aspect of Kia—the Absolute—and even the figure of the Universal Woman was a manifestation of this higher, abstract life-force. Spare's trance method lay in seeking what he called the 'void moment'. He then opened his consciousness to an influx of atavistic automata—residual psychic energies he believed were 'karmas' from his own earlier bird, animal and human incarnations. Spare's occult practice sought to embody these automata through an act of magical 'obsession', a term Spare actually uses to describe his process.[133] While Spare always denied that he was acting like a passive psychic medium, his technique of seeking the 'void moment' and then 'opening the door to the Dwellers on the Threshold' allowed his psyche to be overrun with psychic impressions from his subconscious mind.[134]

Norton, however, did not act in this way. Her trance episodes were willed and consciously determined, and did not involve either magical 'obsession' or 'possession'.[135] Characteristically, none of Norton's drawings was produced using the 'obsessive' technique of automatic art. Spare claimed to be a Surrealist, and was perhaps the *first* Surrealist,[136] but Norton consistently denied that she should be labelled as such, the reason being that her artistic method was not surrealist but descriptive. Norton was essentially a representational artist, portraying in a figurative way the archetypal beings and metaphysical entities encountered on the inner planes of the psyche. Her art is essentially a type of magical reportage.

There is no denying that Norton's magical inclination was towards the 'night' side of the psyche but when she portrayed 'dark forces' they were the *Qliphoth* or 'negative energies' of the Kabbalistic Tree of Life, and she captioned them as such. On the other hand, Spare's 'ugly ecstasies', produced as automatic drawings, are, to use his term, his own karmic atavisms. They are ultimately aspects of himself.

Spare focused both his cosmology and his magic on the potentials of the human organism. In his *Logomachy of Zos* he makes such pronouncements as 'Man is a potentiality of *anything* becoming actuality,'[137] and 'The only attribute of God is man..,'[138] and 'God is absolutely my own Idea; otherwise God cannot exist'.[139] As Gavin Semple has noted, Spare sought through the Death Posture to make a magical sigil out of his own body, to 'flesh' his desires through an act of magical will.[140] As Spare succinctly states: '*All ways to Heaven lead to flesh.*'[141] Spare's method is also essentially retrogressive—his ecstatic journey takes him into his previous incarnations and progressively back to the source of all manifestation: Kia.[142] This is spiritual evolution in reverse. Norton's magical quest is quite different. Having decided that Pan is the overlord of the manifest universe, her task is to pay homage to him as a sacred being, to depict him in her drawings and paintings and in the large mural where he presides over her ritual altar, and to seek his presence on the inner planes of being. Never does she seek to incarnate him *in the flesh*, to use Spare's term. Her drawing of Lucifer as the Adversary, for example, which shows a small, somewhat intimidated human being encountering a much more substantial metaphysical deity,[143] demonstrates that it is ultimately the gods and goddesses who are in control. For Norton the deities are respected as figures of awe; for Spare they are aspects of the life-force to be embodied or 'incarnated'.[144]

*Figure 19: Rosaleen Norton, The Adversary
(courtesy of the estate of Walter Glover)*

Nevertheless, Norton and Spare share one important characteristic: they are both *chthonic* artists—although in different ways. As Marcus M. Jungkurth points out in a recent essay, Spare's artistic *oeuvre* derives, essentially, from the mythological Underworld. Spare's magical name was *Zos vel Thanatos*—'Death is all'—and during his career as a visionary artist and trance magician Spare identified himself with Thanatos, Death, which was one of the bynames of the Greek god of the Underworld, Hades.[145] Spare's images arise from the Underworld of his densely populated psyche. His artistic atavisms are incarnations of his personal karmas that lie just beneath the surface of awareness and through acts of metaphysical ecstasy he induces them to swarm into his art.

Norton's chthonic art, on the other hand, throngs with *Qliphothic* demons and serpentine imagery that emanate from the nether regions of the psyche. Her instinctive *inspirational* attraction is towards the ecstatic Kundalini fire-snake—the latent cosmic power that lies dormant in the primal sex *chakra* at the base of the spine. Like Spare, Norton's artistic sorcery arises from the psychic depths but the thrust of her sexual and magical ecstasy depended first on awakening the fire-serpent and then worshipping Pan as the source and overlord of her primal existence.

References

Agrippa, H.C., 1978 [1533]. *Fourth Book of Occult Philosophy*. London: Askin Publishers.

_____ 1971. *Three Books of Occult Philosophy or Magic* (ed. W.F. Whitehead). London: Aquarian Press.

Anon., 'Inside Rosaleen Norton'. 1965. *Squire*, Sydney, April issue.

Ansell, R. 1988. *The Bookplate Designs of Austin Osman Spare*. London: The Bookplate Society/Keridwen Press.

_____ 2005. (ed.), *Borough Satyr: The Life and Art of Austin Osman Spare*. London: Fulgur.

Beskin, G., and Bonner, J.(eds.). 1987. *Austin Osman Spare 1886-1956: The Divine Draughtsman*, exhibition catalogue. London: Morley Gallery.

_____ (eds.). 1999. *Austin Osman Spare: Artist, Occultist, Sensualist*. London: Beskin Press.

Bogdan, H. 2006. 'Kenneth Grant: Marriage between the West and the East', extract from 'Challenging the Morals of Western Society: the Use of Ritualised Sex in Contemporary Occultism,' *The Pomegranate*, 8, 2. London: Equinox Publishing. Also published on www.fulgur.co.uk

Drury, N. 2011. *Stealing Fire from Heaven: the Rise of Modern Western Magic*. New York: Oxford University Press.

_____ 2012 (forth coming). *Dark Spirits: The Magical Art of Rosaleen Norton and Austin Osman Spare*. Brisbane and Chiang Mai, Thailand: Salamander & Sons.

_____ 2009. *Homage to Pan: the life, art and sex magic of Rosaleen Norton*. London: Creation Oneiros.

_____ 1979. *Inner Visions: Explorations in Magical Consciousness*. London: Routledge & Kegan Paul.

_____ 1988. *Pan's Daughter: the Strange World of Rosaleen Norton*. Sydney: Collins Australia. Republished 1993 by Mandrake, Oxford, UK and reissued in Australia in 2002 as The Witch of Kings Cross. Sydney: Kingsclear. Revised and expanded edition of *Pan's Daughter* to be published by Mandrake, Oxford UK in early 2013.

Drury, N., and Skinner, S. 1972. *The Search for Abraxas*. London: Spearman.

Fortune, D. 1957 [1935]. *The Mystical Qabalah*. London: Benn.

Grant, K. 1975. *Images and Oracles of Austin Osman Spare*. London: Muller.

_____ 1977. *Nightside of Eden*. London: Muller.

Grant, K. and S. 1998. *Zos Speaks!: Encounters with Austin Osman Spare*. London: Fulgur.

Johnson, M. 2002. 'The Witch of Kings Cross: Rosaleen Norton and the

Australian Media', conference presentation, Symbiosis: Institute for Comparative Studies in Science, Myth, Magic and Folklore, University of Newcastle.

_____ 2004. 'The Witching Hour: Sex Magic in 1950s Australia', conference presentation, University of Melbourne.

Jung, C.G. 1919. *Psychology of the Unconscious*. London: Kegan Paul, Trench, Trubner.

_____ 1959.*The Archetypes of the Collective Unconscious*. London: Routledge & Kegan Paul.

Jungkurth, M.M. 1999. 'Neither-Neither: Austin Spare and the Underworld', in G. Beskin and J. Bonner (eds.) *Austin Osman Spare:Artist, Occultist, Sensualist*. London: Beskin Press.

Law, I., 1987. 'Austin Osman Spare' in G. Beskin and J.Bonner (ed.) *Austin Osman Spare 1886-1956: The Divine Draughtsman*, exhibition catalogue. London: Morley Gallery.

_____ 1972. Introduction to A.O. Spare, *A Book of Automatic Drawings*. Stroud, UK: Catalpa Press.

Letchford, F.W. 1995. *From the Inferno to Zos*. Thame, UK: First Impressions.

_____ 1999. 'Memories of a Friendship' in G. Beskin and J. Bonner (eds.), *Austin Osman Spare: Artist, Occultist, Sensualist*. London: Beskin Press.

Marquardt, P.A. 1981.'A Portrait of Hecate', *The American Journal of Philology*, 102, 3, Autumn.

Moore, V. 2004. 'Chthonic: from Beast to Godhead', *Rose Noire*. Published online: www.vadgemoore.com/writings/beast_to_godhead.html

Norton, R. 1949. Exhibition catalogue essay, *The Art of Rosaleen Norton*, Rowden White Library, University of Melbourne, 1-23 August.

_____ 1952. *The Art of Rosaleen Norton*. Sydney: Walter Glover (republished 1982).

_____ 1957.'I was born a Witch'. *Australasian Post*, Sydney, 3 January.

_____ 1984. *Supplement to The Art of Rosaleen Norton*, Walter Glover, Sydney, 1984.

Richmond, K. 2000. *The Occult Visions of Rosaleen Norton*. Sydney: Oceania Lodge of the Ordo Templi Orientis/ Kings Cross Arts Guild.

Semple, G.W. 1995. *Zos-Kia: An Introductory Essay on the Art and Sorcery of Austin Osman Spare*, London: Fulgur.

_____ 1997. 'A Few Leaves from the Devil's Picture Book' in A.O. Spare, *Two Tracts on Cartomancy*. London: Fulgur.

Spare, A.O. 1905. *Earth: Inferno*. London: self-published.

_____ 1907. *A Book of Satyrs*. London: self-published.

_____ 1972 [1925] *A Book of Automatic Drawing*. Stroud: Catalpa Press.

_____1927. *The Anathema of Zos*. London: self-published.

_____ 1913. *The Book of Pleasure (Self-Love): The Psychology of Ecstasy*.

London: self-published. facsimile reprint, 93 Publishing, Montreal.
_____ 1996. *The Book of Ugly Ecstasy*. London: Fulgur.
_____ 1921.*The Focus of Life*. London: self-published. Republished 1976. London: Askin Publishers.
_____ 'Mind to Mind and How' in *Two Tracts on Cartomancy*, Fulgur, London 1997
Spare, A.O., and Carter, F. 1979 [1916]. *Automatic Drawing*. Quebec: 93 Publishing.
Swaffer, H. 2005. 'Artist as Agent of the Unseen' in R. Ansell (ed.), *Borough Satyr: The Life and Art of Austin Osman Spare*. London: Fulgur.
Urban, H.B. 2006. *Magia Sexualis: Sex, Magic and Liberation in Modern Western Esotericism*, Berkeley, California: University of California Press.
Von Rudloff, R. 1999. *Hekate in Ancient Greek Religion*. Victoria, Canada:Horned Owl Publishing.
Wallace, W. 1987. *The Early Work of Austin Osman Spare*. Stroud, UK: Catalpa Press.

Note: The Rosaleen Norton art-works in this book are reproduced courtesy of the estate of the late Walter Glover. Copyright in the art-works of Austin Spare has for many years been regarded as open domain.

Endnotes

1   The first publications to explore Spare's magical approach in depth—N. Drury and S. Skinner, *The Search for Abraxas*, London and K. Grant, *The Magical Revival*, Muller, London—were both published in 1972, twenty years after the publication of *The Art of Rosaleen Norton* and just seven years before Norton's death, and it is unlikely that Norton had access to Spare's privately published books, which for many years have remained extremely rare items in the secondhand book market. Norton does not refer to Spare in her bibliography.

2   The autobiographical essay included in the catalogue accompanying Rosaleen Norton's art exhibition at the University of Melbourne in 1949 shows that she did not believe she had any true artistic 'contemporaries' and she shunned the so-called 'contemporary' trends emerging in Australian art at that time. Similarly, although Spare was briefly fashionable in London's West End early in his career he felt more at home in his vastly less glamorous environment in the slums of south London. See Steffi Grant's personal profile of Spare (whom she first met in the 1940s) in K. and S. Grant, *Zos Speaks!: Encounters with Austin Osman Spare*, Fulgur, London 1998: 13-25. In 1927 Spare also published an invective directed against the 'Mayfair set' titled *The Anathema of Zos: a Sermon to the Hypocrites*. See R.Ansell, *The Bookplate Designs*

    of Austin Osman Spare, The Bookplate Society/Keridwen Press, London 1988: 6.

3   Norton and her lover Gavin Greenlees lived in run-down terrace houses in the Kings Cross and Darlinghurst districts of Sydney and Spare lived for most of his life in confined and impoverished conditions in slum-flats located south of the Thames in the Southwark area of London.

4   Spare held exhibitions at the Elephant and Castle in Southwark and in other 'public houses' in The Borough and Brixton, although he also held exhibitions at mainstream London art galleries, including Bruton Galleries, The Baillie Gallery, The Ryder Gallery, Lefevre Galleries and Archer Gallery. See R. Ansell, *The Bookplate Designs of Austin Osman Spare*, The Bookplate Society/Keridwen Press, London 1988: 6, and W. Wallace, *The Early Work of Austin Osman Spare*, Catalpa Press, Stroud, UK 1987: 20-21. Norton had ongoing 'exhibitions' at the Apollyon and Kashmir coffee-shops in Kings Cross, Sydney.

5   Steffi Grant, a personal friend of Spare, writes that 'He was mad on cats. They crawled all over his place... cosy tame strays wandering straight in and out of the 'kitchen', which was his back room...' See Grant's introduction in K. and S. Grant, *Zos Speaks !: Encounters with Austin Osman Spare*, Fulgur, London 1998: 15. Norton was similarly fond of cats and was photographed with one of her many feline pets in Dave Barnes' article 'Confessions of a Witch', *Australasian Post*, Sydney 15 June 1967: 2.

6   Norton's pantheism was expressed as ritual homage to Pan. Spare declares in *The Logomachy of Zos* ; 'I am a Pantheist...because I can conceive God in You and You in Me... God in us all and in all potencies...' See K. and S. Grant, *Zos Speaks !: Encounters with Austin Osman Spare*, loc cit: 210.

7   According to his close friend, Frank Letchford, Spare read the Theosophical works of Annie Besant and H.P. Blavatsky and was also strongly influenced by Taoism. See F.W .Letchford, *Inferno to Zos*, First Impressions, Thame, UK 1995 :231.

8   Norton acknowledged a specific debt to Jung and his theory of archetypes in *The Art of Rosaleen Norton* [Sydney, 1952] as well as in her interviews with the psychologist L.J. Murphy at the University of Melbourne. Spare appears to have incorporated elements of Freudian psychology into his Zos/Kia conception although Steffi Grant recalls that he used to refer to Freud and Jung as 'Fraud and Junk'. See *Zos Speaks!: Encounters with Austin Osman Spare*, loc cit: 23.

9   Spare joined Crowley's occult order, the Argenteum Astrum, as a probationer in 1909. His magical name was *Yihoveaum*, a combination of the Hebrew JHVH and the Eastern symbol AUM. He also contributed

drawings to Crowley's biennial publication, *The Equinox*. See W. Wallace, *The Early Work of Austin Osman Spare*, loc cit: chronology section (no page number).

10 See www.hekate.timerift.net/whois.htm, W. Burkert, *Ancient Mystery Cults*, Harvard University Press 1987, and J. Sellers, *Qadosh:the Johannite Tradition*, Manutius Press, Oakhurst, California 2006.

11 See W. Burkert, *Ancient Mystery Cults*, Harvard University Press, Cambridge, Massachusetts 1987 and M.W. Meyer (ed.), *The Ancient Mysteries: a Sourcebook*, Harper & Row, San Francisco 1987.

12 V. Moore, 'Chthonic: from Beast to Godhead', *Rose Noire*, 2004, also published on-line at www.vadgemoore.com/writings/beast_to_godhead.html.

13 The Gnostic archon Abraxas was said to rule over 365 heavens and was depicted on numerous charms, amulets and talismans throughout the ancient Middle East in order to attract good fortune.

14 V. Moore, 'Chthonic: from Beast to Godhead', loc cit.

15 Ibid.

16 Ibid.

17 Ibid.

18 His parents were Philip Newton Spare and Eliza Ann Adelaide Osman. Philip Spare was a constable in the City of London police force.

19 Spare lived briefly in Golders Green and later in Bloomsbury but mostly lived south of the Thames. See S. Grant, introduction, *Zos Speaks !: Encounters with Austin Osman Spare*, loc cit: 18.

20 See R. Ansell, *The Bookplate Designs of Austin Osman Spare*, The Bookplate Society / Keridwen Press, London 1988: 1.

21 R. Ansell, *The Bookplate Designs of Austin Osman Spare*, loc.cit: 1.

22 Ibid : 2.

23 See I. Law, 'Austin Osman Spare' in G. Beskin and J. Bonner (ed.) *Austin Osman Spare 1886-1956: The Divine Draughtsman*, exhibition catalogue, The Morley Gallery, London, 1987: 5 and K. Grant, *Images and Oracles of Austin Osman Spare*, Muller, London 1975: 11.

24 R. Ansell, *The Bookplate Designs of Austin Osman Spare*, loc cit: 2.

25 It was published by Otto Schutzer & Co., 1909. See W. Wallace, *The Early Work of Austin Osman Spare*, loc cit 20.

26 See R. Ansell, *The Bookplate Designs of Austin Osman Spare*, loc cit: 5. *The Yellow Book* was published between 1894 and 1897. Henry Harland was its literary editor and Beardsley its art editor until 1896. Spare did not acknowledge any direct influence from Beardsley although he was very familiar with his graphic work.

27 F.W. Letchford, *From the Inferno to Zos*, First Impressions, Thame, UK 1995: 99.

28 *Form* was revived in 1921, but issued in a more modest format.
29 Ibid: 105.
30 *The Golden Hind* was published by Chapman & Hall, London.
31 See K. Grant, introduction to A.O. Spare, *The Book of Pleasure* [1913], facsimile reprint, 93 Publishing, Montreal, Canada 1975.
32 See K. Grant, *Images and Oracles of Austin Osman Spare*, Muller, London 1975: 16. According to Robert Ansell this quote is hearsay and no documentary evidence has so far been produced to support it.
33 K. and S. Grant, *Zos Speaks!: Encounters with Austin Osman Spare*, loc cit: 286-288.
34 R. Ansell, *The Bookplate Designs of Austin Osman Spare*, loc cit: 6. Ansell writes that Spare was acclaimed the 'darling of Mayfair' between 1907 and 1913. The latter date coincides with the release of Spare's most revolutionary and confronting work, *The Book of Pleasure (Self-Love): The Psychology of Ecstasy*.
35 A.O. Spare, *Earth:Inferno*, London 1905: 21.
36 Ibid: 18.
37 A.O. Spare. *The Book of Pleasure (Self-Love): The Psychology of Ecstasy*, London 1913: 45.
38 Ibid: iii.
39 Ibid: 7.
40 G.W. Semple, *Zos-Kia: An Introductory Essay on the Art and Sorcery of Austin Osman Spare*, Fulgur, London 1995: 11.
41 Specifically, S.L. MacGregor Mathers' translation of Knorr Von Rosenroth's selection of key texts from the Zohar, *Kabbala Denudata*, published in an English language edition as *The Kabbalah Unveiled*, Redway, London 1887.
42 F.W. Letchford, *From the Inferno to Zos*, loc cit: 79.
43 G.W. Semple, 'A Few Leaves from the Devil's Picture Book' in A.O. Spare, *Two Tracts on Cartomancy*, Fulgur, London 1997: 21fn.
44 Temurah, or Temura, is a Kabbalistic coding technique intended to work as a disguise. The first half of the Hebrew alphabet is written in reverse order and located above the remaining section so that the letters form vertical pairs: k y th ch z v h d g b a
                  l m n s o p tz q r sh t
    Here k=l, y=m, th=n and so on. A given word can be disguised in Temurah by substituting the code letter in each case. See C. Poncé, *Kabbalah*, Garnstone Press, London 1974: 172.
45 W. Wallace, *The Early Work of Austin Osman Spare*, loc cit: 13.
46 G.G. Scholem, *Major Trends in Jewish Mysticism*, revised edition, Schocken, New York 1961: 240.
47 A.O. Spare, *Axiomata*, Fulgur, London 1992: 9. According to publisher,

Robert Ansell, this work is based on previously unpublished texts from the early 1950s.

48 'Atavistic resurgence' has been defined as 'the return into the sorcerer's consciousness of latent powers and knowledge, resurrecting the 'dead' from the pre-human strata; typically manifesting through bestial and elemental forms, evoked by intense nostalgia.' See G.W. Semple, *Zos-Kia: An Introductory Essay on the Art and Sorcery of Austin Osman Spare*, loc.cit: 48.

49 A.O. Spare, *The Witches' Sabbath*, Fulgur, London 1992:7. This is a posthumously published text, based on manuscripts dating from the early 1950s and is not one of Spare's self-published works.

50 Spare was familiar with the writings of Freud, Krafft-Ebing and Havelock Ellis, all specialist authors in the field of the psychology of sexuality.

51 One of Spare's magical names was *Zos vel Thanatos* which, according to Frank Letchford, was derived 'from the theory posited by Dr Sigmund Freud of the eternal conflict between Eros (love) and Thanatos (the so-called Death-wish).' See F.W. Letchford, *Inferno to Zos*, loc cit: 137. In ancient Greek mythology, Thanatos was the Greek god of Death, the brother of Sleep and the son of Night.

52 According to Frank Letchford, 'The Tao was one of *the* most important influences upon Austin' (see F.W. Letchford, *Inferno to Zos*, loc.cit:231) and it is of interest that the coloured self-portrait of Spare titled *Prayer* [1906], reproduced opposite the title page in William Wallace's *The Early Work of Austin Osman Spare 1900-1919*, loc.cit, shows the artist wearing a Taoist *yin-yang* pendant around his neck. Spare makes a very Taoist remark in his posthumously published text *The Living Word of Zos*: 'I believe in the life; in the flesh of infinite variety. We are eternity, with—as now—a fleeting and fluxing consciousness. Possibilities of being are limitless...' See K. and S. Grant, *Zos Speaks!: Encounters with Austin Osman Spare*, loc cit: 273.

53 For an explanation of 'karma' see fn. 59 below.

54 A.O. Spare, *Axiomata*, loc cit: 19. This publication is not one of Spare's self-published works but a more recent publication based on previously unpublished manuscripts assembled and edited long after his death in 1956.

55 Spare illustrated these 'karmas' in his graphic compositions. Examples may be found in *The Book of Pleasure (Self-Love): The Psychology of Ecstasy* [1913] on pages 49 and 57.

56 A.O. Spare, *The Book of Pleasure (Self-Love): The Psychology of Ecstasy*, loc.cit: 52-53.

57 Letchford provides these dates in his foreword to William Wallace, *The*

Early Work of Austin Osman Spare 1900-1919, loc cit.
58 F.W. Letchford, *From the Inferno to Zos*, loc cit: 161.
59 The Hindu concept of karma is based on the principle of cause and effect, and states that for every action there is an equal and opposite reaction. The renowned Indian spiritual teacher Vivekananda (1862-1902) described karma as 'the eternal assertion of human freedom... our thoughts, our words and deeds are the threads of the net which we throw around ourselves.' In Hindu philosophy the law of karma extends beyond the physical world into the mental, emotional and spiritual aspects of life and applies not only to physical actions but to every conscious thought and action that arises in everyday life. According to the karmic philosophy of life, positive thoughts and actions produce a positive outcome and create good karma. Negative thoughts and actions result in negative outcomes and create bad karma. Austin Spare may have developed his interest in karma through reading the Theosophical writings of Madame H.P. Blavatsky and Annie Besant.
60 K. Grant, *Images and Oracles of Austin Osman Spare*, Muller, London 1975: 9.
61 K. Grant, *Images and Oracles of Austin Osman Spare*, loc cit: 10.
62 Quoted in G.W. Semple, Zos-*Kia: An Introductory Essay on the Art and Sorcery of Austin Osman Spare*, loc.cit: 7
63 K. Grant, *Images and Oracles of Austin Osman Spare*, loc.cit: 21.
64 Grant's close friendship with Spare, and their voluminous correspondence, are documented in K. and S. Grant, *Zos Speaks!: Encounters with Austin Osman Spare*, loc cit.
65 K. Grant, *Images and Oracles of Austin Osman Spare*, loc.cit: 23.
66 A.O. Spare, *Earth: Inferno* [1905], loc cit.
67 K. Grant, *Images and Oracles of Austin Osman Spare*, loc.cit: 71.
68 Ibid: 73.
69 Ibid.
70 A.O. Spare, *The Book of Pleasure (Self-Love): The Psychology of Ecstasy*, loc.cit: 6.
71 Nevertheless, Steffi Grant claims in her Introduction to *Zos Speaks!* that Spare had numerous lovers. Many of them were local women who also modelled for him. Grant writes that 'He said that until he was forty-five he never thought of anything except sex; that he was seriously in love every single week. He must have been very attractive to women, and never found any difficulties in satisfying his desires.' See K. and S. Grant, *Zos Speaks!: Encounters with Austin Osman Spare*, loc cit: 18.
72 To this extent, Spare's approach resembles the Thelemic sex magic of Aleister Crowley. However, Spare was already developing his Zos/Kia cosmology as early as 1906 (elements of it appear in *Earth: Inferno*) so it

would appear that Spare did not derive his sexual practice from Crowley, even though he was briefly a member of Crowley's sex-magic order, the Argenteum Astrum, 1909-1910.

73 K. Grant, *Images and Oracles of Austin Osman Spare*, loc.cit: 61.
74 A.O. Spare, *The Book of Pleasure (Self-Love): The Psychology of Ecstasy*, loc.cit: 48.
75 In *The Focus of Life*, Spare actually defines it in these terms: the Death Posture, he writes is 'a simulation of death by the utter negation of thought.' See A.O. Spare, *The Focus of Life* [1921], Askin Publishers, London 1976:18.
76 A.O. Spare, *Metamorphosis by Death Posture*, quoted in K. Grant, *Images and Oracles of Austin Osman Spare*, loc.cit:61.
77 G.W. Semple, *Zos-Kia: An Introductory Essay on the Art and Sorcery of Austin Osman Spare*, loc.cit: 29.
78 In *The Book of Pleasure*, Spare writes: 'Magical obsession is that state when the mind is illuminated by sub-conscious activity evoked voluntarily by formulae at our own time, etc. for inspiration. It is the condition of Genius.' (p. 41)...The chief cause of genius is realization of "I" by an emotion that allows the lightning assimilation of what is perceived...Its most excellent state is the "Neither-Neither" [Kia], the free or atmospheric "I" (p. 43)...My formula and Sigils for sub-conscious activity are the means of inspiration, capacity or genius, and the means of accelerating evolution.' (p. 48), loc cit.
79 G.W. Semple, *Zos-Kia: An Introductory Essay on the Art and Sorcery of Austin Osman Spare*, loc.cit:26.
80 A.O. Spare, *The Book of Pleasure (Self-Love): The Psychology of Ecstasy*, loc.cit: 7.
81 Ibid.
82 Spare says specifically that the Self is the 'Neither-Neither'. It is the Absolute because it transcends duality. See A.O. Spare, *The Book of Pleasure (Self-Love): The Psychology of Ecstasy*, loc.cit: 33.
83 Ibid: 18.
84 Ibid.
85 Ibid.
86 In *The Book of Pleasure*, Spare writes with regard to the Death Posture: 'Let him practise it daily, accordingly, till he arrives at the centre of desire.' loc.cit:19.
87 F.W. Letchford, *Inferno to Zos*, loc.cit:119.
88 The first publication of one of Spare's pictographic magical sigils appears in the illustration 'Existence', included in *A Book of Satyrs*, 1907. The illustration itself is dated 1906 and also includes the motif of the vulture-head, one of Spare's symbols for Kia. However, as Robert Ansell has

pointed out in a personal communication to the author (June 2007), sigils do not appear in Spare's art throughout his career. For the most part they are a feature of his art between 1909 and 1912, and much later, between 1948 and 1956.

89 As Gavin Semple astutely observes, 'A sigillic language enables the sorcerer to think in symbols... allowing consciousness to pervade hitherto occluded regions; the sigil acts as a "courier" in the transference across the threshold.' See G.W. Semple, *Zos-Kia: An Introductory Essay on the Art and Sorcery of Austin Osman Spare*, Fulgur, London 1995: 33.

90 A.O. Spare, 'Mind to Mind and How' in *Two Tracts on Cartomancy*, Fulgur, London 1997: 32.

91 A.O. Spare, *The Book of Pleasure (Self-Love): The Psychology of Ecstasy*, loc.cit: 48.

92 Gavin W. Semple's edition of Spare's *Two Tracts on Cartomancy* (Fulgur, London 1997) contains a text written by Spare himself. It is titled *Mind to Mind and How* 'by a Sorcerer', and makes reference to the rationale underpinning Spare's magic of Zos/Kia: 'The law of sorcery is its own law, using sympathetic symbols' (p. 31).

93 According to Kenneth Grant, Spare regarded elementals as a 'dissociated part of the subconsciousness'. See K.Grant, *Images and Oracles of Austin Spare*, loc cit: 22. Gavin Semple similarly defines 'elemental automata' as 'residual fragments of consciousness, independent and motivated within a specific field of activity and influence. Once rendered perceptible these are delegated by the sorcerer to new functions according to intent.' See G.W. Semple, *Zos-Kia: An Introductory Essay on the Art and Sorcery of Austin Osman Spare*, Fulgur, London 1995: 48.

94 In his introduction to the 1975 facsmile reprint of *The Book of Pleasure* (93 Publishing, Quebec) Kenneth Grant writes: 'Towards the end of his life, when Spare lived more or less reclusively in a Dickensian South London slum, he was asked whether he regretted his lonely existence. "Lonely!," he exclaimed, and with a sweep of his arm he indicated the host of unseen elementals and familiar spirits that were his constant companions; he had but to turn his head to catch a fleeting glimpse of their subtle presences.'

95 G.W. Semple, 'A Few Leaves from the Devil's Picture Book' in A.O. Spare, *Two Tracts on Cartomancy*, Fulgur, London 1997:21.

96 Cornelius Agrippa (1486-1535) first published his text in 1533 and an English translation appeared in 1651. A revised edition of Book One ('Natural Magic') of *Occult Philosophy or Magic*, edited by Willis F. Whitehead, was published in 1897 and would have been accessible to Spare. This particular edition was subsequently reissued by Aquarian Press, London, in 1971. Agrippa's so-called *Fourth Book of Occult*

Philosophy was issued as a limited-edition facsimile reprint by Askin Publishers, London in 1978.
97   G.W. Semple, ' A Few Leaves from the Devil's Picture Book', loc.cit:21.
98   See H.C. Agrippa, *Three Books of Occult Philosophy or Magic* [1533], ed. W.F. Whitehead, Aquarian Press, London 1971: 113.
99   Ibid.
100 A.O. Spare, *The Book of Pleasure (Self-Love): The Psychology of Ecstasy*, loc.cit: 50.
101 Exhaustion could be brought about in a variety of ways. Spare cites 'Mantras and Posture, Women and Wine, Tennis, and the playing of Patience, or by walking and concentration on the Sigil etc. etc.' See A.O. Spare, *The Book of Pleasure (Self-Love): The Psychology of Ecstasy*, loc. cit: 51.
102 Ibid.
103 Ibid: 45.
104 For Kenneth Grant's account of atavistic resurgence see *Man, Myth and Magic*, vol. 6, Marshall Cavendish, London 1970 and N. Drury and S. Skinner, *The Search for Abraxas*, London 1972: 66.
105 The pastel portrait *Elemental Materialisation* was reproduced in colour as Plate 17 in the gallery catalogue *Austin Osman Spare 1886-1956: The Divine Draughtsman*, prepared by Geraldine Beskin and John Bonner to coincide with an exhibition of Spare's works at the Morley Gallery, London 1987. The pastel is owned by Jimmy Page, guitarist with the well-known rock-group Led Zeppelin.
106 K. Grant, *Images and Oracles of Austin Osman Spare*, loc.cit: 37.
107 Kenneth Grant writes in his introduction to Spare's *Book of Zos vel Thanatos*: 'Spares's relationship to the Surrealist Movement, which he claims to have anticipated by at least a decade, remains to be explained. The Movement was a phenomenon of major occult importance. It not only explored and explicated the creative potential of the subconscious, it also influenced powerfully the direction of the Arts, bringing to the fore the subjective treatment of external 'reality'. The Movement was, of course, intimately related to the researches of Freud, whose exploration of subconscious mechanisms fired the Surrealists to experiment with the method of 'free association'. Freud's *The Interpretation of Dreams* was first published in English translation in 1913, the year in which *The Book of Pleasure* (1909-1913) appeared. The latter showed that Spare's knowledge of the predominating role of the Subconsciousness in Art and Sorcery had already matured and was well in place by the time his book appeared.' See K.and S. Grant, *Zos Speaks! : Encounters with Austin Osman Spare*, loc cit: 158.
108 An observation forwarded by Robert Ansell, June 2007.

109 A.O. Spare, *The Book of Pleasure (Self-Love): The Psychology of Ecstasy*, loc.cit: 47.
110 G.W. Semple, *Zos-Kia: An Introductory Essay on the Art and Sorcery of Austin Osman Spare*, loc cit: 31.
111 A.O. Spare, *The Logomachy of Zos*, an unpublished manuscript quoted in G.W. Semple, *Zos-Kia: An Introductory Essay on the Art and Sorcery of Austin Osman Spare*, loc.cit: 31.
112 F.W. Letchford, *Inferno to Zos*, loc cit: 161-163.
113 G.W. Semple, *Zos-Kia: An Introductory Essay on the Art and Sorcery of Austin Osman Spare*, loc.cit: 37.
114 The article appeared in issue no.1, volume 1 of *Form*, April 1916, and was re-published in a facsmile edition by 93 Publishing, South Stukely, Montreal, in 1979, in an edition of 250 copies.
115 Ibid.
116 I. Law, introduction to A.O.Spare, *A Book of Automatic Drawing*, Catalpa Press, London 1972.
117 See R. Ansell, introduction to A.O.Spare, *The Book of Ugly Ecstasy*, Fulgur, London 1996.
118 A.O. Spare, *The Witches' Sabbath*, Fulgur, London 1992:5.
119 R. Ansell, introduction to A.O.Spare, *The Book of Ugly Ecstasy*, loc cit.
120 Ibid.
121 Ibid.
122 For information on Norton's magical relationships with Greenlees and Goossens see N. Drury, *Homage to Pan, the life, art and sex magic of Rosaleen Norton*, Creation Oneiros, London and Washington DC, 2009.
123 D. Salter, 'The Strange Case of Sir Eugene and the Witch', *Good Weekend/Sydney Morning Herald*, Sydney, 3 July 1999: 17.
124 Norton also received more serious critiques of her visionary art and pagan symbolism in small literary magazines like *Pertinent* and *Arna* but these were specialist publications with low printruns and did not reach the mainstream Australian public.
125 M. Johnson, 'The Witch of Kings Cross: Rosaleen Norton and the Australian Media', conference presentation, Symbiosis: Institute for Comparative Studies in Science, Myth, Magic and Folklore, University of Newcastle, 2002.
126 Ibid: 1.
127 D. Cahill, G. Bouma, H. Dellal and M. Leahy, *Religion, Cultural Diversity and Safeguarding Australia*, Australian Multicultural Foundation, Melbourne 2004: 41.
128 Norton identifies Eloi as such in her unpublished notes that were drawn up and presented to Walter Glover when she was selecting drawings for inclusion in *The Art of Rosaleen Norton*. These notes are now in my

possession.
129 In his autobiographical work, *Memories, Dreams, Reflections*, Jung refers to the mandala as the symbol of individuation : '...the mandala is the centre. It is the exponent of all paths. It is the path to the centre, to individuation....the goal of psychic development is the self.' See C.G. Jung, *Memories, Dreams, Reflections*, Collins / Routledge & Kegan Paul, London 1963: 222.
130 Of the 48 works reproduced in *Supplement to The Art of Rosaleen Norton*, 28 were included in the exhibition at Exiles Gallery, 1-7 October 1982.
131 See T. Owen and D. Dickson, *High Art: A History of the Psychedelic Poster*, Sanctuary Publishing, London 1999.
132 S.L. MacGregor Mathers (trs.), *Goetia: the Lesser Key of Solomon*, De Laurence Scott & Co., Chicago 1916: 33.
133 In *The Book of Pleasure* Spare writes: 'Magical obsession is that state when the mind is illuminated by sub-conscious activity evoked voluntarily by formula at our own time, etc. for inspiration. It is the condition of genius.' A.O. Spare, *The Book of Pleasure*, London 1913: 41.
134 Spare appears to admit this in *The Book of Pleasure* when he writes: 'Depending on its degree of intensity and resistance shown at some time or another, the Ego has or has not knowledge of the obsession; *always is its expression autonomous, divorced from personal control.*' [my emphasis in italics] See A.O. Spare, *The Book of Pleasure*, loc. cit: 41.
135 'Possession' is a term used in both anthropological and esoteric literature to describe a situation where a trance medium believes he or she has become 'possessed' by a spirit or discarnate entity which then takes over aspects of the personality either totally or in part, and appears to operate independently of the person concerned. Spirit possession is a feature of voodoo and modern spiritualism.
136 A claim supported by the distinguished British surrealist, Ithell Colquhuon: note to the author from Robert Ansell, June 2007.
137 A.O. Spare, *The Logomachy of Zos*, in K. and S. Grant, *Zos Speaks! : Encounters with Austin Osman Spare*, Fulgur, London 1998: 184
138 Ibid: 169.
139 Ibid: 168.
140 G.W. Semple, *Zos-Kia: An Introductory Essay on the Art and Sorcery of Austin Osman Spare*, Fulgur, London 1995: 26.
141 A.O. Spare, *The Logomachy of Zos*, loc.cit: 172.
142 Spare writes: 'I believe in the Eternity of the Ego whether I am carnate, discarnate, reincarnate or whatever metamorphosis I suffer. For I am *change* and forever ultimate, however I may appear.' A.O. Spare, *The*

Living Word of Zos, in K.and S. Grant, *Zos Speaks!: Encounters with Austin Osman Spare*, loc.cit: 172

143 This drawing is *The Adversary*, reproduced as Plate XVI in *The Art of Rosaleen Norton*, loc cit: 47.

144 As Spare notes in *The Logomachy of Zos*, 'My gods have grown with me...they are my potentials.' See A.O. Spare, *The Logomachy of Zos*, loc. cit: 188.

145 M.M. Jungkurth, 'Neither-Neither: Austin Spare and the Underworld', in *Austin Osman Spare: Artist, Occultist, Sensualist*, Beskin Press, London 1999.

15
Nothing is True, Everything is Permitted: Chaos Magics in Britain

Dave Evans

> *There is a race of gnomes, so the story goes*
> *who believe that nothing is possible*
> *and there is a sect of magicians who believe*
> *that everything is* [1]

This chapter discusses some elements of the modern emergence of Chaos magics in Britain,[2] which are a loose affiliated collection of relatively new and ahistorical, post-modernist-inspired occult practices which are derived in part of the works of Aleister Crowley (1875-1947) and Austin Osman Spare (1886-1956). The deliberately emphasised plural term 'magicS' used here should be seen as an umbrella classification for a series of generic, fluid and still evolving magical techniques and modes of thought, in much the same way that 'science' is not a subject itself, but a generic term for many sub-disciplines that have some common factors but disparate technical aspects. Much of the work of Spare survives due to the publishing efforts of the magician Kenneth Grant (1924-2011) [3] who was also Crowley's secretary in the last years of his life, so he is also partially responsible for the early *post mortem* publication of much of Crowley's writings.

What's in a Name?

'Chaos magic' is a term subjectively redolent with intrigue and veiled threat, possibly only outdone in perceived sinister negativity by the sobriquet of 'Satanist' in many magical circles.[4] However while there is an element that some Chaos practitioners will indeed gleefully play on any emotional discomfort caused to those with less flexible attitudes by the term, and will experience a deliberate frisson gained by having a 'cool name' for what they do, the deeper meanings are more Taoist and amoral in scope. Chaos is seen as a primordial void, from which existence (and all magic) springs, thus chaos magic can tap into this source, and the notion takes any anthropomorphised godform out of the equation. It also crucially allows control and utter responsibility by the individual magician for what they do, since 'if there is no god, god cannot be blamed if the magic doesn't work'.

Chaos mathematics is also relevant—as in the oft-cited 'Butterfly Effect', for example [5]—although there are averages and medians in the weather, accurate and precise scientific forecasting is made most difficult due to seemingly random tiny variations, which accumulate and influence the future development of a weather system. From this comes the comment to the effect that 'a butterfly flapping its wings in Africa can be the start of a hurricane in America', as every hurricane has to start with a tiny increase in velocity of the air *somewhere*. It is precisely this metaphor of 'small beginnings' that magicians such as the founder of chaos (and considered to be the 'Pope' of the movement) Peter J. Carroll (1953-) regard as easier to influence with magic, in order to have larger ultimate effects in the world: 'it is sometimes possible to bring about the required coincidence by the direct intervention of the will provided that this does not put too great a strain on the universe.'[6]

What is It?

Chaos magic seems to be largely ahistorical and acultural, since it is non-doctrinal and Chaos practitioners are free to delve into a multiplicity of (often highly contradictory and sometimes certainly fictional) sources for ritual inspiration, therefore it is more of an attitude or a philosophy than a recognisable or categorisable belief system *per se*. Thus common ground between practitioners is often rather scarce and importantly the methods described also change far more rapidly over time than other neopagan magical practices. Chaos is influenced by post-modernist ideas of continual change and fluidity, and as described by the magician and author Phil Hine (whose work on Tantra appears elsewhere in this volume), Chaos 'breaks with the modernist idea of progress and historical continuity and ... ransacks all available cultures and time zones' [7] and the techniques used are often highly eclectic, if not sometimes completely contradictory. Hine believes that: 'a great deal of occult memes ... were spawned in the heyday of the Theosophical Society.'[8] That society was most active, or at least most influential in the latter half of the nineteenth century however chaos aims to sweep much of this aside in a drive to modernise the field, as occult writer Nadine Gerkowska remarks:

> ... *approaches of the 19th Century... are not just restrictive, but obsolete... simply because the language and conceptual frames of reference from much of the second millennium have evolved so much, that they are now far removed from gestalts of the last few decades.*[9]

This is an excellent point, since much else from the same period such as the science, medicine, politics and morality has moved on considerably and in many cases been superseded by new ideas or new technology.[10]

It should be no surprise that magic has followed suit—only that it took so long to do so. Hine (again) critically writes of an 'ancient' magical grimoire:

> *Many magical books are dated... in the* Lesser Key of Solomon *... there are demons who specialise in divining the fate of Kings... but you won't find any demons whose provenance relates to debugging a COBOL program or finding lost contact lenses* [11].

Due to the work of various chaos magicians there are now rituals in existence to call upon newly created or modified entities which can allegedly perform such modern tasks.

Academic Approaches

An accurate and comprehensive academic perspective of Chaos has yet to be written,[12] and this act may not yet be possible. Some of the very many problems for the researcher in this very new area are that due to the novel subject and the varied, often contradictory strands within it there are no truly authoritative books on the subject. In studying any other religious belief, spiritual movement or sacred practice there will be an extant 'holy book' (or two), but one reason for the absence of a definitive and authoritative book on Chaos is that it is very much a practical approach rather than relying on expansion of, or preservation of, textual dogma. As Phil Hine points out the major Chaos group the IOT (*Illuminates of*

Thanateros) was founded on the notions of 'doing' magic, rather than just reading about it.[13] When identifying religious adherents, each can be more or less easily identified by particular behaviours they undertake or the symbols they wear (be that clothing, imagery or particular glyphs) or beliefs they hold. These will be different to other groups. For example, strict Muslims can be differentiated from Orthodox Jews by appearance, diet, holy days, holy books, sacred symbols etc. In Chaos magic this is simply not the case—there is no sacred text accepted by all and the sheer eclecticism of behavior and the transience of technique makes it extremely difficult to confidently label *anyone* as a Chaos magician.[14]

Perhaps the only specific imagery for Chaos magic seems to be influenced by a fictional author, the Briton Michael Moorcock (1939-) whose numerous science-fiction/fantasy novels have as their common thread a magical battle of order against chaos. The forces of Chaos in the novels are signified by an 8-pointed star, which has now become a ubiquitous logo of Chaos magicians, as in Figure 1, below.

Figure 1: the Chaos star symbol used by Chaos magicians, derived from the fiction of Michael Moorcock

Anyone bearing or wearing this symbol should not however automatically be considered to be a Chaos magician since the logo has been taken up by various rock groups and so it appears on many more T-shirts and other items of merchandise than would correlate with the numbers of Chaos magicians in existence at any time, in the same way that the plethora of inverted crosses and inverted pentacles exhibited as jewellery and clothing logos by the members of various musical subcultures do not indicate a large number of Satanists and suchlike. It is merely a distracting epiphenomenon of yet another rock band having co-opted a 'scary-looking symbol' in an attempt to shock or attract some *kudos*, while usually having no occult leaning whatsoever. The Chaos magicians themselves will often resist the label simply because being categorised *at all* gives an aura of permanence, which may not be correct, or desired.

This absence of a set and thus accessible, definable *schema* behind Chaos magic both across individuals and within individuals over time and the often rapid changes of perspective cause problems in studying Chaos academically—even at a micro-historical level. In the process of developing a personal magical system the Chaote changes immeasurably and if, as Peter Carroll wrote, 'You cannot be said to possess a personality until you are able to manipulate it or discard it at will'[15] then it therefore is most unlikely that very much accurate, coherent and consistent personal history will be preserved unscathed during such a process. As the modern magician and author 'Jaq Hawkins'[16] points out, Chaos

> *leaves the practitioner free to establish his/her own ideas of method, ethics and appropriate uses of magic…it … transcends tradition and dogma…any and all methods are allowed and encouraged, the only requirement is that it works*[17].

For this reason chaos is also known as 'results magic'. Similarly the Chaos pioneer Ray Sherwin wrote:

> *The individual should experiment with as many techniques as he can find or invent in order to immediately discard those which are obviously not suitable… he can then concentrate his attention on the mastery of the remaining techniques.*[18]

Chaos magic is something that has fully embraced new technology since the primordial chaotic void can also be represented by the infinite possibilities of the internet, as well as allowing rapid promulgation of ideas as ebooks and web postings. Groups working in cyberspace include a loosely affiliated cabal called the z-cluster (zee cluster)[19] who originated in New Orleans but now have worldwide membership and often only meet in virtual space to perform rituals. There are several other internet-only or internet-mainly groups. Other Chaos magicians have embraced new technology in a multitude of forms including devising rites using such 'non-traditional' equipment as cell phones and television screens,[20] 'Techno-paganism' is the subject of a separate chapter in this volume by Nevill Drury. Therefore any credible researches into this area must be of a micro-historical and often individual nature, with the investigator engaging in constant internal reflections, putting in place checks and balances since the work involves talking to people possessed of often tangled narratives, competing agendas and hugely disparate practices. There will also be considerable trawling through competing individual narratives in magazines, correspondence and on websites. In addition, by their very nature Chaos magicians (also known as Chaotes) are fond of deception, playing with the meanings of words and demolishing the nature of belief, which means that the information they sometimes provide (even about themselves) is often skewed and open to academic suspicion. Also they simply construct or co-opt convenient narratives when it suits their purposes—as the Chaos magician Phil Hine writes, in the sphere of occult history it is almost a given that occultists will trawl backwards in time 'selectively editing, and sometimes *fabricating evidence* to support particular models and propositions'.[21] Another problem in historical research in this area is the identification and veracity of sources. For example *The Cardinal Rites of Chaos*[22] was a book published in the 1980s that (falsely) claimed a 1960s genesis of some techniques that figure in current Chaos magic. However, the author 'Paula Pagani' is a pseudonym of the Chaos pioneer Ray Sherwin, who, when writing as Sherwin, not surprisingly reviewed 'Pagani's' book (his own) very favourably in an issue of the IOT in-house journal *Chaos International*.[23]

In addition, one very influential author who is often referred to as the 'Patron Saint of Chaos magic'—Lionel Snell—has published under at least six pseudonyms as well as his 'real' name,[24] and he is far from the only Chaos writer to have more than one publishing or online identity. Thus it is not always easily ascertainable *who is who*, let alone *how many* writers there are in the field. It also means that on researching any particular topic it is difficult to verify if one has actually encountered several different authors expressing true philosophical or practical accord or if it is simply the same author paraphrasing themself under two or more pen names, in order to bolster their own perspective or, perversely, arguing with 'themselves' under different sign-in identities in online *fora* in order to draw attention to their thoughts.

The findings of any such individual microhistorical survey may not then be truly (or in some cases, even remotely) generalisable to any larger population of Chaos magicians. However it is probable that a series of intersecting meta-studies of various competing micro-histories of individuals and small groups within a generic assembly of Chaos magicS could be produced. *Eventually*. The evolution of Chaos methods and the changing personalities who are considered important is also a rapid process thus any academic claim to producing a full report on Chaos magics written in the early 21st century will be possibly be out-dated even by the time it is printed; at present the best we can hope for is a coherent collection of 'snapshots', of which this is one.

Chaos and Punk

In common with many 'challenging new movements' (in any field) Chaotes are often seen by their contemporaries as anarchists or dangerously worrying/threatening revolutionaries. A parallel has been identified between the philosophies and effects of early Chaos magic and the 'Punk' movement in fashion, music and the general *anomie* and societal disaffection of youth.[25] All of these appeared in Western society at around the same time, in the late

1970s, and both the Punks and the Chaotes revolted against the perceived complacency inherent in the current order or 'the system' and in the process caused considerable dismay. However the commonly-voiced soundbyte 'Chaos and Punk arose together and due to each other'—or variations thereof—is a concept that many commentators recycle without any particular evidence to support that view. Chaos theory mathematics was indeed very popular among the intelligentsia at the time, and Punk was certainly a major cultural phenomenon in London, where Chaos magic also partly arose. However it was more a correlation of proximity and era than a causal issue. Many leading lights in early Chaos magic were either stereotypical 'hippies' who were not musically or artistically influenced by Punk or they were Oxbridge scholars and so purely on a social class level thus less likely to be Punks from the outset. The parallel emergence and causal link is perhaps best seen as a convenient meme with some slight element of truth within it. However, since like so many complicated causalities (such as how did World War Two start?) there is no one-line answer.

It should also be remarked that Punk itself was not entirely new, being in many ways a reprise of some of the Dadaist notions of clashing of style, intention to cause outrage and offence rather than aesthetic appreciation and the subversion of authority which had arisen in artistic circles some six decades earlier, and this was to an extent simply rebranded by one of the arch-manipulators of the punk movement, Malcolm MacLaren, who was among other things the manager of the infamous band, The Sex Pistols[26].

Causal Connections

Another academic analytical problem is that of establishing direction of influence. Many new magical techniques seem to have become very popular (or become popular again after a period of decline) at around the same time as chaos magic appeared. The most immediate question is did the broadening appeal of Chaos magic create an environment where other techniques could arise (or be rediscovered) more freely, or did these techniques (such as modern revivals/re-creations of shamanism and western Tantra, as Phil Hine discusses elsewhere in this volume) blend into Chaos, having been revived by Chaos magicians who were in a constant global search for new techniques to sample and to master? Or is the apparent correlation simply that, a coincidence, and acausal in either direction, arising at a time of increased information transfer due to the Internet, etc? It should be remarked that there has always been intermingling of method across neopagan groups, for example the appearance of Tantric elements in Wicca.[27] It is not the case that Chaotes have caused this, more that they have probably exponentially increased the cross-fertilisation.

It is perhaps most likely that Chaos allowed an environment in which experimentation was encouraged more, and among modern occultists it is more often the Chaotes who demonstrate the greater ability to be free thinkers, to be willing to try anything, to attempt to learn more than one belief system at once and to adapt to fluid, challenging and non-linear modes of thinking.

Histories

Jaq Hawkins' (a magician rather than a historian) makes a very creditable attempt at both a brief history of Chaos and an explanation of its methods[28] and provides a probably accurate approximate date (the late 1970s) for when Chaos magic started. She also offers an outline of the history of perhaps the most historically significant Chaos magic group, the *Illuminates of Thanateros* (IOT) and general Chaos magic, but of necessity her short book omits large areas that were influential. It is likely that only with the passage of time and release of privately-held archives that more coherent and useful information will come to light. Hawkins indicates 1970s London and Leeds as the seed beds of Chaos magic; it was in the former location where a loose collective of occultists known as the *Stoke Newington Sorcerers* were in operation, who were disillusioned with what they saw as a staid, stifling and non-progressive environment of 'traditional' magical groups. It is here that Peter Carroll first made his name. Carroll wrote *Liber Null*,[29] arguably the first practitioner-oriented Chaos magic book, which was published in a small print run in 1978, with Ray Sherwin's similar-themed *Book of Results*[30] following soon after. Carroll travelled the world in the late 1970s, forming the short-lived *Church of Chaos* in Australia in 1980.[31] The first British IOT group was formed in Yorkshire soon after, ceasing operation in 1982 after seeding several splinter groups. There have been several notable Chaos groups, for example *The Circle of Chaos* formed in 1984 by Dave Lee [32] and others, lasting approximately three years,[33] during which time the sporadic print journal of the IOT, *Chaos International* [34] currently edited by Ian Read was founded. It has at present run to over 25 issues but may now be a lapsed title.

The geographical element is puzzling. London, Leeds and Bristol seem for some reason to be the hotbeds but why not London, Liverpool and Edinburgh? The Leeds area of Britain is significant as a focus of Chaos magic at least in part due to the proximity of the *Sorcerers Apprentice* occult shop [35] and publishing house who were early champions of the Chaos approaches. The proprietor 'Frater Marabas' (Chris Bray) claims to be one of three founders of the Chaos movement, although this is extremely hard to verify. Carroll ran the *Bristol CHAOS Temple* from 1982-1991, when he entered 'magical retirement'.[36] This was broken by his publishing *Liber Kaos* in 1992 and *PsyberMagick* [37] in 1995, and he is still producing books, magazine articles and compact discs on the subject, teaching online and running a website [38] dealing in part with the magical application of physics.

Chaos is characterised by many transient small groups which form, splinter and reform, often spawning short-lived small circulation magazines about their practices.[39] The fledgling IOT was described by Carroll as 'rarely more than a loose correspondence network and a few people meeting for rituals'[40] but it now comprises a more modern form, having weathered severe internecine conflicts (including the resignation of Carroll during a struggle for leadership with a German contingent) and variable membership numbers, being now a larger international order, with a few hundred members in Europe, the Americas, Africa and the far East. Many significant modern magical writers are or have been members of this group.

Peter Carroll wrote in the late 1970s: 'The IOT continues a tradition perhaps seven thousand years old, yet the Order...has no history.'[41] In 2002 a brief 'history' of the IOT appeared online [42] containing numerous mind games in a book claiming to be 'the truth about the IOT' when to a large extent it simply adds more fuel to the mythic smokescreen. Such semantic games and/or disingenuity are not the sole province of Chaos magicians, for example Aleister Crowley's *Book of Lies* (a selection of mystical aphorisms) published around a century ago was subtitled 'also falsely called breaks...'[43] implying that the title of 'Lies' is itself a lie, and therefore the book reveals various arcane truths. In addition, many modern witches indulge in spurious claims of hereditary provenance for their activities, purely to give themselves some apparent legitimacy, when often they are practising a form of Wicca that is only a few decades old. I have heard of one priestess who calls herself a '14th Generation Witch'; however what this actually means is that *her teacher was initiated by someone who was initiated by someone who*... with 13 more names leading back to Gerald Gardner, the founder of modern Wicca, and so the process can only have occupied 60 years, not fourteen family generations, as the deliberately illegitimate use of the language implies.[44] However, Chaotes excel at such semantic contortions. In 2002 Peter Carroll (supposedly by then long 'retired' from magic) warned me, in response to a research enquiry letter I sent to him: 'Don't waste your life and your academic talents on this muck (Chaos). It's all a total fraud and I should know by now!'[45] However, Carroll's own Chaos magical website [46] was updated with an article written by him less than two months before this comment was made. Less than a month after his letter to me a compact disc, including lectures and a guided magical working commentary, was released under his name [47] and his most recent book *Apophenion* was published in late 2008.[48] It has presumably been in the writing process for some time because it is a complex tome. Carroll has also been teaching the subject online for several years since his comment to me,[49] so as he seems to be still intimately involved with Chaos magic his remarks to me are best appreciated as some kind of Zen humour rather than truly accurate.

Among other notable Chaos groups, *Thee Temple Ov Psychick Youth* (TOPY) [50] were a 'fusion' organisation, creating a crossover of experimental 'industrial' music with linguistic mangling (see their name) and Chaos magical philosophy and practice. The police raided their premises in the 1980s under suspicion of finding video footage of child abuse. It was actually based on misguided perspectives of music videotapes which had been screened on mainstream television five years earlier without protest. However TOPY leader Genesis P. Orridge (Neil Megson, 1950 -) was compelled to leave the UK during the consequent media witch hunt. A subsequent incarnation of TOPY continues, very loosely, as a magical group online without the leadership of Orridge.[51]

Another loose Chaos collective from the 1980s, the *Lincoln Order of Neuromancers* (L.O.O.N), favoured situationist magical workings outside any social norms, for example, a L.O.O.N. banishing ritual comprises simply shouting 'Fuck off you bastards!' at whichever non-human entities were required to depart.[52] Although it has nothing of 'traditional' magical methods [53] it would most likely have a striking effect of banishment, and be extremely amusing as a method of transgression of 'traditional' magical techniques. Humour is an important factor in carnival and misrule and it is not coincidental that 'banishing with laughter' has become a Chaos magical ritual technique.

Many Chaotes do not belong to any kind of group or order, and develop their own individual methods, which potential plethora of individual microhistories can make the academic study and contextualising of their activities difficult. All other magical and mystical approaches found in Britain rely on some form of 'traditional' underpinning to give the notion of authority, often derived from an 'appeal to the power of antiquity' (as discussed with the 14th generation witch above) or that is inferred by any practice being called 'traditional' (even if this is a comparatively recently manufactured tradition such as modern Druidry),[54] and from which an academic starting point can be derived. One liberating bonus of Chaos magic (for the participant) is the freedom from the influence of such dogmatic texts and atmospheres.

What is striking about Chaos is the individual role. Aside from a number of relatively small and often transient groups, the variety of possible practices within chaos magic allows and indeed encourages solo work. It is likely that there are many Chaos magicians who have never been members of a group, nor discussed or published any of their work at all (or if they have, it has been in one of the many small circulation and short-lived Chaos magazines, or on transient websites or newsgroups). Thus is it often purely luck for the academic researcher to discover anything about the numbers, or the work of many Chaos magicians.

Looking at Chaos from the larger perspective of historical change it may be useful to parallel scientific and magical views in different periods of the last one hundred years or so. Around 1910 Freud's psychoanalysis (based on sexuality) was the dominant paradigm while the sex magick of Aleister Crowley was in the vanguard of occultism. Later, Jungian psychology was in the forefront of psychology at roughly the same time as his theories of archetypes were adopted by the 1960s-1970s pagan revival (which was hugely 'psychologised', in parts).[55] The 'new broom; sweeping clean' of Chaos magic has arisen at the same time as post-modernism is deconstructing history, culture, art and philosophy while the new 'indeterminacy' of quantum physics is unravelling science at every level and the 'magical' power of words is being exploited by the behavioural modification techniques of Neuro-Linguistic Programming (NLP). All of it is sweeping aside many old models of our world in wholesale fashion. *Nothing is true...*

The careful reader may notice much use of the male personal pronoun among the predominantly male Chaos writers, and a dearth of female names cited as sources or collaborators. For all the eclecticism and catch-all attitude which propagates among Chaotes there is a singular gap in the ranks for notable female Chaos magicians. Jaq Hawkins is possibly the most notable example (unless there are others hiding behind 'male' pseudonyms?) and it is not immediately obvious why this should be the case, other than it being a reflection of the broad gender imbalance in the breadth of modern magic, which has arguably always been male-dominated. Significant empowered female actors are uncommon. However in Wicca the reverse is the case, with very major female figures such as Doreen Valiente, Janet Farrar, Maxine Sanders and Starhawk being both easy to name and forming the vanguard of the movement, since it is 'goddess-based' and perhaps thus more amenable to female leadership—the reader is referred to the section in this volume on *Wicca and the Sacred Earth* for more information on this area.

Philosophies

Chaos magic makes much use of manipulating beliefs. Cultural and personal beliefs have always had a large part in shaping personal reality—for example, early-modern Catholic Spanish prophets experienced sights of Saints and the Virgin Mary, while in the same time-period and only a few hundred miles north, Lutheran Protestant seers received angelic visions. The nature of the experience followed the dominant religious paradigm during times of conflict and fluid boundaries, so when a territory changed politico-religious hands the styles of visions rapidly changed in parallel with incoming beliefs,[56] which beliefs, as Phil Hine writes, 'structure reality. If you believe in faeries it's much more likely that you're going to be able to see them...' [57] Hine adds:

> *Some people might argue that the older a Mythic cycle is, the more powerful it is. This isn't necessarily true though... old myths have very often been messed about with. Much depends on who's writing them down, and from what angle—myths can be bent by politics.* [58]

Hine also maintains that following the globalisation of the information formerly held in different world cultures, and accelerating transfer and sharing of that information due to the Internet, etc., we are now no longer 'psychically bound to our cultural landscape; we can choose from myriad shards of belief, from the wisdom based on historical traditions, to the myths of rehashed/recovered knowledge.' [59]

The older and more 'traditional' branches of occultism have raised various 'theological' objections to Chaos magic. These are based on the breadth of often seemingly contradictory material that can be, and is, employed and the 'heretical' application of god forms that 'aren't real'. However, pragmatic Chaotes such as Phil Hine hold that 'what matters is the results ... not the "authenticity" of the system used.' For example, a 'more traditional' ceremonial magician who is invoking a deity taken from (for example) the Egyptian pantheon that is perhaps 3000-4000 years old may be enraged by the actions of another 'less traditional' Chaos magician who uses an invocation to a fabricated deity from a fictional novel published within the last fifty or a hundred years,[60] or from a recent TV show or movie,[61] yet who achieves similarly successful 'magical' results as with the Egyptian ritual. There is ultimately no empirical proof for the existence of either a god-form or an agreed measure of a 'successful invocation'. It is merely a matter of perceived antiquity and cultural hegemony that makes the older deity seem more 'real' and 'valid'. The phenomenon itself also implies that magic is purely in the mind if it can be worked with fictional or even newly-fabricated deities, and so maybe there are no gods and they are merely metaphors—a notion that is profoundly challenging and disturbing to many neopagan witches and magicians who tend to have some kind of theistic underpinning (usually pantheistic) to their practices. The magician Stephen Sennitt, writes here about H.P. Lovecraft's work as it is used by magicians, but his remarks are applicable to all use of 'fiction' in magic:

> That a ... 'fictional' mythos can be utilised with such magickal expediency is ... surprising ... to some sceptics... (but) remember ... that even accepted 'facts' have no other purpose than to model reality... accepted 'fiction' can also model reality if it is understood that, like all human-created paradigms, these things have no ultimate meaning in themselves. [62]

Thus Chaotes have plundered the vaults of modern media and cultural memory, devising magical rituals using the motion picture comedians, the Marx Brothers,[63] characters from children's TV programmes (for example *The Teletubbies*[64] and *The Magic Roundabout*[65]) and characters or themes from many films. As Lionel Snell wrote:

> Having ritually invoked not just the great gods of our elders but also Dracula, Mickey Mouse, Hannibal Lecter, Batman (no archetype too vile, trivial or outlandish) I am capable of enjoying almost anything... once I have set my mind to it. [66]

Such 'irreverence' in magic is nothing new, however. In the 1920s Aleister Crowley had experimented with reading profound spiritual messages into children's' nursery rhymes, such as *'Hickory, Dickory, Dock'*.[67] Hine remarks that there is also an illusion in the novelty. However, since 'much of what we see served up on the silver screen is powerful mythic images and situations, repackaged for modern tastes,'[68] for example, 'more people are familiar with the universe of *Star Trek* than with any of the mystery religions.'[69] Many of the plots in *Star Trek* are arguably thematic restatements of such cultural motifs as the Greek myths in any case. Thus it makes perfect sense for the Chaote to tap into those cultural motifs which are historically (for the modern period) more well-known, most accessible and with which people are perhaps more comfortable, than distant and often unfamiliar god-forms. Hine also wrote:

> ...the Mythic world ... is the realm of metaphor and symbol; the larger-than life world of theatre, fantasy, legend and television culture... our ancestors had the deeds of heroes and goddesses, while we have the daily diet of film and television soaps.[70]

The philosopher Karl Popper (1902-1994) derived the so-called Falsification method of philosophical and scientific enquiry after he realised that one cannot 'prove' anything absolutely.[71] All one can do is support a notion by being unable to find contrary evidence, or fail to support a notion by falsifying the logic or assumptions behind it. However as the magician and occult philosopher Lionel Snell wrote, the Chaos magician working with any magical theory should not seek to disprove it as one would with a scientific theory, but to see if you can convince yourself that it is true by acting as if it were true. If this results in the theory 'working', then you rejoice in it as a practical tool. What you do not do is assume... it must be 'true' in any significant sense.[72]

The Chaos approach may seem at first glance to be a convenient or lazy sidestepping of difficult or insoluble philosophical questions and an utter disregard for scientific method (on which most modern academic study is based). However, many of the initial players in Chaos magic were university graduates in 'hard science' subjects such as chemistry, psychology, geology etc, or those requiring significant grasp of complex philosophies, such as theology[73] including Snell, a Cambridge graduate and former Eton mathematics tutor,[74] so they knew Popper inside out but simply chose to subvert the methods. Thus any simplistic labelling of leading Chaotes as naïve or in any way ill-educated, or irrational would be erroneous, insulting and based on poor research. It would be more accurate to infer that they have developed a philosophical system that works, for them, rather than simply chosen to remain within the confines of one of the more (from their perspective) 'limited' magical or mundane world systems.

This Chaos approach may also be seen as a mere restatement of the quote widely attributed to the prolific French writer and philosopher 'Voltaire' (François-Marie Arouet, 1694-1778) that 'If God did not exist it would be necessary to invent him.'[75] However in Chaos theory this is just another device used as a transient belief, or 'paradigm shift'. The paradigm shift technique is used magically in such cases where one assumes the existence of non-human entities such as 'gods' and 'demons' without having a permanent belief in their existence. Such practices are a modern version of Crowley's methods of serial devotion practice; where complete belief in deity 'A' is used during rituals dedicated to them, until contact is made, then the intention to contact deity A is immediately dropped and deity 'B' is chosen (being from a totally different cultural pantheon from deity 'A'), until contact with them is established, and then all efforts are expended to contact deity 'C', who again comes from a different pantheon, and so on, in order to bolster belief in personal ability to contact entities without propagating any one particular deity-centric belief over any other. The reader should note Crowley's pragmatic instructions to his students:

> *It is spoken of the ... Spirits and Conjurations; of Gods ... and many other things which may or may not exist. It is immaterial whether they exist or not. By doing certain things certain results follow; students are most earnestly warned against attributing objective reality or philosophic validity to any of them.*[76]

Unlike traditional forms of magic, in some Chaos circles the ultimate reality of any 'higher beings' is often totally denied, as highlighted by Phil Hine:

> *In attempting to disentangle contemporary magick from the trappings of religiosity ... advocates of the Chaos Current have taken up a pretty hard line... on ... mysticism... while it is permissible to applaud Crowley's practical magick, a hard-line 'Carrollian' chaoist is likely to deplore (Crowley's) mystical writing.*[77]

Although a relatively new movement, Chaos has a robust philosophical underpinning. The rationale behind the movement can perhaps best be summarised by Lionel Snell: 'If you are thinking of adopting a belief you can choose a famous one, or a cranky one... yet most seductive is to invent your own system of beliefs. There are of course no rules for this.'[78] The orthodox academic study of this area being intrinsically rule-driven so far as methodology and disciplinary considerations are concerned, is thus utterly hamstrung. A prime entry criterion for the IOT given in their own introductory manual is that 'the candidate has proven to be open-minded and ... independent and free of dogmatic beliefs'[79] and on initiation he/she must assert that 'there may be no ultimate truth'.[80] That this potential paradox might *itself* be considered a dogmatic belief is not philosophically addressed in their text. This overt stance causes obvious problems for the historian, because something a Chaos magician tells a researcher on one day 'in all honesty' may be comprehensively refuted or contradicted in a subsequent meeting, and yet still be 'in all honesty'. As Chaos pioneer Ray Sherwin wrote, if asked

> *'What do you believe?' the magician, speaking from the central stillness of himself, should be able to reply, in all honesty, 'I believe nothing.' With such a blank slate at his disposal the magician can then adopt and discard beliefs as he sees fit.*[81]

Regarding the underlying philosophies of Chaos magic, Lionel Snell has written:

> *It is desirable to elect beliefs which offer greater scope for Magical results. The belief that our world is but a shadow play of mighty cosmic forces, which can be ... manipulated by human wisdom—that is a pretty good Magical belief... one of the worst possible Magical beliefs is that our world is made of solid matter shaped only by chance, within which human consciousness ... is mere epiphenomena. Magic-wise it's utter useless crap, and yet it is a belief heavily endorsed by our Scientific culture.*[82]

What matters to *most but not all* Chaotes is simply belief, any belief, which can give impetus to their magical work. Academically this facet makes it hard to group Chaos under the umbrella term of a 'new religious movement' (NRM) since due to the removal of extant deities from the concepts many Chaotes would therefore regard themselves as atheists. As Phil Hine has noted, 'Chaos magic is not an overall belief-system in quite the same way (as) other magical belief-systems.'[83] This use of belief as purely a tool is explained by Snell:

> *A statement such as 'Beyond the realm of the senses there exist*

> *dark forces which govern this world, mighty powers mastered by a Priestly caste before the Fall using secret knowledge' ... (is) terrific stuff, and damn good Magic for those ... able to swallow all that. Unfortunately for Magic... our Scientific education has ... constricted the throat...* [84]

Snell has remarked to me that although he greatly admires the academic scholarship involved in the recent advances in studying occultism, such published advances do make honest belief assumptions for magical purposes much harder for the modern mind to take, for example the work of Ronald Hutton in removing the historical foundations for the belief in the notion of a surviving unchanged witch cult since time immemorial.[85] However,

> *...Chaos magic allows for such modern sensibilities by putting the dogma through a blender...(such as) 'Let us adopt a belief system in which...' and then follows the above crap about dark forces. The word 'paradigm' makes a useful blender for over-Scientific sensibilities.*[86]

It is commonly suggested in conversation with occultists that 'if you ask any two occultists a procedural question you may well get three answers.' These answers would, though, be vaguely similar, or at least traceable back to some common factors or principles. However, as Hine writes, 'If you approach two *Chaos* magicians and ask 'em what they're doing ... you're rarely likely to find much ...consensus.'[87] Apart from a general tendency to draw at times from the works of Aleister Crowley and/or Austin Osman Spare, if there is anything else in which Chaotes are in accord (which itself is debatable) it is that 'Anything goes' so far as method and belief is concerned. This can mean a death for organised—and thus more likely to be *recorded* and researchable—spiritual practices. As Jaq Hawkins writes, the Chaos magician 'may choose to direct his/her belief appropriately to the religion in connection with the ritual, but this still is not the same as *belonging* to the religion,'[88] This should not be seen as some off-hand or casual, faddish alignment, or some superficial play-acting or 'pretending to be wizards'. As Phil Hine writes, regardless of one's personal background, it is complete involvement, immersion and relevant behaviour *in the process* of whatever religious practice being employed that is essential: 'You can selectively believe that a particular theory or model of magical action is true *only* for the duration of a particular ritual or phase of work.'[89]

Nothing is True...
A central tenet of Chaos may derive in part from Akron Daraul—who is not regarded as a 'safe' reliable academic source and may well be the duplicitous and slippery Idries Shah writing under a pen name—but who is someone who has been widely read, thus the meme has spread. Daraul wrote that students in Hasan Ibn Sabah's Assassin Sect (an 11th century group operating in the region that is now Afghanistan) had to pass through nine degrees of initiation which progressively eroded their certainty in all conventional ideas of the world and religion, and 'the ninth and last degree brought the revelation ... that there was no such thing as belief: all that mattered was action.'[90] It is perhaps from this that the modern Chaos maxim, 'Nothing is true, everything is permitted' (attributed to Sabah) has arisen, and which provides the title to my chapter. This seemingly amoral, nihilistic motto of Chaos magic was hugely disturbing to onlookers (such as Wiccans who have their own stated and subjectively positive moral code of 'Harm none...'), since as Phil Hine writes: 'The implied criticism was that "Chaos magicians" would become immoral monsters capable of just about anything.'[91]

How Much Blacker Can It Get?
'Traditional' occultists also object to an overt 'dark' side to Chaos. When it was first published, Peter J. Carroll's practical magic book *Psychonaut* was cautiously reviewed by a respected pagan magazine as being very dangerous for the novice,[92] and his *Liber Null* was described as being ethically dubious.[93] Chaos is acknowledged by its practitioners as being 'not for beginners'. This is largely self-evident from talking to practitioners, since much of the effect of Chaos relies on subverting the *status quo*; thus the beginner in Chaos magic should already know and respect these other methods to an extent first both in order to be able to use them well (the IOT insist on the development of technical excellence in several fields for their initiates) before they can be transgressed *in a meaningful way*. As Hawkins writes, 'I don't care if you break the rules... but you've got to know 'em cold if you're going to break them to good effect.'[94] Another factor decried by traditionalists was that contrary to previously 'accepted wisdom' in occultism, *encyclopaedic* knowledge in a relevant subject before performing a Chaos ritual was unnecessary. Instead, what was required was a willingness to experiment, with greater knowledge perhaps coming afterwards. This is in much the same way that it is not necessary to understand every last mechanical, chemical and electrical nuance of how a motor-car functions in order to get in and drive it from A to B.

The common notion that Chaos magicians might in some way be

unintelligent or deranged by definition [95] is perhaps derived in part—as one magician suggested—from their odd behaviour as viewed by the subjective and staid outsider:

> *The problem with us is that we're mercurial—always swapping styles, attitudes, beliefs... and T-shirts! Normal folk tend to be much more habitual and middle-of-the-road—so to them we appear to be rapidly-changing raving schizophrenics!* [96]

What's Your Poison?

Something else that can differentiate Chaos magicians from other occultists is an honesty on 'psychonautical' levels about their use of various substances to explore 'inner space' for magical purposes. These substances vary from arcane botanical entheogenic specimens such as *Ayahuasca* sourced from a far-off tribal shaman down to the latest consciousness-changing 'designer' drugs, usually bearing a complex acronym such as D-OET-25, and invented in Western pharmacology laboratories. Chaotes are as eclectic in their choices of these as they are in any other method, be that a tribal entheogen that has been in use for centuries or something that was perhaps only synthesised last month. The Chaote Julian Vayne, in particular, has written an entire manual on magical drug uses [97] but stresses that employing any drug like any other technique or tool, is a free choice for the individual, and not compulsory—Chaotes are free to do *anything* (everything is permitted...) including *not* indulging in any drugs, ever.[98] It should also be remarked that it is not a simple distinction of 'Chaos magicians take drugs, other occultists do not.' Putting the legal risks about disclosure of using such substances aside it is far more a case of the Chaotes simply tending towards being more open about what they do.

Conclusion: When Chaos becomes the Norm...

Ironically, as Phil Hine points out, it is the very freedom and eclecticism of Chaos that may be its eventual undoing: 'Chaos Culture lacks an overall vision of progression into a shared future... (it) does not have any stated goal to strive for.'[99] The IOT have been criticised by the Chaos magician and writer Joel Biroco for their 'moribund fiddling around' and for their postmodern catch-all technique that may result in a system that has so much choice available that no progress is made in any direction. As Biroco observes: 'Being ahistorical ... means they are doomed to run on the spot, never swelling in progress.'[100] So, ironically for a postmodernist, progressive 'fractal' movement the structure of Chaos magic may have to revert to a core practice using consistent and proven older techniques in order to survive.

As has been seen, what I am referring to as Chaos magics are a complex, generic subject, open to multiple interpretations and internal divisions. The eclecticism and postmodern approach, plus a multitude of pseudonyms, offers much to practitioners but equally the notion of a 'multiplicity of truths' hugely limits the usefulness of many orthodox academic study approaches, where the study even occurs at all. My initial researches in 2002 met with far more resistance from within the academy than without, and it has been the case that 'white folks doing magic' has been a denigrated area of academic research—although, happily, this is changing.[101] The core maxim 'Nothing is true...' presents problems in ascertaining historical facts, as creative disingenuity and false claims abound, often employed as a part of a temporary belief system/paradigm for magical purposes and sometimes simply for sheer amusement or theatre. Thus modern academic studies must understand anything that is said in these terms, and not necessarily in terms of literal verifiable truth, and the investigator must be emotionally and psychologically bolstered to accommodate nested paradoxes and 'strange loops' of information which if pushed too hard with academic measuring instruments (such as surveys, questionnaires, interviews, etc) will lead to unresolveable confounds. It should be a matter of investigating the function of the claim rather than necessarily trying to perfectly verify the entire content of it.

Chaos magics should be seen as an umbrella term for a series of generic, but often distantly related evolving Dada-ist magickal techniques which are in a (Baudrillardian) hyper-real state of constant flux and competing 'reality'. While the Chaos maxim of 'Nothing is true' may seem to some a bleak and nihilistic philosophy it also allows for an infinity of possible temporary truths and thus Chaos offers the practitioner a rich mix of information and practice that would not be possible were they following a more 'monoculture' and prescriptive magical path. Chaos offers the academic a multitude of interesting and rewarding challenges. As a major, influential and fast-moving new development in occultism, Chaos magic cannot be ignored and offers an enticing arena for researchers in finding new, improved research strategies which will hopefully evolve in tandem with the developments in the magical practice itself.

The author is most grateful for the assistance of (in no particular order): Lionel Snell, Ronald Hutton, Dave Lee, Jaq Hawkins, Julian Vayne, Phil Hine, Greg Humphries, Peter J. Carroll, Dave Green, Andy Smith, Matt Lee, and Joel Biroco in the researches which underpinned this chapter.

References

Beyer, J.A. 1996. 'Lubeck prophets in local and Lutheran context', in R. Scribner and T. Johnson, (eds.), *Popular religion in Germany and Central Europe, 1400-1800*. Basingstoke, UK: Macmillan.
Biroco, J. (ed,). 2002. *KAOS 14*. London: KAOS-Babalon Press.
Breakspear, F. 2009. *Toastar! Further Adventures in Chaos Magic*. London: Hidden.
_____ 2007. *Kaostar! Modern Chaos Cunning Craft*. London: Hidden.
Carroll, P.J. 1987 [1978]. *Liber Null & Psychonaut*. York Beach, Maine: Weiser.
_____. Specularium website
_____. 1992. *Liber Kaos*. York Beach, Maine: Weiser.
_____. 1997 [1995]. *PsyberMagick*. Tempe, Arizona: New Falcon.
_____, 2008. *The Apophenion*. Oxford: Mandrake.
Crowley, A. 1973 [1929]. *Magick in Theory and Practice*. London: Routledge & Kegan Paul.
_____ .1981 [1913]. *The Book of Lies*. York Beach, Maine: Weiser.
_____. 1909. 'Liber O Vel Mans Et Sagittae', *The Equinox* 1, 2. London: Simpkin, Marshall, Hamilton, Kent & Co.
Daraul, A. 1965. *Secret Societies*. London: Tandem.
Davis, E. *Calling Cthulhu, Lovecraft's Magick Realism*. Techgnosis website.
Day, J. C. 2003. 'The Shadow over Phillistia, a review of the Cult of Dagon', *J. Academic Study of Magic*, 1.
Dukes, R. 2004. 'Theatre Review: His Dark Materials at the National Theatre', Occultebooks website.
Gerkowska, N. 1999. 'The Latent Self'. *Kaos Magick Journal*, 2,1.
Gleick, J. 1987. *Chaos: Making a New Science*. London: Sphere.
Grant, K. and Grant, S. 1998. *Zos Speaks! Encounters with Austin Osman Spare*. London: Fulgur.
_____.1975. *Images and Oracles of Austin Osman Spare*. London: Muller.
Hale, A. 2009. 'White men can't dance: evaluating Race, Class and Rationality in ethnographies of the esoteric', in D. Evans and D. Green (eds.) *Ten Years of Triumph of the Moon: Academic approaches to studying magic and the occult—examining scholarship into witchcraft and paganism ten years after Ronald Hutton's Triumph of the Moon*. London: Hidden.
Harms, D. and Gonce, J.W. 2003 [1998]. *The Necronomicon Files*. York Beach, Maine: Weiser.
Hawkins, J. 1996. *Understanding Chaos Magic*. Chieveley, Berkshire: Capall Bann.
Hine, P. 1989. *Touched by Fire,* London: Pagan News.
_____ . 1989. *Two Worlds and Inbetween*. London: Pagan News.
_____ . 1991. *Breeding Devils in Chaos: Homosexuality & the Occult*. (Online)

_____. 1992. *Oven Ready Chaos*. London: Chaos International.
_____. 1997. *PerMutations*. London: self-published.
_____. 2002. *Prime Chaos*. Tempe, Arizona: New Falcon.
_____. 1991. 'The physics of evocation—a Mythos perspective' in *Dark Doctrines: The Nox Anthology*. Doncaster, UK: New World.
_____. 1997 [1994]. *The Pseudonomicon*. Irvine, California: Dagon Productions.
Hutton, R. 1999. *The Triumph of the Moon: A History of Modern Pagan Witchcraft*. Oxford: Oxford University Press.
_____.2009. *Blood and Mistletoe: the History of the Druids in Britain*. New Haven: Yale University Press.
Illuminates of Thanateros. 2002. *The Book*. London: IOT.
Johnstone, L. (R. Dukes) ed. 2001 [1974]. *S.S.O.T.B.M.E. An Essay on Magic*. London: El-Cheapo/TMTS.
Joshi, S.T. 2001. *A Dreamer and a Visionary: H. P. Lovecraft in His Time*. Liverpool, UK: Liverpool University Press.
Lee, D. 2001. 'Notes towards a brief history of the IOT.' Unpublished ms.
Lovecraft, H.P. and Conover, W. 2002. *Lovecraft at Last*. New York: Copper Square Press.
L.O.O.N. 1986. *Apikorsus*. E-book, no publisher or location.
Lurhmann, T. M. 1989. *Persuasions of the Witch's Craft: ritual magic in contemporary England*. Cambridge, Massachusetts: Harvard University Press.
Nehring, N. 1993. 'Rock around the Academy', *American Literary History*: 5, 4.
Noland, C. J. 1994. 'Rimbaud and Patti Smith: Style as Social Deviance', *Critical Inquiry*: 21, 3.
Orridge, G. P. ed. 2002. *Painful but Fabulous: the Lives and Art of Genesis P. Orridge*. New York: Soft Skull.
Owen, A. 2004. *The Place of Enchantment: British Occultism and the Culture of the Modern*. Chicago: University of Chicago Press.
Pagani, P. 1984. *The Cardinal Rites of Chaos*. England: Sut Anubis.
Popper, K. 1983 [1934]. *The Logic of Scientific Discovery*. London: Routledge.
Redwood, W. 2003. 'Spiral Bound: Cosmologies, Spatialities and Selves in Contemporary Magick.' London: PhD dissertation, University College, London.
Samuel, G. 2009. 'From Tantric Chakra to Wiccan Circle? Indic borrowings in the Pagan Revival', in D. Evans and D. Green (eds.), *Ten Years of Triumph of the Moon: Academic approaches to studying magic and the occult—examining scholarship into witchcraft and paganism ten years after Ronald Hutton's Triumph of the Moon*. London: Hidden: 168-188.
Sennitt, S. 1997. *Liber Koth*. Mexborough, Yorkshire: Logos Press.
Sherwin, R. 1982. *The Book of Results*. Yorkshire: Morton Press.

_____. 1986. Review of Paula Pagani: *Cardinal Rites of Chaos. Chaos International*, 1.
Thee Temple Ov Psychick Youth. 1988. *Television Magick*. Privately circulated booklet.
Vayne, J. 2005. Lecture at Devon and Cornwall Pagan Federation Conference. Kilkhampton, Devon, March 2005.
_____.2008. *Magick Works*. Oxford: Mandrake.
_____.2006. *Pharmakon: Drugs and the Imagination*. Oxford: Mandrake.
Vayne, J. and Humphries, G. 2004. *Now That's What I Call Chaos Magick*. Oxford: Mandrake/Liminal Space.
Woodman, J. 2004. 'Alien Selves: Modernity and the Social Diagnostics of the Demonic' in "Lovecraftian Magick", *Journal for the Academic Study of Magic*, 2.
_____.2003. 'Modernity, Selfhood, and the Demonic: Anthropological Perspectives on "Chaos Magick" in the United Kingdom'. London: PhD dissertation, Goldsmiths College, University of London.

Endnotes

1. Phil Hine, *Touched by Fire*, (London, Pagan News, 1989) 5 http://www.philhine.org.uk/writings/pdfs/tbfv1.pdf accessed March 1 2010.
2. The emergence in other regions, particularly the Americas is worthy of a book length project on its own.
3. See especially Kenneth & Steffi Grant, *Zos Speaks! Encounters with Austin Osman Spare* (London, Fulgur, 1998) and their *Images and Oracles of Austin Osman Spare* (London, Muller, 1975).
4. There is some crossover between Satanists and Chaos magicians, for more information on the former please see the chapters herein by Jesper Petersen and James R. Lewis.
5. James Gleick, *Chaos, making a New Science* (London, Sphere, 1987) 21-23.
6. Peter J Carroll, *Liber Null & Psychonaut* (York Beach, Maine, Weiser, 1987, Original 1978) 20.
7. Phil Hine, *Prime Chaos* (Tempe, Arizona, New Falcon, 2002) 65.
8. Phil Hine, *Breeding Devils in Chaos: Homosexuality & the Occult*, (Online article) http://www.philhine.org.uk/writings/flsh_breeding.html (1991) accessed March 1 2010. To save the reader ploughing through a dense 3000 pages or so of Theosophical Society works by their leader Madame Blavatsky a summary can be found at the Blavatsky Study Centre Website http://blavatskyarchives.com
9. Nadine Gerkowska, The Latent Self, *Kaos Magick Journal*, 2,1, (1999). http://www.chaosmatrix.org/library/chaos/texts/kmj1999.pdf p 2 Accessed March 1 2010.

10 By comparison steel has replaced cast iron in construction, antibiotics have replaced poultices, computers have replaced the abacus, women now have the vote, air travel is commonplace and many occupations are mechanised or otherwise nonexistent, for example there are no child chimneysweeps in the UK.

11 Phil Hine, *PerMutations* (London, personal publication of E-book, 1997) http://www.philhine.org.uk/writings/pdfs/perm13.pdf Accessed March 1 2010 10

12 This chapter is updated extracts of my PhD thesis which in part attempts to do this. However I should also mention colleagues who have done superb anthropological work in this area, but their entire findings are yet to be published: William Redwood 'Spiral Bound: Cosmologies, Spatialities and Selves in Contemporary Magick', (PhD Diss. 2003); Justin Woodman, 'Modernity, Selfhood, and the Demonic: Anthropological Perspectives on "Chaos Magick" in the United Kingdom', (PhD Diss. 2003). An extract of Justin's work appears as Alien Selves: Modernity and the Social Diagnostics of the Demonic in "Lovecraftian Magick", *J. Academic Study of Magic*, 2 (2004) 13-47

13 Phil Hine, *Oven Ready Chaos*, (London, Chaos International, 1992) http://www.philhine.org.uk/writings/pdfs/orchaos.pdf (Accessed March 1 2010) 5-6

14 Including the author, who will usually tolerate the label rather than welcome it.

15 Peter J Carroll, *Liber Null & Psychonaut* (York Beach, Maine, Weiser, 1987, Original 1978) 48

16 Actually the American film-maker, writer and magician Denise Crehore/Denise Channing

17 Jaq Hawkins, *Understanding chaos magic* (Chieveley, Berkshire, Capall Bann,1996) 5-6, emphasis added

18 Ray Sherwin, *The Book of Results* (Electronic book- Original Yorkshire, Morton Press, 1982) www.hermetism.info/pdf/Chaos%20Magick/The%20Book%20of%20Results%20%28Chaos%20Magick%29.pdf Accessed March 1 2010 Ch 1, emphasis added.

19 The Zees tend to be mobile and transient online, and thus URLs go out of date rapidly—they can best be found by a Google search for 'z cluster chaos' at the time when the reader wishes to find them.

20 For example Thee Temple Ov Psychick Youth, *Television Magick* (TOPY privately circulated booklet, 1988). Francis Breakspear, *Kaostar! Modern Chaos Cunning Craft* (London, Hidden, 2007) 87-89

21 Phil Hine, *Prime Chaos* (Tempe, Arizona, New Falcon, 2002) 60, emphasis added

22 Paula Pagani, *The Cardinal Rites of Chaos* (Electronic book, origi-

nal England, Sut Anubis, 1984) *www.iot.org.br/caostopia/wp-content/the-cardinal-rites-of-chaos.doc Accessed March 1 2010*

23   Ray Sherwin, review of Paula Pagani, Cardinal Rites of Chaos, *Chaos International*, 1 (1986) 48-9

24   These including Adamai Philotinus, Lemuel Johnstone, Ambrose Lea, Liz Angerford, Hugo l'Estrange and Ramsey Dukes, which makes using a coherent academic citation system much harder.

25   Jaq Hawkins, *Understanding Chaos Magic* (Chieveley, Berkshire, Capall Bann,1996:31)

26   There is a wealth of academic material on the punk movement in modern society. The reader is referred to just two useful and accessible examples here: Neil Nehring, Rock around the Academy, *American Literary History*, V 5, N 4 (1993) 764-791 & Carrie Jaures Noland, Rimbaud and Patti Smith: Style as Social Deviance, *Critical Inquiry*, V 21, No. 3, (1994) 581-610. In the odd manner that meaningful coincidences often seem to arise when writing about magic, it was the day after writing this section that the death of Mr. MacLaren from cancer was announced.

27   See for example Geoffrey Samuel, From Tantric Chakra to Wiccan Circle? Indic borrowings in the Pagan Revival, in Dave Evans & Dave Green (eds.) Ten *Years of Triumph of the Moon: Academic approaches to studying magic and the occult—examining scholarship into witchcraft and paganism ten years after Ronald Hutton's Triumph of the Moon* (London, Hidden, 2009) 168-188.

28   Jaq Hawkins, *Understanding chaos magic* (Chieveley, Berkshire, Capall Bann,1996) 31-7

29   Peter J Carroll, *Liber Null & Psychonaut* (York Beach, Maine, Weiser, 1987, Original 1978)

30   Ray Sherwin, *The Book of Results* (Electronic book- Original Yorkshire, Morton Press, 1982) http://www.hermetism.info/pdf/Chaos%20Magick/The%20Book%20of%20Results%20%28Chaos%20Magick%29.pdf Accessed March 1 2010 Ch 2

31   Illuminates of Thanateros, *The Book,* (E-Book, London, IOT, 2002) http://iota.goetia.net/files/the_book_english.pdf Accessed March 1 2010 6

32   Dave Lee, Notes towards a brief history of the IOT, unpublished mss 2001, that became Illuminates of Thanateros, *The Book,* (E-Book, London, IOT, 2002). Dave kindly sent me a pre-publication version of the document in order to assist my researches. The initial manuscript is so close to the published version in content as to make little difference, there are only a few layout and ordering changes. 1.

33   Illuminates of Thanateros, *The Book,* (E-Book, London, IOT, 2002) http://iota.goetia.net/files/the_book_english.pdf Accessed March 1 2010 7

34 Dave Lee, Notes towards a brief history of the IOT, unpublished mss 2001, that became Illuminates of Thanateros, *The Book*, (E-Book, London, IOT, 2002), 1.
35 The Sorcerers Apprentice shop has been in existence for around 35 years see http://www.sorcerers-apprentice.co.uk/
36 Dave Lee, Notes towards a brief history of the IOT, unpublished mss 2001, that became Illuminates of Thanateros, *The Book*, (E-Book, London, IOT, 2002) 2
37 Peter J Carroll, *PsyberMagick*, (Tempe, Arizona, New Falcon, 1997. Original 1995) and his *Liber Kaos* (York Beach, Maine, Weiser, 1992)
38 Peter J Carroll, *Specularium* website http://www.specularium.org/ Accessed April 1 2010
39 For example *Nox* edited by Stephen Sennitt and *Kaos* edited by Joel Biroco
40 Peter Carroll in Dave Lee, Notes towards a brief history of the IOT, unpublished mss 2001, that became Illuminates of Thanateros, *The Book*, (E-Book, London, IOT, 2002) 1
41 Peter J Carroll, *Liber Null & Psychonaut* (York Beach, Maine, Weiser, 1987, Original 1978) 9
42 Illuminates of Thanateros, *The Book*, (E-Book, London, IOT, 2002) http://iota.goetia.net/files/the_book_english.pdf Accessed March 1 2010 1
43 Aleister Crowley, *The book of lies* (York Beach, Maine, Weiser. 1981, Original 1913) flyleaf, emphasis added
44 Ronald Hutton, *The triumph of the Moon: a history of modern pagan witchcraft*. (Oxford, Oxford University Press, 1999) gives a masterful analysis of this phenomenon
45 Peter J Carroll, Personal communication. 2-7-2002.
46 Peter J Carroll, *Specularium* website http://www.specularium.org/ Accessed April 1 2010
47 *New Falcon Publications*, Email Press Release (New Falcon, Tempe, Arizona) 27-7-2002
48 Peter J Carroll, *The Apophenion* (Oxford, Mandrake, 2008)
49 Arcanorium Magical College (website) www.arcanoriumcollege.com/ 2007-present
50 Thee Temple Ov Psychick Youth (Website) www.topy.net Accessed March 1 2010
51 There is not room here for an overview of the fascinating career of Orridge, see Genesis P Orridge, (Ed.), *Painful but Fabulous: the Lives and Art of Genesis P Orridge* (New York, Soft Skull, 2002)
52 L.O.O.N., *Apikorsus*, (E-book, no publisher or location, original 1986) http://www.philhine.org.uk/writings/pdfs/apikorsus.pdf Accessed April 1 2010, 18

53 Involving ritual gestures, possibly using a dagger, special words in appeal to a nebulous deity to magically clear the ritual space, and perhaps the ceremonial application of salt, water or incense, for example
54 For example see Ronald Hutton, *Blood and Misteltoe, The History of the Druids in Britain* (New Haven, Yale University Press, 2009)
55 For a superb summary see Alex Owen, *The Place of Enchantment: British Occultism and the Culture of the Modern* (Chicago, University of Chicago Press, 2004)
56 J. A Beyer, Lubeck prophets in local & Lutheran context, in R Scribner & T Johnson, (Eds.) *Popular religion in Germany and Central Europe, 1400-1800,* (Basingstoke, Macmillan, 1996)
57 Phil Hine, *Prime Chaos* (Tempe, Arizona, New Falcon, 2002) 45
58 Phil Hine, *Two Worlds and Inbetween* (London, Pagan News, 1989) www.philhine.org.uk/writings/pdfs/2worlds.pdf Accessed April 2 2010. 25
59 Phil Hine, *Touched by Fire,* (London, Pagan News 1989) p 7 http://www.philhine.org.uk/writings/pdfs/tbfv1.pdf accessed March 1 2010
60 Chaotes seem particularly fond of working with the fictional 'old gods' in HP Lovecraft, for example see Justin Woodman, 'Alien Selves: Modernity and the Social Diagnostics of the Demonic' in 'Lovecraftian Magick', *Journal for the Academic Study of Magic.* 2 (2004) ; H.P. Lovecraft & W. Conover, *Lovecraft at Last* (New York, Copper Square Press, 2002); ST Joshi, *A Dreamer and A Visionary: H. P. Lovecraft in His Time* (Liverpool, Liverpool University Press, 2001); Phil Hine, 'The Physics of Evocation—a Mythos Perspective', *Dark Doctrines. The Nox anthology* (Doncaster, New World, 1991) 45-59; Phil Hine, *The Pseudonomicon* (Irvine, California, Dagon Productions, 1997, Original 1994); Daniel Harms & John W Gonce, *The Necronomicon Files* (York Beach, Weiser, 2003, original 1998); Erik Davis, 'Calling Cthulhu, Lovecraft's Magick Realism', Techgnosis website http://www.techgnosis.com/lovecraft.html Accessed May 1 2008 ; John C. Day, 'The Shadow over Phillistia, a review of the Cult of Dagon', *J. Academic Study of Magic*, 1, (2003) 33-40
61 For examples of rites based on Buffy the Vampire Slayer, see Julian Vayne & Greg Humphries, *Now That's What I Call Chaos Magick* (Oxford, Mandrake/Liminal Space, 2004) 77-80; or for a ritual using the imagery of Charlie's Angels see Francis Breakspear, *Toastar! Further Adventures in Chaos Magic* (London, Hidden, 2009) 28-40
62 Stephen Sennitt, *Liber Koth* (Mexborough, Yorkshire, Logos Press, 1997) 11
63 Phil Hine, *Prime Chaos* (Tempe, Arizona, New Falcon, 2002) 119
64 Steve Wilson, personal communication, 21-5-2002

65 Ramsey Dukes, conversation, 20-4-2002
66 Ramsey Dukes, Theatre Review: 'His Dark Materials at the National Theatre' (Online) http://www.occultebooks.com/reviews/Review_HisDarkMaterialsattheNationalTheatre.htm Accessed April 1 2010
67 Aleister Crowley, *Magick in theory and practice* (London, Routledge, 1973) 83
68 Phil Hine, *Prime Chaos* (Tempe, Arizona, New Falcon, 2002) 32
69 Phil Hine, *Oven Ready Chaos*, (London, Chaos International, 1992) http://www.philhine.org.uk/writings/pdfs/orchaos.pdf (Accessed March 1 2010) 38
70 Phil Hine, *Two Worlds and Inbetween* (London, Pagan News, 1989) http://www.philhine.org.uk/writings/pdfs/2worlds.pdf Accessed April 2 2010. 5
71 Karl Popper, *The Logic of Scientific Discovery* (London, Routledge, 1983, Original 1934, English edit 1959).
72 Lemuel Johnstone (Ramsey Dukes, Ed.), *S.S.O.T.B.M.E. An Essay on Magic* (London, El-Cheapo/TMTS, 2001, original 1974) 17
73 Jaq Hawkins, *Understanding chaos magic* (Chieveley, Berkshire, Capall Bann,1996) 33
74 Lionel Snell, personal communication, 21-2-2002
75 *Quotations Online*, http://www.quotationspage.com/quotes/Voltaire Accessed April 1 2010
76 Aleister Crowley, 'Liber O Vel Mans Et Sagittae', *The Equinox* 1, 2 (London, Simpkin, Marshall, Hamilton, Kent & Co. Undated facsimile reprint, original 1909)
77 Phil Hine, *PerMutations* (London, personal publication of E-book, 1997) http://www.philhine.org.uk/writings/pdfs/perm13.pdf Accessed March 1 2010 32
78 Angerford & Lea, *Thundersqueak*, p142
79 Illuminates of Thanateros, *The Book*, (E-Book, London, IOT, 2002) http://iota.goetia.net/files/the_book_english.pdf Accessed March 1 2010 15
80 Illuminates of Thanateros, *The Book*, (E-Book, London, IOT, 2002) http://iota.goetia.net/files/the_book_english.pdf Accessed March 1 2010 24
81 Ray Sherwin, *The Book of Results* (Electronic book- Original Yorkshire, Morton Press, 1982) www.hermetism.info/pdf/Chaos%20Magick/The%20Book%20of%20Results%20%28Chaos%20Magick%29.pdf Accessed March 1 2010 Ch 1
82 Lemuel Johnstone (Ramsey Dukes, Ed.), *S.S.O.T.B.M.E. An Essay on Magic* (London, El-Cheapo/TMTS, 2001, original 1974) 103
83 Phil Hine, *Prime Chaos*, (Tempe, Arizona, New Falcon, 2002) 52-53, emphasis added.

84 Personal communication to the author
85 See Ronald Hutton, *The triumph of the Moon: a history of modern pagan witchcraft*. (Oxford, Oxford University Press, 1999)
86 Lemuel Johnstone (Ramsey Dukes, Ed.), *S.S.O.T.B.M.E. An Essay on Magic* (London, El-Cheapo/TMTS, 2001, original 1974) 17, and Lionel Snell, conversation, April 2002.
87 Phil Hine, *Oven Ready Chaos*, (London, Chaos International, 1992) http://www.philhine.org.uk/writings/pdfs/orchaos.pdf (Accessed March 1 2010) 16, emphasis added
88 Jaq Hawkins, *Understanding chaos magic* (Chieveley, Berkshire, Capall Bann,1996) 99, emphasis added
89 Phil Hine, *Prime Chaos*, (Tempe, Arizona, New Falcon, 2002) 27, emphasis added.
90 Akron Daraul, *Secret Societies* (London, Tandem 1965) 13-14
91 Phil Hine, *PerMutations* (London, personal publication of E-book, 1997) http://www.philhine.org.uk/writings/pdfs/perm13.pdf Accessed 1 March 2010: 12
92 Review of Peter J. Carroll, Psychonaut in *Aquarian Arrow*, 16 (1983) 33
93 Review of Peter J Carroll, Liber Null in *Aquarian Arrow*, 18 (1984) 31
94 Hawkins, *Understanding Chaos Magic* (Chieveley, Berkshire, Capall Bann,1996) 109
95 As seems to have been the controversial *a priori* stance of the influential study of London magicians by Tanya M. Lurhmann, *Persuasions of the Witch's craft: ritual magic in contemporary England* (Cambridge, Massachusetts, Harvard University Press, 1989)
96 Anonymised magician, conversation, July 2003.
97 Julian Vayne, *Pharmakon: Drugs and the Imagination* (Oxford, Mandrake, 2006), plus sections of his *Magick Works* (Oxford, Mandrake, 2008)
98 Julian Vayne, lecture at Devon and Cornwall Pagan Federation conference, Kilkhampton, March 2005. Here Julian pointed out that one of his magical colleagues is a complete teetotaller with regard to drugs (legal and illegal) alcohol and tobacco
99 Phil Hine, *PerMutations* (London, personal publication of E-book, 1997) http://www.philhine.org.uk/writings/pdfs/perm13.pdf. Accessed 1 March 2010: 31
100 Joel Biroco, letter in *KAOS 14*, http://www.biroco.com/kaos/ (London, KAOS-Babalon Press, 2002) Accessed 1 April 2010, 11
101 My initial research aims on Chaos were instantly dismissed by a senior and respected academic (who shall remain nameless here) as 'not a subject worthy of academic study'. Amy Hale (who has a chapter in this volume) provides a fascinating review of Western academia and some

negative attitudes to studying our own magics in her chapter 'White men can't dance: evaluating Race, Class and Rationality in ethnographies of the esoteric', in Dave Evans & Dave Green (eds.) *Ten Years of Triumph of the Moon: Academic approaches to studying magic and the occult— examining scholarship into witchcraft and paganism ten years after Ronald Hutton's Triumph of the Moon* (London, Hidden, 2009) 76-96

16
The Computer-Mediated Religious Life of Technoshamans and Cybershamans[1]

Libuše Martínková

The 21st century has brought with it not only a new age of spirituality but also a new kind of shaman. The world-wide-web provides open access to individuals around the globe and the combination of cyberspace and shaman has created the cybershaman.[2] In proposing this term, self-confessed cybershaman Micheal Teal, presents just one of many attempts to define the nature of cybershamanism within the context of contemporary religious postmodernity. However, establishing such a definition is not an easy task. From a scholarly perspective the terms 'technoshamanism' and 'cybershamanism',[3] as well as 'traditional' shamanism itself, from which these new religious movements are derived, are not broadly distinct and transparent.[4] Technoshamans and cybershamans, do not present themselves as a homogenous groups of believers and the borderlines of definition are predictably fuzzy. Nevertheless, what we have here is the application of computer technologies to various forms of shamanic practice—resulting in a new form of postmodern religion.

Across the Internet personal computers play a key role in the religious life of technoshamans and cybershamans, though the *extent* and *modes* of computer use differ considerably from group to group. The technoshamanic or cybershamanic religious experience itself also represents a substantial shift from traditional shamanism. Describing the different ways in which computer technologies are employed in ritual practice is one of the principal themes of this chapter. I also elaborate on the advanced concept of *ritual dynamics* in the context of the new media, especially the Internet.[5] The findings presented here are derived from my own Internet fieldwork which has involved anonymous interviews in real-time chats, as well as web-based discussions and email communications. Most of my conclusions derive from sixteen qualitative interviews conducted in 2004 and 2006 with practitioners of technoshamanism and cybershamanism (as I then understood these terms) although some of these practitioners simply identified themselves as postmodern or electronic shamans. In my research I was obliged to search for relevant websites[6] but I also studied off-line sources as well.[7] The empirical material in my study, which was based on Internet homepages, tended to divide into two categories— those designed to present information *about* technoshamans and cybershamans, and those created *by* the adherents themselves. Both types of Internet presentation were characterized in turn by extreme diversity.

Defining Technoshamanism and Cybershamanism

Drug use, ecstatic dancing, and trance music are well-known elements in the contemporary techno-shamanic subculture, and their use in ritual events binds the various adherents together. According to Erich Schneider one can easily see a mapping between computer networks and the spirit world, and between computers and the powerful entities the traditional shaman interacts with.[8] Schneider is a 'celebrity' among technoshamans and is well known both as a practitioner and for his publications in the field. His views are widely disseminated across the Internet via Usenet articles, and have been forwarded in chain emails by his many admirers since 1993.[9]

One way of defining technoshamanism and cybershamanism is to adopt an emic perspective and consider the views of the followers themselves. One practitioner spoke about 'Redefining ritual for the 21st century... going into ritual trance by use of digital music. [...] Some say that it connects us with God.'[10] This particular remark emerged from a web forum where various social topics were discussed and the focus was not exclusively on religion. However, a sub-group was subsequently established to define 'technoshamanism' itself—and it very quickly became apparent to believers and sympathizers alike that there was considerable diversity in the various forms of technoshamanic practice.

Technoshamanism is located on the fringe of the contemporary pagan revival and appears to be a spiritual hybrid derived from the both the 'Rave' and Internet cultures. It seems clear that technoshamanism itself involves the transgression and dissolution of boundaries—particularly those involving 'culture and Nature' and also 'performance and audience'.[11] However, rather than seeking to establish exactly *who* can be defined as a technoshaman or cybershaman, I have focused my research more specifically on *how* these practitioners employ computers in their religious life. This approach also delineates the categories, as I will show below.

The Role of Computer Technologies in Ritual

Computer mediation is a key element in technoshamanic and cybershamanic spirituality and an analysis of computer use in this context becomes crucial. From an emic perspective the terms technoshaman and cybershaman appear to be interchangeable—these expressions are freely used by the adherents themselves.

Technoshamans view computer technologies as a *tool*—one which is highly effective in providing instantaneous global outcomes in communication with followers or non-adherents alike. Computer technologies also provide data on the various methods utilized to access ecstatic states of consciousness—focusing especially on the spiritual experience of the *journey*, which is itself a key factor in any shamanic religious practice. So what exactly are the tools and methods used for technoshamanic journeying, and how have they become more readily available with the advance of computer technology? While synthetic drug use has nothing to do with computers, *per se*, visual *sensory stimulation*, affecting both individuals and groups, *is* usually carried out by computers and related technologies and involves the use of laser or neon light machines, stroboscope devices, 2D or 3D images projection sets at rave, trance or techno parties. Auditory sensory stimulation can also be provided by computers—creating specific forms of dance music and generating special sounds that affect brain activity.[12] Paradoxically, technoshamanic *sensory deprivation*[13] can also be linked to computers. Many Internet websites advertise special products like sophisticated headphones which eliminate the transmission of external sounds, and which are designed for deep meditation. There are also lucid dream machines and flotation tanks created for home practice, which simulate conditions of complete sensory isolation. At the other end of the spectrum there are devices that have been created to produce loud binaural beats and excessive noise.[14] Dr Dave Green describes these elements in a recent paper on technoshamanic ritual:

> *Technoshamanic culture has, for example, digitised tribal beats,*

> *chants and sounds from the rainforests; replaced psychotropic 'teacher plants' with synthesised highs in the forms of amphetamines, LSD and Ecstasy; substituted the dances of Whirling Dervishes with raves; and swapped ritual bonfires with 'magically' transformative gazes of the strobe, and internet images and computer-generated fractals which are projected onto the walls of the venue.[15]*

Computer technologies, then, have become a key constituent of technoshamanic religious life, substituting the traditional tools and rituals of native shamanism. However, at this point it may be possible etically to distinguish between technoshamans and cybershamans. The latter appear to view computer technologies as a place, environment or more precisely as a *space*.[16] They define this space as an alternative spiritual realm and one they can *journey to*. The cybershamanic religious experience of the journey to 'alternate planes of reality' is also generally based on the assumption that there is a sort of spiritual energy that derives from either the computers or computer networks and which allows cybershamans to interact with it as a power source. Some cybershamans speak explicitly about invisible electronic or digital spirits, 'inhabiting' cyberspace and 'assisting' them on their visionary journeys. A cybershaman known as CyberHeart—also known as C.H. in chat rooms—has sought to describe his spiritual practice in these terms:

> *C.H.: I don't see the stream of numbers, you know, the flow of ones and zeros, the mass of information... It's more like the river, electronic one, or maybe not the river but the wind... No. Something I don't know... Even typing on my keyboard I feel the life, the EnErgy, I see the love, the power...[17]*

Cybershamans sometimes experience a sense of 'immersion' in cyberspace, accompanied by various bodily 'symptoms', as the following text makes clear:

> *Astra: I've started my fire-up ritual by watching the fractal video on the desktop non-stop almost one hour. Maybe more, I don't remember, I definitely did lost the sense of time at first, and then trying to cut off eye-blinks I've lost the peripheral sight... After some time I've registered the distance between me and my computer is changing, the screen was getting closer and closer and I felt something like the immersion to water pool or better comfortable bath filled up all the way up to the top by*

hot water and bath foam... From that moment I knew I am IN THERE, tripping the whole night IN cyberspace, freed from almost all the Earth-based feelings and senses, but enriched by the others, yet unknown.[18]

While technoshamans substitute traditional shamanic rituals and create new ritual practices *with the help of computers*, cybershamans create entirely new rituals that take place *in a computer environment*—that is to say, within cyberspace. In other words, to further understand the crucial role of computers in both technoshamanism and cybershamanism, one has to focus on the concept of *cyberspace* itself. Also, one has to bear in mind that the notion of cyberspace is not inevitably associated with computers linked to the Internet: cyberspace is *where* cybershamans make their spiritual journeys and defines *how* technoshamans set out for their ethereal trips. Allowing for these different modes of computer use by technoshamans and cybershamans, one can then analyze the following quotation from a shaman's 'confession':

I am a Cybershaman—a Shaman and Psychic who uses cyberspace to embrace the 'Infinite Life Force' and open others to a universe of beauty and light. The internet has afforded me the opportunity to bring my unique and treasured purpose to people around the world. On any given day I can offer wisdom and guidance to a housewife in Ireland, a healer in Brazil and a doctor in Japan. The web has become my personal altar where I can share the teachings of the Spirit and explore its unlimited possibilities. My quest for meaning and heart is enhanced by constant access to people and information.[19]

Micheal Teal, the author of this extract, claims he is a cybershaman, but as is apparent from the text, the way he uses computers and the Internet indicates, rather, that he is a technoshaman. Strictly speaking, this is just a portrait of a modern technology tool-user, extending his current religious experience by means of the technological capacity of computers linked via the Internet. Here, for comparison, is a short excerpt from the web presentation of Larry Williamson, also known as 'Schwan-cybershaman'. Williamson clearly demonstrates his cybershamanic orientation:

[...] the basic concept of Webtrance involves netizens from all over the world simultaneously focusing into a mass computer generated trance; thus participating in humanity's digital

reincarnation.[20]

Community, Communication and the Individualization of Rituals

If performance is central to the native shamanic religious experience[21] this particular element is not reflected to the same extent either in technoshamanic or cybershamanic spirituality. The reason is simple—there is no performance without an audience, as long as the term 'performance' is understood here as the act of performing some form of activity *for* and *with* observers. The ritual shift is quite transparent. While the traditional shaman performs his journey into altered spiritual dimensions usually in front of an audience consisting of community members, and the purpose of the shamanic journey is to help the community, the role of a technoshaman in technoshamanic ritual events is somewhat different. Although some technoshamans play leading roles in conducting rave festivals, the notional border between the performer and the audience, i.e. between the producer and the consumer, is progressively fading away. This is made clear in the following extract from an informant called Shana, who is regularly involved in techno parties:

> *Shana: I used to admire him. Popular Techno Shaman. His dj-ing is some way magical...*
> *Shana: I used to listen to him, I was ready to follow him everywhere, you know I mean?*
> *Shana: Later, one day I became a part of the community. I felt so.*
> *Shana: My ego has disappeared, it was part of everybody and every other body was a part of me, but in the same time there still was somehow my self. Was there? I was the Techno Shaman too! Every one was Shaman that night.*[22]

The borders between performance and audience in technoshamanic rave practice are not distinct. Nor is it exactly clear who is the active performer and who is the passive spectator. Instead the participants often claim to be both at the same time—they are both the 'producer' as well as the 'consumer' of the visionary journey experience.

Cybershamans practice their ritual journeying alone, without the presence of other persons. There is no audience; there is no community to assist within the spiritual dimensions of cyberspace. Cybershamans enter their cyber pathways in the isolation of their own homes, or less frequently at other locations where Internet access is available. The cybershamans I was in touch with during my fieldwork did not use terms like 'community', 'group', or 'collective' etc. Instead they were intent on proclaiming their individuality, originality, uniqueness and even anarchy in their ritual practice.

Strictly speaking, to describe the process of individualization in the religious behavior of technoshamans and cybershamans we should distinguish 'primary' individualization—which refers to the change of ritual—and 'secondary' individualization, which refers to the social life of participants.

While primary individualization is quite evidently represented by the shift of rituals as shown above, there is *de facto* no noticeable change in relation to society or community. Technoshamans and cybershamans both require contact with the community - not to conduct the rituals themselves, but in order to share information about rituals, tools, or the shamanic experience.[23]

The function of computer and information technology is obvious here. To connect with the community (however large it is) it does not matter whether it is restricted to an on-line mode, transferred from on-line to off-line, or even configured as off-line-on-line-off-line.[24] The technoshaman RaveRaven[25] serves as a suitable illustration of this interconnectivity between on-line and off-line modes. RaveRaven's relationship is with persons who practice a similar form of spirituality in techno parties conducted at techno clubs. He maintains an email and Internet correspondence with the aim of enlarging his religious horizons theoretically and then meets his contacts again off-line, performing rituals with them in the techno club.

A Change of Time and Place in the Rituals[26]

If we analyze the dynamic structure of technoshamanic and cybershamanic rituals it is clear that elements of these rituals are impacted through computer technologies—especially with regard to the *time* and *place* where they occur. While there is no noticeable change of time setting in technoshamanic rituals—like traditional shamanic rituals they take place mostly at nights—our survey of cybershamanic ritual behavior shows that specific time settings are not significant. What makes the ritual successful here is the possibility of computer and/or Internet access, which could take place at any hour of the day. While trance dance parties, as collective rituals, tend to occur at fixed times the invitees respect this time schedule, cybershamans with constant access to the Internet can perform their individual rituals at any chosen time. As the cybershaman known as Tiger observes in relation to this situation:

> *There is no magick time! Actually there is NO time in Cyber*

Space. Time is the border and there are NO borders in Cyber World...[27]

Nonetheless, it is apparent from my survey of interviews that the majority of cybershamans still set out on their journeys at night-time. There are two main reasons for this: night scheduling of the ritual helps to eliminate potentially distracting factors in one's surroundings and the Internet connection on-line is faster and cheaper at night. For most operators these days the practice of dial-up Internet connection (with different prices at different times of the day) is no longer a feasible option and technoshamans and cybershamans prefer unrestricted on-line access to the Internet.

The aspect of *place* as a dimension of ritual influenced by the use of computer technologies is best understood if we distinguish two sub-categories—the *place of the journey itself* and the *starting point* where participants in the ritual began to experience altered states of consciousness. From a ritual perspective, dance floors in techno clubs are viewed by technoshamans as sacred locations—places where they enter a trance state and where they commence their journeys into spiritual realms.[28] By way of contrast, for the cybershaman rooms containing personal computers at home, in offices, in Internet coffee bars or tearooms, at student residences, or in PC laboratories can all serve as commencement-points for a visionary journey.[29] Cyberspace, as a 'locality' into which one can journey, does not have to be implicitly formed within global computer networks like the Internet or in webs of local character.[30] The subjective experience of 'immersion'—familiar to many cybershamans—was mentioned earlier. But when it comes to basic issues like 'favorite cybershamanic zones' in cyberspace, particular locations for undertaking cybershamanic rituals, the possibility of tracking these locations through URL, or the nature of so called 'avatar identities' (like those found in Second Life), clear points of demarcation emerge. Cybershamans do not occupy exclusive virtual worlds as 'digitalized' residents and they do not dwell in any exclusively cybershamanic MMOGs. This does not mean that cybershamans do not visit these virtual worlds—just that there are just no cybershamanic virtual worlds and game zones on the Internet designed exclusively for them. Nevertheless it would appear that many cybershamans view themselves as 'citizens' of global cyberspace, sometimes using the neologism *netizen* to express their status in these realms. Being a netizen means 'being at home anywhere in cyberspace'.[31] In other words, netizens are not travelling to particular cyber 'destinations', but into cyberspace as a whole. Cyberspace itself, wherever and however it is constituted, represents the altered state—a spiritual realm where one can contact guiding, healing and teaching spirits.

Some cybershamans are especially attracted to fractal art, commencing their trips into cyberspace by visiting favorite pages with fractal photo and video galleries, and sometimes by setting fractal imagery on the initial pages of their Internet browsers.[32] Some practitioners also purchase special computer programs that generate fractal images on their personal computers, while others are themselves skilled computer-program designers,[33] capable of journeying and at the same time programming new fractal sets.[34] The exact location where the cybershaman is surfing at the time of his spiritual journey is not significant — the practitioner can begin, for example, by watching fractal movie sequences set on a desktop and then proceed intentionally to browse websites dedicated to nonlinear studies. Or he may seek to realize his journey by updating web presentations or by playing an off-line chess match with the computer.[35] In general, my research has established that there are no specific cybershamanic ritual pages on the Internet and no special on-line worlds created specifically for cybershamans.

Exploring the Religious Life of Technoshamans and Cybershamans on the Internet

As we have already seen, defining the beliefs and practices of technoshamans and cybershamans is somewhat hampered by the individualized and eclectic character of their religious orientation and in some instances by the absence of virtual worlds with specific Internet locations. With regard to the paradigm proposed by Thomas Luckmann, technoshamanism and cybershamanism may be described as 'invisible religions'.[36] The more familiar, or 'standard' methods employed in examining religious practices on the Internet are insufficient and new methods have to be employed.

For example, if one were to search the world-wide-web using search engines like Google, Yahoo or AltaVista and this did not produce a satisfactory result, it might then be necessary to explore what is known as the Deep Web. The Deep Web, which is also known as the Invisible Web/Net, is estimated to be approximately 500 times larger than the Surface Web.[37] In such instances Deep Web search engines or catalogue directories would have to be utilized. In my research I have used the popular meta-search engine Turbo 10[38] whch is engineered specifically for Deep Net searching. Working with IncyWincy[39] has also been useful and I have found it helpful searching in spiritual catalogue directories like iPadma.[40] Precise combinations of key words may also be required. Entering 'cybershaman' or 'technoshaman' into the search engine would probably be useless, since many believers do not identify themselves in this way. Instead, queries for searching must be expressed in another way—for example, by combining key words like 'shaman', 'cyberspace' and 'journey'. Nevertheless, I have found that searching for technoshamanic and cybershamanic religious data on the Internet (whether on the Surface or Deep Web) and using key words in the search process, as described, has its limitations. Technoshamans and cybershamans often hide their identities behind wider frames of postmodern religion, e.g. neo-paganism, alternative healing methods etc. Browsing multi-religious homepages, as for example Life Positive,[41] can help locate people interested in non-traditional religions, ideas and streams—and this includes technoshamans and cybershamans as well. Another example of a multi-religious framework is the homepage of LDE—the Lucid Dream Exchange—where lucid dreamers publish their experiences.[42] Lucid dreaming—a technique in which the practitioner learns to retain conscious awareness while dreaming—is popular among followers of the neo-pagan movement and yoga practitioners, as well as among techno- and cyber-shamans and for this reason the LDE website is useful in identifying practitioners of these new forms of shamanism. Some technoshamans and cybershamans are also interested in astrophysics, hi-tech philosophy and robotics, and are attracted to the multi-scoped server of The Deoxyribonucleic Hyperdimension, otherwise known as deoxy.[43] Skilled hackers meet here with 'cyberpunks', genetic engineers chat with cyber-sorcerers and various cybershamans can also be discovered among their ranks, sharing their experiences, opinions and information.

Postscript: The Issue of Virtuality

Extending our discussion on cybershamanic discourse and omitting technoshamanism for a moment, I would like to return to my earlier claim that there are no exclusively cybershamanic virtual worlds because cybershamans conduct their rituals within cyberspace *as a whole*. It is important to recognize that cybershamans do not treat cyberspace as a *virtual space* because they do not perceive it as a logical opposite to the real world. Instead, cybershamans view both realms as equally real. Cybershamans do not find occupying cyberspace, and living their virtual life, less valuable than living their real life. Cybershamans use the popular term *flesh space* (or *fleshspace*) to denote the 'opposite' to cyberspace without any sense of bias or qualitative difference.

Finally, it is fair to ask whether technoshamanism and cybershamanism deserve academic examination within the field of religious studies at all. Are there really any established methodological approaches enabling researchers to explore the enormous variety of technoshamanic and cybershamanic religious manifestations? Is it relevant to focus on the 'computer-mediated religious life of technoshamans and cybershamans' and to ignore other aspects of their religious behavior? Do descriptions of computer and Internet use in ritual practice provide actual evidence that these are new religious movements? And do cybershamans really understand virtuality/reality or cyberspace/fleshspace in the way we have described? Scholars interested in this field may be interested to consider the advanced concepts of *Individual Religiousness* and *Individual Rituality*, which are currently being incorporated into a larger framework known as *Ritual Dynamics*.[44] This work is currently being developed at the Heidelberg University Collaborative Research Center in Germany and I have found the application of these innovative approaches very useful for the study of the broad range of religions accessed on the Internet.

References

Bergman, Michael K. (2001): 'The Deep Web: Surfacing Hidden Value', in: *The Journal of Electronic Publishing* Volume 7, Issue 1. Retrieved on March 29, 2007, from: http://www.press.umich.edu/jep/07-01/bergman.html.

Center for Studies on New Religions. Retrieved on March 29, 2007, from: http://www.cesnur.org/.

Green, Dave (2001): *Technoshamanism: Cyber-sorcery and schizophrenia*. Retrieved on March 29, 2007, from: http://www.cesnur.org/2001/london2001/green.htm.

Harvey, Graham (1997): *Listening People, Speaking Earth*. London: Hurst.

Leary, Timothy (1999): *Turn On, Tune In, Drop Out*. Berkeley, California: Ronin Publishing.

Luckmann, Thomas (1967): *The Invisible Religion*. New York: Macmillan.

Schwann (1998): *Webtrance*. Retrieved on March 29, 2007, from: http://www.webtrance.co.za/webtrance.html.

Tambiah, Stanley Jayaraja (1985): *Culture, Thought and Social Action: An Anthropological Perspective*. Cambridge: Harvard University Press.

Teal, Micheal (2005): "Cybershamanism: Shamans on the Internet", in: *Psychic-tymes.com* Vol 6, Issue 17. Retrieved on March 29, 2007, from: http://www.psychic-tymes.com/htm17/shaman17.htm.

Referred Websites:

Website of BrainJav Binaural Beat Generator. Retrieved on March 29, 2007, from: http://pantheon.yale.edu/%7Ebbl2/av/brainjav/BrainJav.htm.

Website of Cybershaman. Retrieved on March 29, 2007, from: http://www.gocs1.com/.

Website of Deoxyribonucleic Hyperdimension. Retrieved on March 29, 2007,

from: http://deoxy.org/.
Website of Fractal Art Galleries. Retrieved on March 29, 2007, from: http://www.fractalus.com/dan/.
Website of Hyperreal. Retrieved on March 29, 2007, from: http://hyperreal.org/.
Website of IncyWincy: The Invisible Web Search Engine. Retrieved on March 29, 2007, from: http://www.incywincy.com/.
Website of iPadma: Spiritual Websearch. Retrieved on March 29, 2007, from: http://www.ipadma.com/.
Website of Life Positive: Your Complete Guide to Holistic Living. Retrieved on March 29, 2007, from: http://www.lifepositive.com/.
Website of the Heidelberg University Collaborative Research Center 619 "Dynamics of Rituals". Retrieved on March 29, 2007, from: http://www.ritualdynamik.uni-hd.de/en/index.htm.
Website of the Heidelberg University Collaborative Research Center 619 "Between Online-Religion and Religion-Online. Constellations of Ritual Transfer within the Medium Internet." Retrieved on March 29, 2007, from: http://www.rituals-online.uni-hd.de/en/.
Website of The Lucid Dream Exchange. Retrieved on March 29, 2007, from: http://www.dreaminglucid.com/.
Website of Mental FX. Retrieved on March 29, 2007, from: http://www.mentalfx.com.
Website of Tetris Zone. Retrieved on March 29, 2007, from: http://www.tetris.com.
Website of The Transparent Corporation. Retrieved on March 29, 2007, from: http://www.transparentcorp.com/.
Website of Tribe. Retrieved on March 29, 2007, from: http://tribes.tribe.net/.
Website of Turbo 10 Search Engine. Retrieved on March 29, 2007, from: http://www.turbo10.com/.
Website of Webtrance. Retrieved on March 29, 2007, from: http://www.webtrance.co.za/webtrance.html.

Endnotes

1   This chapter is based on the results of author's research, included in the project of *"Cultural Turn in the Study of Religion"* supported by GAUK grant project number 535/2004-05 (together with Jiří Gebelt and Lenka Philippová).
2   Teal 2005.
3   I have recognized two linguistic plural forms, occurring in the interviews with the participants of my research or in texts published on the Internet—*technoshamans* and *technoshamen*, and, by extension, *cybershamans* and *cybershamen*. For the purpose of this paper I have adopted the

'terminology' of majority of participants (including those of female sex), denoting themselves in plural *technoshamans* and *cybershamans*.
4   Harvey 1997, 107-108.
5   See the website of the Heidelberg University Collaborative Research Center 619 *"Dynamics of Rituals"*. http://www.ritualdynamik.uni-hd.de/en/index.htm.
6   For example using the Deep Web search engines. See further in the chapter *Exploring Religious Life of Technoshamans and Cybershamans on the Internet*.
7   Real-life meetings with participants, leading to three more interviews.
8   See the website with several definitions of technoshamanism: http://hyperreal.org/raves/spirit/technoshamanism/Technoshaman-Definitions.html. Retrieved from the homepage of *"Hyperreal"* http://hyperreal.org/.
9   See, for example, http://www.bunnysneezes.net/page181.html with exactly the same text of Eric Schneider's definition of technoshamanism.
10 See the message posted by Cozmic Kitty (moderator of the discussion) http://tribes.tribe.net/d7ecdbcd-5ff2-4f62-99ac-5699148dc91b/thread/31346a69-287d-4978-88b2-b31bd4fc2a5d. Retrieved from homepage of *"Tribe"* http://tribes.tribe.net/.
11 Green 2001.
12 See, for example, browser-based binaural beat generator on the website of *"BrainJav Binaural Beat Generator"* http://pantheon.yale.edu/%7Ebbl2/av/brainjav/BrainJav.htm.
13 There are five 'techniques' of sensory deprivation generally known - wall standing, subjection to noise, lack of sleep, food and drinks. Their application concerns wholly different social area—human rights, police interrogation practice and psychic torture. There is an interesting fact of using all these techniques by technoshamans (of course voluntarily), at least by those who practice their spirituality on dance floor in trance and rave celebrations. Instead of wall standing they expose themselves to non-stop dancing, leading to absolute bodily exhaustion, subjection to extremely loud music, perceived not only aurally, is evident here and deprivation of sleep, food and drinks (in duration from one to three days) are just obvious consequences of technoshamanic rave participation. Some technoshamans view these methods, supported massively by the help of computer technology, as a new way of entering the ecstatic states of mind, facilitating (techno)shamanic tripping.
14 See, for example, the homepage of *"The Transparent Corporation"* http://www.transparentcorp.com.
15 Green 2001.
16 I intentionally have omitted here the fact that also cybershamans use the computer technologies with the goal to communicate through this

medium within themselves and with others, because it is quite evident. See the chapter *Community and Communication in the Process of Individualization of the Rituals* further in the text.

17 Interview conducted by author on July 10, 2004.
18 Interview conducted by author on October 31, 2004.
19 Teal 2005.
20 Schwann 1998.
21 See Tambiah 1985.
22 Interview conducted by author on May 15, 2004.
23 Also the process of shaman 'election' or 'installation' could be mentioned here, concerning the course of individualization. While in the original shamanic tradition the shamans are usually chosen by community, in technoshamanism and markedly in cybershamanism, this characteristic is not found, instead self-proclaimed technoshamans and cybershamans are emerging.
24 For further detailed information concerning the offline-online-offline transfers of ritual performance see the concept of *Individual Religiousness as a New Paradigm in the Study of Religions* on the website of the Heidelberg Research Project for Rituals on the Internet. Retrieved on March 29, 2007, from: http://www.rituals-online.uni-hd.de/en/.
25 See the interview conducted by author on July 2, 2006.
26 Also another dimension of ritual was changed—involved 'objects'—although it is to be mentioned here only marginally. Drugs have disappeared from cybershamanic rituals, but caffeine is still very favored, as well as so called energy drinks, helping to keep the travelers awake on their journeys. Also vial of eye drops preventing the red eyes effect is a necessary prop and the change in fashion is evident too—there is no special cybershamanic fashion (on the contrary to the technoshamanic), there are no special 'ritual clothes', since cybershamans make sometimes their journeys even wearing pajamas.
27 Interview conducted by author on July 18, 2006.
28 Green 2001.
29 Unfortunately, I did not collect enough data during the inquiry to be able to gain proper statistic figures in this area.
30 For example LAN (Local Area Network) or MAN (Metropolitan Area Network).
31 Interview conducted by author on July 18, 2006.
32 See, for example, the website of *"Fractal Art Galleries"* http://www.fractalus.com/dan/. Or see the website with number of 'psychedelic trippy animations'- the website of *"Mental FX"* http://www.mentalfx.com.
33 Majority of the cybershamans I have met during the research were

software engineers, computer graphic designers or computer game authors. Also here more data is required before one can present this fact as universally valid.
34 By the way, these sites (or others with similar topics—chaos theories, quantum physics etc.), often located on edu Internet domain, are perhaps the most popular among cybershamans.
35 Other web pages, achieving high popularity among cybershamans, seem to be the homepages providing simple online games like for example Tetris, 2D poker etc. See, for example, website of *"Tetris"* http://www.tetris.com.
36 Luckmann 1967.
37 See Bergman 2001.
38 Website of *"Turbo 10"* http://www.turbo10.com/.
39 Website of *"IncyWincy"* http://www.incywincy.com/.
40 Website of *"iPadma"* http://www.ipadma.com/.
41 Website of *"Life Positive"* http://www.lifepositive.com/.
42 Website of *"The Lucid Dream Exchange"* http://www.dreaminglucid.com/.
43 Website of *"The Deoxyribonucleic Hyperdimension"* http://deoxy.org/.
44 Website of the Heidelberg University Collaborative Research Center 619 *"Dynamics of Rituals"*. http://www.ritualdynamik.uni-hd.de/en/index.htm.

17
The Magic Wonderland of the Senses: Reflections on a Hybridised Tantra Practice

Phil Hine

Introduction

Tantra, as Herbert Guenther put it, is 'one of the haziest misconceptions the Western mind has evolved'. The idea that Tantra exists as a monolithic and separate category to other forms of South Asian religious practice, is itself a product of the Western scholarly (and occult) imagination (see Hugh Urban, 2003, for an overview, also Padoux, 2002). Seeking to understand the manner in which Tantra has been 'imagined' and represented in scholarly, popular and occult discourses has also been a concern of my practice.

Within the subculture of contemporary occultism, this takes a particular form: Tantra is treated as essentially similar in practice and goal to Western Esotericism—at least once its content has been successfully re-interpreted by an author. Generally, there is an emphasis on Tantra as a set of 'techniques' or a 'sacred science' which is open to individuals to varying degrees. The figure of the Tantric practitioner is often portrayed as a kind of Nietzchian superhero, engaging in 'transgressive' practices which serve to take him or her beyond the limits of conventional society.

There is however, very little attention (if any) given to Tantra as a social practice—the practitioner belonging to a particular group, that group's relationship to the wider culture, and the relationship between Tantric practitioners and the state (Tantrics and king-making, for example, or instances where Tantra became a 'state religion'). Often, Western occult authors find it necessary to reinterpret Tantra so that it becomes familiar—comparing it to the Qabalah, or occasionally re-representing Tantric concepts in entirely Western terms. This statement from Christopher Hyatt is not atypical:

> *Thus, do not expect a series of foreign words (some might call it 'Hindu babble') strung together as an answer to a question. To us, such approaches are nothing more than the refusal to answer the question by making the simple complex—for the benefit of the writer's ego. It would be ridiculous for us to answer questions by employing esoteric Eastern concepts. If we did, this book would be of little use for the Western practitioner. We do not pretend to be experts in the phraseology, language, culture, etc. of the Eastern path. What we are expert in is the utilization of their techniques to accomplish the desired ends. In many instances we will deliberately use Western methods and symbols as they are easier for the Western collective unconscious to assimilate and integrate.*[1]

I find this approach to Tantra problematic, as it reduces Tantra to an exoticised support for Western understandings of magic, and ignores much of the rich cultural and theological diversity present in South Asian forms of religiosity. Moreover, it presupposes that 'techniques' can be lifted or adapted from one cultural context to another without considering how those 'techniques' are enmeshed in, and reflect particular cultural practices and understandings. Furthermore, there is a tendency to assume that 'Western' and 'Eastern' paths are fundamentally incommensurable—which ignores the influence of 'Eastern' concepts on Western esotericism over the last two hundred years or so, and takes no account of global exchanges between cultures.

I take a different approach—working from the premise that the historically-originated South Asian practices loosely organised under the category of 'Tantra' are very different from what might be thought of as contemporary Western magic, and that in order to understand and enact them one needs to try and get a handle on the context in which they are embedded. This does require an active commitment to engaging with 'phraseology, language, culture' (and much more besides). I generally refer to this approach as a 'hybridised' Tantra—one that draws from a series of interrelated historically-located practices/texts (notably the

South Asian Sri Vidya, Kaula, and Trika currents) and from contemporary European philosophers (Merleau-Ponty, Deleuze and Guatarri, for example) who are concerned with challenging the binary divisions which have come to dominate our understanding of the world. The tendency to divide mind from body, self from social, subject from object—which has become so central to the Western enterprise—is simply not present in South Asian religiosity in the same way.

Rather than attempting to impose a linear structure on this essay (as in proceeding outwards from a definition) I want instead to discuss what for me are some key themes in my tantra practice.

Wonder

The cultivation of a sustained sense of *Wonder* is both a means, and to some extent, the goal of my Tantra practice. Wonder is often related to the perception of the novel, the unexpected, the inexplicable; it's been linked to what is being increasingly termed a 'spiritual' quest for increased connection—the feeling of belonging, of engaged participation. Wonder can be found in a small moment—the sudden unfamiliarity of any artefact and how it came to be; wonder can be an exhaustive epiphany, something I feel throughout my whole body, something that stays with me. Wonder has been sidelined in contemporary discussions of magic. Wonder is, in many ways, antithetical to utilitarian purposiveness, to the urge to categorise, to order. Wonder propels us towards the unfamiliar, to seek new relations, to revel in dizzying complexity and richness. Wonder pulls us into the world beyond a limited horizon, beyond the certain, the familiar, the possible. Wonder is excessive—and its excessive quality is something that Western philosophy, trailing in the wake of Aristotle, has fought to foreclose—to rein in.

Embodied practice

Tantra is an embodied practice—the body is the primary site for practice—and the means through which the fruits of practice are attained. To speak of the 'body' in Tantra however, is not merely to designate corporeality—Tantric body discourse includes sense-capacities, feelings-thoughts, moral and ethical capacities; the sense of selfhood. The familiar dichotomy between body and mind is absent here. Tantric bodies are open—porous to the world. A body which is a multiplicity of affects; a body which reaches out and is reached out to—a body enmeshed and produced by other bodies through reciprocal relations. The Tantric body is the lived cosmos and it is through the body that the practitioner identifies with the transcendental source which is simultaneously within, without, everywhere—collapsing all distinctions.

Relationality

For me, Tantra is above all, a *relational* practice. At its simplest, it is concerned with how we relate to ourselves, to others (both embodied/unembodied) and to the world in general. To do this requires, I think, both *attention* and *care* towards our relations. Tantra's relationality is baroque in the extreme: every affect or capacity can become — temporarily — a person; a god-goddess; a transactional nexus for worship, reflection, interaction, the joy of self-recognition. Think of yantras, mandalas, mantras as modal states — yantras as shimmering networks of *unfixed* relational points — each point a *Shakti* with the potentiality for exploding outwards into her own yantra, on and on with fractal-like recursion. Consciousness as a flower endlessly unfolding with an infinite number of petals... To dwell within this perspective is to open up to the possibility of engagement.

What is important for me is how to carry these points into *practice*. What is perhaps central to this approach is the negation of the familiar 'magical — mundane' dichotomy. Although I may perform special rituals, alone or with friends much of my Tantra-practice is done on a day-to-day, moment-by-moment basis. Being open to wonder, or being mindful of relationships can be done anywhere, at any time.

The magic wonderland of the senses

What follows is an example of a particular Tantric practice — The Arrow-Shakti rite — which I shall use as a loose framework for discussing how this particular approach that I am developing plays out in practice. This short ritual utilises both external worship (*bahiryaga*) and internal worship (*antaryaga*). In this particular instance, we exteriorise the Sense-Shaktis in order to honour them and engage with them as we would another person, and at the end of the ritual, draw back the Arrow Goddess (who is their condensed form) within the heart-cave which, in some Tantric traditions, is the seat of self. Many Tantric *pujas* (rituals, worship) proceed in this way and make use of various practices and identifications such as mantras and *nyasa* (touching different parts of your body in order to 'place' powers there) and so forth.

Tantric *puja* is modular in its structure — each 'block' can be performed as a particular practice, and *puja* can be extended by adding further blocks. It is important to understand to the underlying principles of the *puja* — many texts stress that mere performance on its own is useless. The central theme in this *puja* is the gift-exchange. Offerings are made to the Sense-Shaktis as goddesses and the Arrow-Shakti (Lalita) who arises out of the total experiences of the senses; the blessing of the deities is received in return — in the form of food or grace (*Prasada*) and through the inter-identification of practitioner and the deities. A central Tantric theme in ritual is that in order to worship a god one must 'become' a god: 'To worship a deity, a man must become the Self of that deity through dedication, breath-control and concentration until his body becomes the deity's abode.'[2]

The visualisation of deities is a central feature of Tantra praxis. There is no connotation that visualisation is primarily imaginative or that it is 'less real' than sense perceptions or that visualisations are separate to an 'external world'. Visualisation is an intensification of experience—a means of reinforcing and *embodying* the symbolic order of the practice. Through the visualisation (of deities, yantras, chakras, etc.) the practitioner inter-identifies the lived body with the symbolic order of the tradition. The basic idea of deity meditation is that by focusing/contemplating the form of a deity (either using an iconic image or a textual description), the practitioner comes to identify with that deity and eventually takes on that deity's qualities or gains that deity's perspective. Generally speaking, there is a progression from meditating on the anthropomorphic image of a deity to meditating on more abstract qualities. In the non-dual Trika movement, visualisation—combined with other practices such as mantra, *nyasa*, etc.—is said to draw the deities near to the practitioner by coalescing their shape or form out of consciousness, whereupon they come to reside in the ritually-prepared body, particularly in the heart. Aspects of Tantra practice are often denoted as being either internally or externally directed. Internal worship might involve, for example, visualising one's chosen deity taking up residence in one's body. External worship might involve worshipping a deity as present within an image. However, these should not be read as opposed practices, but as practices which synergistically support each other—internal practice (that might be construed as 'meditation' in the West) supports and enhances external practice (ritual).

Beginning

I begin by snapping my fingers to the eight directions, above me, and below me.

Western approaches to magic tend to make a distinction between 'sacred' and 'mundane' space—and ritual acts are very often presented in terms of marking a transition from one to the other. In contrast, this Tantric approach holds that *all* space is the body of the goddess; *all* space is Shakti (capacity, power); and ritual acts to further condense or coagulate that Shakti. The emphasis here is thus on the *intensification* of present power. The attention to the eight/ten directions is not concerned with establishing a boundary (as a circle in Western magic is often thought to be) but in reaching outwards and pulling inwards.

Traditionally, snapping the fingers or clapping the hands (accompanied by the appropriate weapon mantras) may have been performed to drive away uninvited or unwanted persons (particularly unembodied persons) from disturbing the ritual. In the present context, this is done to signal the intensification of feeling/attention for the duration of the rite. Clapping the hands or snapping fingers is also more than just making a noise; it's a signal to oneself and others—a signal for attention or invitation.

The directions (eight, nine, or ten) are presided over by groups of deities such as the Lokapalas, the Durgas and the eight forms of Ganesha (there are many more). Worship of these deity-groups could be added to this *puja* at a later stage, according to preference. Note that there is no correspondence made between elements and directions, as one finds commonly in Western esotericism. Eight is generally an auspicious number in South Asia and the eight-direction pattern can also be found in temple and city architecture, and in ceremonies related to kingship (where the ruler's body is ritually made the centre of the eight directions). The eight directions are frequently internalised—for example, as eight cremation grounds, or eight chakras.

Honouring the Guru

I honour my guru, the guru's guru; the Adiguru. I give attention to those who have been teachers for me.

This is a brief moment during the sequence where I acknowledge my debt and relationship to past teachers (and, often, friends who have died)—it's an acknowledgement of the role that others have played in bringing me to this moment. One of the trickiest aspects of Tantra for contemporary Western practitioners is the whole question of having gurus. When I occasionally lecture on the subject of Tantra, I'm often asked if I think a guru is 'necessary' and I usually answer by saying that I don't feel that I would have gained the understanding of Tantra that I feel I have, without the person I refer to as my 'guru'. For me, the necessity of the guru underscores the *relational* aspect of Tantra practice. It is a practice which requires the presence and co-operation of other people—friends, teachers, even (if possible) a loose community or network of other practitioners. As the *Kulanarva Tantra* expresses it: 'Experience and good company are the two clear eyes of the seeker.' My relation with the person who agreed to become my guru—to help me in developing my own practice and approach—is a kind of friendship. It has been intense at times, particularly when we lived in the same city and could meet up fairly regularly. Now we live at different ends of the Earth, and the relationship we have is, of necessity, different. It's not like he even tells me things I should or shouldn't do, or advises me on what to practice, or that we must agree on points of doctrine or theology. Frequently, we don't.

Nyasa

> I salute Shiva Shakti in my heart
> I salute Shiva Shakti on the crown of my head
> I salute Shiva Shakti on the top of my forehead
> I salute Shiva Shakti in my Kavacha
> I salute Shiva Shakti in my three eyes
> I salute Shiva Shakti in my yoni/linga

Nyasa ('placing', 'stamping' or 'imposition') is a major element of Tantric practice, whereby the body is made 'divine' by touching different body regions, visualising a particular God/Goddess (sometimes a God and *Shakti* pairing, also constellations, planets, the letters of the Sanskrit alphabet, sacred sites) often accompanied by mantras. Some *nyasa* sequences are highly complex and can be likened to inscribing a yantra onto one's body. *Nyasa* can be performed as part of *puja* or as a practice in itself. The above is a very simple *nyasa* sequence.

In 'placing' Shiva-Shakti within the body, Shiva-Shakti resides there, and we remind ourselves that we are Shiva-Shakti—or that Shiva-Shakti is our 'source'. We become identical to, or are merged with, the substantive presence of the deity who is the subject of the *puja*. In this approach to *puja*, *nyasa* is one of the processes by which we identify with the subject of the *puja*—simultaneously making our bodies 'divine' and infusing them with the presence of the deity. Following *nyasa*, the deity is often meditated upon as forming within the 'void' in our bodies, and is then externalised (via an out-breath) into a form for worship—either as a visualised form, or a picture, statue, etc.

In this *nyasa*, the *Heart* does not refer to the anatomical organ but to the 'centre' of the body—the dwelling place of deity. The term *Kavacha* ('armour') is used to denote a set of practices related to magical protection—sometimes using amulets, mantra and liturgy to various deities. As to the *Three Eyes*—many Tantric deities are described in texts (and depicted in iconography) as having three eyes (Skt: *Tryambakam* lit: 'three-eyes'). In modern forms of Tantra this is often related to the popular occult notion of the 'third eye' and the Ajna Chakra. There are however, other considerations. In Tantra texts there are many triplicities—inter-related concepts such as the three *Gunas* ('qualities'); three *Shaktis* (Jnana-Iccha-Kriya); three times (past, present, future); three functions (creation, maintenance, destruction); three lights (Sun, Moon,

Fire) and the three worlds. These triplicities are often mapped onto or homologised within the body. There is a popular Puranic story that tells how Parvati, Shiva's spouse, once playfully crept up behind Shiva and covered his eyes with her hands, plunging the Universe into darkness. In order to save the Universe, Shiva opened a 'third eye' between his brows. *Tryambakam* signifies mastery or equipoise between the triplicities.

Eyes are tremendously important in Indian religiosity. *Darsan* (which can be translated as 'to see with reverence') is a central feature in many forms of worship and ritual. In meeting the eyes of a god or goddess (be it through a statue, an auspicious person, or a possessed devotee or a lover) one is said to receive the blessings of that deity. In traditional temple *puja* where deity-images are created, the figure's eyes are the last to be painted. *Darsan* is a communion—an exchange between devotee and deity or, for that matter, a place or an object. *Yoni/Linga* in this context refers to the practitioner's sexual organ.

Shiva-Shakti, in the context of this *nyasa*, is seen as providing the union of consciousness and power. Various textual sources privilege either Shiva or Shakti as the prime cause of the universe, but there is a common tendency in both Trika and Sri Vidya sources to view Shiva-Shakti as a dynamic continuum—reciprocally realising each other. Neither can exist without the other.

The Worship of the Sense-Arrows

I close my eyes and, picking up a freshly-cut flower, inhale its perfume. As I breathe in the scent, I feel close to me the arrow-goddess of the delight of smell.

I reach out and take a grape into my mouth. As its juice floods my mouth I let form before me the shape of the arrow-goddess of the delight of taste.

I press the tips of my fingers together. I direct my attention to how my clothes hang on my body, the feel of the ground beneath me. As I feel these sensations I let the shape form of the arrow-goddess of the delight of touch before me.

I listen to the sounds around me, to the soft breath of those others in this room, to the ticking of a clock, the low hum of electricity, the rumble of traffic outside, the distant bark of a dog. Out of these sounds there forms the arrow-goddess of the delight of hearing.

> *I look about me, settling my gaze on as many places as possible, objects, their shadows, the glinting of lights, textures, surfaces, folds. As my eyes dart about I glimpse the fleeting form of the arrow-goddess of the delight of seeing.*

Here, the senses are personified and worshipped as goddesses—the Arrow-Shaktis. In several Tantric texts (particularly the texts of the Sri Vidya movement) the senses are referred to as flowery arrows, shot from the sugar-cane bow (the mind) and piercing the objects of perception—recalling Puranic tales wherein the God Kama shoots forth an arrow which causes Shiva to be inflamed with desire, so that he acts towards the world. All sense-experiences are divine, opportunities for us to experience wonder, joy, delight. All sensations and all pleasures are emanations of the divine. In cultivating Tantric awareness, the aim is to develop a sensitivity towards the beauty of everything around us and, in so doing, move closer to the sustained awareness of the wonder of the pulsation of consciousness that pervades all experience.

Shakti

Shakti is often translated in popular/occult texts to mean 'energy'. However, it has a wide range of meanings—such as capacity, power, ability, potential. Its verbal root is *sak*—and in its broadest sense it refers to the power to produce an effect. There are a vast variety of ways in which *Shakti* is used. For example, in the Puranas, *Shakti* is often used to denote both a philosophical concept and a goddess simultaneously. She is both the power possessed by the gods and is the transcendental source of the manifest universe—from which all forms emerge and into which, ultimately, they dissolve. *Shakti* is sometimes paired with a male god and portrayed as her consort; at other times, *Shakti* is said to create her male partner from her own body. *Shakti* can imply a relationship between two (or more) points/processes. *Shakti* can be transmitted between persons (embodied or unembodied)—and it can be thought of as a medium of transaction or exchange. *Shakti* can be accumulated through practices—it has moral and ethical aspects. Although *Shakti* is intangible, the degree of *Shakti* a person possesses is said to be reflected in the body as evidence of a practitioner's devotion and self-control (see Alter, 1992). *Shakti* as female power is also related to the belief that women generate more heat than men.

All the powers/abilities of our body/mind complexes can be interacted with as *Shaktis*. The personification and worship of the Sense-Shaktis which take place in this *puja* are of a *temporary* nature. The forms of the deities for ritual and devotion can be abandoned at later stages of practice.

Worship of the Arrow-Shakti

Seated with the five Sense-Shaktis before me, they shimmer and merge in and out of each other, becoming a single figure—their unity.

> *Arrow goddess of the five, clothed in space, of a hue as red as a dawn, drenched in the nectar of ecstasy, holding in her two hands, five arrows and five flowers. She smiles gently, radiating satisfaction and contentment.*
>
> *I make offerings to the Arrow goddess:*
>
> * *Om, this is water, this is for sipping*
> * *Om, this is incense, this is for prayer*
> * *Om, this is perfume, this is for enjoyment*
> * *Om, this is food, this is for sustenance*
> * *Om this is flower, this is for experience*
> * *Om this is fire, this is for sacrifice*
>
> *I contemplate this form, then breathe her into my heart and meditate upon her presence there.*
>
> *Three handclaps to close.*

The offerings made here are the offerings one would make to an honoured guest—they are transactions. The Arrow-Shakti or Arrow-Goddess is a form of the Great Goddess *Lalita Tripurasundari*, who is the central deity of Sri Vidya (see Brooks, 1992). She emerges out of the totality of all sense-perceptions. She is the totality of the sense-perceptions—she is the transcendent source of all experience and all experience is simultaneously a gift *from* Her and an offering *to* Her. She is the Dancing Queen. She delights in all experience and to experience that delight—that wonder—is to *become* Her. The worship of the Arrow-goddess is a reminder—an invitation to contemplate that our senses are not really separate from each other; they cross-talk, play with each other. As much as we think the world in pieces, we experience that which is around us very differently.

Following the offerings and the contemplation of the Arrow-Goddess as separate to oneself, She is—with an in-breath—drawn within, residing in the heart-cave of the self. The *puja* is ended, but the aim, after all, is to shift the practitioner's awareness to being more attentive (and appreciative) of everyday experience—to be open to the wonder of the world around us and through which we move.

> *Let my idle chatter be the muttering of prayer, my every manual movement the execution of ritual gesture, my walking a ceremonial circumambulation, my eating and other acts the rite of sacrifice, my lying down prostration in worship, my every pleasure enjoyed with dedication of myself, let whatever activity is mine be some form of worship of you.*[3]

Conclusion

I was first drawn to Tantra practice in the early 1980s, through a series of recurring dreams in which the goddess Kali loomed large. At that point in my life I was involved in Wicca, and it would have been easy to interpret my dreams of Kali within a Wiccan perspective. But I was looking for something else. Westernised accounts and appropriations of what Tantra is supposedly concerned with are legion. In many ways, one of the largest obstacles I have had to work around over the last thirty years or so, has been moving through the Western representations of Tantra (both occult and scholarly) and discovering the rich and diverse theological approaches in South Asian texts themselves. As I came to grapple with this material, I found that in order to understand it, I had to abandon the Western (imperialist) perspective that asserts that the practices of other cultures can be easily assimilated into Western universalised esoteric schemas and, instead, seek to understand how those practices related to the wider cultural formations of India—both historically and in the contemporary milieu. In doing so, I found myself not only abandoning much of my previous thinking about magical practice, but also focusing towards what for me were increasingly central themes around which I wanted to base my practice—the wonder of life, the act of living from moment to moment, and the myriad ways in which we can experience that through our relations with the world.

References

Alter, J.S. 1992. *The Wrestler's Body: Identity and Ideology in North India*. Berkeley, California: University of California Press.

Brooks, D.R. 1992. *Auspicious Wisdom: The Texts and Traditions of Srividya Sakta Tantrism in South India*. Albany, New York: State University of New York Press.

Brown, W.N. 1966. *Man in the Universe: Some Continuities in Indian Thought*, Berkeley, California: University of California Press.

Daniélou, A. 1991. *The Myths and Gods of India*. Rochester, Vermont: Inner Traditions.

Harper, K.A. and Brown, R.L. (eds.). 2002. *The Roots of Tantra*. Albany, New York: State University of New York Press.

Hyatt, C. S. 1999. *Tantra Without Tears*. Tempe, Arizona: New Falcon Publications.
Padoux, A. 2002, 'What do we mean by Tantrism?' in Harper, K.A. and Brown, R.L. (eds.). 2002. *The Roots of Tantra* Albany, New York: State University of New York Press.
Smith. F. M. 2006. *The Self Possessed: Deity and Spirit Possession in South Asian Literature and Civilisation*. New York: Columbia University Press.
Tigunait, R. 1998. *Sakti: The Power in Tantra — a Scholarly Approach*. Honesdale, Pennsylvania: The Himalayan Institute Press.
Urban, H.B. 2003. *Tantra: Sex Secrecy, Politics and Power in the Study of Religion* Berkeley, California: University of California Press.
Weinstone, A. 2004. *Avatar Bodies: A Tantra for Posthumanism*. Minneapolis: University of Minnesota Press.

Endnotes

1   Christopher S. Hyatt, Tantra Without Tears, New Falcon Publications, 1999, p. 10
2   From the *Gandharva Tantra*, quoted in Alain Daniélou, The Myths and Gods of India, Inner Traditions, 1991, p. 377
3   From the *Saundaryalahari*, quoted in W.N Brown, *Man in the Universe: Some Continuities in Indian Thought*, University of California Press, Berkeley, California, 1966, p. 96.

Contributors

Nikki Bado is an Associate Professor in the Department of Philosophy and Religious Studies at Iowa State University. Bado is co-editor with Chas Clifton of the *Equinox Studies in Contemporary and Historical Paganism* and serves on the editorial board of the *Journal of Magic, Ritual, and Witchcraft*. Her books include *Coming to the Edge of the Circle: A Wiccan Initiation Ritual* (Oxford University Press, 2005) and *Toying With God: The World of Religious Games and Dolls*, with Rebecca Sachs Norris (Baylor, 2010). Bado was recently a Visiting Research Fellow at the Nanzan Institute for Religion and Culture in Nagoya, Japan, where she examined the philosophical implications of ritual praxis and embodiment, and collected footage for a documentary on the Shikoku Pilgrimage.
Email address: nikkibf@iastate.edu

Jenny Blain is Senior Lecturer in Sociology at Sheffield Hallam University, where she leads the cross-disciplinary Master of Research in Social Sciences and specialises in ethnographic research, currently exploring uses of visual ethnography in research on new or 'old' religions and rituals. Dr Blain's recent publications on shamanism, *seidr*, Heathenry and paganisms include *Nine Worlds of Seid-Magic* (Routledge 2002), *Researching Paganisms* (Blain, Ezzy & Harvey, Altamira 2004) and numerous articles and chapters, including 'Now many of those things are shown to me which I was denied before: Seidr, shamanism and journeying, past and present,' for *Studies in Religion / Sciences Religieuses* in 2005. Her book with Robert Wallis on *Sacred Sites Contested Rites/ Rights* was published by Sussex Academic Press in 2007, and current work includes exploration of the importance of 'ancestors' for identities of today—not only ancestors of the far past, but those uncovered through family genealogy.
Email address: j.blain@shu.ac.uk

Nevill Drury is an independent researcher whose specialist interests include contemporary Western magic, shamanism and visionary art. For many years he worked in the Australian book industry as an editor and art book publisher and in 2008 he received his PhD from the University of Newcastle for a dissertation on Rosaleen Norton and the Western esoteric tradition. His most recent publications include *Stealing Fire from Heaven: the Rise of Modern Western Magic* (Oxford University Press, 2011), *Wisdom Seekers: the Rise of the New Spirituality* (O Books, 2011), *Homage to Pan: the Life, Art and Sex Magic of Rosaleen Norton* (Creation Oneiros, 2009) and *The Dictionary of Magic* (Watkins, 2005).
Email address: nevill@nevilldrury.com Website: www.nevilldrury.com

Dave Evans completed his PhD on post-World War Two occultism at the University of Bristol and published it under the title *A History of British Magick after Crowley* (Hidden Publishing, 2007). He writes for numerous magazines and websites in addition to book editing and was the co-founder of the *Journal for the Academic Study of Magic* which ran from 2003-2009. He is an independent multidisciplinary scholar of cultural and social history and is internationally homeless as a wandering teacher.
He can be contacted via a webform at http://daveevansuk.reachby.com

Amy Hale is Adjunct Associate Professor of Humanities at University of Maryland University College. She specializes in contemporary Celtic cultures, primarily the intersection of Cornish identity politics, policy and economic development. In the field of Western Esotericism her specializations include modern British esoteric history and culture, spiritual tourism and methodology. Edited editions include *New Directions in Celtic Studies*, co-edited with Philip Payton (University of Exeter Press, 2000), *Inside Merlin's Cave: A Cornish Arthurian Reader*, co-edited with Alan M. Kent and Tim Saunders. (Francis Boutle Press, 2000), and *Journal of the Academic Study of Magic 5* (Mandrake Press, Oxford 2009) *The Supersensual Life of Ithell Colquhoun: Surrealism, Occultism, Celticism* is forthcoming (Francis Boutle Press).
Email address: Hale.Amy@spcollege.edu

Phil Hine lives and works in London. He has been a magical practitioner and author for over thirty years, and practises a hybridised form of Tantra. He has a particular interest in the history of occultism and how it relates to other cultural formations. He is the author of *Condensed Chaos*, *Prime Chaos* and *The Pseudonomicon* (published by Original Falcon Publications) and has contributed to a wide range of occult journals. His archive of writing can be viewed at: www.philhine.org.uk and he has a new blog project underway: http://enfolding.org

Lynne Hume is Associate Professor and Honorary Research Consultant at the University of Queensland, Australia. Her special interests are in the anthropology of religion and spirituality, alternative spiritualities, consciousness studies, anthropology of the senses, Aboriginal Australian spirituality, and religious dress. She has published in all these areas. Her most recent monographs are *Portals: Opening Doorways to Other Realities through the Senses* (2007) Oxford: Berg; *Ancestral Power: The Dreaming, Consciousness and Aboriginal Australians* (2002) Carlton: Melbourne University Press; and a co-authored book with Nevill Drury, *The Varieties of Magical Experience: Indigenous, Medieval and Modern Magic* (2013) Santa Barbara, CA: Praeger ABC-CLIO .
Email address: l.hume@uq.edu.au

Marguerite Johnson is Senior Lecturer in Classics at The University of Newcastle, Australia. Her primary research interests are in ancient literature with a focus on cultural representations of gender, sexualities and the body. Related to these areas is her work on later engagements with ancient texts and traditions, including examinations of ancient religious and magical practices in modern contexts, particularly issues relating to Hecate, as well as classical references in later European texts such as the *Malleus Maleficarum*. Dr Johnson is the co-author, with Terry Ryan, of *Sexuality in Greek and Roman Society and Literature: a Sourcebook* (Routledge, 2005) and author of *Sappho* (Duckworth, 2006), 'Drawing Down the Goddess: The Ancient (Female) Deities of Modern Paganism' in *Handbook of Contemporary Paganism*, ed. James Lewis and Murphy Pizza (Brill Academic Publishers, 2009), 'The Witching Hour: Sex Magic in 1950s Australia,' *Journal for the Academic Study of Magic* (2009) 5: 234-87, as well as eight entries in *Encyclopedia of Witchcraft*, ed. Richard Golden (ABC-CLIO, 2006).
Email address: Marguerite.Johnson@newcastle.edu.au

Thomas Karlsson founded the esoteric order Dragon Rouge and is author of several articles and books published in more than ten languages, including *Uthark: Nightside of the Runes* (2002); *Qabalah, Qliphoth and Goetic Magic* (2007); *Adul Runa and the Gothic Cabala* (forthcoming in English) and *Astral Travels Out of the Body* (forthcoming in English). Thomas holds a PhD, teaches Western Esotericism at Stockholm University, Sweden, and gives lectures, seminars and workshops on a regular basis. He is also a lyric writer for music bands and is involved in various art projects.
Email address: thomas@dragonrouge.net

James R. Lewis is Associate Professor of Religious Studies at the University of Tromsø, Norway, and Honorary Senior Research Fellow at the University of Wales Lampeter. He edits Brill's Handbooks on Contemporary Religion series. He is an active, well-published scholar of new religious movements. His Brill publications include co-editorship of the *Handbook of New Age* (2007), *Handbook of Contemporary Paganism* (2009), and *Handbook of Religion and the Authority of Science* (2011).
Email address: james.lewis@uit.no

Libuše Martínková is Junior Assistant at Department of the study of religion at the Hussite Theological Faculty of Charles University, Prague, Czech Republic. She received her MA degree in theology and study of religion in 2004. Since 2001 she has been specializing in the relation between the religion and the Internet (*Religious Spam in Email Communication, GSM Technology and its Use in Religious Life, Cyberspace as a Religious Space*). She is currently working on her doctoral project *The Use of New Media in the Vocation of Modern Practical Theology* and lectures in the course *New Media and Christianity* at the Hussite Theological Faculty.
Email address: Libuse.M@seznam.cz

Robert J. Wallis is Professor of Visual Culture and Director of the MA in Art History and Visual Culture at Richmond University, London, and a Visiting Research Fellow in Archaeology at the University of Southampton. His research interests consider indigenous and prehistoric art in shamanist/animist communities, and the re-presentation of the past in the present by contemporary pagans and neoshamans. He has authored *Shamans / neo-Shamans: Ecstasy, Alternative Archaeologies and Contemporary Pagans* (Routledge 2003), co-authored *Sacred Sites, Contested Rites/Rights: Pagan Engagements with Archaeological Monuments* (Sussex Academic Press 2007) and the *Historical Dictionary of Shamanism* (Scarecrow Press 2007), and co-edited *A Permeability of Boundaries: New Approaches to the Archaeology of Art, Religion and Folklore* (Oxford BAR 2001) and, most recently, *Antiquaries and Archaists: The Past in the Past, the Past in the Present* (Spire Press 2009). Wallis co-directs the Sacred Sites Project with Jenny Blain, examining pagan engagements with archaeology. He is a Fellow of the Royal Anthropological Institute and the Society of Antiquaries of London.
Email address: WALLISR@Richmond.ac.uk

Don Webb is the former High Priest of the Temple of Set. His Teacher in the Temple was Dr. Stephen E. Flowers. Don has had over 300 short

stories published, about a hundred poems, three novels and four books on occult topics. He teaches creative writing at UCLA by night and has a screech owl nursery in his backyard. His publications include *Aleister Crowley: The Fire and the Force* (Runa-Raven Press, 2005) and *The Seven Faces of Darkness* (Runa-Raven Press, 1996) and his work has been translated into eleven languages. Like all Texans he has a secret chilli recipe, and unlike most is actually shy in person. Nevertheless, he is pleased to correspond on matters involving the Temple of Set, the interrelationship between occultism and writing, and current magical practice related to the figure of Set-Typhon in Late Antiquity.
Email address: setnakt@austin.rr.com

Dominique Beth Wilson is a PhD candidate at the Department of Studies in Religion at the University of Sydney. Her research interests include pre-Christian mythology, esoteric and New Age beliefs, and the integration these beliefs into new religious movements. Her honour thesis looked at the mythic histories of occult lodges, and her PhD research explores the architecture of the wise man figure with comparative religion.
Email address: shanavyre@hotmail.com

Andrei A. Znamenski has studied history and anthropology both in Russia and the United States. Formerly a resident scholar at the Library of Congress, then a foreign visiting professor at Hokkaido University, Japan, he has taught various courses at Samara Pedagogical University, The University of Toledo, Alabama State University, and the University of Memphis. Among them are World Civilizations and the History of Religions. His major fields of interests include Shamanism, the history of Western esotericism as well as indigenous religions of Siberia and North America. Znamenski lived and travelled extensively in Alaska, Siberia, and Japan. His field and archival research among Athabaskan Indians in Alaska and native people of the Altai (Southern Siberia) resulted in the book *Shamanism and Christianity: Native Responses to Russian Missionaries (1999)* and *Through Orthodox Eyes: Russian Missionary Narratives of Travels to the Dena'ina and Ahtna* (2003). After this, Znamenski became interested in the cultural history of shamanism. Trying to answer a question why shamanism became so popular with Western spiritual seekers since the 1960s, he wrote another book, *The Beauty of the Primitive: Shamanism and Western Imagination* (2007) and edited the three-volume anthology *Shamanism: Critical Concepts* (2004). Simultaneously, he continued to explore shamanism of Siberian indigenous people, travelling to the Altai and surrounding areas, which led to the publication of *Shamanism in Siberia* (2003). Between 2003 and 2004, he resided in

Japan, where along with his Japanese colleague, Professor Koichi Inoue, Znamenski worked with *itako*, blind female healers and mediums from the Amori prefecture.
Email address: andreiznam@yahoo.com

Index

A

Academics: *4, 28, 130, 272, 353*
Acid House: *141*
Adept: *182, 248, 249, 250, 253, 254, 255, 258, 314*
Adjusted styles of communication: *146*
Adlam: *148*
Adler, Margot: *67, 81, 85, 86, 135, 148*
Aghora: *260*
Agrippa, H. Cornelius: *337, 365, 374, 375*
Aiwass: *11, 208, 209, 210, 213, 230, 235*
Alchemy: *310, 314, 315*
Aldhouse-Green: *138, 148*
Alekto: *103*
Allsherjargoði: *176*
Altars: *8, 38, 40, 42, 45, 46, 47, 48, 49, 50, 54, 55, 62, 271*
Altered state of consciousness: *20, 21, 22, 24, 33*
Altered states: *7, 10, 22, 24, 29, 30, 33, 59, 107, 114, 118, 119, 120, 122, 129, 130, 139, 145, 189, 200, 240, 416*
Amazonia: *142*
American Indians: *116, 131, 132, 134, 158*
Ancestors: *10, 54, 116, 139, 147, 162, 169, 170, 171, 392, 437*
Ancestor welfare: *147*
Anglo-American: *130*

Anglo-Saxon: *137, 156, 297*
Animal familiars: *135*
Animal helpers: *130*
Animaphany: *146*
Animic ontologies: *10, 129, 146, 156, 157*
Animism: *10, 42, 127, 129, 144, 145, 146, 147, 148, 157*
Animistic: *28, 146*
Animist ontologies: *10, 128, 145*
Animists: *129, 147*
Anthropologists: *2, 3, 4, 30, 83, 106, 115, 128, 129, 132*
Antinomianism: *249, 252*
Applegrove Community: *293, 294, 304*
Appropriation: *97, 103, 116, 127, 129, 131, 134, 136, 144, 145, 158, 264, 269*
Aquino, Michael: *6, 12, 16, 190, 201, 202, 269, 270, 271, 272, 274, 277, 278, 280, 283, 285, 286, 288, 291, 292, 296, 297, 300, 301, 304*
Archaeological: *94, 136, 138, 147*
Archaic techniques of ecstasy: *108, 130*
Archetypal shaman: *135*
Argenteum Astrum: *11, 213, 214, 215, 241, 244, 368, 373*
Arrow-Shakti: *13, 428, 434*
Artemis: *92*
Art of Rosaleen Norton, The: *327, 347, 351, 352, 353, 354, 355, 356, 357, 358, 359, 365, 366, 367, 368, 376, 377, 378*
Ásatrú: *167, 176, 177*
Asprem: *138, 148*
Astral plane: *22, 192, 237*
Atavistic resurgence: *371*
Athena: *46, 48, 49, 51, 52, 54, 56, 62*
Auditory sensory stimulation: *293, 294, 304*
Autoethnography: *128*
Automatism: *309, 310*
Avatar identities: *416*
Avatars: *128, 142*
Ayahuasca: *293, 294, 304*
Ayahuasceros: *293, 294, 304*
Azazel: *12, 249*

B

Badiou, Alain: *293, 294, 304*
Balzer, Marjorie: *128, 148*
Barrett: *148, 318*

Index 445

Barton, Blanche: *261, 264, 266, 268, 278*
Bataille, Georges: *325*
Bates, Brian: *137, 148*
Beals: *131, 148*
Beardsley, Aubrey: *327, 352, 369*
Belief: *3, 19, 32, 41, 43, 44, 59, 77, 87, 93, 94, 97, 98, 140, 143, 146, 197,*
    205, 230, 284, 288, 298, 317, 321, 329, 338, 341, 380, 381, 384, 386,
    390, 393, 394, 395, 396, 398, 433
Bennett, Allan: *187, 206, 207, 232, 233, 314*
Beshroomed: *146*
Biological determinism: *71*
Bird of Hermes (title): *314, 319, 322*
Birocco, Joel: *158*
Biroco, Joel: *397, 398, 399, 404, 407*
Black Eagle: *143*
Black magic: *12, 89*
Black Pope, The: *266, 269, 278*
Blain, Jenny: *10, 27, 31, 33, 129, 136, 138, 145, 147, 148, 156, 158, 159, 162,*
    165, 167, 169, 170, 172, 176, 177, 178, 437, 440
Blogspots: *142*
Bochner: *129, 150*
Body of light: *190, 191, 192, 193, 234*
Body, reclaiming sacrality of: *69, 73*
Book of Lies (Crowley): *215, 219, 220, 222, 238, 240, 387, 399*
Book of Pleasure (Self-Love): The Psychology of Ecstasy, The (Spare): *327,*
    328, 329, 331, 333, 334, 335, 337, 338, 341, 342, 366, 370, 371, 372,
    373, 374, 375, 376, 377
Book of Settlements: 164
Bourkhoun, Tamara: *315*
Brainwave patterns: *29*
Brandi, Alberto: *248, 259, 260*
Breakspear, Francis: *399, 402, 405*
Breton, André: *203, 259, 308, 309, 310, 312, 320*
Brighid: *51*
British Circle of the Universal Bond: *315*
British Druid Order: *138*
Brodie-Innes, John W.: *184, 190, 201, 202*
Brown, Michael F.: *3, 142, 149, 435, 436*
Budapest, Z.: *67, 86*
Buffy the Vampire Slayer: *88, 102, 405*
Bythos: *255*

C

Campbell, Joseph: *88, 130, 138, 149*
Cardinal Rites of Chaos, The: *400, 401, 402, 403*
Carroll, Peter J.: *143, 149, 380, 383, 386, 387, 388, 396, 398, 399, 401, 402, 403, 404, 407*
Castaneda, Carlos: *9, 106, 107, 113, 122, 123, 130, 131, 149, 150, 154, 155*
Categories, conceal as much as reveal: *79, 80*
Cave art: *134*
Cave artists: *135*
Celebration: *38, 42, 43, 44, 48, 51, 52, 69, 94, 139, 353*
Celtic: *41, 45, 51, 55, 59, 61, 138, 139, 140, 141, 149, 150, 152, 153, 154, 184, 186, 319, 320, 321, 438*
Celtic shamanism: *138, 139, 140*
Celts: *54, 138, 149, 152, 319*
Ceremonial magic: *10, 11, 12, 98, 143, 183, 184, 186, 205, 209, 233, 319*
Ceremony: *5, 25, 208, 214, 220, 221, 237, 271*
Changing ones: *136*
Changing the weather: *130*
Chaos International: *384, 387, 400, 401, 402, 403, 406, 407*
Chaos Magic (Kaos Magick/Magik): *142, 149, 151, 285, 399, 403, 405, 407*
Chaos Magick or Vampiric Sorcery: *90*
Chapman: *138, 149, 370*
Charing, Howard: *132*
Charisma: *263, 265*
Charms: *136, 240, 331, 369*
Christianity: *55, 58, 62, 79, 93, 96, 99, 100, 113, 121, 165, 174, 183, 197, 210, 211, 235, 261, 264, 265, 268, 273, 320, 440, 441*
Christian Science: *263, 264*
Chthonic deities: *94, 324, 325*
Churchill, Ward: *149*
Church of Chaos: *387*
Church of Satan: *12, 17, 261, 262, 263, 264, 265, 266, 267, 268, 269, 270, 271, 273, 274, 275, 276, 277, 278, 279, 280, 285, 290, 291, 292, 301, 303, 305*
Church of Satanic Brotherhood, The: *268*
Circle of Chaos, The: *387*
Clan totems: *135*
Clark: *141, 149*
Clifton, Chas: *85, 86, 131, 149, 152, 437*
Clyde Beatty Circus, Anton La Vey and the: *266*
Colonialism: *127, 133*

Index

Colour: *12, 26, 27, 29, 46, 53, 224, 287, 297, 299, 301, 315, 316, 317, 318, 321, 353, 359, 375*
Colquhoun, Ithell: *12, 186, 199, 237, 307, 308, 309, 310, 311, 312, 313, 314, 315, 316, 317, 318, 319, 320, 321, 322, 438*
Co-Masonry: *315*
Communities, human and non-human: *8, 10, 59, 70, 73, 108, 117, 129, 131, 134, 135, 141, 143, 145, 147, 159, 160, 164, 165, 172, 175, 314, 440*
Computers, computer-generated music: *411*
Computer technologies: *13, 409, 410, 411, 412, 415, 416, 421*
Computer use: *410, 411, 413*
Consciousness: *3, 5, 6, 7, 10, 11, 15, 16, 19, 20, 21, 22, 24, 27, 28, 29, 30, 31, 33, 34, 44, 59, 70, 105, 109, 113, 116, 119, 120, 123, 127, 129, 130, 143, 145, 146, 147, 160, 169, 171, 172, 183, 184, 186, 188, 189, 190, 191, 192, 193, 194, 200, 220, 222, 226, 227, 232, 234, 236, 240, 250, 253, 256, 283, 284, 285, 288, 291, 292, 303, 310, 325, 329, 336, 337, 339, 342, 343, 349, 350, 357, 362, 371, 374, 394, 397, 411, 416, 429, 432, 433, 439*
Context: *6, 9, 11, 13, 22, 39, 44, 45, 47, 68, 71, 93, 114, 117, 129, 130, 132, 133, 136, 159, 165, 175, 186, 190, 221, 223, 278, 280, 302, 324, 327, 328, 348, 399, 405, 409, 410, 411, 426, 430, 432*
Conway: *70, 85, 86, 138, 139, 149*
Cornish: *320, 321, 438*
Cornwall: *314, 319, 320, 321, 401, 407*
Corvis Nocturnum: 87
Cosmopolitan: *115, 141*
Costumes: *41, 45, 52, 53, 54*
Coughlin, Timothy Roderick: *87, 88, 89, 101*
Cowan, Thomas: *138, 139, 149*
Creeping Toad: *158*
Crowley, Aleister: *4, 6, 11, 13, 26, 44, 92, 97, 103, 181, 184, 186, 187, 188, 199, 202, 205, 210, 216, 226, 232, 234, 235, 236, 237, 238, 243, 244, 245, 270, 285, 288, 300, 305, 314, 324, 349, 372, 379, 387, 389, 391, 395, 404, 406, 441*
Crowley, Rose: *131, 154, 188, 198, 207, 208, 209, 213, 214, 215, 219, 220, 221, 224, 316, 366, 369*
Cruden, Lauren: *115, 116, 129, 149*
Csikszentmihalyi: *21*
Cú Chulainn: *138*
Cultural imperialism: *134*
Culture-historians: *138*
Culture-vultures: *144*
Cunningham: *55, 61, 135, 149*

Curwen, David: *231, 232*
CyberHeart: *412*
Cyberia: *142, 154*
Cyberpunks: *418*
Cybershamans: *412, 414, 416, 417, 418, 421*
Cyber-sorcerers: *418*
Cyberspace: *13, 142, 383, 409, 412, 413, 414, 416, 417, 418, 419*

D

Dada: *398*
Daly, Mary: *96, 101*
Dance (or 'rave') culture; as illegal: *141, 142*
Daraul, Akron: *396, 399, 407*
Darkchilde.777, Lilith: *98, 99*
Dark Goddess: *8, 94, 101, 256*
Darwinism: *264*
Davidson, Peter: *227, 228, 243*
Davis, Erik: *55, 60, 399, 405*
Davis, John C.: *276, 277*
Davis, Jr. Sammy, Anton La Vey and: *267*
Davy: *43*
Day, John: *399, 405*
Death posture (Spare): *143*
DeCecco, Robert: *274*
Deep Web, The: 417, 418, 419, 421
Deloria, jr., Vine: *117, 125*
Del Renzio, Toni: *308, 309, 314, 322*
Demeter: *95, 96, 97, 101, 103, 324, 325*
Demetra: *93*
De Mille, Richard: *131, 149*
Demiurge: *255*
Deoxyribonucleic Hyperdimension, The: 418, 419, 423
Desmond, Arthur: *270*
Devil: *103, 262, 265, 267, 273, 278, 279, 280, 348, 353, 366, 370, 374, 375*
Devil's Avenger, The (Burton Wolfe): *266*
Diagnostic and Statistical Manual of Mental Disorders (DSM): 158
Dichotomous thinking: *65, 73*
Dietler: *138, 149*
Difference: *6, 24, 69, 84, 90, 92, 128, 254, 263, 309, 311, 403, 418*
Digitalis, Ravien: *9, 87, 88, 89, 90, 93, 101, 102*
Digital music: *410*

Digital spirits: *412*
Diversity: *4, 128, 295, 296, 410, 426*
Divination: *9, 89, 113, 119, 135, 137, 160, 174, 177, 242, 303, 315*
DJ's: *141*
D-OET-25: *397*
Dordogne: *134*
Double-beings: *131*
Dourley: *150*
Dowson, Thomas A.: *128*
Draconian tradition: *248, 250, 251*
Dragon Rouge: *11, 12, 102, 137, 150, 247, 248, 249, 250, 251, 252, 254, 255, 256, 257, 258, 259, 439*
Dragon, symbolism of the: *11, 12, 102, 137, 150, 245, 247, 248, 249, 250, 251, 252, 254, 255, 256, 257, 258, 259, 439*
Drugs: *28, 130, 141, 142, 146, 359, 397, 407*
Druid: *140*
Druidry: *42, 139, 315, 319, 320, 389*
Drum: *108, 109, 110, 133, 139, 167*
Drumming circles: *131*
Drury, Nevill: *1, 123, 134, 150, 181, 200, 202, 205, 323, 365, 367, 375, 376, 384, 438*
Dualism: *259, 260*
Dukes, Ramsey: *399, 400, 403, 406, 407*
Dumas, Denise: *97*
Dumnonioi, Touta: *141*
Dundes, Alan: *79, 80, 81, 85, 86*
Durkheim, Emil: *3, 39, 58*

E

Eagle's Wing College of Shamanic Medicine (formerly Eagle's Wing for Contemporary Shamanism): *132*
Eclectic: *13, 38, 45, 93, 119, 132, 136, 141, 227, 381, 397, 417*
Eclectics: *92, 93*
Eco-nanny: *140*
Ecstasies: *127, 130, 145, 363*
Ecstatic states of consciousness: *411*
Edda, poetic: *167, 178, 179*
Edda, prose: *168*
Eighteenth century: *127, 128*
Eirik the Red: *178*
Eliade, Mircea: *9, 39, 55, 58, 59, 107, 109, 115, 122, 130, 132, 138, 143, 150,*

172, 178, 228, 243, 244, 304
Ellis: *129, 150, 271, 279, 327, 371*
Email lists: *142*
Emotions: *7, 21, 25, 30, 53, 54, 83, 99, 200, 296, 297*
Empowerment: *88, 100, 128, 132, 142, 297*
Energy: *7, 16, 20, 22, 23, 24, 25, 28, 31, 68, 87, 88, 97, 197, 213, 222, 232, 233, 234, 241, 256, 259, 285, 286, 287, 288, 293, 318, 319, 321, 330, 340, 412, 422, 433*
England: *4, 14, 27, 137, 153, 196, 198, 199, 202, 207, 214, 224, 233, 236, 237, 400, 407*
Enochian Keys: *270*
Enochian magic: *214, 237, 314, 315*
Entheogen: *144, 146, 397*
Entheogenic: *20, 146, 397*
Entheogens: *7, 24, 27, 28*
Entheogen tourism: *144*
Enuma Elish: *255, 256*
Epicureanism: *262*
Epistemology: *33, 140, 146*
Ergi: *148, 166, 167, 174, 175, 176, 178*
Erowid: *142*
Esotericism: *1, 10, 55, 56, 60, 106, 110, 118, 122, 181, 216, 239, 242, 243, 247, 249, 251, 252, 253, 256, 259, 367, 425, 426, 430, 438, 439, 441*
Essentialism: *69, 78, 80*
Ethnographic records: *128*
Europe: *9, 27, 109, 117, 121, 123, 127, 130, 131, 132, 133, 134, 135, 136, 137, 138, 141, 142, 144, 145, 148, 149, 155, 160, 170, 171, 176, 177, 178, 186, 216, 224, 228, 327, 387, 399, 405*
European prehistory: *135*
Evola, Julius: *254, 259, 260*
Extra pay, to shamanisms: *144*

F

Fake Indians: *131*
Fallen Angels: *12, 249*
Farrar: *86, 135, 150, 390*
Fellowship of Isis: *315, 319*
Feminism: *72, 78, 100*
Fikes: *122, 123, 131, 150*
Fitche, Johann Gottlieb: *289, 291, 292, 304*
Flaherty, Gloria: *128, 150*

Flesh space / fleshspace: *418, 419*
Flotation tanks: *411*
Flow: *20, 21, 34, 68, 74, 287, 288, 301, 318, 330, 344, 412*
Fluffy Bunnies: *9, 89*
Fluid boundaries: *128, 390*
Flying Rolls: *189, 201*
Folk traditions: *144*
Ford, Michael W.: *90, 91, 92, 93, 97, 98, 101, 103*
Fortune, Dion: *4, 6, 15, 16, 183, 184, 191, 201, 202, 203, 315, 349, 365*
Foundation for Shamanic Studies (see also Harner, Michael): *9, 108, 133, 158*
Fractal imagery: *417*
France: *134, 208, 224, 240, 327*
Frater Marabas (aka Chris Bray): *387*
Free belief: *143*
Frequencies: *20*
Freud, Sigmund: *3, 310, 324, 368, 371, 375, 389*
Fries, Jan: *137, 138, 139, 140, 144, 150*

G

Galdr: *137, 166*
Galdrbok: *137, 152*
Gallagher, Anne-Marie: *138, 150*
Gardell: *150*
Garden of Eden: *247, 248, 256*
Gardner, Gerald: *314, 315, 388*
Garstin, Edward Langsford: *314*
Gender: *72, 74, 75, 83, 93, 117, 136, 174, 176, 178, 308, 312, 313, 390, 439*
Genesis P. Orridge (aka Neil Megson): *388, 400, 404*
George, Demetra: *93, 95, 96, 101, 103*
Gerkowska, Nadine: *381, 399, 401*
Germany: *137, 197, 230, 244, 295, 399, 405, 419*
Gilmore, Peter H.: *280*
Globalised: *128, 142, 143*
Gnosis: *56, 60, 183, 189, 223, 231, 236, 238*
God: *4, 5, 11, 12, 15, 38, 39, 45, 48, 53, 61, 67, 68, 72, 73, 77, 78, 81, 86, 96, 125, 134, 146, 154, 168, 171, 178, 182, 183, 188, 189, 191, 192, 194, 195, 196, 197, 198, 206, 207, 208, 212, 218, 220, 222, 233, 235, 239, 248, 249, 254, 255, 256, 257, 258, 259, 279, 281, 284, 286, 287, 288, 289, 290, 292, 293, 302, 303, 305, 313, 325, 349, 350, 356, 362, 363, 364, 368, 371, 380, 391, 392, 393, 410, 428, 429, 431, 432, 433, 437*
Goddess spirituality: *8, 9, 11, 95, 181*

Gods: *6, 15, 34, 40, 41, 42, 43, 46, 48, 49, 52, 56, 61, 67, 68, 72, 73, 74, 78, 82, 91, 93, 100, 139, 150, 153, 156, 168, 183, 186, 188, 189, 191, 193, 208, 210, 211, 226, 234, 249, 250, 284, 285, 288, 289, 302, 312, 322, 324, 325, 330, 331, 346, 349, 350, 362, 363, 378, 391, 393, 405, 433, 435, 436*
Goetia: *12, 324, 337, 360, 377, 403, 404, 406*
Golden Dawn: *4, 5, 6, 10, 11, 12, 16, 181, 182, 183, 184, 185, 186, 187, 188, 189, 190, 191, 192, 193, 194, 195, 196, 197, 198, 199, 200, 201, 202, 203, 206, 207, 209, 213, 215, 224, 227, 232, 235, 237, 242, 312, 314, 315, 316, 317, 318, 320*
Golden Hind, The: 327, 370
Gonce, John: *399, 405*
Goodman, Felicitas: *119*
Goodrick-Clarke, Nick: *138, 150, 196, 202*
Goose of Hermogenes (title): *314, 318, 319, 322*
Goossens, Sir Eugene: *348, 376*
Granholm, Kennet: *137, 150, 259, 260*
Grant, Kenneth: *11, 132, 210, 211, 231, 232, 234, 235, 236, 237, 238, 244, 245, 259, 327, 332, 339, 340, 341, 365, 367, 368, 369, 370, 371, 372, 373, 374, 375, 377, 378, 379, 399, 401*
Graves, Robert: *67, 86, 321*
Grayston, Lorraine: *132*
Great Beast: *208, 211, 235, 238*
Great God Pan: *325, 349*
Green, Dave: *56, 61, 85, 131, 138, 148, 150, 369, 398, 399, 400, 403, 408, 411, 419, 421, 422*
Greenlandic: *134*
Greenlees, Gavin: *347, 350, 352, 353, 354, 357, 368, 376*
Greenwood, Susan: *1, 4, 14, 30, 31, 34, 55, 61, 150, 158*
Grey Owl: *131*
Grundy, Stephan: *172, 178*
Guardian spirit: *23, 111*
Guðríðr: 162
Guenther, Herbert: *425*
Gunnhildr: 164

H

Hallucinations: *129, 145, 146*
Hallucinogen: *109, 146*
Hanged Man, The, Tarot image of: *259*
Hardman, Charlotte: *151*

Index 453

Harmony, facilitation of by shamans: *129*
Harms, Daniel: *399, 405*
Harner, Michael: *9, 10, 16, 24, 31, 34, 107, 108, 109, 110, 111, 112, 113, 114,*
    115, 119, 122, 123, 124, 130, 133, 134, 135, 136, 138, 140, 143, 144,
    147, 151
Harner Shamanic Counseling Training: *133*
Harnessing game: *130*
Harvey, Graham: *25, 34, 56, 57, 85, 86, 95, 99, 100, 101, 103, 129, 132, 141,*
    143, 144, 145, 147, 148, 149, 151, 156, 158, 272, 419, 421, 437
Hastrup, Kristen: *163, 164, 174, 178*
Hawkins, Jaq: *383, 386, 390, 395, 396, 398, 399, 402, 403, 406, 407*
Hayden: *151, 238*
Healing: *10, 20, 22, 23, 25, 26, 31, 33, 51, 61, 72, 88, 101, 109, 115, 121, 123,*
    124, 125, 129, 130, 133, 135, 137, 139, 141, 143, 148, 151, 152, 153,
    155, 160, 170, 171, 174, 175, 177, 197, 241, 242, 284, 315, 417, 418
Heathen: *137*
Heathenry: *42, 141, 149, 159, 176, 177, 178, 437*
Hecate: *9, 12, 87, 90, 91, 92, 93, 94, 95, 96, 97, 101, 103, 187, 249, 302, 324,*
    325, 349, 360, 366, 367, 439
Hegarty, Diane: *266*
Heidelberg University Collaborative Research Center: *419, 420, 421, 423*
Heinze, Ruth Inge: *125, 129, 151*
Helios: *96*
Helpers: *130, 133, 143*
Herakleitos: *251*
Hermes Trismegistus: *20*
Hermetic Brotherhood of Luxor: *216, 224, 227, 228, 243*
Hesiod: *90, 101*
Heterosexist stereotypes: *136*
Heterotopic space: *141*
High seat or ritual platform: *136, 161, 167, 169*
High-seat seidr: *136*
Hindu philosophy: *143, 372*
Hine, Phil: *13, 143, 151, 380, 381, 384, 386, 390, 391, 392, 393, 394, 395,*
    396, 397, 398, 399, 401, 402, 405, 406, 407, 425, 438
Historic: *133, 162, 188, 196*
Holographic entry point: *41, 49, 59*
Holy: *37, 39, 40, 42, 57, 58, 62, 68, 69, 93, 96, 218, 226, 294, 381, 382*
Holy Guardian Angel: *4, 207, 292*
Holyoak: *148, 151*
Honouring the Ancient Dead (HAD): *147*
Hoppál, Mihaly: *133, 144, 151, 178*

Horned god of the witches: *134*
Høst, Annette: *160*
Hrafnar (see also Paxton, Diana): *10, 118, 119, 160, 167, 168, 170, 171, 177*
Human-animal therianthropic figures: *134*
Human-people: *129, 147*
Human remains: *147, 156*
Human world: *129, 146, 147, 282*
Humphrey, Caroline: *143, 155*
Humphries, Greg: *398, 401, 405*
Hungary: *144, 153, 216*
Hutson: *141, 151*
Hutton, Ronald: *1, 14, 67, 85, 86, 130, 134, 135, 138, 140, 151, 395, 398, 399, 400, 403, 404, 405, 407, 408*
Huxley, Thomas: *132, 154, 327*
Hyatt, Christopher: *426, 436*
Hyle: *256, 257*

I

Ibn Sabah, Hasan: *396*
Iceland: *161, 162, 163, 165, 171, 172, 176, 178*
Ideology: *117, 137, 141*
Imagination: *5, 6, 7, 13, 20, 24, 25, 26, 28, 29, 30, 39, 46, 77, 94, 97, 110, 120, 186, 188, 189, 190, 191, 241, 425*
Indigenous shamans: *28, 127, 128, 133, 136*
Individualise: *143*
Individuals-practicing: *66*
Initiation: *12, 14, 29, 33, 41, 65, 66, 67, 72, 80, 86, 130, 133, 184, 207, 210, 231, 232, 236, 242, 252, 253, 254, 281, 288, 319, 320, 394, 396, 437*
Initiation paradigm, problems with: *80*
Inner visions: *129, 130*
In Pursuit of Satan (Robert Hicks): *272*
Insider anthropology: *129*
Insider/outsider problems in religious studies: *65, 66*
Internet: *142, 166, 261, 383, 384, 412, 413*
Intuition: *2, 32, 288*
Invisible religions: *417*
IOT (Illuminates of Thanateros): *381, 384, 386, 387, 394, 396, 397, 400, 403, 404, 406*
Ipsissimus: *296, 297, 300, 301*
Irish: *55, 59, 138, 156, 184*
Iron Age: *138, 154, 179*

J

Jackson: *129, 152*
Jahweh-in-drag: *81*
Jakobsen, Merete D.: *129, 134, 152*
James: *12, 58, 60, 67, 102, 138, 152, 261, 296, 300, 301, 304, 313, 401, 439, 440*
Jilek: *130, 152*
Jivaro (see also Harner, Michael): *115, 140*
Johnson, Nathan: *8, 9, 87, 90, 91, 92, 102, 137, 152, 215, 348, 365, 376, 399, 405, 439*
Journal of Shamanic Practice: *132*
Journeying: *129, 130, 133, 134, 135, 142, 160, 166, 170, 175, 177, 411, 414, 417, 437*
Journeying, technoshamanic: *142, 411, 414*
Jung, Carl: *70, 88, 93, 102, 118, 130, 150, 188, 199, 200, 202, 289, 324, 349, 358, 366, 368, 377*
Justice (personification, goddess): *91, 92*

K

Kabbalah: *119, 181, 184, 187, 206, 218, 227, 258, 259, 260, 314, 315, 320, 324, 329, 357, 370*
Kabbalistic Tree of Life: *16, 181, 183, 184, 185, 186, 194, 195, 196, 197, 198, 213, 237, 318, 363*
Kali: *9, 12, 87, 90, 92, 94, 234, 245, 249, 250, 255, 256, 332, 435*
Karlsson, Thomas: *11, 12, 137, 152, 247, 259, 260, 439*
Karmic bonds: *254*
Kasulis, Thomas: *41, 54, 56, 58, 59, 63, 79*
Katz, Richard: *128, 152*
Kehoe, Alice B.: *129, 131, 134, 152*
Kellner, Carl: *216, 217, 223, 227, 228, 239*
Key of Solomon: *337, 360, 377, 381*
King, Francis: *16, 138, 152, 185, 189, 198, 199, 200, 201, 202, 203, 215, 236, 237, 238, 239, 318*
Kinsella, Thomas: *138, 152*
Koenig, P-R.: *216, 217, 228, 230, 239, 243, 244*
Konstantinos, John: *87, 88, 93, 102*
Kormáks saga: *162, 173*
Kripal, Jeffrey J.: *123, 248, 260*
Kundalini: *232, 234, 245, 254, 255, 256, 260, 357, 360, 364*
Kundalini serpent: *232, 234*

Kundalini Yoga: *357*
Kürti: *152*

L

Lalita: *428, 434*
Lascaux: *134*
Laura, Judith: *70*
LaVey, Anton: *12, 261, 262, 264, 265, 266, 267, 268, 269, 270, 271, 273, 274, 275, 276, 277, 278, 279, 280, 290, 291, 300*
Laxdæla saga: 165
Lee, Dave: *387, 398, 400, 403, 404*
Lee, Matt: *398*
Left-Hand Path: *11, 12, 13, 87, 94, 99, 247, 248, 259, 260, 279, 283, 302, 303*
Les Trois Freres: *134*
Letcher, Andy: *28, 31, 34, 146, 147, 153*
Letchford, Frank: *330, 336, 342, 366, 368, 369, 370, 371, 372, 373, 376*
Lévi, Eliphas: *189, 224, 239, 310*
Lewis-Williams, David J.: *128, 129, 153*
Liber 777 (Crowley): *187, 188, 199, 200, 202*
Liberal: *121, 137*
Liber AL vel Legis (The Book of the Law): *209, 210, 211, 212, 213, 214, 230, 235, 236, 237*
Lilith: *9, 87, 90, 92, 94, 96, 97, 98, 99, 102, 250, 255, 256, 274, 297, 300, 349, 356, 357, 359, 360*
Lincoln Order of Neuromancers (L.O.O.N): *388*
Lindquist, Galina: *124, 129, 153, 159, 170, 171, 178*
Literalism, problems of: *73, 75, 76, 77, 78*
Loke: *12, 249*
London: *57, 101, 122, 125, 132, 142, 143, 148, 150, 151, 153, 154, 155, 166, 177, 178, 182, 184, 185, 187, 199, 200, 201, 202, 203, 206, 215, 227, 237, 238, 239, 279, 308, 314, 319, 320, 326, 337, 344, 345, 365, 367, 368, 369, 370, 373, 374, 375, 376, 377, 385, 386, 387, 400, 402, 403, 407, 419, 438, 440*
Lovecraft, H.P.: *297, 301, 391, 399, 400, 405*
Lucid Dream Exchange: *418, 420, 423*
Lucid dream machines: *411*
Lucifer: *12, 249, 274, 278, 349, 353, 354, 355, 363*
Luckmann, Thomas: *33, 417, 419, 423*
Luhrmann, Tanya: *1, 3, 4, 14, 135, 153*

M

MacCumhail, Fionn: *138*
MacEowan: *124, 138*
MacLaren, Malcolm: *385, 403*
MacLellan, Gordon 'the Toad': *147, 158*
Maga: *300*
Magical consciousness: *19, 22, 24, 29, 194, 325*
Magical grimoires: *12, 324, 337, 360*
Magical sigils: *217, 328, 329, 334, 337, 339, 373*
Magical will: *5, 6, 183, 208, 213, 329, 330, 333, 338, 341, 342, 363*
Magick in Theory and Practice (Crowley): *4, 15, 187, 188, 200, 202, 206, 209, 234, 236, 399*
Magic / magick: *1, 3, 4, 5, 6, 7, 8, 9, 10, 11, 12, 13, 14, 15, 19, 20, 25, 27, 28, 29, 30, 31, 33, 42, 43, 44, 45, 53, 54, 72, 79, 80, 87, 88, 89, 90, 91, 92, 93, 94, 97, 98, 100, 101, 103, 129, 135, 136, 137, 138, 142, 143, 146, 148, 160, 161, 162, 163, 164, 165, 166, 167, 171, 173, 175, 177, 181, 183, 184, 186, 188, 189, 190, 199, 201, 205, 206, 207, 208, 209, 211, 212, 213, 214, 215, 216, 217, 218, 219, 220, 221, 222, 223, 224, 225, 226, 227, 228, 230, 231, 232, 233, 234, 235, 237, 240, 241, 243, 244, 249, 252, 258, 262, 266, 269, 282, 284, 285, 286, 287, 289, 293, 294, 296, 297, 298, 299, 303, 304, 314, 315, 319, 323, 324, 327, 328, 332, 334, 335, 348, 360, 362, 363, 365, 372, 373, 374, 376, 380, 381, 382, 383, 384, 385, 386, 387, 388, 389, 390, 391, 392, 393, 394, 395, 396, 397, 398, 399, 400, 402, 403, 406, 407, 408, 415, 426, 427, 428, 429, 438*
Magic mushrooms (Psilocybin): *146*
Magic; sympathetic: *44, 45, 53*
Magister: *299*
Magus: *299, 300, 318*
Mahakala: *254*
Mansfield, Jayne, Anton La Vey and: *267*
Marduk: *255*
Materialist discourse: *146*
Mathers, Moina: *184, 192, 193, 198, 237, 314*
Mathers, Samuel Liddell: *182, 184*
Matt, Daniel C.: *257, 260, 398*
Matter: *8, 21, 83, 87, 92, 112, 124, 129, 144, 145, 185, 212, 214, 228, 250, 251, 255, 256, 257, 258, 283, 287, 345, 391, 394, 398, 415, 432*
Matthews, Caitlin & John: *138, 140, 153*
Max.555, Joseph: *98, 99*
Mayer, Peter: *32, 34, 269*

McClenon: *153*
McKenna, Terence: *142*
MDMA: *141*
Medicine Wheel: *62, 132*
Medieval: *121, 134, 135, 138, 163, 178, 179, 181, 182, 223, 297, 300, 303, 324, 337, 354, 357, 360*
Medieval manuscripts: *138*
Medieval witches: *135*
Meditation: *9, 21, 24, 42, 44, 89, 95, 103, 108, 171, 188, 196, 329, 411, 429*
Megaira: *92, 103*
Meister Eckhart: *258*
Mental imagery: *25, 26*
Merkur, Dan: *194, 195, 201, 203*
Metamorphosis: *23, 377*
Mexico: *23, 131, 155, 208, 272*
Might is Right (Arthur Desmond): *269, 270, 279*
Migration age: *135*
Miles: *143, 153, 287*
Missionary: *133*
Mobile phone technology: *142*
Modern pagan witchcraft: *9, 14, 404, 407*
Monaghan, Patricia: *83, 84, 86*
Monotheistic Goddess: *81*
Monroe, Marilyn, Anton La Vey and: *266, 267*
Moorcock, Michael: *382*
Moore, Vadge: *312, 322, 324, 325, 366, 369*
Muni: *254*
Murray, Margaret: *134, 154, 320*
Mycospirituality: *146*
Mysterium tremendum: *8, 37, 38, 39, 40, 41, 45, 49, 51, 52, 53, 54, 298*
Mysticism: *4, 9, 89, 181, 207, 216, 255, 257, 258, 260, 324, 370, 393*
Mythology: *10, 27, 38, 41, 49, 137, 171, 209, 288, 330, 332, 357, 371, 441*

N

NAFPS (New Age Frauds and Plastic Shamans): *157, 158*
Nagual: *131*
Nagual dreaming woman: *131*
Nagualism: *131*
Narby, Jeremy: *132, 154*
Nath: *254*
Nationalism: *2, 137, 141, 144*

Index 459

Nationhood: *138*
Native Americana: *106, 116, 117, 125*
Natural world, as resources: *147*
Nazi rituals: *266*
Near East: *134*
Necchi, Joe: *276, 279*
Nemo: *275, 276, 279*
Neo-colonialism: *127*
Neopaganism: *56, 60, 86, 273*
Neoshamanism: *149, 152*
Neoshamanisms: *158*
Netizens: *413, 416*
Neuburg, Victor: *213, 214, 215, 226, 237, 238*
Neuro-Linguistic Programming (NLP): *389*
Neurologically: *145*
New Age: *55, 56, 60, 88, 93, 94, 116, 117, 123, 132, 157, 158, 255, 440, 441*
New-primitive: *141*
New religious movement (NRM): *394*
New Toltequity: *131*
Nine Satanic Statements (Anton La Vey): *270, 271*
Nineteenth century: *106, 145, 291, 381*
Noble savage: *144*
Nocturnal Magic: *9, 87, 88, 89, 90, 91, 93*
Noel, Daniel: *130, 131, 154*
Nordic *Sejd* tradition: *248*
Norse: *125, 135, 148, 164, 167, 169, 171, 172, 173, 177, 178, 179*
Norse myths and sagas: *135*
North America: *86, 114, 116, 121, 123, 130, 131, 132, 157, 167, 170, 171, 176, 224, 441*
Northern Europe: *135, 136, 137, 160, 178*
North Scandinavia: *133*
Norton, Rosaleen: *12, 323, 324, 325, 327, 347, 348, 349, 350, 351, 352, 353, 354, 355, 356, 357, 358, 359, 360, 361, 362, 363, 364, 365, 366, 367, 368, 376, 377, 378, 438*
Nothing is True, Everything is Permitted: *143*
Nox, Orphic principle of: *251, 256, 257, 258, 400, 404, 405*
Numinous/numen: *37, 39, 40, 56, 57, 58, 61*
Nyx, Lori: *97, 101*

Objective universe: *7, 283*

Objectivity: *1, 128*
Odin: *163, 166, 174, 259*
Old Stone Age: *134*
Ontologies: *10, 128, 129, 130, 136, 145, 146, 156, 157*
Ontology: *129, 140, 146, 148*
Ophitian Gnosticism: *248*
Ordo Templi Orientis (O.T.O.): *11, 17, 212, 215, 216, 217, 218, 219, 220, 221, 223, 224, 227, 228, 230, 231, 233, 234, 236, 238, 239, 240, 243, 244, 315, 366*
Ordo Templi Satanis: *268*
Origin of religion: *134*
Orr, Emma Restall: *147, 154*
Örvar-odds saga: 163
Other-than-human-people: *129*
Otherworld: *14, 34, 41, 57, 59, 140*
Otto, Rudolf: *37, 38, 39, 41, 53, 54, 56, 57, 58, 59, 63, 369*
Ouija board: *142*
Ouroboros: *251, 255, 260*

P

Pagan: *7, 8, 9, 14, 31, 37, 38, 40, 41, 42, 43, 44, 45, 49, 51, 52, 53, 54, 55, 56, 57, 58, 59, 60, 61, 62, 67, 68, 70, 72, 73, 80, 86, 88, 89, 92, 97, 101, 118, 121, 127, 134, 135, 136, 137, 138, 147, 148, 149, 150, 151, 153, 154, 155, 156, 315, 320, 347, 348, 349, 376, 389, 396, 399, 400, 401, 403, 404, 405, 406, 407, 410, 418, 440*
Pagan animist: *147*
Pagani, Paula (pseudonym of Ray Sherwin): *384, 400, 401, 402, 403*
Paganism: *14, 17, 23, 31, 33, 34, 40, 42, 43, 44, 46, 50, 55, 56, 57, 58, 59, 60, 62, 65, 86, 88, 89, 90, 92, 94, 96, 99, 100, 101, 102, 125, 148, 149, 151, 152, 155, 159, 177, 178, 319, 320, 437, 439, 440*
Paganism: ancient European: *42, 43*
Pain: *15, 20, 69*
Palo Mayombe: *248*
Papyri Graecae Magicae (Greek Magical Papyri): 91
Paradigms, power of: *78, 79, 80, 81, 82*
Paradigms, problems with: *70*
Participant observation: *30, 31*
Party-drugs: *141*
Pathological: *28, 146*
Paxton, Diana: *10, 118, 125, 167, 168*
Pearce: *129, 153*

Performance: *15, 75, 77, 98, 103, 141, 142, 144, 177, 189, 207, 309, 411, 414, 422, 428*
Persecuted: *128*
Persecution: *94, 134*
Persephone: *92, 95, 96, 97, 103, 324*
Personal growth: *132, 133*
Personal healing: *133*
Personal responsibility: *12, 249*
Personal transformation: *137*
Persons: *10, 39, 42, 129, 145, 146, 156, 253, 278, 414, 415, 430, 433*
Peters: *154, 157*
Pethro Vodou: 248
Peyote: *34, 142*
Peyote Church, The: *142*
Pharmacology: *142, 397*
Pipe ceremonies: *131*
Plastic shamans: *116, 117, 131*
Plato: *69, 84, 296*
Platonic solids: *317*
Playgans: *9, 89*
Pleroma: *255*
Popper, Karl: *392, 400, 406*
Positivist: *75, 145*
Post-Communist Siberia: *128*
Post-modernist: *379, 380*
Post-Soviet: *144*
Price: *135, 154, 156, 159, 165, 179, 303*
Price, Neil: *51, 52, 53, 54*
Priest: *12, 24, 53, 67, 68, 72, 73, 114, 152, 209, 211, 212, 215, 220, 221, 222, 232, 238, 274, 277, 280, 282, 296, 297, 299, 300, 304, 440*
Priestess: *4, 8, 14, 45, 61, 72, 85, 147, 201, 203, 215, 221, 222, 238, 274, 276, 296, 298, 299, 360, 388*
Priesthood: *295, 296, 298*
Primitive: *3, 107, 116, 121, 141, 144, 145, 325*
Prior, Bernie: *22, 120, 131, 272*
Prohibitive: *146*
Prometheus: *12, 249*
Psychedelic: *7, 28, 108, 141, 146, 359, 360, 422*
Psychic awareness: *24*
Psychoactive plants: *27, 28, 199*
Psychological: *5, 19, 24, 26, 28, 29, 34, 69, 98, 137, 146, 188, 251, 328, 358*
Psychosis: *146*

Psytrance (psychedelic trance music): *141*
Puja: *428, 430, 431, 432, 433, 434*
Punk: *385, 403*

Q
Qliphoth: *195, 249, 255, 256, 257, 259, 260, 353, 363, 439*
Quantum physics: *22, 33, 143, 389, 423*

R
Race: *138, 150, 288, 379*
Radical empiricism: *31*
Raine, Kathleen: *183, 198, 203*
Rand, Ayn: *262, 270, 271, 279*
Randolph, Paschal Beverly: *216, 224, 225, 226, 227, 228, 241, 242, 243*
Rave festivals: *414*
RaveRaven: *415*
Ravers: *141*
Read, Ian: *387*
Real and imagined: *127, 143*
Reconstructionists: *92*
Recreational: *146*
Redbeard, Ragnar (Arthur Desmond): *270, 279*
Redwood, Bill: *400, 402*
Reed-Danahay: *129, 154*
Reflexive scholarship: *82*
Regardie, Israel: *5, 6, 11, 15, 16, 183, 186, 187, 189, 196, 200, 201, 203*
Reindeer herders: *133*
Religion: *3, 8, 13, 32, 38, 39, 40, 42, 53, 65, 66, 77, 78, 82, 85, 88, 89, 92, 93, 95, 100, 106, 107, 117, 121, 127, 129, 130, 134, 135, 137, 140, 143, 144, 160, 164, 167, 170, 177, 178, 183, 247, 248, 249, 263, 264, 269, 271, 272, 273, 277, 282, 283, 284, 297, 300, 315, 324, 330, 395, 396, 399, 405, 409, 410, 418, 426, 439, 440, 441*
Religious postmodernity: *409*
Resistive discourses: *28, 146*
Reuss, Theodor: *11, 215, 216, 217, 218, 219, 224, 227, 228, 230, 236, 239*
Right-Hand Path: *286*
Right-wing politics: *138, 140, 141*
Rios, Marlene Dobkin de: *154, 200, 202*
Rishi: 254
Rites of passage: *80, 139, 195*

Ritual: *7, 8, 23, 31, 39, 40, 42, 43, 44, 45, 47, 48, 50, 51, 52, 53, 54, 62, 65, 66, 68, 74, 75, 77, 82, 85, 97, 98, 99, 103, 109, 122, 136, 137, 139, 159, 161, 168, 169, 170, 175, 181, 183, 184, 185, 186, 188, 189, 192, 195, 198, 199, 207, 212, 213, 214, 215, 217, 221, 222, 225, 226, 228, 229, 230, 233, 236, 237, 240, 243, 262, 269, 271, 272, 283, 291, 298, 300, 301, 311, 324, 360, 363, 368, 380, 388, 389, 391, 395, 396, 400, 405, 407, 410, 411, 412, 413, 414, 415, 416, 417, 419, 422, 428, 429, 430, 432, 433, 435, 437*
Ritual dynamics: *410*
Ritual magic: *137, 262, 269, 400, 407*
Rock art; shamanistic approach: *128, 156*
Romance: *45, 121, 131*
Roman ethnographers: *138*
Root, Deborah: *131, 154*
Rosemary's Baby: *267, 269*
Rosenkreutz, Christian: *183, 197, 199*
Ross: *138, 149, 154*
Rountree, Kathryn: *69, 85, 86*
Ruith, Mog: *138*
Runes: *137*
Runic John: *137, 154*
Russell, Dawn: *132, 326*
Rutherford, Leo: *132, 155*

S

Saami: *133, 178*
Sabbats: *45, 48*
Sacred geometry: *317, 318*
Sacred spaces: *46, 50, 54*
Sahasrara: *254*
Saining: *139*
Saints and Sinners (Lawrence Wright): *267*
Sakha: *115*
Sakti (Shakti): 13, 233, 256, 428, 429, 431, 432, 433, 434, 436
Saler: *131, 155*
Sámi shamanism: *159, 172*
San/Bushman: *128*
Sanchez, Victor: *131, 155*
San Francisco Ballet Orchestra, The, Anton La Vey and: *266, 267*
San Pedro: *142*
Sanson: *155*

Santo Daime: *142*
Satanic Bible, The: *12, 261, 262, 265, 268, 269, 270, 271, 272, 273, 274, 275, 276, 277, 278, 279*
Satanism: *12, 90, 255, 261, 262, 264, 265, 266, 268, 269, 271, 272, 273, 274, 275, 276, 278, 279, 280, 291*
Saxons: *135*
Scandinavian Center for Shamanic Studies: *115, 135*
Scarlet Woman: *97, 208, 209, 211, 214, 232, 233, 235, 236*
Schneider, Erich: *410, 421*
Scholem, Gershom: *258, 260, 370*
Schreck, Nikolas: *267, 270, 279*
Schreck, Zeena: *267, 270, 275, 279*
Schutz: *21, 33, 34*
Scientology: *263, 264*
Scrying: *99, 137*
Second Life: *128, 157, 158, 416*
Secret Life of a Satanist (Blanche Barton): *266, 278*
See as others do: *129*
Seeing as others do: *145*
Seeress: *10, 27, 131, 136, 160, 161, 162, 164, 165, 167, 168, 169, 170, 171, 173, 174*
Seership: *139*
Seething: *137*
Seidhfeuer' network: *137*
Seiðr: *10, 125, 135, 137, 148, 154, 155, 158, 159, 160, 164, 167, 171, 174, 176, 177, 437*
Seiðr, men and: *174, 176, 177*
Seidr-séance: *136*
Selene: *92*
Self-deification: *12, 248, 255, 302, 303*
Self-hypnosis: *12, 323, 324, 342, 349, 352*
Self-sacrifice: *251*
Semen: *212, 213, 217, 218, 219, 220, 222, 223, 228, 229, 230, 233, 234, 243*
Semple, Gavin: *143, 155, 328, 329, 334, 335, 338, 363, 366, 370, 371, 372, 373, 374, 375, 376, 377*
Sennitt, Stephen: *391, 400, 404, 405*
Sensory deprivation: *421*
Sephiroth: *185*
Serpent: *91, 232, 234, 248, 251, 255, 256, 288, 360, 365*
Serpent, symbolism of the: *137, 150, 195, 201, 222, 232, 248, 251, 255, 256, 258, 259, 260*
Setian: *281, 282, 283, 284, 285, 286, 287, 288, 289, 290, 291, 292, 293, 294,*

Index 465

  295, 296, 297, 298, 299, 300, 302
Set of techniques: *130, 143*
Sex magick (Crowley): *11, 205, 208, 222, 224, 228, 230, 231, 232, 233, 243, 389*
Shadow Magic: *9, 87, 96, 99, 100, 102*
Shah, Idries: *396*
Shallcrass, Philip 'Greywolf': *138, 139, 144*
Shamanic Craft: *135*
Shamanic trembling: *137*
Shamanic vision: *26, 140*
Shamanic Wicca: *135*
Shamanism: *9, 10, 14, 16, 22, 105, 106, 107, 108, 109, 110, 111, 112, 113, 114, 115, 116, 118, 119, 120, 121, 122, 123, 125, 127, 128, 129, 130, 131, 132, 133, 134, 135, 136, 137, 138, 139, 140, 141, 142, 143, 144, 145, 147, 148, 155, 156, 158, 159, 168, 172, 177, 178, 200, 386, 409, 410, 412, 418, 437, 438, 441*
Shamanisms: *127, 134*
Shamanistic: *9, 127, 128, 129, 133, 135, 137, 138, 141, 143, 144, 159, 167, 171, 172, 177*
Shamanistic worldviews: *129*
Shamen, The: *142*
Shape-shifting: *23, 163*
Sherwin, Ray: *383, 384, 386, 394, 400, 402, 403, 406*
Shiva: *76, 94, 233, 254, 303, 431, 432, 433*
Shnirelman: *144, 155*
Shunya: *254*
Siberia: *110, 128, 139, 148, 441*
Sickness: *133*
Sigil magic: *143, 327, 328*
Sigils: *12, 143, 217, 223, 324, 328, 329, 330, 334, 337, 338, 339, 373, 374*
Silverman, Julian: *107, 123*
Sinclair, Lilith: *274*
Sixth sense: *32*
Smith: *131, 153, 155, 230, 271, 280, 398, 400, 403, 436*
Smith, Andy: *398*
Smudging: *139*
Snell, Lionel: *384, 391, 392, 393, 394, 395, 398, 406, 407*
Societas Rosicruciana in Anglia (SRIA): *182, 184, 196, 197*
Somataphobia: *69, 78*
Sonoran Desert: *131*
Sorcerer: *134, 283, 346, 371, 374*
Sorcerers Apprentice: *387, 404*

Sorcery: *12, 133, 135, 161, 162, 163, 223, 302, 303, 337, 348, 364, 374, 419*
Soul: *15, 38, 114, 135, 140, 160, 175, 190, 195, 254, 300, 329, 330, 357*
Southern Africa: *128*
Soviet Union: *144*
Spae-working: *162, 163, 175*
Spare, Austin Osman: *12, 13, 143, 153, 155, 215, 220, 225, 238, 315, 323, 324, 325, 326, 327, 328, 329, 330, 331, 332, 333, 334, 335, 336, 337, 338, 339, 340, 341, 342, 343, 344, 345, 346, 362, 363, 364, 365, 366, 367, 368, 369, 370, 371, 372, 373, 374, 375, 376, 377, 378, 379, 395, 399, 401*
Spermo-Gnostics: *228, 239, 243, 244*
Spiral Tribe: *141*
Spirit: *6, 10, 13, 15, 20, 23, 26, 28, 30, 31, 39, 83, 88, 97, 98, 99, 109, 110, 111, 112, 116, 121, 124, 125, 129, 130, 131, 135, 139, 140, 141, 142, 143, 145, 146, 149, 169, 174, 177, 190, 191, 193, 197, 206, 207, 214, 228, 250, 251, 256, 258, 259, 284, 298, 307, 324, 329, 331, 346, 349, 356, 377, 410, 421*
Spirit-energy: *31*
Spirit-helpers: *143*
Spirit-quest: *140*
Spirits: *10, 15, 23, 27, 28, 33, 49, 59, 103, 110, 111, 112, 114, 116, 120, 130, 133, 135, 136, 139, 143, 145, 146, 161, 162, 163, 164, 165, 168, 170, 171, 175, 197, 218, 310, 324, 337, 338, 349, 357, 361, 374, 412, 417*
Spiritual tourists: *128*
Spirit world: *26, 110, 130, 131, 139, 141, 142, 174, 410*
Sri Vidya: *427, 432, 433, 434*
Staff: *54, 135, 136, 161, 165, 171*
Starhawk: *7, 16, 26, 28, 34, 66, 67, 68, 69, 85, 86, 94, 135, 155, 390*
Star Trek: *392*
Statnekov, Daniel: *119, 120, 125*
Stone, Merlin: *67, 86, 96, 121, 134, 219, 223, 253, 267, 280, 319, 321*
Struggle with spirits: *130*
Stucken, Hans: *137, 155*
Sturluson, Snorri: *166, 168, 178, 179*
Subjective universe: *6, 7, 190, 283*
Supernatural: *37, 39, 49, 54, 59, 94, 135, 138, 164, 175, 263, 264, 269, 277, 349, 352, 358*
Surrealism: *307, 308, 309, 310, 311, 313, 314, 319, 322, 438*
Sutin, Lawrence: *212, 232, 233, 234, 235, 236, 238, 243, 244, 245*
Swaffer, Hannen: *342, 367*
Sweat lodge: *30, 116*

T

Táin Bó Cúailnge: 138
Talamantez: *130*
Taliesin: *138, 140, 153*
Tantra: *13, 97, 101, 216, 231, 233, 234, 255, 380, 386, 425, 426, 427, 428, 429, 430, 431, 435, 436, 438*
Tantric traditions: *254, 428*
Taoism: *251, 330, 368*
Tarot cards: *192, 311, 316*
Tattva symbols: *190, 193*
Taussig, Michael: *132, 155*
Teal, Micheal: *409, 413, 419, 420, 422*
Technoshamans: *409, 410, 412, 413, 414, 415, 416, 417, 418, 419, 420, 421, 422*
Tehom: 255, 256, 257, 258, 259
Temple of Lylyth: *261, 262, 280*
Temple of Set: *6, 12, 16, 17, 277, 281, 282, 285, 288, 294, 295, 298, 300, 301, 302, 303, 304, 305, 440, 441*
Tesseract: *317, 319*
Thee Temple Ov Psychick Youth (TOPY): *388, 401, 402, 404*
Thelema: *11, 205, 208, 209, 211, 216, 217, 243, 244, 300, 315*
Théon, Max: *227, 243*
Theosophical Society: *196, 381, 401*
Theosophy: *105, 123, 324, 341, 357*
Theurgy: *218, 219, 220, 240, 243*
Third gender: *136*
Thirteenth century: *136*
Þorbjörg: *161, 162, 167*
Thorsson, Edred: *137, 155, 260*
Thought-forms: *190, 331*
Tiamat: *255, 256, 257, 258*
Time: *5, 8, 15, 20, 21, 22, 23, 24, 26, 27, 32, 40, 41, 42, 45, 48, 52, 58, 65, 67, 68, 69, 70, 71, 72, 73, 74, 75, 76, 77, 78, 85, 90, 95, 96, 97, 98, 105, 106, 110, 111, 113, 114, 117, 119, 122, 128, 133, 137, 139, 143, 145, 147, 162, 164, 165, 167, 172, 174, 176, 184, 188, 199, 205, 206, 207, 211, 216, 217, 218, 221, 225, 227, 230, 233, 243, 250, 253, 254, 255, 257, 261, 264, 266, 268, 269, 273, 290, 293, 294, 298, 301, 302, 308, 314, 316, 321, 326, 327, 328, 336, 339, 343, 347, 348, 358, 367, 373, 375, 377, 380, 383, 384, 385, 386, 387, 388, 389, 390, 395, 402, 410, 412, 414, 415, 416, 417, 428*
Tipi: *131*

Toltec seeress: *131*
Toltec Warriors: *131*
Townsend, Joan: *114, 124, 129, 133, 155*
Trance: *7, 10, 11, 21, 23, 24, 25, 27, 43, 59, 99, 128, 131, 135, 137, 139, 141, 146, 160, 161, 168, 169, 170, 174, 175, 176, 188, 189, 196, 197, 220, 224, 225, 237, 242, 323, 324, 334, 335, 349, 350, 352, 362, 363, 364, 377, 410, 411, 413, 415, 416, 421*
Trance dances: *128*
Trance magic: *323, 324, 362*
Tranquillity: *133*
Tree of Life, Kabbalistic: *16, 181, 183, 184, 185, 186, 188, 189, 193, 194, 195, 196, 197, 198, 200, 203, 213, 237, 256, 257, 318, 363*
Trias, Eugenio: *252*
Trichotomy: *79, 80*
Tripartite cosmology: *10, 129*
Triple Goddess paradigm, inadequacy of: *70, 71*
Triple Goddess paradigm, problems with literal interpretation: *78*
Truth-value of science: *146*
Tunneshende, Merilyn: *131, 155*
Turner, Edith: *23, 27, 31, 35, 146, 156, 283*
Twentieth-century: *44, 133*
Twenty-first century: *38, 52, 128, 145, 148*
Twitter: *142*

U

UK: *132, 141, 147, 197, 200, 201, 231, 368, 388, 399, 400, 402*
Ulfhednr: *137*
Umweldt: *22, 28*
Under the cloak: *165, 174*
Universalise: *130, 143*
Universalising: *130, 133*
Upper, middle and lower worlds: *10, 129*
Upper Palaeolithic: *134*
USA: *102, 130, 141*

V

Vamachara: *248, 255*
Vama Marg: *255*
Vayne, Julian: *397, 398, 401, 405, 407*
Vibrations: *20, 232*

Victorian: *14, 129, 197, 242, 353, 354*
Virtuality: *419*
Virtual space: *383, 418*
Vision quests: *116, 121, 132*
Visualization: *26, 28*
Vitebsky, Piers: *141, 156*
Void moment (Spare): *329, 333, 339, 362, 363*
Voltaire (François-Marie Arouet): *393, 406*
Völuspá: 168, 179
Voodoo: *349, 357*

W

Waite, Arthur Edward: *183, 184, 197, 198, 199, 202, 203*
Wallis, Robert J.: *9, 10, 15, 31, 122, 127, 128, 131, 132, 133, 134, 136, 137, 138, 139, 144, 145, 147, 148, 151, 152, 156, 157, 158, 159, 167, 172, 178, 179, 291, 437, 440*
Wannabes: *131*
Way of the Shaman, The (see also Harner, Michael): *16, 34, 108, 109, 111, 112, 119, 122, 123, 124, 133, 151*
Way of Wyrd, The: 137, 148
Web: *121, 128, 142, 383, 409, 410, 411, 413, 417, 423*
Webb: *12, 129, 157, 281, 296, 300, 301, 302, 305, 440*
Weber, Max: *263, 264, 265, 280*
Welsh: *138, 140*
Westcott: *182, 184, 185, 186, 187, 199*
Western lens: *130*
Wheel of the Year: *44, 45, 51, 61, 68*
Whistling bottles (see also Statnekov, Daniel): *119*
White: *6, 9, 62, 67, 86, 89, 90, 101, 103, 138, 150, 153, 219, 222, 225, 228, 245, 283, 284, 296, 305, 321, 350, 353, 354, 355, 359, 366, 399, 408*
White-lighters: *9, 89*
White Magic: *225, 228, 283, 284*
Whore of Babalon: *208, 211*
Wicca: *4, 7, 8, 9, 11, 14, 42, 44, 48, 55, 59, 60, 61, 62, 65, 66, 67, 68, 71, 80, 82, 85, 87, 90, 92, 93, 99, 119, 121, 135, 149, 181, 386, 388, 390, 435*
Wiccan Rede: *9, 87, 88, 89, 103*
Wiccan-shamanism: *135*
Wider-than-human world: *129, 147*
Williamson, Larry: *413*
Willpower: *29*
Witchcraft: *11, 14, 16, 17, 34, 38, 42, 44, 55, 56, 58, 60, 61, 62, 63, 66, 72,*

85, 86, 87, 89, 92, 93, 99, 101, 102, 103, 122, 125, 134, 149, 150, 151, 152, 155, 178, 243, 244, 400, 437, 439
Witches: *43, 44, 50, 60, 96, 134, 135, 354, 388, 391*
Wolfe, Burton: *231, 266, 280*
Wonder: *32, 76, 283, 295, 302, 427, 428, 433, 434, 435*
Woodman, Justin: *401, 402, 405*
Woodman, William Robert: *182, 184, 185, 186*
Working (Setian): *147, 190, 238, 285, 291, 298, 305, 417*
Workshops: *45, 108, 114, 131, 132, 135, 140, 158, 439*
Wright, Lawrence: *266, 267, 280*

X

Xeper: *291, 293, 300*
Xloptuny Curse: *276, 277, 279*

Y

Yakut (Sakha): *115*
Yale: *133*
Yaqui Indian: *131*
Yeats, William Butler: *184, 198, 199, 202, 203, 207, 320, 322*
Yorke, Gerald: *183, 198*

Z

Z-cluster: *383*
Znamenski: *9, 105, 122, 157, 441, 442*
Zohar, The: *257, 329, 370*
Zos/Kia cosmology (Spare): *324, 341, 372*

About Concrescent Scholars

Concrescent Scholars is dedicated to peer-reviewed works of scholarship in the fields of Esotericism, Pagan religion and culture, Magic, and the Occult from within, and without, the Academy.

These young scholarly fields intersect in real lives today and need a forum in which to mature. This is one such forum where the voices of both academic and the practitioner will be heard in new collections, monographs, and translations that further the discipline.

We take advantage of the recent revolution in publishing technology and economics to bring forth works that, previously, might only have been circulated privately, or been prohibitively expensive.

Now, we are growing the future together.

Colophon

This book is made of Times and Didot, using Adobe InDesign. The cover was designed and the body was set by Sam Webster.

Visit our website at
www.Concrescent.net

www.ingramcontent.com/pod-product-compliance
Lightning Source LLC
Chambersburg PA
CBHW021813300426
44114CB00009BA/156